A Guide to Modern Econometrics

Fifth Edition

Marno Verbeek

Rotterdam School of Management, Erasmus University, Rotterdam

Wiley Custom

ISBN: 9781119472117

This book was set in 10/12, TimesLTStd by SPi Global.

Printed and bound in the United Kingdom by CPI Antony Rowe, Ltd.

Contents

Preface

Emperor Joseph II: "*Your work is ingenious. It's quality work. And there are simply too many notes, that's all. Just cut a few and it will be perfect.*"

Wolfgang Amadeus Mozart: "*Which few did you have in mind, Majesty?*"

from the movie *Amadeus*, 1984 (directed by Milos Forman)

The field of econometrics has developed rapidly in the last three decades, while the use of up-to-date econometric techniques has become more and more standard practice in empirical work in many fields of economics. Typical topics include unit root tests, cointegration, estimation by the generalized method of moments, heteroskedasticity and autocorrelation consistent standard errors, modelling conditional heteroskedasticity, causal inference and the estimation of treatment effects, models based on panel data, models with limited dependent variables, endogenous regressors and sample selection. At the same time econometrics software has become more and more user friendly and up-to-date. As a consequence, users are able to implement fairly advanced techniques even without a basic understanding of the underlying theory and without realizing potential drawbacks or dangers. In contrast, many introductory econometrics textbooks pay a disproportionate amount of attention to the standard linear regression model under the strongest set of assumptions. Needless to say that these assumptions are hardly satisfied in practice (but not really needed either). On the other hand, the more advanced econometrics textbooks are often too technical or too detailed for the average economist to grasp the essential ideas and to extract the information that is needed. This book tries to fill this gap.

The goal of this book is to familiarize the reader with a wide range of topics in modern econometrics, focusing on what is important for doing and understanding empirical work. This means that the text is a guide to (rather than an overview of) alternative techniques. Consequently, it does not concentrate on the formulae behind each technique (although the necessary ones are given) nor on formal proofs, but on the intuition behind the approaches and their practical relevance. The book covers a wide range of topics that is usually not found in textbooks at this level. In particular, attention is paid to cointegration, the generalized method of moments, models with limited dependent variables and panel data models. As a result, the book discusses developments in time series analysis, cross-sectional methods as well as panel data modelling. More than 25 full-scale empirical illustrations are provided in separate sections and subsections, taken from fields like labour economics, finance, international economics, consumer behaviour, environmental economics and macro-economics. These illustrations carefully discuss and interpret econometric analyses of relevant economic problems, and each of them covers between two and nine pages of the text. As before, data sets are available through the supporting website of this book. In addition, a number of exercises are of an empirical nature and require the use of actual data.

This fifth edition builds upon the success of its predecessors. The text has been carefully checked and updated, taking into account recent developments and insights. It includes new material on causal inference, the use and limitations of p-values, instrumental variables estimation and its implementation, regression discontinuity design, standardized coefficients, and the presentation of estimation results. Several empirical illustrations are new or updated. For example, Section 5.7 is added containing a new illustration on the causal effect of institutions on economic development, to illustrate the use of instrumental variables. Overall, the presentation is meant to be concise and intuitive, providing references to primary sources wherever possible. Where relevant, I pay particular attention to implementation concerns, for example, relating to identification issues. A large number of new references has been added in this edition to reflect the changes in the text. Increasingly, the literature provides critical surveys and practical guides on how more advanced econometric techniques, like robust standard errors, sample selection models or causal inference methods, are used in specific areas, and I have tried to refer to them in the text too.

This text originates from lecture notes used for courses in Applied Econometrics in the M.Sc. programmes in Economics at K. U. Leuven and Tilburg University. It is written for an intended audience of economists and economics students that would like to become familiar with up-to-date econometric approaches and techniques, important for doing, understanding and evaluating empirical work. It is very well suited for courses in applied econometrics at the master's or graduate level. At some schools this book will be suited for one or more courses at the undergraduate level, provided students have a sufficient background in statistics. Some of the later chapters can be used in more advanced courses covering particular topics, for example, panel data, limited dependent variable models or time series analysis. In addition, this book can serve as a guide for managers, research economists and practitioners who want to update their insufficient or outdated knowledge of econometrics. Throughout, the use of matrix algebra is limited.

I am very much indebted to Arie Kapteyn, Bertrand Melenberg, Theo Nijman and Arthur van Soest, who all have contributed to my understanding of econometrics and have shaped my way of thinking about many issues. The fact that some of their ideas have materialized in this text is a tribute to their efforts. I also owe many thanks to several generations of students who helped me to shape this text into its current form. I am very grateful to a large number of people who read through parts of the manuscript and provided me with comments and suggestions on the basis of the first three editions. In particular, I wish to thank Niklas Ahlgren, Sascha Becker, Peter Boswijk, Bart Capéau, Geert Dhaene, Tom Doan, Peter de Goeij, Joop Huij, Ben Jacobsen, Jan Kiviet, Wim Koevoets, Erik Kole, Marco Lyrio, Konstantijn Maes, Wessel Marquering, Bertrand Melenberg, Paulo Nunes, Anatoly Peresetsky, Francesco Ravazzolo, Regina Riphahn, Max van de Sande Bakhuyzen, Erik Schokkaert, Peter Sephton, Arthur van Soest, Ben Tims, Frederic Vermeulen, Patrick Verwijmeren, Guglielmo Weber, Olivier Wolthoorn, Kuo-chun Yeh and a number of anonymous reviewers. Of course I retain sole responsibility for any remaining errors. Special thanks go to Jean-Francois Flechet for his help with many empirical illustrations and his constructive comments on many early drafts. Finally, I want to thank my wife Marcella and our three children, Timo, Thalia and Tamara, for their patience and understanding for all the times that my mind was with this book when it should have been with them.

1 Introduction

1.1 About Econometrics

Economists are frequently interested in relationships between different quantities, for example between individual wages and the level of schooling. The most important job of econometrics is to quantify these relationships on the basis of available data and using statistical techniques, and to interpret, use or exploit the resulting outcomes appropriately. Consequently, econometrics is the interaction of economic theory, observed data and statistical methods. It is the interaction of these three that makes econometrics interesting, challenging and, perhaps, difficult. In the words of a seminar speaker, several years ago: 'Econometrics is much easier without data'.

Traditionally econometrics has focused upon aggregate economic relationships. Macro-economic models consisting of several up to many hundreds of equations were specified, estimated and used for policy evaluation and forecasting. The recent theoretical developments in this area, most importantly the concept of cointegration, have generated increased attention to the modelling of macro-economic relationships and their dynamics, although typically focusing on particular aspects of the economy. Since the 1970s econometric methods have increasingly been employed in micro-economic models describing individual, household or firm behaviour, stimulated by the development of appropriate econometric models and estimators that take into account problems like discrete dependent variables and sample selection, by the availability of large survey data sets and by the increasing computational possibilities. More recently, the empirical analysis of financial markets has required and stimulated many theoretical developments in econometrics. Currently econometrics plays a major role in empirical work in all fields of economics, almost without exception, and in most cases it is no longer sufficient to be able to run a few regressions and interpret the results. As a result, introductory econometrics textbooks usually provide insufficient coverage for applied researchers. On the other hand, the more advanced econometrics textbooks are often too technical or too detailed for the average economist to grasp the essential ideas and to extract the information that is needed. Thus there is a need for an accessible textbook that discusses the recent and relatively more advanced developments.

The relationships that economists are interested in are formally specified in mathematical terms, which lead to econometric or statistical models. In such models there is room for deviations from the strict theoretical relationships owing to, for example, measurement errors, unpredictable behaviour, optimization errors or unexpected events. Broadly, econometric models can be classified into a number of categories.

A first class of models describes relationships between present and past. For example, how does the short-term interest rate depend on its own history? This type of model, typically referred to as a time series model, usually lacks any economic theory and is mainly built to get forecasts for future values and the corresponding uncertainty or volatility.

A second type of model considers relationships between economic quantities over a certain time period. These relationships give us information on how (aggregate) economic quantities fluctuate over time in relation to other quantities. For example, what happens to the long-term interest rate if the monetary authority adjusts the short-term one? These models often give insight into the economic processes that are operating.

Thirdly, there are models that describe relationships between different variables measured at a given point in time for different units (e.g. households or firms). Most of the time, this type of relationship is meant to explain why these units are different or behave differently. For example, one can analyse to what extent differences in household savings can be attributed to differences in household income. Under particular conditions, these cross-sectional relationships can be used to analyse 'what if' questions. For example, how much more would a given household, or the average household, save if income were to increase by 1%?

Finally, one can consider relationships between different variables measured for different units over a longer time span (at least two periods). These relationships simultaneously describe differences between different individuals (why does person 1 save much more than person 2?), and differences in behaviour of a given individual over time (why does person 1 save more in 1992 than in 1990?). This type of model usually requires panel data, repeated observations over the same units. They are ideally suited for analysing policy changes on an individual level, provided that it can be assumed that the structure of the model is constant into the (near) future.

The job of econometrics is to specify and quantify these relationships. That is, econometricians formulate a statistical model, usually based on economic theory, confront it with the data and try to come up with a specification that meets the required goals. The unknown elements in the specification, the parameters, are *estimated* from a sample of available data. Another job of the econometrician is to judge whether the resulting model is 'appropriate'. That is, to check whether the assumptions made to motivate the estimators (and their properties) are correct, and to check whether the model can be used for its intended purpose. For example, can it be used for prediction or analysing policy changes? Often, economic theory implies that certain restrictions apply to the model that is estimated. For example, the efficient market hypothesis implies that stock market returns are not predictable from their own past. An important goal of econometrics is to formulate such hypotheses in terms of the parameters in the model and to test their validity.

The number of econometric techniques that can be used is numerous, and their validity often depends crucially upon the validity of the underlying assumptions. This book attempts to guide the reader through this forest of estimation and testing procedures, not by describing the beauty of all possible trees, but by walking through this forest in a structured way, skipping unnecessary side-paths, stressing the similarity of the different species that are encountered and pointing out dangerous pitfalls. The resulting walk is hopefully enjoyable and prevents the reader from getting lost in the econometric forest.

1.2 The Structure of This Book

The first part of this book consists of Chapters 2, 3 and 4. Like most textbooks, it starts with discussing the linear regression model and the OLS estimation method. Chapter 2 presents the basics of this important estimation method, with some emphasis on its validity under fairly weak conditions, while Chapter 3 focuses on the interpretation of the models and the comparison of alternative specifications. Chapter 4 considers two particular deviations from the standard assumptions of the linear model: autocorrelation and heteroskedasticity of the error terms. It is discussed how one can test for these phenomena, how they affect the validity of the OLS estimator and how this can be corrected. This includes a critical inspection of the model specification, the use of adjusted standard errors for the OLS estimator and the use of alternative (GLS) estimators. These three chapters are essential for the remaining part of this book and should be the starting point in any course.

In Chapter 5 another deviation from the standard assumptions of the linear model is discussed, which is, however, fatal for the OLS estimator. As soon as the error term in the model is correlated with one or more of the explanatory variables, all good properties of the OLS estimator disappear, and we necessarily have to use alternative approaches. This raises the challenge of identifying causal effects with nonexperimental data. The chapter discusses instrumental variable (IV) estimators and, more generally, the generalized method of moments (GMM). This chapter, at least its earlier sections, is also recommended as an essential part of any econometrics course.

Chapter 6 is mainly theoretical and discusses maximum likelihood (ML) estimation. Because in empirical work maximum likelihood is often criticized for its dependence upon distributional assumptions, it is not discussed in the earlier chapters where alternatives are readily available that are either more robust than maximum likelihood or (asymptotically) equivalent to it. Particular emphasis in Chapter 6 is on misspecification tests based upon the Lagrange multiplier principle. While many empirical studies tend to take the distributional assumptions for granted, their validity is crucial for consistency of the estimators that are employed and should therefore be tested. Often these tests are relatively easy to perform, although most software does not routinely provide them (yet). Chapter 6 is crucial for understanding Chapter 7 on limited dependent variable models and for a small number of sections in Chapters 8 to 10.

The last part of this book contains four chapters. Chapter 7 presents models that are typically (though not exclusively) used in micro-economics, where the dependent variable is discrete (e.g. zero or one), partly discrete (e.g. zero or positive) or a duration. This chapter covers probit, logit and tobit models and their extensions, as well as models for count data and duration models. It also includes a critical discussion of the sample selection problem. Particular attention is paid to alternative approaches to estimate the causal impact of a treatment upon an outcome variable in case the treatment is not randomly assigned ('treatment effects').

Chapters 8 and 9 discuss time series modelling including unit roots, cointegration and error-correction models. These chapters can be read immediately after Chapter 4 or 5, with the exception of a few parts that relate to maximum likelihood estimation. The theoretical developments in this area over the last three decades have been substantial, and many recent textbooks seem to focus upon it almost exclusively. Univariate time series models are covered in Chapter 8. In this case, models are developed that explain an economic variable from its own past. These include ARIMA models, as well as GARCH models for the conditional variance of a series. Multivariate time series models that consider several variables simultaneously are discussed in Chapter 9. These include vector autoregressive models, cointegration and error-correction models.

Finally, Chapter 10 covers models based on panel data. Panel data are available if we have repeated observations of the same units (e.g. households, firms or countries). Over recent decades the use of panel data has become important in many areas of economics. Micro-economic panels of households and firms are readily available and, given the increase in computing resources, more manageable than in the past. In addition, it has become increasingly common to pool time series of several countries. One of the reasons for this may be that researchers believe that a cross-sectional comparison of countries provides interesting information, in addition to a historical comparison of a country with its own past. This chapter also discusses the recent developments on unit roots and cointegration in a panel data setting. Furthermore, a separate section is devoted to repeated cross-sections and pseudo panel data.

At the end of the book the reader will find two short appendices discussing mathematical and statistical results that are used in several places in the book. This includes a discussion of some relevant matrix algebra and distribution theory. In particular, a discussion of properties of the (bivariate) normal distribution, including conditional expectations, variances and truncation, is provided.

In my experience the material in this book is too much to be covered in a single course. Different courses can be scheduled on the basis of the chapters that follow. For example, a typical graduate course in applied econometrics would cover Chapters 2, 3, 4 and parts of Chapter 5, and then continue with selected parts of Chapters 8 and 9 if the focus is on time series analysis, or continue with Section 6.1 and Chapter 7 if the focus is on cross-sectional models. A more advanced undergraduate or graduate course may focus attention on the time series chapters (Chapters 8 and 9), the micro-econometric chapters (Chapters 6 and 7) or panel data (Chapter 10 with some selected parts from Chapters 6 and 7).

Given the focus and length of this book, I had to make many choices concerning which material to present or not. As a general rule I did not want to bother the reader with details that I considered not essential or not to have empirical relevance. The main goal was to give a general and comprehensive overview of the different methodologies and approaches, focusing on what is relevant for doing and understanding empirical work. Some topics are only very briefly mentioned, and no attempt is made to discuss them at any length. To compensate for this I have tried to give references in appropriate places to other sources, including specialized textbooks, survey articles and chapters, and guides with advice for practitioners.

1.3 Illustrations and Exercises

In most chapters a variety of empirical illustrations are provided in separate sections or subsections. While it is possible to skip these illustrations essentially without losing continuity, these sections do provide important aspects concerning the implementation of the methodology discussed in the preceding text. In addition, I have attempted to provide illustrations that are of economic interest in themselves, using data that are typical of current empirical work and cover a wide range of different areas. This means that most data sets are used in recently published empirical work and are fairly large, both in terms of number of observations and in terms of number of variables. Given the current state of computing facilities, it is usually not a problem to handle such large data sets empirically.

Learning econometrics is not just a matter of studying a textbook. Hands-on experience is crucial in the process of understanding the different methods and how and when to implement them. Therefore, readers are strongly encouraged to get their hands dirty and to estimate a number of models using appropriate or inappropriate methods, and to perform a number of alternative specification tests. With modern software becoming more and more user friendly, the actual computation of even the more complicated estimators and test statistics is often surprisingly simple, sometimes dangerously simple. That is, even with the wrong data, the wrong model and the wrong methodology, programmes may come up with results that are seemingly all right. At least some expertise is required to prevent the practitioner from such situations, and this book plays an important role in this.

To stimulate the reader to use actual data and estimate some models, almost all data sets used in this text are available through the website www.wileyeurope.com/college/verbeek. Readers are encouraged to re-estimate the models reported in this text and check whether their results are the same, as well as to experiment with alternative specifications or methods. Some of the exercises make use of the same or additional data sets and provide a number of specific issues to consider. It should be stressed that, for estimation methods that require numerical optimization, alternative programmes, algorithms or settings may give slightly different outcomes. However, you should get results that are close to the ones reported.

I do not advocate the use of any particular software package. For the linear regression model any package will do, while for the more advanced techniques each package has its particular advantages and disadvantages. There is typically a trade-off between user-friendliness and flexibility. Menu-driven packages often do not allow you to compute anything other than what's on the menu, but, if the menu is sufficiently rich, that may not be a problem. Command-driven packages require somewhat more input from the user, but are typically quite flexible. For the illustrations in the text, I made use of Eviews, RATS and Stata. Several alternative econometrics programmes are available, including MicroFit, PcGive, TSP and SHAZAM; for more advanced or tailored methods, econometricians make use of GAUSS, Matlab, Ox, S-Plus and many other programmes, as well as specialized software for specific methods or types of model. Journals like the *Journal of Applied Econometrics* and the *Journal of Economic Surveys* regularly publish software reviews.

The exercises included at the end of each chapter consist of a number of questions that are primarily intended to check whether the reader has grasped the most important concepts. Therefore, they typically do not go into technical details or ask for derivations or proofs. In addition, several exercises are of an empirical nature and require the reader to use actual data, made available through the book's website.

2 An Introduction to Linear Regression

The linear regression model in combination with the method of ordinary least squares (OLS) is one of the cornerstones of econometrics. In the first part of this book we shall review the linear regression model with its assumptions, how it can be estimated, evaluated and interpreted and how it can be used for generating predictions and for testing economic hypotheses.

This chapter starts by introducing the ordinary least squares method as an algebraic tool, rather than a statistical one. This is because OLS has the attractive property of providing a best linear approximation, irrespective of the way in which the data are generated, or any assumptions imposed. The linear regression model is then introduced in Section 2.2, while Section 2.3 discusses the properties of the OLS estimator in this model under the so-called Gauss–Markov assumptions. Section 2.4 discusses goodness-of-fit measures for the linear model, and hypothesis testing is treated in Section 2.5. In Section 2.6, we move to cases where the Gauss–Markov conditions are not necessarily satisfied and the small sample properties of the OLS estimator are unknown. In such cases, the limiting behaviour of the OLS estimator when – hypothetically – the sample size becomes infinitely large is commonly used to approximate its small sample properties. An empirical example concerning the capital asset pricing model (CAPM) is provided in Section 2.7. Sections 2.8 and 2.9 discuss data problems related to multicollinearity, outliers and missing observations, while Section 2.10 pays attention to prediction using a linear regression model. Throughout, an empirical example concerning individual wages is used to illustrate the main issues. Additional discussion on how to interpret the coefficients in the linear model, how to test some of the model's assumptions and how to compare alternative models is provided in Chapter 3, which also contains three extensive empirical illustrations.

2.1 Ordinary Least Squares as an Algebraic Tool

2.1.1 Ordinary Least Squares

Suppose we have a sample with N observations on individual wages and a number of background characteristics, like gender, years of education and experience. Our main interest lies in the question as to how *in this sample* wages are related to the other observables. Let us denote wages by y (the regressand) and the other $K-1$ characteristics by $x_2, \ldots, x_K$ (the regressors). It will become clear below why this numbering of variables is convenient. Now we may ask the question: which linear combination of $x_2, \ldots, x_K$ and a constant gives a good approximation of y? To answer this question, first consider an arbitrary linear combination, including a constant, which can be written as

$$\tilde{\beta}_1 + \tilde{\beta}_2 x_2 + \cdots + \tilde{\beta}_K x_K, \tag{2.1}$$

where $\tilde{\beta}_1, \ldots, \tilde{\beta}_K$ are constants to be chosen. Let us index the observations by i such that $i = 1, \ldots, N$. Now, the difference between an observed value y_i and its linear approximation is

$$y_i - [\tilde{\beta}_1 + \tilde{\beta}_2 x_{i2} + \cdots + \tilde{\beta}_K x_{iK}]. \tag{2.2}$$

To simplify the derivations we shall introduce some shorthand notation. Appendix A provides additional details for readers unfamiliar with the use of vector notation. The special case of $K = 2$ is discussed in the next subsection. For general K we collect the x-values for individual i in a vector x_i, which includes the constant. That is,

$$x_i = (1 \quad x_{i2} \quad x_{i3} \ldots x_{iK})'$$

where $'$ is used to denote a transpose. Collecting the $\tilde{\beta}$ coefficients in a K-dimensional vector $\tilde{\beta} = (\tilde{\beta}_1 \ldots \tilde{\beta}_K)'$, we can briefly write (2.2) as

$$y_i - x_i'\tilde{\beta}. \tag{2.3}$$

Clearly, we would like to choose values for $\tilde{\beta}_1, \ldots, \tilde{\beta}_K$ such that these differences are small. Although different measures can be used to define what we mean by 'small', the most common approach is to choose $\tilde{\beta}$ such that the sum of squared differences is as small as possible. In this case we determine $\tilde{\beta}$ to minimize the following objective function:

$$S(\tilde{\beta}) \equiv \sum_{i=1}^{N} (y_i - x_i'\tilde{\beta})^2. \tag{2.4}$$

That is, we minimize the sum of squared approximation errors. This approach is referred to as the **ordinary least squares** or **OLS** approach. Taking squares makes sure that positive and negative deviations do not cancel out when taking the summation.

To solve the minimization problem, we consider the first-order conditions, obtained by differentiating $S(\tilde{\beta})$ with respect to the vector $\tilde{\beta}$. (Appendix A discusses some rules on how to differentiate a scalar expression, like (2.4), with respect to a vector.)

This gives the following system of K conditions:

$$-2\sum_{i=1}^{N} x_i(y_i - x_i'\tilde{\beta}) = 0 \tag{2.5}$$

or

$$\left(\sum_{i=1}^{N} x_i x_i'\right)\tilde{\beta} = \sum_{i=1}^{N} x_i y_i. \tag{2.6}$$

These equations are sometimes referred to as **normal equations**. As this system has K unknowns, one can obtain a unique solution for $\tilde{\beta}$ provided that the symmetric matrix $\sum_{i=1}^{N} x_i x_i'$, which contains sums of squares and cross-products of the regressors x_i, can be inverted. For the moment, we shall assume that this is the case. The solution to the minimization problem, which we shall denote by b, is then given by

$$b = \left(\sum_{i=1}^{N} x_i x_i'\right)^{-1} \sum_{i=1}^{N} x_i y_i. \tag{2.7}$$

By checking the second-order conditions, it is easily verified that b indeed corresponds to a minimum of (2.4).

The resulting linear combination of x_i is thus given by

$$\hat{y}_i = x_i' b,$$

which is the **best linear approximation** of y from $x_2, \ldots, x_K$ and a constant. The phrase 'best' refers to the fact that the sum of squared differences between the observed values y_i and fitted values $\hat{y}_i$ is minimal for the least squares solution b.

In deriving the linear approximation, we have not used any economic or statistical theory. It is simply an algebraic tool, and it holds irrespective of the way the data are generated. That is, given a set of variables we can always determine the best linear approximation of one variable using the other variables. The only assumption that we had to make (which is directly checked from the data) is that the $K \times K$ matrix $\sum_{i=1}^{N} x_i x_i'$ is invertible. This says that none of the x_{ik}s is an *exact* linear combination of the other ones and thus redundant. This is usually referred to as the **no-multicollinearity assumption**. It should be stressed that the linear approximation is an *in-sample* result (i.e. in principle it does not give information about observations (individuals) that are not included in the sample) and, in general, there is no direct interpretation of the coefficients.

Despite these limitations, the algebraic results on the least squares method are very useful. Defining a **residual** e_i as the difference between the observed and the approximated value, $e_i = y_i - \hat{y}_i = y_i - x_i' b$, we can decompose the observed y_i as

$$y_i = \hat{y}_i + e_i = x_i' b + e_i. \tag{2.8}$$

This allows us to write the minimum value for the objective function as

$$S(b) = \sum_{i=1}^{N} e_i^2, \tag{2.9}$$

which is referred to as the **residual sum of squares**. It can be shown that the approximated value $x_i'b$ and the residual e_i satisfy certain properties by construction. For example, if we rewrite (2.5), substituting the OLS solution b, we obtain

$$\sum_{i=1}^{N} x_i(y_i - x_i'b) = \sum_{i=1}^{N} x_i e_i = 0. \tag{2.10}$$

This means that the vector $e = (e_1, \ldots, e_N)'$ is orthogonal[1] to each vector of observations on an x-variable. For example, if x_i contains a constant, it implies that $\sum_{i=1}^{N} e_i = 0$. That is, the average residual is zero. This is an intuitively appealing result. If the average residual were nonzero, this would mean that we could improve upon the approximation by adding or subtracting the same constant for each observation, that is, by changing b_1. Consequently, for the average observation it follows that

$$\bar{y} = \bar{x}'b, \tag{2.11}$$

where $\bar{y} = (1/N)\sum_{i=1}^{N} y_i$ and $\bar{x} = (1/N)\sum_{i=1}^{N} x_i$, a K-dimensional vector of sample means. This shows that for the average observation there is no approximation error. Similar interpretations hold for the other regressors: if the derivative of the sum of squared approximation errors with respect to $\tilde{\beta}_k$ is positive, that is if $\sum_{i=1}^{N} x_{ik} e_i > 0$, it means that we can improve the objective function in (2.4) by decreasing $\tilde{\beta}_k$. Equation (2.8) thus decomposes the observed value of y_i into two orthogonal components: the fitted value (related to x_i) and the residual.

2.1.2 Simple Linear Regression

In the case where $K = 2$ we only have one regressor and a constant. In this case, the observations[2] (y_i, x_i) can be drawn in a two-dimensional graph with x-values on the horizontal axis and y-values on the vertical one. This is done in Figure 2.1 for a hypothetical data set. The best linear approximation of y from x and a constant is obtained by minimizing the sum of squared residuals, which – in this two-dimensional case – equals the vertical distances between an observation and the fitted value. All fitted values are on a straight line, the **regression line**.

Because a 2×2 matrix can be inverted analytically, we can derive solutions for b_1 and b_2 in this special case from the general expression for b above. Equivalently, we can minimize the residual sum of squares with respect to the unknowns directly. Thus we have

$$S(\tilde{\beta}_1, \tilde{\beta}_2) = \sum_{i=1}^{N} (y_i - \tilde{\beta}_1 - \tilde{\beta}_2 x_i)^2. \tag{2.12}$$

The basic elements in the derivation of the OLS solutions are the first-order conditions

$$\frac{\partial S(\tilde{\beta}_1, \tilde{\beta}_2)}{\partial \tilde{\beta}_1} = -2\sum_{i=1}^{N} (y_i - \tilde{\beta}_1 - \tilde{\beta}_2 x_i) = 0, \tag{2.13}$$

[1] Two vectors x and y are said to be orthogonal if $x'y = 0$, that is if $\sum_i x_i y_i = 0$ (see Appendix A).

[2] In this subsection, x_i will be used to denote the single regressor, so that it does not include the constant.

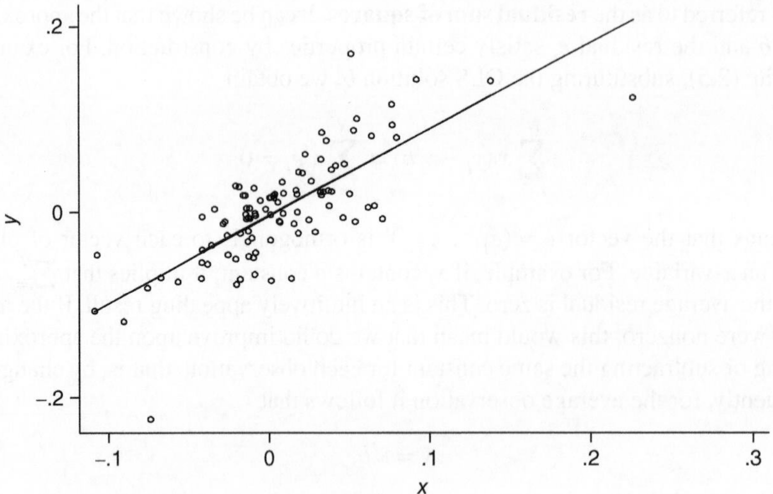

Figure 2.1 Simple linear regression: fitted line and observation points.

$$\frac{\partial S(\tilde{\beta}_1, \tilde{\beta}_2)}{\partial \tilde{\beta}_2} = -2 \sum_{i=1}^{N} x_i(y_i - \tilde{\beta}_1 - \tilde{\beta}_2 x_i) = 0. \tag{2.14}$$

From (2.13) we can write

$$b_1 = \frac{1}{N} \sum_{i=1}^{N} y_i - b_2 \frac{1}{N} \sum_{i=1}^{N} x_i = \bar{y} - b_2 \bar{x}, \tag{2.15}$$

where b_2 is solved from combining (2.14) and (2.15). First, from (2.14) we write

$$\sum_{i=1}^{N} x_i y_i - b_1 \sum_{i=1}^{N} x_i - \left(\sum_{i=1}^{N} x_i^2 \right) b_2 = 0$$

and then substitute (2.15) to obtain

$$\sum_{i=1}^{N} x_i y_i - N \bar{x} \bar{y} - \left(\sum_{i=1}^{N} x_i^2 - N \bar{x}^2 \right) b_2 = 0$$

such that we can solve for the slope coefficient b_2 as

$$b_2 = \frac{\sum_{i=1}^{N} (x_i - \bar{x})(y_i - \bar{y})}{\sum_{i=1}^{N} (x_i - \bar{x})^2}. \tag{2.16}$$

By dividing both numerator and denominator by $N - 1$ it appears that the OLS solution b_2 is the ratio of the sample covariance between x and y and the sample variance of x. From (2.15), the intercept is determined so as to make the average approximation error (residual) equal to zero.

2.1.3 Example: Individual Wages

An example that will appear at several places in this chapter is based on a sample of individual wages with background characteristics, like gender, race and years of schooling. We use a subsample of the US National Longitudinal Survey (NLS) that relates to 1987, and we have a sample of 3294 young working individuals, of which 1569 are females. The average hourly wage rate in this sample equals \$6.31 for males and \$5.15 for females. Now suppose we try to approximate wages by a linear combination of a constant and a 0–1 variable denoting whether the individual is male. That is, $x_i = 1$ if individual i is male and zero otherwise. Such a variable that can only take on the values of zero and one is called a **dummy variable**. Using the OLS approach the result is

$$\hat{y}_i = 5.15 + 1.17x_i.$$

This means that for females our best approximation is \$5.15 and for males it is \$5.15 + \$1.17 = \$6.31. It is not a coincidence that these numbers are exactly equal to the sample means in the two subsamples. It is easily verified from the results above that

$$b_1 = \bar{y}_f$$
$$b_2 = \bar{y}_m - \bar{y}_f$$

where $\bar{y}_m = \sum_i x_i y_i / \sum_i x_i$ is the sample average of the wage for males, and $\bar{y}_f = \sum_i (1 - x_i) y_i / \sum_i (1 - x_i)$ is the average for females.

2.1.4 Matrix Notation

Because econometricians make frequent use of matrix expressions as shorthand notation, some familiarity with this matrix 'language' is a prerequisite to reading the econometrics literature. In this text, we shall regularly rephrase results using matrix notation, and occasionally, when the alternative is extremely cumbersome, restrict attention to matrix expressions only. Using matrices, deriving the least squares solution is faster, but it requires some knowledge of matrix differential calculus. We introduce the following notation:

$$X = \begin{pmatrix} 1 & x_{12} & \dots & x_{1K} \\ \vdots & \vdots & & \vdots \\ 1 & x_{N2} & \dots & x_{NK} \end{pmatrix} = \begin{pmatrix} x_1' \\ \vdots \\ x_N' \end{pmatrix}, \quad y = \begin{pmatrix} y_1 \\ \vdots \\ y_N \end{pmatrix}.$$

So, in the $N \times K$ matrix X the ith row refers to observation i, and the kth column refers to the kth explanatory variable (regressor). The criterion to be minimized, as given in (2.4), can be rewritten in matrix notation using the fact that the inner product of a vector a with itself ($a'a$) is the sum of its squared elements (see Appendix A). That is,

$$S(\tilde{\beta}) = (y - X\tilde{\beta})'(y - X\tilde{\beta}) = y'y - 2y'X\tilde{\beta} + \tilde{\beta}'X'X\tilde{\beta}, \tag{2.17}$$

from which the least squares solution follows from differentiating[3] with respect to $\tilde{\beta}$ and setting the result to zero:

$$\frac{\partial S(\tilde{\beta})}{\partial \tilde{\beta}} = -2(X'y - X'X\tilde{\beta}) = 0. \tag{2.18}$$

[3] See Appendix A for some rules for differentiating matrix expressions with respect to vectors.

Solving (2.18) gives the OLS solution

$$b = (X'X)^{-1}X'y, \tag{2.19}$$

which is exactly the same as the one derived in (2.7) but now written in matrix notation. Note that we again have to assume that $X'X = \sum_{i=1}^{N} x_i x_i'$ is invertible, that is, there is no exact (or perfect) multicollinearity.

As before, we can decompose y as

$$y = Xb + e, \tag{2.20}$$

where e is an N-dimensional vector of residuals. The first-order conditions imply that $X'(y - Xb) = 0$ or

$$X'e = 0, \tag{2.21}$$

which means that each column of the matrix X is orthogonal to the vector of residuals. With (2.19) we can also write (2.20) as

$$y = Xb + e = X(X'X)^{-1}X'y + e = \hat{y} + e \tag{2.22}$$

so that the predicted value for y is given by

$$\hat{y} = Xb = X(X'X)^{-1}X'y = P_X y. \tag{2.23}$$

In linear algebra, the matrix $P_X \equiv X(X'X)^{-1}X'$ is known as a projection matrix (see Appendix A). It projects the vector y upon the columns of X (the column space of X). This is just the geometric translation of finding the best linear approximation of y from the columns (regressors) in X. The matrix P_X is also referred to as the 'hat matrix' because it transforms y into $\hat{y}$ ('y hat'). The residual vector of the projection $e = y - Xb = (I - P_X)y = M_X y$ is the orthogonal complement. It is a projection of y upon the space orthogonal to the one spanned by the columns of X. This interpretation is sometimes useful. For example, projecting twice on the same space should leave the result unaffected, so that it holds that $P_X P_X = P_X$ and $M_X M_X = M_X$. More importantly, it holds that $M_X P_X = 0$ as the column space of X and its orthogonal complement do not have anything in common (except the null vector). This is an alternative way to interpret the result that $\hat{y}$ and e and also X and e are orthogonal. The interested reader is referred to Davidson and MacKinnon (2004, Chapter 2) for an excellent discussion on the geometry of least squares.

2.2 The Linear Regression Model

Usually, economists want more than just finding the best linear approximation of one variable given a set of others. They want economic relationships that are more generally valid than the sample they happen to have. They want to draw conclusions about what happens if one of the variables actually changes. That is, they want to say something about values that are not (yet) included in the sample. For example, we may want to predict the wage of an individual on the basis of his or her background characteristics and determine how it would be different if this person had more years of education. In this case, we want the relationship that is found to be more than just a historical coincidence; it should reflect a fundamental relationship. To do this it is assumed that there is a general relationship that is valid for all possible observations from a well-defined population (e.g. all individuals with a paid job on a given date, or all firms in a certain industry). Restricting attention to linear relationships, we specify a **statistical model** as

$$y_i = \beta_1 + \beta_2 x_{i2} + \cdots + \beta_K x_{iK} + \varepsilon_i \tag{2.24}$$

or

$$y_i = x_i'\beta + \varepsilon_i, \tag{2.25}$$

where y_i and x_i are observable variables and ε_i is unobserved and referred to as an **error term** or disturbance term. In this context, y_i is referred to as the dependent variable and the variables in x_i are called independent variables, explanatory variables, regressors or – occasionally – covariates. The elements in β are unknown population parameters. The equality in (2.25) is supposed to hold for any possible observation, whereas we only observe a **sample** of N observations. We consider this sample as one realization of all potential samples of size N that could have been drawn from the same population. In this way y_i and ε_i (and often x_i) can be considered as **random variables**. Each observation corresponds to a realization of these random variables. Again we can use matrix notation and stack all observations to write

$$y = X\beta + \varepsilon, \tag{2.26}$$

where y and ε are N-dimensional vectors and X, as before, is of dimension $N \times K$. Notice the difference between this equation and (2.20).

In contrast to (2.8) and (2.20), (2.25) and (2.26) are population relationships, where β is a vector of unknown parameters characterizing the population. The **sampling process** describes how the sample is taken from the population and, as a result, determines the randomness of the sample. In a first view, the x_i variables are considered as fixed and nonstochastic, which means that every new sample will have the same X matrix. In this case one refers to x_i as being **deterministic**. A new sample only implies new values for ε_i, or – equivalently – for y_i. The only relevant case where the x_is are truly deterministic is in a laboratory setting, where a researcher can set the conditions of a given experiment (e.g. temperature, air pressure). In economics we will typically have to work with nonexperimental data.[4] Despite this, it is convenient and in particular cases appropriate in an economic context to act as if the x_i variables are deterministic. In this case, we will have to make some assumptions about the sampling distribution of ε_i. A convenient one corresponds to **random sampling** where each error ε_i is a random drawing from the population distribution, independent of the other error terms. We shall return to this issue below.

In a second view, a new sample implies new values for both x_i and ε_i, so that each time a new set of N observations for (y_i, x_i) is drawn. In this case random sampling means that each set (y_i, x_i) is a random drawing from the population distribution. In this context, it will turn out to be important to make assumptions about the joint distribution of x_i and ε_i, in particular regarding the extent to which the distribution of ε_i is allowed to depend upon X. The idea of a (random) sample is most easily understood in a cross-sectional

[4] In recent years, the use of field experiments in economics has gained popularity, see, for example, Levitt and List (2009).

context, where interest lies in a large and fixed population, for example all UK households in January 2015, or all stocks listed at the New York Stock Exchange on a given date. In a time series context, different observations refer to different time periods, and it does not make sense to assume that we have a random sample of time periods. Instead, we shall take the view that the sample we have is just one realization of what could have happened in a given time span and the randomness refers to alternative states of the world. In such a case we will need to make some assumptions about the way the data are generated (rather than the way the data are sampled).

It is important to realize that without additional restrictions the *statistical* model in (2.25) is a tautology: for any value of β one can always define a set of ε_is such that (2.25) holds exactly for each observation. We thus need to impose some assumptions to give the model a meaning. A common assumption is that the expected value of ε_i given all the explanatory variables in x_i is zero, that is, $E\{\varepsilon_i|x_i\} = 0$. Usually, people refer to this assumption by saying that the explanatory variables are **exogenous**. Under this assumption it holds that

$$E\{y_i|x_i\} = x_i'\beta, \tag{2.27}$$

so that the (population) regression line $x_i'\beta$ describes the conditional expectation of y_i given the values for x_i. The coefficients β_k measure how the expected value of y_i is affected if the value of x_{ik} is changed, keeping the other elements in x_i constant (the **ceteris paribus** condition). Economic theory, however, often suggests that the model in (2.25) describes a causal relationship, in which the β coefficients measure the changes in y_i *caused* by a ceteris paribus change in x_{ik}. In such cases, ε_i has an economic interpretation (not just a statistical one) and imposing that it is uncorrelated with x_i, as we do by imposing $E\{\varepsilon_i|x_i\} = 0$, may not be justified. Because in many applications it can be argued that unobservables in the error term are related to observables in x_i, we should be cautious interpreting our regression coefficients as measuring causal effects. We shall come back to these issues in Section 3.1 and, in more detail, in Chapter 5 ('endogenous regressors').

Now that our β coefficients have a meaning, we can try to use the sample (y_i, x_i), $i = 1, \ldots, N$, to say something about them. The rule that says how a given sample is translated into an approximate value for β is referred to as an **estimator**. The result for a given sample is called an **estimate**. The *estimator* is a vector of random variables, because the sample may change. The *estimate* is a vector of numbers. The most widely used estimator in econometrics is the **ordinary least squares (OLS)** estimator. This is just the ordinary least squares rule described in Section 2.1 applied to the available sample. The OLS estimator for β is thus given by

$$b = \left(\sum_{i=1}^{N} x_i x_i'\right)^{-1} \sum_{i=1}^{N} x_i y_i. \tag{2.28}$$

Because we have assumed an underlying 'true' model (2.25), combined with a sampling scheme, b is now a vector of random variables. Our interest lies in the true unknown parameter vector β, and b is considered an approximation to it. Whereas a given sample only produces a single estimate, we evaluate the quality of it through the properties of the underlying estimator. The estimator b has a sampling distribution because its value depends upon the sample that is taken (randomly) from the population.

It is extremely important to understand the difference between the estimator b and the true population coefficients β. The first is a vector of random variables, the outcome of which depends upon the sample that is employed (and, in the more general case, upon the estimation method that is used). The second is a set of fixed unknown numbers, characterizing the population model (2.25). Likewise, the distinction between the error terms ε_i and the residuals e_i is important. Error terms are unobserved, and distributional assumptions about them are necessary to derive the sampling properties of estimators for β. We will see this in the next section. The residuals are obtained after estimation, and their values depend upon the *estimated* value for β and therefore depend upon the sample and the estimation method. The properties of the error terms ε_i and the residuals e_i are not the same and occasionally very different. For example, (2.10) is typically not satisfied when the residuals are replaced by the error terms. Empirical papers are often rather sloppy in their terminology, referring to the error terms as being 'residuals' or using the two terms interchangeably. In this text, we will be more precise and use 'error term' or occasionally 'disturbance term' for ε_i and 'residuals' for e_i.

2.3 Small Sample Properties of the OLS Estimator

2.3.1 The Gauss–Markov Assumptions

Whether or not the OLS estimator b provides a good approximation to the unknown parameter vector β depends crucially upon the assumptions that are made about the distribution of ε_i and its relation to x_i. A standard case in which the OLS estimator has good properties is characterised by the Gauss–Markov conditions. Later, in Section 2.6, Chapter 4 and Section 5.1, we shall consider weaker conditions under which OLS still has some attractive properties. For now, it is important to realize that the Gauss–Markov conditions are not all strictly needed to justify the use of the ordinary least squares estimator. They just constitute a simple case in which the small sample properties of b are easily derived.

For the linear regression model in (2.25), given by

$$y_i = x_i'\beta + \varepsilon_i,$$

the **Gauss–Markov conditions** are

$$E\{\varepsilon_i\} = 0, \quad i = 1, \ldots, N \tag{A1}$$

$$\{\varepsilon_1, \ldots, \varepsilon_N\} \text{ and } \{x_1, \ldots, x_N\} \text{ are independent} \tag{A2}$$

$$V\{\varepsilon_i\} = \sigma^2, \quad i = 1, \ldots, N \tag{A3}$$

$$\text{cov}\{\varepsilon_i, \varepsilon_j\} = 0, \quad i,j = 1, \ldots, N,\ i \neq j. \tag{A4}$$

Assumption (A1) says that the expected value of the error term is zero, which means that, *on average*, the regression line should be correct. Assumption (A3) states that all error terms have the same variance, which is referred to as **homoskedasticity**, while assumption (A4) imposes zero correlation between different error terms. This excludes any form of **autocorrelation**. Taken together, (A1), (A3) and (A4) imply that the error terms are uncorrelated drawings from a distribution with expectation zero and constant variance σ^2. Using the matrix notation introduced earlier, it is possible to rewrite these three conditions as

$$E\{\varepsilon\} = 0 \text{ and } V\{\varepsilon\} = \sigma^2 I_N, \tag{2.29}$$

where I_N is the $N \times N$ identity matrix. This says that the covariance matrix of the vector of error terms ε is a diagonal matrix with σ^2 on the diagonal. Assumption (A2) implies that X and ε are independent. Loosely speaking, this means that knowing X does not tell us anything about the distribution of the error terms in ε. This is a fairly strong assumption. It implies that

$$E\{\varepsilon|X\} = E\{\varepsilon\} = 0 \tag{2.30}$$

and

$$V\{\varepsilon|X\} = V\{\varepsilon\} = \sigma^2 I_N. \tag{2.31}$$

That is, the matrix of regressor values X does not provide any information about the expected values of the error terms or their (co)variances. The two conditions (2.30) and (2.31) combine the necessary elements from the Gauss–Markov assumptions needed for the results below to hold. By conditioning on X, we may act as if X were nonstochastic. The reason for this is that the outcomes in the matrix X can be taken as given without affecting the properties of ε, that is, one can derive all properties conditional upon X. For simplicity, we shall take this approach in this section and Section 2.5. Under the Gauss–Markov assumptions (A1) and (A2), the linear model can be interpreted as the conditional expectation of y_i given x_i, that is, $E\{y_i|x_i\} = x_i'\beta$. This is a direct implication of (2.30).

2.3.2 Properties of the OLS Estimator

Under assumptions (A1)–(A4), the OLS estimator b for β has several desirable properties. First of all, it is **unbiased**. This means that, in repeated sampling, we can expect that the OLS estimator is on average equal to the true value β. We formulate this as $E\{b\} = \beta$. It is instructive to see the proof:

$$\begin{aligned} E\{b\} &= E\{(X'X)^{-1}X'y\} = E\{\beta + (X'X)^{-1}X'\varepsilon\} \\ &= \beta + E\{(X'X)^{-1}X'\varepsilon\} = \beta. \end{aligned}$$

In the second step we have substituted (2.26). The final step is the essential one and follows from

$$E\{(X'X)^{-1}X'\varepsilon\} = E\{(X'X)^{-1}X'\}E\{\varepsilon\} = 0,$$

because, from assumption (A2), X and ε are independent and, from (A1), $E\{\varepsilon\} = 0$. Note that we did not use assumptions (A3) and (A4) in the proof. This shows that the OLS estimator is unbiased as long as the error terms are mean zero and independent of all explanatory variables, even if heteroskedasticity or autocorrelation are present. We shall come back to this issue in Chapter 4. If an estimator is unbiased, this means that its probability distribution has an expected value that is equal to the true unknown parameter it is estimating.

In addition to knowing that we are, on average, correct, we would also like to make statements about how (un)likely it is to be far off in a given sample. This means we would like to know the distribution of b (around its mean β). First of all, the variance of b (conditional upon X) is given by

$$V\{b|X\} = \sigma^2(X'X)^{-1} = \sigma^2\left(\sum_{i=1}^{N} x_i x_i'\right)^{-1}, \tag{2.32}$$

which, for simplicity, we shall denote by $V\{b\}$. The $K \times K$ matrix $V\{b\}$ is a variance–covariance matrix, containing the variances of $b_1, b_2, \ldots, b_K$ on the diagonal, and their covariances as off-diagonal elements. The proof is fairly easy and goes as follows:

$$\begin{aligned} V\{b\} &= E\{(b-\beta)(b-\beta)'\} = E\{(X'X)^{-1}X'\varepsilon\varepsilon'X(X'X)^{-1}\} \\ &= (X'X)^{-1}X'(\sigma^2 I_N)X(X'X)^{-1} = \sigma^2(X'X)^{-1}. \end{aligned}$$

Without using matrix notation the proof goes as follows:

$$\begin{aligned} V\{b\} &= V\left\{\left(\sum_i x_i x_i'\right)^{-1} \sum_i x_i \varepsilon_i\right\} = \left(\sum_i x_i x_i'\right)^{-1} V\left\{\sum_i x_i \varepsilon_i\right\}\left(\sum_i x_i x_i'\right)^{-1} \\ &= \left(\sum_i x_i x_i'\right)^{-1} \sigma^2 \left(\sum_i x_i x_i'\right)\left(\sum_i x_i x_i'\right)^{-1} = \sigma^2\left(\sum_i x_i x_i'\right)^{-1}. \end{aligned} \tag{2.33}$$

This requires assumptions (A1)–(A4).

The last result is collected in the **Gauss–Markov theorem**, which says that under assumptions (A1)–(A4) the OLS estimator b is the **best linear unbiased estimator** for β. In short we say that b is BLUE for β. To appreciate this result, consider the class of linear unbiased estimators. A linear estimator is a linear function of the elements in y and can be written as $\tilde{b} = Ay$, where A is a $K \times N$ matrix. The estimator is unbiased if $E\{Ay\} = \beta$. (Note that the OLS estimator is obtained for $A = (X'X)^{-1}X'$.) Then the theorem states that the difference between the covariance matrices of $\tilde{b} = Ay$ and the OLS estimator b is always positive semi-definite. What does this mean? Suppose we are interested in some linear combination of β coefficients, given by $d'\beta$, where d is a K-dimensional vector. Then the Gauss–Markov result implies that the variance of the OLS estimator $d'b$ for $d'\beta$ is not larger than the variance of any other linear unbiased estimator $d'\tilde{b}$, that is,

$$V\{d'\tilde{b}\} \geq V\{d'b\} \text{ for any vector } d.$$

As a special case this holds for the kth element and we have

$$V\{\tilde{b}_k\} \geq V\{b_k\}.$$

Thus, under the Gauss–Markov assumptions, the OLS estimator is the most accurate (linear) unbiased estimator for β. More details on the Gauss–Markov result can be found in Greene (2012, Section 4.3).

To estimate the variance of b we need to replace the unknown error variance σ^2 with an estimate. An obvious candidate is the sample variance of the **residuals** $e_i = y_i - x_i'b$, that is,

$$\tilde{s}^2 = \frac{1}{N-1}\sum_{i=1}^{N} e_i^2 \tag{2.34}$$

(recalling that the average residual is zero). However, because e_i is different from ε_i, it can be shown that this estimator is biased for σ^2. An unbiased estimator is given by

$$s^2 = \frac{1}{N-K}\sum_{i=1}^{N} e_i^2. \tag{2.35}$$

This estimator has a degrees of freedom correction as it divides by the number of observations minus the number of regressors (including the intercept). An intuitive argument for this is that K parameters were chosen so as to minimize the residual sum of squares and thus to minimize the sample variance of the residuals. Consequently, $\tilde{s}^2$ is expected to underestimate the variance of the error term σ^2. The estimator s^2, with a degrees of freedom correction, is unbiased under assumptions (A1)–(A4); see Greene (2012, Section 4.3) for a proof. The variance of b can thus be estimated by

$$V\{b\} = s^2(X'X)^{-1} = s^2\left(\sum_{i=1}^{N} x_i x_i'\right)^{-1}. \tag{2.36}$$

The estimated variance of an element b_k is given by $s^2 c_{kk}$, where c_{kk} is the (k, k) element in $(\Sigma_i x_i x_i')^{-1}$. The square root of this estimated variance is usually referred to as the **standard error** of b_k. We shall denote it as se(b_k). It is the *estimated* standard deviation of b_k and is a measure for the accuracy of the estimator. Under assumptions (A1)–(A4), it holds that se$(b_k) = s\sqrt{c_{kk}}$. When the error terms are not homoskedastic or exhibit autocorrelation, the standard error of the OLS estimator b_k will have to be computed in a different way (see Chapter 4).

In general the expression for the estimated covariance matrix in (2.36) does not allow derivation of analytical expressions for the standard error of a single element b_k. As an illustration, however, let us consider the regression model with two explanatory variables and a constant:

$$y_i = \beta_1 + \beta_2 x_{i2} + \beta_3 x_{i3} + \varepsilon_i.$$

In this case it is possible to derive that the variance of the OLS estimator b_2 for β_2 is given by

$$V\{b_2\} = \frac{\sigma^2}{1-r_{23}^2}\left[\sum_{i=1}^{N}(x_{i2}-\bar{x}_2)^2\right]^{-1},$$

where r_{23} is the sample correlation coefficient between x_{i2} and x_{i3}, and $\bar{x}_2$ is the sample average of x_{i2}. We can rewrite this as

$$V\{b_2\} = \frac{\sigma^2}{1-r_{23}^2}\frac{1}{N}\left[\frac{1}{N}\sum_{i=1}^{N}(x_{i2}-\bar{x}_2)^2\right]^{-1}. \tag{2.37}$$

This shows that the variance of b_2 is driven by four elements. First, the term in square brackets denotes the sample variance of x_2: more variation in the regressor values leads to a more accurate estimator. Second, the term $\frac{1}{N}$ is inversely related to the sample size: having more observations increases precision. Third, the larger the error variance σ^2, the larger the variance of the estimator. A low value for σ^2 implies that observations are typically close to the regression line, which obviously makes it easier to estimate it. Finally, the variance is driven by the correlation between the regressors. The variance of b_2 is inflated if the correlation between x_{i2} and x_{i3} is high (either positive or negative). In the extreme case where $r_{23} = 1$ or -1, x_{i2} and x_{i3} are perfectly correlated and the above variance becomes infinitely large. This is the case of perfect collinearity, and the OLS estimator in (2.7) cannot be computed (see Section 2.8).

Assumptions (A1)–(A4) state that the error terms ε_i are mutually uncorrelated, are independent of X, have zero mean and have a constant variance, but do not specify the shape of the distribution. For exact statistical inference from a given sample of N observations, explicit distributional assumptions have to be made.[5] The most common assumption is that the errors are jointly normally distributed.[6] In this case the uncorrelatedness of (A4) is equivalent to independence of all error terms. The precise assumption is as follows:

$$\varepsilon \sim \mathcal{N}(0, \sigma^2 I_N), \tag{A5}$$

saying that the vector of error terms ε has an N-variate normal distribution with mean vector 0 and covariance matrix $\sigma^2 I_N$. Assumption (A5) thus replaces (A1), (A3) and (A4). An alternative way of formulating (A5) is

$$\varepsilon_i \sim NID(0, \sigma^2), \tag{A5$'$}$$

which is a shorthand way of saying that the error terms ε_i are independent drawings from a normal distribution ('normally and independently distributed', or n.i.d.) with mean zero and variance σ^2. Even though error terms are unobserved, this does not mean that we are free to make any assumption we like. For example, if error terms are assumed to follow a normal distribution, this means that y_i (for given values of x_i) also follows a normal distribution. Clearly, we can think of many variables whose distribution (conditional upon a given set of x_i variables) is not normal, in which case the assumption of normal error terms is inappropriate. Fortunately, not all assumptions are equally crucial for the validity of the results that follow and, moreover, the majority of the assumptions can be tested empirically; see Chapters 3, 4 and 6.

To make things simpler, let us consider the X matrix as fixed and deterministic or, alternatively, let us work conditionally upon the outcomes X. Then the following result holds. Under assumptions (A2) and (A5) the OLS estimator b is normally distributed with mean vector β and covariance matrix $\sigma^2(X'X)^{-1}$, that is,

$$b \sim \mathcal{N}(\beta, \sigma^2(X'X)^{-1}). \tag{2.38}$$

The proof of this follows directly from the result that b is a linear combination of all ε_i and is omitted here. The result in (2.38) implies that each element in b is normally distributed, for example

$$b_k \sim \mathcal{N}(\beta_k, \sigma^2 c_{kk}), \tag{2.39}$$

where, as before, c_{kk} is the (k, k) element in $(X'X)^{-1}$. These results provide the basis for statistical tests based upon the OLS estimator b.

[5] Later we shall see that for approximate inference in large samples this is not necessary.

[6] The distributions used in this text are explained in Appendix B.

2.3.3 Example: Individual Wages (Continued)

Let us now turn back to our wage example. We can formulate a (fairly trivial) econometric model as

$$wage_i = \beta_1 + \beta_2 male_i + \varepsilon_i,$$

where $wage_i$ denotes the hourly wage rate of individual i and $male_i = 1$ if i is male and 0 otherwise. Imposing that $E\{\varepsilon_i\} = 0$ and $E\{\varepsilon_i|male_i\} = 0$ gives β_1 the interpretation of the expected wage rate for females, while $E\{wage_i|male_i = 1\} = \beta_1 + \beta_2$ is the expected wage rate for males. Thus, β_2 is the expected wage differential between an arbitrary male and female. These parameters are unknown population quantities, and we may wish to estimate them. Assume that we have a random sample, implying that different observations are independent. Also assume that ε_i is independent of the regressors, in particular, that the variance of ε_i does not depend upon gender ($male_i$). Then the OLS estimator for β is unbiased and its covariance matrix is given by (2.32). The estimation results are given in Table 2.1. In addition to the OLS estimates, identical to those presented before, we now also know something about the accuracy of the estimates, as reflected in the reported standard errors. We can now say that our estimate of the expected hourly wage differential β_2 between males and females is \$1.17 with a standard error of \$0.11. Combined with the normal distribution, this allows us to make statements about β_2. For example, we can test the hypothesis that $\beta_2 = 0$. If this hypothesis is true, the wage differential between males and females in our sample is nonzero only by chance. Section 2.5 discusses how to test hypotheses regarding β.

2.4 Goodness-of-Fit

Having estimated a particular linear model, a natural question that comes up is: how well does the estimated regression line fit the observations? A popular measure for the goodness-of-fit of a regression model is the proportion of the (sample) variance of y that is explained by the model. This variable is called the R^2 (R squared) and is defined as

$$R^2 = \frac{\hat{V}\{\hat{y}_i\}}{\hat{V}\{y_i\}} = \frac{1/(N-1)\sum_{i=1}^{N}(\hat{y}_i - \bar{y})^2}{1/(N-1)\sum_{i=1}^{N}(y_i - \bar{y})^2}, \tag{2.40}$$

where $\hat{y}_i = x_i'b$ and $\bar{y} = (1/N)\sum_i y_i$ denotes the sample mean of y_i. Note that $\bar{y}$ also corresponds to the sample mean of $\hat{y}_i$, because of (2.11).

Table 2.1 OLS results wage equation

Dependent variable: *wage*

Variable	Estimate	Standard error
constant	5.1469	0.0812
male	1.1661	0.1122

$s = 3.2174$ $R^2 = 0.0317$ $F = 107.93$

From the first-order conditions (compare (2.10)) it follows directly that

$$\sum_{i=1}^{N} e_i x_{ik} = 0, \quad k = 1, \ldots, K.$$

Consequently, we can write $y_i = \hat{y}_i + e_i$, where $\sum_i e_i \hat{y}_i = 0$. In the most relevant case where the model contains an intercept term, it holds that

$$\hat{V}\{y_i\} = \hat{V}\{\hat{y}_i\} + \hat{V}\{e_i\}, \tag{2.41}$$

where $\hat{V}\{e_i\} = \tilde{s}^2$. Using this, the R^2 can be rewritten as

$$R^2 = 1 - \frac{\hat{V}\{e_i\}}{\hat{V}\{y_i\}} = 1 - \frac{1/(N-1)\sum_{i=1}^{N} e_i^2}{1/(N-1)\sum_{i=1}^{N} (y_i - \bar{y})^2}. \tag{2.42}$$

Equation (2.41) shows how the sample variance of y_i can be decomposed into the sum of the sample variances of two orthogonal components: the predictor $\hat{y}_i$ and the residual e_i. The R^2 thus indicates which proportion of the sample variation in y_i is explained by the model.

If the model of interest contains an intercept term, the two expressions for R^2 in (2.40) and (2.42) are equivalent. Moreover, in this case it can be shown that $0 \leq R^2 \leq 1$. Only if all $e_i = 0$ does it hold that $R^2 = 1$, whereas the R^2 is zero if the model does not explain anything in addition to the sample mean of y_i. That is, the R^2 of a model with just an intercept term is zero by construction. In this sense, the R^2 indicates how much better the model fits the data than a trivial model with only a constant term.

From the results in Table 2.1, we see that the R^2 of the very simple wage equation is only 0.0317. This means that only approximately 3.2% of the variation in individual wages can be attributed to gender differences. Apparently, many other observable and unobservable factors affect a person's wage besides gender. This does not automatically imply that the model that was estimated in Table 2.1 is incorrect or useless: it just indicates the relative (un)importance of gender in explaining individual wage variation.

In the exceptional cases where the model does *not* contain an intercept term, the two expressions for R^2 are not equivalent. The reason is that (2.41) is violated because $\sum_{i=1}^{N} e_i$ is no longer equal to zero. In this situation it is possible that the R^2 computed from (2.42) becomes negative. An alternative measure, which is routinely computed by some software packages if there is no intercept, is the uncentred R^2, which is defined as

$$\text{uncentred } R^2 = \frac{\sum_{i=1}^{N} \hat{y}_i^2}{\sum_{i=1}^{N} y_i^2} = 1 - \frac{\sum_{i=1}^{N} e_i^2}{\sum_{i=1}^{N} y_i^2}. \tag{2.43}$$

Generally, the uncentred R^2 is higher than the standard R^2.

Because the R^2 measures the explained variation in y_i, it is also sensitive to the definition of this variable. For example, explaining wages is different to explaining log wages, and the R^2s will be different. Similarly, models explaining consumption, changes in consumption or consumption growth will not be directly comparable in terms of their R^2s. It is clear that some sources of variation are much harder to explain than others. For example, variation in aggregate consumption for a given country is usually easier to explain than the cross-sectional variation in consumption over individual households. Consequently, there is no absolute benchmark to say that an R^2 is 'high' or 'low'. A value of 0.2 may be high in certain applications but low in others, and even a value of 0.95 may be low in certain contexts.

Sometimes the R^2 is suggested to measure the quality of the econometric model, whereas it measures nothing more than the quality of the linear approximation. As the OLS approach is developed to give the best linear approximation, irrespective of the 'true' model and the validity of its assumptions, estimating a linear model by OLS will always give the best R^2 possible. Any other estimation method, and we will see several below, will lead to lower R^2 values even though the corresponding estimator may have much better statistical properties under the assumptions of the model. Even worse, when the model is not estimated by OLS the two definitions (2.40) and (2.42) are not equivalent and it is not obvious how an R^2 should be defined. For later use, we shall present an alternative definition of the R^2, which for OLS is equivalent to (2.40) and (2.42), and for any other estimator is guaranteed to be between zero and one. It is given by

$$R^2 = \text{corr}^2\{y_i, \hat{y}_i\} = \frac{\left(\sum_{i=1}^{N}(y_i - \bar{y})(\hat{y}_i - \bar{y})\right)^2}{\left(\sum_{i=1}^{N}(y_i - \bar{y})^2\right)\left(\sum_{i=1}^{N}(\hat{y}_i - \bar{y})^2\right)}, \tag{2.44}$$

which denotes the squared (sample) correlation coefficient between the actual and fitted values. Using (2.41) it is easily verified that, for the OLS estimator, (2.44) is equivalent to (2.40). Written in this way, the R^2 can be interpreted to measure how well the variation in $\hat{y}_i$ relates to variation in y_i. Despite this alternative definition, the R^2 reflects the quality of the linear approximation and not necessarily that of the statistical model in which we are interested. Accordingly, the R^2 is typically not the most important aspect of our estimation results.

Another drawback of the R^2 is that it will never decrease if the number of regressors is increased, even if the additional variables have no real explanatory power. A common way to solve this is to correct the variance estimates in (2.42) for the degrees of freedom. This gives the so-called **adjusted** R^2, or $\bar{R}^2$, defined as

$$\bar{R}^2 = 1 - \frac{1/(N-K)\sum_{i=1}^{N} e_i^2}{1/(N-1)\sum_{i=1}^{N}(y_i - \bar{y})^2}. \tag{2.45}$$

This goodness-of-fit measure has some punishment for the inclusion of additional explanatory variables in the model and therefore does not automatically increase when regressors are added to the model (see Chapter 3). In fact, it may decline when a variable is added to the set of regressors. Note that, in extreme cases, the $\bar{R}^2$ may become negative. Also note that the adjusted R^2 is strictly smaller than R^2 unless $K = 1$ and the model only includes an intercept.

2.5 Hypothesis Testing

Under the Gauss–Markov assumptions (A1)–(A4) and normality of the error terms (A5), we saw that the OLS estimator b has a normal distribution with mean β and covariance matrix $\sigma^2(X'X)^{-1}$. We can use this result to develop tests for hypotheses regarding the unknown population parameters β. Starting from (2.39), it follows that the variable

$$z = \frac{b_k - \beta_k}{\sigma\sqrt{c_{kk}}} \tag{2.46}$$

has a standard normal distribution (i.e. a normal distribution with mean 0 and variance 1). If we replace the unknown σ by its estimate s, this is no longer exactly true. It can be shown[7] that the unbiased estimator s^2 defined in (2.35) is independent of b and has a Chi-squared distribution with $N - K$ degrees of freedom. In particular,[8]

$$(N - K)s^2/\sigma^2 \sim \chi^2_{N-K}. \tag{2.47}$$

Consequently, the random variable

$$t_k = \frac{b_k - \beta_k}{s\sqrt{c_{kk}}} \tag{2.48}$$

is the ratio of a standard normal variable and the square root of an independent Chi-squared variable and therefore follows Student's t distribution with $N - K$ degrees of freedom. The t distribution is close to the standard normal distribution except that it has fatter tails, particularly when the number of degrees of freedom $N - K$ is small. The larger the $N - K$, the more closely the t distribution resembles the standard normal, and for sufficiently large $N - K$ the two distributions are identical.

2.5.1 A Simple t-Test

The result above can be used to construct test statistics and confidence intervals. The general idea of hypothesis testing is as follows. Starting from a given hypothesis, the **null hypothesis**, a **test statistic** is computed that has a known distribution *under the assumption that the null hypothesis is valid*. Next, it is decided whether the computed value of the test statistic is unlikely to come from this distribution, which indicates that the null hypothesis is unlikely to hold. Let us illustrate this with an example. Suppose we have a null hypothesis that specifies the value of β_k, say H_0: $\beta_k = \beta_k^0$, where β_k^0 is a specific value chosen by the researcher. If this hypothesis is true, we know that the statistic

$$t_k = \frac{b_k - \beta_k^0}{\text{se}(b_k)} \tag{2.49}$$

has a t distribution with $N - K$ degrees of freedom. If the null hypothesis is not true, the alternative hypothesis H_1: $\beta_k \neq \beta_k^0$ holds. The quantity in (2.49) is a **test statistic** and is computed from the estimate b_k, its standard error $\text{se}(b_k)$, and the hypothesized value β_k^0

[7] The proof of this is beyond the scope of this text. The basic idea is that a sum of squared normals is Chi-squared distributed (see Appendix B).

[8] See Appendix B for details about the distributions in this section.

under the null hypothesis. If the test statistic realizes a value that is very unlikely under the null distribution, we reject the null hypothesis. This corresponds to having very large values for t_k, either positive or negative. To be precise, one rejects the null hypothesis if the probability of observing a value of $|t_k|$ or larger is smaller than a given **significance level** α, often 5%. From this, one can define the **critical values** $t_{N-K;\alpha/2}$ using

$$P\{|t_k| > t_{N-K;\alpha/2}\} = \alpha.$$

For $N - K$ not too small, these critical values are only slightly larger than those of the standard normal distribution, for which the two-tailed critical value for $\alpha = 0.05$ is 1.96. Consequently, at the 5% level the null hypothesis will be rejected if

$$|t_k| > 1.96.$$

The above test is referred to as a **two-sided test** because the alternative hypothesis allows for values of β_k on both sides of β_k^0. Occasionally, the alternative hypothesis is one-sided, for example: the expected wage for a man is larger than that for a woman. Formally, we define the null hypothesis as H_0: $\beta_k \leq \beta_k^0$ with alternative H_1: $\beta_k > \beta_k^0$. Next we consider the distribution of the test statistic t_k at the boundary of the null hypothesis (i.e. under $\beta_k = \beta_k^0$, as before) and we reject the null hypothesis if t_k is too large (note that large values for b_k lead to large values for t_k). Large negative values for t_k are compatible with the null hypothesis and do not lead to its rejection. Thus for this **one-sided test** the critical value is determined from

$$P\{t_k > t_{N-K;\alpha}\} = \alpha.$$

Using the standard normal approximation again, we reject the null hypothesis at the 5% level if

$$t_k > 1.64.$$

Regression packages typically report the following t-value:

$$t_k = \frac{b_k}{\text{se}(b_k)},$$

sometimes referred to as the t-ratio, which is the point estimate divided by its standard error. The t-ratio is the t-statistic one would compute to test the null hypothesis that $\beta_k = 0$, which may be a hypothesis that is of economic interest as well. If it is rejected, it is said that 'b_k differs significantly from zero', or that the corresponding variable 'x_{ik} has a statistically significant impact on y_i'. Often we simply say that (the effect of) 'x_{ik} is statistically significant'. If an explanatory variable is statistically significant, this does not necessarily imply that its impact is economically meaningful. Sometimes, particularly with large data sets, a coefficient can be estimated very accurately, and we reject the hypothesis that it is zero, although the economic magnitude of its effect is very small. Conversely, if a variable is insignificant this does not necessarily mean that it has no impact. Insignificance can result from absence of the effect, or from imprecision, particularly if the sample is small or exhibits little variation. It is good practice to pay attention to the magnitude of the estimated coefficients as well as to their statistical significance. Confidence intervals are also very useful, as they combine information about the economic magnitude of an effect as well as its precision.

A **confidence interval** can be defined as the interval of all values for β_k^0 for which the null hypothesis that $\beta_k = \beta_k^0$ is not rejected by the t-tests. Loosely speaking, given the estimate b_k and its associated standard error, a confidence interval gives a range of values that are likely to contain the true value β_k. It is derived from the fact that the following inequalities hold with probability $1 - \alpha$:

$$-t_{N-K;\alpha/2} < \frac{b_k - \beta_k}{\mathrm{se}(b_k)} < t_{N-K;\alpha/2}, \tag{2.50}$$

or

$$b_k - t_{N-K;\alpha/2}\mathrm{se}(b_k) < \beta_k < b_k + t_{N-K;\alpha/2}\mathrm{se}(b_k). \tag{2.51}$$

Consequently, using the standard normal approximation, a 95% confidence interval (setting $\alpha = 0.05$) for β_k is given by the interval

$$[b_k - 1.96\mathrm{se}(b_k), b_k + 1.96\mathrm{se}(b_k)]. \tag{2.52}$$

In repeated sampling, 95% of these intervals will contain the true value β_k which is a fixed but unknown number (and thus not stochastic). Shorter intervals (corresponding to lower standard errors) are obviously more informative, as they narrow down the range of plausible values for the true parameter β_k.

2.5.2 Example: Individual Wages (Continued)

From the results in Table 2.1 we can compute t-ratios and perform simple tests. For example, if we want to test whether $\beta_2 = 0$, we construct the t-statistic as the estimate divided by its standard error to get $t = 10.38$. Given the large number of observations, the appropriate t distribution is virtually identical to the standard normal one, so the 5% two-tailed critical value is 1.96. This means that we clearly reject the null hypothesis that $\beta_2 = 0$. That is, we reject that in the population the expected wage differential between males and females is zero. We can also compute a confidence interval, which has bounds $1.17 \pm 1.96 \times 0.11$. This means that with 95% confidence we can say that over the entire population the expected wage differential between males and females is between \$0.95 and \$1.39 per hour. Our sample thus provides a reasonably accurate estimate of the wage differential, suggesting that an economically meaningful difference exists between (average) wages for males and females.

2.5.3 Testing One Linear Restriction

The test discussed above involves a restriction on a single coefficient. Often, a hypothesis of economic interest implies a linear restriction on more than one coefficient, such as[9] $\beta_2 + \beta_3 + \cdots + \beta_K = 1$. In general, we can formulate such a linear hypothesis as

$$H_0: \; r_1\beta_1 + \cdots + r_K\beta_K = r'\beta = q, \tag{2.53}$$

for some scalar value q and a K-dimensional vector r. We can test the hypothesis in (2.53) using the result that $r'b$ is the BLUE for $r'\beta$ with variance $V\{r'b\} = r'V\{b\}r$. Replacing

[9] For example, in a Cobb–Douglas production function, written as a linear regression model in logs, constant returns to scale corresponds to the sum of all slope parameters (the coefficients for all log inputs) being equal to one.

σ^2 in the covariance matrix $V\{b\}$ by its estimate s^2 produces the estimated covariance matrix, denoted as $\hat{V}\{b\}$. Consequently, the standard error of the linear combination $r'b$ is $\text{se}(r'b) = \sqrt{r'\hat{V}\{b\}r}$. As b is K-variate normal, $r'b$ is normal as well (see Appendix B), so we have

$$\frac{r'b - r'\beta}{\text{se}(r'b)} \sim t_{N-K}, \tag{2.54}$$

which is a straightforward generalization of (2.48).[10] The test statistic for H_0 follows as

$$t = \frac{r'b - q}{\text{se}(r'b)}, \tag{2.55}$$

which has a t_{N-K} distribution *under the null hypothesis*. At the 5% level, absolute values of t in excess of 1.96 (the normal approximation) lead to rejection of the null. This represents the most general version of the ***t*-test**. Any modern software package will provide easy ways to calculate (2.55), with (2.49) as a special case.

2.5.4 A Joint Test of Significance of Regression Coefficients

A standard test that is typically automatically supplied by a regression package is a test for the joint hypothesis that all coefficients, except the intercept β_1, are equal to zero. We shall discuss this procedure slightly more generally by testing the null that J of the K coefficients are equal to zero ($J < K$). Without loss of generality, assume that these are the last J coefficients in the model

$$H_0: \ \beta_{K-J+1} = \cdots = \beta_K = 0. \tag{2.56}$$

The alternative hypothesis in this case is that H_0 is not true, that is, at least one of these J coefficients is not equal to zero.

The easiest test procedure in this case is to compare the sum of squared residuals of the full model with the sum of squared residuals of the restricted model (which is the model with the last J regressors omitted). Denote the residual sum of squares of the full model by S_1 and that of the restricted model by S_0. If the null hypothesis is correct, one would expect that the sum of squares with the restriction imposed is only slightly larger than that in the unrestricted case. A test statistic can be obtained by using the following result, which we present without proof. Under the null hypothesis and assumptions (A1)–(A5) it holds that

$$\frac{S_0 - S_1}{\sigma^2} \sim \chi^2_J. \tag{2.57}$$

From earlier results we know that $(N-K)s^2/\sigma^2 = S_1/\sigma^2 \sim \chi^2_{N-K}$. Moreover, under the null hypothesis it can be shown that $S_0 - S_1$ and s^2 are independent. Consequently, we can define the following test statistic:

$$F = \frac{(S_0 - S_1)/J}{S_1/(N-K)}. \tag{2.58}$$

[10] The statistic is the same if r is a K-dimensional vector of zeros with a 1 on the kth position.

Under the null hypothesis, F has an F distribution with J and $N - K$ degrees of freedom, denoted as F^J_{N-K}. If we use the definition of the R^2 from (2.42), we can also write this F-statistic as

$$F = \frac{(R_1^2 - R_0^2)/J}{(1 - R_1^2)/(N - K)}, \tag{2.59}$$

where R_1^2 and R_0^2 are the usual goodness-of-fit measures for the unrestricted and the restricted models, respectively. This shows that the test can be interpreted as testing whether the increase in R^2 moving from the restricted model to the more general model is significant.

It is clear that in this case only very large values for the test statistic imply rejection of the null hypothesis. Despite the two-sided alternative hypothesis, the critical values $F^J_{N-K;\alpha}$ for this test are one-sided and defined by the following equality:

$$P\{F > F^J_{N-K;\alpha}\} = \alpha,$$

where α is the significance level of the test. For example, if $N - K = 60$ and $J = 3$ the critical value at the 5% level is 2.76. The resulting test is referred to as the ***F*-test**.

In most applications the estimators for different elements in the parameter vector will be correlated, which means that the explanatory powers of the explanatory variables overlap. Consequently, the marginal contribution of each explanatory variable, when added last, may be quite small. Hence, it is perfectly possible for the t-tests on each variable's coefficient to be insignificant, while the combined F-test for a number of these coefficients is highly significant. That is, it is possible that the null hypothesis $\beta_1 = 0$ is as such not unlikely, that the null $\beta_2 = 0$ is not unlikely, but that the joint null $\beta_1 = \beta_2 = 0$ is quite unlikely to be true. As a consequence, in general, t-tests on each restriction separately may not reject, while a joint F-test does. The converse is also true: it is possible that individual t-tests do reject the null, while the joint test does not. The section on multicollinearity below illustrates this point. Section 3.6 provides an empirical illustration.

A special case of this F-test is sometimes misleadingly referred to as the model test,[11] where one tests the significance of all regressors, that is, one tests $H_0 : \beta_2 = \beta_3 = \cdots = \beta_K = 0$, meaning that all partial slope coefficients are equal to zero. The appropriate test statistic in this case is

$$F = \frac{(S_0 - S_1)/(K - 1)}{S_1/(N - K)}, \tag{2.60}$$

where S_1 is the residual sum of squares of the model, that is $S_1 = \sum_i e_i^2$, and S_0 is the residual sum of squares of the restricted model containing only an intercept term, that is, $S_0 = \sum_i (y_i - \bar{y})^2$.[12] Because the restricted model has an R^2 of zero by construction, the test statistic can also be written as

$$F = \frac{R^2/(K - 1)}{(1 - R^2)/(N - K)}. \tag{2.61}$$

[11] This terminology is misleading as it does not in any way test whether the restrictions imposed by the model are correct. The only thing tested is whether all coefficients, excluding the intercept, are equal to zero, in which case one would have a trivial model with an R^2 of zero. As shown in (2.61), the test statistic associated with the model test is simply a function of the R^2.

[12] Using the definition of the OLS estimator, it is easily verified that the intercept term in a model without regressors is estimated as the sample average $\bar{y}$. Any other choice would result in a larger S value.

This F-statistic is routinely provided by the majority of all regression packages. Note that it is a simple function of the R^2 of the model. If the test based on F does not reject the null hypothesis, one can conclude that the model performs rather poorly: a 'model' with just an intercept term would not do significantly worse. However, the converse is certainly not true: if the test does reject the null, one cannot conclude that the model is good, perfect, valid or correct. An alternative model may perform much better. Chapter 3 pays more attention to this issue.

2.5.5 Example: Individual Wages (Continued)

The fact that we concluded previously that there was a significant difference between expected wage rates for males and females does not necessarily point to discrimination. It is possible that working males and females differ in terms of their characteristics, for example their years of schooling. To analyse this, we can extend the regression model with additional explanatory variables, for example $school_i$, which denotes the years of schooling, and $exper_i$, which denotes experience in years. The model is now interpreted to describe the conditional expected wage of an individual given his or her gender, years of schooling and experience, and can be written as

$$wage_i = \beta_1 + \beta_2 male_i + \beta_3 school_i + \beta_4 exper_i + \varepsilon_i.$$

The coefficient β_2 for $male_i$ now measures the difference in expected wage between a male and a female *with the same schooling and experience*. Similarly, the coefficient β_3 for $school_i$ gives the expected wage difference between two individuals with the same experience and gender where one has an additional year of schooling. In general, the coefficients in a multiple regression model can only be interpreted under a **ceteris paribus condition**, which says that the other variables that are included in the model are constant.

Estimation by OLS produces the results given in Table 2.2. The coefficient for $male_i$ now suggests that, if we compare an arbitrary male and female with the same years of schooling and experience, the expected wage differential is \$1.34 compared with \$1.17 before. With a standard error of \$0.11, this difference is still statistically highly significant. The null hypothesis that schooling has no effect on a person's wage, given gender and experience, can be tested using the t-test described previously, with a test statistic of 19.48. Clearly the null hypothesis is rejected at any reasonable level of significance. The estimated wage increase from one additional year of schooling, keeping years of experience fixed, is \$0.64. It should not be surprising, given these results, that the joint hypothesis that all three partial slope coefficients are zero, that is, wages are not affected

Table 2.2 OLS results wage equation

Dependent variable: *wage*

Variable	Estimate	Standard error	t-ratio
constant	−3.3800	0.4650	−17.2692
male	1.3444	0.1077	12.4853
school	0.6388	0.0328	19.4780
exper	0.1248	0.0238	5.2530

$s = 3.0462$ $R^2 = 0.1326$ $\bar{R}^2 = 0.1318$ $F = 167.63$

by gender, schooling or experience, is rejected as well. The F-statistic takes the value of 167.6, the appropriate 5% critical value being 2.60.

Finally, we can use the above results to compare this model with the simpler one in Table 2.1. The R^2 has increased from 0.0317 to 0.1326, which means that the current model is able to explain 13.3% of the within-sample variation in wages. We can perform a joint test on the hypothesis that the two additional variables, schooling and experience, both have zero coefficients, by performing the F-test described above. The test statistic in (2.59) can be computed from the R^2s reported in Tables 2.1 and 2.2 as

$$F = \frac{(0.1326 - 0.0317)/2}{(1 - 0.1326)/(3294 - 4)} = 191.35.$$

With a 5% critical value of 3.00, the null hypothesis is obviously rejected. We can thus conclude that the model that includes gender, schooling and experience performs significantly better than the model that only includes gender.

2.5.6 The General Case

The most general linear null hypothesis is a combination of the previous two cases and comprises a set of J linear restrictions on the coefficients. We can formulate these restrictions as

$$R\beta = q,$$

where R is a $J \times K$ matrix, assumed to be of full row rank,[13] and q is a J-dimensional vector. An example of this is the set of restrictions $\beta_2 + \beta_3 + \cdots + \beta_K = 1$ and $\beta_2 = \beta_3$, in which case $J = 2$ and

$$R = \begin{pmatrix} 0 & 1 & 1 & \cdots & \cdots & 1 \\ 0 & 1 & -1 & 0 & \cdots & 0 \end{pmatrix}, \quad q = \begin{pmatrix} 1 \\ 0 \end{pmatrix}.$$

In principle it is possible to estimate the model imposing the above restrictions, such that the test procedure of Subsection 2.5.4 can be employed. In this case, the F-test in (2.59) can be used, where R_0^2 denotes the R^2 of the restricted model with $R\beta = q$ imposed.

For later use, it is instructive to discuss an alternative formulation of the F-test that does not require explicit estimation of the restricted model. This alternative derivation starts from the result that, under assumptions (A1)–(A5), Rb has a normal distribution with mean vector $R\beta$ and covariance matrix $V\{Rb\} = RV\{b\}R'$ (compare (2.38)). As a result, under the null hypothesis the quadratic form

$$(Rb - q)'V\{Rb\}^{-1}(Rb - q) \tag{2.62}$$

has a Chi-squared distribution with J degrees of freedom. Because the covariance matrix in (2.62) is unknown, we replace it with an estimate by substituting s^2 for σ^2. The resulting test statistic is given by

$$\xi = (Rb - q)'[R\hat{V}\{b\}R']^{-1}(Rb - q), \tag{2.63}$$

where $\hat{V}\{b\}$ is given in (2.36). In large samples, the difference between σ^2 and s^2 has little impact and the test statistic in (2.63) approximately has a Chi-squared distribution

[13] Full row rank implies that the restrictions do not exhibit any linear dependencies.

(under the null hypothesis).[14] The corresponding test is sometimes referred to as the Chi-squared version of the F-test. In fact, (2.63) presents the general structure of the **Wald test** on a set of linear restrictions and is easily extended to cover more general situations. We will use this structure below for cases where the Gauss–Markov assumptions are not all satisfied, and where the model deviates from the linear regression model.

To obtain the exact sampling distribution under assumptions (A1)–(A5), we can use (2.47) again such that a test statistic can be obtained as the ratio of two independent Chi-squared variables (divided by their degrees of freedom). This leads to $F = \xi/J$ or

$$F = \frac{(Rb - q)'(R(X'X)^{-1}R')^{-1}(Rb - q)}{Js^2}, \tag{2.64}$$

which, under H_0, follows an F distribution with J and $N - K$ degrees of freedom. As before, large values of F lead to rejection of the null. It can be shown that the F-statistic in (2.64) is algebraically identical to the ones in (2.58) and (2.59) and most modern software packages will provide easy ways to calculate them. When we are testing one linear restriction ($J = 1$), it can be shown that (2.64) is the square of the corresponding t-statistic, as given in (2.55), and the two tests are equivalent. Some software packages tend to report the F-version of the test, even with one linear restriction. The disadvantage of this is that the sign of the t-statistic is not immediately clear, making one-sided hypothesis testing a bit more cumbersome. It is recommended (and customary) to report t-statistics in these cases.

2.5.7 Size, Power and p-Values

When a hypothesis is statistically tested, two types of errors can be made. The first one is that we reject the null hypothesis while it is actually true, and is referred to as a **type I error** ('a false positive'). The second one, a **type II error** ('a false negative'), is that the null hypothesis is not rejected while the alternative is true. The probability of a type I error is directly controlled by researchers through their choice of the significance level α. When a test is performed at the 5% level, the probability of rejecting the null hypothesis while it is true is 5%. This probability (significance level) is often referred to as the **size** of the test. The probability of a type II error depends upon the true parameter values. Intuitively, if the truth deviates much from the stated null hypothesis, the probability of such an error will be relatively small, while it will be quite large if the null hypothesis is close to the truth. The reverse probability, that is, the probability of rejecting the null hypothesis when it is false, is known as the **power** of the test. It indicates how 'powerful' a test is in finding deviations from the null hypothesis (depending upon the true parameter value). In general, reducing the size of a test will decrease its power, so that there is a trade-off between type I and type II errors.

Suppose that we are testing the hypothesis that $\beta_2 = 0$, whereas its true value is 0.1. It is clear that the probability that we reject the null hypothesis depends upon the standard error of our OLS estimator b_2 and thus, among other things, upon the sample size. The larger the sample, the smaller is the standard error and the more likely we are to reject. This implies that type II errors become increasingly unlikely if we have large samples.

[14] The approximate result is obtained from the asymptotic distribution, and also holds if normality of the error terms is not imposed (see Subsection 2.6.2). The approximation is more accurate if the sample size is large.

To compensate for this, researchers typically reduce the probability of type I errors (i.e. of incorrectly rejecting the null hypothesis) by lowering the size α of their tests. This explains why in large samples it is more appropriate to choose a size of 1% or less rather than the 'traditional' 5%. Similarly, in very small samples we may prefer to work with a significance level of 10%.

Commonly, the null hypothesis that is chosen is assumed to be true unless there is convincing evidence to the contrary. This suggests that, if a test does not reject, for whatever reason, we stick to the null hypothesis. This view is not completely appropriate. A range of alternative hypotheses could be tested (e.g. $\beta_2 = 0$, $\beta_2 = 0.1$ and $\beta_2 = 0.5$) with the result that none of them is rejected. Obviously, concluding that these three null hypotheses are simultaneously true would be ridiculous. The only appropriate conclusion is that we *cannot reject* that β_2 is 0, nor that it is 0.1 or 0.5. Sometimes econometric tests are simply not very powerful, and very large sample sizes are needed to reject a given hypothesis. Calculating a confidence interval will help to see this. If the confidence bounds are wide, a wide range of parameter values are consistent with the data.

Most software packages routinely provide p-values with any test statistic that is calculated. A p-value denotes the probability, under the null hypothesis, to find the reported value of the test statistic or a more extreme one. If the p-value is smaller than the significance level a, the null hypothesis is rejected. Checking p-values allows researchers to draw their conclusions without consulting the appropriate critical values, making them a 'convenient' source of information. It also shows the sensitivity of the decision to reject the null hypothesis with respect to the choice of significance level. For example, a p-value of 0.08 indicates that the null hypothesis is rejected at the 10% significance level, but not at the 5% level. However, p-values are often misinterpreted or misused, as stressed by a recent statement of the American Statistical Association (Wasserstein and Lazar, 2016). For example, it is inappropriate (though a common mistake) to interpret a p-value as giving the probability that the null hypothesis is true. The p-value gives the probability of getting certain results if the null is true, not the probability that the null is true if we have obtained certain results (see Cumming, 2012, Chapter 2, for more discussion).

The fact that p-values are easily available allows researchers to perform statistical tests without the necessity to evaluate test statistics or confidence bounds, and without the necessity to even understand the test that is performed. Focusing just on p-values is not recommended, as one may easily confuse statistical significance with economic significance.[15] Moreover, p-values are random variables, just like test statistics. In a new sample, the inferred level of significance will therefore be different. Again, calculating confidence intervals is more informative (see Cumming, 2012, for an extensive discussion on this issue).

Unfortunately, in empirical work some researchers are overly obsessed with obtaining 'significant' results and finding p-values smaller than 0.05 (and this also extends to journal editors). If publication decisions depend on the statistical significance of research findings, the literature as a whole will overstate the size of the true effect. This is referred to as publication bias (or 'file drawer' bias). Masicampo and Lalande (2012) talk about 'a peculiar prevalence of p-values just below 0.05' in the psychology literature.

[15] 'A common problem is that researchers misinterpret p-values by equating small p-values with important or reproducible findings' (Starbuck, 2016). As stressed by Wasserstein and Lazar (2016), 'any effect, no matter how tiny, can produce a small p-value if the sample size or measurement precision is high enough'.

Ashenfelter, Harmon and Oosterbeek (1999) provide an analysis of this problem in the empirical literature estimating the relationship between schooling and wages. Investigating more than 50 000 tests published in three leading economic journals, Brodeur et al. (2015) conclude that the distribution of *p*-values indicates both selection by journals as well as a tendency of researchers to inflate the value of almost-rejected tests by choosing slightly more 'significant' specifications. See also the discussion on data mining in Subsection 3.2.2.

2.5.8 Reporting Regression Results

To conclude this section, let us briefly discuss how to report regression results. Importantly, it should be clear from a table, or from the notes to a table, what exactly is the dependent variable. Readers do not wish to have to read through several pages of text to identify what a model tries to explain. If relevant, be also specific on the units of measurement (or transformations of the dependent variable), so that coefficient estimates can be interpreted more easily. For example, when estimating a wage equation, it is helpful to know whether the dependent variable is an hourly wage rage, a monthly wage rate, or the natural logarithm of either of these. In all cases the coefficient estimates should be reported, at least for the main variables of interest. To save space, coefficients for control variables (e.g. time dummies, industry dummies) are often suppressed. If so, make clear in the reporting that these variables are included in the model anyway.

It is also useful to report at least the most basic statistics of the regression, like the number of observations and the (adjusted) R^2. Depending on the context, additional statistics can be reported that facilitate comparison of alternative model specifications, or that allow one to check the validity of the model assumptions. Examples of these will be discussed later. Regarding estimation precision and statistical significance, standard errors, *t*-values and/or *p*-values could be reported. Most articles report either standard errors or *t*-values (in parentheses); because there is no easy way to identify which of the two options is chosen, it is convenient to add a note to the results stating, for example, 'standard errors in parentheses'. Because standard errors are also useful to test a hypothesis other than some effect being zero (e.g. $\beta_k = 1$), they are slightly preferred to *t*-values, although the latter choice makes it easy to quickly establish statistical significance (particularly in cases where, for example, a coefficient estimate is reported as 0.02 with a standard error of 0.01). Standard errors can be complemented with asterisks to indicate significance at 1, 5 or 10% levels. When reporting *p*-values, it is recommended to report exact *p*-values, not just '$p < 0.05$'. Finally, you should report all results with a 'reasonable' number of digits. For example, reporting an estimate as 0.81853086 suggests a much larger degree of precision than is warranted. On the other hand, reporting it as 0.8 would be rather imprecise. In the text you can use rounded numbers, like 'the estimated wage differential due to one more year of education is $0.82 per hour', while reporting more precise numbers in the tables. When relevant, add the units of measurement when interpreting an estimated coefficient.

Note that OLS is an estimation method, not a model. On the one hand, we can talk about a model like (2.24), its assumptions and how its specification is linked to economic theory, without using any data at all. This is because the econometric model is assumed to apply to a well-defined population, and its unknown coefficients reflect relationships in the population. On the other hand, the linear regression model can be estimated making alternative sets of assumptions and using other methods than OLS. Therefore, it is not recommended to report that you have estimated 'an OLS model'. It is better to state that you have estimated a linear regression model, using ordinary least squares, and specifying the crucial assumptions made (e.g. random sample and homoskedasticity). Of course, if you use OLS as an algebraic tool only (to obtain the best linear approximation), there is no underlying population regression model.

2.6 Asymptotic Properties of the OLS Estimator

In many cases, the small sample properties of the OLS estimator may deviate from those discussed above. For example, if the error terms in the linear model ε_i do not follow a normal distribution, it is no longer the case that the sampling distribution of the OLS estimator b is normal. If assumption (A2) of the Gauss–Markov conditions is violated, it can no longer be shown that b has an expected value of β. In fact, the linear regression model under the Gauss–Markov assumptions and with normal error terms is one of the very few cases in econometrics where the exact sampling distribution of the estimator is known. As soon as we relax some of these assumptions or move to alternative models, the small sample properties of the estimator are typically unknown. In such cases we use an alternative approach to evaluate the quality of an estimator, which is based on asymptotic theory. Asymptotic theory refers to the question as to what happens if, hypothetically, the sample size grows infinitely large. Asymptotically, econometric estimators usually have nice properties, like normality, and we use the asymptotic properties to approximate the properties in the finite sample that we happen to have. This section presents a first discussion of the asymptotic properties of the OLS estimator. More details are provided in Pesaran (2015, Chapter 8).

2.6.1 Consistency

Let us start with the linear model under the Gauss–Markov assumptions. In this case we know that the OLS estimator b has the following first two moments:

$$E\{b\} = \beta \tag{2.65}$$

$$V\{b\} = \sigma^2\left(\sum_{i=1}^{N} x_i x_i'\right)^{-1} = \sigma^2(X'X)^{-1}. \tag{2.66}$$

Unless we assume that the error terms are normal, the shape of the distribution of b is unknown. It is, however, possible to say something about the distribution of b, at least approximately. A first starting point is the so-called **Chebyshev's inequality**, which says that the probability that a random variable z deviates more than a positive number δ from its mean is bounded by its variance divided by δ^2, that is,

$$P\{|z - E\{z\}| > \delta\} < \frac{V\{z\}}{\delta^2}, \quad \text{for all} \quad \delta > 0. \tag{2.67}$$

For the OLS estimator this implies that its kth element satisfies

$$P\{|b_k - \beta_k| > \delta\} < \frac{V\{b_k\}}{\delta^2} = \frac{\sigma^2 c_{kk}}{\delta^2} \quad \text{for all} \quad \delta > 0, \tag{2.68}$$

where c_{kk}, as before, is the (k, k) element in $(X'X)^{-1} = (\sum_{i=1}^{N} x_i x_i')^{-1}$. This inequality becomes useful if we fix δ at some small positive number, and then let, in our mind, the sample size N grow to infinity. Then what happens? It is clear that $\sum_{i=1}^{N} x_i x_i'$ increases as the number of terms grows, so that the variance of b decreases as the sample size increases. If we assume that[16]

$$\frac{1}{N}\sum_{i=1}^{N} x_i x_i' \text{ converges to a finite nonsingular matrix } \Sigma_{xx} \tag{A6}$$

if the sample size N becomes infinitely large, it follows directly from the above inequality that

$$\lim_{N\to\infty} P\{|b_k - \beta_k| > \delta\} = 0 \text{ for all } \delta > 0. \tag{2.69}$$

This says that, asymptotically, the probability that the OLS estimator deviates more than δ from the true parameter value is zero. We usually refer to this property as 'the probability limit of b is β', or 'b converges in probability to β', or just[17]

$$\operatorname{plim} b = \beta. \tag{2.70}$$

Note that b is a vector of random variables whose distribution depends on N, and β is a vector of fixed (unknown) numbers. When an estimator for β converges to the true value, we say that it is a **consistent estimator**. Any estimator that satisfies (2.69) is a consistent estimator for β, even if it is biased.

Consistency is a large sample property and, loosely speaking, says that, if we obtain more and more observations, the probability that our estimator is some positive number away from the true value β becomes smaller and smaller. Values that b may take that are not close to β become increasingly unlikely. In many cases, one cannot prove that an estimator is unbiased, and it is possible that no unbiased estimator exists (e.g. in nonlinear or dynamic models). In these cases, a minimum requirement for an estimator to be useful is that it is consistent. We shall therefore mainly be concerned with consistency of an estimator, not with its (un)biasedness in small samples.

A useful property of probability limits (plims) is the following. If plim $b = \beta$ and g(.) is a continuous function, it also holds that

$$\operatorname{plim} g(b) = g(\beta). \tag{2.71}$$

This guarantees that the parameterization employed is irrelevant for consistency. For example, if s^2 is a consistent estimator for σ^2, then s is a consistent estimator for σ. Note that this result does not hold for unbiasedness, as $E\{s\}^2 \neq E\{s^2\}$ (see Appendix B).

[16] The nonsingularity of Σ_{xx} requires that, asymptotically, there is no multicollinearity. The requirement that the limit is finite is a 'regularity' condition, which will be satisfied in most empirical applications. A sufficient condition is that the regressors are independent drawings from the same distribution with a finite variance. Violations typically occur in time series contexts where one or more of the x-variables may be trended. We shall return to this issue in Chapters 8 and 9.

[17] Unless indicated otherwise, lim and plim refer to the (probability) limit for the sample size N going to infinity ($N \to \infty$).

The OLS estimator is consistent under substantially weaker conditions than the Gauss–Markov assumptions employed earlier. To see this, let us write the OLS estimator as

$$b = \left(\frac{1}{N} \sum_{i=1}^{N} x_i x_i' \right)^{-1} \frac{1}{N} \sum_{i=1}^{N} x_i y_i = \beta + \left(\frac{1}{N} \sum_{i=1}^{N} x_i x_i' \right)^{-1} \frac{1}{N} \sum_{i=1}^{N} x_i \varepsilon_i. \tag{2.72}$$

This expression states that the OLS estimator b equals the vector of true population coefficients β plus a vector of estimation errors that depend upon the sample averages of $x_i x_i'$ and $x_i \varepsilon_i$. This decomposition plays a key role in establishing the properties of the OLS estimator and stresses again that this requires assumptions on ε_i and its relation with the explanatory variables. If the sample size increases, the sample averages in (2.72) are taken over increasingly more observations. It seems reasonable to assume, and it can be shown to be true under very weak conditions,[18] that in the limit these sample averages converge to the corresponding population means. Then, under assumption (A6), we have

$$\text{plim}(b - \beta) = \Sigma_{xx}^{-1} E\{x_i \varepsilon_i\}, \tag{2.73}$$

which shows that the OLS estimator is consistent if it holds that

$$E\{x_i \varepsilon_i\} = 0. \tag{A7}$$

This condition simply says that the error term is mean zero and uncorrelated with any of the explanatory variables. Note that $E\{\varepsilon_i | x_i\} = 0$ implies (A7), while the converse is not necessarily true.[19] Thus we can conclude that the OLS estimator b is consistent for β under conditions (A6) and (A7), which are much weaker than the Gauss–Markov conditions (A1)–(A4) required for unbiasedness. We shall discuss the relevance of this below.

Similarly, the least squares estimator s^2 for the error variance σ^2 is consistent under conditions (A6), (A7) and (A3) (and some weak regularity conditions). The intuition is that, with b converging to β, the residuals e_i become asymptotically equivalent to the error terms ε_i, so that the sample variance of e_i will converge to the error variance σ^2, as defined in (A3).

2.6.2 Asymptotic Normality

If the small sample distribution of an estimator is unknown, the best we can do is try to find some approximation. In most cases, one uses an asymptotic approximation (for N going to infinity) based on the **asymptotic distribution**. Most estimators in econometrics can be shown to be asymptotically normally distributed (under weak regularity conditions). By the asymptotic distribution of a consistent estimator $\hat{\beta}$ we mean the distribution of $\sqrt{N}(\hat{\beta} - \beta)$ as N goes to infinity. The reason for the factor $\sqrt{N}$ is that asymptotically $\hat{\beta}$ is equal to β with probability one for all consistent estimators. That is, $\hat{\beta} - \beta$ has a degenerate distribution for $N \to \infty$ with all probability mass at zero.

---

[18] The result that sample averages converge to population means is provided in several versions of the **law of large numbers** (see Davidson and MacKinnon, 2004, Section 4.5 or Greene, 2012, Appendix D).

[19] To be precise, $E\{\varepsilon_i | x_i\} = 0$ implies that $E\{\varepsilon_i g(x_i)\} = 0$ for *any* function g (see Appendix B).

If we multiply by $\sqrt{N}$ and consider the asymptotic distribution of $\sqrt{N}(\hat{\beta} - \beta)$, this will usually be a nondegenerate normal distribution. In that case $\sqrt{N}$ is referred to as the **rate of convergence**, and it is sometimes said that the corresponding estimator is root-N-consistent. In later chapters we shall see a few cases where the rate of convergence differs from root N.

For the OLS estimator it can be shown that under the Gauss–Markov conditions (A1)–(A4) combined with (A6) we have

$$\sqrt{N}(b - \beta) \to \mathcal{N}(0, \sigma^2 \Sigma_{xx}^{-1}), \tag{2.74}$$

where $\to$ means 'is asymptotically distributed as'. Thus, the OLS estimator b is consistent and asymptotically normal (CAN), with variance–covariance matrix $\sigma^2 \Sigma_{xx}^{-1}$. In practice, where we necessarily have a finite sample, we can use this result to approximate the distribution of b as

$$b \overset{a}{\sim} \mathcal{N}(\beta, \sigma^2 \Sigma_{xx}^{-1}/N), \tag{2.75}$$

where $\overset{a}{\sim}$ means 'is approximately distributed as'.

Because the unknown matrix Σ_{xx} will be consistently estimated by the sample mean $(1/N)\sum_{i=1}^{N} x_i x_i'$, this approximate distribution is estimated as

$$b \overset{a}{\sim} \mathcal{N}\left(\beta, s^2 \left(\sum_{i=1}^{N} x_i x_i'\right)^{-1}\right). \tag{2.76}$$

This provides a distributional result for the OLS estimator b based upon asymptotic theory, which is approximately valid in small samples. The quality of the approximation increases as the sample size grows, and in a given application it is typically hoped that the sample size will be sufficiently large for the approximation to be reasonably accurate. Because the result in (2.76) corresponds exactly to what is used in the case of the Gauss–Markov assumptions combined with the assumption of normal error terms, it follows that all the distributional results for the OLS estimator reported above, including those for t- and F-statistics, are approximately valid, *even if the errors are not normally distributed*.

Because, asymptotically, a t_{N-K} distributed variable converges to a standard normal one, it is not uncommon to use the critical values from a standard normal distribution (like the 1.96 at the 5% level) for all inferences, while not imposing normality of the errors. Thus, to test the hypothesis that $\beta_k = \beta_k^0$ for some given value β_k^0, we proceed on the basis that (see (2.44))

$$t_k = \frac{b_k - \beta_k^0}{\mathrm{se}(b_k)}$$

approximately has a standard normal distribution (under the null), under assumptions (A1)–(A4) and (A6). Similarly, to test the multiple restrictions $R\beta = q$, we proceed on the basis that (see (2.62))

$$\xi = (Rb - q)' \hat{V}\{Rb\}^{-1}(Rb - q)$$

has an approximate Chi-squared distribution with J degrees of freedom, where J is the number of restrictions that is tested.

It is possible further to relax the assumptions without affecting the validity of the results in (2.74) and (2.76). In particular, we can relax assumption (A2) to

$$x_i \text{ and } \varepsilon_i \text{ are independent.} \tag{A8}$$

This condition does not rule out a dependence between x_i and ε_j for $i \neq j$, which is of interest for models with lagged dependent variables. Note that (A8) implies (A7). Further discussion on the asymptotic distribution of the OLS estimator and how it can be estimated is provided in Chapters 4 and 5.

2.6.3 Small Samples and Asymptotic Theory

The linear regression model under the Gauss–Markov conditions is one of the very few cases in which the finite sample properties of the estimator and test statistics are known. In many other circumstances and models it is not possible or extremely difficult to derive small sample properties of an econometric estimator. In such cases, most econometricians are (necessarily) satisfied with knowing 'approximate' properties. As discussed above, such approximate properties are typically derived from asymptotic theory in which one considers what happens to an estimator or test statistic if the size of the sample is (hypothetically) growing to infinity. As a result, one expects that approximate properties based on asymptotic theory will work reasonably well if the sample size is sufficiently large.

Unfortunately, there is no unambiguous definition of what is 'sufficiently large'. In simple circumstances a sample size of 30 may be sufficient, whereas in more complicated or extreme cases a sample of 1000 may still be insufficient for the asymptotic approximation to be reasonably accurate. To obtain some idea about the small sample properties, Monte Carlo simulation studies are often performed. In a **Monte Carlo study**, a large number (e.g. 1000) of simulated samples are drawn from a data generating process, specified by the researcher. Each random sample is used to compute an estimator and/or a test statistic, and the distributional characteristics over the different replications are analysed.

As an illustration, consider the data generating process

$$y_i = \beta_1 + \beta_2 x_i + \varepsilon_i,$$

corresponding to the simple linear regression model. To conduct a simulation, we need to choose the distribution of x_i, or fix a set of values for x_i, we need to specify the values for β_1 and β_2 and we need to specify the distribution of ε_i. Suppose we consider samples of size N, with fixed values $x_i = 1$ for $i = 1, \ldots, N/2$ (males, say) and $x_i = 0$ otherwise (females).[20] If $\varepsilon_i \sim NID(0, 1)$, independently of x_i, the endogenous variable y_i is also normally distributed with mean $\beta_1 + \beta_2 x_i$ and unit variance. Given these assumptions, a computer can easily generate a sample of N values for y_i. Next, we use this sample to compute the OLS estimator. Replicating this R times, with R newly drawn samples, produces R estimates for β, $b^{(1)}, \ldots, b^{(R)}$, say. Assuming $\beta_1 = 0$ and $\beta_2 = 1$, Figure 2.2 presents a histogram of $R = 1000$ OLS estimates for β_2 based on 1000 simulated samples of size $N = 100$. Because we know that the OLS estimator is unbiased under these assumptions, we expect that $b^{(r)}$ is, on average, close to the true value of 1. Moreover, from the results

[20] N is taken to be an even number.

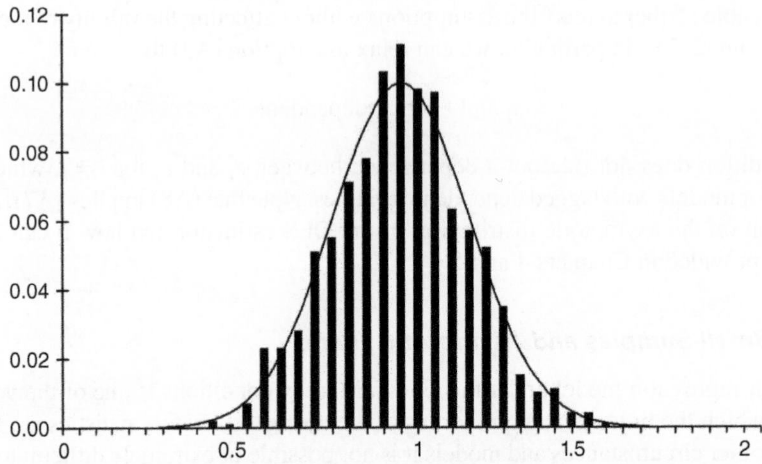

Figure 2.2 Histogram of 1000 OLS estimates with normal density (Monte Carlo results).

in Subsection 2.3.2, and because the R replications are generated independently, we know that the slope coefficient in $b^{(r)}$ is distributed as

$$b_2^{(r)} \sim NID(\beta_2, c_{22}),$$

where $\beta_2 = 1$ and

$$c_{22} = \left[\sum_{i=1}^{N} (x_i - \bar{x})^2\right]^{-1} = 4/N.$$

The larger the number of replications, the more the histogram in Figure 2.2 will resemble the normal distribution. For ease of comparison, the normal density is also drawn.

A Monte Carlo study allows us to investigate the exact sampling distribution of an estimator or a test statistic as a function of the way in which the data are generated. This is useful in cases where one of the model assumptions (A2), (A3), (A4) or (A5) is violated and exact distributional results are unavailable. For example, a consistent estimator may exhibit small sample biases, and a Monte Carlo study may help us in identifying cases in which this small sample bias is substantial and other cases where it can be ignored. When the distribution of a test statistic is approximated on the basis of asymptotic theory, the significance level of the test (e.g. 5%) also holds approximately. The chosen level is then referred to as the nominal significance level or nominal size, while the actual probability of a type I error may be quite different (often larger). A Monte Carlo study allows us to investigate the difference between the nominal and actual significance levels. In addition, we can use a Monte Carlo experiment to analyse the distribution of a test statistic when the null hypothesis is false. This way we can investigate the power of a test. That is, what is the probability of rejecting the null hypothesis when it is actually false. For example, we may analyse the probability that the null hypothesis that $\beta_2 = 0.5$ is rejected as a function of the true value of β_2 (and the sample size N). If the true value is 0.5 this gives us the (actual) size of the test, whereas for $\beta_2 \neq 0.5$ we obtain the power of the test. Finally, we can use a simulation study to analyse the properties of an estimator on the basis of a model that deviates from the data generating process, for example a model that omits a relevant explanatory variable.

While Monte Carlo studies are useful, their results usually strongly depend upon the choices for x_i, β, σ^2 and the sample size N, and therefore cannot necessarily be extrapolated to different settings. Nevertheless, they provide interesting information about the statistical properties of an estimator or test statistic under controlled circumstances. Fortunately, for the linear regression model the asymptotic approximation usually works quite well. As a result, for most applications it is reasonably safe to state that the OLS estimator is approximately normally distributed. More information about Monte Carlo experiments is provided in Davidson and MacKinnon (1993, Chapter 21), while a simple illustration is provided in Patterson (2000, Section 8.2).

2.7 Illustration: The Capital Asset Pricing Model

One of the most important models in finance is the Capital Asset Pricing Model (CAPM). The CAPM is an equilibrium model that assumes that all investors compose their asset portfolio on the basis of a trade-off between the expected return and the variance of the return on their portfolio. This implies that each investor holds a so-called **mean variance efficient** portfolio, a portfolio that gives maximum expected return for a given variance (level of risk). If all investors hold the same beliefs about expected returns and (co)variances of individual assets, and in the absence of transaction costs, taxes and trading restrictions of any kind, it is also the case that the aggregate of all individual portfolios, the **market portfolio**, is mean variance efficient. In this case it can be shown that expected returns on individual assets are linearly related to the expected return on the market portfolio. In particular, it holds that[21]

$$E\{r_{jt} - r_f\} = \beta_j E\{r_{mt} - r_f\}, \tag{2.77}$$

where r_{jt} is the risky return on asset j in period t, r_{mt} is the risky return on the market portfolio and r_f denotes the riskless return, which we assume to be time invariant for simplicity. The proportionality factor β_j is given by

$$\beta_j = \frac{\text{cov}\{r_{jt}, r_{mt}\}}{V\{r_{mt}\}} \tag{2.78}$$

and indicates how strong fluctuations in the returns on asset j are related to movements of the market as a whole. As such, it is a measure of systematic risk (or market risk). Because it is impossible to eliminate systematic risk through a diversification of one's portfolio without affecting the expected return, investors are compensated for bearing this source of risk through a risk premium $E\{r_{mt} - r_f\} > 0$. Accordingly, (2.77) tells us that the expected return on any risky asset, in excess of the riskless rate, is proportional to its 'beta'.

In this section, we consider the CAPM and see how it can be rewritten as a linear regression model, which allows us to estimate and test it. In Subsection 2.6.3 we use the CAPM to analyse the (fraudulent) returns on Bernard Madoff's investment fund.

[21] Because the data correspond to different time periods, we index the observations by t, $t = 1, 2, \ldots, T$, rather than i.

A more extensive discussion of empirical issues related to the CAPM can be found in Berndt (1991) or, more technically, in Campbell, Lo and MacKinlay (1997, Chapter 5) and Gouriéroux and Jasiak (2001, Section 4.2). More details on the CAPM can be found in finance textbooks, for example Elton, Gruber, Brown and Goetzmann (2014, Chapter 13).

2.7.1 The CAPM as a Regression Model

The relationship in (2.77) is an *ex ante* equality in terms of unobserved expectations. Ex post, we only observe realized returns on the different assets over a number of periods. If, however, we make the usual assumption that expectations are rational, so that expectations of economic agents correspond to mathematical expectations, we can derive a relationship from (2.77) that involves actual returns. To see this, let us define the unexpected returns on asset j as

$$u_{jt} = r_{jt} - E\{r_{jt}\},$$

and the unexpected returns on the market portfolio as

$$u_{mt} = r_{mt} - E\{r_{mt}\}.$$

Then, it is possible to rewrite (2.77) as

$$r_{jt} - r_f = \beta_j(r_{mt} - r_f) + \varepsilon_{jt}, \tag{2.79}$$

where

$$\varepsilon_{jt} = u_{jt} - \beta_j u_{mt}.$$

Equation (2.79) is a regression model, without an intercept, where ε_{jt} is treated as an error term. This error term is not something that is just added to the model, but it has a meaning, being a function of unexpected returns. It is easy to show, however, that it satisfies some minimal requirements for a regression error term, as given in (A7). For example, it follows directly from the definitions of u_{mt} and u_{jt} that it is mean zero, that is,

$$E\{\varepsilon_{jt}\} = E\{u_{jt}\} - \beta_j E\{u_{mt}\} = 0. \tag{2.80}$$

Furthermore, it is uncorrelated with the regressor $r_{mt} - r_f$. This follows from the definition of β_j, which can be written as

$$\beta_j = \frac{E\{u_{jt}u_{mt}\}}{V\{u_{mt}\}}$$

(note that r_f is not stochastic), and the result that

$$E\{\varepsilon_{jt}(r_{mt} - r_f)\} = E\{(u_{jt} - \beta_j u_{mt})u_{mt}\} = E\{u_{jt}u_{mt}\} - \beta_j E\{u_{mt}^2\} = 0.$$

From the previous section it then follows that OLS provides a consistent estimator for β_j. If, in addition, we impose assumption (A8) that ε_{jt} is independent of $r_{mt} - r_f$ and assumptions (A3) and (A4) stating that ε_{jt} does not exhibit autocorrelation or heteroskedasticity, we can use the asymptotic result in (2.74) and the approximate distributional result in (2.76). This implies that routinely computed OLS estimates, standard errors and tests are appropriate by virtue of the asymptotic approximation.

2.7.2 Estimating and Testing the CAPM

The CAPM describes the expected returns on any asset or portfolio of assets as a function of the (expected) return on the market portfolio. In this subsection, we consider the returns on three different industry portfolios while approximating the return on the market portfolio by the return on a value-weighted stock market index. Returns for the period January 1960 to December 2014 (660 months) for the food, consumer durables and construction industries were obtained from the Center for Research in Security Prices (CRSP). The industry portfolios are value weighted and are rebalanced once every year. While theoretically the market portfolio should include all tradeable assets, we shall assume that the CRSP value-weighted index is a good approximation. The riskless rate is approximated by the return on 1-month treasury bills. Although this return is time varying, it is known to investors while making their decisions. All returns are expressed in percentage per month.

First, we estimate the CAPM relationship (2.79) for these three industry portfolios. We thus regress excess returns on the industry portfolios (returns in excess of the riskless rate) upon excess returns on the market index proxy, not including an intercept. This produces the results presented in Table 2.3. The estimated beta coefficients indicate how sensitive the value of the industry portfolios are to general market movements. This sensitivity is relatively low for the food industry, but fairly high for construction: an excess return on the market of, say, 10% corresponds to an expected excess return on the food and construction portfolios of 7.6 and 11.7%, respectively. It is not surprising to see that the durables and construction industries are more sensitive to overall market movements than is the food industry. Assuming that the conditions required for the distributional results of the OLS estimator are satisfied, we can directly test the hypothesis (which has some economic interest) that $\beta_j = 1$ for each of the three industry portfolios. This results in t-values of -10.00, 2.46 and 7.04, respectively, so that we reject the null hypothesis for each of the three industries. Because the intercept terms are suppressed, the goodness-of-fit measures in Table 2.3 are uncentred R^2s as defined in (2.43). Some regression packages would nevertheless report R^2s based on (2.42) in such cases. Occasionally, this can lead to negative values.

As the CAPM implies that the only relevant variable in the regression is the excess return on the market portfolio, any other variable (known to the investor when making his or her decisions) should have a zero coefficient. This also holds for a constant term. To check whether this is the case, we can re-estimate the above models while including an intercept term. This produces the results in Table 2.4. From these results, we can test the

Table 2.3 CAPM regressions (without intercept)

Dependent variable: *excess industry portfolio returns*			
Industry	Food	Durables	Construction
excess market return	0.755	1.066	1.174
	(0.025)	(0.027)	(0.025)
uncentred R^2	0.590	0.706	0.774
s	2.812	3.072	2.831

Note: Standard errors in parentheses.

Table 2.4 CAPM regressions (with intercept)

Dependent variable: *excess industry portfolio returns*			
Industry	Food	Durables	Construction
constant	0.320	−0.120	−0.027
	(0.110)	(0.120)	(0.111)
excess market return	0.747	1.069	1.174
	(0.025)	(0.027)	(0.025)
R^2	0.585	0.705	0.772
s	2.796	3.072	2.833

Note: Standard errors in parentheses.

validity of the CAPM by testing whether the intercept term is zero. For food, the appropriate t-statistic is 2.92, which implies that we reject the validity of the CAPM at the 5% level. The point estimate of 0.320 implies that the food industry portfolio is expected to have a return that is 0.32% per month higher than the CAPM predicts. The 95% confidence interval for this 'abnormal return' is given by (−0.106%, 0.535%). Note that the estimated beta coefficients are very similar to those in Table 2.3 and that the R^2s are close to the uncentred R^2s.

The R^2s in these regressions have an interesting economic interpretation. Equation (2.79) allows us to write

$$V\{r_{jt}\} = \beta_j^2 V\{r_{mt}\} + V\{\varepsilon_{jt}\},$$

which shows that the variance of the return on a stock (portfolio) consists of two parts: a part related to the variance of the market index and an idiosyncratic part. In economic terms, this says that total risk equals market risk plus idiosyncratic risk. Market risk is determined by β_j and is rewarded: stocks with a higher β_j provide higher expected returns because of (2.77). Idiosyncratic risk is not rewarded because it can be eliminated by diversification: if we construct a portfolio that is well diversified, it will consist of a large number of assets, with different characteristics, so that most of the idiosyncratic risk will cancel out and mainly market risk matters. The R^2, being the proportion of explained variation in total variation, is an estimate of the relative importance of market risk for each of the industry portfolios. For example, it is estimated that 58.5% of the risk (variance) of the food industry portfolio is due to the market as a whole, while 41.5% is idiosyncratic (industry-specific) risk. Because of their larger R^2s, the durables and construction industries appear to be better diversified.

Finally, we consider one deviation from the CAPM that is often found in empirical work: the existence of a January effect. There is some evidence that, ceteris paribus, returns in January are higher than in any of the other months. We can test this within the CAPM framework by including a dummy in the model for January and testing whether it is significant. By doing this, we obtain the results in Table 2.5. Computing the t-statistics corresponding to the January dummy shows that for two of the three industry portfolios we do not reject the absence of a January effect at the 5% level. For the food industry, however, the January effect appears to be negative and statistically significant at the 5% level (with a t-value of −2.47). Consequently, the results do not provide support for the existence of a positive January effect.

Table 2.5 CAPM regressions (with intercept and January dummy)

Dependent variable: *excess industry portfolio returns*			
Industry	Food	Durables	Construction
constant	0.400	−0.126	−0.077
	(0.114)	(0.126)	(0.116)
January dummy	−0.971	0.081	0.605
	(0.393)	(0.433)	(0.399)
excess market return	0.749	1.069	1.173
	(0.024)	(0.027)	(0.025)
R^2	0.589	0.705	0.773
s	2.786	3.074	2.830

Note: Standard errors in parentheses.

2.7.3 The World's Largest Hedge Fund

The Capital Asset Pricing Model is commonly used in academic studies to evaluate the performance of professional money managers. In these cases, the intercept of the CAPM is interpreted as a risk-adjusted performance measure. A positive intercept, typically referred to as 'alpha', reflects superior skill or information of the investment manager. For example, Malkiel (1995) uses the CAPM to evaluate the performance of all equity mutual funds that existed in the period 1971–1991 and finds that, on average, mutual funds have a negative alpha (i.e. a negative estimated intercept), and that the proportion of funds with a significantly positive alpha is very small. Malkiel concludes that mutual funds tend to underperform the market, which is consistent with the idea that financial markets are very efficient.

Hedge funds typically challenge this view and argue that they can produce excess performance (positive alpha). Unfortunately, the performance data for hedge funds are less readily available than for mutual funds, over shorter histories, and are potentially subject to manipulation or even fraudulent. Bollen and Pool (2012) examine whether the presence of suspicious patterns in hedge fund returns raises the probability of fraud. One of their potential red flags is a low correlation of hedge fund returns with standard asset classes.

In this subsection we illustrate this by considering the returns produced by Bernard Madoff. A former chairman of the board of directors of the NASDAQ stock market, Madoff used to be a well-respected person on Wall Street. Madoff Investment Securities was effectively running one of the largest hedge funds in the world. Many years in a row, the returns reported by Madoff were incredibly good. However, already in 1999, Harry Markopolos, who presented evidence of the Madoff Ponzi scheme to the Securities and Exchange Commission (SEC), suspected that the Madoff returns were not real and that the world's largest hedge fund was a fraud. Despite the many red flags, the SEC did not uncover the massive fraud.[22] One of the red flags described by Markopolos is that Madoff's returns had a correlation of only 0.06 with the S&P 500, whereas the supposed

[22] See Markopolos (2010) for an account of how Markopolos uncovered Madoff's scam, years before it actually fell apart.

Table 2.6 CAPM regression (with intercept) Madoff's returns

Dependent variable: *excess returns Fairfield Sentry Ltd.*			
Variable	Estimate	Standard error	t-ratio
constant	0.5050	0.0467	11.049
excess market return	0.0409	0.0107	3.813

$s = 0.6658$ $R^2 = 0.0639$ $\bar{R}^2 = 0.0595$ $F = 14.54$

split-strike conversion strategy should feature a correlation close to 0.50. We consider the returns on Fairfield Sentry Ltd, which was one of the feeder funds of Madoff Investment Securities. Even a simple inspection of the return series produces some suspicious results. Over the period December 1990–October 2008 ($T = 215$), the average monthly return was 0.842% with a surprisingly low standard deviation of only 0.709%. Moreover, the number of months with a negative return was as low as 16, corresponding to less than 7.5% of the periods. In comparison, during the same period the stock market index produced a negative return in 39% of the months.

We shall now investigate to what extent the CAPM is able to explain Madoff's returns, realizing that large positive intercept terms, that is, large alphas, are excluded by the CAPM and quite unlikely in practice. To do so we regress the excess returns on Fairfield Sentry upon a constant and the excess returns on the market portfolio. The results are given in Table 2.6.

Indeed, the Madoff fund has an extremely low exposure to the stock market, with an estimated beta coefficient of only 0.04. This is confirmed by the extremely low R^2 of 6.4%. The fund also produces a high intercept term of 0.505% per month, with a suspiciously high t-ratio of 11.05, corresponding to a very narrow 95% confidence interval of (0.415%, 0.595%). This suggests that Madoff's fund was able to reliably outperform the market by 5.0 to 7.1% per year. Despite the fact that the CAPM explains very little of the variation in Madoff's returns, the estimated standard deviation of the error term, s, is as low as 0.67%. Apparently, both the systematic risk of the fund is low, as well as its idiosyncratic risk, but nevertheless its returns are very high. From many perspectives, the returns on this fund were too good to be true, and in fact they were not real either.

On December 10, 2008, Madoff's sons told authorities that their father had confessed to them that Madoff Investment Securities was a fraud and 'one big lie.' Bernard Madoff was arrested by the FBI on the following day. In 2009, he was sentenced to 150 years in prison.

2.8 Multicollinearity

In general, there is nothing wrong with including variables in your model that are correlated. In fact, an important reason to use *multiple* linear regression is that explanatory variables affecting y_i are mutually correlated. In an individual wage equation, for example, we may want to include both age and experience, although it can be expected that older persons, on average, have more experience. However, if the correlation between two variables is too high, this may lead to problems. Technically, the problem is that the matrix $X'X$ is close to being not invertible. This may lead to unreliable estimates with high standard errors and of unexpected sign or magnitude. Intuitively, the problem is also clear. If age and experience are highly correlated it may be hard for the model to identify the *individual* impact of these two variables, which is exactly what we are trying to do. In such a case, a large number of observations with sufficient variation in both age and experience may help us to get sensible answers. If this is not the case and we do get poor estimates (e.g. t-tests show that neither age nor experience are individually significant), we can only conclude that there is insufficient information in the sample to identify the effects we would like to identify. In the wage equation, we wish to estimate the effect of age, keeping experience and the other included variables constant, as well as the effect of experience, keeping age and the other variables constant (the ceteris paribus condition). It is clear that in the extreme case where people of the same age have the same years of experience we would not be able to identify these effects. In the case where age and experience are highly but not perfectly correlated, the estimated effects are likely to be highly inaccurate.

In general, the term **multicollinearity** is used to describe the problem when an approximate linear relationship among the explanatory variables leads to unreliable regression estimates. This approximate relationship is not restricted to two variables but can involve more regressors. In the wage equation, for example, the problems may be aggravated if we include years of schooling in addition to age and years of experience. To illustrate the problem, consider the general expression for the variance of the OLS estimator of a single coefficient β_k in a multiple regression framework with an intercept. It can be shown, generalizing (2.37), that

$$V\{b_k\} = \frac{\sigma^2}{1-R_k^2}\frac{1}{N}\left[\frac{1}{N}\sum_{i=1}^{N}(x_{ik}-\bar{x}_k)^2\right]^{-1}, \quad k = 2,\ldots,K, \tag{2.81}$$

where R_k^2 denotes the squared multiple correlation coefficient between x_{ik} and the other explanatory variables (i.e. the R^2 from regressing x_{ik} upon the remaining regressors and a constant). If R_k^2 is close to one, x_{ik} can be closely approximated by a linear combination of the other regressors, and the variance of b_k will be large. However, if there is enough variation in x_{ik}, the sample is sufficiently large and the variance of the error term is sufficiently small, a large value of R_k^2 need not cause a problem.

The **variance inflation factor** (VIF) is sometimes used to detect multicollinearity. It is given by

$$VIF(b_k) = \frac{1}{1-R_k^2}$$

and indicates the factor by which the variance of b_k is inflated compared with the hypothetical situation when there is no correlation between x_{ik} and any of the other explanatory variables. As stressed by Maddala and Lahiri (2009, Chapter 7), this comparison is not very useful and does not provide us with guidance as to what to do with the problem. Clearly, $1/(1-R_k^2)$ is not the only factor determining whether multicollinearity is a problem. Although some textbooks suggest as a rule of thumb that a variance inflation factor of 10 or more (corresponding to $R_k^2 > 0.9$) is 'too high', it will depend upon the other elements in (2.81) whether or not this is problematic; see Wooldridge (2012, Section 3.4) for more discussion. The VIF is not a formal test for multicollinearity, and mechanically excluding variables from a model with 'too large VIFs' is not recommended. Nevertheless, an inspection of VIFs may be helpful if estimation results are unsatisfactory and suspected to be affected by multicollinearity.

Equation (2.81) also shows that multicollinearity may affect only a subset of the estimation results, perhaps those that we are less interested in. For example, suppose we estimate a linear regression model with three explanatory variables

$$y_i = \beta_1 + \beta_2 x_{i2} + \beta_3 x_{i3} + \beta_4 x_{i4} + \varepsilon_i,$$

where x_{i3} and x_{i4} are highly correlated, but where our main parameter of interest is β_2. As long as x_{i2} is uncorrelated with both x_{i3} and x_{i4}, the amount of correlation between x_{i3} and x_{i4} has no impact on the standard error of our estimator for β_2. In this case $VIF(b_2) = 1$, while $VIF(b_3)$ and $VIF(b_4)$ can be almost arbitrarily high.

In the extreme case, one explanatory variable is an exact linear combination of one or more other explanatory variables (including the intercept). This is usually referred to as **exact multicollinearity**, in which case the OLS estimator is not uniquely defined from the first-order conditions of the least squares problem given in (2.6) (the matrix $X'X$ is not invertible). The use of too many dummy variables (which are either zero or one) is a typical cause for exact multicollinearity. Consider the case where we would like to include a dummy for males ($male_i$), a dummy for females ($female_i$) as well as a constant. Because $male_i + female_i = 1$ for each observation (and 1 is included as the constant), the $X'X$ matrix becomes singular. Exact multicollinearity is easily solved by excluding one of the variables from the model and estimating the model including either $male_i$ and a constant, $female_i$ and a constant, or both $male_i$ and $female_i$ but no constant. The latter approach is not recommended because standard software may compute statistics like the R^2 and the F-statistic in a different way if the constant is suppressed. Another useful example of exact multicollinearity in this context is the inclusion of the variables age, years of schooling and potential experience, defined as age minus years of schooling minus six. Clearly, this leads to a singular $X'X$ matrix if a constant is included in the model (see Section 5.4 for an illustration).

To illustrate the effect of multicollinearity on the OLS estimator in more detail, consider the following example. Let the following regression model be estimated:

$$y_i = \beta_1 + \beta_2 x_{i2} + \beta_3 x_{i3} + \varepsilon_i,$$

where the explanatory variables are scaled such that their sample variances are equal to one. Denoting the sample correlation coefficient between x_{i2} and x_{i3} by r_{23}, the covariance matrix of the OLS estimator for β_2 and β_3 can be written as

$$\sigma^2 \frac{1}{N} \begin{pmatrix} 1 & r_{23} \\ r_{23} & 1 \end{pmatrix}^{-1} = \frac{\sigma^2/N}{1 - r_{23}^2} \begin{pmatrix} 1 & -r_{23} \\ -r_{23} & 1 \end{pmatrix}.$$

This formula shows that not only the variance of both b_2 and b_3 increases if the absolute value of the correlation coefficient between x_{i2} and x_{i3} increases, but also their covariance is affected by r_{23}. If x_{i2} and x_{i3} show a (strong) positive correlation, the estimators b_2 and b_3 will be (strongly) negatively correlated.

Another consequence of multicollinearity is that some linear combinations of the parameters are pretty accurately estimated, while other linear combinations are highly inaccurate. Usually, when regressors are positively correlated, the sum of the regression coefficients can be rather precisely determined, while the difference cannot. In the previous example, the variance of $b_2 + b_3$ is given by

$$V\{b_2 + b_3\} = \frac{\sigma^2/N}{1 - r_{23}^2}(2 - 2r_{23}) = 2\frac{\sigma^2/N}{1 + r_{23}},$$

while the variance of the difference equals

$$V\{b_2 - b_3\} = \frac{\sigma^2/N}{1 - r_{23}^2}(2 + 2r_{23}) = 2\frac{\sigma^2/N}{1 - r_{23}}.$$

So, if r_{23} is close to 1, the variance of $b_2 - b_3$ is many times higher than the variance of $b_2 + b_3$. For example, if $r_{23} = 0.95$ the ratio of the two variances is 39. An important consequence of this result is that for prediction purposes, in particular the accuracy of prediction, multicollinearity typically has little impact. This is a reflection of the fact that the 'total impact' of all explanatory variables is accurately identified. This result will only hold if the combination of regressor values for which we wish to generate the prediction are not 'atypical' for the estimation sample.

In summary, high correlations between (linear combinations of) explanatory variables may result in multicollinearity problems. If this happens, one or more parameters in which we are interested are estimated highly inaccurately. Essentially, this means that our sample does not provide sufficient information about these parameters. To alleviate the problem, we are therefore forced to use more information, for example by imposing some a priori restrictions on the vector of parameters. Commonly, this means that one or more variables are omitted from the model. Another solution, which is typically not practical, is to extend the sample size. As illustrated by the above example, all variances decrease as the sample size increases. An extensive and critical survey of the multicollinearity problem, and the (in)appropriateness of some mechanical procedures to solve it, is provided in Maddala and Lahiri (2009, Chapter 7).

2.8.1 Example: Individual Wages (Continued)

Let us go back to the simple wage equation of Subsection 2.3.3. As explained previously, the addition of a female dummy to the model would cause exact multicollinearity. Intuitively, it is also obvious that, with only two groups of people, one dummy variable and a constant are sufficient to capture them. The choice of whether to include the male or the female dummy is arbitrary. The fact that the two dummy variables add up to one for each observation does not imply multicollinearity if the model does not contain an intercept term. Consequently, it is possible to include both dummies while excluding the intercept term. To illustrate the consequences of these alternative choices, consider the estimation results in Table 2.7.

As before, the coefficient for the male dummy in specification A denotes the expected wage differential between men and women. Similarly, the coefficient for the female dummy in the second specification denotes the expected wage differential between women and men. For specification C, however, the coefficients for *male* and *female* reflect the expected wage for men and women, respectively. It is quite clear that all three specifications are equivalent, while their parameterization is different.

Table 2.7 Alternative specifications with dummy variables

Dependent variable: *wage*			
Specification	A	B	C
constant	5.147	6.313	–
	(0.081)	(0.078)	
male	1.166	–	6.313
	(0.112)		(0.078)
female	–	−1.166	5.147
		(0.112)	(0.081)
R^2	0.0317	0.0317	0.0317

Note: Standard errors in parentheses.

2.9 Missing Data, Outliers and Influential Observations

In calculating the OLS estimate b some observations may have a much bigger impact than others. If one or a few observations are extremely influential, it is advisable to check them to make sure they are not due to erroneous data (e.g. misplacement of a decimal point) or relate to some atypical cases (e.g. including the CEO of Apple in your sample of wages). More generally, it makes sense to check the sensitivity of your estimation results with respect to (seemingly) small changes in your sample or sample period. In some cases, it is advisable to use more robust estimation methods rather than OLS. Another problem that arises in many situations is that of missing observations. For example, years of experience may not be observed for a subset of individuals. The easy solution is to drop individuals with incomplete information from the sample and estimate the wage equation using complete cases only, but this is only innocuous when the observations are missing in a random way. In this section, we discuss these two problems in a bit more detail, including some pragmatic ways of dealing with them.

2.9.1 Outliers and Influential Observations

Loosely speaking, an outlier is an observation that deviates markedly from the rest of the sample. In the context of a linear regression, an outlier is an observation that is far away from the (true) regression line. Outliers may be due to measurement errors in the data, but can also occur by chance in any distribution, particularly if it has fat tails. If outliers correspond to measurement errors, the preferred solution is to discard the corresponding unit from the sample (or correct the measurement error if the problem is obvious). If outliers are correct data points, it is less obvious what to do. Recall from the discussion in Subsection 2.3.2 that variation in the explanatory variables is a key factor in determining the precision of the OLS estimator, so that outlying observations may be very valuable (and throwing them away is not a good idea).

The problem with outliers is not so much that they deviate from the rest of the sample, but rather that the outcomes of estimation methods, like ordinary least squares, can be very sensitive to one or more outliers. In such cases, an outlier becomes an 'influential observation'. There is, however, no simple mathematical definition of what exactly is an outlier. Nevertheless, it is highly advisable to compute summary statistics of all relevant variables in your sample before performing any estimation. This also provides a quick

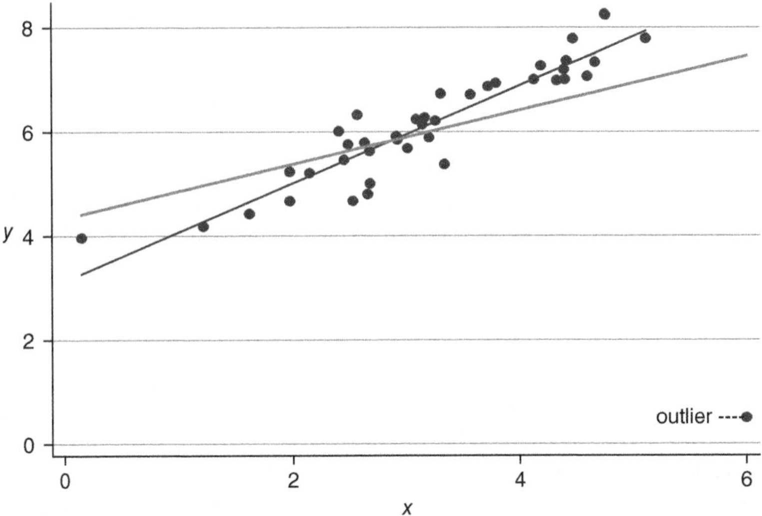

Figure 2.3 The impact of estimating with and without an outlying observation.

way to identify potential mistakes or problems in your data. For example, for some units in the sample the value of some variable could be several orders of magnitude too large to be plausibly correct. Data items that by definition cannot be negative are sometimes coded as negative. In addition, statistical agencies may code missing values as −99 or −999.

To illustrate the potential impact of outliers, consider the example in Figure 2.3. The basic sample contains 40 simulated observations based on $y_i = \beta_1 + \beta_2 x_i + \varepsilon_i$, where $\beta_1 = 3$ and $\beta_2 = 1$, and x_i is drawn from a normal distribution with mean 3 and unit variance. However, we have manually added an outlying observation corresponding to $x = 6$ and $y = 0.5$. The two lines in Figure 2.3 depict the fitted regression lines (estimated by OLS) with and without the outlier included. Clearly, the inclusion of the outlier pulls down the regression line. The estimated slope coefficient when the outlier is included is 0.52 (with a standard error of 0.18), and the R^2 is only 0.18. When the outlier is dropped, the estimated slope coefficient increases to 0.94 (with a standard error of 0.06), and the R^2 increases to 0.86. It is clear in this case that one extreme observation has a severe impact on the estimation results. In reality we cannot always be sure which regression line is closer to the true relationship, but even if the influential observation is correct, the interpretation of the regression results may change if it is known that only a few observations are primarily responsible for them.

A first tool to obtain some idea about the possible presence of outliers in a regression context is provided by inspecting the OLS residuals, where all of the observations are used. This, however, is not necessarily helpful. Recall that OLS is based on minimizing the residual sum of squares, given in (2.4),

$$S(\tilde{\beta}) = \sum_{i=1}^{N} (y_i - x_i'\tilde{\beta})^2, \tag{2.82}$$

which implies that large residuals are penalized more than proportionally. Accordingly, OLS tries to prevent very large residuals. This is illustrated by the fact that an outlier, as in Figure 2.3, can substantially affect the estimated regression line. It is therefore a better option to investigate the residual of an observation when the model coefficients are estimated using only the rest of the sample. Denoting the full sample OLS estimate for β by b, as before, we denote the OLS estimate after excluding observation j from the sample by $b^{(j)}$. An easy way to calculate $b^{(j)}$ is to augment the original model with a dummy variable that is equal to one for observation j and 0 otherwise. This effectively discards observation j. The resulting model is given by

$$y_i = x_i'\beta + \gamma d_{ij} + \varepsilon_i, \tag{2.83}$$

where $d_{ij} = 1$ if $i = j$ and 0 otherwise. The OLS estimate for β from this regression corresponds to the OLS estimate in the original model when observation j is dropped. The estimated value of γ corresponds to the residual $y_j - x_j'b^{(j)}$ when the model is estimated excluding observation j and the routinely calculated t-ratio of γ is referred to as the studentized residual. The studentized residuals are approximately standard normally distributed (under the null hypothesis that $\gamma = 0$) and can be used to judge whether an observation is an outlier. Rather than using conventional significance levels (and a critical value of 1.96), one should pay attention to large outliers (t-ratios much larger than 2) and try to understand the cause of them. Are the outliers correctly reported and, if yes, can they be explained by one or more additional explanatory variables? Davidson and MacKinnon (1993, Section 1.6) provide more discussion and background. A classic reference is Belsley, Kuh and Welsh (1980).

2.9.2 Robust Estimation Methods

As mentioned above, OLS can be very sensitive to the presence of one or more extreme observations. This is due to the fact that it is based on minimizing the sum of squared residuals in (2.82) where each observation is weighted equally. Alternative estimation methods are available that are less sensitive to outliers, and a relatively popular approach is called **least absolute deviations** or LAD. Its objective function is given by

$$S_{LAD}(\tilde{\beta}) = \sum_{i=1}^{N} |y_i - x_i'\tilde{\beta}|, \tag{2.84}$$

which replaces the squared terms by their absolute values. There is no closed-form solution to minimizing (2.84) and the LAD estimator for β would have to be determined using numerical optimization. This is a special case of a so-called quantile regression and procedures are readily available in recent software packages, like Eviews and Stata. In fact, LAD is designed to estimate the conditional median (of y_i given x_i) rather than the conditional mean, and we know medians are less sensitive to outliers than are averages. The statistical properties of the LAD estimator are only available for large samples (see Koenker, 2005, for a comprehensive treatment). Under assumptions (A1)–(A4), the LAD estimator is consistent for the conditional mean parameters β in (2.25) under weak regularity conditions.

Sometimes applied researchers choose for a more pragmatic approach. For example, in corporate finance studies it has become relatively common to 'winsorize' the data before performing a regression. Winsorizing means that the tails of the distribution of each variable are adjusted. For example, a 99% winsorization would set all data below the 1st percentile equal to the 1st percentile, and all data above the 99th percentile to the 99th percentile. In essence this amounts to saying 'I do not believe the data are correct, but I know that the data exist. So instead of completely ignoring the data item, I will replace it with something a bit more reasonable' (Frank and Goyal, 2008). Estimation is done by standard methods, like ordinary least squares, treating the winsorized observations as if they are genuine observations. Note that winsorizing is different from dropping the extreme observations.

Another alternative is the use of **trimmed least squares** (or least trimmed squares). This corresponds to minimizing the residual sum of squares, but with the most extreme (e.g. 5%) observations – in terms of their residuals – omitted. Because the values of the residuals depend upon the estimated coefficients, the objective function is no longer a quadratic function of $\tilde{\beta}$ and the estimator would have to be determined numerically; see Rousseeuw and Leroy (2003, Chapter 3).

Frequently, modelling logs rather than levels also helps to reduce the sensitivity of the estimation results to extreme values. For example, variables like wages, total expenditures or wealth are typically included in natural logarithms in individual-level models (see Section 3.1). With country-level data, using per capita values can also be helpful in this respect.

2.9.3 Missing Observations

A frequently encountered problem in empirical work, particularly with micro-economic data, is that of missing observations. For example, when estimating a wage equation it is possible that years of schooling are not available for a subset of the individuals. Or, when estimating a model explaining firm performance, expenditures on research and development may be unobserved for some firms. Abrevaya and Donald (2011) report that nearly 40% of all papers recently published in four top empirical economics journals have data missingness. In such cases, a first requirement is to make sure that the missing data are properly indicated in the data set. It is not uncommon to have missing values being coded as a large (negative) number, for example −999, or simply as zero. Obviously, it is incorrect to treat these 'numbers' as if they are actual observations. When missing data are properly indicated, regression software will automatically calculate the OLS estimator using the complete cases only. Although this involves a loss of efficiency compared to the hypothetical case when there are no missing observations, it is often the best one can do.

However, missing observations are more problematic if they are not missing at random. In this case the sample available for estimation may not be a random sample of the population of interest and the OLS estimator may be subject to **sample selection bias**. Let r_i be a dummy variable indicating whether unit i is in the estimation sample and thus has no missing data. Then the key condition for not having a bias in estimating the regression model explaining y_i from x_i, is that the conditional expectation of y_i given x_i is not affected by conditioning upon the requirement that unit i is in the sample. Mathematically, this means that the following equality holds:

$$E\{y_i|x_i, r_i = 1\} = E\{y_i|x_i\}. \tag{2.85}$$

What we can estimate from the available sample is the left-hand side of (2.85), whereas we are interested in the right-hand side, corresponding to (2.27), and therefore we want the two terms to coincide. The condition in (2.85) is satisfied if the probability distribution of r_i given x_i does not depend upon y_i. This means that selection in the sample is allowed to depend upon the explanatory variables x_i, but not upon the unobservables ε_i in the regression model. For example, if we only observe wages above a certain threshold and have missing values otherwise, the OLS estimator in the wage equation will suffer from selection bias. On the other hand, when some levels of schooling are overrepresented in the sample this does not bias the results as long as years of schooling is a regressor in the model. We will defer a full treatment of the sample selection problem and some approaches of dealing with it to Sections 7.5 and 7.6.

Suppose we have a sample of 1000 individuals, observing their wages, schooling, experience and some other background characteristics. We also observe their place of residence, but this information is missing for half of the sample. This means that we can estimate a wage equation using 1000 observations, but if we wish to control for place of residence the effective sample reduces to 500. In this case we have to make a trade-off between the ability to control for place of residence in the model and the efficiency gain of using twice as many observations. In such cases, it is not uncommon to report estimation results for both model specifications using the largest possible sample. The estimation results for the two specifications will be different not only because they are based on a different set of regressor variables, but also because the samples used in estimating them are different. In the ideal case, the difference in estimation samples has no systematic impact. To check this, it makes sense to also estimate the different specifications using the same data sample. This sample will contain the cases that are common across the different subsamples (in this case 500 observations). If the results for the same model are significantly different between the samples of 500 and 1000 individuals, this suggests that condition (2.85) is violated, and further investigation into the missing data problem is warranted. The above arguments are even more important when there are missing data for several of the explanatory variables for different subsets of the original sample.

A pragmatic, but inappropriate, solution to deal with missing data is to replace the missing data by some number, for example zero or the sample average, and augment the regression model with a missing data indicator, equal to one if the original data was missing and zero otherwise. This way the complete sample can be used again. While this approach is simple and intuitively appealing, it can be shown to produce biased estimates, even if the data are missing at random (see Jones, 1996).

Imputation means that missing values are replaced by one or more imputed values. Simple ad hoc imputation methods are typically not recommended. For example, replacing missing values by the sample average of the available cases will clearly distort the marginal distribution of the variable of interest as well as its covariances with other variables. Hot deck imputation, which means that missing values are replaced by random draws from the available observed values, also destroys the relationships with other variables. Little and Rubin (2002) provide an extensive treatment of missing data problems and solutions, including imputation methods. Cameron and Trivedi (2005, Chapter 27) provide more discussion of missing data and imputation in a regression context. In general, any statistical analysis that follows after missing data are imputed should take into account the approximation errors made in the imputation process. That is, imputed data cannot be treated simply as if they are genuinely observed data (although this is commonly what happens, particularly if the proportion of imputed values is small). Dardanoni, Modica and Peracchi (2011) provide an insightful analysis of this problem.

2.10 Prediction

An econometrician's work does not end after having produced the coefficient estimates and corresponding standard errors. A next step is to interpret the results and to use the model for its intended goals. One of these goals, particularly with time series data, is prediction. In this section we consider prediction using the regression model, that is, we want to predict the value for the dependent variable at a given value for the explanatory variables, x_0. Given that the model is assumed to hold for all potential observations, it will also hold that

$$y_0 = x_0'\beta + \varepsilon_0,$$

where ε_0 satisfies the same properties as all other error terms. This assumes that the model parameters in the prediction sample are the same as those in the estimation sample. The obvious predictor for y_0 is $\hat{y}_0 = x_0'b$. As $E\{b\} = \beta$, it is easily verified that this is an **unbiased predictor**, that is,[23] $E\{\hat{y}_0 - y_0\} = 0$. Under assumptions (A1)–(A4), the variance of the predictor is given by

$$V\{\hat{y}_0\} = V\{x_0'b\} = x_0'V\{b\}x_0 = \sigma^2 x_0'(X'X)^{-1}x_0. \tag{2.86}$$

This variance, however, is only an indication of the variation in the predictor if different samples were drawn, that is, the variation in the predictor owing to variation in b. To analyse how accurate the predictor is, we need the variance of the **prediction error**, which is defined as

$$\hat{y}_0 - y_0 = x_0'b - x_0'\beta - \varepsilon_0 = x_0'(b - \beta) - \varepsilon_0. \tag{2.87}$$

The prediction error has variance

$$V\{\hat{y}_0 - y_0\} = \sigma^2 + \sigma^2 x_0'(X'X)^{-1}x_0 \tag{2.88}$$

provided that it can be assumed that b and ε_0 are uncorrelated. This is usually not a problem because ε_0 is not used in the estimation of β. The most important component in the prediction error variance is σ^2, the error variance of the model. The second component is due to the estimation error in b, which leads to sampling error in the predictor $\hat{y}_0$. In the simple regression model (with one explanatory variable x_i), one can rewrite the above expression as (see Maddala and Lahiri, 2009, Section 3.7)

$$V\{\hat{y}_0 - y_0\} = \sigma^2 + \sigma^2\left(\frac{1}{N} + \frac{(x_0 - \bar{x})^2}{\sum_i (x_i - \bar{x})^2}\right).$$

Consequently, the further the value of x_0 is from the sample mean $\bar{x}$, the larger the variance of the prediction error. This is a sensible result: if we want to predict y for extreme values of x, we cannot expect it to be very accurate.

[23] In this expectation, both $\hat{y}_0$ and y_0 are treated as random variables.

The accuracy of the prediction is reflected in a so-called **prediction interval**. A 95% prediction interval for y_0 is given by

$$\left[x_0'b - 1.96s\sqrt{1 + x_0'(X'X)^{-1}x_0},\quad x_0'b + 1.96s\sqrt{1 + x_0'(X'X)^{-1}x_0}\right], \tag{2.89}$$

where, as before, 1.96 is the critical value of a standard normal distribution, and s is defined in (2.35). With a probability of 95%, this interval contains the true unobserved value y_0.

Econometric predictions are useful in different ways. First, they can be employed to determine the expected value of y for a unit that is not included in the sample. For example, we can determine the expected sales price of a house given its characteristics, based on a regression model estimated using a sample of houses that have actually been sold. Section 3.4 provides an example of such a model. Second, we can predict the value of y under alternative (potentially not yet observed) values of x. For example, we could try to predict the reduction in cigarette consumption if the sales tax on cigarettes would be increased by 50 cents per package. Third, we can simply try to predict a future outcome of y given currently observed values of x, using a time series model. For example, we can try to predict next month's stock market returns given historical returns and other information variables. This is illustrated in Section 3.5, where we also pay attention to forecast evaluation.

We shall come back to the prediction issue at different places in this book. Because dynamic models are often used for prediction purposes, Chapter 8 pays particular attention to dynamic forecasting.

Wrap-up

This chapter provided a concise introduction to the linear regression model and the ordinary least squares estimation technique, which are the most important workhorses in econometrics. The mechanics of ordinary least squares (OLS) are discussed more extensively in Davidson and MacKinnon (2004, Chapter 2) and Greene (2012, Chapter 3). Under a relatively strong set of assumptions, the OLS estimator in the linear model has many desirable properties, including unbiasedness and efficiency. Asymptotic properties, like consistency, can be derived under weaker conditions. The assumptions of the linear model will be further relaxed in Chapters 4 and 5. Under appropriate assumptions, hypotheses regarding the model coefficients can be tested by means of a t-test or, in case of multiple restrictions, an F-test. The R^2 measures how well the estimated model fits the data, but is often not the most important criterion to evaluate a model. In empirical work we frequently encounter complicating issues, like multicollinearity, missing observations and outliers. Dealing with these issues requires expertise and, occasionally, some pragmatism. The discussion in this chapter assumed that the model specification was more or less given. In the next chapter, we will elaborate more on interpretation, model selection, specification search and misspecification issues.

Exercises

Exercise 2.1 (Regression)

Consider the following linear regression model:

$$y_i = \beta_1 + \beta_2 x_{i2} + \beta_3 x_{i3} + \varepsilon_i = x_i'\beta + \varepsilon_i.$$

a. Explain how the ordinary least squares estimator for β is determined, and derive an expression for b.

b. Which assumptions are needed to make b an unbiased estimator for β?

c. Explain how a confidence interval for β_2 can be constructed. Which additional assumptions are needed?

d. Explain how one can test the hypothesis that $\beta_3 = 1$.

e. Explain how one can test the hypothesis that $\beta_2 + \beta_3 = 0$.

f. Explain how one can test the hypothesis that $\beta_2 = \beta_3 = 0$.

g. Which assumptions are needed to make b a consistent estimator for β?

h. Suppose that $x_{i2} = 2 + 3x_{i3}$. What will happen if you try to estimate the above model?

i. Suppose that the model is estimated with $x_{i2}^* = 2x_{i2} - 2$ included rather than x_{i2}. How are the coefficients in this model related to those in the original model? And the R^2s?

j. Suppose that $x_{i2} = x_{i3} + u_i$, where u_i and x_{i3} are uncorrelated. Suppose that the model is estimated with u_i included rather than x_{i2}. How are the coefficients in this model related to those in the original model? And the R^2s?

Exercise 2.2 (Individual Wages)

Using a sample of 545 full-time workers in the USA, a researcher is interested in the question as to whether women are systematically underpaid compared with men. First, she estimates the average hourly wages in the sample for men and women, which are \$5.91 and \$5.09, respectively.

a. Do these numbers give an answer to the question of interest? Why not? How could one (at least partially) correct for this?

The researcher also runs a simple regression of an individual's wage on a male dummy, equal to 1 for males and 0 for females. This gives the results reported in Table 2.8.

Table 2.8 Hourly wages explained from gender: OLS results

Variable	Estimate	Standard error	t-ratio
constant	5.09	0.58	8.78
male	0.82	0.15	5.47

$N = 545$ $s = 2.17$ $R^2 = 0.26$

b. How can you interpret the coefficient estimate of 0.82? How do you interpret the estimated intercept of 5.09?

c. How do you interpret the R^2 of 0.26?

d. Explain the relationship between the coefficient estimates in the table and the average wage rates of males and females.

e. A student is unhappy with this model as 'a female dummy is omitted from the model'. Comment upon this criticism.

f. Test, using the above results, the hypothesis that men and women have, on average, the same wage rate, against the *one-sided* alternative that women earn less. State the assumptions required for this test to be valid.

g. Construct a 95% confidence interval for the average wage differential between males and females in the population.

Subsequently, the above 'model' is extended to include differences in age and education by including the variables *age* (age in years) and *educ* (education level, from 1 to 5). Simultaneously, the endogenous variable is adjusted to be the *natural logarithm* of the hourly wage rate. The results are reported in Table 2.9.

Table 2.9 Log hourly wages explained from gender, age and education level: OLS results

Variable	Estimate	Standard error	t-ratio
constant	−1.09	0.38	2.88
male	0.13	0.03	4.47
age	0.09	0.02	4.38
educ	0.18	0.05	3.66

$N = 545 \quad s = 0.24 \quad R^2 = 0.691 \quad \bar{R}^2 = 0.682$

h. How do you interpret the coefficients of 0.13 for the male dummy and 0.09 for age?

i. Test the joint hypothesis that gender, age and education do not affect a person's wage.

j. A student is unhappy with this model as 'the effect of education is rather restrictive'. Can you explain this criticism? How could the model be extended or changed to meet the above criticism? How can you test whether the extension has been useful?

The researcher re-estimates the above model including age^2 as an additional regressor. The t-value on this new variable becomes −1.14, while $R^2 = 0.699$ and $\bar{R}^2$ increases to 0.683.

k. Could you give a reason why the inclusion of age^2 might be appropriate?

l. Would you retain this new variable given the R^2 and the $\bar{R}^2$ measures? Would you retain age^2 given its t-value? Explain this apparent conflict in conclusions.

Exercise 2.3 (Asset Pricing – Empirical)

In the recent finance literature it is suggested that asset prices are fairly well described by a so-called factor model, where excess returns are linearly explained from excess returns on a number of 'factor portfolios'. As in the CAPM, the intercept term should be zero, just like the coefficient for any other variable included in the model the value of which is known in advance (e.g. a January dummy). The data set for this exercise contains excess returns on four factor portfolios for January 1960 to December 2014[24]:

rmrf : excess return on a value-weighted market proxy

smb : return on a small-stock portfolio minus the return on a large-stock portfolio (Small minus Big)

hml : return on a value-stock portfolio minus the return on a growth-stock portfolio (High minus Low)

umd : return on a high prior return portfolio minus the return on a low prior return portfolio (Up minus Down)

All data are for the USA. Each of the last three variables denotes the difference in returns on two hypothetical portfolios of stocks. These portfolios are re-formed each month on the basis of the most recent available information on firm size, book-to-market value of equity and historical returns, respectively. The *hml* factor is based on the ratio of book value to market value of equity, and reflects the difference in returns between a portfolio of stocks with a high book-to-market ratio (value stocks) and a portfolio of stocks with a low book-to-market ratio (growth stocks). The factors are motivated by empirically found anomalies of the CAPM (e.g. small firms appear to have higher returns than large ones, even after the CAPM risk correction).

In addition to the excess returns on these four factors, we have observations on the returns on ten different 'assets', which are ten portfolios of stocks, maintained by the Center for Research in Security Prices (CRSP). These portfolios are size based, which means that portfolio 1 contains the 10% smallest firms listed at the New York Stock Exchange and portfolio 10 contains the 10% largest firms that are listed. Excess returns (in excess of the risk-free rate) on these portfolios are denoted by $r1$ to $r10$, respectively.

In answering the following questions, use $r1$, $r10$ and the returns on two additional portfolios that you select.

a. Regress the excess returns on your four portfolios upon the excess return on the market portfolio (proxy), noting that this corresponds to the CAPM. Include a constant in these regressions.

b. Give an economic interpretation of the estimated β coefficients.

c. Give an economic and a statistical interpretation of the R^2s.

[24] All data for this exercise are taken from the website of Kenneth French; see http://mba.tuck.dartmouth.edu/pages/faculty/ken.french.

d. Test the hypothesis that $\beta_j = 1$ for each of the four portfolios. State the assumptions you need to make for the tests to be (asymptotically) valid.

e. Test the validity of the CAPM by testing whether the constant terms in the four regressions are zero.

f. Test for a January effect in each of the four regressions.

g. Next, estimate the four-factor model

$$r_{jt} = \alpha_j + \beta_{j1} rmrf_t + \beta_{j2} smb_t + \beta_{j3} hml_t + \beta_{j4} umd_t + \varepsilon_{jt}$$

by OLS. Compare the estimation results with those obtained from the one-factor (CAPM) model. Pay attention to the estimated partial slope coefficients and the R^2s.

h. Perform F-tests for the hypothesis that the coefficients for the three new factors are jointly equal to zero.

i. Test the validity of the four-factor model by testing whether the constant terms in the four regressions are zero. Compare your conclusions with those obtained from the CAPM.

Exercise 2.4 (Regression – True or False?)

Carefully read the following statements. Are they true or false? Explain.

a. Under the Gauss–Markov conditions, OLS can be shown to be BLUE. The phrase 'linear' in this acronym refers to the fact that we are estimating a linear model.

b. In order to apply a t-test, the Gauss–Markov conditions are strictly required.

c. A regression of the OLS residual upon the regressors included in the model by construction yields an R^2 of zero.

d. The hypothesis that the OLS estimator is equal to zero can be tested by means of a t-test.

e. From asymptotic theory, we learn that – under appropriate conditions – the error terms in a regression model will be approximately normally distributed if the sample size is sufficiently large.

f. If the absolute t-value of a coefficient is smaller than 1.96, we accept the null hypothesis that the coefficient is zero, with 95% confidence.

g. Because OLS provides the *best* linear approximation of a variable y from a set of regressors, OLS also gives *best* linear unbiased estimators for the coefficients of these regressors.

h. If a variable in a model is significant at the 10% level, it is also significant at the 5% level.

i. For hypothesis testing, the p-value is more informative than a confidence interval.

j. It is advisable to remove outliers from a data set as this leads to lower standard errors for the OLS estimator.

k. The p-value of a test corresponds to the probability that the null hypothesis is true.

l. To prevent multicollinearity, two explanatory variables with a correlation of 0.9 should not be included in the same regression model.

m. Consider a regression model with two explanatory variables, x_2 and x_3, and a constant. Other things equal, the variance of the OLS estimator b_2 for β_2 is larger if x_2 and x_3 are moderately negatively correlated than if they are uncorrelated.

n. Suppose we are interested in the impact of beauty upon a person's wage (the 'beauty premium', see Hamermesh and Biddle, 1994). If a beauty premium exists, we should find a positive and statistically significant estimate for its coefficient in a wage equation.

3 Interpreting and Comparing Regression Models

In Chapter 2 attention was paid to the estimation of linear regression models. In particular, the ordinary least squares approach was discussed, including its properties under several sets of assumptions. This allowed us to estimate the vector of unknown parameters β and to test parametric restrictions, like $\beta_k = 0$. In the first section of this chapter we pay additional attention to the interpretation of regression models and their coefficients. In Section 3.2, we discuss how we can select the set of regressors to be used in our model and what the consequences are if we misspecify this set. This also involves comparing alternative models. Section 3.3 discusses the assumption of linearity and how it can be tested. To illustrate the main issues, this chapter is concluded with three empirical examples. Section 3.4 describes a model to explain house prices, Section 3.5 discusses linear forecasting models to predict stock market returns, while Section 3.6 considers the estimation and specification of an individual wage equation.

3.1 Interpreting the Linear Model

As already stressed in Chapter 2, the linear model

$$y_i = x_i'\beta + \varepsilon_i \tag{3.1}$$

has little meaning unless we complement it with additional assumptions on ε_i. It is common to state that ε_i has expectation zero and that the x_is are taken as given. A formal way of stating this is that it is assumed that the expected value of ε_i given X (the collection of all x_is, $i = 1, \dots, N$), or the expected value of ε_i given x_i, is zero, that is,

$$E\{\varepsilon_i|X\} = 0 \quad \text{or} \quad E\{\varepsilon_i|x_i\} = 0 \tag{3.2}$$

respectively, where the latter condition is implied by the first. Under $E\{\varepsilon_i|x_i\} = 0$, we can interpret the regression model as describing the conditional expected value of y_i given values for the explanatory variables x_i. For example, what is the expected wage for an *arbitrary* woman of age 40, with a university education and 14 years of experience? Or, what is the expected unemployment rate given wage rates, inflation and total output in the economy? The first consequence of (3.2) is the interpretation of the individual β coefficients. For example, β_k measures the expected change in y_i if x_{ik} changes with one unit, whereas the other variables in x_i do not change. That is,

$$\frac{\partial E\{y_i|x_i\}}{\partial x_{ik}} = \beta_k. \tag{3.3}$$

It is important to realize that we had to state explicitly that the other variables in x_i did not change. This is the so-called **ceteris paribus condition**. In a multiple regression model, single coefficients can only be interpreted under ceteris paribus conditions. For example, β_k could measure the effect of age on the expected wage of a woman, if the education level and years of experience are kept constant. An important consequence of the ceteris paribus condition is that *it is not possible to interpret a single coefficient in a regression model without knowing what the other variables in the model are.* If interest is focused on the relationship between y_i and x_{ik}, the other variables in x_i act as **control variables**. For example, we may be interested in the relationship between house prices and the number of bedrooms, controlling for differences in lot size and location. Depending upon the question of interest, we may decide to control for some factors but not for all (see Wooldridge, 2012, Section 6.3, for more discussion).

Sometimes these ceteris paribus conditions are hard to maintain. For example, in the wage equation case, it may be very common that a changing age almost always corresponds to changing years of experience. Although the β_k coefficient in this case still measures the effect of age, keeping years of experience (and the other variables) fixed, it may not be very well identified from a given sample owing to the collinearity between the two variables. In some cases it is just impossible to maintain the ceteris paribus condition, for example if x_i includes both age and age-squared. Clearly, it is ridiculous to say that a coefficient β_k measures the effect of age given that age-squared is constant. In this case, one should go back to the derivative (3.3). If $x_i'\beta$ includes, say, $age_i\beta_2 + age_i^2\beta_3$, we can derive

$$\frac{\partial E\{y_i|x_i\}}{\partial age_i} = \beta_2 + 2\, age_i\beta_3, \tag{3.4}$$

which can be interpreted as the marginal effect of a changing age if the other variables in x_i (excluding age_i^2) are kept constant. This shows how the marginal effects of explanatory variables can be allowed to vary over the observations by including additional terms involving these variables (in this case age_i^2). For example, we can allow the effect of age to be different for men and women by including an interaction term $age_i male_i$ in the regression, where $male_i$ is a dummy for males. Thus, if the model includes $age_i\beta_2 + age_i male_i\beta_3$, the effect of a changing age is

$$\frac{\partial E\{y_i|x_i\}}{\partial age_i} = \beta_2 + male_i\beta_3, \tag{3.5}$$

which is β_2 for females and $\beta_2 + \beta_3$ for males. Sections 3.4 and 3.6 will illustrate the use of such interaction terms.

In general, the inclusion of (many) interaction terms complicates direct interpretation of the regression coefficients. For example, when the model of interest contains the interaction term $x_{i2}x_{i3}$, the coefficient for x_{i2} measures the partial effect of x_{i2} when $x_{i3} = 0$, which may be irrelevant or uninteresting. When the model is expanded to include $x_{i2}x_{i4}$, interpretation becomes even more involved. This does not imply that we should not use interaction terms. Instead, we should be careful with the interpretation of our estimation results (and make sure that all relevant interaction terms are clearly reported).

When interaction terms are used, it is typically recommended to also include the original variables themselves in the regression model, unless there is a very good reason not to do so. That is, when $x_{i2}x_{i3}$ is included in the model, so should be x_{i2} and x_{i3}. If not, the interaction term may pick up the effect of the original variables – see the discussion on omitted variables in the next section.

The economic interpretation of the regression coefficient β_k in (3.3) depends upon the units in which y_i and x_{ik} are measured. If the variables are rescaled the magnitude of the coefficient and its estimate change accordingly. For example, if x_{ik} is measured in 1000s of euros rather than euros, its coefficient will be 1000 times smaller, such that the economic interpretation is equivalent. Moreover, the coefficient estimate and its standard error will also change proportionally, such that the t-statistic and statistical significance are unaffected. In general, if x_{ik} is multiplied by a constant c, its coefficient is divided by c. If y_i is multiplied by c, all coefficients are multiplied by c, whereas t-statistics, F-statistics and R^2 are unaffected. It may be attractive to scale the variables in a model such that the order of magnitude of the coefficients is reasonably similar. Adding or subtracting a constant from a variable does not affect the slope coefficients in a regression, whereas the intercept will adapt. For example, replacing x_{ik} by $x_{ik} - d$ increases the intercept by $\beta_k d$.

Occasionally, researchers 'standardize' the variables in a regression model. This means that each variable is replaced by a standardized version obtained by subtracting the sample average and dividing by the sample standard deviation. Whereas this does not affect statistical significance, the resulting regression coefficients now measure the expected change in y_i related to a change in x_{ik} in 'units of standard deviation'. For example, if x_{ik} changes by one standard deviation, we expect y_i to increase by β_k standard deviations. The regression coefficients in this case are referred to as **standardized coefficients** and can be compared more easily across explanatory variables.[1] Note that standardization does not make too much sense when explanatory variables are dummy variables, variables with a small number of discrete outcomes or interaction variables. Standardization is particularly useful when an explanatory variable is measured on a scale that may be difficult to interpret (e.g. test scores, or measures of concepts like happiness and satisfaction).

The interpretation of (3.1) as a conditional expectation does not necessarily imply that we can interpret the parameters in β as measuring the *causal* effect of x_i upon y_i. For example, it is not unlikely that expected wage rates vary between married and unmarried workers, even after controlling for many other factors, but it is not very likely that being married causes people to have higher wages. Rather, marital status proxies for a variety of (un)observable characteristics that also affect a person's wage. Similarly, if you try to relate regional crime rates to, say, the number of police officers, you will probably find a positive relationship. This is because regions with more crime tend to

[1] See Bring (1994) for a critical note on the interpretation of standardized coefficients as a measure for the relative importance of explanatory variables.

spend more money on law enforcement and therefore have more police, not because the police are *causing* the crime. Angrist and Pischke (2009) provide an excellent discussion of the challenges of identifying causal effects in empirical work. If we wish to interpret coefficients causally, the ceteris paribus condition should include all other (observable and unobservable) factors, not just the observed variables that we happen to include in our model. Whether or not such an extended interpretation of the ceteris paribus condition makes sense – and a causal interpretation is appropriate – depends crucially upon the economic context. Unfortunately, statistical tests provide very little guidance on this issue. Accordingly, we should be very careful attaching a causal interpretation to estimated coefficients. In Chapter 5 we shall come back to this issue.

Frequently, economists are interested in elasticities rather than marginal effects. An **elasticity** measures the *relative* change in the dependent variable owing to a *relative* change in one of the x_i variables. Often, elasticities are estimated directly from a linear regression model involving the (natural) logarithms of most explanatory variables (excluding dummy variables), that is,

$$\log y_i = (\log x_i)'\gamma + \upsilon_i, \tag{3.6}$$

where $\log x_i$ is shorthand notation for a vector with elements $(1, \log x_{i2}, \dots, \log x_{iK})'$ and it is assumed that $E\{\upsilon_i | \log x_i\} = 0$. We shall call this a **loglinear model**. In this case,

$$\frac{\partial E\{y_i|x_i\}}{\partial x_{ik}} \cdot \frac{x_{ik}}{E\{y_i|x_i\}} \approx \frac{\partial E\{\log y_i | \log x_i\}}{\partial \log x_{ik}} = \gamma_k, \tag{3.7}$$

where the $\approx$ is due to the fact that $E\{\log y_i | \log x_i\} = E\{\log y_i | x_i\} \neq \log E\{y_i|x_i\}$. Note that (3.3) implies that in the linear model

$$\frac{\partial E\{y_i|x_i\}}{\partial x_{ik}} \cdot \frac{x_{ik}}{E\{y_i|x_i\}} = \frac{x_{ik}}{x_i'\beta}\beta_k, \tag{3.8}$$

which shows that the linear model implies that elasticities are *nonconstant* and vary with x_i, whereas the loglinear model imposes *constant* elasticities. Although in many cases the choice of functional form is dictated by convenience in economic interpretation, other considerations may play a role. For example, explaining $\log y_i$ rather than y_i often helps to reduce heteroskedasticity problems, as illustrated in Sections 3.6 and 4.5. Note that elasticities are independent of the scaling of the variables. In Section 3.3 we shall briefly consider statistical tests for a linear versus a loglinear specification.

If x_{ik} is a dummy variable (or another variable that may take nonpositive values), we cannot take its logarithm and we include the original variable in the model. Thus we estimate

$$\log y_i = x_i'\beta + \varepsilon_i. \tag{3.9}$$

Of course, it is possible to include some explanatory variables in logs and some in levels. In (3.9) the interpretation of a coefficient β_k is the *relative* change in the expected value of y_i owing to an *absolute* change of one unit in x_{ik}. This is referred to as a **semi-elasticity**. For example, if x_{ik} is a dummy for males, $\beta_k = 0.10$ tells us that the (ceteris paribus) relative wage differential between men and women is 10%. Again, this holds only approximately (see Subsection 3.6.2). The use of the *natural* logarithm in (3.9), rather than the log with base 10, is essential for this interpretation.

The inequality of $E\{\log y_i|x_i\}$ and $\log E\{y_i|x_i\}$ also has some consequences for prediction purposes. Suppose we start from the loglinear model (3.6) with $E\{\upsilon_i|\log x_i\} = 0$. Then, we can determine the predicted value of $\log y_i$ as $(\log x_i)'\gamma$. However, if we are interested in predicting y_i rather than $\log y_i$, it is not the case that $\exp\{(\log x_i)'\gamma\}$ is a good predictor for y_i in the sense that it corresponds to the expected value of y_i, given x_i. That is, $E\{y_i|x_i\} \geq \exp\{E\{\log y_i|x_i\}\} = \exp\{(\log x_i)'\gamma\}$. This inequality is referred to as Jensen's inequality and will be important when the variance of υ_i is not very small. The reason is that taking logarithms is a nonlinear transformation, whereas the expected value of a nonlinear function is not this nonlinear function of the expected value. The only way to get around this problem is to make distributional assumptions. If, for example, it can be assumed that υ_i in (3.6) is normally distributed with mean zero and variance σ_υ^2, it implies that the conditional distribution of y_i is lognormal (see Appendix B) with mean

$$E\{y_i|x_i\} = \exp\left\{E\{\log y_i|x_i\} + \tfrac{1}{2}\sigma_\upsilon^2\right\} = \exp\left\{(\log x_i)'\gamma + \tfrac{1}{2}\sigma_\upsilon^2\right\}. \tag{3.10}$$

Sometimes, the additional half-variance term is also added when the error terms are not assumed to be normal. Often, it is simply omitted. Additional discussion on predicting y_i when the dependent variable is $\log y_i$ is provided in Wooldridge (2012, Section 6.4).

The logarithmic transformation cannot be used if a variable is negative or equal to zero. An alternative transformation that is occasionally used, also when $y_i \leq 0$, is the inverse hyperbolic sine transformation (see Burbidge, Magee and Robb, 1988), given by

$$\text{ihs}(y_i) = \log\left(y_i + \sqrt{y_i^2 + 1}\right).$$

Although this looks complicated, the inverse sine is approximately equal to $\log(2) + \log(y_i)$ for y_i larger than 4, so estimation results can be interpreted pretty much in the same way as with a standard logarithmic dependent variable. When y_i is close to zero, the transformation is almost linear. Alternatively, authors often use $\log(c + y_i)$ in cases where y_i can be zero or very close to zero, for some small constant c, even though results will be sensitive to the choice of c.

Another consequence of (3.2) is often overlooked. If we change the set of explanatory variables x_i to z_i, say, and estimate another regression model,

$$y_i = z_i'\gamma + \upsilon_i \tag{3.11}$$

with the interpretation that $E\{y_i|z_i\} = z_i'\gamma$, there is no conflict with the previous model stating that $E\{y_i|x_i\} = x_i'\beta$. Because the conditioning variables are different, both conditional expectations can be correct in the sense that both are linear in the conditioning variables. Consequently, if we interpret the regression models as describing the conditional expectation given the variables that are included, there can never be any conflict between them. They are just two different things in which we might be interested. For example, we may be interested in the expected wage as a function of gender only, but also in the expected wage as a function of gender, education and experience. Note that, because of a different ceteris paribus condition, the coefficients for gender in these two models do not have the same interpretation. Often, researchers implicitly or explicitly make the assumption that the set of conditioning variables is larger than those that are included. Sometimes it is suggested that the model contains all relevant observable variables (implying that observables that are not included in the model are in the conditioning set but irrelevant). If it is argued, for example, that the two linear models presented earlier should be interpreted as

$$E\{y_i|x_i, z_i\} = z_i'\gamma$$

and

$$E\{y_i|x_i, z_i\} = x_i'\beta$$

respectively, then the two models *are* typically in conflict and at most one of them can be correct.[2] Only in such cases does it make sense to compare the two models statistically and to test, for example, which model is correct and which one is not. We come back to this issue in Subsection 3.2.3.

3.2 Selecting the Set of Regressors

3.2.1 Misspecifying the Set of Regressors

If one is (implicitly) assuming that the conditioning set of the model contains more variables than the ones that are included, it is possible that the set of explanatory variables is 'misspecified'. This means that one or more of the omitted variables are relevant, that is, they have nonzero coefficients. This raises two questions: what happens when a relevant variable is excluded from the model, and what happens when an irrelevant variable is included in the model? To illustrate this, consider the following two models:

$$y_i = x_i'\beta + z_i'\gamma + \varepsilon_i, \tag{3.12}$$

and

$$y_i = x_i'\beta + v_i, \tag{3.13}$$

both interpreted as describing the conditional expectation of y_i given x_i, z_i (and maybe some additional variables). The model in (3.13) is nested in (3.12) and implicitly assumes that z_i is irrelevant ($\gamma = 0$). What happens if we estimate model (3.13) whereas model (3.12) is the correct model? That is, what happens when we omit z_i from the set of regressors?

The OLS estimator for β based on (3.13), denoted as b_2, is given by

$$b_2 = \left(\sum_{i=1}^{N} x_i x_i'\right)^{-1} \sum_{i=1}^{N} x_i y_i. \tag{3.14}$$

The properties of this estimator under model (3.12) can be determined by substituting (3.12) into (3.14) to obtain

$$b_2 = \beta + \left(\sum_{i=1}^{N} x_i x_i'\right)^{-1} \sum_{i=1}^{N} x_i z_i'\gamma + \left(\sum_{i=1}^{N} x_i x_i'\right)^{-1} \sum_{i=1}^{N} x_i \varepsilon_i. \tag{3.15}$$

Depending upon the assumptions made for model (3.12), the last term in this expression will have an expectation or probability limit of zero.[3] The second term on the right-hand side, however, corresponds to a bias (or asymptotic bias) in the OLS estimator owing to

[2] We abstract from trivial exceptions, like $x_i = -z_i$ and $\beta = -\gamma$.

[3] Compare the derivations of the properties of the OLS estimator in Section 2.6.

estimating the incorrect model (3.13). This is referred to as an **omitted variable bias**. As expected, there will be no bias if $\gamma = 0$ (implying that the two models are identical), but there is one more case in which the estimator for β will not be biased and that is when $\sum_{i=1}^{N} x_i z_i' = 0$, or, asymptotically, when $E\{x_i z_i'\} = 0$. If this happens we say that x_i and z_i are **orthogonal**. This does not happen very often in economic applications. Note, for example, that the presence of an intercept in x_i implies that $E\{z_i\}$ should be zero.

The converse is less of a problem. If we were to estimate model (3.12) while in fact model (3.13) was appropriate, that is, we needlessly included the irrelevant variables z_i, we would simply be estimating the γ coefficients, which in reality are zero. In this case, however, it would be preferable to estimate β from the restricted model (3.13) rather than from (3.12) because the latter estimator for β will usually have a higher variance and thus be less reliable. While the derivation of this result requires some tedious matrix manipulations, it is intuitively obvious: model (3.13) imposes more information, so that we can expect that the estimator that exploits this information is, on average, more accurate than one that does not. Thus, including irrelevant variables in your model, even though they have a zero coefficient, will typically increase the variance of the estimators for the other model parameters. Including as many variables as possible in a model is thus not a good strategy, while including too few variables has the danger of biased estimates. This means we need some guidance on how to select the set of regressors.

3.2.2 Selecting Regressors

Again, it should be stressed that, if we interpret the regression model as describing the conditional expectation of y_i given the *included* variables x_i, there is no issue of a misspecified set of regressors, although there might be a problem of functional form (see the next section). This implies that statistically there is nothing to test here. The set of x_i variables will be chosen on the basis of what we find interesting, and often economic theory or common sense guides us in our choice. Interpreting the model in a broader sense implies that there may be relevant regressors that are excluded or irrelevant ones that are included. To find potentially relevant variables, we can use economic theory again. For example, when specifying an individual wage equation, we may use the human capital theory, which essentially says that everything that affects a person's productivity will affect his or her wage. In addition, we may use job characteristics (blue or white collar, shift work, public or private sector, etc.) and general labour market conditions (e.g. sectorial unemployment).

It is good practice to select the set of *potentially* relevant variables on the basis of economic arguments rather than statistical ones. Although it is sometimes suggested otherwise, statistical arguments are never certainty arguments. That is, there is always a small (but not ignorable) probability of drawing the wrong conclusion. For example, there is always a probability (corresponding to the size of the test) of rejecting the null hypothesis that a coefficient is zero, while the null is actually true. Such type I errors are rather likely to happen if we use a sequence of many tests to select the regressors to include in the model. This process is referred to as **data snooping, data mining** or ***p*-hacking** (see Leamer, 1978; Lovell, 1983; or Charemza and Deadman, 1999, Chapter 2), and in economics it is not a compliment if someone accuses you of doing it.[4] In general, data snooping refers to the fact that a given set of data is used more than once to choose a model specification and to test hypotheses. You can imagine, for example, that, if you have a set of 20 potential regressors and you try each one of them, it is quite likely to conclude that one of them is 'significant', even though there is no true relationship between any of these regressors and the variable you are explaining. Although statistical software packages sometimes provide mechanical routines to select regressors, these are typically *not recommended* in economic work. The probability of making incorrect choices is high, and it is not unlikely that your 'model' captures some peculiarities in the data that have no real meaning.[5] In practice, however, it is hard to prevent some amount of data snooping from entering your work. Even if you do not perform your own specification search and happen to 'know' which model to estimate, this 'knowledge' may be based upon the successes and failures of past investigations. Nevertheless, it is important to be aware of the problem. In recent years, the possibility of data snooping biases has played an important role in empirical studies modelling stock returns. Lo and MacKinlay (1990), for example, analyse such biases in tests of financial asset pricing models, while Sullivan, Timmermann and White (2001) analyse the extent to which the presence of calendar effects in stock returns, like the January effect discussed in Section 2.7, can be attributed to data snooping.

To illustrate the data snooping problem, let us consider the following example (Lovell, 1983). Suppose that an investigator wants to specify a linear regression model for next month's stock returns from a number of equally plausible candidate explanatory variables. The model is restricted to have at most two explanatory variables. What are the implications of searching for the best two candidate regressors when the null hypothesis is true that stock prices follow a random walk and all explanatory variables are actually irrelevant? Because statistical tests are always subject to type I errors (rejecting the null hypothesis while it is actually true), the probability of such errors accumulates rapidly if a large sequence of tests is performed. When the claimed confidence level is 95%, the probability of incorrectly rejecting the null in the above example increases to approximately $1 - 0.95^{k/2}$, where k is the number of candidate regressors. For example, if all candidate regressors are uncorrelated, the probability of finding t-values larger than 1.96 when the best two out of 20 regressors are selected is as large as 40%, while in fact all true coefficients are zero. This probability increases to more than 92% if the best two out of 100 candidates have been selected.

The danger of data mining is particularly high if the specification search is from simple to general. In this approach, you start with a simple model, and you include additional variables or lags of variables until the specification appears adequate. That is, until the restrictions imposed by the model are no longer rejected and you are happy with the signs of the coefficient estimates and their significance. Clearly, such a procedure may involve a very large number of tests. Stepwise regression, an automated version of such a specific-to-general approach, is bad practice and can easily lead to inappropriate model

[4] In computer science and big data analytics, the term data mining is used to describe the (useful) process of summarizing and finding interesting patterns in huge data sets (Varian, 2014).

[5] For example, when searching long enough, one can document "relationships" between the number of people who died by falling into a swimming pool and the number of films that Nicolas Cage appeared in, or between mozzarella cheese consumption and the number of civil engineering doctorates; see Vigen (2015) for a humorous account of such spurious correlations.

specifications, particularly if the candidate explanatory variables are not orthogonal; see Doornik (2008) for a recent example. An alternative is the **general-to-specific modelling** approach, advocated by Professor David Hendry and others, typically referred to as the **LSE methodology**.[6] This approach starts by estimating a general unrestricted model (GUM), which is subsequently reduced in size and complexity by testing restrictions that can be imposed; see Charemza and Deadman (1999) for an extensive treatment. The idea behind this approach is appealing. Assuming that a sufficiently general and complicated model can describe reality, any more parsimonious model is an improvement if it conveys all of the same information in a simpler, more compact form. The art of model specification in the LSE approach is to find models that are valid restrictions of the GUM, and that cannot be reduced to even more parsimonious models that are also valid restrictions. Although the LSE methodology involves a large number of (mis)specification tests, it can be argued to be relatively insensitive to data-mining problems. The basic argument, formalized by White (1990), is that, as the sample size grows to infinity, only the true specification will survive all specification tests. This assumes that the 'true specification' is a special case of the GUM with which a researcher starts. Rather than ending up with a specification that is most likely incorrect, owing to an accumulation of type I and type II errors, the general-to-specific approach in the long run would result in the correct specification. While this asymptotic result is insufficient to assure that the LSE approach works well with sample sizes typical for empirical work, Hoover and Perez (1999) show that it may work pretty well in practice in the sense that the methodology recovers the correct specification (or a closely related specification) most of the time. An automated version of the general-to-specific approach is developed by Krolzig and Hendry (2001) and is available in PcGets (Owen, 2003) and, with some refinements, in Autometrics (Doornik, 2009). Hendry (2009) discusses the role of model selection in applied econometrics and provides an illustration. Castle, Qin and Reed (2013) review and compare a large number of model selection algorithms. The use of automatic model selection procedures in empirical work is not widespread, although the recent emergence of 'big data' generates new interest in this issue, particularly for large dimensional problems (see Varian, 2014).[7]

In practice, most applied researchers will start somewhere 'in the middle' with a specification that could be appropriate and, ideally, then test (1) whether restrictions imposed by the model are correct and (2) whether restrictions not imposed by the model could be imposed. In the first category are misspecification tests for omitted variables, but also for autocorrelation and heteroskedasticity (see Chapter 4). In the second category are tests of parametric restrictions, for example that one or more explanatory variables have zero coefficients.

While the current chapter provides useful tests and procedures for specifying and estimating an econometric model, there is no golden rule to find an acceptable specification in a given application. Important reasons for this are that specification is simply

[6] The adjective LSE derives from the fact that there is a strong tradition of time series econometrics at the London School of Economics (LSE), starting in the 1960s (see Mizon, 1995). Currently, the practitioners of LSE econometrics are widely dispersed among institutions throughout the world.

[7] A reasonably popular approach in economic applications is the LASSO ('Least absolute shrinkage and selection operator'), developed by Tibshirani (1996). This combines estimation and variable selection in large-dimensional problems (e.g. when there are more regressors than observations) by minimizing the usual sum of squared residuals, but imposing a bound on the sum of the absolute values of the coefficients. Several variants and extensions have been developed. Ng (2013) reviews recent advances in variable selection methods in predictive regressions.

not easy, that only a limited amount of reliable data is available and that theories are often highly abstract or controversial (see Hendry and Richard, 1983). This makes specification of a model partly an imaginative process for which it is hard to write down rules. Or, as formulated somewhat bluntly in Chapter 1, econometrics is much easier without data. Kennedy (2008, Chapters 5 and 22) provides a very useful discussion of specification searches in practice, combined with the 'ten commandments of applied econometrics'.

In presenting your estimation results, it is not a 'sin' to have insignificant variables included in your specification. The fact that your results do not show a significant effect on y_i of some variable x_{ik} is informative to the reader, and there is no reason to hide it by re-estimating the model while excluding x_{ik}. It is also recommended that an intercept term be kept in the model, even if it appears insignificant. Of course, you should be careful including many variables in your model that are multicollinear so that, in the end, almost none of the variables appears individually significant.

Besides formal statistical tests there are other criteria that are sometimes used to select a set of regressors. First of all, the R^2, discussed in Section 2.4, measures the proportion of the sample variation in y_i that is explained by variation in x_i. It is clear that, if we were to extend the model by including z_i in the set of regressors, the explained variation would never decrease, so that also the R^2 would never decrease if we included additional variables in the model. Using the R^2 as the criterion would thus favour models with as many explanatory variables as possible. This is certainly not optimal, because with too many variables we will not be able to say very much about the model's coefficients, as they may be estimated rather inaccurately. Because the R^2 does not 'punish' the inclusion of many variables, it would be better to use a measure that incorporates a trade-off between goodness-of-fit and the number of regressors employed in the model. One way to do this is to use the adjusted R^2 (or $\bar{R}^2$), as discussed in Chapter 2. Writing it as

$$\bar{R}^2 = 1 - \frac{1/(N-K)\sum_{i=1}^{N} e_i^2}{1/(N-1)\sum_{i=1}^{N} (y_i - \bar{y})^2}, \tag{3.16}$$

and noting that the denominator in this expression is unaffected by the model under consideration, shows that the adjusted R^2 provides a trade-off between goodness-of-fit, as measured by $\sum_{i=1}^{N} e_i^2$, and the simplicity or parsimony of the model, as measured by the number of parameters K. There exist a number of alternative criteria that provide such a trade-off, the most common ones being **Akaike's Information Criterion** (AIC), proposed by Akaike (1983), given by

$$AIC = \log \frac{1}{N} \sum_{i=1}^{N} e_i^2 + \frac{2K}{N}, \tag{3.17}$$

and the **Schwarz Bayesian Information Criterion** (BIC), proposed by Schwarz (1978), which is given by

$$BIC = \log \frac{1}{N} \sum_{i=1}^{N} e_i^2 + \frac{K}{N} \log N. \tag{3.18}$$

Models with a lower AIC or BIC are typically preferred. Note that both criteria add a penalty that increases with the number of regressors. Because the penalty is larger for

BIC, the latter criterion tends to favour more parsimonious models than *AIC*. The *BIC* can be shown to be consistent in the sense that, asymptotically, it will select the true model provided the true model is among the set being considered. In small samples however, Monte Carlo evidence shows that AIC can work better. The use of either of these criteria is usually restricted to cases where alternative models are not nested (see Subsection 3.2.3), and economic theory provides no guidance on selecting the appropriate model. A typical situation is the search for a parsimonious model that describes the dynamic process of a particular variable (see Chapter 8); Section 3.5 provides an illustration.

Alternatively, it is possible to test whether the increase in R^2 is statistically significant. Testing this is exactly the same as testing whether the coefficients for the newly added variables z_i are all equal to zero, and we have seen a test for that in Chapter 2. Recall from (2.59) that the appropriate F-statistic can be written as

$$F = \frac{(R_1^2 - R_0^2)/J}{(1 - R_1^2)/(N - K)}, \tag{3.19}$$

where R_1^2 and R_0^2 denote the R^2 in the model with and without z_i, respectively, and J is the number of variables in z_i. Under the null hypothesis that z_i has zero coefficients, the F-statistic has an F distribution with J and $N - K$ degrees of freedom, provided we can impose conditions (A1)–(A5) from Chapter 2. The F-test thus provides a statistical answer to the question as to whether the increase in R^2 as a result of including z_i in the model was significant or not. It is also possible to rewrite F in terms of adjusted R^2s. This would show that $\bar{R}_1^2 > \bar{R}_0^2$ if and only if F exceeds a certain threshold. In general, these thresholds do not correspond to 5% or 10% critical values of the F distribution, but are substantially smaller. In particular, it can be shown that $\bar{R}_1^2 > \bar{R}_0^2$ if and only if the F-statistic is larger than one. For a single variable ($J = 1$) this implies that the adjusted R^2 will increase if the additional variable has a t-ratio with an absolute value larger than unity. (Recall that, for a single restriction, $t^2 = F$.) This reveals that the use of the adjusted R^2 as a tool to select regressors leads to the inclusion of more variables than standard t- or F-tests.

Direct tests of the hypothesis that the coefficients γ for z_i are zero can be obtained from the t- and F-tests discussed in Chapter 2. Compared with F above, a test statistic can be derived that is more generally appropriate. Let $\hat{\gamma}$ denote the OLS estimator for γ and let $\hat{V}\{\hat{\gamma}\}$ denote an estimated covariance matrix for $\hat{\gamma}$. Then, it can be shown that, under the null hypothesis that $\gamma = 0$, the test statistic

$$\xi = \hat{\gamma}'\hat{V}\{\hat{\gamma}\}^{-1}\hat{\gamma} \tag{3.20}$$

has an asymptotic χ^2 distribution with J degrees of freedom. This is similar to the Wald test described in Chapter 2 (compare (2.63)). The form of the covariance matrix of $\hat{\gamma}$ depends upon the assumptions we are willing to make. Under the Gauss–Markov assumptions, we would obtain a statistic that satisfies $\xi = JF$.

It is important to recall that two single tests are not equivalent to one joint test. For example, if we are considering the exclusion of two single variables with coefficients γ_1 and γ_2, the individual t-tests may reject neither $\gamma_1 = 0$ nor $\gamma_2 = 0$, whereas the joint F-test (or Wald test) rejects the joint restriction $\gamma_1 = \gamma_2 = 0$. The message here is that, if we want to drop two variables from the model *at the same time*, we should be looking at a joint test rather than at two separate tests. Once the first variable is omitted from the model, the second one may appear significant. This is particularly of importance if collinearity exists between the two variables.

3.2.3 Comparing Non-nested Models

Sometimes econometricians want to compare two different models that are not nested. In this case neither of the two models is obtained as a special case of the other. Such a situation may arise if two alternative economic theories lead to different models for the same phenomenon. Let us consider the following two alternative specifications:

$$\text{Model A: } y_i = x_i'\beta + \varepsilon_i \tag{3.21}$$

and

$$\text{Model B: } y_i = z_i'\gamma + v_i, \tag{3.22}$$

where both are interpreted as describing the conditional expectation of y_i given x_i and z_i. The two models are non-nested if z_i includes a variable that is not in x_i, and vice versa. Because both models are explaining the same endogenous variable, it is possible to use the $\bar{R}^2$, *AIC* or *BIC* criteria discussed in the previous subsection. An alternative and more formal idea that can be used to compare the two models is that of **encompassing** (see Mizon, 1984; Mizon and Richard, 1986): if model A is believed to be the correct model, it must be able to encompass model B, that is, it must be able to explain model B's results. If model A is unable to do so, it has to be rejected. Vice versa, if model B is unable to encompass model A, it should be rejected as well. Consequently, it is possible that both models are rejected, because neither of them is correct. If model A is not rejected, we can test it against another rival model and maintain it as long as it is not rejected.

The encompassing principle is very general and it is legitimate to require a model to encompass its rivals. If these rival models are nested within the current model, they are automatically encompassed by it, because a more general model is always able to explain results of simpler models (compare (3.15)). If the models are not nested, encompassing is nontrivial. Unfortunately, encompassing tests for general models are fairly complicated, but for the regression models above things are relatively simple.

We shall consider two alternative tests. The first is the **non-nested *F*-test** or encompassing F-test. Writing $x_i' = (x_{1i}', x_{2i}')$, where x_{1i} is included in z_i (and x_{2i} is not), model B can be tested by constructing a so-called artificial nesting model as

$$y_i = z_i'\gamma + x_{2i}'\delta_A + v_i. \tag{3.23}$$

This model typically has no economic rationale, but reduces to model B if $\delta_A = 0$. Thus, the validity of model B (model B encompasses model A) can be tested using an F-test for the restrictions $\delta_A = 0$. In a similar fashion, we can test the validity of model A by testing $\delta_B = 0$ in

$$y_i = x_i'\beta + z_{2i}'\delta_B + \varepsilon_i, \tag{3.24}$$

where z_{2i} contains the variables from z_i that are not included in x_i. The null hypotheses that are tested here state that one model encompasses the other. The outcome of the two tests may be that both models have to be rejected. On the other hand, it is also possible that neither of the two models is rejected. Thus the fact that model A is rejected should not be interpreted as evidence in favour of model B. It just indicates that something is captured by model B that is not adequately taken into account in model A.

A more parsimonious non-nested test is the ***J*-test**. Let us start again from an artificial nesting model that nests both model A and model B, given by

$$y_i = (1 - \delta)x_i'\beta + \delta z_i'\gamma + u_i, \tag{3.25}$$

where δ is a scalar parameter and u_i denotes the error term. If $\delta = 0$, (3.25) corresponds to model A, and if $\delta = 1$ it reduces to model B. Unfortunately, the nesting model (3.25) cannot be estimated because in general β, γ and δ cannot be separately identified. One solution to this problem (suggested by Davidson and MacKinnon,1981) is to replace the unknown parameters γ with $\hat{\gamma}$, the OLS estimates from model B, and to test the hypothesis that $\delta = 0$ in

$$y_i = x_i'\beta^* + \delta z_i'\hat{\gamma} + u_i = x_i'\beta^* + \delta \hat{y}_{iB} + u_i, \tag{3.26}$$

where $\hat{y}_{iB}$ is the predicted value from model B and $\beta^* = (1 - \delta)\beta$. The J-test for the validity of model A uses the t-statistic for $\delta = 0$ in this last regression. Computationally, it simply means that the fitted value from the rival model is added to the model that we are testing and that we test whether its coefficient is zero using a standard t-test. Compared with the non-nested F-test, the J-test involves only one restriction. This means that the J-test may be more attractive (have more power) if the number of additional regressors in the non-nested F-test is large. If the non-nested F-test involves only one additional regressor, it is equivalent to the J-test. More details on non-nested testing can be found in Davidson and MacKinnon (2004, Section 10.8) and the references therein.

Another relevant case with two alternative models that are non-nested is the choice between a linear and loglinear functional form. Because the dependent variable is different (y_i and $\log y_i$ respectively), a comparison on the basis of goodness-of-fit measures, including *AIC* and *BIC*, is inappropriate. One way to test the appropriateness of the linear and loglinear models involves nesting them in a more general model using the so-called Box–Cox transformation (see Davidson and MacKinnon, 2004, Section 10.8) and comparing them against this more general alternative. Alternatively, an approach similar to the encompassing approach above can be chosen by making use of an artificial nesting model. A very simple procedure is the PE test, suggested by MacKinnon, White and Davidson (1983). First, estimate both the linear and loglinear models by OLS. Denote the predicted values by $\hat{y}_i$ and $\log \tilde{y}_i$, respectively. Then the linear model can be tested against its loglinear alternative by testing the null hypothesis that $\delta_{LIN} = 0$ in the test regression

$$y_i = x_i'\beta + \delta_{LIN}(\log \hat{y}_i - \log \tilde{y}_i) + u_i.$$

Similarly, the loglinear model corresponds to the null hypothesis $\delta_{LOG} = 0$ in

$$\log y_i = (\log x_i)'\gamma + \delta_{LOG}(\hat{y}_i - \exp\{\log \tilde{y}_i\}) + u_i.$$

Both tests can simply be based on the standard t-statistics, which under the null hypothesis have an approximate standard normal distribution. If $\delta_{LIN} = 0$ is not rejected, the linear model may be preferred. If $\delta_{LOG} = 0$ is not rejected, the loglinear model is preferred. If both hypotheses are rejected, neither of the two models appears to be appropriate and a more general model should be considered, for example, by generalizing the functional form of the x_i variables in either the linear or the loglinear model.[8] An empirical illustration using the PE test is provided in Section 3.4.

3.3 Misspecifying the Functional Form

When we interpret the linear regression model as describing the conditional expected value of y_i given x_i, that is, $E\{y_i|x_i\} = x_i'\beta$, we are implicitly assuming that no other functions of x_i are relevant. This is restrictive, and it makes sense to test this restriction, or to compare the linear model against more general alternatives. In this section, we discuss some tests on the functional form of the model, and introduce a class of nonlinear models that can be estimated using a nonlinear least squares approach. Subsection 3.3.3 presents a test for testing whether the model coefficients are constant across two (or more) subgroups in the sample, typically referred to as a test for a structural break.

3.3.1 Nonlinear Models

Nonlinearities can arise in two different ways. In the first case, the model is still linear in the parameters but nonlinear in its explanatory variables. This means that we include nonlinear functions of x_i as additional explanatory variables, for example, the variables age_i^2 and $age_i male_i$ could be included in an individual wage equation. The resulting model is still linear in the parameters and can still be estimated by ordinary least squares. In the second case, the model is nonlinear in its parameters and estimation is less easy. In general, this means that $E\{y_i|x_i\} = g(x_i, \beta)$, where $g(.)$ is a regression function nonlinear in β. For example, for a scalar x_i we could have

$$g(x_i, \beta) = \beta_1 + \beta_2 x_i^{\beta_3} \tag{3.27}$$

or for a two-dimensional x_i

$$g(x_i, \beta) = \beta_1 x_{i1}^{\beta_2} x_{i2}^{\beta_3}, \tag{3.28}$$

which corresponds to a Cobb–Douglas production function with two inputs. As the second function is linear in parameters after taking logarithms (assuming $\beta_1 > 0$), it is a common strategy in this case to model $\log y_i$ rather than y_i. This does not work for the first example.

Nonlinear models can also be estimated by a nonlinear version of the least squares method, by minimizing the objective function

$$S(\tilde{\beta}) = \sum_{i=1}^{N} (y_i - g(x_i, \tilde{\beta}))^2 \tag{3.29}$$

with respect to $\tilde{\beta}$. This is called **nonlinear least squares** estimation. Unlike in the linear case, it is generally not possible analytically to solve for the value of $\tilde{\beta}$ that minimizes $S(\tilde{\beta})$, and we need to use numerical procedures to obtain the nonlinear least

[8] It may be noted that with sufficiently general functional forms it is possible to obtain models for y_i and $\log y_i$ that are both correct in the sense that they represent $E\{y_i|x_i\}$ and $E\{\log y_i|x_i\}$, respectively. It is not possible, however, that both specifications have a homoskedastic error term (see the example in Section 3.6).

squares estimator. A necessary condition for consistency is that there exists a *unique* global minimum for $S(\tilde{\beta})$, which means that the model is identified. An excellent treatment of such nonlinear models is given in Davidson and MacKinnon (1993), and we will not pursue it here.

It is possible to rule out functional form misspecifications completely, by saying that one is interested in the *linear* function of x_i that approximates y_i as well as possible. This goes back to the initial interpretation of ordinary least squares as determining the linear combination of x variables that approximates a variable y as well as possible. We can do the same thing in a statistical setting by relaxing the assumption that $E\{\varepsilon_i|x_i\} = 0$ to $E\{\varepsilon_i x_i\} = 0$. Recall that $E\{\varepsilon_i|x_i\} = 0$ implies that $E\{\varepsilon_i g(x_i)\} = 0$ for any function g (see Appendix B.5), showing that imposing $E\{\varepsilon_i x_i\} = 0$ is indeed weaker. In this case, we can interpret the linear regression model as describing the best linear approximation of y_i from x_i. In many cases, we would interpret the linear approximation as an estimate for its population equivalent rather than just an in-sample result. Note that the condition $E\{\varepsilon_i x_i\} = 0$ corresponds to condition (A7) from Chapter 2 and is necessary for consistency of the OLS estimator.

3.3.2 Testing the Functional Form

A simple way to test the functional form of

$$E\{y_i|x_i\} = x_i'\beta \tag{3.30}$$

would be to test whether additional nonlinear terms in x_i are significant. This can be done using standard t-tests, F-tests, or, more generally, Wald tests. For example, to test whether individual wages depend linearly upon experience, one can test the significance of squared experience. Such an approach only works if one can be specific about the alternative. If the number of variables in x_i is large, the number of possible tests is also large.

Ramsey (1969) has suggested a test based upon the idea that, under the null hypothesis, nonlinear functions of $\hat{y}_i = x_i'b$ should not help in explaining y_i. In particular, he tests whether powers of $\hat{y}_i$ have nonzero coefficients in the auxiliary regression

$$y_i = x_i'\beta + \alpha_2\hat{y}_i^2 + \alpha_3\hat{y}_i^3 + \cdots + \alpha_Q\hat{y}_i^Q + v_i. \tag{3.31}$$

An **auxiliary regression**, and we shall see several below, is typically used to compute a test statistic only, and is not meant to represent a meaningful model. In this case we can use a standard F-test for the $Q-1$ restrictions in H_0: $\alpha_2 = \cdots = \alpha_Q = 0$, or a more general Wald test (with an asymptotic χ^2 distribution with $Q-1$ degrees of freedom). These tests are usually referred to as **RESET tests** (Regression Equation Specification Error Tests). Often, a test is performed for $Q = 2$ only. It is not unlikely that a RESET test rejects because of the omission of relevant variables from the model (in the sense defined earlier) rather than just a functional form misspecification. That is, the inclusion of an additional variable may capture the nonlinearities indicated by the test.

3.3.3 Testing for a Structural Break

So far, we have assumed that the functional form of the model is the same for all observations in the sample. As shown in Section 3.1, interacting dummy variables with other explanatory variables provides a useful tool to allow the marginal effects in the model to be different across subsamples. Sometimes it is interesting to consider an alternative specification in which all the coefficients are different across two or more subsamples. In a cross-sectional context, we can think of subsamples containing males and females or married and unmarried workers. In a time series application, the subsamples are typically defined by time. For example, the coefficients in the model may be different before and after a major change in macro-economic policy. In such cases, the change in regression coefficients is referred to as a **structural break**.

Let us consider an alternative specification consisting of two groups, indicated by $g_i = 0$ and $g_i = 1$, respectively. A convenient way to express the general specification is given by

$$y_i = x_i'\beta + g_i x_i'\gamma + \varepsilon_i, \tag{3.32}$$

where the K-dimensional vector $g_i x_i$ contains all explanatory variables (including the intercept), interacted with the indicator variable g_i. This equation says that the coefficient vector for group 0 is β, whereas for group 1 it is $\beta + \gamma$. The null hypothesis is $\gamma = 0$, in which case the model reduces to the restricted model.

A first way to test $\gamma = 0$ is obtained by using the F-test from Subsection 2.5.4. Its test statistic is given by

$$F = \frac{(S_R - S_{UR})/K}{S_{UR}/(N - 2K)},$$

where K is the number of regressors in the restricted model (including the intercept) and S_{UR} and S_R denote the residual sums of squares of the unrestricted and the restricted model, respectively. Alternatively, the general unrestricted model can be estimated by running a separate regression for each subsample. This leads to identical coefficient estimates as in (3.32), and consequently the unrestricted residual sum of squares can be obtained as $S_{UR} = S_0 + S_1$, where S_g denotes the residual sum of squares in subsample g; see Section 3.6 for an illustration. The above F-test is typically referred to as the **Chow test** for structural change (Chow, 1960).[9] When using (3.32), it can easily be adjusted to check for a break in a subset of the coefficients by including only those interactions in the general model. Note that the degrees of freedom of the test should be adjusted accordingly.

Application of the Chow test is useful if one has some a priori idea that the regression coefficients may be different across two well-defined subsamples. In a time series application, this requires a known break date, that is, a time period that indicates when the structural change occurred. Sometimes there are good economic reasons to identify the break dates, for example, the German unification in 1990, or the end of the Bretton Woods system of fixed exchange rates in 1973. If the date of a possible break is not known exactly, it is possible to adjust the Chow test by testing for all possible breaks in a given time interval. Although the test statistic is easily obtained as the maximum of all F-statistics, its distribution is nonstandard; see Stock and Watson (2007, Section 14.7) for additional discussion.

[9] The above version of the Chow test assumes homoskedastic error terms under the null hypothesis. That is, it assumes that the variance of ε_i is constant and does not vary across subsamples or with x_i. A version that allows for heteroskedasticity can be obtained by applying the Wald test to (3.32), combined with a heteroskedasticity-robust covariance matrix; see Subsections 4.3.2 and 4.3.4.

3.4 Illustration: Explaining House Prices

In this section we consider an empirical illustration concerning the relationship between sale prices of houses and their characteristics. The resulting price function can be referred to as a **hedonic price function**, because it allows the estimation of hedonic prices (see Rosen, 1974). A hedonic price refers to the implicit price of a certain attribute (e.g. the number of bedrooms) as revealed by the sale price of a house. In this context, a house is considered as a bundle of such attributes. Typical products for which hedonic price functions are estimated are computers, cars and houses. For our purpose, the important conclusion is that a hedonic price function describes the expected price (or log price) as a function of a number of characteristics. Berndt (1991, Chapter 4) discusses additional economic and econometric issues relating to the use, interpretation and estimation of such price functions.

The data we use are taken from a study by Anglin and Gençay (1996) and contain sale prices of 546 houses, sold during July, August and September of 1987, in the city of Windsor, Canada, along with their important features. The following characteristics are available: the lot size of the property in square feet, the numbers of bedrooms, full bathrooms and garage places and the number of stories. In addition there are dummy variables for the presence of a driveway, recreational room, full basement and central air conditioning, for being located in a preferred area and for using gas for hot water heating. To start our analysis, we shall first estimate a model that explains the log of the sale price from the log of the lot size, the numbers of bedrooms and bathrooms and the presence of air conditioning. OLS estimation produces the results in Table 3.1. These results indicate a reasonably high R^2 of 0.57 and fairly high t-ratios for all coefficients. The coefficient for the air conditioning dummy indicates that a house that has central air conditioning is expected to sell at a 21% higher price than a house without it, both houses having the same number of bedrooms and bathrooms and the same lot size. A 10% larger lot, ceteris paribus, increases the expected sale price by about 4%, while an additional bedroom is estimated to raise the price by almost 8%. The expected log sale price of a house with four bedrooms, one full bathroom, a lot size of 5000 sq. ft and no air conditioning can be computed as

$$7.094 + 0.400 \log(5000) + 0.078 \times 4 + 0.216 = 11.028,$$

which corresponds to an expected price of $\exp\{11.028 + 0.5 \times 0.2456^2\} = 63\,460$ Canadian dollars. The latter term in this expression corresponds to one-half of the

Table 3.1 OLS results hedonic price function

Dependent variable: log(*price*)			
Variable	Estimate	Standard error	t-ratio
constant	7.094	0.232	30.636
log(*lotsize*)	0.400	0.028	14.397
bedrooms	0.078	0.015	5.017
bathrooms	0.216	0.023	9.386
air conditioning	0.212	0.024	8.923

$s = 0.2456$ $R^2 = 0.5674$ $\bar{R}^2 = 0.5642$ $F = 177.41$

estimated error variance (s^2) and is based upon the assumption that the error term is normally distributed (see (3.10)). Omitting this term produces an expected price of only 61 575 dollars. To appreciate the half-variance term, consider the fitted values of our model. Taking the exponential of these fitted values produces predicted prices for the houses in our sample. The average predicted price is 66 679 dollars, while the sample average of actual prices is 68 122. This indicates that without any corrections we would systematically underpredict prices. When the half-variance term is added, the average predicted price based on the model explaining log prices increases to 68 190, which is fairly close to the actual average.

To test the functional form of this simple specification, we can use the RESET test. This means that we generate predicted values from our model, take powers of them, include them in the original equation and test their significance. Note that these latter regressions are run for testing purposes only and are not meant to produce a meaningful model. Including the squared fitted value produces a t-statistic of 0.514 ($p = 0.61$), and including the squared and cubed fitted values gives an F-statistic of 0.56 ($p = 0.57$). Neither test indicates particular misspecifications of our model. Nevertheless, we may be interested in including additional variables in our model because prices may also be affected by characteristics like the number of garage places or the location of the house. To this end, we include all other variables in our model to obtain the specification that is reported in Table 3.2. Given that the R^2 increases to 0.68 and that all the individual t-statistics are larger than 2, this extended specification appears to perform significantly better in explaining house prices than the previous one. A joint test on the hypothesis that all seven additional variables have a zero coefficient is provided by the F-test, where the test statistic is computed on the basis of the respective R^2s as

$$F = \frac{(0.6865 - 0.5674)/7}{(1 - 0.6865)/(546 - 12)} = 28.99,$$

which is highly significant for an F distribution with 7 and 532 degrees of freedom ($p = 0.000$). Looking at the point estimates, the ceteris paribus effect of a 10% larger lot size is

Table 3.2 OLS results hedonic price function, extended model

Dependent variable: log(*price*)

Variable	Estimate	Standard error	t-ratio
constant	7.745	0.216	35.801
log(*lotsize*)	0.303	0.027	11.356
bedrooms	0.034	0.014	2.410
bathrooms	0.166	0.020	8.154
air conditioning	0.166	0.021	7.799
driveway	0.110	0.028	3.904
recreational room	0.058	0.026	2.225
full basement	0.104	0.022	4.817
gas for hot water	0.179	0.044	4.079
garage places	0.048	0.011	4.178
preferred area	0.132	0.023	5.816
stories	0.092	0.013	7.268

$s = 0.2104$ $R^2 = 0.6865$ $\bar{R}^2 = 0.6801$ $F = 106.33$

now estimated to be only 3%. This is almost certainly due to the change in ceteris paribus condition, for example houses with larger lot sizes tend to have a driveway relatively more often.[10] Similarly, the estimated impact of the other variables is reduced compared with the estimates in Table 3.1. As expected, all coefficient estimates are positive and relatively straightforward to interpret. Ceteris paribus, a house in a preferred neighbourhood of the city is expected to sell at a 13% higher price than a house located elsewhere.

As before we can test the functional form of the specification by performing one or more RESET tests. With a t-value of 0.06 for the squared fitted values and an F-statistic of 0.04 for the squared and cubed terms, there is again no evidence of misspecification of the functional form. An inspection of the auxiliary regression results, though, suggests that this may be attributable to a lack of power owing to multicollinearity. Instead, it is possible to consider more specific alternatives when testing the functional form. For example, one could hypothesize that an additional bedroom implies a larger price increase when the house is in a preferred neighbourhood. If this is the case, the model should include an interaction term between the location dummy and the number of bedrooms. If the model is extended to include this interaction term, the t-test on the new variable produces a highly insignificant value of −0.131. Overall, the current model appears surprisingly well specified.

The model allows us to compute the expected log sale price of an arbitrary house in Windsor. If you own a two-storeyed house on a lot of 10 000 square feet, located in a preferred neighbourhood of the city, with four bedrooms, one bathroom, two garage places, a driveway, a recreational room, air conditioning and a full and finished basement, using gas for water heating, the expected log price is 11.87. This indicates that the hypothetical price of your house, if sold in the summer of 1987, is estimated to be slightly more than 146 000 Canadian dollars.

Instead of modelling log prices, we could also consider explaining prices. Table 3.3 reports the results of a regression model where prices are explained as a linear function

Table 3.3 OLS results hedonic price function, linear model

Dependent variable: *price*

Variable	Estimate	Standard error	t-ratio
constant	−4038.35	3409.47	−1.184
lot size	3.546	0.350	10.124
bedrooms	1832.00	1047.00	1.750
bathrooms	14 335.56	1 489.92	9.622
air conditioning	12 632.89	1555.02	8.124
driveway	6687.78	2045.25	3.270
recreational room	4511.28	1899.96	2.374
full basement	5452.39	1588.02	3.433
gas for hot water	12 831.41	3217.60	3.988
garage places	4244.83	840.54	5.050
preferred area	9369.51	1669.09	5.614
stories	6556.95	925.29	7.086

$s = 15\,423$ $R^2 = 0.6731$ $\bar{R}^2 = 0.6664$ $F = 99.97$

[10] The sample correlation coefficient between log lot size and the driveway dummy is 0.33.

of lot size and all other variables. Compared with the previous model, the coefficients now reflect absolute differences in prices rather than relative differences. For example, the presence of a driveway (ceteris paribus) is expected to increase the house price by 6 688 dollars, while Table 3.2 implies an estimated increase of 11%. It is not directly clear from a comparison of the results in Tables 3.2 and 3.3 which of the two specifications is preferable. Recall that the R^2 does not provide an appropriate means of comparison. As discussed in Subsection 3.2.3, it is possible to test these two non-nested models against each other. Using the PE test we can test the two hypotheses that the linear model is appropriate and that the loglinear model is appropriate. When testing the linear model, we obtain a test statistic of −6.196. Given the critical values of a standard normal distribution, this implies that the specification in Table 3.3 has to be rejected. This does not automatically imply that the specification in Table 3.2 is appropriate. Nevertheless, when testing the loglinear model (where only price and lot size are in logs) we find a test statistic of −0.569, so that it is not rejected.

3.5 Illustration: Predicting Stock Index Returns

A linear regression model can be used to generate an out-of-sample forecast provided that the values of the right-hand side variables are known at the time when making the forecast. The forecast is then simply the linear combination of the forecast variables multiplied by the estimated regression coefficients; see Section 2.10. In the current section we use linear regression models to forecast future stock market returns. We do so by estimating several alternative models using data up to December 2003, and we then generate (one-month ahead) forecasts for the subsequent 120 months, taking the estimated models as given and using the actual values for the forecasting variables. We pay attention to the specification of the forecasting model, particularly to the use of mechanical procedures to select regressors, and to the evaluation of out-of-sample forecasts.

In the academic literature on stock market predictability, the prevalent view until the 1970s was that stock prices are very closely described by a random walk and that no economically exploitable predictable patterns exist. In this case, the stock market is said to be efficient and returns y_t in period t are described by a trivial regression model

$$y_t = \beta_1 + \varepsilon_t, \tag{3.33}$$

where ε_t is mean zero and uncorrelated over time. Denoting a K-dimensional vector of forecasting variables, known before the start of period t, by x_t (including a constant), market efficiency implies that the slope coefficients $\beta_2, \ldots, \beta_K$ in

$$y_t = x_t'\beta + \varepsilon_t$$

are equal to zero. Given a choice for x_t, this hypothesis can easily be tested using a standard F-test or Wald test, assuming that the relevant assumptions are satisfied. As discussed in Subsection 2.6.2, the F-test is approximately valid if x_t and ε_t are independent (assumption (A8)) and if ε_t are independent drawings from a distribution with mean zero and constant variance.

Several recent studies report evidence that stock returns are to some extent predictable, either from their own past or from other publicly available information, like dividend yields, price–earnings ratios, interest rates or simply from calendar dummies. However, many studies report regression results estimated on the basis of the entire sample period of observations. Accordingly, forecasting models are formulated and estimated with the benefit of hindsight, and the results are inappropriate to evaluate the economic value of the predictions for the purpose of trading. Moreover, some model specifications may be the result of an extensive specification search and as such may suffer from data snooping. If this is the case, the estimated model may pick up accidental historical patterns that have no predictive value outside the employed sample period.

3.5.1 Model Selection

In this section we consider models that try to predict the return on the S&P 500 index in excess of the risk-free rate (T-bill return). We have a base set of forecasting variables similar to those used in Goyal and Welch (2008) and Rapach and Zhou (2013), extended with a dummy variable equal to one during winter months (November–April), based on the 'Halloween anomaly' of Bouman and Jacobsen (2002). The following variables are available:

$exret_t$:	excess return on S&P 500 index (including dividends) in month t
b/m_{t-1}:	ratio of book value to market value for the Dow Jones Industrial Average, lagged 1 month
dfr_{t-1}:	default return spread, lagged 1 month (difference between long-term corporate bond and long-term government bond returns)
dfy_{t-1}:	default yield spread, lagged 1 month (difference between BAA and AAA-rated corporate bond yields)
$\log(dp_{t-1})$:	log(dividend price ratio), lagged 1 month
$\log(dy_{t-1})$:	log(dividend yield), lagged 1 month
$\log(ep_{t-1})$:	log(earnings price ratio), lagged 1 month
$infl_{t-2}$:	inflation rate (CPI), lagged 2 months
ltr_{t-1}:	long-term rate of return (government bonds), lagged 1 month
lty_{t-1}:	long-term yield, lagged 1 month
tms_{t-1}:	term spread, lagged 1 month (difference between long-term yield on government bonds and the Treasury bill)
$winter_t$:	dummy variable, 1 if t is November to April, 0 otherwise

Due to delay in releases of the consumer price index, the inflation variable is lagged twice, whereas all other financial variables are lagged once.

The available data cover the period January 1950 until December 2013. We will use the first 54 years, until December 2003, to specify and estimate a regression equation, and use the last 120 months of our sample period to evaluate the out-of-sample forecasting power of each specification. That is, the data used for evaluating the model's forecasting performance cover a different period than those used to specify and estimate the model. In the first specification we include all variables listed above. Because this specification is not based on any statistical test or model selection criterion, the model is not subject to data snooping in a strict sense. However, the choice of variables included in the analysis is a potential source of indirect data snooping bias, because it is partly based on what other studies have found using similar data. Although the inclusion of business cycle indicators to forecast stock returns has some rationale, little theory or guidance exists on the choice of forecasting variables in x_t. This makes the model specification search very much an empirical exercise. Accordingly, in addition to the full specification, we also perform four different specification searches. Keeping in mind the reservations mentioned in Subsection 3.2.2, we use a number of mechanical procedures to select the subset of regressors. Having eleven candidate regressors implies that more than 2000 different regression models can be specified ($2^{11} = 2048$). From this large set of alternative specifications we select those models that have either the highest $\bar{R}^2$, the lowest Akaike information criterion (AIC) or the lowest Schwartz information criterion (BIC). Further, we choose a specification based on a general-to-specific approach by stepwise deleting explanatory variables that have a t-ratio smaller than 1.96 (starting from the most general specification including all explanatory variables). The constant term is always retained. Table 3.4 provides the OLS estimation results of four specifications; the specification that maximizes the adjusted R^2 happens to be identical to the one with the lowest AIC.

Table 3.4 Forecasting equation S&P 500 excess returns

Dependent variable: *excess return S&P 500 index* (Jan 1950–Dec 2003)

	Full	Max $\bar{R}^2$/Min AIC	Min BIC	Stepwise
constant	0.201	0.204	0.095	0.210
	(0.063)	(0.054)	(0.024)	(0.054)
b/m_{t-1}	−0.037	−0.039	–	−0.042
	(0.018)	(0.016)		(0.016)
dfr_{t-1}	0.174	–	–	–
	(0.168)			
dfy_{t-1}	1.706	1.747	–	2.023
	(0.687)	(0.668)		(0.654)
$\log(dp_{t-1})$	0.052	–	–	–
	(0.042)			
$\log(dy_{t-1})$	−0.055	–	–	–
	(0.041)			
$\log(ep_{t-1})$	0.038	0.035	0.017	0.036
	(0.012)	(0.009)	(0.004)	(0.009)
$infl_{t-2}$	−0.361	–	–	–
	(0.648)			
ltr_{t-1}	0.176	0.122	0.158	–
	(0.076)	(0.063)	(0.062)	
lty_{t-1}	−0.350	−0.354	−0.213	−0.370
	(0.098)	(0.087)	(0.063)	(0.087)
tms_{t-1}	0.414	0.419	0.513	0.402
	(0.149)	(0.135)	(0.131)	(0.135)
$winter_t$	0.010	0.009	0.010	0.009
	(0.003)	(0.003)	(0.003)	(0.003)
s	0.0409	0.0409	0.0411	0.0410
R^2	0.0749	0.0710	0.0581	0.0655
$\bar{R}^2$	0.0589	0.0608	0.0508	0.0568
AIC	−3.5367	−3.5449	−3.5373	−3.5421
BIC	−3.4537	−3.4895	−3.4958	−3.4937
F	4.6691	6.9632	7.900	7.470
p-value	0	0	0	0

A number of remarks can be made about these estimation results. Relative to the adjusted R^2 and AIC criteria, model selection based on the Schwartz criterion (BIC) is more conservative. Because BIC has the heaviest penalty for additional model parameters, it tends to favour more parsimonious models. Interestingly, the model from the stepwise selection procedure has the same number of parameters but does not include the same regressors as the BIC specification. The R^2s are fairly low for each of the models, reflecting that stock returns are hard to predict, even within a given sample.

The table reports standard errors and F-statistics without taking into account that the model specifications are the result of a specification search based on the same data. Strictly speaking, this makes them inappropriate because the distribution of the test statistics is conditional upon the outcomes of the specification search and therefore no longer a t or F distribution. For example, it is not surprising to see that the stepwise approach results in a model where all t-ratios are larger than 2, because the model was constructed to satisfy this condition. Similarly, it can be expected that the F-statistic increases once 'less important' explanatory variables are dropped. The 'true' significance of the explanatory variables should also take into account the selection process, although in general this is nontrivial; see, for example, Lovell (1983) and Sullivan, Timmermann and White (2001) for some approaches to this problem.

3.5.2 Forecast Evaluation

In the current application our final task is not to make precise statistical statements about the model parameters but to generate forecasts. We can use the estimated coefficients for any of the four models above to predict the excess return on the S&P 500 index over the period January 2004 to December 2013. We do this following the procedure described in Section 2.10. For example, for the full specification the prediction for January 2004 (using the observed values of the explanatory variables) is 2.83%. The corresponding prediction interval is fairly wide and has boundaries $2.83\% \pm 1.96 \times 4.09\%$ or $(-5.19\%,\ 10.85\%)$. For the model based on the BIC criterion, the forecast for January 2004 is 2.27% with a prediction interval of $(-5.78\%,\ 10.33\%)$, which substantially overlaps with the first. (The actual excess return in this month is 1.83%.) The width of these intervals reflects the large uncertainty inherent in stock market returns. Nevertheless, an investor taking the point forecasts as given may make very different trading decisions on these two predictions.

It is not obvious a priori which of the four models will produce the best out-of-sample forecasts. This, among other things, will depend on the question as to whether the 'true' set of regressors is changing over time and/or the 'true' model coefficients are time invariant. As stressed by Rossi (2013), 'in-sample predictive content does not necessarily translate into out-of-sample predictive ability'. To evaluate the out-of-sample forecasting performance, we compute predictions for each month in the period January 2004 to December 2013, using the observed regressor values, while taking the coefficient estimates based on the period January 1950 to December 2003 as given. This way we construct 120 one-month-ahead predictions. There are several ways to measure the accuracy of the forecasts, all of which are based on a comparison of the generated predictions with the ex post realizations. Denoting the series of predictions by $\hat{y}_{T+h}$, $h = 1, 2, \dots, H$, where T reflects the final period of the estimation sample and H the number of forecasting periods, a first measure is the mean absolute forecast error, or **mean absolute deviation**, given by

$$MAD = \frac{1}{H}\sum_{h=1}^{H} |\hat{y}_{T+h} - y_{T+h}|, \tag{3.34}$$

where y_{T+h} are the observed values. This measure is appropriate if the costs of making a wrong forecast are proportional to the absolute size of the forecast error. If the *relative* forecast error is more relevant, one can use the **mean absolute percentage error**, given by

$$MAPE = 100\frac{1}{H}\sum_{h=1}^{H} \frac{|\hat{y}_{T+h} - y_{T+h}|}{y_{T+h}}.$$

This measure does not make sense in the current example, where the dependent variable is already a percentage (a return) and can take on positive and negative values.

A relatively popular approach is based on a 'quadratic loss function', where larger forecast errors, either positive or negative, are punished more heavily. This leads to the root mean squared error, given by

$$RMSE = \sqrt{\frac{1}{H}\sum_{h=1}^{H} (\hat{y}_{T+h} - y_{T+h})^2}. \tag{3.35}$$

Both MAD and RMSE are expressed in the same units as the dependent variable. Typically, they are compared with the corresponding values based on some (simple) benchmark model. In the stock return forecasting literature, an often used benchmark is the historical average return. This allows us to define an out-of-sample R^2 statistic, which summarizes the models' forecasting performance. Based on (2.42) it is given by

$$R^2_{os1} = 1 - \frac{\sum_{h=1}^{H} (\hat{y}_{T+h} - y_{T+h})^2}{\sum_{h=1}^{H} (\bar{y} - y_{T+h})^2}, \tag{3.36}$$

where $\bar{y}$ is the historical average return, in this case estimated over the period up to T. A positive out-of-sample R^2 indicates that the predictive regression has a lower mean squared prediction error than the historical average return. This measure is used in Campbell and Thompson (2008), Goyal and Welch (2008) and Rapach and Zhou (2013). Alternatively an out-of-sample R^2 is based on the squared correlation coefficient between the forecasts and the realized values. Using the definition in (2.44), this leads to

$$R^2_{os2} = \text{corr}^2\{\hat{y}_{T+h}, y_{T+h}\}, \tag{3.37}$$

which produces a number between 0 and 1. It tells us which percentage of the variation in y_{T+h} can be 'explained' by the forecast $\hat{y}_{T+h}$, and it can be contrasted with the in-sample R^2s reported in Table 3.4. This measure is employed in Pesaran and Timmermann (1995).

All of the above measures are symmetric, in the sense that positive and negative forecasting errors of the same size (or same relative size for MAPE) are punished equally. If it is clear that positive forecast errors have more severe consequences than negative forecast errors (or vice versa), it is possible to use asymmetric measures. Ideally, the purpose for which the forecast is made should play a role in the evaluation criterion;

see Granger and Pesaran (2000), who argue in favour of a closer link between the decision and the forecast evaluation problems, and Elliott and Timmermann (2016, Chapter 2), who discuss the central role of the loss function for the construction and evaluation of forecasts. In the current context, it would make sense to develop one or more trading rules based on the return forecasts and evaluate these trading strategies using economic criteria. If such a trading strategy corresponds to a switching rule (moving in and out of the stock market depending upon the sign of the return forecast), a simple measure of forecast accuracy is the hit ratio, defined as the proportion of correct predictions for the sign of y_{T+h}. In Subsection 7.1.5 we discuss some alternative measures to evaluate the forecasting performance for a binary variable.

The results for several of the above forecasting performance measures in the current application are given in Table 3.5, where we have added, as a benchmark, a simple forecast based upon the historical average over the estimation sample. This corresponds to using (3.33) as a (trivial) forecasting model. The relative out-of-sample forecasting performance of the regression models differs widely across the alternative evaluation measures. The out-of-sample R^2_{os1}s are all negative, which is driven by the relatively low root mean squared forecast error (RMSE) of the historical average, whereas the out-of-sample R^2_{os2}s, which are in the [0,1] range by construction, are small and below the in-sample R^2s. The full model containing all variables does not perform very well, most likely because due to in-sample overfitting it is picking up patterns that have no predictive power outside the estimation period. The model based upon the minimum BIC criterion has better values for RSME and MAD, but still performs worse than the historical average. The hit rates seem reasonable and suggest that the models are to some extent able to forecast the sign of the excess market return, but – again – the historical average does a better job here. Because in 62.5% of the months between January 2004 and December 2013 the excess return was positive, a simple historical average has the right sign in 62.5% of the cases.

The results in Table 3.5 illustrate that different evaluation criteria can lead to different conclusions regarding forecasting performance. In general, they paint a pessimistic picture of the ability of regression models to produce reliable out-of-sample forecasts for future stock market returns. When the parameter estimates of the regression models are updated more frequently, for example every month, the out-of-sample predictive accuracy improves somewhat. We leave this as an exercise to the reader. Pesaran and Timmermann (1995, 2000) allow the model selection criteria to choose a different specification each month and then analyse the forecasting performance. The general message from this section, however, is that the R^2s reported in Table 3.4 appear to be overstating the out-of-sample predictability of returns on the S&P 500 index. Goyal and Welch (2008)

Table 3.5 Out-of-sample forecasting performance Jan 2004–Dec 2013

	Full	Max R^2	Min BIC	Stepwise	Constant
RMSE	4.800%	4.733%	4.307%	4.796%	4.188%
MAD	3.416%	3.348%	3.108%	3.410%	3.078%
R^2_{os1}	−31.4%	−27.7%	−5.76%	−31.1%	0
R^2_{os2}	1.35%	1.48%	4.76%	1.01%	0
hit rate	58.3%	59.2%	56.7%	60.0%	62.5%

emphasize that predictive regressions for stock index returns often perform very poorly out-of-sample and find that historical average returns almost always generate superior return forecasts. This view is challenged by Campbell and Thompson (2008), who argue that many predictive regressions beat the historical average return once weak restrictions are imposed on the signs of coefficients and return forecasts. Rapach and Zhou (2013) provide a recent survey on stock return forecasting and note that even a small degree of return predictability can translate into sizeable utility gains for an investor.

3.6 Illustration: Explaining Individual Wages

It is a well-known fact that the average hourly wage rates of males are higher than those of females in almost all industrialized countries. In this section, we analyse this phenomenon for Belgium. In particular, we want to find out whether factors such as education level and experience can explain the wage differential. For this purpose we use a data set consisting of 1472 individuals, randomly sampled from the working population in Belgium for the year 1994. The data set, taken from the Belgian part of the European Community Household Panel, contains 893 males and 579 females. The analysis is based on the following four variables:

wage before-tax hourly wage rate, in euros per hour
male 1 if male, 0 if female
educ education level, 1 = primary school,
2 = lower vocational training, 3 = intermediate level,
4 = higher vocational training, 5 = university level
exper experience in years

Some summary statistics of these variables are given in Table 3.6. We see, for example, that the average wage rate for men is €11.56 per hour, whereas for women it is only €10.26 per hour, which corresponds to a difference of €1.30 or almost 13%. Because the average years of experience in the sample is lower for women than for men, this does not necessarily imply wage discrimination against women.

3.6.1 Linear Models

A first model to estimate the effect of gender on the hourly wage rate, correcting for differences in experience and education level, is obtained by regressing *wage* upon *male*, *exper* and *educ*, the results of which are given in Table 3.7. If we interpret this model as describing the expected wage given gender, experience and education level, the ceteris

Table 3.6 Summary statistics, 1472 individuals

	Males		Females	
	Mean	Standard dev.	Mean	Standard dev.
wage	11.56	4.75	10.26	3.81
educ	3.24	1.26	3.59	1.09
exper	18.52	10.25	15.20	9.70

Table 3.7 OLS results specification 1

Dependent variable: *wage*			
Variable	Estimate	Standard error	t-ratio
constant	0.214	0.387	0.552
male	1.346	0.193	6.984
educ	1.986	0.081	24.629
exper	0.192	0.010	20.064

$s = 3.55$ $R^2 = 0.3656$ $\bar{R}^2 = 0.3643$ $F = 281.98$

paribus effect of gender is virtually identical to the average wage differential. Apparently, adjusting for differences in education and experience does not change the expected wage differential between males and females. Note that the difference is statistically highly significant, with a t-ratio of 6.984. As expected, the effect of experience, keeping the education level fixed, is positive: an additional year of experience increases the expected wage by somewhat more than €0.19 per hour. Similarly, higher education levels substantially increase the expected wage. If we compare two people with two adjacent education levels but of the same gender and having the same experience, the expected wage differential is approximately €1.99 per hour. Given the high t-ratios, both the effects of *exper* and *educ* are statistically highly significant. The R^2 of the estimated model is 0.3656, which implies that more than 36% of the variation in individual wages can be attributed (linearly) to differences in gender, experience and education.

It could be argued that experience affects a person's wage nonlinearly: after many years of experience, the effect of an additional year on one's wage may become increasingly smaller. To model this, we can include the square of experience in the model, which we expect to have a negative coefficient. The results of this are given in Table 3.8. The additional variable $exper^2$ has a coefficient that is estimated to be negative, as expected. With a t-ratio of −5.487 we can safely reject the null hypothesis that squared experience has a zero coefficient, and we can conclude that including $exper^2$ significantly improves the model. Note that the adjusted R^2 has increased from 0.3643 to 0.3766. Given the presence of both experience and its square in the specification, we cannot interpret their coefficients in isolation. One way to describe the effect of experience is to say that the expected wage difference through a marginal increase of experience is, ceteris paribus, given by

Table 3.8 OLS results specification 2

Dependent variable: *wage*			
Variable	Estimate	Standard error	t-ratio
constant	−0.892	0.433	−2.062
male	1.334	0.191	6.988
educ	1.988	0.080	24.897
exper	0.358	0.032	11.309
$exper^2$	−0.0044	0.0008	−5.487

$s = 3.51$ $R^2 = 0.3783$ $\bar{R}^2 = 0.3766$ $F = 223.20$

(differentiate with respect to experience as in (3.4))

$$0.358 - 0.0044 \times 2 \times exper_i,$$

which shows that the effect of experience differs with its level. Initially, it is as big as €0.36 per hour, but it reduces to less than €0.10 for a person with 30 years of experience. Alternatively, we can simply compare predicted wages for a person with, say, 30 years of experience and one with 31 years. The estimated wage difference is then given by

$$0.358 - 0.0044(31^2 - 30^2) = 0.091$$

which produces a slightly lower estimate. The difference is caused by the fact that the first number is based on the effect of a 'marginal' change in experience (it is a derivative), while an increase of 1 year is not really marginal.

Before continuing our statistical analysis, it is important to analyse to what extent the assumptions regarding the error terms are satisfied in this example. Recall that, for the standard errors and statistical tests to be valid, we need to exclude both autocorrelation and heteroskedasticity. Given that there is no natural ordering in the data and individuals are randomly sampled, autocorrelation is not an issue, but heteroskedasticity could be problematic. While we shall see some formal tests for heteroskedasticity in Chapter 4, a quick way to get some insight into the likelihood of the failure of the homoskedasticity assumption is to make a graph of the residuals of the model against the predicted values. If there is no heteroskedasticity, we can expect the dispersion of residuals not to vary with different levels of the fitted values. For the model in Table 3.8, we present such a graph in Figure 3.1.

Figure 3.1 clearly shows an increased variation in the residuals for larger fitted values and thus casts serious doubt on the assumption of homoskedasticity. This implies that the routinely computed standard errors and corresponding t-tests are not appropriate.

One way to eliminate or reduce the heteroskedasticity problem is provided by changing the functional form and use log wages rather than wages as the explanatory variable.

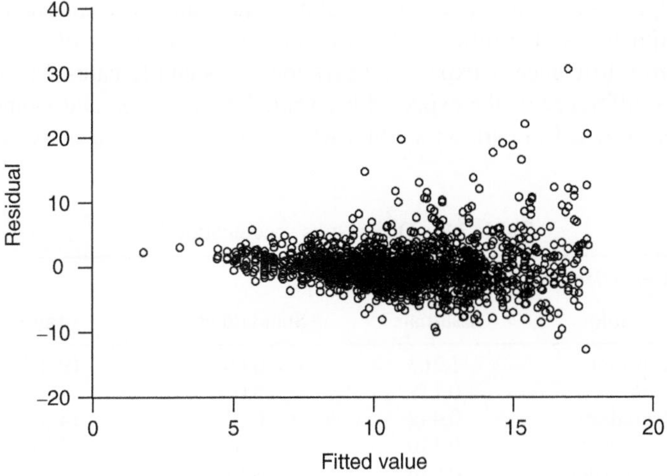

Figure 3.1 Residuals versus fitted values, linear model.

Why this may help in solving the problem can be seen as follows. Let us denote the current model as

$$w_i = g(x_i) + \varepsilon_i, \tag{3.38}$$

where $g(x_i)$ is a function of x_i that predicts the wage w_i (e.g. $x_i'\beta$) and ε_i is an error term that has mean zero (conditional upon x_i). This is an additive model in the sense that the error term is added to the predicted value. It is also possible to consider a multiplicative model of the form

$$w_i = g(x_i) \exp\{\eta_i\}, \tag{3.39}$$

where η_i is an error term that has mean zero (conditional upon x_i). It is easily verified that the two models are equivalent if $g(x_i)[\exp\{\eta_i\} - 1] = \varepsilon_i$. If η_i is homoskedastic, it is clear that ε_i is heteroskedastic with a variance that depends upon $g(x_i)$. If we thus find heteroskedasticity in the additive model, it could be the case that a multiplicative model is appropriate with a homoskedastic error term. The multiplicative model can easily be written as an additive model, with an additive error term, by taking (natural) logarithms. This gives

$$\log w_i = \log g(x_i) + \eta_i = f(x_i) + \eta_i. \tag{3.40}$$

In our case $g(x_i) = x_i'\beta$. Estimation of (3.40) becomes simple if we assume that the function f is such that $\log g(x_i)$ is a linear function of the parameters. Typically, this involves the inclusion of logs of the x variables (excluding dummy variables), so that we obtain a loglinear model (compare (3.6)).

3.6.2 Loglinear Models

For our next specification, we estimate a loglinear model that explains the log of the hourly wage rate from gender, the log of experience, the squared log of experience and the log of education. (Note that the log of experience-squared is perfectly collinear with the log of experience.) This gives the results in Table 3.9. Because the endogenous variable is different, the R^2 is not really comparable with those for the models that explain the hourly wage rate, but it happens to be almost the same. The interpretation of the coefficient estimates is also different from before. The coefficient of *male* now measures the *relative* difference in expected wages for males and females. In particular, the ceteris paribus difference of the expected log wage between men and women is 0.118. If a woman is expected to earn an amount w^*, a comparable man is expected to earn

Table 3.9 OLS results specification 3

Dependent variable: log(*wage*)

Variable	Estimate	Standard error	t-ratio
constant	1.263	0.066	19.033
male	0.118	0.016	7.574
log(*educ*)	0.442	0.018	24.306
log(*exper*)	0.110	0.054	2.019
$\log^2$(*exper*)	0.026	0.011	2.266

$s = 0.286$ $R^2 = 0.3783$ $\bar{R}^2 = 0.3766$ $F = 223.13$ $S = 120.20$

$\exp\{\log w^* + 0.118\} = w^* \exp\{0.118\} = w^* 1.125$, which corresponds to a difference of approximately 12%. Because $\exp(a) \approx 1 + a$ if a is close to zero, it is common in loglinear models to make the direct transformation from the estimated coefficients to percentage changes. Thus a coefficient of 0.118 for males is interpreted as an expected wage differential of approximately 11.8%.

Before continuing, let us consider the issue of heteroskedasticity again. A plot of the residuals of the loglinear model against the predicted log wages is provided in Figure 3.2. Although there appear to be some traces of heteroskedasticity still, the graph is much less pronounced than for the additive model. Therefore, we shall continue to work with specifications that explain log wages rather than wages and, where needed, assume that the errors are homoskedastic. In particular, we shall assume that standard errors and routinely computed t- and F-tests are appropriate. Chapter 4 provides some additional discussion on tests for heteroskedasticity and how it can be handled.

The coefficients for log experience and its square are somewhat hard to interpret. If $\log^2(exper)$ were excluded, the estimated coefficient for $\log(exper)$ would simply imply an expected wage increase of approximately 0.11% for an experience increase of 1%. In the current case, we can estimate the elasticity as

$$0.110 + 2 \times 0.026 \log(exper).$$

It is surprising to see that this elasticity is increasing with experience. This, however, is not in conflict with our earlier finding that suggested that the effect of experience is positive but decreasing with its level. The effects of $\log(exper)$ and $\log^2(exper)$ are, individually, marginally significant at the 5% level but insignificant at the 1% level. (Note that, given the large number of observations, a size of 1% may be considered more appropriate.) This does not necessarily mean that experience has no significant effect upon wages. To that end, we need to consider a joint test for the two restrictions. The test statistic can be computed from the R^2s of the above model and a restricted model that excludes both

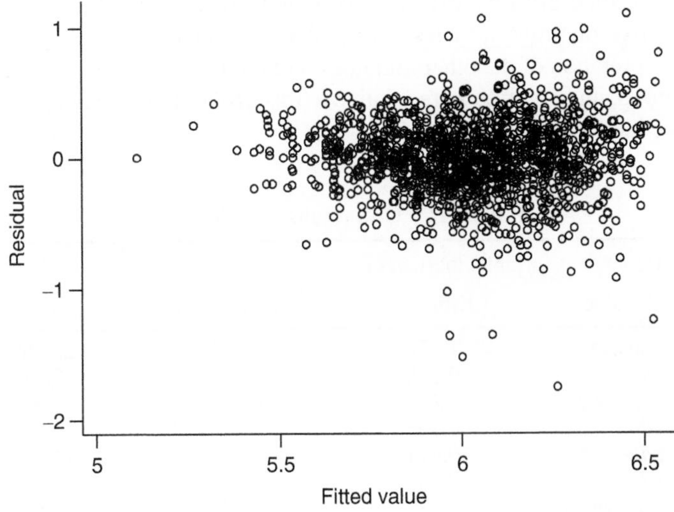

Figure 3.2 Residuals against fitted values, loglinear model.

Table 3.10 OLS results specification 4

Dependent variable: log(*wage*)

Variable	Estimate	Standard error	t-ratio
constant	1.145	0.041	27.798
male	0.120	0.016	7.715
log(*educ*)	0.437	0.018	24.188
log(*exper*)	0.231	0.011	21.488

$s = 0.287$ $R^2 = 0.3761$ $\bar{R}^2 = 0.3748$ $F = 294.96$ $S = 120.63$

log(*exper*) and $\log^2(exper)$. This restricted model has an R^2 of only 0.1798, such that an F-statistic can be computed as

$$F = \frac{(0.3783 - 0.1798)/2}{(1 - 0.3783)/(1472 - 5)} = 234.2, \tag{3.41}$$

which indicates a remarkably strong rejection. Because the two variables that involve experience are individually insignificant at the 1% level, we could consider dropping one of them. If we drop $\log^2(exper)$, we obtain the results in Table 3.10, which show that the resulting model only has a slightly worse fit.

Let us consider this reduced specification in more detail. Because the effect of education is restricted to be linear in the log of the education level, the ceteris paribus difference in expected log wages between two persons with education levels *educ*1 and *educ*2, respectively, is 0.437(log(*educ*1) − log(*educ*2)). So compared with the lowest education level 1, the effects of levels 2 to 5 are estimated as 0.30, 0.48, 0.61 and 0.70, respectively. It is also possible unrestrictedly to estimate these four effects by including four dummy variables corresponding to the four higher education levels. The results of this are provided in Table 3.11. Note that, with five educational levels, the inclusion of four dummies is sufficient to capture all effects. By including five dummies, we would fall into the so-called **dummy variable trap**, and exact multicollinearity would arise. Which of the five dummy variables is excluded is immaterial; it only matters for the economic interpretation of the other dummies' coefficients. The omitted category acts as a reference group, and all effects are relative to this group. In this example, the reference category has education level one.

Table 3.11 OLS results specification 5

Dependent variable: log(*wage*)

Variable	Estimate	Standard error	t-ratio
constant	1.272	0.045	28.369
male	0.118	0.015	7.610
educ = 2	0.144	0.033	4.306
educ = 3	0.305	0.032	9.521
educ = 4	0.474	0.033	14.366
educ = 5	0.639	0.033	19.237
log(*exper*)	0.230	0.011	21.804

$s = 0.282$ $R^2 = 0.3976$ $\bar{R}^2 = 0.3951$ $F = 161.14$ $S = 116.47$

Looking at the results in Table 3.11, we see that each of the four dummy variables is individually highly significant, with coefficients that deviate somewhat from the effects estimated on the basis of the restricted model. In fact, the previous model is nested within the current model and imposes three restrictions. Although it is somewhat complicated to determine analytical expressions for these three restrictions, we can easily test them using the R^2 version of the F-test. This gives

$$F = \frac{(0.3976 - 0.3761)/3}{(1 - 0.3976)/(1472 - 7)} = 17.358. \tag{3.42}$$

As the 1% critical value for an F distribution with 3 and 1465 degrees of freedom is given by 3.78, the null hypothesis has to be rejected. That is, specification 5 with educational dummies is a significant improvement over specification 4 with the log education level.

3.6.3 The Effects of Gender

Until now the effect of gender was assumed to be constant, irrespective of a person's experience or education level. As it is possible, for example, that men are differently rewarded than women for having more education, this may be restrictive. It is possible to allow for such differences by interacting each of the explanatory variables with the gender dummy. One way to do so is to include the original regressor variables as well as the regressors multiplied by *male*. This way the coefficients for the latter set of variables measure to what extent the effect is different for males.

Including interactions for all five variables produces the results in Table 3.12. This is the unrestricted specification used in the Chow test, discussed in Subsection 3.3.3. An exactly equivalent set of results would have been obtained if we had estimated the model separately for the two subsamples of males and females. The only advantage of estimating over the subsamples is the fact that in computing the standard errors it is assumed that the error terms are homoskedastic *within each subsample*, while the pooled model in Table 3.12 imposes homoskedasticity over the entire sample. This explains why

Table 3.12 OLS results specification 6

Dependent variable: log(*wage*)

Variable	Estimate	Standard error	t-ratio
constant	1.216	0.078	15.653
male	0.154	0.095	1.615
educ = 2	0.224	0.068	3.316
educ = 3	0.433	0.063	6.851
educ = 4	0.602	0.063	9.585
educ = 5	0.755	0.065	11.673
log(*exper*)	0.207	0.017	12.535
educ = 2 × *male*	−0.097	0.078	−1.242
educ = 3 × *male*	−0.167	0.073	−2.272
educ = 4 × *male*	−0.172	0.074	−2.317
educ = 5 × *male*	−0.146	0.076	−1.935
log(*exper*) × *male*	0.041	0.021	1.891

$s = 0.281$ $R^2 = 0.4032$ $\bar{R}^2 = 0.3988$ $F = 89.69$ $S = 115.37$

estimated standard errors will be different, a large difference corresponding to strong heteroskedasticity. The coefficient estimates are exactly identical. This follows directly from the definition of the OLS estimator: minimizing the sum of squared residuals with different coefficients for two subsamples is exactly equivalent to minimizing for each subsample separately.

The results in Table 3.12 do not indicate important significant differences between men and women in the effect of experience. There are some indications, however, that the effect of education is lower for men than for women, as two of the four education dummies interacted with *male* are significant at the 5% level, though not at the 1% level. Note that the coefficient for *male* no longer reflects the gender effect, as the other variables are a function of gender as well. The estimated wage differential between a male and a female of, say, 20 years of experience and education level 2 can be computed as

$$0.154 + 0.041 \log(20) - 0.097 = 0.180,$$

corresponding to somewhat more than 18%. To test statistically the joint hypothesis that each of the five coefficients of the variables interacted with *male* are zero, we can easily compute an F-test from the R^2s in Tables 3.12 and 3.11. This is equivalent to the Chow test for a structural break (between the two subsamples defined by gender). This results in

$$F = \frac{(0.4032 - 0.3976)/5}{(1 - 0.4032)/(1472 - 12)} = 2.7399,$$

which does not exceed the 1% critical value of 3.01, but does reject at the 5% level. As a more general specification test, we can perform Ramsey's RESET test. Including the square of the fitted value to the specification in Table 3.12 produces a t-statistic of 3.989, which implies rejection at both the 5% and 1% level.

A final specification that we explore involves interaction terms between experience and education, which allows the effect of education to be different across education levels and at the same time allows the effects of different education levels to vary with experience. To do so, we interacted log(*exper*) with each of the four education dummies. The results are reported in Table 3.13. The coefficient for log(*exper*) interacted with $educ = 2$ measures to what extent the effect of experience is different for education level 2 in comparison with the reference category, that is, education level 1. The results do not indicate any important interaction effects between experience and education. Individually, each of the four coefficients does not differ significantly from zero, and jointly the F-test produces the insignificant value of 2.196.

Apparently, this last specification suffers from multicollinearity. Almost none of the individual coefficients is significant, while the R^2 is reasonably large. Note that a joint test on all coefficients, except the intercept, being zero, produces the highly significant value of 97.90. Finally, we perform a RESET test (with $Q = 2$) on this model, which produces a t-value of 2.13, which is insignificant at the 1% level. Nevertheless, specification 6 in Table 3.12 seems more appropriate than the current one.

3.6.4 Some Words of Warning

Despite our relatively careful statistical analysis, we still have to be cautious in interpreting the resulting estimates economically. The educational level, for example, will to a large extent capture differences in the type of jobs in which people are employed.

Table 3.13 OLS results specification 7

Dependent variable: log(*wage*)			
Variable	Estimate	Standard error	t-ratio
constant	1.489	0.212	7.022
male	0.116	0.015	7.493
$educ = 2$	0.067	0.226	0.297
$educ = 3$	0.135	0.219	0.618
$educ = 4$	0.205	0.219	0.934
$educ = 5$	0.341	0.218	1.565
$\log(exper)$	0.163	0.065	2.494
$\log(exper) \times educ = 2$	0.019	0.070	0.274
$\log(exper) \times educ = 3$	0.050	0.068	0.731
$\log(exper) \times educ = 4$	0.088	0.069	1.277
$\log(exper) \times educ = 5$	0.100	0.068	1.465

$s = 0.281$ $R^2 = 0.4012$ $\bar{R}^2 = 0.3971$ $F = 97.90$ $S = 115.76$

That is, the effect of education, as measured by the models' coefficients, will typically operate through a person's job characteristics. Thus the educational effect cannot be interpreted to hold for people *who have the same job*, besides having the same experience and gender. Of course, this is a direct consequence of not including 'job type' in the model, such that it is not captured by our ceteris paribus condition.

Another issue is that the model is only estimated for the subpopulation of working males and females. There is no reason why it would be valid to extend the estimation results also to explain wages of nonworkers who consider entering the labour market. It may well be the case that selection into the labour market is nonrandom and depends upon potential wages, which would lead to a so-called selection bias in the OLS estimator. To take this into account, it is possible to model wages jointly with the decision to join the labour market, and we shall discuss a class of models for such problems in Chapter 7.

We should also be careful of interpreting the coefficient for education as measuring the *causal* effect. That is, if we increase the education level of an arbitrary person in the sample, the expected effect upon his or her wage may not correspond to the estimated coefficient. The reason is that education is typically correlated with unobserved characteristics (intelligence, ability) that also determine a person's wage. In this sense, the effect of education as estimated by OLS is partly due to differences in unobserved characteristics of people attaining the different education levels. Chapter 5 comes back to this problem.

Wrap-up

The multiple linear regression model allows one to investigate the impact of a variable upon the dependent variable, while controlling for other factors. Omitted variable bias arises when a relevant explanatory variable that is correlated with the included regressors is excluded from the model. The most common interpretation of the linear model is in terms of a conditional expectation, noting that this does not automatically imply that the model coefficients reflect causal effects. Specification searches are among the difficult jobs in econometrics, where a trade-off has to be made between explanatory power and parsimony, taking into account economic interpretability and problems like data mining and multicollinearity. A general-to-specific approach is preferred to a specific-to-general procedure and to mechanical stepwise procedures. Specification tests are helpful in this process. In this chapter we have considered three empirical illustrations that help to highlight practical issues regarding interpretation, model selection and testing. Among other things, we have discussed the choice between a linear and a loglinear model, out-of-sample forecast evaluation, the use of interaction terms and subsample estimation and the possibility of heteroskedasticity. Berndt (1991) provides an excellent coverage of econometric modelling in the context of a dozen empirical examples. Kennedy (2008, Chapter 22) has a very useful discussion of the ten commandments of applied econometrics. The next chapter will more formally discuss heteroskedasticity and serial correlation in the error terms, and make a first step in relaxing the Gauss–Markov conditions.

Exercises

Exercise 3.1 (Specification Issues)

a. Explain what is meant by 'data mining'.

b. Explain why it is inappropriate to drop two variables from the model at the same time on the basis of their *t*-ratios only.

c. Explain the usefulness of the $\bar{R}^2$, *AIC* and *BIC* criteria to compare two models that are nested.

d. Consider two non-nested regression models explaining the same variable y_i. How can you test one against the other?

e. Explain why a functional form test (like Ramsey's RESET test) may indicate an omitted variable problem.

Exercise 3.2 (Regression – Empirical)

For this exercise we use data on sales, size and other characteristics of 400 Dutch men's fashion stores. The goal is to explain sales per square metre (*sales*) from the characteristics of the shop (number of owners, full-time and part-time workers, number of hours worked, shop size, etc.).

a. Estimate a linear model (model A) that explains *sales* from total number of hours worked (*hoursw*), shop size in square metres (*ssize*) and a constant. Interpret the results.

b. Perform Ramsey's RESET test with $Q = 2$.

c. Test whether the number of owners (*nown*) affects shop sales, conditional upon *hoursw* and *ssize*.

d. Also test whether the inclusion of the number of part-time workers (*npart*) improves the model.

e. Estimate a linear model (model B) that explains *sales* from the number of owners, full-time workers (*nfull*), part-time workers and shop size. Interpret the results.

f. Compare model A and model B on the basis of $\bar{R}^2$, AIC and BIC.

g. Perform a non-nested F-test of model A against model B. Perform a non-nested F-test of model B against model A. What do you conclude?

h. Repeat the above test using the J-test. Does your conclusion change?

i. Include the numbers of full-time and part-time workers in model A to obtain model C. Estimate this model. Interpret the results and perform a RESET test. Are you satisfied with this specification?

Exercise 3.3 (Regression – Empirical)

This exercise uses the data set with house prices of Section 3.4.

a. Create four dummy variables relating to the number of bedrooms, corresponding to 2 or less, 3, 4 and 5 or more. Estimate a model for log prices that includes log lot size, the number of bathrooms, the air conditioning dummy and three of these dummies. Interpret the results.

b. Why is the model under **a** not nested in the specification that is reported in Table 3.1?

c. Perform two non-nested F-tests to test these two specifications against each other. What do you conclude?

d. Include all four dummies in the model and re-estimate it. What happens? Why?

e. Suppose that lot size were measured in square metres rather than square feet. How would this affect the estimation results in Table 3.2? Pay attention to the coefficient estimates, the standard errors and the R^2. How would the results in Table 3.3 be affected by this? Note: the conversion is 1 m^2 = 10.76 ft^2.

Exercise 3.4 (Regression – Empirical)

The data set for this exercise contains 545 observations of young working males in the USA with some professional and personal characteristics for the year 1987. The following variables are available:

logwage	natural logarithm of the wage rate per hour (in US$)
union	dummy variable, 1 if union member
mar	dummy variable, 1 if married
school	schooling in years
exper	experience (in years)
black	dummy variable, 1 if black
hisp	dummy variable, 1 if Hispanic

We want to explain log wages from the other available variables using the following linear model:

$$\begin{aligned} logwage_i = \beta_1 + \beta_2 school_i + \beta_3 exper_i + \beta_4 union_i \\ + \beta_5 mar_i + \beta_6 black_i + \beta_7 hisp_i + \varepsilon_i. \end{aligned} \quad (3.43)$$

We assume that all ε_i and all explanatory variables are independent and that the ε_i are independently distributed with expectation 0 and variance σ^2.

a. Compute summary statistics of all variables in the model, and provide a brief interpretation.

b. Estimate the parameters by OLS. Report and interpret the estimation results, including the R^2. Pay attention to economic interpretations as well as statistical significance.

c. Test, on the basis of the results of **b**, the null hypotheses that being a union member, ceteris paribus, affects a person's expected wage by 5%. Also test the joint hypothesis that race does not affect wages. In each case, formulate the null and alternative hypotheses, present the test statistic and how you compute it.

d. Consider a more general model than (3.43) that also includes $exper_i^2$. Compare this model with the specification in (3.43) on the basis of (i) R^2, (ii) adjusted R^2, (iii) the AIC, and (iv) a t-test. What is your conclusion, and which method do you prefer? (Note: irrespective of your conclusion, continue your analysis with specification (3.43).)

e. Save the OLS residuals from (3.43). Run a regression where you try to explain the residuals from the explanatory variables in (3.43). What do you find? Interpret.

f. How would you extend the above model to allow for the possibility that black union members benefit more from union membership than do non-black union members? Estimate this extended model, and test the hypothesis.

g. Compute and report White standard errors for your OLS results. Compare them with the routinely computed standard errors. What do you conclude? (Note: this covers material from Chapter 4.)

h. Perform a Breusch–Pagan test for heteroskedasticity. Assume that the heteroskedasticity may be related to *all* the explanatory variables in x_i. Interpret the result. (Note: this covers material from Chapter 4.)

4 Heteroskedasticity and Autocorrelation

In many empirical cases, the Gauss–Markov conditions (A1)–(A4) from Chapter 2 will not all be satisfied. As we have seen in Subsection 2.6.1, this is not necessarily fatal for the OLS estimator in the sense that it is consistent under fairly weak conditions. In this chapter we will discuss the consequences of heteroskedasticity and autocorrelation, which imply that the error terms in the model are no longer independently and identically distributed. In such cases, the OLS estimator may still be unbiased or consistent, but its covariance matrix is different from the one derived in Chapter 2. Moreover, the OLS estimator may be relatively inefficient and no longer have the property of being best linear unbiased (BLUE).

In Section 4.1, we discuss the general consequences for the OLS estimator of an error covariance matrix that is not a constant times the identity matrix, while Section 4.2 presents, in a general matrix notation, an alternative estimator that is best linear unbiased in this more general case. Heteroskedasticity is treated in Sections 4.3–4.5, while the remaining sections of this chapter are devoted to autocorrelation. Examples of heteroskedastcity, its consequences and potential solutions are discussed in Section 4.3. This includes the use of heteroskedasticity-consistent standard errors in combination with OLS. Section 4.4 discusses a number of alternative tests that can be used to detect heteroskedasticity. An empirical illustration involving a labour demand equation with heteroskedastic error terms is presented in Section 4.5.

The basics of autocorrelation are treated in Sections 4.6 and 4.7, while a fairly simple illustration is given in Section 4.8. In Sections 4.9 and 4.10 attention is paid to some additional issues concerning autocorrelation, which includes a discussion of moving average error terms and the use of standard errors that are robust to both heteroskedasticity and autocorrelation. Finally, Section 4.11 has an extensive illustration on uncovered interest rate parity, which involves autocorrelation due to a so-called overlapping samples problem.

4.1 Consequences for the OLS Estimator

The model of interest is unchanged and given by

$$y_i = x_i'\beta + \varepsilon_i, \tag{4.1}$$

which can be written as

$$y = X\beta + \varepsilon. \tag{4.2}$$

The essential Gauss–Markov assumptions from (A1)–(A4) can be summarized as

$$E\{\varepsilon|X\} = E\{\varepsilon\} = 0 \tag{4.3}$$

$$V\{\varepsilon|X\} = V\{\varepsilon\} = \sigma^2 I, \tag{4.4}$$

which say that the conditional distribution of the errors given the matrix of explanatory variables has zero means, constant variances and zero covariances. In particular this means that each error term has the same variance and that two different error terms are uncorrelated. These assumptions imply that $E\{\varepsilon_i|x_i\} = 0$, so that the model corresponds to the conditional expectation of y_i given x_i. Moreover, under these assumptions the OLS estimator was shown to be the best linear unbiased estimator for β.

Both heteroskedasticity and autocorrelation imply that (4.4) no longer holds. Heteroskedasticity arises if different error terms do not have identical variances, so that the diagonal elements of the covariance matrix are not the same. For example, it is possible that different groups in the sample (e.g. males and females) have different variances. It can also be expected that the variation of unexplained household savings increases with income, just as the level of savings will increase with income. Autocorrelation typically arises in cases where the data have a time dimension. It implies that the covariance matrix is nondiagonal such that different error terms are correlated. The reason could be persistence in the unexplained part of the model. Both of these problems will be discussed in more detail below. For the moment it is important to note that they both violate (4.4). Let us assume that the error covariance matrix can more generally be written as

$$V\{\varepsilon|X\} = \sigma^2\Psi, \tag{4.5}$$

where Ψ is a positive definite matrix, which, for the sake of argument, we will sometimes assume to be known. It is clear from the above that it may depend upon X. Cases where Ψ does not equal the identity matrix are sometimes referred to as having 'nonspherical error terms'.

If we reconsider the proof of unbiasedness of the OLS estimator, it is immediately clear that only assumption (4.3) was used. As this assumption is still imposed, assuming (4.5) instead of (4.4) will not change the result that the OLS estimator b is an unbiased estimator for β. However, the simple expression for the covariance matrix of b is no longer valid. Recall that the OLS estimator can be written as $b = (X'X)^{-1}X'y = \beta + (X'X)^{-1}X'\varepsilon$. Conditional upon X, the covariance matrix of b thus depends upon the conditional covariance matrix of ε, given in (4.5). In particular, we obtain (for a given matrix X)

$$\begin{aligned} V\{b|X\} &= V\{(X'X)^{-1}X'\varepsilon|X\} = (X'X)^{-1}X'V\{\varepsilon|X\}X(X'X)^{-1} \\ &= \sigma^2(X'X)^{-1}X'\Psi X(X'X)^{-1}, \end{aligned} \tag{4.6}$$

which only reduces to the simpler expression $\sigma^2(X'X)^{-1}$ in (2.32) if Ψ is the identity matrix. Consequently, although the OLS estimator is still unbiased, its routinely computed variance and standard errors will be based on the wrong expression. Thus, standard t- and F-tests will no longer be valid, and statistical inferences will be misleading. In addition, the proof of the Gauss–Markov result that the OLS estimator is BLUE also breaks down, so that the OLS estimator is unbiased but no longer best.

These consequences indicate two ways of handling the problems of heteroskedasticity and autocorrelation. The first implies the derivation of an alternative estimator that is best linear unbiased. The second implies sticking to the OLS estimator but somehow adjusting its standard errors to allow for heteroskedasticity and/or autocorrelation. In fact, there is also a third way of eliminating the problems. The reason is that in many cases you may find heteroskedasticity and (particularly) autocorrelation because the model you are estimating is misspecified in one way or the other. If this is the case, detecting heteroskedasticity or autocorrelation should lead you to reconsider the model and evaluate to what extent you are confident in its specification. Examples of this will be discussed below.

For pedagogical purposes we shall first, in the next section, consider the derivation of an alternative estimator. It should be stressed, however, that this is in many cases not the most natural thing to do.

4.2 Deriving an Alternative Estimator

In this section we shall derive the best linear unbiased estimator for β under assumption (4.5) assuming that Ψ is completely known. The idea behind the derivation is that we know the best linear unbiased estimator under the Gauss–Markov assumptions (A1)–(A4), so that we transform the model such that it satisfies the Gauss–Markov conditions again, that is, such that we obtain error terms that are homoskedastic and exhibit no autocorrelation. We start this by writing

$$\Psi^{-1} = P'P, \tag{4.7}$$

for some square, nonsingular matrix P, not necessarily unique. For the moment, it is not important how to find such a matrix P. It suffices to note that because Ψ is positive definite there will always exist a matrix P that satisfies (4.7). Using (4.7) it is possible to write

$$\Psi = (P'P)^{-1} = P^{-1}(P')^{-1}$$
$$P\Psi P' = PP^{-1}(P')^{-1}P' = I.$$

Consequently, it holds for the error term vector ε premultiplied by the transformation matrix P that

$$E\{P\varepsilon|X\} = PE\{\varepsilon|X\} = 0$$
$$V\{P\varepsilon|X\} = PV\{\varepsilon|X\}P' = \sigma^2 P\Psi P' = \sigma^2 I.$$

In other words, $P\varepsilon$ satisfies the Gauss–Markov conditions. Consequently, we can transform the entire model by this P matrix to obtain

$$Py = PX\beta + P\varepsilon \quad \text{or} \quad y^* = X^*\beta + \varepsilon^*, \tag{4.8}$$

where the error term vector ε^* satisfies the Gauss–Markov conditions.[1] We know that applying ordinary least squares in this transformed model produces the best linear unbiased estimator for β. This, therefore, is automatically the best linear unbiased estimator for β in the original model with assumptions (4.3) and (4.5). The resulting estimator is given by

$$\hat{\beta} = (X^{*\prime}X^*)^{-1}X^{*\prime}y^* = (X'\Psi^{-1}X)^{-1}X'\Psi^{-1}y. \tag{4.9}$$

This estimator is referred to as the **generalized least squares (GLS) estimator**. It is easily seen that it reduces to the OLS estimator if $\Psi = I$. Moreover, the choice of P is irrelevant for the estimator; only Ψ^{-1} matters. We shall see several examples of GLS estimators below that are easier to interpret than this general formula. The point to remember from this expression is that all the GLS estimators that we will see below are special cases of (4.9).

Clearly, we can only compute the GLS estimator if the matrix Ψ is known. In practice this will typically not be the case, and Ψ will have to be estimated first. Using an estimated version of Ψ in (4.9) results in a **feasible generalized least squares** estimator for β, typically referred to as **FGLS** or **EGLS** (with the 'E' for estimated). This raises some additional issues that we will consider below.

The transformed model in (4.8) only plays a role in our construction of an alternative to OLS and is not of economic interest in itself. Nevertheless, the interpretation of (feasible) GLS as OLS in an appropriately transformed model is useful, because it easily allows us to derive the properties of the GLS estimator $\hat{\beta}$ by taking all the standard OLS results after replacing the original variables with their transformed counterparts. For example, the covariance matrix of $\hat{\beta}$ (for a given X) is given by

$$V\{\hat{\beta}\} = \sigma^2(X^{*\prime}X^*)^{-1} = \sigma^2(X'\Psi^{-1}X)^{-1}, \tag{4.10}$$

where σ^2 can be estimated by dividing the residual sum of squares by the number of observations minus the number of regressors, that is,

$$\hat{\sigma}^2 = \frac{1}{N-K}(y^* - X^*\hat{\beta})'(y^* - X^*\hat{\beta}) = \frac{1}{N-K}(y - X\hat{\beta})'\Psi^{-1}(y - X\hat{\beta}). \tag{4.11}$$

The fact that $\hat{\beta}$ is BLUE implies that it has a smaller variance than the OLS estimator b. Indeed, it can be shown that the OLS covariance matrix (4.6) is larger than the GLS covariance matrix (4.10), in the sense that the matrix difference is positive semi-definite.

4.3 Heteroskedasticity

4.3.1 Introduction

The case where $V\{\varepsilon|X\}$ is diagonal, but not equal to σ^2 times the identity matrix, is referred to as **heteroskedasticity**. It means that the error terms are mutually uncorrelated, while the variance of ε_i may vary over the observations. This problem is frequently encountered in cross-sectional models. For example, consider the case where y_i denotes

[1] Alternative transformation matrices P can be found such that the vector $P\varepsilon$ does not exhibit autocorrelation or heteroskedasticity. The requirement that P is nonsingular guarantees that no information is lost in the transformation.

expenditures on food and x_i consists of a constant and disposable income dpi_i. An Engel curve for food is expected to be upward sloping. Thus, on average higher income corresponds to higher expenditure on food. In addition, one can expect that the variation in food expenditures among high-income households is much larger than the variation among low-income households. If this is the case, the variance of ε_i increases with income. Figure 4.1 illustrates this typical case with hypothetical data. Larger values for disposable income correspond to higher expected food expenditures, but also have a higher variance. Observations in the right part of the graph are – on average – further from the true regression line than those in the left part. That is, they have larger absolute values of the error term.

The heteroskedasticity in Figure 4.1 could be modelled as

$$V\{\varepsilon_i|dpi_i\} = \sigma_i^2 = \sigma^2 \exp\{\alpha_2 dpi_i\} = \exp\{\alpha_1 + \alpha_2 dpi_i\} \tag{4.12}$$

for some α_2 and $\alpha_1 = \log \sigma^2$. For the moment, we will not make additional assumptions about the form of heteroskedasticity. We just assume that

$$V\{\varepsilon_i|X\} = V\{\varepsilon_i|x_i\} = \sigma^2 h_i^2, \tag{4.13}$$

where all h_i^2 are known and positive. Combining this with the assumed absence of autocorrelation, we can formulate the new assumption as

$$V\{\varepsilon|X\} = \sigma^2 Diag\{h_i^2\} = \sigma^2 \Psi, \tag{A9}$$

where $Diag\{h_i^2\}$ is a diagonal matrix with elements $h_1^2, \ldots, h_N^2$. Assumption (A9) replaces assumptions (A3) and (A4) from Chapter 2. Clearly, if the variances of the error terms depend upon the explanatory variables, we can no longer assume independence, as in

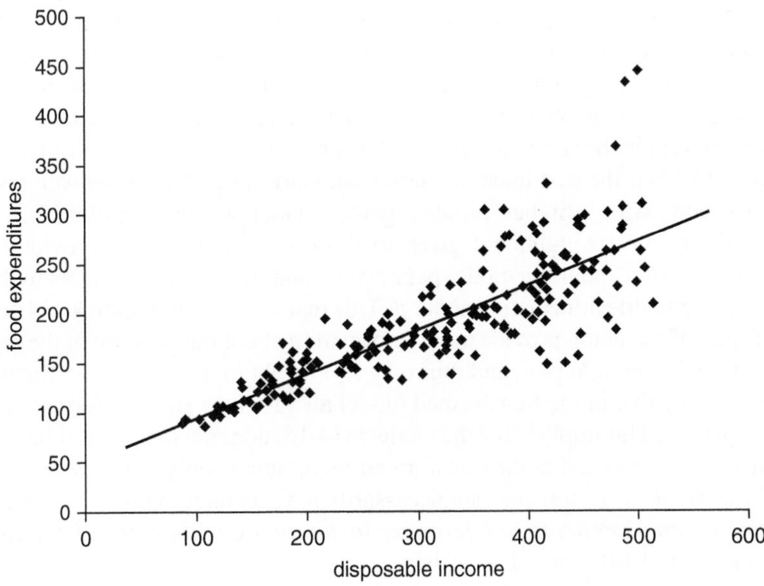

Figure 4.1 An Engel curve with heteroskedasticity.

(A2). Therefore, we replace assumptions (A1) and (A2) with a weaker one, given in (2.30) and (4.3) before. That is, we impose

$$E\{\varepsilon|X\} = 0. \tag{A10}$$

Condition (A10) states that ε is conditionally mean independent of X. This is substantially stronger than condition (A7), which only requires ε_i and x_i to be uncorrelated.

We are interested in the best linear unbiased estimator for β in the model

$$y_i = x_i'\beta + \varepsilon_i, \quad i = 1, \ldots, N \tag{4.14}$$

under assumptions (A9) and (A10). To this end, we can use the general matrix expressions from above. From the structure of Ψ it is easily seen that an appropriate transformation matrix P is a diagonal matrix with elements $h_1^{-1}, \ldots, h_N^{-1}$. Typical elements in the transformed data vector Py are thus $y_i^* = y_i/h_i$ (and similar for the elements in x_i and ε_i). The GLS estimator for β is thus obtained by applying OLS to the following transformed model:

$$y_i^* = x_i^{*\prime}\beta + \varepsilon_i^* \tag{4.15}$$

or

$$\frac{y_i}{h_i} = \left(\frac{x_i}{h_i}\right)'\beta + \frac{\varepsilon_i}{h_i}. \tag{4.16}$$

It is easily seen that the transformed error term is homoskedastic. The resulting least squares estimator is given by

$$\hat{\beta} = \left(\sum_{i=1}^{N} h_i^{-2} x_i x_i'\right)^{-1} \sum_{i=1}^{N} h_i^{-2} x_i y_i. \tag{4.17}$$

(Note that this is a special case of (4.9).) This GLS estimator is sometimes referred to as a **weighted least squares** estimator, because it is a least squares estimator in which each observation is weighted by (a factor proportional to) the inverse of the error variance. It can be derived directly from minimizing the residual sum of squares in (2.4) after dividing each term in the summation by h_i^2. Under assumptions (A9) and (A10), the GLS estimator in (4.17) is the best linear unbiased estimator for β. The use of weights implies that observations with a higher variance get a smaller weight in estimation. Loosely speaking, the greatest weights are given to those observations that provide the most accurate information about the model parameters, and the smallest weights to those that provide relatively little information about β. This makes sense; in Figure 4.1 observations in the left part of the graph provide more information about the position of the regression line than those in the right part, and thus they should get more weight in estimation. It is important to note that in the transformed model all variables are transformed, including the intercept term. This implies that the model in (4.16) does not contain an intercept term. It should also be stressed that the transformed regression is only employed to determine the GLS estimator easily and does not necessarily have an interpretation of itself. That is, *the parameter estimates are to be interpreted in the context of the original untransformed model*, that is, in (4.14) rather than (4.16).

4.3.2 Estimator Properties and Hypothesis Testing

Because the GLS estimator is simply an OLS estimator in a transformed model that satisfies the Gauss–Markov properties, we can immediately determine the properties of $\hat{\beta}$ from the standard properties of the OLS estimator, after replacing all variables with their transformed counterparts. For example, the covariance matrix of $\hat{\beta}$ is given by

$$V\{\hat{\beta}\} = \sigma^2 \left(\sum_{i=1}^{N} h_i^{-2} x_i x_i' \right)^{-1}, \tag{4.18}$$

where the unknown error variance σ^2 can be estimated unbiasedly by

$$\hat{\sigma}^2 = \frac{1}{N-K} \sum_{i=1}^{N} h_i^{-2} (y_i - x_i'\hat{\beta})^2. \tag{4.19}$$

If, in addition to assumptions (A9) and (A10), we assume normality of the error terms as in (A5), it also follows that $\hat{\beta}$ has a normal distribution with mean β and variance (4.18). This can be used to derive tests for linear restrictions on the β coefficients. For example, to test the hypothesis H_0: $\beta_2 = 1$ against H_1: $\beta_2 \neq 1$, we can use the t-statistic given by

$$t_2 = \frac{\hat{\beta}_2 - 1}{\text{se}(\hat{\beta}_2)}, \tag{4.20}$$

where se$(\hat{\beta}_2)$ denotes the standard error of $\hat{\beta}_2$ based on (4.18) and (4.19).

Because we assumed that all h_i^2s are known, estimating the error variance by $\hat{\sigma}^2$ has the usual consequence of changing the standard normal distribution into a t_{N-K} distribution. If normality of the errors is not assumed, the normal distribution is only asymptotically valid. The null hypothesis would be rejected at the 5% level if $|t_2|$ were larger than the critical value of the standard normal distribution, which is 1.96.

As before, the F-test can be used to test a number of linear restrictions on β, summarized as H_0: $R\beta = q$, where R is of dimension $J \times K$. For example, we could test $\beta_2 + \beta_3 + \beta_4 = 1$ and $\beta_5 = 0$ simultaneously ($J = 2$). The alternative is H_1: $R\beta \neq q$ (which means that the equality sign does not hold for at least one element). The test statistic is based upon the GLS estimator $\hat{\beta}$ and requires the (estimated) variance of $R\hat{\beta}$, which is given by $V\{R\hat{\beta}\} = RV\{\hat{\beta}\}R'$. It is similar to (2.63) and is given by

$$\xi = (R\hat{\beta} - q)'(R\hat{V}\{\hat{\beta}\}R')^{-1}(R\hat{\beta} - q). \tag{4.21}$$

Under H_0 this statistic has an asymptotic χ^2 distribution with J degrees of freedom. This test is usually referred to as a **Wald test** (compare Chapters 2 and 3). Because $\hat{V}\{\hat{\beta}\}$ is obtained from $V\{\hat{\beta}\}$ by replacing σ^2 with its estimate $\hat{\sigma}^2$, we can also construct a version of this test that has an exact F distribution (imposing normality of the error terms), as in the standard case (compare Subsection 2.5.6). The test statistic is given by $F = \xi/J$, which under the null hypothesis has an F distribution with J and $N - K$ degrees of freedom.

4.3.3 When the Variances Are Unknown

Obviously, it is hard to think of any economic example in which the variances of the error terms would be known up to a proportionality factor. One example arises when the available data are a cross-section of group averages with different group sizes (e.g. averages within birth cohorts). If the relationship is homoskedastic at the individual level (and individual observations are independent), the variance of the error term of the relationship in terms of the group averages is inversely related to the number of observations per group. That is,

$$V\{\varepsilon_i|x_i\} = \sigma^2 n_i^{-1}, \tag{4.22}$$

where n_i is the number of individuals in group i. In this case, the transformed regression model is given by

$$\sqrt{n_i} y_i = \sqrt{n_i} x_i'\beta + \sqrt{n_i}\varepsilon_i, \tag{4.23}$$

the error term of which is homoskedastic.[2] The weighted least squares estimator then gives higher weight to groups with more observations, which makes sense intuitively.

If the h_is in (4.13) are unknown, it is no longer possible to compute the GLS estimator. In this case $\hat{\beta}$ is only of theoretical interest. The obvious solution seems to be to replace the unknown h_i^2s with unbiased or consistent estimates and hope that this does not affect the properties of the estimator for β. This is not as simple as it seems. The main problem is that there are N unknown h_i^2s and only N observations to estimate them. In particular, for any observation i there is only one residual e_i to estimate the variance of ε_i. As a consequence, we cannot expect to find consistent estimators for the h_i^2s unless additional assumptions are made. These assumptions relate to the form of heteroskedasticity and will usually specify the N unknown variances as a function of observed (exogenous) variables and a small number of unknown parameters. Using consistent estimators for these parameters, we can determine $\hat{h}_i^2$, which in turn is a consistent estimator for h_i^2, and subsequently compute the estimator

$$\hat{\beta}^* = \left(\sum_{i=1}^N \hat{h}_i^{-2} x_i x_i'\right)^{-1} \sum_{i=1}^N \hat{h}_i^{-2} x_i y_i. \tag{4.24}$$

This estimator is a **feasible** (or estimated) **generalized least squares estimator** (FGLS, EGLS), because it is based on estimated values for h_i^2. Provided the unknown parameters in h_i^2 are consistently estimated, it holds (under some weak regularity conditions) that the EGLS estimator $\hat{\beta}^*$ and the GLS estimator $\hat{\beta}$ are asymptotically equivalent. This just means that asymptotically we can ignore the fact that the unknown weights are replaced by consistent estimates. Unfortunately, the EGLS estimator does not share the small sample properties of the GLS estimator, so that we cannot say that $\hat{\beta}^*$ is BLUE. In fact, $\hat{\beta}^*$ will usually be a nonlinear estimator as $\hat{h}_i^2$ is a nonlinear function of y_is. Thus, although we can expect that in reasonably large samples the behaviour of the EGLS and the GLS estimators are fairly similar, there is no guarantee that the EGLS estimator outperforms the OLS estimator in small samples (although usually it does).

[2] In the presence of 'group effects' in the unobservables, the individual error terms are correlated within groups, and weighting group averages by the square root of n_i does not necessarily produce homoskedastic error terms.

What we can conclude is that under assumptions (A9) and (A10), together with an assumption about the form of heteroskedasticity, the feasible GLS estimator is consistent for β and asymptotically best (asymptotically efficient). Its covariance matrix can be estimated by

$$\hat{V}\{\hat{\beta}^*\} = \hat{\sigma}^2\left(\sum_{i=1}^{N} \hat{h}_i^{-2} x_i x_i'\right)^{-1}, \tag{4.25}$$

where $\hat{\sigma}^2$ is the standard estimator for the error variance from the transformed regression (based on (4.19) but replacing $\hat{\beta}$ with $\hat{\beta}^*$).

In the remaining part of our discussion on heteroskedasticity, we shall pay attention to four issues. First, we shall see that we can apply ordinary least squares and adjust its standard errors for heteroskedasticity, without making any assumptions about its form. Second, we shall see how assumptions on the form of heteroskedasticity can be exploited to consistently estimate the unknown parameters in h_i^2 in order to determine the EGLS estimator. Third, we briefly discuss the general role of weighted estimation. Finally, in Section 4.4, we discuss a range of alternative tests for the detection of heteroskedasticity.

4.3.4 Heteroskedasticity-consistent Standard Errors for OLS

Reconsider the model with heteroskedastic errors,

$$y_i = x_i'\beta + \varepsilon_i, \tag{4.26}$$

with $E\{\varepsilon_i|X\} = 0$ and $V\{\varepsilon_i|X\} = \sigma_i^2$. If we apply ordinary least squares in this model, we know from the general results above that this estimator is unbiased and consistent for β. From (4.6), the appropriate covariance matrix is given by

$$V\{b|X\} = \left(\sum_{i=1}^{N} x_i x_i'\right)^{-1}\left(\sum_{i=1}^{N} \sigma_i^2 x_i x_i'\right)\left(\sum_{i=1}^{N} x_i x_i'\right)^{-1}. \tag{4.27}$$

It seems that to estimate this covariance matrix we also need to estimate all σ_i^2s, which is impossible without additional assumptions. However, as argued by White (1980), only a consistent estimator of the $K \times K$ matrix

$$\Sigma \equiv \frac{1}{N}\sum_{i=1}^{N} \sigma_i^2 x_i x_i' \tag{4.28}$$

is required. Under very general conditions it can be shown that

$$S \equiv \frac{1}{N}\sum_{i=1}^{N} e_i^2 x_i x_i', \tag{4.29}$$

where e_i is the OLS residual, is a consistent[3] estimator for Σ. Therefore,

$$\hat{V}\{b\} = \left(\sum_{i=1}^{N} x_i x_i'\right)^{-1}\left(\sum_{i=1}^{N} e_i^2 x_i x_i'\right)\left(\sum_{i=1}^{N} x_i x_i'\right)^{-1} \tag{4.30}$$

[3] To be precise, the probability limit of $S - \Sigma$ equals a null matrix.

can be used as an estimate of the true variance of the OLS estimator. This result shows that we can still make appropriate inferences based upon b without actually specifying the type of heteroskedasticity. All we have to do is replace the standard formula for computing the OLS covariance matrix with the one in (4.30), which is a simple option in most modern software packages. Standard errors computed as the square root of the diagonal elements in (4.30) are usually referred to as **heteroskedasticity-consistent standard errors** or simply White standard errors.[4] The use of such robust standard errors has become a standard practice in many areas of application. Because the resulting test statistics are (asymptotically) appropriate, whether or not the errors have a constant variance, this is referred to as 'heteroskedasticity-robust inference'. In most empirical applications the robust standard errors are larger than their homoskedastic counterparts.

The estimator in (4.30) uses squared OLS residuals to estimate σ_i^2. Because OLS tends to make the residuals as small as possible, this induces a bias in the covariance matrix estimator, somewhat similar to the problem discussed in Subsection 2.3.2. Some modifications of (4.29) have been proposed that are suggested to have better small sample properties (see Davidson and MacKinnon, 2004, Section 5.5). A popular one includes a degrees of freedom correction and employs

$$S^* = \frac{1}{N-K} \sum_{i=1}^{N} e_i^2 x_i x_i' \tag{4.31}$$

rather than (4.29). Despite this adjustment, the calculation of heteroskedasticity-consistent standard errors relies upon asymptotic properties, and their performance in relatively small samples may not be very accurate (see MacKinnon and White, 1985).

If you have some idea about the form of heteroskedasticity (i.e. how h_i depends upon observables and unknown parameters), feasible generalized least squares may provide a more efficient estimator. The following subsection provides an example of this.

4.3.5 Multiplicative Heteroskedasticity

A common form of heteroskedasticity employed in practice is that of **multiplicative heteroskedasticity**. Here it is assumed that the error variance is related to a number of exogenous variables, gathered in a J-dimensional vector z_i (not including a constant). To guarantee positivity of the error variance for all parameter values, an exponential function is used. In particular, it is assumed that

$$V\{\varepsilon_i | x_i\} = \sigma_i^2 = \sigma^2 \exp\{\alpha_1 z_{i1} + \cdots + \alpha_J z_{iJ}\} = \sigma^2 \exp\{z_i'\alpha\}, \tag{4.32}$$

where z_i is a vector of observed variables that is a function of x_i (usually a subset of x_i variables or transformations thereof). In this model the error variance is related to one or more exogenous variables, as in the Engel curve example above.

To be able to compute the EGLS estimator, we need consistent estimators for the unknown parameters α in $h_i^2 = \exp\{z_i'\alpha\}$, which can be based upon the OLS residuals. To see how, first note that $\log \sigma_i^2 = \log \sigma^2 + z_i'\alpha$. One can expect that the OLS residuals

[4] This covariance matrix estimate is also attributed to Eicker (1967), so that some authors refer to the corresponding standard errors as the Eicker–White standard errors.

$e_i = y_i - x_i'b$ have something to tell about σ_i^2. Indeed it can be shown that

$$\log e_i^2 = \log \sigma^2 + z_i'\alpha + \upsilon_i, \qquad (4.33)$$

where $\upsilon_i = \log(e_i^2/\sigma_i^2)$ is an error term that is (asymptotically) homoskedastic and uncorrelated with z_i. One problem is that υ_i does not have zero expectation (not even asymptotically). However, this will only affect the estimation of the constant $\log \sigma^2$, which is irrelevant for our purpose. Consequently, the EGLS estimator for β can be obtained along the following steps.

1. Estimate the model with OLS. This gives the least squares estimator b.
2. Compute $\log e_i^2 = \log (y_i - x_i'b)^2$ from the least squares residuals.
3. Estimate (4.33) with least squares, that is, regress $\log e_i^2$ upon z_i and a constant. This gives consistent estimators $\hat{\alpha}$ for α.
4. Compute $\hat{h}_i^2 = \exp\{z_i'\hat{\alpha}\}$ and transform all observations to obtain

$$y_i/\hat{h}_i = (x_i/\hat{h}_i)'\beta + (\varepsilon_i/\hat{h}_i),$$

   and apply OLS to the transformed model. Do not forget to transform the constant. This yields the EGLS estimator $\hat{\beta}^*$ for β.
5. The scalar σ^2 can be estimated consistently by

$$\hat{\sigma}^2 = \frac{1}{N-K} \sum_{i=1}^{N} \frac{(y_i - x_i'\hat{\beta}^*)^2}{\hat{h}_i^2}.$$

6. Finally, a consistent estimator for the covariance matrix of $\hat{\beta}^*$ is given by

$$\hat{V}\{\hat{\beta}^*\} = \hat{\sigma}^2 \left(\sum_{i=1}^{N} \frac{x_i x_i'}{\hat{h}_i^2} \right)^{-1}.$$

   This corresponds to the least squares covariance matrix in the transformed regression that is automatically computed in regression packages.

4.3.6 Weighted Least Squares with Arbitrary Weights

Occasionally, there are reasons to use a weighted least squares estimator where the weights do not necessarily correspond to the inverse of the error variances. Consider the situation where we have grouped or aggregated data and the number of units per group is different. In this case, we may decide to weight the observations by the number of units in each group, as an attempt to correct for heteroskedasticity, even though we are not sure that the error variance is proportional to the inverse of the group size (it is under some restrictive assumptions). Let us denote the general weighted least squares estimator as

$$\hat{\beta}_w = \left(\sum_{i=1}^{N} w_i x_i x_i' \right)^{-1} \sum_{i=1}^{N} w_i x_i y_i, \qquad (4.34)$$

where $w_i > 0$ is an observed weight variable. If the weights are exogenous, the estimator in (4.34) is unbiased and consistent for β under the same conditions as the OLS estimator

b. However, if the weights in (4.34) are not the optimal weights, corresponding to $1/h_i^2$, the WLS estimator will not be BLUE. Moreover, routinely computed standard errors (based on (4.10)) will be incorrect. Nevertheless, $\hat{\beta}_w$ may be more efficient than OLS. Its covariance matrix is given by

$$V\{\hat{\beta}_w\} = \left(\sum_{i=1}^{N} w_i x_i x_i'\right)^{-1} \sum_{i=1}^{N} \sigma_i^2 w_i^2 x_i x_i' \left(\sum_{i=1}^{N} w_i x_i x_i'\right)^{-1}, \tag{4.35}$$

where $\sigma_i^2 = V\{\varepsilon_i\}$, as before. This can be estimated consistently by using a variant of the heteroskedasticity-consistent covariance matrix discussed in Subsection 4.3.4.

If the weights in (4.34) more or less have a monotonic relationship with the inverse of the error variance, we may prefer to use the weighted least squares estimator, even though the resulting estimator is not the optimal GLS estimator. In this case, we apply the weighting approach to increase the efficiency of our estimator for β and combine it with the use of heteroskedasticity-consistent standard errors, to make sure that our inference is correct even if we do not know the correct form of heteroskedasticity. This way, our results are more efficient than OLS (corresponding to $w_i = 1$), but robust to general forms of heteroskedasticity. Weighted least squares can also be used in cases of stratified sampling, where the weights are used to compensate for the fact that some strata are underrepresented in a sample (e.g. an unrepresentative racial composition); see Cameron and Trivedi (2005, Section 24.3) for more discussion.

4.4 Testing for Heteroskedasticity

In order to judge whether in a given model the OLS results are misleading because of inappropriate standard errors due to heteroskedasticity, a number of alternative tests are available. If these tests do not reject the null, there is no need to suspect the OLS results. If rejections are found, we may consider the use of an EGLS estimator, heteroskedasticity-consistent standard errors for the OLS estimator, or we may revise the specification of our model. In this section, we discuss several tests that are designed to test the null hypothesis of homoskedasticity against a variety of alternative hypotheses of heteroskedasticity.

4.4.1 Testing for Multiplicative Heteroskedasticity

For the first test the alternative hypothesis is well specified and is given by (4.32), that is,

$$\sigma_i^2 = \sigma^2 \exp\{z_i'\alpha\}, \tag{4.36}$$

where z_i is a J-dimensional vector as before. The null hypothesis of homoskedasticity corresponds to $\alpha = 0$, so the problem under test is

$$H_0: \alpha = 0 \quad \text{versus} \quad H_1: \alpha \neq 0.$$

This hypothesis can be tested using the results of the least squares regression in (4.33). There are several (asymptotically equivalent) ways to perform this test, but the simplest one is based on the standard F-test in (4.33) for the hypothesis that all coefficients, except the constant, are equal to zero. This statistic is usually automatically provided in a regression package. Because the error term in (4.33) does not satisfy the Gauss–Markov conditions exactly, the F distribution (with J and $N - J - 1$ degrees of freedom) holds only by approximation. Another approximation is based on the asymptotic χ^2 distribution (with J degrees of freedom) of the test statistic after multiplication by J (compare Subsection 2.5.6).

4.4.2 The Breusch–Pagan Test

In this test, proposed by Breusch and Pagan (1980), the alternative hypothesis is less specific and generalizes (4.32). It is given by

$$\sigma_i^2 = \sigma^2 h(z_i'\alpha), \tag{4.37}$$

where h is an unknown, continuously differentiable function (that does not depend on i), such that $h(.) > 0$ and $h(0) = 1$. As a special case (if $h(t) = \exp\{t\}$) we obtain (4.36). A test for H_0: $\alpha = 0$ versus H_1: $\alpha \neq 0$ can be derived independently of the function h. The simplest variant of the Breusch–Pagan test can be computed as the number of observations multiplied by the R^2 of an auxiliary regression, regressing e_i^2 (the squared OLS residuals) on z_i and a constant. The resulting test statistic, given by $\xi = NR^2$, is asymptotically χ^2 distributed with J degrees of freedom. The Breusch–Pagan test is a **Lagrange multiplier test** for heteroskedasticity. The main characteristics of Lagrange multiplier tests are that they do not require the model to be estimated under the alternative and that they are often simply computed from the R^2 of some auxiliary regression. Chapter 6 provides a general discussion of Lagrange Multiplier tests.

4.4.3 The White Test

All tests for heteroskedasticity above test for deviations from the null of homoskedasticity in particular directions. That is, it is necessary to specify the nature of heteroskedasticity one is testing for. The White test (White, 1980) does not require additional structure on the alternative hypothesis and exploits further the idea of a heteroskedasticity-consistent covariance matrix for the OLS estimator. As we have seen, the correct covariance matrix of the least squares estimator is given by (4.27), which can be estimated by (4.30). The conventional estimator is

$$\hat{V}\{b\} = s^2 \left(\sum_{i=1}^{N} x_i x_i' \right)^{-1}. \tag{4.38}$$

If there is no heteroskedasticity, (4.38) will give a consistent estimator of $V\{b\}$, while if there is, it will not. White has devised a statistical test based on this observation. A simple operational version of this test is carried out by obtaining NR^2 in the regression of e_i^2 on a constant and all (unique) first moments, second moments and cross-products of the original regressors. The test statistic is asymptotically distributed as Chi-squared with P degrees of freedom, where P is the number of regressors in the auxiliary regression, excluding the intercept.

The White test is a generalization of the Breusch–Pagan test, which also involves an auxiliary regression of squared residuals, but excludes any higher-order terms. Consequently, the White test may detect more general forms of heteroskedasticity than the Breusch–Pagan test. In fact, the White test is extremely general. Although this is a virtue, it is, at the same time, a potentially serious shortcoming. The test may reveal heteroskedasticity, but it may instead simply identify some other specification error (such as an incorrect functional form). Moreover, the power of the White test may be rather low against certain alternatives, particularly if the number of observations is small.

4.4.4 Which Test?

In practice, the choice of an appropriate test for heteroskedasticity is determined by how explicit we want to be about the form of heteroskedasticity. In general, the more explicit we are, the more powerful the test will be, that is, the more likely it is that the test will correctly reject the null hypothesis. However, if the true heteroskedasticity is of a different form, the chosen test may not indicate the presence of heteroskedasticity at all. The most general test, the White test, has limited power against a large number of alternatives, whereas a specific test, like the one for multiplicative heteroskedasticity, has more power but only against a limited number of alternatives. In some cases, a visual inspection of the residuals (e.g. a plot of OLS residuals against one or more exogenous variables) or economic theory can help us in choosing the appropriate alternative. You may also refer to the graphs presented in Section 3.6.

4.5 Illustration: Explaining Labour Demand

In this section we consider a simple model to explain labour demand of Belgian firms. To this end, we have a cross-sectional data set of 569 firms that includes information for 1996 on the total number of employees, their average wage, the amount of capital and a measure of output. The following four variables play a role:

labour	total employment (number of workers)
capital	total fixed assets (in million euro)
wage	total wage costs divided by number of workers (in 1000 euro)
output	value added (in million euro)

To set ideas, let us start from a simple production function[5]

$$Q = f(K, L),$$

where Q denotes output and K and L denote the capital and labour input, respectively. The total production costs are $rK + wL$, where r denotes the costs of capital and w denotes the wage rate. Taking r and w and the output level Q as given, minimizing total costs (with respect to K and L) subject to the production function results in demand functions for capital and labour. In general form, the labour demand function can be written as

$$L = g(Q, r, w)$$

for some function g. Because observations on the costs of capital are not easily available and typically do not exhibit much cross-sectional variation, we will, in estimation,

[5] An excellent overview of production functions with cost minimization, in an applied econometrics context, is given in Wallis (1979).

Table 4.1 OLS results linear model

Dependent variable: *labour*			
Variable	Estimate	Standard error	t-ratio
constant	287.72	19.64	14.648
wage	−6.742	0.501	−13.446
output	15.40	0.356	43.304
capital	−4.590	0.269	−17.067

$s = 156.26$ $R^2 = 0.9352$ $\bar{R}^2 = 0.9348$ $F = 2716.02$

approximate r by the capital stock K. The inclusion of capital stock in a labour demand equation may also be motivated by more advanced theoretical models (see Layard and Nickell, 1986).

First, we shall assume that the function g is linear in its arguments and add an additive error term. Estimating the resulting linear regression model using the sample of 569 firms yields the results reported in Table 4.1. The coefficient estimates all have the expected sign: higher wages ceteris paribus lead to a reduction of labour input, while more output requires more labour.

Before interpreting the associated standard errors and other statistics, it is useful to check for the possibility of heteroskedasticity. We do this by performing a Breusch–Pagan test using the alternative hypothesis that the error variance depends upon the three explanatory variables. Running an auxiliary regression of the squared OLS residuals upon *wage, output* and *capital*, including a constant, leads to the results in Table 4.2. The high t-ratios as well as the relatively high R^2 are striking and indicate that the error variance is unlikely to be constant. We can compute the Breusch–Pagan test statistic by computing $N = 569$ times the R^2 of this auxiliary regression, which gives 331.0. As the asymptotic distribution under the null hypothesis is a Chi-squared with three degrees of freedom, this implies a very sound rejection of homoskedasticity.

It is actually quite common to find heteroskedasticity in situations like this, in which the size of the observational units differs substantially. For example, our sample contains firms with one employee and firms with over 1000 employees. We can expect that large firms have larger absolute values of all variables in the model, including the unobservables collected in the error term. A common approach to alleviate this problem is to use logarithms of all variables rather than their levels (compare Section 3.6). Consequently, our first step in handling the heteroskedasticity problem is to consider a loglinear model.

Table 4.2 Auxiliary regression Breusch–Pagan test

Dependent variable: e_i^2			
Variable	Estimate	Standard error	t-ratio
constant	−22719.51	11838.88	−1.919
wage	228.86	302.22	0.757
output	5362.21	214.35	25.015
capital	−3543.51	162.12	−21.858

$s = 94\,182$ $R^2 = 0.5818$ $\bar{R}^2 = 0.5796$ $F = 262.05$

Table 4.3 OLS results loglinear model

Dependent variable: log(*labour*)

Variable	Estimate	Standard error	t-ratio
constant	6.177	0.246	25.089
log(*wage*)	−0.928	0.071	−12.993
log(*output*)	0.990	0.026	37.487
log(*capital*)	−0.004	0.019	−0.197

$s = 0.465$ $R^2 = 0.8430$ $\bar{R}^2 = 0.8421$ $F = 1011.02$

It can be shown that the loglinear model is obtained if the production function is of the Cobb–Douglas type, that is, $Q = AK^{\alpha}L^{\beta}$.

The OLS estimation results for the loglinear model are given in Table 4.3. Recall that in the loglinear model the coefficients have the interpretation of elasticities. The wage elasticity of labour demand is estimated to be −0.93, which is fairly high. It implies that a 1% increase in wages, ceteris paribus, results in almost a 1% decrease in labour demand. The elasticity of the demand for labour with respect to output has an estimate of approximately unity, so that 1% more output requires 1% more labour input.

If the error term in the loglinear model is heteroskedastic, the standard errors and t-ratios in Table 4.3 are not appropriate. We can perform a Breusch–Pagan test in a similar way as before: the auxiliary regression of squared OLS residuals upon the three explanatory variables (in logs) leads to an R^2 of 0.0136. The resulting test statistic is 7.74, which is on the margin of being significant at the 5% level. A more general test is the White test. To compute the test statistic, we run an auxiliary regression of squared OLS residuals upon all original regressors, their squares and all their interactions. The results are presented in Table 4.4. With an R^2 of 0.1029, the test statistic takes the value of 58.5, which is highly significant for a Chi-squared variable with nine degrees of freedom. Looking at the t-ratios in this regression, the variance of the error term appears to be significantly related to output and capital.

Table 4.4 Auxiliary regression White test

Dependent variable: e_i^2

Variable	Estimate	Standard error	t-ratio
constant	2.545	3.003	0.847
log(*wage*)	−1.299	1.753	−0.741
log(*output*)	−0.904	0.560	−1.614
log(*capital*)	1.142	0.376	3.039
$\log^2$(*wage*)	0.193	0.259	0.744
$\log^2$(*output*)	0.138	0.036	3.877
$\log^2$(*capital*)	0.090	0.014	6.401
log(*wage*)log(*output*)	0.138	0.163	0.849
log(*wage*)log(*capital*)	−0.252	0.105	−2.399
log(*output*)log(*capital*)	−0.192	0.037	−5.197

$s = 0.851$ $R^2 = 0.1029$ $\bar{R}^2 = 0.0884$ $F = 7.12$

Table 4.5 OLS results loglinear model with White standard errors

Dependent variable: log(*labour*)			
		Heteroskedasticity-consistent	
Variable	Estimate	Standard error	t-ratio
constant	6.177	0.294	21.019
log(*wage*)	−0.928	0.087	−10.706
log(*output*)	0.990	0.047	21.159
log(*capital*)	−0.004	0.038	−0.098

$s = 0.465$ $R^2 = 0.8430$ $\bar{R}^2 = 0.8421$ $F = 544.73$

As the White test strongly indicates the presence of heteroskedasticity, it seems appropriate to compute heteroskedasticity-consistent standard errors for the OLS estimator. This is a standard option in most modern software packages, and the results are presented in Table 4.5. Clearly, the adjusted standard errors are larger than the incorrect ones, reported in Table 4.3. Note that the F-statistic is also adjusted and uses the heteroskedasticity-consistent covariance matrix. (Some software packages simply reproduce the F-statistic from Table 4.3.) Qualitatively, the conclusions are not changed: wages and output are significant in explaining labour demand, capital is not.

If we are willing to make assumptions about the form of heteroskedasticity, the use of the more efficient EGLS estimator is an option. Let us consider the multiplicative form in (4.32), where we choose $z_i = x_i$. That is, the variance of ε_i depends upon log(*wage*), log(*output*) and log(*capital*). We can estimate the parameters of the multiplicative heteroskedasticity by computing the log of the squared OLS residuals and then estimating a regression of $\log e_i^2$ upon z_i and a constant. This gives the results in Table 4.6. The variables log(*capital*) and log(*output*) appear to be important in explaining the variance of the error term. Also note that the F-value of this auxiliary regression leads to rejection of the null hypothesis of homoskedasticity. To check whether this specification for the form of heteroskedasticity is not too restrictive, we estimated a version where the three squared terms are also included. An F-test on the three restrictions implied by the model presented in Table 4.6 produced an F-statistic of 1.85 ($p = 0.137$), so that the null hypothesis is not rejected.

Recall that the previous regression produces consistent estimates for the parameters describing the multiplicative heteroskedasticity, excluding the constant. The exponential of the predicted values of the regression can be used to transform the original data.

Table 4.6 Auxiliary regression multiplicative heteroskedasticity

Dependent variable: $\log e_i^2$			
Variable	Estimate	Standard error	t-ratio
constant	−3.254	1.185	−2.745
log(*wage*)	−0.061	0.344	−0.178
log(*output*)	0.267	0.127	2.099
log(*capital*)	−0.331	0.090	−3.659

$s = 2.241$ $R^2 = 0.0245$ $\bar{R}^2 = 0.0193$ $F = 4.73$

Table 4.7 EGLS results loglinear model

Dependent variable: log(*labour*)			
Variable	Estimate	Standard error	t-ratio
constant	5.895	0.248	23.806
log(*wage*)	−0.856	0.072	−11.903
log(*output*)	1.035	0.027	37.890
log(*capital*)	−0.057	0.022	−2.636

$s = 2.509$ $R^2 = 0.9903$ $\bar{R}^2 = 0.9902$ $F = 14401.3$

As the inconsistency of the constant affects all variables equiproportionally, it does not affect the estimation results based on the transformed data. Transforming all variables and using an OLS procedure on the transformed equation yields the EGLS estimates presented in Table 4.7. If we compare the results in Table 4.7 with the OLS results with heteroskedasticity-consistent standard errors in Table 4.5, we see that the efficiency gain is substantial. The standard errors for the EGLS approach are much smaller. Note that a comparison with the results in Table 4.3 is not appropriate, as the standard errors in the latter table are only valid in the absence of heteroskedasticity. The EGLS coefficient estimates are fairly close to the OLS ones. A remarkable difference is that the effect of capital is now significant at the 5% level, whereas we did not find statistical evidence for this effect before. We can test the hypothesis that the wage elasticity equals minus one by computing the t-statistic $(-0.856 + 1)/0.072 = 2.01$, which implies a (marginal) rejection at the 5% level. A 95% confidence interval for the wage elasticity is given by $(-0.997, -0.715)$.

The fact that the R^2 in Table 4.7 is larger than in the OLS case is misleading for two reasons. First, the transformed model does not contain an intercept term so that the uncentred R^2 is computed. Second, the R^2 is computed for the transformed model with a transformed endogenous variable. If one were to compute the implied R^2 for the original model, it would be smaller than the one obtained by running OLS. It is known from Chapter 2 that the alternative definitions of the R^2 do not give the same outcome if the model is not estimated by OLS. Using the definition that

$$R^2 = \text{corr}^2\{y_i, \hat{y}_i\}, \tag{4.39}$$

where $\hat{y}_i = x_i'\hat{\beta}^*$, the above example produces an R^2 of 0.8403, which is only slightly lower than the OLS value. Because OLS is defined to minimize the residual sum of squares, it automatically maximizes the R^2. Consequently, the use of any other estimator will never increase the R^2, and the R^2 is not a good criterion to compare alternative estimators. (Of course, there are more important things in an econometrician's life than a high R^2.)

4.6 Autocorrelation

We will now look at another case where $V\{\varepsilon\} = \sigma^2 I$ is violated, namely when the covariances between different error terms are not all equal to zero. The most relevant example of this occurs when two or more consecutive error terms are correlated, and we say that the error term is subject to **autocorrelation** or **serial correlation**. Given our general discussion earlier, as long as it can be assumed that $E\{\varepsilon|X\} = 0$ (assumption (A10)), the consequences of autocorrelation are similar to those of heteroskedasticity: OLS remains unbiased, but it becomes inefficient and its standard errors are estimated in the wrong way.

There are many instances where we expect that error terms of different observations are correlated. The most common case occurs with time series data, where the error terms of one or more consecutive periods are correlated. Recall that the error term captures all (unobservable) factors affecting the dependent variable that the model has not accounted for. It is not unlikely that some persistence exists in these unobservables, leading to serial correlation in the error term. With cross-sectional data, random sampling guarantees that different error terms are mutually independent, and autocorrelation is not an issue. However, when a sample is constructed in a particular (nonrandom) way, correlation between different observations may arise. For example, if our data set contains repeated observations on the same individuals, so-called panel data, we can expect the different error terms of an individual to be correlated. This situation is discussed in Chapter 10. A related situation arises when the data are collected at different hierarchical levels, for example, students within schools, or patients within hospitals. This type of correlation is usually handled in so-called multilevel models. Another case where observations could be correlated cross-sectionally is with spatial data, where the observations correspond to different points in space (e.g. cities). Spatial dependence arises when the error term of one location depends upon values of the neighbouring locations. Lesage and Pace (2009) provide an introduction to spatial econometrics and we shall not pursue it here.

In this chapter, we focus on autocorrelation in time series data. To stress this, we shall follow the literature and index the observations from $t = 1, 2, \ldots, T$ rather than from $i = 1, 2, \ldots, N$. The most important difference is that now the order of the observations does matter and the index reflects a natural ordering. In general, the error term ε_t picks up the influence of all relevant variables that have not been included in the model. Persistence of the effects of excluded variables is therefore a frequent cause of positive autocorrelation. If such excluded variables are observed and could have been included in the model, we can also interpret the resulting autocorrelation as an indication of a misspecified model. This explains why tests for autocorrelation are very often interpreted as misspecification tests. Incorrect functional forms, omitted variables and an inadequate dynamic specification of the model may all lead to findings of autocorrelation.

Suppose you are using monthly data to estimate a model that explains the demand for ice cream. Typically, the state of the weather will be an important factor hidden in the error term ε_t. In this case, you are likely to find a pattern of observations that is like the one in Figure 4.2. In this figure we plot ice cream consumption against time, while the connected points describe the fitted values of a regression model that explains ice cream consumption from aggregate income and a price index.[6] Clearly, positive and negative residuals group together. In macro-economic analyses, business cycle movements may have very similar effects. In most economic applications, autocorrelation is positive, but sometimes it will be negative: a positive error for one observation is likely to be followed by a negative error for the next, and vice versa.

[6] The data used in this figure are taken from Hildreth and Lu (1960); see also Section 4.8.

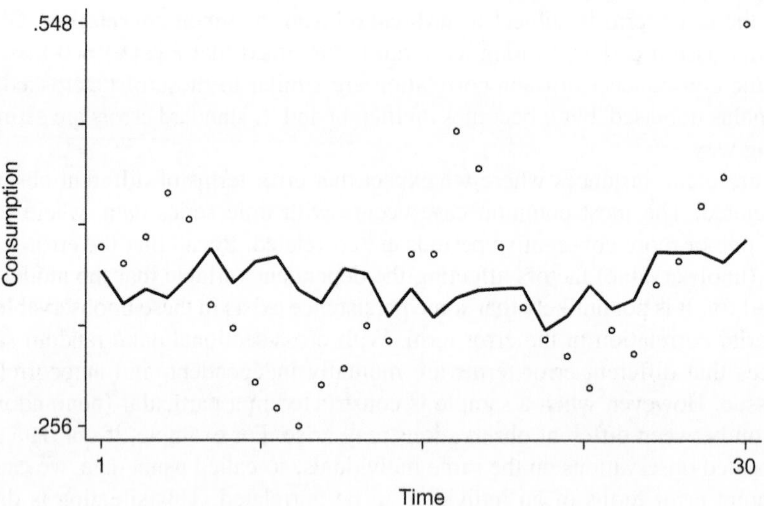

Figure 4.2 Actual and fitted consumption of ice cream, March 1951–July 1953.

4.6.1 First-order Autocorrelation

There are many forms of autocorrelation, and each one leads to a different structure for the error covariance matrix $V\{\varepsilon\}$. The most popular form is known as a first-order autoregressive process, also referred to as $AR(1)$. In this case the error term in

$$y_t = x_t'\beta + \varepsilon_t \tag{4.40}$$

is assumed to depend upon its predecessor as follows:

$$\varepsilon_t = \rho\varepsilon_{t-1} + \upsilon_t, \tag{4.41}$$

where υ_t is an error term with mean zero and constant variance σ_υ^2 that exhibits no serial correlation. This assumes that the value of the error term in any observation is equal to ρ times its value in the previous observation plus a fresh component υ_t, which is independent over time. Furthermore, assumption (A2) from Chapter 2 is imposed, which implies that all explanatory variables are independent of all error terms. The parameters ρ and σ_υ^2 are typically unknown, and, along with β, we may wish to estimate them. Note that the statistical properties of υ_t are the same as those assumed for ε_t in the standard case: thus if $\rho = 0$, $\varepsilon_t = \upsilon_t$ and the standard Gauss–Markov conditions (A1)–(A4) from Chapter 2 are satisfied.

To derive the covariance matrix of the error term vector ε, we need to make an assumption about the distribution of the initial period error, ε_1. Most commonly, it is assumed that ε_1 is mean zero with the same variance as all other ε_ts. This is consistent with the idea that the process has been operating for a long period in the past and that $|\rho| < 1$. When the condition $|\rho| < 1$ is satisfied, we say that the first-order autoregressive process is **stationary**. A stationary process is such that the mean, variances and covariances of ε_t do not change over time (see Chapter 8). Imposing stationarity, it easily follows from

$$E\{\varepsilon_t\} = \rho E\{\varepsilon_{t-1}\} + E\{\upsilon_t\}$$

that $E\{\varepsilon_t\} = 0$. Further, from

$$V\{\varepsilon_t\} = V\{\rho\varepsilon_{t-1} + \upsilon_t\} = \rho^2 V\{\varepsilon_{t-1}\} + \sigma_\upsilon^2$$

we establish that the variance of ε_t, denoted as σ_ε^2, is given by

$$\sigma_\varepsilon^2 = V\{\varepsilon_t\} = \frac{\sigma_\upsilon^2}{1-\rho^2}. \tag{4.42}$$

The nondiagonal elements in the variance–covariance matrix of ε follow from

$$\text{cov}\{\varepsilon_t, \varepsilon_{t-1}\} = E\{\varepsilon_t\varepsilon_{t-1}\} = \rho E\{\varepsilon_{t-1}^2\} + E\{\varepsilon_{t-1}\upsilon_t\} = \rho\frac{\sigma_\upsilon^2}{1-\rho^2}. \tag{4.43}$$

The covariance between error terms two periods apart is

$$E\{\varepsilon_t\varepsilon_{t-2}\} = \rho E\{\varepsilon_{t-1}\varepsilon_{t-2}\} + E\{\varepsilon_{t-2}\upsilon_t\} = \rho^2\frac{\sigma_\upsilon^2}{1-\rho^2}, \tag{4.44}$$

and in general we have, for non-negative values of s,

$$E\{\varepsilon_t\varepsilon_{t-s}\} = \rho^s\frac{\sigma_\upsilon^2}{1-\rho^2}. \tag{4.45}$$

This shows that for $0 < |\rho| < 1$ all elements in the error term vector ε are mutually correlated with a decreasing covariance if the distance in time gets large (i.e. if s gets large). The covariance matrix of ε is thus a full matrix (a matrix without zero elements).

If the model specified in (4.40) is beyond doubt, it is possible to derive a GLS estimator for β that is more efficient than OLS. Using the general discussion in Section 4.2, the required transformation matrix can be derived. However, looking at (4.40) and (4.41) directly, it is immediately apparent which transformation is appropriate. Because $\varepsilon_t = \rho\varepsilon_{t-1} + \upsilon_t$, where υ_t satisfies the Gauss–Markov conditions, it is obvious that a transformation like $\varepsilon_t - \rho\varepsilon_{t-1}$ will generate homoskedastic nonautocorrelated errors. That is, all observations should be transformed as $y_t - \rho y_{t-1}$ and $x_t - \rho x_{t-1}$. Consequently, the transformed model is given by

$$y_t - \rho y_{t-1} = (x_t - \rho x_{t-1})'\beta + \upsilon_t, \quad t = 2, 3, \ldots, T. \tag{4.46}$$

Because this model satisfies the Gauss–Markov conditions, estimation of (4.46) with OLS yields the GLS estimator (assuming ρ is known). However, this statement is not entirely correct, since the transformation in (4.46) cannot be applied to the first observation (because y_0 and x_0 are not observed). The information in this first observation is lost, and OLS in (4.46) produces only an approximate GLS estimator.[7]

The first observation can be rescued by noting that the error term for the first observation, ε_1, is uncorrelated with all υ_ts, $t = 2, \ldots, T$. However, the variance of ε_1 (given in (4.42)) is much larger than the variance of the transformed errors ($\upsilon_2, \ldots, \upsilon_T$), particularly when ρ is close to unity. To obtain homoskedastic and nonautocorrelated errors in a transformed model (which includes the first observation), this first observation should

[7] Technically, the implicit transformation matrix P that is used here is not a square matrix and thus not invertible.

be transformed by multiplying it by $\sqrt{1-\rho^2}$. The complete transformed model is thus given by

$$\sqrt{1-\rho^2}y_1 = \sqrt{1-\rho^2}x_1'\beta + \sqrt{1-\rho^2}\varepsilon_1, \tag{4.47}$$

and by (4.46) for observations 2 to T. It is easily verified that the transformed error in (4.47) has the same variance as υ_t. OLS applied on (4.46) and (4.47) produces the GLS estimator $\hat{\beta}$, which is the best linear unbiased estimator (BLUE) for β.

In early work (Cochrane and Orcutt, 1949) it was common to drop the first (transformed) observation and to estimate β from the remaining $T-1$ transformed observations. As said, this yields only an approximate GLS estimator, and it will not be as efficient as the estimator using all T observations. However, if T is large, the difference between the two estimators is negligible. Estimators not using the first transformed observations are often referred to as Cochrane–Orcutt estimators. Similarly, the transformation not including the first observation is referred to as the Cochrane–Orcutt transformation. The estimator that uses all transformed observations is sometimes called the Prais–Winsten (1954) estimator.

4.6.2 Unknown ρ

In practice it is highly uncommon that the value of ρ is known. This means we will have to estimate it. Starting from

$$\varepsilon_t = \rho\varepsilon_{t-1} + \upsilon_t, \tag{4.48}$$

where υ_t satisfies the usual assumptions, it seems natural to estimate ρ from a regression of the OLS residual e_t on e_{t-1}. The resulting OLS estimator for ρ is given by

$$\hat{\rho} = \left(\sum_{t=2}^{T} e_{t-1}^2\right)^{-1}\left(\sum_{t=2}^{T} e_t e_{t-1}\right). \tag{4.49}$$

This estimator for ρ is typically biased, because (4.48) is a dynamic model (violating assumption (A2)) and because the unobserved error terms are replaced by residuals. Nevertheless, it is consistent under weak regularity conditions. If we use $\hat{\rho}$ instead of ρ to compute the feasible GLS (EGLS) estimator $\hat{\beta}^*$, the BLUE property is no longer retained. Under the same conditions as before, it holds that the EGLS estimator $\hat{\beta}^*$ is asymptotically equivalent to the GLS estimator $\hat{\beta}$. That is, for large sample sizes we can ignore the fact that ρ is estimated.

A related estimation procedure is the so-called iterative Cochrane–Orcutt procedure, which is applied in many software packages. In this procedure, ρ and β are recursively estimated until convergence, that is, having estimated β with EGLS (by $\hat{\beta}^*$), the residuals are recomputed and ρ is estimated again using the residuals from the EGLS step. With this new estimate of ρ, EGLS is applied again, and one obtains a new estimate of β. This procedure goes on until convergence, that is, until both the estimate for ρ and the estimate for β do not change anymore. One can expect that this procedure increases the efficiency (i.e. decreases the variance) of the estimator for ρ. However, there is no guarantee that it will increase the efficiency of the estimator for β as well. We know that asymptotically it does not matter that we estimate ρ, and – consequently – it does not matter (asymptotically) how we estimate it either, as long as it is estimated consistently. In small samples, however, iterated EGLS typically performs somewhat better than its two-step variant.

In many cases, the presence of autocorrelation is an indication that the model is misspecified, for example, suffering from omitted variables. In these cases, the natural approach is to try to improve the specification of the model rather than to change the estimator from OLS to EGLS. We discuss this in more detail in Section 4.10.

4.7 Testing for First-order Autocorrelation

When $\rho = 0$ no autocorrelation is present and OLS is BLUE. If $\rho \neq 0$, inferences based on the OLS estimator will be misleading because standard errors will be based on the wrong formula. More generally, autocorrelation is often seen as a sign of misspecification. Accordingly, it is common practice with time series data to test for autocorrelation in the error term. Suppose we want to test for first-order autocorrelation indicated by $\rho \neq 0$ in (4.41). We will present several alternative tests for autocorrelation below. The first set of tests are relatively simple and based on asymptotic approximations, whereas the last test has a known small sample distribution.

4.7.1 *Asymptotic Tests*

The OLS residuals from (4.40) provide useful information about the possible presence of serial correlation in the equation's error term. An intuitively appealing starting point is to consider the regression of the OLS residual e_t upon its lag e_{t-1}. This regression may be done with or without an intercept term (leading to marginally different results). This auxiliary regression not only produces an estimate for the first-order autocorrelation coefficient, $\hat{\rho}$, but also routinely provides a standard error to this estimate. In the absence of lagged dependent variables in (4.40), the corresponding t-test is asymptotically valid. In fact, the resulting test statistic can be shown to be approximately equal to

$$t \approx \sqrt{T}\hat{\rho}, \tag{4.50}$$

which provides an alternative way of computing the test statistic. Consequently, at the 5% significance level we reject the null hypothesis of no autocorrelation against a two-sided alternative if $|t| > 1.96$. If the alternative hypothesis is positive autocorrelation ($\rho > 0$), which is often expected a priori, the null hypothesis is rejected at the 5% level if $t > 1.64$ (compare Subsection 2.5.1).

Another alternative is based upon the R^2 of the auxiliary regression (including an intercept term). If we take the R^2 of this regression and multiply it by the effective number of observations $T - 1$, we obtain a test statistic that, under the null hypothesis, has a Chi-squared distribution with one degree of freedom. Clearly an R^2 close to zero in this regression implies that lagged residuals are not explaining current residuals and a simple way to test $\rho = 0$ is by computing $(T - 1)R^2$. This test is a special case of the Breusch (1978)–Godfrey (1978) Lagrange multiplier test (see Chapter 6) and is easily extended to higher orders of autocorrelation (by including additional lags of the residual and adjusting the degrees of freedom accordingly).

If the model of interest includes a lagged dependent variable (or other explanatory variables that are correlated with lagged error terms), the above tests are still appropriate provided that the regressors x_t are included in the auxiliary regression. This takes account of the possibility that x_t and υ_{t-1} are correlated, and makes sure that the test statistics have the appropriate approximate distribution. When it is suspected that the error term in the equation of interest is heteroskedastic, such that the variance of ε_t depends upon x_t, the t-versions of the autocorrelation tests can be made heteroskedasticity consistent by using White standard errors (see Subsection 4.3.4) in the auxiliary regression to construct the test statistics.

4.7.2 The Durbin–Watson Test

A popular test for first-order autocorrelation is the Durbin–Watson test (Durbin and Watson, 1950), which has a known small sample distribution under a restrictive set of conditions. Two important assumptions underlying this test are that we can treat the x_ts as deterministic and that x_t contains an intercept term. The first assumption is important because it requires that all error terms are independent of *all* explanatory variables (assumption (A2)). Most importantly, this excludes the inclusion of lagged dependent variables in the model.

The Durbin–Watson test statistic is given by

$$dw = \frac{\sum_{t=2}^{T} (e_t - e_{t-1})^2}{\sum_{t=1}^{T} e_t^2}, \qquad (4.51)$$

where e_t is the OLS residual (notice the different indices for the summations). Straightforward algebra shows that

$$dw \approx 2 - 2\hat{\rho}, \qquad (4.52)$$

where the approximation sign is due to small differences in the observations over which summations are taken. Consequently, a value of dw close to 2 indicates that the first-order autocorrelation coefficient ρ is close to zero. If dw is 'much smaller' than 2, this is an indication for positive autocorrelation ($\rho > 0$); if dw is much larger than 2, then $\rho < 0$. Even under H_0: $\rho = 0$, the distribution of dw depends not only upon the sample size T and the number of variables K in x_t but also upon the actual values of the x_ts. Consequently, critical values cannot be tabulated for general use. Fortunately, it is possible to compute upper and lower limits for the critical values of dw that depend only upon sample size T and number of variables K in x_t. These values, d_L and d_U, were tabulated by Durbin and Watson (1950) and Savin and White (1950) and are partly reproduced in Table 4.8.

Table 4.8 Lower and upper bounds for 5% critical values of the Durbin–Watson test (Savin and White, 1977)

Number of observations	Number of regressors (incl. intercept)							
	$K=3$		$K=5$		$K=7$		$K=9$	
	d_L	d_U	d_L	d_U	d_L	d_U	d_L	d_U
$T=25$	1.206	1.550	1.038	1.767	0.868	2.012	0.702	2.280
$T=50$	1.462	1.628	1.378	1.721	1.291	1.822	1.201	1.930
$T=75$	1.571	1.680	1.515	1.739	1.458	1.801	1.399	1.867
$T=100$	1.634	1.715	1.592	1.758	1.550	1.803	1.506	1.850
$T=200$	1.748	1.789	1.728	1.810	1.707	1.831	1.686	1.852

The true critical value d_{crit} is between the bounds that are tabulated, that is, $d_L < d_{crit} < d_U$. Under H_0 we thus have (at the 5% level)

$$P\{dw < d_L\} \leq P\{dw < d_{crit}\} = 0.05 \leq P\{dw < d_U\}.$$

For a one-sided test against positive autocorrelation ($\rho > 0$), there are three possibilities:

a. dw is less than d_L. In this case, it is certainly lower than the true critical value d_{crit}, so you would reject H_0.
b. dw is larger than d_U. In this case, it is certainly larger than d_{crit} and you would not reject H_0.
c. dw lies between d_L and d_U. In this case it might be larger or smaller than the critical value. Because you cannot tell which, you are unable to accept or reject H_0. This is the so-called 'inconclusive region'.

The larger the sample size, the smaller is the inconclusive region. For $K = 5$ and $T = 25$ we have $d_{L;5\%} = 1.038$ and $d_{U;5\%} = 1.767$; for $T = 100$ these numbers are 1.592 and 1.758.

The existence of an inclusive region and the requirement that the Gauss–Markov conditions, including normality of the error terms, are satisfied are important drawbacks of the Durbin–Watson test. Nevertheless, because it is routinely supplied by most regression packages, it typically provides a quick indication of the potential presence of autocorrelation. Because the distribution depends upon the regressor values, most software packages do not provide a p-value though. Values of dw substantially less than 2 are an indication of positive autocorrelation (as they correspond to $\hat{\rho} > 0$). Note that the asymptotic tests are approximately valid, even without normal error terms, and can be extended to allow for the presence of lagged dependent variables in x_t.

In the less common case where the alternative hypothesis is the presence of negative autocorrelation ($\rho < 0$), the true critical value is between $4 - d_U$ and $4 - d_L$, so that no additional tables are required.

4.8 Illustration: The Demand for Ice Cream

This empirical illustration is based on one of the founding articles on autocorrelation, namely Hildreth and Lu (1960). The data used in this study are time series data with 30 four-weekly observations from 18 March 1951 to 11 July 1953 on the following variables:

cons	consumption of ice cream per head (in pints)
income	average family income per week (in US dollars)
price	price of ice cream (per pint)
temp	average temperature (in Fahrenheit)

A graphical illustration of the data is given in Figure 4.3, where we see the time series patterns of consumption, price and temperature (divided by 100). The graph clearly suggests that the temperature is an important determinant for the consumption of ice cream, which supports our expectations.

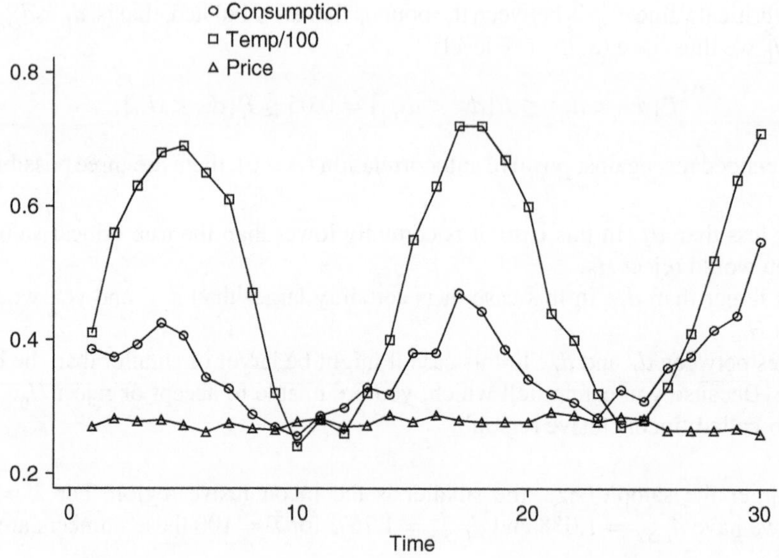

Figure 4.3 Ice cream consumption, price and temperature/100.

The model used to explain consumption of ice cream is a linear regression model with *income*, *price* and *temp* as explanatory variables. The results of a first OLS regression are given in Table 4.9. While the coefficient estimates have the expected signs, the Durbin–Watson statistic is computed as 1.0212. For a one-sided Durbin–Watson test for H_0: $\rho = 0$, against the alternative of positive autocorrelation, at the 5% level ($\alpha = 0.05$) we have $d_L = 1.21$ ($T = 30, K = 4$) and $d_U = 1.65$. The value of 1.02 clearly implies that the null hypothesis should be rejected against the alternative of positive autocorrelation. When we plot the observed values of *cons* and the predicted values according to the model, as in Figure 4.4, we see that positive (negative) values for the error term are more likely to be followed by positive (negative) values. Apparently, the inclusion of *temp* in the model is insufficient to capture the seasonal fluctuation in ice cream consumption.

The first-order autocorrelation coefficient in

$$\varepsilon_t = \rho\varepsilon_{t-1} + \upsilon_t$$

Table 4.9 OLS results

Dependent variable: *cons*

Variable	Estimate	Standard error	t-ratio
constant	0.197	0.270	0.730
price	−1.044	0.834	−1.252
income	0.00331	0.00117	2.824
temp	0.00345	0.00045	7.762

$s = 0.0368$ $R^2 = 0.7190$ $\bar{R}^2 = 0.6866$ $F = 22.175$ $dw = 1.0212$

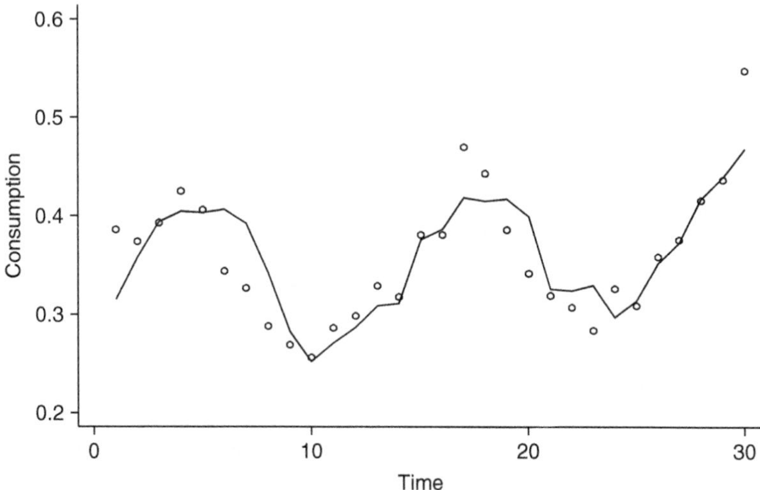

Figure 4.4 Actual and fitted values (connected) of ice cream consumption.

is easily estimated by saving the residuals from the previous regression and running a least squares regression of e_t on e_{t-1} (without a constant).[8] This gives an estimate $\hat{\rho} = 0.401$ with an R^2 of 0.149. The asymptotic test for H_0: $\rho = 0$ against first-order autocorrelation is based on $\sqrt{T}\hat{\rho} = 2.19$. This is larger than the 5% critical value from the standard normal distribution given by 1.96, so again we have to reject the null hypothesis of no serial correlation. The Breusch–Godfrey test produces a test statistic of $(T-1)R^2 = 4.32$, which exceeds the 5% critical value of 3.84 of a Chi-squared distribution with one degree of freedom.

These rejections imply that OLS is no longer the best linear unbiased estimator for β and, most importantly, that the routinely computed standard errors are not correct. It is possible to make correct and more accurate statements about the price elasticity of ice cream if we choose a more efficient estimation method, like (estimated) GLS. The iterative Cochrane–Orcutt method yields the results presented in Table 4.10. Note that the EGLS results confirm our earlier results, which indicate that income and temperature

Table 4.10 EGLS (iterative Cochrane–Orcutt) results

Dependent variable: *cons*			
Variable	Estimate	Standard error	t-ratio
constant	0.157	0.300	0.524
price	−0.892	0.830	−1.076
income	0.00320	0.00159	2.005
temp	0.00356	0.00061	5.800
$\hat{\rho}$	0.401	0.2079	1.927

$s = 0.0326^*$ $R^2 = 0.7961^*$ $\bar{R}^2 = 0.7621^*$ $F = 23.419$ $dw = 1.5486^*$

[8] There is no need to include a constant because the average OLS residual is zero.

Table 4.11 OLS results extended specification

Dependent variable: *cons*

Variable	Estimate	Standard error	t-ratio
constant	0.189	0.232	0.816
price	−0.838	0.688	−1.218
income	0.00287	0.00105	2.722
temp	0.00533	0.00067	7.953
$temp_{t-1}$	−0.00220	0.00073	−3.016

$s = 0.0299$ $R^2 = 0.8285$ $\bar{R}^2 = 0.7999$ $F = 28.979$ $dw = 1.5822$

are important determinants in the consumption function. It should be stressed that the statistics in Table 4.10 that are indicated by an asterisk correspond to the transformed model and are not directly comparable with their equivalents in Table 4.9, which reflect the untransformed model. This also holds for the Durbin–Watson statistic, which is no longer appropriate in Table 4.10.

As mentioned before, the finding of autocorrelation may be an indication that there is something wrong with the model, like the functional form or the dynamic specification. A possible way to eliminate the problem of autocorrelation is to change the specification of the model. It seems natural to consider including one or more lagged variables in the model. In particular, we will include the lagged temperature $temp_{t-1}$. OLS in this extended model produces the results in Table 4.11.

Compared with Table 4.9, the Durbin–Watson test statistic has increased to 1.58, which is in the inconclusive region ($\alpha = 0.05$) given by (1.14, 1.74). As the value is fairly close to the upper bound, we may choose not to reject the null of no autocorrelation. Apparently, lagged temperature has a significant negative effect on ice cream consumption, whereas the current temperature has a positive effect. This may indicate an increase in demand when the temperature rises, which is not fully consumed and reduces expenditures one period later.[9]

4.9 Alternative Autocorrelation Patterns

4.9.1 Higher-order Autocorrelation

First-order autoregressive errors are not uncommon in macro-economic time series models, and in most cases allowing for first-order autocorrelation will eliminate the problem. However, when we have quarterly or monthly data, for example, it is possible that there is a periodic (quarterly or monthly) effect that is causing the errors across the same periods but in different years to be correlated. For example, we could have (in the case of quarterly data)

$$\varepsilon_t = \gamma \varepsilon_{t-4} + \upsilon_t, \tag{4.53}$$

or, more generally,

$$\varepsilon_t = \gamma_1 \varepsilon_{t-1} + \gamma_2 \varepsilon_{t-2} + \gamma_3 \varepsilon_{t-3} + \gamma_4 \varepsilon_{t-4} + \upsilon_t, \tag{4.54}$$

[9] What is measured by *cons* is expenditures on ice cream, not actual consumption.

which is known as fourth-order autocorrelation. Essentially, this is a straightforward generalization of the first-order process. It is possible to test for higher orders of serial correlation using the Breusch–Godfrey test of Subsection 4.7.1. As long as the explanatory variables are uncorrelated with all error terms, the auxiliary regressions correspond to OLS applied to (4.53) or (4.54), where the errors ε_t are replaced by the OLS residuals e_t. Application of EGLS follows along the same lines as with $AR(1)$ errors, where the appropriate transformations will be clear from (4.53) and (4.54).

4.9.2 Moving Average Errors

As discussed, an autoregressive specification of the errors, as in (4.41), (4.53) or (4.54), implies that all error terms are mutually correlated, although the correlation between terms that are many periods apart will be negligibly small. In some cases, (economic) theory suggests a different form of autocorrelation, in which only particular error terms are correlated, while all others have a zero correlation. This can be modelled by a so-called **moving average** error process. Moving average structures often arise when the sampling interval (e.g. 1 month) is smaller than the interval for which the variables are defined (e.g. 1 quarter). Consider the problem of estimating an equation to explain the value of some financial instrument such as 90-day treasury bills or 3-month forward contracts on foreign exchange. If one uses monthly data, then any innovation occurring in month t would affect the value of instruments maturing in months t, $t+1$ and $t+2$ but would not affect the value of instruments maturing later, because the latter would not yet have been issued. This suggests correlation between the error terms 1 and 2 months apart, but zero correlation between terms further apart.

Another example is the explanation of the yearly change in prices (inflation) observed every 6 months. Suppose we have observations on the change in consumer prices compared with the level 1 year ago, at 1 January and 1 July. Also suppose that background variables (e.g. money supply) included in x_t are observed half-yearly. If the 'true' model is given by

$$y_t = x_t'\beta + \upsilon_t, \quad t = 1, 2, \ldots, T \text{ (half-yearly)}, \tag{4.55}$$

where y_t is the half-yearly change in prices and the error term υ_t satisfies the Gauss–Markov conditions, it holds for the change on a yearly level, $y_t^* = y_t + y_{t-1}$, that

$$y_t^* = (x_t + x_{t-1})'\beta + \upsilon_t + \upsilon_{t-1}, \quad t = 1, 2, \ldots, T, \tag{4.56}$$

or

$$y_t^* = x_t^{*\prime}\beta + \varepsilon_t, \quad t = 1, 2, \ldots, T, \tag{4.57}$$

where $\varepsilon_t = \upsilon_t + \upsilon_{t-1}$ and $x_t^* = x_t + x_{t-1}$. If we assume that υ_t has a variance σ_υ^2, the properties of the error term in (4.57) are as follows:

$$\begin{aligned}
E\{\varepsilon_t\} &= E\{\upsilon_t\} + E\{\upsilon_{t-1}\} = 0 \\
V\{\varepsilon_t\} &= V\{\upsilon_t + \upsilon_{t-1}\} = 2\sigma_\upsilon^2 \\
\text{cov}\{\varepsilon_t, \varepsilon_{t-1}\} &= \text{cov}\{\upsilon_t + \upsilon_{t-1}, \upsilon_{t-1} + \upsilon_{t-2}\} = \sigma_\upsilon^2 \\
\text{cov}\{\varepsilon_t, \varepsilon_{t-s}\} &= \text{cov}\{\upsilon_t + \upsilon_{t-1}, \upsilon_{t-s} + \upsilon_{t-1-s}\} = 0, \quad s = 2, 3, \ldots
\end{aligned}$$

Consequently, the covariance matrix of the error term vector contains a large number of zeros. On the diagonal we have $2\sigma_v^2$ (the variance), and just below and above the diagonal we have σ_v^2 (the first-order autocovariance), while all other covariances are equal to zero. We call this a first-order moving average process, or, in short, an $MA(1)$ process, for ε_t. In fact, this is a restricted version because the correlation coefficient between ε_t and ε_{t-1} is a priori fixed at 0.5. A general first-order moving average process would be specified as

$$\varepsilon_t = v_t + \alpha v_{t-1}$$

for some α, $|\alpha| < 1$; see the discussion in Chapter 8 on time series models.

It is generally somewhat harder to apply EGLS with moving average errors than with autoregressive errors. This is because the transformation generating 'Gauss–Markov errors' is complicated. Some software packages have specialized procedures available, but, if appropriate software is lacking, estimation can be quite difficult. An attractive solution is to apply ordinary least squares while correcting standard errors for the presence of autocorrelation (of whatever nature) in ε_t. This will be discussed in the next section. An empirical example involving moving average errors is provided in Section 4.11.

4.10 What to Do When You Find Autocorrelation?

As stressed above, in many cases the finding of autocorrelation is an indication that the model is misspecified. If this is the case, the most natural route is *not* to change the *estimator* (from OLS to EGLS) but to change the *model*. Typically, three (interrelated) types of misspecification may lead to a finding of autocorrelation in the OLS residuals: dynamic misspecification, omitted variables and functional form misspecification.

If we leave the case where the error term is independent of all explanatory variables, there is another reason why GLS or EGLS may be inappropriate. In particular, it is possible that the GLS estimator is inconsistent because the transformed model does not satisfy the minimal requirements for the OLS estimator to be consistent. This situation can arise even if OLS applied to the original equation *is* consistent. Section 4.11 provides an empirical example of this issue.

4.10.1 Misspecification

Let us start with functional form misspecification. Suppose that the true linear relationship is between y_t and $\log x_t$ as

$$y_t = \beta_1 + \beta_2 \log x_t + \varepsilon_t,$$

and suppose, for illustrative purposes, that x_t increases with t. If we nevertheless estimate a linear model that explains y_t from x_t, we could find a situation as depicted in Figure 4.5. In this figure, based upon simulated data with $x_t = t$ and $y_t = 0.5 \log x_t$ plus a small error, the fitted values of a linear model are connected while the actual values are not. Very clearly, residuals of the same sign group together. The Durbin–Watson statistic corresponding to this example is as small as 0.193. The solution in this case is not to re-estimate the linear model using feasible generalized least squares but to change the functional form and include $\log x_t$ rather than x_t.

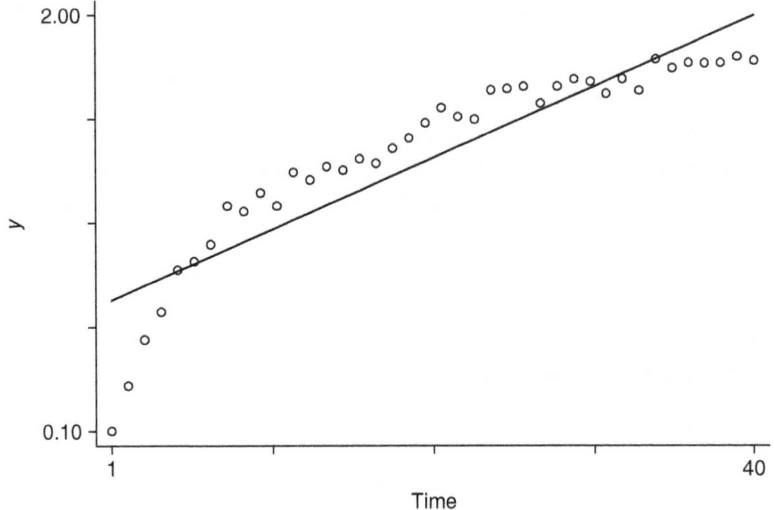

Figure 4.5 Actual and fitted values when true model is $y_t = 0.5 \log t + \varepsilon_t$.

As discussed previously, the omission of a relevant explanatory variable may also lead to a finding of autocorrelation. For example, in Section 4.8 we saw that excluding sufficient variables that reflect the seasonal variation of ice cream consumption resulted in such a case. In a similar fashion, an incorrect dynamic specification may result in autocorrelation. In such cases, we have to decide whether the model of interest is supposed to be static or dynamic. To illustrate this, start from the (static) model

$$y_t = x_t'\beta + \varepsilon_t \tag{4.58}$$

with first-order autocorrelation $\varepsilon_t = \rho\varepsilon_{t-1} + \upsilon_t$. We can interpret the above model as describing $E\{y_t|x_t\} = x_t'\beta$. However, we may also be interested in forecasting on the basis of current x_t values as well as lagged observations on x_{t-1} and y_{t-1}, that is, $E\{y_t|x_t, x_{t-1}, y_{t-1}\}$. For the above model, we obtain

$$E\{y_t|x_t, x_{t-1}, y_{t-1}\} = x_t'\beta + \rho(y_{t-1} - x_{t-1}'\beta) \tag{4.59}$$

and we can write a dynamic model as

$$y_t = x_t'\beta + \rho y_{t-1} - \rho x_{t-1}'\beta + \upsilon_t, \tag{4.60}$$

the error term of which does not exhibit any autocorrelation. The model in (4.60) shows that the inclusion of a lagged dependent variable and lagged exogenous variables results in a specification that does not suffer from autocorrelation. Conversely, we may find autocorrelation in (4.58) if the dynamic specification is similar to (4.60) but includes, for example, only y_{t-1} or some elements of x_{t-1}. In such cases, the inclusion of these 'omitted' variables will resolve the autocorrelation problem.

The static model (4.58) with first-order autocorrelation provides us with $E\{y_t|x_t\}$ as well as the dynamic forecast $E\{y_t|x_t, x_{t-1}, y_{t-1}\}$ and may be more parsimonious compared with a full dynamic model with several lagged variables included (with unrestricted coefficients). It is a matter of choice whether we are interested in $E\{y_t|x_t\}$ or $E\{y_t|x_t, x_{t-1}, y_{t-1}\}$ or both. For example, explaining a person's wage from his or her wage in the previous year may be fairly easy, but may not provide answers to the questions in which we are interested. In many applications, though, the inclusion of a lagged dependent variable in the model will eliminate the autocorrelation problem. It should be emphasized, though, that the Durbin–Watson test is inappropriate in a model where a lagged dependent variable is present. In Subsection 5.2.1, particular attention is paid to models with both autocorrelation and a lagged dependent variable.

4.10.2 Heteroskedasticity-and-autocorrelation-consistent Standard Errors for OLS

Let us reconsider our basic model

$$y_t = x_t'\beta + \varepsilon_t, \tag{4.61}$$

where ε_t is subject to autocorrelation. If this is the model in which we are interested, for example because we want to know the conditional expectation of y_t given a well-specified x_t, we can choose to apply the GLS approach or apply ordinary least squares while adjusting its standard errors. This last approach is particularly useful when the correlation between ε_t and ε_{t-s} can be argued to be (virtually) zero after some lag length H and/or when the conditions for consistency of the GLS estimator happen to be violated.

If $E\{x_t\varepsilon_t\} = 0$ and $E\{\varepsilon_t\varepsilon_{t-s}\} = 0$ for $s = H, H+1, \ldots$, the OLS estimator is consistent, and its covariance matrix can be estimated by

$$\hat{V}^*\{b\} = \left(\sum_{t=1}^{T} x_t x_t'\right)^{-1} TS^* \left(\sum_{t=1}^{T} x_t x_t'\right)^{-1}, \tag{4.62}$$

where

$$S^* = \frac{1}{T}\sum_{t=1}^{T} e_t^2 x_t x_t' + \frac{1}{T}\sum_{j=1}^{H-1} w_j \sum_{s=j+1}^{T} e_s e_{s-j}(x_s x_{s-j}' + x_{s-j} x_s'). \tag{4.63}$$

Note that we obtain the White covariance matrix, as discussed in Subsection 4.3.4, if $w_j = 0$, so that (4.62) generalizes (4.30). In the standard case $w_j = 1$, but this may lead to an estimated covariance matrix in finite samples that is not positive definite. To prevent this, it is common to use Bartlett weights, as suggested by Newey and West (1987). These weights decrease linearly with j as $w_j = 1 - j/H$. The use of such a set of weights is compatible with the idea that the impact of the autocorrelation of order j diminishes with $|j|$. Standard errors computed from (4.62) are referred to as **heteroskedasticity-and-autocorrelation-consistent (HAC) standard errors** or simply **Newey–West standard errors**. With $w_j = 1$ they are referred to as Hansen–White standard errors. HAC standard errors may also be used when the autocorrelation is, strictly speaking, not restricted to H lags, for example with an autoregressive structure. Theoretically, this can be justified by applying an asymptotic argument that H increases with T as T goes to infinity (but not as fast as T). Empirically, this may not work very well in small samples. Modern econometric software packages provide alternative ways to implement HAC standard errors.

Either the researcher should specify the maximum lag length H a priori, or the package selects H as a function of the sample size (e.g. $H = T^{1/4}$). In some programmes, $H + 1$ is referred to as the 'bandwidth'. The Bartlett weights guarantee that the estimator S^* is positive definite in every sample.

4.11 Illustration: Risk Premia in Foreign Exchange Markets

A trader who orders goods abroad that have to be paid for at some later date can settle his required payments in different ways. As an example, consider a European trader who at the end of the current month buys an amount of coffee at the price of US$100 000, to be paid by the end of next month. A first strategy to settle his account is to buy dollars now and hold these in deposit until the end of next month. This has the obvious consequence that the trader does not get the European (1 month) interest rate during this month, but the US one (assuming he holds the dollar amount in a US deposit). A second strategy is to buy dollars at the so-called forward market. There a price (exchange rate) is determined, which has to be paid for in dollars when delivered at the end of next month. This **forward rate** is agreed upon in the current period and has to be paid at delivery (1 month from now). Assuming that the forward contract is riskless (ignoring default risk, which is usually very small), the trader will be indifferent between the two strategies. Both possibilities are without risk, and therefore it is expected that both yield the same return at the end of next month. If not, arbitrage possibilities would generate riskless profits. The implied equality of the interest rate differential (European and US rates) and the difference between the forward rate and the spot rate is known as the **covered interest rate parity** (CIP) condition.

A third possibility for the trader to pay his bill in dollars is simply to wait until the end of next month and then buy US dollars at a yet unknown exchange rate. If the usual assumption is made that the trader is risk averse, it will only be attractive to take the additional exchange rate risk if it can be expected that the future spot rate (expressed in dollars per euro) is higher than the forward rate. If this is the case, we say that the market is willing to pay a **risk premium**. In the absence of a risk premium (the forward rate equals the expected spot rate), the covered interest rate parity implies the **uncovered interest rate parity** (UIP), which says that the interest rate differential between two countries equals the expected relative change in the exchange rate. In this section we consider tests for the existence of risk premia in the forward exchange market, based upon regression models.

4.11.1 Notation

For a European investor it is possible to hedge against currency risk by buying at time t the necessary amount of US dollars for delivery at time $t + 1$ against a known rate F_t, the forward exchange rate. Thus, F_t is the rate at time t against which dollars can be bought and sold (through a forward contract) at time $t + 1$. The riskless interest rates for Europe and the US are given by $R^E_{f,t+1}$ and $R^{US}_{f,t+1}$, respectively. For the European investor, the investment in US deposits can be made riskless through hedging on the forward exchange market. That is, a riskless investment for the European investor would give return

$$R^{US}_{f,t+1} + \log F_t - \log S_t, \tag{4.64}$$

where S_t is the current spot (exchange) rate. To avoid riskless arbitrage opportunities (and unlimited profits for investors), this return should equal the riskless return on European deposits, that is, it should hold that

$$R^{E}_{f,t+1} - R^{US}_{f,t+1} = \log F_t - \log S_t. \tag{4.65}$$

The right-hand side of (4.65) is known as the (negative of the) forward discount, while the left-hand side is referred to as the interest differential. Condition (4.65) is known as covered interest rate parity and is a pure no-arbitrage condition that is therefore almost surely satisfied in practice (if transaction costs are negligible).

An alternative investment corresponds to an investment in US deposits without hedging the currency risk. The return on this risky investment is

$$R^{US}_{f,t+1} + \log S_{t+1} - \log S_t, \tag{4.66}$$

the expected value of which equals (4.64) if

$$E_t\{\log S_{t+1}\} = \log F_t \quad \text{or} \quad E_t\{s_{t+1}\} = f_t,$$

where small letters denote the log of capital letters, and $E_t\{.\}$ denotes the conditional expectation given all available information at time t. The equality $E_t\{s_{t+1}\} = f_t$ together with covered interest rate parity implies the uncovered interest rate parity condition, which says that the interest differential between two countries equals the expected exchange rate change, that is,

$$R^{E}_{f,t+1} - R^{US}_{f,t+1} = E_t\{\log S_{t+1}\} - \log S_t. \tag{4.67}$$

Many macro-economic models employ this UIP condition. One of its consequences is that a small country cannot control both its domestic interest rate level and its exchange rates. Below, attention will be paid to the question as to whether uncovered interest rate parity holds, that is whether risk premia on the forward exchange markets exist.

The reason why the expected future spot rate $E_t\{s_{t+1}\}$ may differ from the forward rate f_t is the existence of a risk premium. It is possible that the market is willing to pay a risk premium for taking the exchange rate risk in (4.66). In the absence of a risk premium, hedging against currency risk is free, and any investor can eliminate his or her exchange rate risk completely without costs. Because the existence of a positive risk premium for a European investor implies that a US investor can hedge exchange rate risk against the euro while receiving a discount, it is not uncommon to assume that neither investor pays a risk premium. In this case, the foreign exchange market is often referred to as being (risk-neutral) 'efficient' (see Taylor, 1995).

Note that the risk premium is defined as the difference between the expected log of the future spot rate and the log of the forward rate. Dropping the logarithm has the important objection that expressing exchange rates in one or the other currency is no longer irrelevant. In the logarithmic case this is irrelevant because $E_t\{\log S^{-1}_{t+1}\} - \log F^{-1}_t = -E_t\{\log S_{t+1}\} + \log F_t$.

4.11.2 Tests for Risk Premia in the 1-Month Market

One approach to test for the presence of risk premia is based on a simple regression framework. In this subsection we shall discuss tests for the presence of a risk premium in the 1-month forward market using monthly data. That is, the sampling frequency corresponds exactly to the length of the term contract. Empirical results will be presented for 1-month forwards on the US$/€ and US$/£ Sterling exchange rates, using monthly data from January 1979 to December 2001. The pre-euro exchange rates are based on the German mark. The use of monthly data to test for risk premia on the 3-month forward market is discussed in the next subsection.

The hypothesis that there is no risk premium can be written as

$$H_0\colon E_{t-1}\{s_t\} = f_{t-1}. \tag{4.68}$$

A simple way to test this hypothesis exploits the well-known result that the difference between a random variable and its conditional expectation given a certain information set is uncorrelated with any variable from this information set, that is,

$$E\{(s_t - E_{t-1}\{s_t\})x_{t-1}\} = 0 \tag{4.69}$$

for any x_{t-1} that is known at time $t - 1$. From this we can write the following regression model:

$$s_t - f_{t-1} = x'_{t-1}\beta + \varepsilon_t, \tag{4.70}$$

where $\varepsilon_t = s_t - E_{t-1}\{s_t\}$. If H_0 is correct and if x_{t-1} is known at time $t - 1$, it should hold that $\beta = 0$. Consequently, H_0 is easily tested by testing whether $\beta = 0$ for a given choice of x_{t-1} variables. Below we shall choose as elements in x_{t-1} a constant and the forward discount $s_{t-1} - f_{t-1}$.

Because $s_{t-1} - f_{t-2}$ is observed in period $t - 1, \varepsilon_{t-1}$ is also an element of the information set at time $t - 1$. Therefore, (4.69) also implies that under H_0 the error terms in (4.70) exhibit no autocorrelation. Autocorrelation in ε_t is thus an indication for the existence of a risk premium. Note that the hypothesis does not imply anything about the variance of ε_t, which suggests that imposing homoskedasticity may not be appropriate and heteroskedasticity-consistent standard errors could be employed.

The data employed are taken from Datastream and cover the period January 1979–December 2001. We use the US$/€ rate and the US$/£ rate, which are visualized in Figure 4.6. From this figure we can infer the strength of the US dollar in 1985 and in 2000/2001. In Figure 4.7 the monthly forward discount $s_t - f_t$ is plotted for both exchange rates. Typically, the forward discount is smaller than 1% in absolute value. For the euro, the dollar spot rate is in almost all months below the forward rate, which implies, given the covered interest rate parity argument, that the US nominal interest rate exceeds the European one. Only during 1993–1994 and at the end of 2001 the converse appears to be the case.

Next, (4.70) is estimated by OLS taking $x_{t-1} = (1, s_{t-1} - f_{t-1})'$. The results for the US$/£ rate are given in Table 4.12. Because the forward discount has the properties of a lagged dependent variable ($s_{t-1} - f_{t-1}$ is correlated with ε_{t-1}), the Durbin–Watson test is not appropriate. The simplest alternative is to use the Breusch–Godfrey test, which is based upon an auxiliary regression of e_t upon $e_{t-1}, s_{t-1} - f_{t-1}$ and a constant (see above)

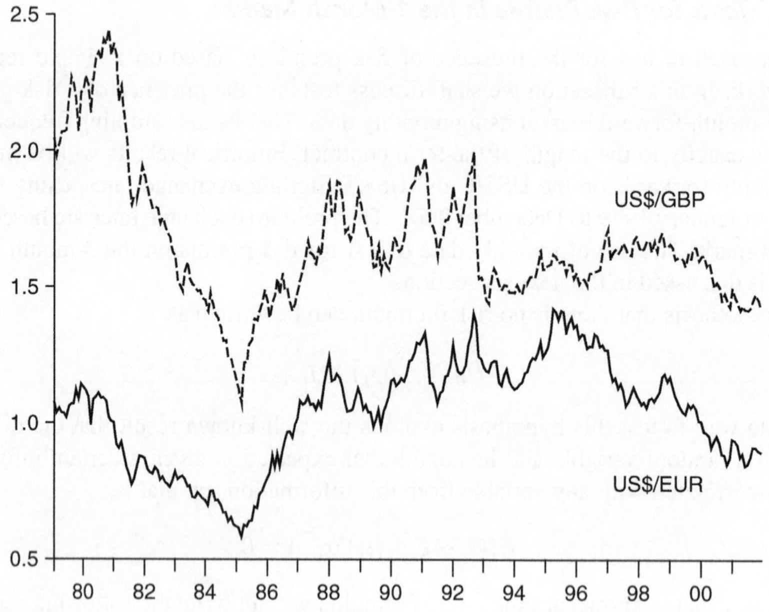

Figure 4.6 US$/EUR and US$/GBP exchange rates, January 1979–December 2001.

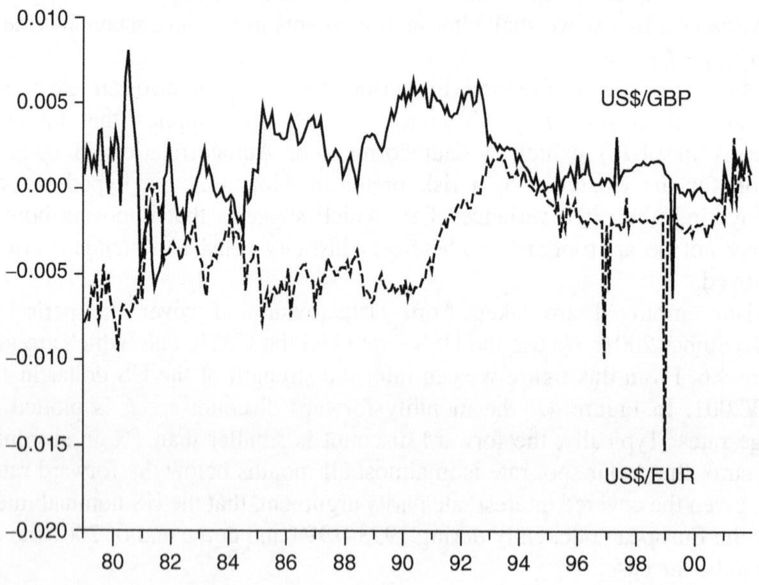

Figure 4.7 Forward discount, US$/EUR and US$/GBP, January 1979–December 2001.

Table 4.12 OLS results US$/£Sterling

Dependent variable: $s_t - f_{t-1}$			
Variable	Estimate	Standard error	t-ratio
constant	−0.0051	0.0024	−2.162
$s_{t-1} - f_{t-1}$	3.2122	0.8175	3.929

$s = 0.0315$ $R^2 = 0.0535$ $\bar{R}^2 = 0.0501$ $F = 15.440$

and then taking[10] TR^2. We can test for higher-order autocorrelations by including additional lags, like e_{t-2} and e_{t-3}. This way, the null hypothesis of no autocorrelation can be tested against the alternatives of first- and (up to) twelfth-order autocorrelation, with test statistics of 0.22 and 10.26. With 5% critical values of 3.84 and 21.0 (for an χ^2_1 and χ^2_{12}, respectively), this does not imply rejection of the null hypotheses. The t-statistics in the regression indicate that the intercept term is significantly different from zero, while the forward discount has a significantly positive coefficient. A joint test on the two restrictions $\beta = 0$ results in an F-statistic of 7.74 ($p = 0.0005$), so that the null hypothesis of no risk premium is rejected. The numbers imply that, if the nominal UK interest rate exceeds the US interest rate such that the forward discount $s_{t-1} - f_{t-1}$ exceeds 0.16% (e.g. in the early 1990s), it is found that $E_{t-1}\{s_t\} - f_{t-1}$ is positive. Thus, UK investors can sell their pounds on the forward market at a rate of, say, \$1.75, while the expected spot rate is, say, \$1.77. UK importers wanting to hedge against exchange rate risk for their orders in the US have to pay a risk premium. On the other hand, US traders profit from this; they can hedge against currency risk and cash (!) a risk premium at the same time.[11]

The t-tests employed above are only asymptotically valid if ε_t exhibits no autocorrelation, which is guaranteed by (4.69), and if ε_t is homoskedastic. The Breusch–Pagan test statistic for heteroskedasticity can be computed as TR^2 of an auxiliary regression of e_t^2 upon a constant and $s_{t-1} - f_{t-1}$, which yields a value of 7.26, implying a clear rejection of the null hypothesis. The use of more appropriate heteroskedasticity-consistent standard errors does not result in qualitatively different conclusions.

In a similar way we can test for a risk premium in the US$/€ forward rate. The results of this regression are as follows:

$$s_t - f_{t-1} = \underset{(0.0031)}{-0.0023} + \underset{(0.766)}{0.485}(s_{t-1} - f_{t-1}) + e_t, \quad R^2 = 0.0015$$

$$BG(1) = 0.12, \quad BG(12) = 14.12.$$

Here $BG(h)$ denotes the Breusch–Godfrey test statistic for up to hth-order autocorrelation. For the US$/€ rate, no risk premium is found: both the regression coefficients are not significantly different from zero and the hypothesis of no autocorrelation is not rejected.

[10] Below we use the effective number of observations in the auxiliary regressions to determine T in TR^2.

[11] There is no fundamental problem with the risk premium being negative. While this means that the expected return is lower than that of a riskless investment, the actual return may still exceed the riskless rate in situations that are particularly interesting to the investor. For example, a fire insurance on your house typically has a negative expected return, but a large positive return in the particular case that your house burns down.

4.11.3 Tests for Risk Premia Using Overlapping Samples

The previous subsection was limited to an analysis of the 1-month forward market for foreign exchange. Of course, forward markets exist with other maturities, for example 3 months or 6 months. In this subsection we shall pay attention to the question of the extent to which the techniques discussed in the previous section can be used to test for the presence of a risk premium in the 3-month forward market. The frequency of observation is, still, 1 month.

Let us denote the log price of a 3-month forward contract by f_t^3. The null hypothesis of no risk premium can then be formulated as

$$H_0\colon\ E_{t-3}\{s_t\} = f_{t-3}^3. \tag{4.71}$$

Using similar arguments to before, a regression model similar to (4.70) can be written as

$$s_t - f_{t-3}^3 = x_{t-3}'\beta + \varepsilon_t, \tag{4.72}$$

where $\varepsilon_t = s_t - E_{t-3}\{s_t\}$. If x_{t-3} is observed at time $t-3$, the vector β in (4.72) should equal zero under H_0. Simply using OLS to estimate the parameters in (4.72) with $x_{t-3} = (1, s_{t-3} - f_{t-3})'$ gives the following results for the US\$/£ rate:

$$\begin{aligned} s_t - f_{t-3}^3 &= -0.014 + 3.135\,(s_{t-3} - f_{t-3}^3) + e_t, \quad R^2 = 0.1146 \\ &\quad\ (0.004) \quad (0.529) \\ &\quad BG(1) = 119.69, \quad BG(12) = 173.67, \end{aligned}$$

and for the US\$/€ rate:

$$\begin{aligned} s_t - f_{t-3}^3 &= -0.011 + 0.006\,(s_{t-3} - f_{t-3}^3) + e_t, \quad R^2 = 0.0000 \\ &\quad\ (0.006) \quad (0.535) \\ &\quad BG(1) = 130.16, \quad BG(12) = 177.76. \end{aligned}$$

These results seem to suggest the clear presence of a risk premium in both markets: the Breusch–Godfrey tests for autocorrelation indicate strong autocorrelation, while the regression coefficients for the US\$/£ exchange market are highly significant. *These conclusions are, however, incorrect.*

The assumption that the error terms exhibit no autocorrelation was based on the observation that (4.69) also holds for $x_{t-1} = \varepsilon_{t-1}$ such that ε_{t+1} and ε_t are uncorrelated. However, this result is only valid if the frequency of the data coincides with the maturity of the contract. In the present case, we have monthly data for 3-month contracts. The analogue of (4.69) now is

$$E\{(s_t - E_{t-3}\{s_t\})x_{t-3}\} = 0 \text{ for any } x_{t-3} \text{ known at time } t-3. \tag{4.73}$$

Consequently, this implies that ε_t and ε_{t-j} $(j = 3, 4, 5, \ldots)$ are uncorrelated but does not imply that ε_t and ε_{t-1} or ε_{t-2} are uncorrelated. On the contrary, these errors are likely to be highly correlated.

Consider an illustrative case where (log) exchange rates are generated by a so-called random walk[12] process, that is, $s_t = s_{t-1} + \eta_t$, where the η_t are independent and identically

---

[12] More details on random walk processes are provided in Chapter 8.

distributed with mean zero and variance σ_η^2 and where no risk premia exist, that is, $f_{t-3}^3 = E_{t-3}\{s_t\}$. Then it is easily shown that

$$\varepsilon_t = s_t - E_{t-3}\{s_t\} = \eta_t + \eta_{t-1} + \eta_{t-2}.$$

Consequently, the error term ε_t is described by a moving average autocorrelation pattern of order 2. When log exchange rates are not random walks, the error term ε_t will comprise 'news' from periods $t, t-1$ and $t-2$, and therefore ε_t will be a moving average even in the more general case. This autocorrelation problem is due to the so-called overlapping samples problem, where the frequency of observation (monthly) is higher than the frequency of the data (quarterly). If we test whether the autocorrelation goes beyond the first two lags, that is, whether ε_t is correlated with ε_{t-3} up to ε_{t-12}, we can do so by running a regression of the OLS residual e_t upon $e_{t-3}, \ldots, e_{t-12}$ and the regressors from (4.72). This results in Breusch–Godfrey test statistics of 7.85 and 9.04, respectively, both of which are insignificant for a Chi-squared distribution with 10 degrees of freedom.

The fact that the first two autocorrelations of the error terms in the regressions above are nonzero implies that the regression results are not informative about the existence of a risk premium: standard errors are computed in an incorrect way and, moreover, the Breusch–Godfrey tests for autocorrelation may have rejected because of the first two autocorrelations being nonzero, which is not in conflict with the absence of a risk premium. Note that the OLS estimator is still consistent, even with a moving average error term.

One way to 'solve' the problem of autocorrelation is simply dropping two-thirds of the information by using the observations from 3-month intervals only. This is unsatisfactory, because of the loss of information and therefore the potential loss of power of the tests. Two alternatives may come to mind: (i) using GLS (hopefully) to estimate the model more efficiently, and (ii) using OLS while computing corrected (Newey–West) standard errors. Unfortunately, the first option is not appropriate here because the transformed data will not satisfy the conditions for consistency and GLS will be inconsistent. This is due to the fact that the regressor $s_{t-3} - f_{t-3}^3$ is correlated with lagged error terms.

We shall therefore consider the OLS estimation results again, but compute HAC standard errors. Note that $H = 3$ is sufficient. Recall that these standard errors also allow for heteroskedasticity. The results can be summarized as follows. For the US$/£ rate we have

$$\underset{}{s_t - f_{t-3}^3} = \underset{[0.005]}{-0.014} + \underset{[0.663]}{3.135}\,(s_{t-3} - f_{t-3}^3) + e_t, \quad R^2 = 0.1146,$$

and for the US$/€ rate

$$s_t - f_{t-3}^3 = \underset{[0.008]}{-0.011} + \underset{[0.523]}{0.006}\,(s_{t-3} - f_{t-3}^3) + e_t, \quad R^2 = 0.0000,$$

where the standard errors within square brackets are the Newey–West standard errors with $H = 3$. Qualitatively, the conclusions do not change: for the 3-month US$/£ market, uncovered interest rate parity has to be rejected. Because covered interest rate parity implies that

$$s_t - f_t = R_{f,t+1}^* - R_{f,t+1},$$

where * denotes the foreign country and the exchange rates are measured, as before, in units of home currency for one unit of foreign currency, the results imply that, at times when the US interest rate is high relative to the UK one, UK investors pay a risk premium to US traders. For the European/US market, the existence of a risk premium was not found in the data.

Wrap-up

Heteroskedasticity is a very common violation of the Gauss–Markov conditions. Its presence invalidates the routinely calculated standard errors for OLS, and implies that OLS is no longer the best linear unbiased estimator for the linear model. If the specification of the model is non-suspect, a convenient way to deal with heteroskedasticity is to calculate heteroskedasticity-robust standard errors. If efficiency is an issue, one may consider the use of generalized least squares, although this comes at the cost of imposing additional assumptions about the form of heteroskedasticity. Several tests are available to test for the presence of heteroskedasticity, including the Breusch–Pagan test and the White test. Changing the functional form of the model, for example by transforming the dependent variable in logs, may help to reduce or eliminate the heteroskedasticity problem. Serial correlation is a concern in time series applications, and is typically interpreted as a sign of misspecification. The Durbin–Watson test provides a quick way to assess the likelihood of first-order serial correlation, but several alternative tests are available that are more generally applicable. If the serial correlation cannot be removed by changing the specification of the model, it can be dealt with by calculating Newey–West standard errors. A typical situation where this is required is when we have an overlapping samples problem. In exceptional cases, the use of GLS can be considered. Time series models will be discussed in more detail in Chapters 8 and 9.

Exercises

Exercise 4.1 (Heteroskedasticity – Empirical)

This exercise uses data for 30 standard metropolitan statistical areas (SMSAs) in California for 1972 on the following variables:

airq	indicator for air quality (the lower the better)
vala	value added of companies (in 1000 US$)
rain	amount of rain (in inches)
coas	dummy variable, 1 for SMSAs at the coast; 0 for others
dens	population density (per square mile)
medi	average income per head (in US$)

a. Estimate a linear regression model that explains *airq* from the other variables using ordinary least squares. Interpret the coefficient estimates.

b. Test the null hypothesis that average income does not affect the air quality. Test the joint hypothesis that none of the variables has an effect upon air quality.

c. Perform a Breusch–Pagan test for heteroskedasticity related to all five explanatory variables.

d. Perform a White test for heteroskedasticity. Comment upon the appropriateness of the White test in light of the number of observations and the degrees of freedom of the test.

e. Assuming that we have multiplicative heteroskedasticity related to *coas* and *medi*, estimate the coefficients by running a regression of $\log e_i^2$ upon these two variables. Test the null hypothesis of homoskedasticity on the basis of this auxiliary regression.

f. Using the results from **e**, compute an EGLS estimator for the linear model. Compare your results with those obtained under **a**. Redo the tests from **b**.

g. Comment upon the appropriateness of the R^2 in the regression of **f**.

Exercise 4.2 (Autocorrelation – Empirical)

Consider the data and model of Section 4.8 (the demand for ice cream). Extend the model by including lagged consumption (rather than lagged temperature). Perform a test for first-order autocorrelation in this extended model.

Exercise 4.3 (Autocorrelation Theory)

a. Explain what is meant by the 'inconclusive region' of the Durbin–Watson test.

b. Explain why autocorrelation may arise as the result of an incorrect functional form.

c. Explain why autocorrelation may arise because of an omitted variable.

d. Explain why adding a lagged dependent variable and lagged explanatory variables to the model eliminates the problem of first-order autocorrelation. Give at least two reasons why this is not necessarily a preferred solution.

e. Explain what is meant by an 'overlapping samples' problem. What is the problem?

f. Give an example where first-order autocorrelation leads to an inconsistent OLS estimator.

g. Explain when you would use Newey–West standard errors.

h. Describe in steps how you would compute the feasible GLS estimator for β in the standard model with (second-order) autocorrelation of the form $\varepsilon_t = \rho_1\varepsilon_{t-1} + \rho_2\varepsilon_{t-2} + \upsilon_t$. (You do not have to worry about the initial observation(s).)

Exercise 4.4 (Overlapping Samples – Empirical)

The data set FORWARD2 also contains exchange rates for the pound sterling against the euro, for the period January 1979 to December 2001. Pre-euro exchange rates are computed from the German mark.

a. Produce a graph of the £/€ exchange rate.

b. Compute the 1-month and 3-month forward discount for this market and produce a graph.

c. Test for the existence of a risk premium on the 1-month horizon using (4.70), including the lagged forward discount as a regressor.

d. Test for autocorrelation in this model using the Breusch–Godfrey test. Use a few different values for the maximum lag length. Why is the Durbin–Watson test not valid in this case?

e. Test for the existence of a risk premium on the 3-month horizon using (4.72), including the 3-month forward discount, lagged 3 months, as a regressor.

f. Test for autocorrelation in this model using the Breusch–Godfrey test for up to two lags and for up to 12 lags.

g. Test for autocorrelation in this model for lags 3 to 12.

h. Compute HAC standard errors for the 3-month risk premium regression.

i. Interpret your results and compare with those reported in Section 4.11.

5 Endogenous Regressors, Instrumental Variables and GMM

Until now, it was assumed that the error terms in the linear regression model were contemporaneously uncorrelated with the explanatory variables, or – even stronger – that they were *independent* of *all* explanatory variables.[1] As a result, the linear model could be interpreted as describing the conditional expectation of y_t given a set of variables x_t. In this chapter we shall discuss cases in which it is unrealistic or impossible to treat the explanatory variables in a model as given or exogenous. In such cases, it can be argued that some of the explanatory variables are correlated with the equation's error term, such that the OLS estimator is biased and inconsistent. There are different reasons why one may argue that error terms are contemporaneously correlated with one or more of the explanatory variables, but the common aspect is that the linear model no longer corresponds to a conditional expectation or a best linear approximation.

In Section 5.1, we start with a review of the properties of the OLS estimator in the linear model under different sets of assumptions. Section 5.2 discusses cases where the OLS estimator cannot be shown to be unbiased or consistent. In such cases, we need to look for alternative estimators. The instrumental variables estimator is considered in Sections 5.3 and 5.6, while in Section 5.8 we extend this class of instrumental variables estimators to the generalized method of moments (GMM), which also allows estimation of nonlinear models. Given the increased popularity of causal inference in empirical work, Section 5.5 briefly discusses other approaches than instrumental variables for this purpose. Empirical illustrations concerning the returns to schooling, the impact of institutions on economic

[1] Recall that independence is stronger than uncorrelatedness (see Appendix B).

development and the estimation of intertemporal asset pricing models are provided in Sections 5.4, 5.7 and 5.9, respectively.

5.1 A Review of the Properties of the OLS Estimator

Let us consider the linear model again

$$y_t = x_t'\beta + \varepsilon_t, \quad t = 1, 2, \ldots, T, \tag{5.1}$$

or, in matrix notation,

$$y = X\beta + \varepsilon. \tag{5.2}$$

In Chapters 2 and 4 we saw that the OLS estimator b is unbiased for β if it can be assumed that ε is mean zero and conditional mean independent of X, that is, if $E\{\varepsilon|X\} = 0$ (assumption (A10) from Chapter 4). This says that knowing any of the explanatory variables is uninformative about the expected value of any of the error terms. Independence of X and ε with $E\{\varepsilon\} = 0$ (assumptions (A1) and (A2) from Section 2.3) implies that $E\{\varepsilon|X\} = 0$ but is stronger, as it does not allow the variance of ε to depend upon X either.

In many cases, the assumption that ε is conditionally mean independent of X is too strong. To illustrate this, let us start with a motivating example. The efficient market hypothesis (under constant expected returns) implies that the returns on any asset are unpredictable from any publicly available information. Under the so-called weak form of the efficient market hypothesis, asset returns cannot be predicted from their own past (see Fama, 1991). This hypothesis can be tested statistically using a regression model and testing whether lagged returns explain current returns. That is, in the model

$$y_t = \beta_1 + \beta_2 y_{t-1} + \beta_3 y_{t-2} + \varepsilon_t, \tag{5.3}$$

where y_t denotes the return in period t, the null hypothesis of weak form efficiency implies that $\beta_2 = \beta_3 = 0$. Because the explanatory variables are lagged dependent variables (which are a function of lagged error terms), the assumption $E\{\varepsilon|X\} = 0$ is inappropriate. Nevertheless, we can make weaker assumptions under which the OLS estimator is consistent for $\beta = (\beta_1, \beta_2, \beta_3)'$.

In the notation of the more general model (5.1), consider the following set of assumptions:

$$x_t \text{ and } \varepsilon_t \text{ are independent (for each } t) \tag{A8}$$

$$\varepsilon_t \sim IID(0, \sigma^2), \tag{A11}$$

where the notation in (A11) is shorthand for saying that the error terms ε_t are independent and identically distributed (i.i.d.) with mean zero and variance σ^2. Under some additional regularity conditions,[2] the OLS estimator b is consistent for β and asymptotically normally distributed (CAN) with covariance matrix $\sigma^2\Sigma_{xx}^{-1}$, with

$$\Sigma_{xx} = \underset{T\to\infty}{\text{plim}} \frac{1}{T} \sum_{t=1}^{T} x_t x_t'.$$

[2] We shall not present any proofs or derivations here. The interested reader is referred to more advanced textbooks, like Hamilton (1994, Chapter 8). The most important 'regularity condition' is that Σ_{xx} is finite and invertible (compare assumption (A6) from Section 2.6).

Formally it holds that

$$\sqrt{T}(b-\beta) \to \mathcal{N}(0, \sigma^2\Sigma_{xx}^{-1}), \tag{5.4}$$

which corresponds to (2.74) from Chapter 2. In small samples, it thus holds approximately that

$$b \overset{a}{\sim} \mathcal{N}\left(\beta, \sigma^2\left(\sum_{t=1}^{T} x_t x_t'\right)^{-1}\right). \tag{5.5}$$

This distributional result for the OLS estimator is the same as that obtained under the Gauss–Markov assumptions (A1)–(A4), combined with normality of the error terms in (A5), albeit that (5.5) only holds approximately by virtue of the asymptotic result in (5.4). This means that *all standard tests in the linear model* (t-tests, F-tests and Wald tests) *are valid by approximation, provided assumptions (A8) and (A11) are satisfied.* For the asymptotic distribution in (5.4) to be valid we have to assume that x_t and ε_t are independent (for each t). This means that x_s is allowed to depend upon ε_t as long as $s \neq t$. The inclusion of a lagged dependent variable as in (5.3) is the most important example of such a situation. The current result shows that, as long as the error terms are independently and identically distributed, the presence of a lagged dependent variable in x_t only affects the small sample properties of the OLS estimator but not the asymptotic distribution. Under assumptions (A6), (A8) and (A11), the OLS estimator is consistent, asymptotically normally distributed (CAN) and asymptotically efficient.

Assumption (A11) excludes autocorrelation and heteroskedasticity in ε_t. In the example above, autocorrelation can be excluded as it is a violation of market efficiency (returns should be unpredictable). The homoskedasticity assumption is more problematic. Heteroskedasticity may arise when the error term is more likely to take on extreme values for particular values of one or more of the regressors. In this case the variance of ε_t depends upon x_t. Similarly, shocks in financial time series are usually clustered over time, that is, big shocks are likely to be followed by big shocks, in either direction. An example of this is that, in periods of financial turbulence, it is hard to predict whether stock prices will go up or down, but it is clear that there is much more uncertainty in the market than in other periods. In this case, the variance of ε_t depends upon historical innovations $\varepsilon_{t-1}, \varepsilon_{t-2}, \ldots$. Such cases are referred to as conditional heteroskedasticity, or sometimes just as ARCH or GARCH, which are particular specifications to model this phenomenon.[3]

When assumption (A11) is dropped, it can no longer be claimed that $\sigma^2\Sigma_{xx}^{-1}$ is the appropriate covariance matrix, nor that (5.5) holds by approximation. This means that routinely computed standard errors are incorrect. In general, however, consistency and asymptotic normality of b are not affected. Moreover, asymptotically valid inferences can be made if we estimate the covariance matrix in a different way. Let us relax assumptions (A8) and (A11) to

$$E\{x_t\varepsilon_t\} = 0 \text{ for each } t \tag{A7}$$

$$\varepsilon_t \text{ are serially uncorrelated with expectation zero.} \tag{A12}$$

[3] ARCH is short for AutoRegressive Conditional Heteroskedasticity, and GARCH is a Generalized form of that. We shall discuss this in more detail in Chapter 8.

Assumption (A7) imposes that x_t is uncorrelated[4] with ε_t, while (A12) allows for heteroskedasticity in the error term, but excludes autocorrelation. Under some additional regularity conditions, it can be shown that the OLS estimator b is consistent for β and asymptotically normal according to

$$\sqrt{T}(b - \beta) \to \mathcal{N}(0, \Sigma_{xx}^{-1}\Sigma\Sigma_{xx}^{-1}), \tag{5.6}$$

where

$$\Sigma \equiv \text{plim}\ \frac{1}{T}\sum_{t=1}^{T} \varepsilon_t^2 x_t x_t'.$$

In this case, the asymptotic covariance matrix can be estimated following the method of White (see Subsection 4.3.4), and

$$\hat{V}\{b\} = \left(\sum_{t=1}^{T} x_t x_t'\right)^{-1} \sum_{t=1}^{T} e_t^2 x_t x_t' \left(\sum_{t=1}^{T} x_t x_t'\right)^{-1}, \tag{5.7}$$

where e_t denotes the OLS residual, is a consistent estimator for the true covariance matrix of the OLS estimator under assumptions (A6), (A7) and (A12). Consequently, all standard tests for the linear model are asymptotically valid in the presence of heteroskedasticity of unknown form if the test statistics are adjusted by replacing the standard estimate for the OLS covariance matrix with the heteroskedasticity-consistent estimate from (5.7).

Suppose one is interested in predictability of long-horizon returns, for example over a horizon of several years. In principle, tests of long-term predictability can be carried out along the same lines as short-term predictability tests. However, for horizons of 5 years, say, this would imply that only a limited number of 5-year returns can be analysed, even if the sample period covers several decades. Therefore, tests of predictability of long-horizon returns have typically tried to make more efficient use of the available information by using overlapping samples (compare Subsection 4.11.3); see Fama and French (1988) for an application. In this case, 5-year returns are computed over all periods of five consecutive years. Ignoring second-order effects, the return over 5 years is simply the sum of five annual returns, so that the return over 1990–1994 partly overlaps with, for example, the returns over 1991–1995 and 1992–1996. Denoting the return in year t as y_t, the 5-year return over the years t to $t + 4$ is given by $Y_t = \sum_{j=0}^{4} y_{t+j}$. To test the predictability of these 5-year returns, suppose we estimate a model that explains Y_t from its value in the previous 5-year period (Y_{t-5}) using data for every year, that is,

$$Y_t = \delta_5 + \theta_5 Y_{t-5} + \varepsilon_t, \quad t = 1, \ldots, T \text{ years}. \tag{5.8}$$

All T *annual* observations in the sample on *5-year* returns are regressed on a constant and the 5-year return *lagged 5 years*. In this model the error term exhibits *autocorrelation* because of the overlapping samples problem. In order to explain this issue, assume that the following model holds for annual returns

$$y_t = \delta_1 + \theta_1 y_{t-1} + u_t, \tag{5.9}$$

where u_t exhibits no autocorrelation. Under the null hypothesis that $\theta_1 = 0$, it can be shown that $\delta_5 = 5\delta_1$ and $\theta_5 = 0$, while $\varepsilon_t = \sum_{j=0}^{4} u_{t+j}$. Consequently, the covariance

[4] Note that $E\{x_t z_t\} = \text{cov}\{x_t, z_t\}$ if either x_t or z_t has a zero mean (see Appendix B).

between ε_t and ε_{t-j} is nonzero as long as $j < 5$. From Chapter 4 we know that the presence of autocorrelation invalidates routinely computed standard errors, including those based on the heteroskedasticity-consistent covariance matrix in (5.7). However, if we can still assume that $E\{\varepsilon_t\} = 0$, the regressors are contemporaneously uncorrelated with the error terms (condition (A7)), and the autocorrelation is zero after H periods, it can be shown that all results based on assumptions (A7) and (A12) hold true if the covariance matrix of the OLS estimator is estimated by the Newey–West (1987) estimator presented in Subsection 4.10.2. Then,

$$\hat{V}^*\{b\} = \left(\sum_{t=1}^{T} x_t x_t'\right)^{-1} TS^* \left(\sum_{t=1}^{T} x_t x_t'\right)^{-1}, \tag{5.10}$$

where

$$S^* = \frac{1}{T}\sum_{t=1}^{T} e_t^2 x_t x_t' + \frac{1}{T}\sum_{j=1}^{H-1} w_j \sum_{s=j+1}^{T} e_s e_{s-j}(x_s x_{s-j}' + x_{s-j} x_s') \tag{5.11}$$

with $w_j = 1 - j/H$. Note that in the above example H equals 5. As a consequence, the standard tests from the linear model are asymptotically valid in the presence of heteroskedasticity and autocorrelation (up to a finite number of lags) if we replace the standard covariance matrix estimate with the heteroskedasticity- and autocorrelation-consistent estimate from (5.10).

5.2 Cases Where the OLS Estimator Cannot Be Saved

The previous section shows that we can go as far as assumption (A7) and impose $E\{\varepsilon_t x_t\} = 0$, essentially without affecting the consistency of the OLS estimator. If the autocorrelation in the error term is somehow restricted, it is still possible to make appropriate inferences in this case, using the White or Newey–West estimates for the covariance matrix. The assumption that $E\{\varepsilon_t x_t\} = 0$ says that error terms and explanatory variables are *contemporaneously uncorrelated*. Sometimes there are statistical or economic reasons why we would not want to impose this condition. In such cases, we can no longer argue that the OLS estimator is unbiased or consistent, and we need to consider alternative estimators. Some examples of such situations are the presence of a lagged dependent variable and autocorrelation in the error term, **measurement errors** in the regressors, and **simultaneity** or **endogeneity** of regressors. Let us now consider examples of these situations in turn.

5.2.1 *Autocorrelation with a Lagged Dependent Variable*

Suppose the model of interest is given by

$$y_t = \beta_1 + \beta_2 x_t + \beta_3 y_{t-1} + \varepsilon_t, \tag{5.12}$$

where x_t is a single variable. Recall that, as long as we can assume that $E\{x_t\varepsilon_t\} = 0$ and $E\{y_{t-1}\varepsilon_t\} = 0$ for all t, the OLS estimator for β is consistent (provided that some regularity conditions are met). However, suppose that ε_t is subject to first-order autocorrelation as in (4.41), that is,

$$\varepsilon_t = \rho\varepsilon_{t-1} + \upsilon_t. \tag{5.13}$$

Now, we can rewrite the model as

$$y_t = \beta_1 + \beta_2 x_t + \beta_3 y_{t-1} + \rho\varepsilon_{t-1} + \upsilon_t. \tag{5.14}$$

But it also holds that

$$y_{t-1} = \beta_1 + \beta_2 x_{t-1} + \beta_3 y_{t-2} + \varepsilon_{t-1}, \tag{5.15}$$

from which it follows immediately that the error term ε_t is correlated with y_{t-1}. Thus, if $\rho \neq 0$, OLS no longer yields consistent estimators for the regression parameters in (5.12). A possible solution is the use of maximum likelihood or instrumental variables techniques, which will be discussed below; Stewart and Gill (1998, Section 7.4) provide additional discussion and details. Note that the Durbin–Watson test is not valid to test for autocorrelation in model (5.12), because the condition that the explanatory variables can be treated as deterministic is violated. An alternative test is provided by the Breusch–Godfrey Lagrange multiplier test for autocorrelation (see Section 4.7, or Chapter 6 for a general discussion on Lagrange multiplier tests). This test statistic can be computed as T times the R^2 of a regression of the least squares residuals e_t on e_{t-1} and all included explanatory variables (including the relevant lagged values of y_t). Under H_0, the test statistic asymptotically has a Chi-squared distribution with one degree of freedom.

In the above example the linear regression model does not correspond to the conditional expectation of y_t given x_t and y_{t-1}. Because knowledge of y_{t-1} tells us something about the expected value of the error term ε_t, it will be the case that $E\{\varepsilon_t|x_t, y_{t-1}\}$ is a function of y_{t-1}. Consequently, the last term in

$$E\{y_t|x_t, y_{t-1}\} = \beta_1 + \beta_2 x_t + \beta_3 y_{t-1} + E\{\varepsilon_t|x_t, y_{t-1}\} \tag{5.16}$$

will be nonzero. As we know that OLS is generally consistent when estimating a conditional expectation, we may suspect that OLS is inconsistent whenever the model we are estimating does not correspond to a conditional expectation. A lagged dependent variable, combined with autocorrelation of the error term, is such a case.

5.2.2 Measurement Error in an Explanatory Variable

Another situation where the OLS estimator is likely to be inconsistent arises when an explanatory variable is subject to measurement error. Suppose that a variable y_t depends upon a variable w_t according to

$$y_t = \beta_1 + \beta_2 w_t + \upsilon_t, \tag{5.17}$$

where υ_t is an error term with zero mean and variance σ_υ^2. It is assumed that $E\{\upsilon_t|w_t\} = 0$, such that the model describes the expected value of y_t given w_t,

$$E\{y_t|w_t\} = \beta_1 + \beta_2 w_t.$$

As an example, think of y_t denoting household savings and w_t denoting disposable income. Suppose that w_t cannot be measured absolutely accurately (e.g. because of misreporting) and let us denote the *measured* value for w_t by x_t. For each observation, x_t equals – by construction – the true value w_t plus the **measurement error** u_t, that is,

$$x_t = w_t + u_t. \tag{5.18}$$

Let us consider the following set of assumptions, which may be reasonable in certain applications. First, it is assumed that the measurement error u_t is mean zero with constant variance σ_u^2. Second, u_t is assumed to be independent of the error term v_t in the model. Third, and most importantly, the measurement error is independent of the underlying true value w_t. This means that the true level of disposable income (in our example) does not reveal any information about the size, sign or value of the measurement error. Substituting (5.18) into (5.17), we obtain

$$y_t = \beta_1 + \beta_2 x_t + \varepsilon_t, \tag{5.19}$$

where $\varepsilon_t = v_t - \beta_2 u_t$.

Equation (5.19) presents a linear model in terms of the observables y_t and x_t with an error term ε_t. If we use the available data on y_t and x_t, and unsuspectingly regress y_t upon x_t and a constant, the OLS estimator b is inconsistent for $\beta = (\beta_1, \beta_2)'$, because x_t depends on u_t and so does ε_t. That is, $E\{x_t \varepsilon_t\} \neq 0$ and one of the necessary conditions for consistency of b is violated. Suppose that $\beta_2 > 0$. When the measurement error in an observation is positive, two things happen: x_t has a positive component u_t, and ε_t has a negative component $-\beta_2 u_t$. Consequently, x_t and ε_t are negatively correlated, $E\{x_t \varepsilon_t\} = \text{cov}\{x_t, \varepsilon_t\} < 0$, and it follows that the OLS estimator is inconsistent for β. When $\beta_2 < 0$, x_t and ε_t are positively correlated.

To illustrate the inconsistency of the OLS estimator, write the estimator for β_2 as (compare Subsection 2.1.2)

$$b_2 = \frac{\sum_{t=1}^{T} (x_t - \bar{x})(y_t - \bar{y})}{\sum_{t=1}^{T} (x_t - \bar{x})^2}, \tag{5.20}$$

where $\bar{x}$ denotes the sample mean of x_t. Substituting (5.19), this can be written as

$$b_2 = \beta_2 + \frac{(1/T) \sum_{t=1}^{T} (x_t - \bar{x})(\varepsilon_t - \bar{\varepsilon})}{(1/T) \sum_{t=1}^{T} (x_t - \bar{x})^2}. \tag{5.21}$$

As the sample size increases to infinity, sample moments converge to population moments. Thus

$$\text{plim}\, b_2 = \beta_2 + \frac{\text{plim}(1/T) \sum_{t=1}^{T} (x_t - \bar{x})(\varepsilon_t - \bar{\varepsilon})}{\text{plim}(1/T) \sum_{t=1}^{T} (x_t - \bar{x})^2} = \beta_2 + \frac{E\{x_t \varepsilon_t\}}{V\{x_t\}}, \tag{5.22}$$

where the second equality uses $E\{\varepsilon_t\} = 0$. The last term in this probability limit is nonzero. First,

$$E\{x_t \varepsilon_t\} = E\{(w_t + u_t)(v_t - \beta_2 u_t)\} = -\beta_2 \sigma_u^2,$$

and, second,

$$V\{x_t\} = V\{w_t + u_t\} = \sigma_w^2 + \sigma_u^2,$$

where $\sigma_w^2 = V\{w_t\}$. Consequently,

$$\text{plim}\, b_2 = \beta_2 \left(1 - \frac{\sigma_u^2}{\sigma_w^2 + \sigma_u^2} \right). \tag{5.23}$$

So, b_2 is consistent only if $\sigma_u^2 = 0$, that is, if there is no measurement error. It is asymptotically biased towards zero if σ_u^2 is positive, with a larger bias if the measurement error is large relative to the variance in the true variable w_t. The ratio σ_u^2/σ_w^2 may be referred to as a noise-to-signal ratio because it gives the variance of the measurement error (the noise) in relation to the variance of the true values (the signal). If this ratio is small, we have a small bias, if it is large, the bias is also large. In general, the OLS estimator underestimates the effect of true disposable income if reported disposable income is subject to measurement error unrelated to the true level.

It is important to note that the inconsistency of b_2 carries over to the estimator b_1 for the constant term $\beta_1 = E\{y_t - \beta_2 x_t\}$. In particular,

$$\begin{aligned}\text{plim}(b_1 - \beta_1) &= \text{plim}(\bar{y} - b_2\bar{x} - E\{y_t\} + \beta_2 E\{x_t\}) \\ &= -\text{plim}(b_2 - \beta_2)E\{x_t\}. \end{aligned} \tag{5.24}$$

So, if $E\{x_t\} > 0$ an overestimation of the slope parameter corresponds to an underestimated intercept. This is a general result: *inconsistency of one element in b usually carries over to all other elements.*

Again, the model of interest in this case does not correspond to the conditional expectation of y_t given x_t. From (5.19) we can derive that

$$E\{y_t|x_t\} = \beta_1 + \beta_2 x_t - \beta_2 E\{u_t|x_t\},$$

where the latter term is nonzero because of (5.18). If we assume joint normality of u_t, w_t and x_t, it follows that (see Appendix B)

$$E\{u_t|x_t\} = \frac{\sigma_u^2}{\sigma_w^2 + \sigma_u^2}(x_t - E\{x_t\}).$$

Combining the last two equations and using (5.23) shows that the OLS estimator, though inconsistent for β_2, is consistent for the coefficients in the conditional expectation of savings y_t given *reported* disposable income x_t, but this is not what we are interested in. Nevertheless, this result may be useful because it implies that we can ignore the measurement error problem if we interpret the coefficients in terms of the effects of reported variables rather than their true underlying values. Although this would often not make sense economically, there is no statistical problem in doing so.

5.2.3 Endogeneity and Omitted Variable Bias

In Section 3.2 we have discussed the issue of omitted variable bias, which arises if a relevant explanatory variable, correlated with the included regressors, is omitted from the model. Implicitly this assumes that the conditioning set of the model is larger than the set of right-hand-side variables in the equation. Omitted variable bias also arises if there are *unobservable* omitted factors in the model that happen to be correlated with one or more of the explanatory variables. This bias is of particular concern when we wish to attach a causal interpretation to our model coefficients, in which case the ceteris paribus condition includes all other factors that have an impact on the outcome variable y_i, whether observed or unobserved. The presence of an unobserved component in the equation that is potentially correlated with the observed regressors is also referred to as 'unobserved heterogeneity'. It means that the observational units differ in many other respects than is observable for a researcher. The problem is that OLS does not control for these differences and may therefore attach the wrong importance to differences in the observed explanatory variables. Angrist and Pischke (2009) provide a very useful overview of the challenges of causal inference in econometrics. Among other things, they discuss the role of controlling for confounding variables in the regression to reduce the omitted variable bias problem.

As an example, consider an individual wage equation, specified as

$$y_i = x_{1i}'\beta_1 + x_{2i}\beta_2 + u_i\gamma + v_i, \tag{5.25}$$

where y_i denotes a person's log wage, x_{1i} is a vector of individual characteristics, including an intercept term, and x_{2i} denotes years of schooling. Further, u_i is an unobserved variable reflecting a person's ability. Persons with higher levels of ability tend to have higher wages ($\gamma > 0$), but are also more likely to have more schooling. Thus, we would expect that $\text{cov}\{x_{2i}, u_i\} > 0$. Because u_i is unobserved, the econometrician simply estimates

$$y_i = x_i'\beta + \varepsilon_i,$$

where $x_i' = (x_{1i}', x_{2i})$, $\beta' = (\beta_1', \beta_2)$ and $\varepsilon_i = u_i\gamma + v_i$. Following the derivations in Subsection 3.2.1, it can be shown that the OLS estimator for β satisfies

$$b = \beta + \left(\sum_{i=1}^{N} x_i x_i'\right)^{-1} \sum_{i=1}^{N} x_i u_i \gamma + \left(\sum_{i=1}^{N} x_i x_i'\right)^{-1} \sum_{i=1}^{N} x_i v_i.$$

Assuming $E\{x_i v_i\} = 0$, this allows us to show that the probability limit of b is given by

$$\text{plim}\, b = \beta + \Sigma_{xx}^{-1} E\{x_i u_i\}\gamma. \tag{5.26}$$

Accordingly, when $\gamma \neq 0$, consistency of the OLS estimator for β requires $E\{x_i u_i\} = 0$. That is, the unobserved ability should be uncorrelated with schooling and the other explanatory variables in the model.

Assuming $E\{x_i u_i\} > 0$, we expect that OLS overestimates the returns to schooling. What is OLS estimating in this case? It is telling us how much the expected wages of two persons differ if one has 1 year more of schooling than the other, while having identical values for x_{1i}. This is not a causal effect. It just tells us that people with more education are expected to have higher wages. Part of this effect may be due to the fact that people attaining different years of schooling also have different unobserved characteristics (like ability, ambition, intelligence, ...). The wage differential that is *caused* by the difference in schooling (the effect of x_{2i} keeping x_{1i} and u_i fixed) may actually be much smaller than what OLS is estimating.

In general, explanatory variables in x_i that are correlated with the equation's error term ε_i are said to be **endogenous**. Those uncorrelated are called exogenous. In many applications we have to worry about endogeneity of regressors, and OLS results are prone to suffer from endogeneity bias. Often it is likely that unobservable heterogeneity exists that is correlated with observed regressors. For example, with firm level data, managerial quality is often unobserved but affecting both the outcome (e.g. a measure of firm performance) and the regressor of interest (e.g. a measure of governance).

5.2.4 Simultaneity and Reverse Causality

Another form of the endogeneity problem is **reverse causality**. It refers to the possibility that not only x_i has an impact on y_i but at the same time y_i has an impact on one or more elements of x_i, say x_{2i}. For example, the level of criminal activity in a city will be affected by the amount spent on law enforcement, while city officials may decide upon the budget for law enforcement partly by the expected level of criminal activity. Estimating the causal impact of law enforcement upon criminal activity using a cross-section of cities is therefore subject to endogeneity bias.

A situation of reverse causality naturally arises when y and x_2 are simultaneously determined. In macro-economics there is a wide range of models consisting of a system of equations that simultaneously determine a number of endogenous variables. Consider, for example, a demand equation and a supply equation, both depending upon prices, and an equilibrium condition that says that demand and supply should be equal. The resulting system simultaneously determines quantities and prices, and it can typically not be said that prices determine quantities or quantities determine prices.

In this subsection, we consider a simple example of a simultaneous equations model. The equation of interest is a Keynesian consumption function relating per capita consumption y_t of a country to per capita income x_{2t}, given by

$$y_t = \beta_1 + \beta_2 x_{2t} + \varepsilon_t, \tag{5.27}$$

where $t = 1, \ldots, T$ (years). The coefficient β_2 is interpreted as the marginal propensity to consume, and we expect $0 < \beta_2 < 1$. This is a causal interpretation describing the impact of income upon consumption: how much more will people consume if their income increases by one unit? However, aggregate income x_{2t} is not exogenously given as it will be determined by the identity

$$x_{2t} = y_t + z_{2t}, \tag{5.28}$$

where z_{2t} denotes per capita investment.[5] This equation is a definition equation for a closed economy without a government. It says that total consumption plus total investment should equal total income. We assume that investment is exogenous, which means that z_{2t} and ε_t are uncorrelated, that is,

$$E\{z_{2t}\varepsilon_t\} = 0. \tag{5.29}$$

This means that z_{2t} is determined outside the model. In contrast, both y_t and x_{2t} are endogenous variables, which are jointly determined in the model. The model in (5.27)–(5.28) is a very simple simultaneous equations model in **structural form** (or in short: a structural model).

The fact that x_{2t} is endogenous has its consequences for the estimation of the consumption function (5.27). Because y_t influences x_{2t} through (5.28), we can no longer argue that x_{2t} and ε_t are uncorrelated. Consequently, the OLS estimator for β_2 will be biased and inconsistent. To elaborate upon this, it is useful to consider the **reduced form** of this

[5] The numbering of the variables is chosen to match the general notation of Section 5.3.

model, in which the endogenous variables y_t and x_{2t} are expressed as a function of the exogenous variable z_{2t} and unobservable error terms. Solving (5.27) and (5.28) for y_t and x_{2t}, we obtain the reduced-form equations

$$x_{2t} = \frac{\beta_1}{1-\beta_2} + \frac{1}{1-\beta_2} z_{2t} + \frac{1}{1-\beta_2}\varepsilon_t, \tag{5.30}$$

$$y_t = \frac{\beta_1}{1-\beta_2} + \frac{\beta_2}{1-\beta_2} z_{2t} + \frac{1}{1-\beta_2}\varepsilon_t. \tag{5.31}$$

From the first of these two equations it follows that

$$\text{cov}\{x_{2t}, \varepsilon_t\} = \frac{1}{1-\beta_2}\text{cov}\{z_{2t}, \varepsilon_t\} + \frac{1}{1-\beta_2}V\{\varepsilon_t\} = \frac{\sigma^2}{1-\beta_2}.$$

Consequently, (5.27) presents a linear model where the regressor x_{2t} is correlated with the error term ε_t. As a result, OLS applied to (5.27) will be biased and inconsistent. Similarly to the earlier derivation, it holds that

$$\text{plim } b_2 = \beta_2 + \frac{\text{cov}\{x_{2t}, \varepsilon_t\}}{V\{x_{2t}\}},$$

where

$$V\{x_{2t}\} = V\left\{\frac{1}{1-\beta_2} z_{2t} + \frac{1}{1-\beta_2}\varepsilon_t\right\} = \frac{1}{(1-\beta_2)^2}(V\{z_{2t}\} + \sigma^2),$$

so that we finally find that

$$\text{plim } b_2 = \beta_2 + (1-\beta_2)\frac{\sigma^2}{V\{z_{2t}\} + \sigma^2}. \tag{5.32}$$

As $0 < \beta_2 < 1$, and $\sigma^2 > 0$, the OLS estimator will *overestimate* the true value β_2. Although we have only shown the inconsistency of the estimator for the slope coefficient, the intercept term will in general also be estimated inconsistently (compare (5.24)).

The simple model in this subsection illustrates a common problem in macro- or microeconomic models. If we consider an equation where one or more of the explanatory variables is jointly determined with the left-hand-side variable, the OLS estimator will typically provide inconsistent estimators for the behavioural parameters in this equation. Statistically, this means that the equation we have written down does not correspond to a conditional expectation so that the usual assumptions on the error term cannot be imposed.

In the next sections we shall consider alternative approaches to estimating a single equation with endogenous regressors, using so-called instrumental variables. While relaxing the exogeneity assumption in (A7), we shall stress that these approaches require the imposition of alternative assumptions, such as (5.29), which may or may not be valid in practice. This implies that instrumental variables estimators have to be used with care.

5.3 The Instrumental Variables Estimator

If one or more explanatory variables in a regression model are endogenous, that is, correlated with the error term, the OLS estimator is biased and inconsistent. In these cases there is need for an alternative estimator. In the current section, we shall discuss the instrumental variables estimator using the wage equation from Subsection 5.2.3 as motivation.

5.3.1 *Estimation with a Single Endogenous Regressor and a Single Instrument*

Suppose we explain an individual's log wage y_i from a number of personal characteristics, x_{1i}, as well as the years of schooling, x_{2i}, by means of a linear model

$$y_i = x'_{1i}\beta_1 + x_{2i}\beta_2 + \varepsilon_i. \tag{5.33}$$

We know from Chapter 2 that this model has no interpretation unless we make some assumptions about ε_i. Otherwise, we could just set β_1 and β_2 to arbitrary values and define ε_i such that the equality in (5.33) holds for every observation. The most common interpretation so far is that (5.33) describes the conditional expectation or the best linear approximation of y_i given x_{1i} and x_{2i}. This requires us to impose that

$$E\{\varepsilon_i x_{1i}\} = 0 \tag{5.34}$$

$$E\{\varepsilon_i x_{2i}\} = 0, \tag{5.35}$$

which are the necessary conditions for consistency of the OLS estimator. As soon as we relax any of these conditions, the model no longer corresponds to the conditional expectation of y_i given x_{1i} and x_{2i}.

In the above wage equation, ε_i includes all unobservable factors that affect a person's wage, including things like 'ability' or 'intelligence'. Typically, it is argued that years of schooling of a person also depend upon these unobserved characteristics. If this is the case, OLS is *consistently* estimating the conditional expected value of a person's wage given, among other things, years of schooling, but *not consistently* estimating the causal effect of schooling. That is, the OLS estimate for β_2 would reflect the difference in expected wages of two arbitrary persons with the same observed characteristics in x_{1i}, but with x_2 and $x_2 + 1$ years of schooling, respectively. It does not, however, measure the expected wage difference if an arbitrary person (for some exogenous reason) decides to increase his or her schooling from x_2 to $x_2 + 1$ years. The reason is that, when interpreting the model as a conditional expectation, the unobservable factors affecting a person's wage are not assumed to be constant across the two persons, whereas in the causal interpretation the unobservables are kept unchanged. Put differently, when we interpret the model as a conditional expectation, the ceteris paribus condition only refers to the included variables in x_{1i}, whereas for a causal interpretation it also includes the unobservables (omitted variables) in the error term.

Quite often, coefficients in a regression model are interpreted as measuring causal effects. In such cases, it makes sense to discuss the validity of conditions like (5.34) and (5.35). If $E\{\varepsilon_i x_{2i}\} \neq 0$, we say that x_{2i} is endogenous (with respect to the causal effect β_2). For micro-economic wage equations, it is often argued that many explanatory variables are potentially endogenous, including education level, union status, sickness, industry and marital status. To illustrate this, it is not uncommon (for USA data) to find that expected wages are about 10% higher if a person is married. Quite clearly, this is not reflecting the causal effect of being married, but the consequence of differences in unobservable characteristics of married and unmarried people.

If it is no longer imposed that $E\{\varepsilon_i x_{2i}\} = 0$, the OLS method produces a biased and inconsistent estimator for the parameters in the model. The solution requires an alternative estimation method. To derive a consistent estimator, it is necessary that we make sure that our model is statistically identified. This means that we need to impose additional assumptions; otherwise the model is not identified, and any estimator is necessarily inconsistent. To see this, let us go back to the conditions (5.34) and (5.35). These conditions are so-called **moment conditions**, conditions in terms of expectations (moments) that are implied by the model. These conditions should be sufficient to identify the unknown parameters in the model. That is, the K parameters in β_1 and β_2 should be such that the following K equalities hold:

$$E\{(y_i - x_{1i}'\beta_1 - x_{2i}\beta_2)x_{1i}\} = 0 \tag{5.36}$$

$$E\{(y_i - x_{1i}'\beta_1 - x_{2i}\beta_2)x_{2i}\} = 0. \tag{5.37}$$

When estimating the model by OLS we impose these conditions on the estimator through the corresponding sample moments. That is, the OLS estimator $b = (b_1', b_2)'$ for $\beta = (\beta_1', \beta_2)'$ is solved from

$$\frac{1}{N}\sum_{i=1}^{N}(y_i - x_{1i}'b_1 - x_{2i}b_2)x_{1i} = 0 \tag{5.38}$$

$$\frac{1}{N}\sum_{i=1}^{N}(y_i - x_{1i}'b_1 - x_{2i}b_2)x_{2i} = 0. \tag{5.39}$$

In fact, these are the first-order conditions for the minimization of the least squares criterion. The number of conditions exactly equals the number of unknown parameters, so that b_1 and b_2 can be solved uniquely from (5.38) and (5.39). However, as soon as (5.35) is violated, condition (5.39) drops out, and we can no longer solve for b_1 and b_2. This means that β_1 and β_2 are no longer identified.

To identify β_1 and β_2 in the more general case, we need at least one additional moment condition. Such a moment condition is usually derived from the availability of an **instrument** or **instrumental variable**. An instrumental variable z_{2i}, say, is a variable that can be assumed to be uncorrelated with the model's error ε_i but correlated with the endogenous regressor x_{2i}.[6] If such an instrument can be found, condition (5.37) can be replaced by

$$E\{(y_i - x_{1i}'\beta_1 - x_{2i}\beta_2)z_{2i}\} = 0. \tag{5.40}$$

An instrument that is uncorrelated with the equation's error term and satisfies (5.40) is referred to as 'exogenous'. Provided the moment condition in (5.40) is not a combination

[6] The assumption that the instrument is correlated with x_{2i} is needed for identification. If there is no correlation the additional moment does not provide any (identifying) information on β_2.

of the other ones (z_{2i} is not a linear combination of x_{1i}s), this is sufficient to identify the K parameters β_1 and β_2. The condition in (5.40) is referred to as an **exclusion restriction**, which reflects the implicit assumption that z_{2i} is validly excluded from the model of interest in (5.33).

The **instrumental variables estimator** $\hat{\beta}_{IV}$ can then be solved from

$$\frac{1}{N}\sum_{i=1}^{N}(y_i - x_{1i}'\hat{\beta}_{1,IV} - x_{2i}\hat{\beta}_{2,IV})x_{1i} = 0 \tag{5.41}$$

$$\frac{1}{N}\sum_{i=1}^{N}(y_i - x_{1i}'\hat{\beta}_{1,IV} - x_{2i}\hat{\beta}_{2,IV})z_{2i} = 0. \tag{5.42}$$

The solution can be determined analytically and leads to the following expression for the IV estimator

$$\hat{\beta}_{IV} = \left(\sum_{i=1}^{N} z_i x_i'\right)^{-1} \sum_{i=1}^{N} z_i y_i, \tag{5.43}$$

where $x_i' = (x_{1i}', x_{2i})$ and $z_i' = (x_{1i}', z_{2i})$. Clearly, if $z_{2i} = x_{2i}$, this expression reduces to the OLS estimator.

Identification of the model and consistency of the IV estimator requires that the moment conditions uniquely identify the parameters of interest. This requires that the $K \times K$ matrix

$$\text{plim}\,\frac{1}{N}\sum_{i=1}^{N} z_i x_i' = \Sigma_{zx} \tag{5.44}$$

is finite and invertible. This means that the partial correlation between the instrument and the endogenous variable is nonzero. To be precise, it requires the coefficient π_2 in the reduced form equation

$$x_{2i} = x_{1i}'\pi_1 + z_{2i}\pi_2 + v_i$$

to be different from zero, which says that the endogenous regressor x_{2i} and the instrument z_{2i} have nonzero correlation, after netting out the effects of all other exogenous variables in the model. Note that this also requires that z_{2i} is not a linear combination of the elements in x_{1i}. If this condition is satisfied we call the instrument 'relevant'. The requirement that an instrument be relevant is not a trivial regularity condition and in many applications is a point of concern (see below).

The asymptotic covariance matrix of $\hat{\beta}_{IV}$ depends upon the assumptions we make about the distribution of ε_i. Under assumptions (5.36), (5.40) (valid instrument) and (5.44) (relevant instrument), and assuming ε_i is $IID(0, \sigma^2)$, independently of z_i, it can be shown that

$$\sqrt{N}(\hat{\beta}_{IV} - \beta) \to \mathcal{N}(0, \sigma^2(\Sigma_{xz}\Sigma_{zz}^{-1}\Sigma_{zx})^{-1}), \tag{5.45}$$

where the symmetric $K \times K$ matrix

$$\Sigma_{zz} \equiv \text{plim}\,\frac{1}{N}\sum_{i=1}^{N} z_i z_i'$$

is assumed to be invertible, and $\Sigma_{zx} = \Sigma'_{xz}$. Nonsingularity of Σ_{zz} requires that there is no multicollinearity among the K elements in the vector z_i. In finite samples we can estimate the covariance matrix of $\hat{\beta}_{IV}$ by

$$\hat{V}\{\hat{\beta}_{IV}\} = \hat{\sigma}^2\left(\left(\sum_{i=1}^{N} x_i z_i'\right)\left(\sum_{i=1}^{N} z_i z_i'\right)^{-1}\left(\sum_{i=1}^{N} z_i x_i'\right)\right)^{-1}, \tag{5.46}$$

where $\hat{\sigma}^2$ is a consistent estimator for σ^2 based upon the residual sum of squares, for example,

$$\hat{\sigma}^2 = \frac{1}{N-K}\sum_{i=1}^{N}(y_i - x_i'\hat{\beta}_{IV})^2. \tag{5.47}$$

Similarly to OLS, it is also possible to compute a heteroskedasticity-consistent covariance matrix for the IV estimator. Accordingly, it is very easy to calculate standard errors for the IV estimator that are robust to heteroskedasticity of unknown form; see Davidson and MacKinnon (2004, Section 8.5).

The above results show that it is possible to consistently estimate the coefficients in a linear regression model when one of the regressors is correlated with the error term, provided that we can find an instrumental variable that is both relevant and exogenous. The problem for the practitioner is that it is often far from obvious to find variables that could serve as valid instruments, or to establish whether a chosen instrument is indeed exogenous. The requirement that an instrument is relevant is relatively easy. It requires that the instrument is correlated with the endogenous regressor, conditional upon the other regressors in the equation. This correlation should be sufficiently strong to increase statistical power and to avoid a so-called weak instruments problem. If the instrument is only weakly correlated with the endogenous regressor, this means that the R^2 of the reduced form increases only marginally when the instrument is added. In this case, the instrumental variables estimator has poor properties (see Subsection 5.6.4). Evaluating the significance of the instrument in the reduced form is a helpful exercise. The usual rule of thumb is that an instrumental variable should have an F-statistic in the reduced form larger than 10, corresponding to a t-ratio exceeding 3.16 (Stock and Watson, 2007, Chapter 12).

The requirement that an instrumental variable is exogenous is more complicated. As stressed by Angrist and Pischke (2009, Chapter 4) this actually requires two things. One is that the instrument is as good as randomly assigned and cannot be influenced by the dependent variable y_i (conditional upon the other regressors). Second is an 'only through' condition and requires that the instrument predicts the dependent variable y_i only though the instrumented variable (x_{2i}), conditional upon the other regressors, not directly or through a third unobserved variable. This is often called 'an exclusion restriction', and it requires that the instrument itself is appropriately excluded from the equation of interest.

In the above wage equation example, we require an instrumental variable that is correlated with years of schooling x_{2i} but uncorrelated with wages directly or with the unobserved 'ability' factors that are included in ε_i. This requires a variable that is correlated with the costs of schooling, or the likelihood of having certain levels of schooling, while being unrelated to a person's ability. Potential instruments relate to differences in costs due to loan policies or other subsidies that vary independently of ability or earnings potential, or to variation in institutional constraints, like changes in compulsory schooling laws; we come back to this example in Section 5.4.

Unlike the relevance condition, the exclusion or exogeneity condition cannot be tested. This is because ε_i is unobserved. Essentially, when using instrumental variables we are replacing one untestable assumption $E\{\varepsilon_i x_{2i}\} = 0$ with another untestable assumption $E\{\varepsilon_i z_{2i}\} = 0$ (imposing $E\{\varepsilon_i x_{1i}\} = 0$ in both cases). In other words, in both cases the moment conditions we impose are identifying conditions. Accordingly, they cannot be tested statistically. The only case where moment conditions are partially testable is when there are more conditions than actually needed for identification, that is, when we have more instrumental variables than endogenous regressors. In this case, one can test the so-called overidentifying restrictions, without, however, being able to specify which of the moment conditions corresponds to these restrictions (see below). The fact that the scope for testing the validity of instruments is very limited indicates that researchers should pay careful attention to the justification of their instruments, paying attention to theoretical arguments or institutional background. The reliability of an instrument relies on argumentation, not on empirical testing.

Another drawback of instrumental variables estimation is that the standard errors of an IV estimator are typically quite high compared to those of the OLS estimator. The most important reason for this is that instrument and regressor have a low correlation; see Wooldridge (2010, Subsection 5.2.6) for more discussion. Due to the concerns above, some authors argue that under poor conditions instrumental variable estimates are more likely to provide the wrong statistical inference than simple OLS estimates that make no correction for endogeneity (Larcker and Rusticus, 2010).

Keeping in mind the above, the endogeneity of x_{2i} can be tested provided we assume that the instrument z_{2i} is valid. Hausman (1978) proposes to compare the OLS and IV estimators for β. Assuming (5.44) and $E\{\varepsilon_i z_i\} = 0$, the IV estimator is consistent. If, in addition, $E\{\varepsilon_i x_{2i}\} = 0$, the OLS estimator is also consistent and should differ from the IV one by sampling error only. A computationally attractive version of the **Hausman test** for endogeneity (often referred to as the Durbin–Wu–Hausman test) can be based upon a simple auxiliary regression. First, estimate a regression explaining x_{2i} from x_{1i} and z_{2i}, and save the residuals, say $\hat{v}_i$. This is the reduced-form equation. Next, add the residuals to the model of interest and estimate

$$y_i = x_{1i}'\beta_1 + x_{2i}\beta_2 + \hat{v}_i\gamma + e_i$$

by OLS. This reproduces[7] the IV estimator for β_1 and β_2, but also produces an estimate for γ. If $\gamma = 0$, x_{2i} is exogenous. Consequently, we can easily test the endogeneity of x_{2i} by performing a standard t-test on $\gamma = 0$ in the above regression. Note that the endogeneity test requires the assumption that the instrument is exogenous and therefore does not help to determine which identifying moment condition, $E\{\varepsilon_i x_{2i}\} = 0$ or $E\{\varepsilon_i z_{2i}\} = 0$, is appropriate.

The concerns with instrumental variables approaches, or with causal inference more generally, have received substantial attention recently, with Angrist and Pischke (2009) as a prominent example. Larcker and Rusticus (2010) are very critical on the use of instrumental variables in accounting research. After inspecting a number of recently published

[7] Although the estimates for β_1 and β_2 will be identical to the IV estimates, the standard errors will not be appropriate; see Wooldridge (2010, Section 6.2).

studies, they conclude that the variables selected as instruments seem largely arbitrary and not justified by any rigorous theoretical discussion. According to them, many IV applications in accounting are likely to produce highly misleading parameter estimates and test statistics. In a similar vein, Roberts and Whited (2013) argue that truly exogenous instruments are extremely difficult to find in corporate finance research and conclude that 'many papers in corporate finance discuss only the relevance of the instrument and ignore any exclusion restrictions'. Sovey and Green (2011) show that many of the articles in political science do a poor job in providing argumentation for the validity of instruments. Atanasov and Black (2016) focus on shock-based instrumental variables in corporate finance and accounting, which rely on an external shock as the basis for causal inference, for example a change of governance rules imposed by governments. They conclude that only a small minority of the studies they investigated have convincing causal inference strategies. Similarly, Durlauf, Johnson and Temple (2005) state that many IV procedures in the empirical growth literature are 'undermined by the failure to address properly the question of whether these instruments are valid, i.e., whether they may be plausibly argued to be uncorrelated with the error term in a growth regression'. Bazzi and Clemens (2013) also demonstrate that invalid and weak instruments are commonly used, even in the more recent growth literature.[8] See Section 5.7 for an empirical illustration in this context.

5.3.2 Back to the Keynesian Model

The problem for the practitioner is thus to find suitable instruments. In most cases, this means that somehow our knowledge of economic theory has to be exploited. In a complete simultaneous equations model (that specifies relationships for all endogenous variables), this problem can be solved because any exogenous variable in the system that is not included in the equation of interest can be used as an instrument. More precisely, any exogenous variable that has an effect on the endogenous regressor can be used as an instrument. Information on this is obtained from the reduced form for the endogenous regressor. For the Keynesian model, this implies that investments z_{2t} provide a valid instrument for income x_{2t}. The resulting instrumental variable estimator is then given by

$$\hat{\beta}_{IV} = \left[\sum_{t=1}^{T} \begin{pmatrix} 1 \\ z_{2t} \end{pmatrix} (1 \;\; x_{2t})\right]^{-1} \sum_{t=1}^{T} \begin{pmatrix} 1 \\ z_{2t} \end{pmatrix} y_t,$$

which we can solve for $\hat{\beta}_{2,IV}$ as

$$\hat{\beta}_{2,IV} = \frac{\sum_{t=1}^{T}(z_{2t} - \bar{z}_2)(y_t - \bar{y})}{\sum_{t=1}^{T}(z_{2t} - \bar{z}_2)(x_{2t} - \bar{x}_2)}, \tag{5.48}$$

where $\bar{z}_2$, $\bar{y}$ and $\bar{x}_2$ denote the sample averages.

An alternative way to see that the estimator (5.48) works is to start from (5.27) and take the covariance with our instrument z_{2t} on both sides of the equality sign. This gives

$$\text{cov}\{y_t, z_{2t}\} = \beta_2 \text{cov}\{x_{2t}, z_{2t}\} + \text{cov}\{\varepsilon_t, z_{2t}\}. \tag{5.49}$$

[8] Most of this literature uses panel data, which we discuss in Chapter 10.

Exogeneity of the instrument z_{2t} implies that the last term in this equality is zero. Further, when the instrument is relevant, $\text{cov}\{x_{2t}, z_{2t}\} \neq 0$, and we can solve for β_2 as

$$\beta_2 = \frac{\text{cov}\{z_{2t}, y_t\}}{\text{cov}\{z_{2t}, x_{2t}\}}. \tag{5.50}$$

This relationship suggests an estimator for β_2 by replacing the population covariances with their sample counterparts. This gives the instrumental variables estimator we have seen above:

$$\hat{\beta}_{2,IV} = \frac{(1/T)\sum_{t=1}^{T}(z_{2t} - \bar{z}_2)(y_t - \bar{y})}{(1/T)\sum_{t=1}^{T}(z_{2t} - \bar{z}_2)(x_{2t} - \bar{x}_2)}. \tag{5.51}$$

Consistency follows directly from the general result that, under weak regularity conditions, sample moments converge to population moments.

5.3.3 Back to the Measurement Error Problem

The model is given by

$$y_t = \beta_1 + \beta_2 x_t + \varepsilon_t,$$

where (as an interpretation) y_t denotes savings and x_t denotes *observed* disposable income, which equals true disposable income plus a random measurement error. The presence of this measurement error induces correlation between x_t and ε_t.

Given this model, no obvious instruments arise. In fact, this is a common problem in models with measurement errors due to inaccurate recording. The task is to find an observed variable that is (1) correlated with income x_t but (2) not correlated with u_t, the measurement error in income (nor with ε_t). If we can find such a variable, we can apply instrumental variables estimation. Mainly because of the problem of finding suitable instruments, the problem of measurement error is often ignored in empirical work.

5.3.4 Multiple Endogenous Regressors

If more than one explanatory variable is considered to be endogenous, the dimension of x_{2i} is increased accordingly, and the model reads

$$y_i = x_{1i}'\beta_1 + x_{2i}'\beta_2 + \varepsilon_i.$$

To estimate this equation, we need an instrument for each element in x_{2i}. This means that, if we have five endogenous regressors, we need at least five different instruments. Denoting the instruments by the vector z_{2i}, the instrumental variables estimator can again be written as in (5.43),

$$\hat{\beta}_{IV} = \left(\sum_{i=1}^{N} z_i x_i'\right)^{-1} \sum_{i=1}^{N} z_i y_i,$$

where now $x_i' = (x_{1i}', x_{2i}')$ and $z_i' = (x_{1i}', z_{2i}')$.

It is sometimes convenient to refer to the entire vector z_i as the vector of instruments. If a variable in x_i is assumed to be exogenous, we do not need to find an instrument for it. Alternatively and equivalently, this variable is used as its own instrument. This means that the vector of exogenous variables x_{1i} is included in the K-dimensional vector of instruments z_i. If all the variables are exogenous, $z_i = x_i$ and we obtain the OLS estimator, where 'each variable is instrumented by itself'.

In a simultaneous equations context, the exogenous variables from elsewhere in the system are candidate instrumental variables. The so-called 'order condition for identification' (see Greene, 2012, Section 10.6) essentially says that sufficient instruments should be available in the system. If, for example, there are five exogenous variables in the system that are not included in the equation of interest, we can have up to five endogenous regressors. If there is only one endogenous regressor, we have five different instruments to choose from. It is also possible and advisable to estimate more efficiently by using all the available instruments simultaneously. This is discussed in Section 5.6. First, however, we shall discuss an empirical illustration concerning the estimation of the causal effect of schooling on earnings.

5.4 Illustration: Estimating the Returns to Schooling

It is quite clear that, on average, people with more education have higher wages. It is less clear, however, whether this positive correlation reflects a causal effect of schooling, or that individuals with a greater earnings capacity have chosen more years of schooling. If the latter possibility is true, the OLS estimates on the returns to schooling simply reflect differences in unobserved characteristics of working individuals, and an increase in a person's schooling owing to an exogenous shock will have no effect on this person's wage. The problem of estimating the causal effect of schooling upon earnings has therefore attracted substantive attention in the literature; see Card (1999) for a survey.

Most studies are based upon the human capital earnings function, which says that

$$w_i = \beta_1 + \beta_2 S_i + \beta_3 E_i + \beta_4 E_i^2 + \varepsilon_i,$$

where w_i denotes the log of individual earnings, S_i denotes years of schooling and E_i denotes years of experience. In the absence of information on actual experience, E_i is sometimes replaced by 'potential experience', measured as $age_i - S_i - 6$, assuming people start school at the age of 6. This specification is usually augmented with additional explanatory variables that one wants to control for, like regional, gender and racial dummies. In addition, it is sometimes argued that the returns to education vary across individuals. With this in mind, let us reformulate the wage equation as

$$\begin{aligned} w_i &= z_i'\beta + \gamma_i S_i + u_i \\ &= z_i'\beta + \gamma S_i + \varepsilon_i, \end{aligned} \tag{5.52}$$

where $\varepsilon_i = u_i + (\gamma_i - \gamma)S_i$, and z_i includes all observable variables (except S_i), including the experience variables and a constant. It is assumed that $E\{\varepsilon_i z_i\} = 0$. The coefficient γ has the interpretation of the average return to (an additional year of) schooling $E\{\gamma_i\} = \gamma$ and is our parameter of interest. In addition, we specify a reduced form for S_i as

$$S_i = z_i'\pi + v_i, \tag{5.53}$$

where $E\{v_i z_i\} = 0$. This reduced form is simply a best linear approximation of S_i and does not necessarily have an economic interpretation. OLS estimation of β and

γ in (5.52) is consistent only if $E\{\varepsilon_i S_i\} = E\{\varepsilon_i \upsilon_i\} = 0$. This means that there are no unobservable characteristics that both affect a person's choice of schooling and his or her (later) earnings.

As discussed in Card (1995), there are different reasons why schooling may be correlated with ε_i. An important one is 'ability bias' (see Griliches, 1977). Suppose that some individuals have unobserved characteristics (ability) that enable them to get higher earnings. If these individuals also have above-average schooling levels, this implies a positive correlation between ε_i and υ_i and an OLS estimator that is *upward* biased. Another reason why ε_i and υ_i may be correlated is the existence of measurement error in the schooling measure. As discussed in Subsection 5.2.2, this induces a negative correlation between ε_i and υ_i and, consequently, a *downward* bias in the OLS estimator for γ. Finally, if the individual specific returns to schooling (γ_i) are higher for individuals with low levels of schooling, the unobserved component $(\gamma_i - \gamma)S_i$ will be negatively correlated with S_i, which, again, induces a *downward* bias in the OLS estimator.

In the above formulation there are no instruments available for schooling as all potential candidates are included in the wage equation. Put differently, the number of moment conditions in

$$E\{\varepsilon_i z_i\} = E\{(w_i - z_i'\beta - \gamma S_i)z_i\} = 0$$

is one short to identify β and γ. However, if we can think of a variable in z_i (z_{2i}, say) that affects schooling but not wages, this variable can be excluded from the wage equation so as to reduce the number of unknown parameters by 1, thereby making the model exactly identified. In this case the instrumental variables estimator for[9] β and γ, using z_{2i} as an instrument, is a consistent estimator.

A continuing discussion in labour economics is the question as to which variable can legitimately serve as an instrument. Typically, an instrument is thought of as a variable that affects the costs of schooling (and thus the choice of schooling) but not earnings. There is a long tradition of using family background variables, for example the number of siblings or parents' education, as instruments. As Card (1999) notes, the interest in family background is driven by the fact that children's schooling choices are highly correlated with the characteristics of their parents. More recently, institutional factors of the schooling system are exploited as potential instruments. For example, Angrist and Krueger (1991) use an individual's quarter of birth as an instrument for schooling. Using an extremely large data set of men born from 1930 to 1959, they find that people with birth dates earlier in the year have slightly less schooling than those born later in the year. Assuming that quarter of birth is independent of unobservable taste and ability factors, it can be used as an instrument to estimate the returns to schooling. Card (1995) uses the presence of a nearby college as an instrument that can validly be excluded from the wage equation. Students who grow up in an area without a college face a higher cost of college education, while one would expect that higher costs, on average, reduce the years of schooling, particularly in low-income families. Evans and Montgomery (1994) and Dickson (2013), among others, use early smoking habits as an instrument for schooling. They argue that the choice to smoke at a young age is related to an individual's rate of time preference and therefore correlated with schooling, making the instrument relevant. Moreover, smoking behaviour is unlikely to have a direct impact on a person's earnings at higher ages, which – when true – would make the instrument exogenous.

[9] Note that z_{2i} is excluded from the wage equation so that the element in β corresponding to z_{2i} is set to zero.

In this section we use data on 3010 men taken from the US National Longitudinal Survey of Young Men, also employed in Card (1995). In this panel survey, a group of individuals was followed from 1966 when they were aged 14–24, and interviewed in a number of consecutive years. The labour market information that we use covers 1976. In this year, the average years of schooling in this sample is somewhat more than 13 years, with a maximum of 18. Average experience in 1976, when this group of men was between 24 and 34 years old, is 8.86 years, while the average hourly raw wage is $5.77.

Table 5.1 reports the results of an OLS regression of an individual's log hourly wage upon years of schooling, experience and experience-squared and three dummy variables indicating whether the individual was black, lived in a metropolitan area (*smsa*) and lived in the south. The OLS estimator implies estimated average returns to schooling of approximately 7.4% per year.[10] The inclusion of additional variables, like region of residence in 1966 and family background characteristics, in some cases significantly improved the model but hardly affected the coefficients for the variables reported in Table 5.1 (see Card, 1995), so that we shall continue with this fairly simple specification.

If schooling is endogenous, then experience and its square are by construction also endogenous, given that age is not a choice variable and therefore unambiguously exogenous. This means that our linear model may suffer from three endogenous regressors so that we need (at least) three instruments. For experience and its square, age and age-squared are obvious candidates. As discussed previously, for schooling the solution is less trivial. Card (1995) argues that the presence of a nearby college in 1966 may provide a valid instrument. A necessary (but not sufficient) condition for this is that college proximity in 1966 affects the schooling variable, conditional upon the other exogenous variables. To see whether this is the case, we estimate a reduced form, where schooling is explained by age and age-squared, the three dummy variables from the wage equation and a dummy indicating whether an individual lived near a college in 1966. The results, by OLS, are reported in Table 5.2. Recall that this reduced form is not an economic or causal model to explain schooling choice. It is just a statistical reduced form corresponding to the best linear approximation of schooling.

The fact that the lived near college dummy is significant in this reduced form is reassuring. It indicates that, ceteris paribus, students who lived near a college in 1966 have

Table 5.1 Wage equation estimated by OLS

Dependent variable: log(*wage*)

Variable	Estimate	Standard error	t-ratio
constant	4.7337	0.0676	70.022
schooling	0.0740	0.0035	21.113
exper	0.0836	0.0066	12.575
$exper^2$	−0.0022	0.0003	−7.050
black	−0.1896	0.0176	−10.758
smsa	0.1614	0.0156	10.365
south	−0.1249	0.0151	−8.259

$s = 0.374$ $R^2 = 0.2905$ $\bar{R}^2 = 0.2891$ $F = 204.93$

[10] Because the dependent variable is in logs, a coefficient of 0.074 corresponds to a relative difference of approximately 7.4%; see Chapter 3.

Table 5.2 Reduced form for schooling, estimated by OLS

Dependent variable: *schooling*

Variable	Estimate	Standard error	t-ratio
constant	−1.8695	4.2984	−0.435
age	1.0614	0.3014	3.522
age^2	−0.0188	0.0052	−3.386
black	−1.4684	0.1154	−12.719
smsa	0.8354	0.1093	7.647
south	−0.4597	0.1024	−4.488
lived near college	0.3471	0.1070	3.244

$s = 2.5158$ $R^2 = 0.1185$ $\bar{R}^2 = 0.1168$ $F = 67.29$

on average 0.35 years more schooling. Recall that a valid instrument is required to be exogenous and relevant. Relevance requires that the candidate instrument is correlated with schooling but not a linear combination of the other variables of the model. This can be checked by evaluating the reduced form. Exogeneity of the instrument requires that it is uncorrelated with the error term in the wage equation and cannot be tested. It would only be possible to test for such a correlation if we have a consistent estimator for β and γ first, but we can only find a consistent estimator if we impose that our instrument is valid. Accordingly, the exogeneity of instruments can only be tested, to some extent, if the model is overidentified; see Section 5.6. In the present case we need to trust economic arguments, rather than statistical ones, to rely upon the instrument that is chosen.

Using age, age-squared and the lived near college dummy as instruments for experience, experience-squared and schooling,[11] we obtain the estimation results reported in Table 5.3. The estimated returns to schooling are over 13%, with a relatively large standard error of somewhat more than 5%. Although the estimate is substantially higher than the OLS one, its inaccuracy is such that this difference could just be due to sampling error. Nevertheless, the value of the IV estimate is fairly robust to changes in the

Table 5.3 Wage equation estimated by IV

Dependent variable: log(*wage*)

Variable	Estimate	Standard error	t-ratio
constant	4.0656	0.6085	6.682
schooling	0.1329	0.0514	2.588
exper	0.0560	0.0260	2.153
exper^2	−0.0008	0.0013	−0.594
black	−0.1031	0.0774	−1.333
smsa	0.1080	0.0050	2.171
south	−0.0982	0.0288	−3.413

Instruments: *age*, *age*^{2} and *lived near college*
used for: *exper*, *exper*^{2} and *schooling*

[11] Although the formulation suggests otherwise, it is not the case that instruments have a one-to-one correspondence with the endogenous regressors. Implicitly, all instruments are jointly used for all variables.

specification (e.g. the inclusion of regional indicators or family background variables). The fact that the IV estimator suffers from such large standard errors is due to the fairly low correlation between the instruments and the endogenous regressors. This is reflected in the R^2 of the reduced form for schooling, which is only 0.1185.[12] Although in general the instrumental variables estimator is less accurate than the OLS estimator (which may be inconsistent), the loss in efficiency is particularly large if the instruments are only weakly correlated with the endogenous regressors.

Table 5.3 does not report any goodness-of-fit statistics. The reason is that there is no unique definition of an R^2 or adjusted R^2 if the model is not estimated by ordinary least squares. More importantly, the fact that we estimate the model by instrumental variables methods indicates that goodness-of-fit is not what we are after. Our goal was to obtain a consistent estimator for the causal effect of schooling upon earnings, and that is exactly what instrumental variables methods are trying to do. Again, this reflects that the R^2 plays no role whatsoever in comparing alternative estimators.

If college proximity is to be a valid instrument for schooling, it has to be the case that it has no direct effect on earnings. As with most instruments, this is a point of discussion (see Card, 1995). For example, it is possible that families that place a strong emphasis on education choose to live near a college, while children of such families have a higher 'ability' or are more motivated to achieve labour market success (as measured by earnings). Unfortunately, as said before, the current, exactly identified, specification does not allow us to test the exogeneity of the instruments.

The fact that the IV estimate of the returns to schooling is higher than the OLS one suggests that OLS underestimates the true causal effect of schooling. This is at odds with the most common argument against the exogeneity of schooling, namely 'ability bias', but in line with the more recent empirical studies on the returns to schooling (including, for example, Angrist and Krueger, 1991). The downward bias of OLS could be due to measurement error, or – as argued by Card (1995) – to the possibility that the true returns to schooling vary across individuals, negatively related to schooling. A model where the returns to schooling are heterogeneous, and where individuals make educational choices comparing their individual returns and costs, is obviously more involved than (5.52); see Card (1999) or Heckman (2001). In such a model, an instrumental variables estimator is typically inconsistent for estimating the 'average return to schooling' for the entire population. However, it can be argued to estimate the average return to schooling for a person whose schooling was influenced by the instrument, that is, for a person who acquires more schooling because he or she lives near college. This is known as the 'local average treatment effect' (Imbens and Angrist, 1994). This interpretation, however, still requires the instrument to be both exogenous and relevant. Section 7.7 discusses the estimation of average treatment effects in more detail. Carneiro and Heckman (2002) claim that the literature on estimating the returns to schooling is plagued by bad instruments. In particular, they demonstrate that some often-used instruments, like distance to college and number of siblings, are correlated with proxies for innate ability.

---

[12] The R^2s for the reduced forms for experience and experience-squared (not reported) are both larger than 0.60.

5.5 Alternative Approaches to Estimate Causal Effects

The identification of causal effects is among the most crucial issues in (microeconometric) empirical work. The challenge here is to answer 'what-if' questions, which basically involve a comparison of actual with counterfactual states of the world. For example, would a firm perform better if CEO pay has a larger performance-related component (e.g. stock options)? Do unemployed people find a job more easily if they take part in a specific training programme? Would infant mortality in a country improve if per capita income goes up? Or, what would the earnings of a person be had she taken one more year of schooling? The problem is that we only observe actual outcomes, not counterfactual ones. For example, we only observe earnings of persons that actually took one more year of schooling, but these persons may be (and are likely to be) different from those who did not. That is, we compare earnings of groups of individuals with, say, 10 and 11 years of schooling, and we would like to interpret this difference as the expected change in earnings if a given person (or a random person) with 10 years of schooling would actually have had 11 years of schooling (other things equal).

The ideal solution to this problem is the use of randomized trials. In this case, people are randomly assigned to alternative values of the regressor of interest. For example, when the efficacy and safety of new drugs are investigated, this is done by randomly assigning the drug to a treatment group and a placebo to a control group. Unfortunately, in economics we often do not have the opportunity to randomize variables like schooling and union status for individuals, or taxes and governance for firms. Nevertheless, experimental research has gained popularity also in economics, both in and outside laboratory contexts. For example, in the 1970s the US government has initiated several social experiments to analyse the effect of, for example, potential tax policies, health insurance plans and housing subsidies (see Hausman and Wise, 1985). An influential one was the RAND Health Insurance Experiment, which randomly assigned families to different health insurance plans (see Aron-Dine, Einav and Finkelstein, 2013, for a reexamination of the analysis from this experiment). A recent survey of field experiments in economics, including a discussion of strengths and weaknesses, is given in Levitt and List (2009). See also List (2011). Laboratory experiments, and what they reveal about the real world, are discussed in Levitt and List (2007).

Angrist and Krueger (1999) and Angrist and Pischke (2015) list four approaches to identify causal effects in the absence of true randomization and controlled experiments. Besides instrumental variables discussed in this chapter, a useful (and simpler) approach is to try to control for confounding variables as much as possible. For example, several studies investigating the causal effect of schooling upon earnings have tried to control for ability (e.g. by including scores on SAT or IQ tests) and family background. As discussed previously, this is a useful way to reduce the omitted variable bias in the OLS estimates. If regression estimates are very sensitive to the choice of control variables, the choice of regressors is obviously crucial, and there is reason to wonder whether there might be an unobserved characteristic that would change the estimates even further (thus invalidating this approach). Also note that some control variables may be endogenous themselves. For example, test scores may be affected by schooling. Moreover, adding control variables does not address problems due to measurement error in the regressor of interest. Controlling for confounding variables is therefore often a good first step, but typically insufficient to convincingly identify causal effects.

A third approach to control for unobservable differences involves the use of fixed effects or related panel data techniques, including differences-in-differences approaches. We shall discuss this in more detail in Chapter 10. In this case, we have multiple observations on the same individual or firm, and it is possible to control for unobserved time-invariant heterogeneity. A related approach uses sibling or twins data to estimate the causal effect of schooling (see, e.g., Griliches, 1979). It is also possible to use some sort of matching model. In this case, an individual or firm is compared with a matched counterpart that is as similar as possible (but with a different value for the regressor of interest); see, for example, Heckman, Ichimura and Todd (1998) and Section 7.7.

A final approach that has gained much popularity recently, particularly in labour economics, is the use of regression discontinuity designs. The idea here is that there is some kind of threshold in an observed variable, and we compare individuals just below and above this threshold. Around the threshold, individuals are (assumed to be) roughly the same. Due to the discontinuity at the threshold, this allows identification of a causal effect. We discuss this approach in more detail in Subsection 7.7.2.

In the absence of truly randomized experiments and truly exogenous instruments, the estimation of causal effects remains challenging. All the above approaches are potentially useful in certain contexts, but there is no universal approach that solves endogeneity issues in all circumstances. Useful overviews on dealing with endogeneity and identifying causal effects are given in Roberts and Whited (2013) for empirical corporate finance and Angrist and Pischke (2015) for labour economics, health economics and related areas. Much of the recent literature places the discussion of causal inference in the context of the estimation of treatment effects, and we defer discussion of this to Section 7.7.

5.6 The Generalized Instrumental Variables Estimator

In Section 5.3 we considered the linear model where for each explanatory variable exactly one instrument is available, which could equal the variable itself if it were assumed exogenous. In this section we generalize this by allowing the use of an arbitrary number of instruments.

5.6.1 Multiple Endogenous Regressors with an Arbitrary Number of Instruments

Let us, in general, consider the following model

$$y_i = x_i'\beta + \varepsilon_i, \tag{5.54}$$

where x_i is of dimension K. The OLS estimator is based upon the K moment conditions

$$E\{\varepsilon_i x_i\} = E\{(y_i - x_i'\beta)x_i\} = 0.$$

More generally, let us assume that there are R instruments available in the vector z_i, which may overlap with x_i. The relevant moment conditions are then given by the following R restrictions

$$E\{\varepsilon_i z_i\} = E\{(y_i - x_i'\beta)z_i\} = 0. \tag{5.55}$$

If $R = K$, we are back in the previous situation and the instrumental variables estimator can be solved from the sample moment conditions

$$\frac{1}{N}\sum_{i=1}^{N}(y_i - x_i'\hat{\beta}_{IV})z_i = 0$$

and we obtain

$$\hat{\beta}_{IV} = \left(\sum_{i=1}^{N} z_i x_i'\right)^{-1} \sum_{i=1}^{N} z_i y_i.$$

If the model is written in matrix notation

$$y = X\beta + \varepsilon$$

and the matrix Z is the $N \times R$ matrix of values for the instruments, this instrumental variables estimator can also be written as

$$\hat{\beta}_{IV} = (Z'X)^{-1}Z'y. \tag{5.56}$$

If $R > K$ there are more instruments than regressors. In this case it is not possible to solve for an estimate of β by replacing (5.55) with its sample counterpart. The reason for this is that there would be more equations than unknowns. Instead of dropping instruments (and losing efficiency), one therefore chooses β in such a way that the R sample moments

$$\frac{1}{N}\sum_{i=1}^{N}(y_i - x_i'\beta)z_i$$

are as close as possible to zero. This is done by minimizing the following quadratic form

$$Q_N(\beta) = \left[\frac{1}{N}\sum_{i=1}^{N}(y_i - x_i'\beta)z_i\right]' W_N \left[\frac{1}{N}\sum_{i=1}^{N}(y_i - x_i'\beta)z_i\right], \tag{5.57}$$

where W_N is an $R \times R$ positive definite symmetric matrix. This matrix is a weighting matrix and tells us how much weight to attach to which (linear combinations of the) sample moments. In general it may depend upon the sample size N because it may itself be an estimate. For the asymptotic properties of the resulting estimator for β, the probability limit of W_N, denoted by $W = \text{plim } W_N$, is important. This matrix W should be positive definite and symmetric. Using matrix notation for convenience, we can rewrite (5.57) as

$$Q_N(\beta) = \left[\frac{1}{N}Z'(y - X\beta)\right]' W_N \left[\frac{1}{N}Z'(y - X\beta)\right]. \tag{5.58}$$

Differentiating this with respect to β (see Appendix A) gives the first-order conditions

$$-2X'ZW_NZ'y + 2X'ZW_NZ'X\hat{\beta}_{IV} = 0,$$

which in turn imply

$$X'ZW_NZ'y = X'ZW_NZ'X\hat{\beta}_{IV}. \tag{5.59}$$

This is a system with K equations and K unknown elements in $\hat{\beta}_{IV}$, where $X'Z$ is of dimension $K \times R$ and $Z'y$ is $R \times 1$. Provided the matrix $X'Z$ is of rank K, the solution to (5.59) is

$$\hat{\beta}_{IV} = (X'ZW_NZ'X)^{-1}X'ZW_NZ'y, \tag{5.60}$$

which, in general, depends upon the weighting matrix W_N.

If $R = K$, the matrix $X'Z$ is square and (by assumption) invertible. This allows us to write

$$\begin{aligned}\hat{\beta}_{IV} &= (Z'X)^{-1}W_N^{-1}(X'Z)^{-1}X'ZW_NZ'y \\ &= (Z'X)^{-1}Z'y,\end{aligned}$$

which corresponds to (5.56), the weighting matrix being irrelevant. In this situation, the number of moment conditions is exactly equal to the number of parameters to be estimated. One can think of this as a situation where β is 'exactly identified' because we have just enough information (i.e. moment conditions) to estimate β. An immediate consequence of this is that the minimum of (5.58) is zero, implying that all sample moments can be set to zero by choosing β appropriately. That is, $Q_N(\hat{\beta}_{IV})$ is equal to zero. In this case $\hat{\beta}_{IV}$ does not depend upon W_N and the same estimator is obtained regardless of the choice of weighting matrix.

If $R < K$, the number of parameters to be estimated exceeds the number of moment conditions. In this case β is 'underidentified' (not identified) because there is insufficient information (i.e. moment conditions) from which to estimate β uniquely. Technically, this means that the inverse in (5.60) does not exist, and an infinite number of solutions satisfy the first-order conditions in (5.59). Unless we can come up with additional moment conditions, this identification problem is fatal in the sense that no consistent estimator for β exists. Any estimator is necessarily inconsistent.

If $R > K$, the number of moment conditions exceeds the number of parameters to be estimated. As a result, β is 'overidentified' because there is more information than is necessary to obtain a consistent estimate of β. In this case we have a range of estimators for β, corresponding to alternative choices for the weighting matrix W_N. As long as the weighting matrix is (asymptotically) positive definite, the resulting estimators are all consistent for β. The idea behind the consistency result is that we are minimizing a quadratic loss function in a set of sample moments that asymptotically converge to the corresponding population moments, which are equal to zero for the true parameter values. This is the basic principle behind the so-called method of moments, which will be discussed in more detail in Section 5.8.

Different weighting matrices W_N lead to different consistent estimators with generally different asymptotic covariance matrices. This allows us to choose an optimal weighting matrix that leads to the most efficient instrumental variables estimator. It can be shown that the optimal weighting matrix is proportional to the inverse of the covariance matrix of the sample moments. Intuitively, this means that sample moments with a small variance, which consequently provide accurate information about the unknown parameters in β, get more weight in estimation than the sample moments with a large variance. Essentially, this is the same idea as the weighted least squares approach discussed in Chapter 4, albeit that the weights now reflect different sample moments rather than different observations.

Of course the covariance matrix of the sample moments

$$\frac{1}{N}\sum_{i=1}^{N} \varepsilon_i z_i$$

depends upon the assumptions we make about ε_i and z_i. If, as before, we assume that ε_i is $IID(0, \sigma^2)$ and independent of z_i, the asymptotic covariance matrix of the sample moments is given by

$$\sigma^2 \Sigma_{zz} = \sigma^2 \text{ plim } \frac{1}{N}\sum_{i=1}^{N} z_i z_i'.$$

Consequently, an optimal weighting matrix is obtained as

$$W_N^{opt} = \left(\frac{1}{N}\sum_{i=1}^{N} z_i z_i'\right)^{-1} = \left(\frac{1}{N} Z'Z\right)^{-1},$$

and the resulting IV estimator is

$$\hat{\beta}_{IV} = (X'Z(Z'Z)^{-1}Z'X)^{-1}X'Z(Z'Z)^{-1}Z'y. \tag{5.61}$$

This is the expression that is found in most textbooks (see, e.g., Greene, 2012, Section 8.3). The estimator is sometimes referred to as the **generalized instrumental variables estimator** (GIVE). It is also known as the two-stage least squares or 2SLS estimator (see below). If ε_i is heteroskedastic or exhibits autocorrelation, the optimal weighting matrix should be adjusted accordingly. How this is done follows from the general discussion in Section 5.8.

The asymptotic distribution of $\hat{\beta}_{IV}$ is given by

$$\sqrt{N}(\hat{\beta}_{IV} - \beta) \to \mathcal{N}(0, \sigma^2(\Sigma_{xz}\Sigma_{zz}^{-1}\Sigma_{zx})^{-1}),$$

which is the same expression as given in Section 5.3. The only difference is in the dimensions of the matrices Σ_{xz} and Σ_{zz}. An estimator for the covariance matrix is easily obtained by replacing the asymptotic limits with their small-sample counterparts. This gives

$$\hat{V}\{\hat{\beta}_{IV}\} = \hat{\sigma}^2(X'Z(Z'Z)^{-1}Z'X)^{-1}, \tag{5.62}$$

where the estimator for σ^2 is obtained from the IV residuals $\hat{\varepsilon}_i = y_i - x_i'\hat{\beta}_{IV}$ as

$$\hat{\sigma}^2 = \frac{1}{N-K}\sum_{i=1}^{N} \hat{\varepsilon}_i^2.$$

Starting from (5.61) is it also relatively easy to derive the asymptotic covariance matrix of $\hat{\beta}_{IV}$ in the case where the error terms are not homoskedastic. A heteroskedasticity-consistent covariance matrix can be estimated in a similar fashion as discussed in Subsection 4.3.4 (see Davidson and MacKinnon, 2004, Section 8.5).

5.6.2 Two-stage Least Squares and the Keynesian Model Again

The estimator in (5.61) is often used in the context of a simultaneous equations system and then has the name of the **two-stage least squares (2SLS) estimator**. Essentially, this interpretation says that the same estimator can be obtained in two steps, both of which can be estimated by least squares. In the first step the reduced form is estimated by OLS (i.e. a regression of each endogenous regressor upon all instruments). In the second step the original structural equations are estimated by OLS, while replacing all endogenous variables on the right-hand side with their predicted values from the reduced form equations.

To illustrate this, let the reduced form of the kth explanatory variable be given by (in vector notation)

$$x_k = Z\pi_k + v_k.$$

OLS in this equation produces predicted values $\hat{x}_k = Z(Z'Z)^{-1}Z'x_k$. If x_k is a column in Z, we will automatically have $\hat{x}_k = x_k$. Consequently, the matrix of explanatory variables in the second step can be written as $\hat{X}$ which has the columns $\hat{x}_k, k = 1, \ldots, K$, where

$$\hat{X} = Z(Z'Z)^{-1}Z'X.$$

The OLS estimator in the second step is thus given by

$$\hat{\beta}_{IV} = (\hat{X}'\hat{X})^{-1}\hat{X}'y, \tag{5.63}$$

which can easily be shown to be identical to (5.61). The advantage of this approach is that the estimator can be computed using standard OLS software. In the second step, OLS is applied to the original model where all endogenous regressors are replaced by their predicted values on the basis of the instruments. It is a common mistake that the instruments themselves are included in the second stage. This is incorrect. One should include the fitted values from the reduced forms, which are linear combinations of all instruments. While the two-stage approach reproduces the IV estimator, the second stage does not automatically provide the correct standard errors (see Maddala and Lahiri, 2009, Section 9.6, for details).

The use of $\hat{X}$ also allows us to write the generalized instrumental variables estimator in terms of the standard formula in (5.56) if we redefine our matrix of instruments. If we use the K columns of $\hat{X}$ as instruments in the standard formula (5.56), we obtain

$$\hat{\beta}_{IV} = (\hat{X}'X)^{-1}\hat{X}'y,$$

which is identical to (5.61). It shows that one can also interpret $\hat{X}$ as the matrix of instruments (which is sometimes done).

To go back to our Keynesian model, let us now assume that the economy includes a government and a private sector, with private investment z_{2t} and government expenditures z_{3t}, both of which are assumed exogenous. The definition equation now reads

$$x_{2t} = y_t + z_{2t} + z_{3t}.$$

This implies that both z_{2t} and z_{3t} are now valid instruments to use for income x_{2t} in the consumption function. Although it is possible to define simple IV estimators similarly to (5.51) using either z_{2t} or z_{3t} as instrument, the most efficient estimator uses both instruments simultaneously. The generalized instrumental variables estimator is thus given by

$$\hat{\beta}_{IV} = (X'Z(Z'Z)^{-1}Z'X)^{-1}X'Z(Z'Z)^{-1}Z'y,$$

where the rows in Z and X are given by $z_t' = (1, z_{2t}, z_{3t})$ and $x_t' = (1, x_{2t})$, respectively.

5.6.3 Specification Tests

The results on consistency and the asymptotic distribution of the generalized instrumental variables estimator are based on the assumption that the model is correctly specified. As the estimator is only based on the model's moment conditions, it is required that the moment conditions be correct. It is therefore important to test whether the data are consistent with these moment conditions. In the 'exactly identified' case, $(1/N)\sum_i \hat{\varepsilon}_i z_i = 0$ by construction, regardless of whether or not the population moment conditions are true. Consequently, one cannot derive a useful test from the corresponding sample moments. Put differently, these $K = R$ identifying restrictions are not testable. However, if β is overidentified, it is clear that only K (linear combinations) of the R elements in $(1/N)\sum_i \hat{\varepsilon}_i z_i$ are set equal to zero. If the population moment conditions were true, one would expect the elements in the vector $(1/N)\sum_i \hat{\varepsilon}_i z_i$ all to be sufficiently close to zero (as they should converge to zero asymptotically). This provides a basis for a test of the model specification. It can be shown that (under (5.55)) the statistic (based on the GIV estimator with the optimal weighting matrix)

$$\xi = NQ_N(\hat{\beta}_{IV}) = \left(\sum_{i=1}^{N} \hat{\varepsilon}_i z_i\right)' \left(\hat{\sigma}^2 \sum_{i=1}^{N} z_i z_i'\right)^{-1} \left(\sum_{i=1}^{N} \hat{\varepsilon}_i z_i\right) \tag{5.64}$$

has an asymptotic Chi-squared distribution with $R - K$ degrees of freedom. Note that the number of degrees of freedom equals the number of moment conditions minus the number of parameters to be estimated. This is the case because only $R - K$ of the sample moment conditions $(1/N)\sum_i \hat{\varepsilon}_i z_i$ are free on account of the K restrictions imposed by the first-order conditions for $\hat{\beta}_{IV}$ in (5.59). A test based on (5.64) is usually referred to as an **overidentifying restrictions test** or Sargan test. A simple way to compute (5.64) is by taking N times the R^2 of an auxiliary regression of IV residuals $\hat{\varepsilon}_i$ upon the full set of instruments z_i. If the test rejects, the specification of the model is rejected in the sense that the sample evidence is inconsistent with the joint validity of all R moment conditions. Without additional information it is not possible to determine which of the moments are incorrect, that is, which of the instruments are invalid.[13] Roberts and Whited (2013) are therefore critical on the usefulness of this test because it assumes that a sufficient number of instruments are valid, yet which ones and why is left unspecified. Moreover, the test may lack power if many instruments are used that are uncorrelated with ε_i but add little explanatory power to the reduced forms.

If a subset of the instruments is known to satisfy the moment conditions, it is possible to test the validity of the remaining instruments or moments provided that the model is identified on the basis of the nonsuspect instruments. Assume that $R_1 \geq K$ moment conditions are nonsuspect and we want to test the validity of the remaining $R - R_1$ moment

[13] Suppose a pub allows you to buy three beers but pay for only two. Can you tell which of the three beers is the free one?

conditions. To compute the test statistic, estimate the model using all R instruments and compute the overidentifying restrictions test statistic ξ. Next, estimate the model using only the R_1 nonsuspect instruments. Typically, this will lead to a lower value for the overidentifying restrictions test, ξ_1, say. The test statistic to test the suspect moment conditions is easily obtained as $\xi - \xi_1$, which, under the null hypothesis, has an approximate Chi-squared distribution with $R - R_1$ degrees of freedom. In the special case that $R_1 = K$, this test reduces to the overidentifying restrictions test in (5.64), and the test statistic is independent of the choice of the R_1 instruments that are said to be nonsuspect.

5.6.4 Weak Instruments

A problem with instrumental variables estimation that has received considerable attention recently is that of 'weak instruments'. The problem is that the properties of the IV estimator can be very poor, and the estimator can be severely biased, if the instruments exhibit only weak correlation with the endogenous regressor(s). In these cases, the normal distribution provides a very poor approximation to the true distribution of the IV estimator, even if the sample size is large. As a result, the standard IV estimator is biased, its standard errors are misleading and hypothesis tests are unreliable. To illustrate the problem, let us consider the IV estimator for the case of a single regressor and a constant. If $\tilde{x}_i = x_i - \bar{x}$ denotes the regressor values in deviation from the sample mean, and similarly for $\tilde{y}_i$ and $\tilde{z}_i$, the IV estimator for β_2 can be written as (compare (5.51))

$$\hat{\beta}_{2,IV} = \frac{(1/N)\sum_{i=1}^{N} \tilde{z}_i\tilde{y}_i}{(1/N)\sum_{i=1}^{N} \tilde{z}_i\tilde{x}_i}.$$

If the instrument is valid (and under weak regularity conditions), the estimator is consistent and converges to

$$\beta_2 = \frac{\text{cov}\{z_i, y_i\}}{\text{cov}\{z_i, x_i\}}.$$

However, if the instrument is not correlated with the regressor, the denominator of this expression is zero. In this case, the IV estimator is inconsistent and the asymptotic distribution of $\hat{\beta}_{2,IV}$ deviates substantially from a normal distribution. The instrument is weak if there is some correlation between z_i and x_i, but not enough to make the asymptotic normal distribution provide a good approximation in finite (potentially very large) samples. For example, Bound, Jaeger and Baker (1995) show that part of the results of Angrist and Krueger (1991), who use quarter of birth to instrument for schooling in a wage equation, suffers from the weak instruments problem. Even with samples of more than 300 000 (!) individuals, the IV estimator appeared to be unreliable and misleading.

To figure out whether you have weak instruments, it is useful to examine the reduced-form regression and evaluate the explanatory power of the additional instruments that are not included in the equation of interest. Consider the linear model with one endogenous regressor

$$y_i = x_{1i}'\beta_1 + x_{2i}\beta_2 + \varepsilon_i,$$

where $E\{x_{1i}\varepsilon_i\} = 0$ and where additional instruments z_{2i} (for x_{2i}) satisfy $E\{z_{2i}\varepsilon_i\} = 0$. The appropriate reduced form is given by

$$x_{2i} = x_{1i}'\pi_1 + z_{2i}'\pi_2 + v_i.$$

If $\pi_2 = 0$, the instruments in z_{2i} are irrelevant and the IV estimator is inconsistent. If π_2 is 'close to zero', the instruments are weak. The value of the F-statistic for $\pi_2 = 0$ is a measure for the information content contained in the instruments. Staiger and Stock (1997) provide a theoretical analysis of the properties of the IV estimator and provide some guidelines about how large the F-statistic should be for the IV estimator to have good properties. As a simple rule-of-thumb, Stock and Watson (2007, Chapter 12) suggest that you do not have to worry about weak instruments if the F-statistic exceeds 10. The implicit null hypothesis here is not that $\pi_2 = 0$, but that the bias in the resulting IV estimator is 'small'. Stock and Yogo (2005) show that critical values larger than 10 are appropriate when there are more than two instruments. In any case, it is a good practice to compute and present the F-statistic of the reduced form in empirical work. If the F-statistic for the significance of the instruments in the reduced form is too small, you should not put much confidence in the IV results. If you have many instruments available, it may be a good strategy to use the most relevant subset and drop the 'weak' ones. Donald and Newey (2001) propose a way to choose among many valid instruments by minimizing the (finite sample) mean square error of the estimator. Cameron and Trivedi (2005, Subsection 6.4.4) discuss leading alternative estimators that have received renewed interest given the poor finite-sample properties of the standard IV estimator with weak instruments. See also Stock, Wright and Yogo (2002), Hahn and Hausman (2003) and Stock and Yogo (2005) for more discussion. Hahn, Han and Moon (2011) show that the standard Hausman test of Subsection 5.3.1 is invalid in the case of weak instruments, and provide an alternative version that is valid even when the instruments are weak.

5.6.5 Implementing and Reporting Instrumental Variables Estimators

Clearly, using instrumental variables estimators rather than OLS is more involved than pressing another button in Eviews or Stata, and writing a paper stating that you 'addressed the endogeneity problem by using instrumental variables', without further explanation or details, is not acceptable. A first step, recommended by Larcker and Rusticus (2010) is to describe the economic theories the research questions are based on. For example, the endogeneity problem could be due to an important control variable that is not available (a confounding variable), the regressor of interest could be the outcome of a choice that individuals or firms are making, partly based upon the costs and benefits of such a choice, the direction of causality could be unclear, or there may be good reason to suspect measurement errors. With a more detailed description of the endogeneity problem, its background and potential alternative theories, a researcher is better equipped to select an empirical approach, and readers are more able to evaluate whether the approach is appropriate. As stated by Roberts and Whited (2013), the only way to find a good instrument is to understand the economics of the question at hand.

An obvious requirement in an empirical study is to state explicitly what the instruments are. This sounds trivial, but this is often overlooked, implicit or hidden in an appendix. There should also be a discussion of why these instruments are valid, most importantly why they would satisfy the exogeneity requirement. It is rarely the case that instruments are entirely convincing, in the sense that all potential reviewers and discussants would accept them, but that does not imply that one should not try to give convincing arguments. It is also advisable to anticipate the potential reasons why the instrument is not exogenous and demonstrate that these effects are either very small or controlled for by inclusion of other variables in the model (see Larcker and Rusticus, 2010).

Another recommendation is to also report the first-stage regression results, like those in Table 5.2, including some relevant statistics. This allows one to see which instruments are weak and which instruments are crucial in driving the results. Importantly, it should be clear from these results that the instruments are relevant. Check, for example, whether the F-test of the instrumental variables exceeds 10. If instruments are only weakly related to the endogenous regressor, instrumental variables estimates will be highly imprecise, or – even worse – suffer from a weak instruments problem. Make sure that the first-stage regression includes all exogenous regressors from the model as well as all instruments.

Third, it is advised to also report OLS results along with the IV ones. This provides a benchmark and allows comparison, for example, to see whether the difference between the results is consistent with the underlying theory and the hypothesized source of endogeneity. It is typically a bad idea to immediately jump to instrumental variables estimation without having looked at OLS results. Finding that OLS results and IV results are very similar does not necessarily indicate that there are no endogeneity concerns. It could also be that the IV approach is done inappropriately, for example, by using an instrument that is highly correlated with the endogenous regressor and is endogenous itself.

Finally, researchers should provide some robustness checks on the chosen instruments and report tests for appropriateness of the instrumental variables. For example, when relevant, the overidentifying restriction test should be reported, despite its limitations.

5.7 Institutions and Economic Development

Economic development differs widely across countries, and it is an interesting and relevant question what drives these differences. For example, geographical and ecological variables, like climate zone, latitude or distance from the coast, are highly correlated with GDP per capita. It is possible, however, that the effects of these variables upon GDP per capita work mainly indirectly through the choice of political and economic institutions (e.g. property rights enforcement, rule of law). A problem with investigating the impact of institutions on GDP is that institutional quality is potentially correlated with omitted variables, might be measured with error and may itself be partly driven by GDP (reverse causality). In a highly cited article, Acemoglu, Johnson and Robinson (2001) use an innovative instrument to address these endogeneity problems: early settler mortality. Their logic is that mortality rates faced by settlers more than 100 years ago are correlated with current institutional quality and can be assumed to have no direct effect on a country's GDP today.

In this section we use data and insights of Acemoglu, Johnson and Robinson (2001) to highlight the practical implementation of instrumental variables estimation. The main equation of interest is

$$\log(GDP_i) = \beta_1 + QI_i\beta_2 + x_i'\beta_3 + \varepsilon_i,$$

where $\log(GDP_i)$ denotes the logarithm of GDP per capita in country i, QI_i is a measure of the quality of institutions, whereas x_i is a vector of other characteristics that are assumed to be exogenous, for example, related to climate or geography. The base sample contains 64 countries that were ex-colonies and for which the relevant data are available.

The dependent variable is GDP per capita in 1995, adjusted for purchasing power parity. QI_i measures the risk of confiscation and forced nationalization of property, ranging from 0 to 10, where a higher score means less risk.

We first estimate the model by ordinary least squares, with two alternative choices for x_i. This provides a benchmark for the results to come. The first specification includes only one control variable, *latitude*, a measure of distance to the equator, scaled from 0 to 1. The second specification also includes dummies for Africa and Asia, as well as a measure of malaria risk, *malfal94*, the proportion of the population living where falciparum malaria is endemic. The results are given in Table 5.4. Because there is no information on *malfal94* for Malta and the Bahamas, the sample size reduces to 62 for the latter specification. The table reports routinely calculated standard errors assuming homoskedasticity. Heteroskedasticity-consistent standard errors are reasonably similar.

In interpreting these results, one should keep in mind that the sample is relatively small and that many of the variables tend to be correlated. For example, the malaria variable has a correlation of 0.45 with latitude, whereas African countries tend to be closer to the equator. As a result, estimation results may change quite a bit from one specification to the other, depending upon which explanatory variables are included. Overall, the results in the table show a strong correlation between institutions, as measured by QI, and economic performance.

We also observe a significant relationship between GDP per capita and latitude in specification (1), which essentially disappears in specification (2) when other control variables related to location and malaria risk are included. As argued by Acemoglu, Johnson and Robinson (2001), there are several reasons for not interpreting the relationship between GDP and institutions as causal. Most important, there are many omitted determinants of income differences that will naturally be correlated with institutions. Further, the institutions variable may be measured with considerable error. Finally, it is possible that richer economies are able to afford better institutions, leading to reverse causality. All of these problems can be solved with an appropriate instrument for institutions.

Table 5.4 OLS results explaining GDP per capita

Dependent variable: log(*GDP*)		
Variable	(1)	(2)
constant	4.728	6.178
	(0.397)	(0.404)
QI	0.468	0.364
	(0.064)	(0.056)
latitude	1.577	0.234
	(0.710)	(0.625)
africa		−0.414
		(0.226)
asia		−0.457
		(0.221)
malfal94		−0.788
		(0.278)
R^2	0.575	0.740
Number of observations	64	62

The main instrument exploited by Acemoglu, Johnson and Robinson (2001) is the logarithm of the mortality rate expected by the first European settlers in the colonies, *logem4*. Their argument is that settler mortality rates were a major determinant of settlements, which – in turn – were a major determinant of early institutions. Because there is a strong correlation between current institutions and earlier ones, this implies that early settler mortality rates are likely to be correlated with institutions, making the instrument relevant. The exclusion restriction (or exogeneity condition) requires that, conditional on the controls in the model, the mortality rates of European settlers more than a century ago have no effect on GDP per capita today. The major concern with this is the possibility that early mortality rates are correlated with the current disease environment, which may have a direct effect on economic performance. Acemoglu, Johnson and Robinson (2001) argue that this is unlikely to be the case. As a second instrument we consider the percentage of the population from European descent in 1900, *euro1900*. Starting from the two different specifications of our main equation of interest, this leads to four different reduced forms: one set where *logem4* is used as instrument, and one set where both *logem4* and *euro1900* are used as instruments. The latter specification involves one overidentifying restriction, which is empirically testable. Table 5.5 presents the (OLS) estimates of the reduced forms.

The results for specifications (1a) and (1b) show that settler mortality, *logem4*, is significantly and negatively related to institutions. However, in the extended specifications (2a) and (2b), the role of this variable is much weaker. Judging from the low F-test for (2a), it could even be a weak instrument in this case. Our second instrument, *euro1900*, is significant in each case and contributing substantially to an increase of the R^2s. If this instrument is truly exogenous, we should therefore put more confidence in the IV results using both variables as instruments.

Table 5.5 OLS results reduced form (QI explained from exogenous variables)

Dependent variable: *QI*				
Variable	(1a)	(1b)	(2a)	(2b)
constant	8.529	7.853	7.872	5.861
	(0.812)	(0.831)	(0.963)	(0.962)
logem4 (instrument)	−0.510	−0.368	−0.328	−0.031
	(0.141)	(0.149)	(0.199)	(0.187)
euro1900 (instrument)	–	0.021	–	0.044
		(0.008)		(0.010)
latitude	2.002	0.200	1.888	−1.654
	(1.337)	(1.495)	(1.457)	(1.515)
africa			0.135	1.272
			(0.527)	(0.531)
asia			0.487	1.989
			(0.519)	(0.572)
malfal94			−0.774	−1.241
			(0.695)	(0.617)
R^2	0.296	0.367	0.322	0.493
F-test on instrument(s)	13.09	10.52	2.72	11.03
Number of observations	64	63	62	62

Table 5.6 IV results explaining GDP per capita

Dependent variable: log(*GDP*)				
Variable	(1a)	(1b)	(2a)	(2b)
constant	1.692	1.995	2.772	4.991
	(1.293)	(1.018)	(2.717)	(0.764)
QI (instrumented)	0.996	0.946	0.893	0.548
	(0.222)	(0.173)	(0.420)	(0.115)
latitude	−0.647	−0.597	−1.070	−0.220
	(1.335)	(1.186)	(1.425)	(0.723)
africa			−0.445	−0.425
			(0.365)	(0.247)
asia			−0.825	−0.585
			(0.455)	(0.250)
malfal94			−0.106	−0.550
			(0.691)	(0.328)
Instruments	*logem4*	*logem4 euro1900*	*logem4*	*logem4 euro1900*
Overidentifying restrictions test	−	0.069	−	1.928
(*p*-value)		(0.791)		(0.165)
Durbin–Wu–Hausman test	−4.33	−5.37	−2.14	−2.14
(*p*-value)	(0.000)	(0.000)	(0.037)	(0.037)
Number of observations	64	63	62	62

Relative to OLS, the instrumental variable estimation results, presented in Table 5.6, show a larger impact of institutions on log(*GDP*). For all specifications the estimated impact is statistically significant, with *t*-statistics varying between 2.13 and 5.45. Somewhat surprisingly, the coefficient on *QI* appears to be underestimated by OLS. This suggests that measurement error is more important than reverse causality and omitted variable biases, which can both be expected to lead to overestimation by OLS of the causal impact of institutions. For example, the ecological climate of a country may be correlated in the same direction with both the quality of institutions and GDP per capita.

Once the endogeneity of *QI* is controlled for, the significance of latitude disappears. Similarly, in specifications (2a) and (2b), the effects of malaria risk and being an African country are no longer significant in explaining GDP per capita. This suggests that geography is only relevant in explaining the cross-sectional variation in GDP per capita through the choice of institutions, with little or no direct effect. Acemoglu, Johnson and Robinson (2005) conclude from this that differences in economic institutions are the fundamental cause of differences in economic development. This conclusion is debated, for example, by Sachs (2003). His main argument is that the estimated model appears overly simplistic with no attention to the dynamic evolution of institutions and GDP over time. Moreover, the choice and measurement of some of the control variables, like the proxy for malaria risk, are disputed. There is a huge literature on the important role of institutions in economic development. In a recent overview, Fernández and Tamayo (2017) present an integrated account of the interlinkages between institutions, finance and growth.

Table 5.6 also presents the results for the overidentifying restrictions tests for the two specifications that are overidentified. It is calculated as N times the R^2 of an auxiliary regression of the IV residuals upon all instruments and exogenous variables, as explained in Subsection 5.6.3. Under the null hypothesis that all imposed moment conditions are jointly valid, the test statistic has an asymptotic Chi-squared distribution with one degree of freedom. It can be interpreted as testing the exogeneity of *euro1900* under the condition that *logem4* is truly exogenous (or the other way around). The test results support the overidentifying restrictions imposed by the two instruments. It is possible, however, that the test does not reject due to low power, particularly given the small sample. The Durbin–Wu–Hausman test tests the endogeneity of *QI* by (indirectly) comparing the OLS and IV estimates. It is calculated by adding the reduced form residuals to the equation of interest, which is then estimated by OLS. The table presents the corresponding t-statistics. In all cases, the null hypothesis is rejected, most strongly in the model with few control variables. If we believe that the instrumental variables are valid, this indicates that the OLS results are biased due to the endogeneity of institutions.

5.8 The Generalized Method of Moments

The approaches sketched above are special cases of an approach proposed by Hansen (1982), usually referred to as the generalized method of moments (GMM). This approach estimates the model parameters directly from the moment conditions that are imposed by the model. These conditions can be linear in the parameters (as in the above examples) but quite often are nonlinear. To enable identification, the number of moment conditions should be at least as large as the number of unknown parameters. The present section provides a fairly intuitive discussion of the generalized method of moments. First, in the next subsection, we start with a motivating example that illustrates how economic theory can imply nonlinear moment conditions. An extensive, not too technical, overview of GIVE and GMM methodology is given in Hall (1993); Hall (2005) provides more details.

5.8.1 Example

The following example is based on Hansen and Singleton (1982) and illustrates how an economic model of individual behaviour can imply a set of moment conditions that can be exploited to estimate the unknown parameters. It also illustrates how valid instruments may follow from economic theory. Consider an individual agent who maximizes the expected utility of current and future consumption by solving

$$\max E_t \left\{ \sum_{s=0}^{S} \delta^s U(C_{t+s}) \right\}, \tag{5.65}$$

where C_{t+s} denotes consumption in period $t+s$, $U(C_{t+s})$ is the utility attached to this consumption level, which is discounted by the discount factor δ ($0 < \delta \leq 1$) and E_t is the expectation operator conditional upon all information available at time t. Associated with this problem is a set of intertemporal budget constraints of the form

$$C_{t+s} + q_{t+s} = w_{t+s} + (1 + r_{t+s})q_{t+s-1}, \tag{5.66}$$

where q_{t+s} denotes financial wealth at the end of period $t+s$, r_{t+s} is the return on financial wealth (invested in a portfolio of assets) and w_{t+s} denotes labour income. The budget constraint says that labour income plus asset income should be spent on consumption C_{t+s} or saved in q_{t+s}. This maximization problem is hard to solve analytically. Nevertheless, it is still possible to estimate the unknown parameters involved through the first-order conditions. The first-order conditions of (5.65) subject to (5.66) imply that

$$E_t\{\delta U'(C_{t+1})(1 + r_{t+1})\} = U'(C_t),$$

where U' is the first derivative of U. The right-hand side of this equality denotes the marginal utility of one additional dollar consumed today, while the left-hand side gives the expected marginal utility of saving this dollar until the next period (so that it becomes $1 + r_{t+1}$ dollars) and consuming it then. Optimality thus implies that (expected) marginal utilities are equalized.

As a next step, we can rewrite this equation as

$$E_t\left\{\frac{\delta U'(C_{t+1})}{U'(C_t)}(1 + r_{t+1}) - 1\right\} = 0. \tag{5.67}$$

Essentially, this is a (conditional) moment condition that can be exploited to estimate the unknown parameters if we make some assumption about the utility function U. We can do this by transforming (5.67) into a set of unconditional moment conditions. Suppose z_t is included in the information set. This implies that z_t does not provide any information about the expected value of

$$\frac{\delta U'(C_{t+1})}{U'(C_t)}(1 + r_{t+1}) - 1$$

so that it also holds that[14]

$$E\left\{\left(\frac{\delta U'(C_{t+1})}{U'(C_t)}(1 + r_{t+1}) - 1\right) z_t\right\} = 0. \tag{5.68}$$

Thus we can interpret z_t as a vector of instruments, valid by the assumption of optimal behaviour (rational expectations) of the agent. For simplicity, let us assume that the utility function is of the power form, that is,

$$U(C) = \frac{C^{1-\gamma}}{1-\gamma},$$

where γ denotes the (constant) coefficient of relative risk aversion, where higher values of γ correspond to a more risk-averse agent. Then we can write (5.68) as

$$E\left\{\left(\delta\left(\frac{C_{t+1}}{C_t}\right)^{-\gamma}(1 + r_{t+1}) - 1\right) z_t\right\} = 0. \tag{5.69}$$

We now have a set of moment conditions that identify the unknown parameters δ and γ, and, given observations on C_{t+1}/C_t, r_{t+1} and z_t, allow us to estimate them consistently. This requires an extension of the earlier approach to nonlinear functions.

[14] We use the general result that $E\{x_1|x_2\} = 0$ implies that $E\{x_1 g(x_2)\} = 0$ for any function g (see Appendix B).

5.8.2 The Generalized Method of Moments

Let us, in general, consider a model that is characterized by a set of R moment conditions as

$$E\{f(w_t, z_t, \theta)\} = 0, \tag{5.70}$$

where f is a vector function with R elements, θ is a K-dimensional vector containing all unknown parameters, w_t is a vector of observable variables that could be endogenous or exogenous and z_t is the vector of instruments. In the example of the previous subsection, $w_t' = (C_{t+1}/C_t, r_{t+1})$; and in the linear model of Section 5.6, $w_t' = (y_t, x_t')$.

To estimate θ we take the same approach as before and consider the sample equivalent of (5.70) given by

$$g_T(\theta) \equiv \frac{1}{T}\sum_{t=1}^{T} f(w_t, z_t, \theta). \tag{5.71}$$

If the number of moment conditions R equals the number of unknown parameters K, it would be possible to set the R elements in (5.71) to zero and to solve for θ to obtain a unique consistent estimator. If f is nonlinear in θ, an analytical solution may not be available. If the number of moment conditions is less than the number of parameters, the parameter vector θ is not identified. If the number of moment conditions is larger, we cannot solve uniquely for the unknown parameters by setting (5.71) to zero. Instead, we choose our estimator for θ such that the vector of sample moments is as close as possible to zero, in the sense that a quadratic form in $g_T(\theta)$ is minimized. That is,

$$\min_\theta Q_T(\theta) = \min_\theta g_T(\theta)' W_T g_T(\theta), \tag{5.72}$$

where, as before, W_T is a positive definite matrix with plim $W_T = W$. The solution to this problem provides the **generalized method of moments** or GMM estimator $\hat{\theta}$. Although we cannot obtain an analytical solution for the GMM estimator in the general case, it can be shown that it is consistent and asymptotically normal (CAN) under some weak regularity conditions. The heuristic argument presented for the generalized instrumental variables estimator in the linear model extends to this more general setting. Because sample averages converge to population means, which are zero for the true parameter values, an estimator chosen to make these sample moments as close to zero as possible (as defined by (5.72)) will converge to the true value and will thus be consistent. In practice, the GMM estimator is obtained by numerically solving the minimization problem in (5.72), for which a variety of algorithms is available; see Wooldridge (2010, Section 12.7) or Greene (2012, Appendix E) for a general discussion.

As before, different weighting matrices W_T lead to different consistent estimators with different asymptotic covariance matrices. The optimal weighting matrix, which leads to the smallest covariance matrix for the GMM estimator, is the inverse of the covariance matrix of the sample moments. In the absence of autocorrelation it is given by

$$W^{opt} = (E\{f(w_t, z_t, \theta) f(w_t, z_t, \theta)'\})^{-1}.$$

In general this matrix depends upon the unknown parameter vector θ, which presents a problem that we did not encounter in the linear model. The solution is to adopt a multistep estimation procedure. In the first step we use a suboptimal choice of W_T that does not depend upon θ (e.g. the identity matrix) to obtain a first consistent estimator $\hat{\theta}_{[1]}$, say. Then, we can consistently estimate the optimal weighting matrix by[15]

$$W_T^{opt} = \left(\frac{1}{T} \sum_{t=1}^{T} f(w_t, z_t, \hat{\theta}_{[1]}) f(w_t, z_t, \hat{\theta}_{[1]})' \right)^{-1}. \tag{5.73}$$

In the second step one obtains the asymptotically efficient (optimal) GMM estimator $\hat{\theta}_{GMM}$. Its asymptotic distribution is given by

$$\sqrt{T}(\hat{\theta}_{GMM} - \theta) \to \mathcal{N}(0, V), \tag{5.74}$$

where the asymptotic covariance matrix V is given by

$$V = (DW^{opt}D')^{-1}, \tag{5.75}$$

where D is the $K \times R$ derivative matrix

$$D = E\left\{ \frac{\partial f(w_t, z_t, \theta)}{\partial \theta'} \right\}. \tag{5.76}$$

Intuitively, the elements in D measure how sensitive a particular moment is with respect to small changes in θ. If the sensitivity with respect to a given element in θ is large, small changes in this element lead to relatively large changes in the objective function $Q_T(\theta)$ and the particular element in θ is relatively accurately estimated. As usual, the covariance matrix in (5.75) can be estimated by replacing the population moments in D and W^{opt} with their sample equivalents, evaluated at $\hat{\theta}_{GMM}$.

The GMM estimator described above is a two-step estimator. Alternatively, it is possible to employ the so-called iterated GMM estimator. This estimator has the same asymptotic properties as the two-step one, but is sometimes argued to have better small-sample performance. It is obtained by computing a new optimal weighting matrix using the two-step estimator, and using this to obtain a next estimator, $\hat{\theta}_{[3]}$, say, which in turn is used in a weighting matrix to obtain $\hat{\theta}_{[4]}$. This procedure is repeated until convergence.

The great advantages of the generalized method of moments are that (1) it does not require distributional assumptions, like normality, (2) it can allow for heteroskedasticity of unknown form and (3) it can estimate parameters even if the model cannot be solved analytically from the first-order conditions. Unlike most of the cases we discussed before, the exogeneity of the instruments in z_t is beyond doubt if the model leads to a conditional moment restriction (as in (5.67)) and z_t is in the conditioning set. For example, if at time t the agent maximizes expected utility given all publicly available information, then any variable that is observed (to the agent) at time t provides an exogenous instrument. Obviously, the instrument only helps to estimate θ if it is relevant. In the example, this requires that the instrument has some relation with the arguments in the agent's utility function (future returns or consumption growth).

Finally, we consider the extension of the **overidentifying restrictions test** to nonlinear models. Following the intuition from the linear model, it would be anticipated that, if the population moment conditions $E\{f(w_t, z_t, \theta)\} = 0$ are correct, then $g_T(\hat{\theta}_{GMM}) \approx 0$.

[15] If there is autocorrelation in $f(w_t, z_t, \theta)$ up to a limited order, the optimal weighting matrix can be estimated using a variant of the Newey–West estimator discussed in Section 5.1; see Greene (2012, Section 13.6).

Therefore, the sample moments provide a convenient test of the model specification. Provided that all moment conditions are correct, the test statistic

$$\xi = T g_T(\hat{\theta}_{GMM})' W_T^{opt} g_T(\hat{\theta}_{GMM}),$$

where $\hat{\theta}_{GMM}$ is the optimal GMM estimator and W_T^{opt} is the optimal weighting matrix given in (5.73) (based upon a consistent estimator for θ), is asymptotically Chi-squared distributed with $R - K$ degrees of freedom. Recall that, for the exactly identified case, there are zero degrees of freedom, and there is nothing that can be tested.

In the next section we present an empirical illustration using GMM to estimate intertemporal asset pricing models. In Section 10.5 we shall consider another example of GMM, where it is used to estimate a dynamic panel data model. First, we consider a few simple examples.

5.8.3 Some Simple Examples

As a very simple example, assume we are interested in estimating the population mean μ of a variable y_i on the basis of a sample of N observations ($i = 1, 2, \ldots, N$). The moment condition of this 'model' is given by

$$E\{y_i - \mu\} = 0,$$

with sample equivalent

$$\frac{1}{N}\sum_{i=1}^{N}(y_i - \mu).$$

By setting this to zero and solving for μ, we obtain a method of moments estimator

$$\hat{\mu} = \frac{1}{N}\sum_{i=1}^{N} y_i,$$

which is just the sample average.

If we consider the linear model

$$y_i = x_i'\beta + \varepsilon_i$$

with instrument vector z_i, the moment conditions are

$$E\{\varepsilon_i z_i\} = E\{(y_i - x_i'\beta)z_i\} = 0.$$

If ε_i is i.i.d., the optimal GMM estimator is the instrumental variables estimator given in (5.43) or (5.61). More generally, the optimal weighting matrix is given by

$$W^{opt} = (E\{\varepsilon_i^2 z_i z_i'\})^{-1},$$

which is estimated unrestrictedly as

$$W_N^{opt} = \left(\frac{1}{N}\sum_{i=1}^{N} \hat{\varepsilon}_i^2 z_i z_i'\right)^{-1},$$

where $\hat{\varepsilon}_i$ is the residual based upon an initial consistent estimator. When it is imposed that ε_i is i.i.d., we can simply use

$$W_N^{opt} = \left(\frac{1}{N}\sum_{i=1}^{N} z_i z_i'\right)^{-1}.$$

The $K \times R$ derivative matrix is given by

$$D = E\{x_i z_i'\},$$

which we can estimate consistently by

$$D_N = \frac{1}{N}\sum_{i=1}^{N} x_i z_i'.$$

In general, the covariance matrix of the *optimal* GMM or GIV estimator $\hat{\beta}$ for β can be estimated as

$$\hat{V}\{\hat{\beta}\} = \left(\sum_{i=1}^{N} x_i z_i'\right)^{-1} \sum_{i=1}^{N} \hat{\varepsilon}_i^2 z_i z_i' \left(\sum_{i=1}^{N} z_i x_i'\right)^{-1}. \tag{5.77}$$

This estimator generalizes (5.62) just as the White heteroskedasticity-consistent covariance matrix generalizes the standard OLS expression. Thus, the general GMM set-up allows for heteroskedasticity of ε_i automatically.

5.8.4 Weak Identification

Unfortunately, there is considerable evidence that the asymptotic distribution in (5.74) often provides a poor approximation to the sampling distribution of the GMM estimator in samples that are typical for empirical work (see, e.g., Hansen, Heaton and Yaron, 1996). The problem of weak instruments, as discussed in Subsection 5.6.4, also extends to the generalized method of moments. To understand the problem, consider the general set of moment conditions in (5.70). The parameters of interest are identified under the assumption that

$$E\{f(w_t, z_t, \theta_0)\} = 0,$$

where θ_0 is the true value of θ, and that

$$E\{f(w_t, z_t, \theta)\} \neq 0$$

for $\theta \neq \theta_0$. That is, the moment conditions are only satisfied for the true parameter values. The latter condition states that the moment conditions are 'relevant', and is necessary for identification (and consistency of the GMM estimator). It tells us that it is not sufficient to have enough moment conditions ($R \geq K$), but also that the moment conditions should provide relevant information about the parameters of interest. If $E\{f(w_t, z_t, \theta)\}$ is nearly zero for $\theta \neq \theta_0$, then θ can be thought of as being weakly identified.

As mentioned by Stock, Wright and Yogo (2002), an implication of weak identification is that the GMM estimator can exhibit a variety of pathologies. For example, the two-step estimator and the iterated GMM estimator may lead to quite different estimates and confidence intervals. Or the GMM estimator may be very sensitive to the addition of one or more instruments, or to changes in the sample. All these features may indicate a weak identification problem.

Stock and Wright (2000) explore the distribution theory for GMM estimators when some or all of the parameters are weakly identified, paying particular attention to variants of the nonlinear model discussed in Subsection 5.8.1.

5.9 Illustration: Estimating Intertemporal Asset Pricing Models

In the finance literature, the GMM framework is frequently used to estimate and test asset pricing models. An asset pricing model, for example the CAPM discussed in Section 2.7, should explain the variation in expected returns for different risky investments. Because some investments are more risky than others, investors may require compensation for bearing this risk by means of a risk premium. This leads to variation in expected returns across different assets. An extensive treatment of asset pricing models and their link with the generalized method of moments is provided in Cochrane (2005).

In this section we consider the consumption-based asset pricing model. This model is derived from the framework sketched in Subsection 5.8.1 by introducing a number of alternative investment opportunities for financial wealth. Assume that there are J alternative risky assets available that the agent can invest in, with returns $r_{j,t+1}$, $j = 1, \ldots, J$, as well as a riskless asset with certain return $r_{f,t+1}$. Assuming that the agent optimally chooses his or her portfolio of assets, the first-order conditions of the problem now imply that

$$E_t\{\delta U'(C_{t+1})(1 + r_{f,t+1})\} = U'(C_t)$$
$$E_t\{\delta U'(C_{t+1})(1 + r_{j,t+1})\} = U'(C_t), \quad j = 1, \ldots, J.$$

This says that the expected marginal utility of investing one additional dollar in asset j is equal for all assets and equal to the marginal utility of consuming this additional dollar today. Assuming power utility, as before, and restricting attention to unconditional expectations,[16] the first-order conditions can be rewritten as

$$E\left\{\delta\left(\frac{C_{t+1}}{C_t}\right)^{-\gamma}(1 + r_{f,t+1})\right\} = 1 \tag{5.78}$$

$$E\left\{\delta\left(\frac{C_{t+1}}{C_t}\right)^{-\gamma}(r_{j,t+1} - r_{f,t+1})\right\} = 0, \quad j = 1, \ldots, J, \tag{5.79}$$

where the second set of conditions is written in terms of excess returns, that is, returns in excess of the risk-free rate.

Let us, for convenience, define the intertemporal marginal rate of substitution

$$m_{t+1}(\theta) \equiv \delta\left(\frac{C_{t+1}}{C_t}\right)^{-\gamma},$$

[16] This means that we restrict attention to moments using instrument $z_t = 1$ only.

where θ contains all unknown parameters. In finance, $m_{t+1}(\theta)$ is often referred to as a stochastic discount factor or a pricing kernel (see Campbell, Lo and MacKinlay, 1997, Chapter 8, or Cochrane, 2005). Alternative asset pricing models are described by alternative specifications for the pricing kernel $m_{t+1}(\theta)$. To see how a choice for $m_{t+1}(\theta)$ provides a model that describes expected returns, we use the fact that for two arbitrary random variables $E\{xy\} = \text{cov}\{x, y\} + E\{x\}E\{y\}$ (see Appendix B), from which it follows that

$$\text{cov}\{m_{t+1}(\theta), r_{j,t+1} - r_{f,t+1}\} + E\{m_{t+1}(\theta)\}E\{r_{j,t+1} - r_{f,t+1}\} = 0.$$

This allows us to write

$$E\{r_{j,t+1} - r_{f,t+1}\} = -\frac{\text{cov}\{m_{t+1}(\theta), r_{j,t+1} - r_{f,t+1}\}}{E\{m_{t+1}(\theta)\}}, \tag{5.80}$$

which says that the expected excess return on any asset j is equal to a risk premium that depends linearly upon the covariance between the asset's excess return and the stochastic discount factor. Knowledge of $m_{t+1}(\theta)$ allows us to describe or explain the cross-sectional variation of expected returns across different assets. In the consumption-based model, this tells us that assets that have a positive covariance with consumption growth (and thus make future consumption more volatile) must promise higher expected returns to induce investors to hold them. Conversely, assets that covary negatively with consumption growth can offer expected returns that are lower than the risk-free rate.[17]

The moment conditions in (5.78) and (5.79) can be used to estimate the unknown parameters δ and γ. In this section we use data that cover monthly returns over the period February 1959–November 1993. The basic assets we consider are 10 portfolios of stocks, maintained by the Center for Research in Security Prices at the University of Chicago. These portfolios are size-based, which means that portfolio 1 contains the 10% smallest firms listed at the New York Stock Exchange, while portfolio 10 contains the 10% largest firms that are listed. The riskless return is approximated by the monthly return on a 3-month US Treasury Bill, which does not vary much over time. For consumption we use total US personal consumption expenditures on nondurables and services. It is assumed that the model is valid for a representative agent whose consumption corresponds to this measure of aggregate per capita consumption. Data on size-based portfolios are used because most asset pricing models tend to underpredict the returns on the stocks of small firms. This is the so-called small-firm effect (see Banz, 1981, or Campbell, Lo and MacKinlay, 1997, p. 211).

With one riskless asset and 10 risky portfolios, (5.78) and (5.79) provide 11 moment conditions with only two parameters to estimate. These parameters can be estimated using the identity matrix as a suboptimal weighting matrix, using the efficient two-step GMM estimator or the iterated GMM estimator. Table 5.7 presents the estimation results on the basis of the monthly returns from February 1959 to November 1993 using one-step and iterated GMM.[18] The γ estimates are huge and rather imprecise. For the iterated GMM procedure, for example, a 95% confidence interval for γ based upon the approximate normal distribution is as large as (−9.67, 124.47). The estimated risk aversion coefficients of 57.4

[17] For example, you may reward a particular asset if it delivers a high return in the situation where you happen to get unemployed.

[18] For the one-step GMM estimator the standard errors and the overidentifying restrictions test are computed in a nonstandard way. The formulae given in the text do not apply because the optimal weighting matrix is not used. See Cochrane (2005, Chapter 11) for the appropriate expressions.

Table 5.7 GMM estimation results consumption-based asset pricing model

	One-step GMM		Iterated GMM	
	Estimate	Standard error	Estimate	Standard error
δ	0.6996	(0.1436)	0.8273	(0.1162)
γ	91.4097	(38.1178)	57.3992	(34.2203)
ξ $(df = 9)$	4.401	$(p = 0.88)$	5.685	$(p = 0.77)$

and 91.4 are much higher than what is considered economically plausible. This finding illustrates the so-called equity premium puzzle (see Mehra and Prescott, 1985), which reflects that the high-risk premia on risky assets (equity) can only be explained in this model if agents are extremely risk averse (compare Campbell, Lo and MacKinlay, 1997, Section 8.2). Looking at the overidentifying restrictions tests, we see, somewhat surprisingly, that they do not reject the joint validity of the imposed moment conditions. This means that the consumption-based asset pricing model is statistically not rejected by the data. This is solely due to the high imprecision of the estimates. Unfortunately this is only a statistical satisfaction and certainly does not imply that the model is economically valuable. The gain in efficiency from the use of the optimal weighting matrix appears to be fairly limited, with standard errors that are only up to 20% smaller than for the one-step method.

To investigate the economic value of the above model, it is possible to compute so-called pricing errors (compare Cochrane, 1996). One can directly compute the average expected excess return according to the model, simply by replacing the population moments in (5.80) by the corresponding sample moments and using the estimated values for δ and γ. On the other hand the average excess returns on asset j can be directly computed from the data. In Figure 5.1, we plot the average excess returns against the predicted average excess returns, as well as a 45° line. We do this for the one-step estimator only because, as argued by Cochrane (1996), this estimator minimizes the vector of pricing errors of the 11 assets. Points on the 45° line indicate that the average pricing error is zero. Points above this line indicate that the return of the corresponding asset is underpredicted by the model. The figure confirms our idea that the economic performance of the model is somewhat disappointing. Clearly, the model is unable fully to capture the cross-sectional variation in expected excess returns. The two portfolios with the smallest firms have the highest mean excess return and are both above the 45° line. The model apparently does not solve the small-firm effect as the returns on these portfolios are underpredicted.

The unsatisfactory performance of the consumption-based asset pricing model has led to a wide range of adjustments and alternative models. Cochrane (1996), for example, proposes an investment-based asset pricing model, which performs much better than the model discussed above. Other approaches exploit alternative specifications for investor preferences or incorporate transaction costs in the model. The consumption-based model states that expected asset returns are driven by their covariance with consumption risk. Empirically, the problem is that aggregate per capita consumption growth is too smooth to explain the risk premium, so that unrealistically high estimates for γ are required. Several papers have explored alternative measures of consumption risk. Parker and Julliard (2005), for example, measure the risk of a portfolio by its ultimate risk to consumption, defined as the covariance of its return and consumption growth over

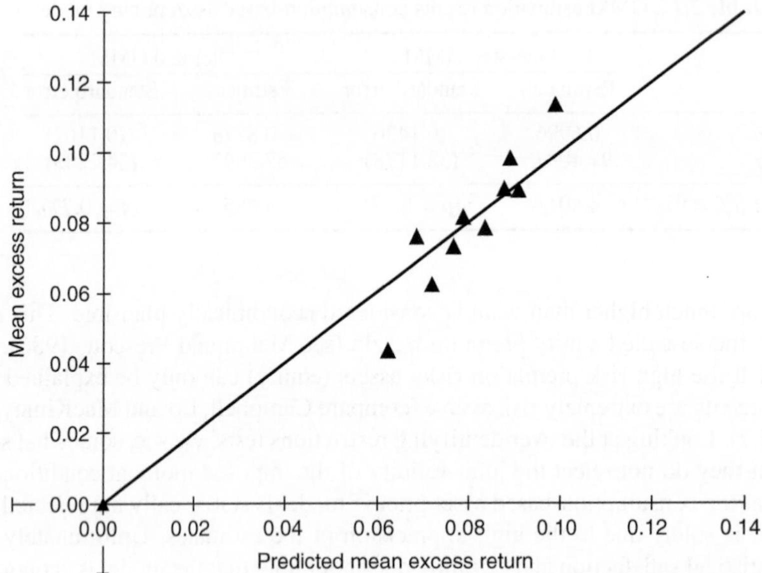

Figure 5.1 Actual versus predicted mean excess returns of size-based portfolios.

the quarter of the return and many following quarters ('ultimate consumption'). Their argument is that the contemporaneous covariance of consumption and wealth understates the true risk of a portfolio if consumption responds with a lag to changes in wealth. Jagannathan and Wang (2007) argue that investors are likely to review their decisions only at intervals determined by culture or institutional features of the economy, such as when profits and losses have to be realized for tax purposes. They then use the growth rate in average per capita expenditures from the end of the calendar year to the next. More recently, Savov (2011) uses municipal solid waste ('garbage') as a new measure of consumption. His argument is that almost all forms of consumption produce waste, and they do so at the time of consumption. Therefore, rates of garbage generation should be informative about rates of consumption. A useful overview of the growing body of empirical work on consumption-based asset pricing models, with an emphasis on method of moments estimation, is given in Ludvigson (2013).

Wrap-up

A common problem in linear regression is that one or more regressors are endogenous, which means they are correlated with the equation's error term. This arises when the regression model does not correspond to a conditional expectation. Important causes for this are measurement error, reverse causality and omitted variable bias. Causal parameters can be estimated by means of instrumental variables techniques, provided it is possible to find valid instruments. In many applications this is challenging, and the choice of instruments is often criticized in empirical work. We saw how instrumental variables estimation exploits different moment conditions compared to the OLS estimator. If more moment conditions are imposed than there are unknown parameters, we can use a generalized instrumental variables estimator, which is a special case of the generalized method of moments (GMM). We discussed the use of GMM, illustrating it with the estimation of an intertemporal asset pricing model. In dynamic models one usually has the advantage that the choice of instruments is less suspect: lagged values can be assumed to be uncorrelated with current innovations. An important advantage of GMM is that it can estimate the parameters in a model without having to solve the model analytically. Practically, IV and GMM estimation are often hampered by a weak instruments problem. Chapter 10 will discuss the use of GMM estimation for dynamic panel data models.

Exercises

Exercise 5.1 (Instrumental Variables)

Consider the following model

$$y_i = \beta_1 + \beta_2 x_{i2} + \beta_3 x_{i3} + \varepsilon_i, \quad i = 1, \dots, N, \tag{5.81}$$

where (y_i, x_{i2}, x_{i3}) are observed and have finite moments, and ε_i is an unobserved error term. Suppose this model is estimated by ordinary least squares. Denote the OLS estimator by b.

a. What are the *essential* conditions required for unbiasedness of b? What are the *essential* conditions required for consistency of b? Explain the difference between unbiasedness and consistency.

b. Show how the conditions for consistency can be written as moment conditions (if you have not done so already). Explain how a method of moments estimator can be derived from these moment conditions. Is the resulting estimator any different from the OLS one?

Now suppose that $\text{cov}\{\varepsilon_i, x_{i3}\} \neq 0$

c. Give two examples of cases where one can expect a nonzero correlation between a regressor, x_{i3}, and the error ε_i.

d. In this case, is it possible still to make appropriate inferences based on the OLS estimator while adjusting the standard errors appropriately?

e. Explain how an instrumental variable, z_i, say, leads to a new moment condition and, consequently, an alternative estimator for β.

f. Why does this alternative estimator lead to a smaller R^2 than the OLS one? What does this say of the R^2 as a measure for the adequacy of the model?

g. Why can we not choose $z_i = x_{i2}$ as an instrument for x_{i3}, even if $E\{x_{i2}\varepsilon_i\} = 0$? Would it be possible to use x_{i2}^2 as an instrument for x_{i3}?

Exercise 5.2 (Returns to Schooling – Empirical)

Consider the data used in Section 5.4. The purpose of this exercise is to explore the role of parents' education as instruments to estimate the returns to schooling.

a. Estimate a reduced form for schooling, as reported in Table 5.2, but include mother's and father's education levels, instead of the lived near college dummy. What do these results indicate about the possibility of using parents' education as instruments?

b. Estimate the returns to schooling, on the basis of the same specification as in Section 5.4, using mother's and father's education as instruments (and age and age-squared as instruments for experience and its square).

c. Test the overidentifying restriction.

d. Re-estimate the model using also the lived near college dummy and test the two overidentifying restrictions.

e. Compare and interpret the different estimates on the returns to schooling from Table 5.3, and parts **b** and **d** of this exercise.

Exercise 5.3 (GMM)

An intertemporal utility maximization problem gives the following first-order condition

$$E_t\left\{\delta\left(\frac{C_{t+1}}{C_t}\right)^{-\gamma}(1+r_{t+1})\right\}=1,$$

where E_t denotes the expectation operator conditional upon time t information, C_t denotes consumption in period t, r_{t+1} is the return on financial wealth, δ is a discount rate and γ is the coefficient of relative risk aversion. Assume that we have a time series of observations on consumption levels, returns and instrumental variables z_t.

a. Show how the above condition can be written as a set of *unconditional* moment conditions. Explain how we can estimate δ and γ consistently from these moment conditions.

b. What is the minimum number of moment conditions that is required? What do we (potentially) gain by having more moment conditions?

c. How can we improve the efficiency of the estimator for a given set of moment conditions? In which case does this not work?

d. Explain what we mean by 'overidentifying restrictions'. Is this a good or a bad thing?

e. Explain how the overidentifying restrictions test is performed. What is the null hypothesis that is tested? What do you conclude if the test rejects?

6 Maximum Likelihood Estimation and Specification Tests

In Chapter 5 we paid attention to the generalized method of moments. In the GMM approach the model imposes assumptions about a number of expectations (moments) that involve observable data and unknown coefficients, which are exploited in estimation. In this chapter we consider an estimation approach that typically makes stronger assumptions, because it assumes knowledge of the entire distribution, not just of a number of its moments. If the distribution of a variable y_i conditional upon a number of variables x_i is known up to a small number of unknown coefficients, we can use this to estimate these unknown parameters by choosing them in such a way that the resulting distribution corresponds as well as possible, in a way to be defined more precisely below, to the observed data. This is, somewhat loosely formulated, the method of maximum likelihood.

In certain applications and models, distributional assumptions like normality are commonly imposed because estimation strategies that do not require such assumptions are complex or unavailable. If the distributional assumptions are correct, the maximum likelihood estimator is, under weak regularity conditions, consistent and asymptotically normal. Moreover, it fully exploits the assumptions about the distribution so that the estimator is asymptotically efficient. This means that alternative consistent estimators will have an asymptotic covariance matrix that is at least as large (in a matrix sense) as that of the maximum likelihood estimator.

This chapter starts with an introduction to maximum likelihood estimation. Section 6.1 describes the approach starting with some simple examples and concluding with some general results and discussion. Because the distributional assumptions are typically crucial for the consistency and efficiency of the maximum likelihood estimator, it is important to be able to test these assumptions. This is discussed in Section 6.2, while Section 6.3 focuses on the implementation of the Lagrange multiplier tests for particular hypotheses, mostly in the context of the linear regression model. Section 6.4 explores the link with the generalized method of moments (GMM) to introduce quasi-maximum likelihood estimation and to extend the class of Lagrange multiplier tests to moment conditions tests. Knowledge of the issues in Section 6.1 is crucial for understanding Chapter 7 and some specific sections of Chapters 8, 9 and 10. The remaining sections of this chapter cover issues relating to specification tests and are somewhat more technical. They are a prerequisite for some specific sections of Chapter 7 that can be skipped without loss of continuity. The material in Section 6.4 is used in Section 7.3 (count data models) and Section 8.11 (GARCH models).

6.1 An Introduction to Maximum Likelihood

The starting point of maximum likelihood estimation is the assumption that the (conditional) distribution of an observed phenomenon (the endogenous variable) is known, except for a finite number of unknown parameters. These parameters will be estimated by taking those values for them that give the observed values the highest probability, the highest likelihood. The **maximum likelihood** method thus provides a means of estimating a set of parameters characterizing a distribution, if we know, or assume we know, the form of this distribution. For example, we could characterize the distribution of some variable y_i (for given x_i) as normal with mean $\beta_1 + \beta_2 x_i$ and variance σ^2. This corresponds to the simple linear regression model with normal error terms.

6.1.1 Some Examples

The principle of maximum likelihood is most easily introduced in a discrete setting where y_i only has a finite number of outcomes; see Buse (1982) for an intuitive exposition. As an example, consider a large pool filled with red and yellow balls. We are interested in the fraction p of red balls in this pool ($0 < p < 1$). To obtain information on p, we take a random sample of N balls (and do not look at all the other balls). Let us denote $y_i = 1$ if ball i is red and $y_i = 0$ if it is not. Then it holds by assumption[1] that $P\{y_i = 1\} = p$. Suppose our sample contains $N_1 = \sum_i y_i$ red and $N - N_1$ yellow balls. The probability of obtaining such a sample (in a given order) is given by

$$P\{N_1 \text{ red balls, } N - N_1 \text{ yellow balls}\} = p^{N_1}(1-p)^{N-N_1}. \tag{6.1}$$

The expression in (6.1), interpreted as a function of the unknown parameter p, is referred to as the **likelihood function**. Maximum likelihood estimation for p implies that we choose a value for p such that (6.1) is maximal. This gives the maximum likelihood estimator $\hat{p}$. For computational purposes it is often more convenient to maximize the (natural) logarithm of (6.1), which is a monotone transformation. This gives the **loglikelihood function**

$$\log L(p) = N_1 \log(p) + (N - N_1)\log(1-p). \tag{6.2}$$

[1] We assume that sampling takes place with replacement. Alternatively, one can assume that the number of balls in the pool is infinitely large, such that previous draws do not affect the probability of drawing a red ball.

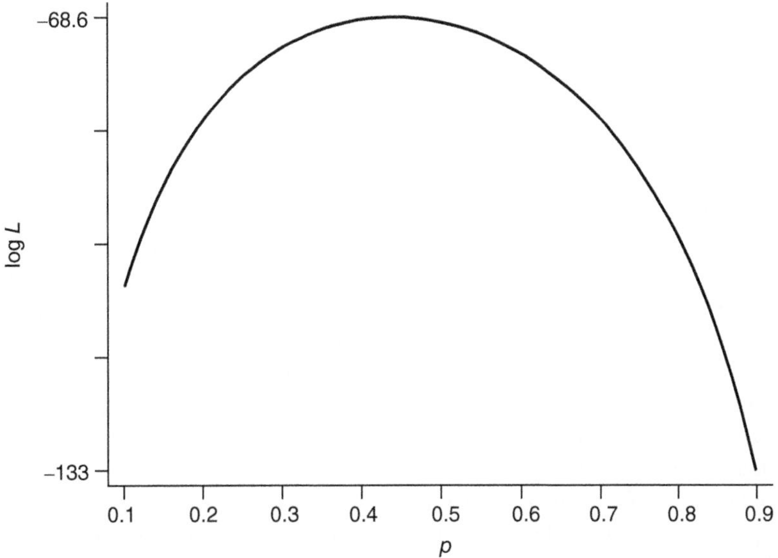

Figure 6.1 Sample loglikelihood function for $N = 100$ and $N_1 = 44$.

For a sample of size 100 with 44 red balls ($N_1 = 44$), Figure 6.1 displays the loglikelihood function for values of p between 0.1 and 0.9. Maximizing (6.2) gives the first-order condition

$$\frac{d \log L(p)}{dp} = \frac{N_1}{p} - \frac{N - N_1}{1 - p} = 0, \tag{6.3}$$

which, solving for p, gives the maximum likelihood (ML) estimator

$$\hat{p} = N_1/N. \tag{6.4}$$

The ML estimator thus corresponds to the sample proportion of red balls and probably also corresponds to your best guess for p based on the sample that was drawn. In principle, we also need to check the second-order condition to make sure that the solution we have corresponds to a maximum, although in this case it is obvious from Figure 6.1. This gives

$$\frac{d^2 \log L(p)}{dp^2} = -\frac{N_1}{p^2} - \frac{N - N_1}{(1 - p)^2} < 0, \tag{6.5}$$

showing, indeed, that we have found a maximum.

So the intuition of the maximum likelihood principle is as follows. From the (assumed) distribution of the data (e.g. y_i), we determine the likelihood of observing the sample that we happen to observe as a function of the unknown parameters that characterize the distribution. Next, we choose as our maximum likelihood estimates those values for the unknown parameters that give us the highest likelihood. It is clear that this approach makes sense in the above example. The usefulness of the maximum likelihood method is more general, as it can be shown that – under suitable regularity conditions – the maximum likelihood estimator is generally consistent for the true underlying parameters. The ML estimator has several other attractive properties, which we shall discuss below.

As a next illustration, consider the simple regression model

$$y_i = \beta_1 + \beta_2 x_i + \varepsilon_i, \tag{6.6}$$

where we make assumptions (A1)–(A4) from Chapter 2. These assumptions state that ε_i has mean zero, is homoskedastic, has no autocorrelation and is independent of all x_i $(i = 1, \ldots, N)$. While these assumptions imply that $E\{y_i|x_i\} = \beta_1 + \beta_2 x_i$ and $V\{y_i|x_i\} = \sigma^2$, they do not impose a particular distribution. To enable maximum likelihood estimation, we thus need to augment the above assumptions with an assumption about the shape of the distribution. The most common assumption is that ε_i is normal, as in assumption (A5) from Chapter 2. We can summarize these assumptions by saying that the error terms ε_i are normally and independently distributed (n.i.d.) with mean zero and variance σ^2, or $\varepsilon_i \sim NID(0, \sigma^2)$.

The probability of observing a particular outcome y for y_i is, however, zero for any y, because y_i has a continuous distribution. Therefore the contribution of observation i to the likelihood function is the value of the *density* function at the observed point y_i. For the normal distribution (see Appendix B) this gives

$$f(y_i|x_i; \beta, \sigma^2) = \frac{1}{\sqrt{2\pi\sigma^2}} \exp\left\{-\frac{1}{2}\frac{(y_i - \beta_1 - \beta_2 x_i)^2}{\sigma^2}\right\}, \tag{6.7}$$

where $\beta = (\beta_1, \beta_2)'$. Because of the independence assumption, the joint density of $y_1, \ldots, y_N$ (conditional on $X = (x_1, \ldots, x_N)'$) is given by

$$\begin{aligned} f(y_1, \ldots, y_N|X; \beta, \sigma^2) &= \prod_{i=1}^{N} f(y_i|x_i; \beta, \sigma^2) \\ &= \left(\frac{1}{\sqrt{2\pi\sigma^2}}\right)^N \prod_{i=1}^{N} \exp\left\{-\frac{1}{2}\frac{(y_i - \beta_1 - \beta_2 x_i)^2}{\sigma^2}\right\}. \end{aligned} \tag{6.8}$$

The likelihood function is identical to the joint density function of $y_1, \ldots, y_N$, but it is considered as a function of the unknown parameters β, σ^2. Consequently, we can write the loglikelihood function as

$$\log L(\beta, \sigma^2) = -\frac{N}{2}\log(2\pi\sigma^2) - \frac{1}{2}\sum_{i=1}^{N}\frac{(y_i - \beta_1 - \beta_2 x_i)^2}{\sigma^2}. \tag{6.9}$$

As the first term in this expression does not depend upon β, it is easily seen that maximizing (6.9) with respect to β_1 and β_2 corresponds to minimizing the residual sum of squares $S(\beta)$, as defined in Section 2.1. That is, the maximum likelihood estimators for β_1 and β_2 are identical to the OLS estimators. Denoting these estimators by $\hat{\beta}_1$ and $\hat{\beta}_2$, and defining the residuals $e_i = y_i - \hat{\beta}_1 - \hat{\beta}_2 x_i$, we can go on and maximize (6.9) with respect to σ^2. Substituting the ML solutions for β_1 and β_2 and differentiating[2] with

[2] We shall consider σ^2 as an unknown parameter, so that we differentiate with respect to σ^2 rather than σ. The resulting estimator is invariant to this choice.

respect to σ^2, we obtain the first-order condition

$$-\frac{N}{2}\frac{2\pi}{2\pi\sigma^2} + \frac{1}{2}\sum_{i=1}^{N}\frac{e_i^2}{\sigma^4} = 0. \tag{6.10}$$

Solving this for σ^2 gives the maximum likelihood estimator for σ^2 as

$$\hat{\sigma}^2 = \frac{1}{N}\sum_{i=1}^{N} e_i^2. \tag{6.11}$$

This estimator is a consistent estimator for σ^2. It does not, however, correspond to the unbiased estimator for σ^2 that was derived in the context of the OLS estimator (see Chapter 2), given by

$$s^2 = \frac{1}{N-K}\sum_{i=1}^{N} e_i^2,$$

where K is the number of regressors (including the intercept). The difference lies in the degrees of freedom correction in s^2. Because s^2 is unbiased, the ML estimator $\hat{\sigma}^2$ will be biased in finite samples. Asymptotically, $(N-K)/N$ converges to 1 and the bias disappears, so that the ML estimator is consistent, the degrees of freedom correction being a small-sample issue.

In this particular example the maximum likelihood estimator for β happens to reproduce the OLS estimator and consequently has the small-sample properties of the OLS estimator. The fact that the ML estimator for σ^2 deviates from the unbiased estimator s^2 indicates that this is not a general result. In small samples the latter estimator has better properties than the ML estimator. In many relevant cases, the ML estimator cannot be shown to be unbiased, and its small-sample properties are unknown. This means that in general the maximum likelihood approach can be defended only on asymptotic grounds, the ML estimator being consistent, asymptotically normal (CAN) and asymptotically efficient. Furthermore, it is typically not possible to derive a closed-form expression for the ML estimator, except in a number of special cases (like those considered above).

If the error terms ε_i in this example are non-normal or heteroskedastic, the loglikelihood function given in (6.9) is incorrect, that is, does not correspond to the true distribution of y_i given x_i. In such a case the estimator derived from maximizing the incorrect loglikelihood function (6.9) is not the maximum likelihood estimator in a strict sense, and there is no guarantee that it will have good properties. In some particular cases consistency can still be achieved by maximizing an incorrect likelihood function, in which case it is common to refer to the estimator as a quasi-ML estimator. This example illustrates this point, because the (quasi-)ML estimator for β equals the OLS estimator b, which is consistent under much weaker conditions. Again, this is not a general result, and it is not appropriate in general to rely upon such an argument to defend the use of maximum likelihood. Section 6.4 presents some additional discussion on this issue.

6.1.2 General Properties

To define the maximum likelihood estimator in a more general situation, suppose that interest lies in the conditional distribution of y_i given x_i. Let the density or probability mass function be given by $f(y_i|x_i;\theta)$, where θ is a K-dimensional vector of unknown parameters, and assume that observations are mutually independent. In this situation the joint density or probability mass function of the sample $y_1,\ldots,y_N$ (conditional upon $X=(x_1,\ldots,x_N)'$) is given by[3]

$$f(y_1,\ldots,y_N|X;\theta)=\prod_{i=1}^{N}f(y_i|x_i;\theta).$$

The likelihood function for the available sample is then given by

$$L(\theta|y,X)=\prod_{i=1}^{N}L_i(\theta|y_i,x_i)=\prod_{i=1}^{N}f(y_i|x_i;\theta),$$

which is a function of θ. For several purposes it is convenient to employ the **likelihood contributions**, denoted by $L_i(\theta|y_i,x_i)$, which reflect how much observation i contributes to the likelihood function. The maximum likelihood estimator $\hat{\theta}$ for θ is the solution to

$$\max_{\theta}\log L(\theta)=\max_{\theta}\sum_{i=1}^{N}\log L_i(\theta), \tag{6.12}$$

where $\log L(\theta)$ is the loglikelihood function, and for simplicity we dropped the other arguments. The first-order conditions of this problem imply that

$$\left.\frac{\partial \log L(\theta)}{\partial\theta}\right|_{\hat{\theta}}=\sum_{i=1}^{N}\left.\frac{\partial \log L_i(\theta)}{\partial\theta}\right|_{\hat{\theta}}=0, \tag{6.13}$$

where $|_{\hat{\theta}}$ indicates that the expression is evaluated at $\theta=\hat{\theta}$. If the loglikelihood function is globally concave there is a unique global maximum, and the maximum likelihood estimator is uniquely determined by these first-order conditions. Only in special cases can the ML estimator be determined analytically. In general, numerical optimization is required (see Cameron and Trivedi, 2005, Chapter 10 or Greene, 2012, Appendix E, for a discussion). Fortunately, for many standard models, efficient algorithms are available in recent software packages.

For notational convenience, we shall denote the vector of first derivatives of the loglikelihood function, also known as the **score vector**, as

$$s(\theta)\equiv\frac{\partial \log L(\theta)}{\partial\theta}=\sum_{i=1}^{N}\frac{\partial \log L_i(\theta)}{\partial\theta}\equiv\sum_{i=1}^{N}s_i(\theta), \tag{6.14}$$

which also defines the individual score contributions $s_i(\theta)$. The first-order conditions

$$s(\hat{\theta})=\sum_{i=1}^{N}s_i(\hat{\theta})=0$$

thus say that the K sample averages of the score contributions, evaluated at the ML estimate $\hat{\theta}$, should be zero.

[3] We use $f(.)$ as generic notation for a (multivariate) density or probability mass function.

Provided that the likelihood function is correctly specified, it can be shown under weak regularity conditions that:

1. The maximum likelihood estimator is **consistent** for θ (plim $\hat{\theta} = \theta$);
2. The maximum likelihood estimator is **asymptotically efficient** (i.e. asymptotically the ML estimator has the 'smallest' variance among all consistent asymptotically normal estimators);
3. The maximum likelihood estimator is **asymptotically normally distributed**, according to
$$\sqrt{N}(\hat{\theta} - \theta) \to \mathcal{N}(0, V), \tag{6.15}$$
where V is the asymptotic covariance matrix.

The covariance matrix V is determined by the shape of the loglikelihood function. To describe it in the general case, we define the information in observation i as

$$I_i(\theta) \equiv -E\left\{\frac{\partial^2 \log L_i(\theta)}{\partial\theta\,\partial\theta'}\right\}, \tag{6.16}$$

which is a symmetric $K \times K$ matrix. Loosely speaking, this matrix summarizes the expected amount of information about θ contained in observation i. The average information matrix for a sample of size N is defined as

$$\bar{I}_N(\theta) \equiv \frac{1}{N}\sum_{i=1}^{N} I_i(\theta) = -E\left\{\frac{1}{N}\frac{\partial^2 \log L(\theta)}{\partial\theta\,\partial\theta'}\right\}, \tag{6.17}$$

while the limiting **information matrix** is defined as $I(\theta) \equiv \lim_{N\to\infty}\bar{I}_N(\theta)$. In the special case where the observations are independently and identically distributed, it follows that $I_i(\theta) = \bar{I}_N(\theta) = I(\theta)$. Under appropriate regularity conditions, the asymptotic covariance matrix of the maximum likelihood estimator can be shown to equal the inverse of the information matrix, that is,

$$V = I(\theta)^{-1}. \tag{6.18}$$

The term on the right-hand side of (6.17) is the expected value of the matrix of second-order derivatives, scaled by the number of observations and reflects the curvature of the loglikelihood function. Clearly, if the loglikelihood function is highly curved around its maximum, the second derivative is large, the variance is small and the maximum likelihood estimator is relatively accurate. If the function is less curved, the variance will be larger. Given the asymptotic efficiency of the maximum likelihood estimator, the inverse of the information matrix $I(\theta)^{-1}$ provides a lower bound on the asymptotic covariance matrix for any consistent asymptotically normal estimator for θ. The ML estimator is asymptotically efficient because it attains this bound, often referred to as the **Cramèr–Rao lower bound**.

In practice the covariance matrix V can be estimated consistently by replacing the expectations operator with a sample average and replacing the unknown coefficients with the maximum likelihood estimates. That is,

$$\hat{V}_H = \left(-\frac{1}{N}\sum_{i=1}^{N}\left.\frac{\partial^2 \log L_i(\theta)}{\partial\theta\,\partial\theta'}\right|_{\hat{\theta}}\right)^{-1}, \tag{6.19}$$

where we take derivatives first and in the result replace the unknown θ with $\hat{\theta}$. The suffix H is used to stress that the estimator for V is based upon the Hessian matrix, the matrix of second derivatives.

An alternative expression for the information matrix can be obtained from the result that the matrix

$$J_i(\theta) \equiv E\{s_i(\theta)s_i(\theta)'\}, \tag{6.20}$$

with $s_i(\theta)$ defined in (6.14), is identical to $I_i(\theta)$, provided that the likelihood function is correctly specified. In Section 6.4, we shall return to the possibility that the likelihood function is misspecified and that the matrices $I_i(\theta)$ and $J_i(\theta)$ are different. For the moment, we shall use $I(\theta)$ to denote the information matrix based on either definition. The result in (6.20) indicates that V can also be estimated from the first-order derivatives of the loglikelihood function as

$$\hat{V}_G = \left(\frac{1}{N} \sum_{i=1}^{N} s_i(\hat{\theta})s_i(\hat{\theta})' \right)^{-1}, \tag{6.21}$$

where the suffix G reflects that the estimator employs the outer product of the gradients (first derivatives). This estimator for V was suggested by Berndt, Hall, Hall and Hausman (1974) and is sometimes referred to as the BHHH estimator. It is important to note that computation of the latter expression requires the individual likelihood contributions. In general, the two covariance matrix estimates $\hat{V}_H$ and $\hat{V}_G$ will not be identical. The first estimator typically has somewhat better properties in small samples.

The presentation and derivations in this chapter are limited to the case of independent observations. Maximum likelihood estimation is also possible in case of heterogeneous and dependent observations. In this case the likelihood function is based on the joint distribution of $y_i, \ldots, y_N$ (conditional upon exogenous variables); see Pesaran (2015, Chapter 9) for more discussion.

To illustrate the maximum likelihood principle, Subsection 6.1.3 again considers the simple example of the pool with balls, while Subsection 6.1.4 treats the linear regression model with normal errors. The stochastic frontier model, which has an asymmetric error term, is presented in Subsection 6.1.5. Models with limited dependent variables that are typically estimated by maximum likelihood are presented in Chapter 7 and, for panel data, in Section 10.7. The remainder of this chapter discusses issues relating to specification and misspecification tests. Although this is not without importance, it is somewhat more technical, and some readers may prefer to skip these sections on first reading and continue with Chapter 7. Section 6.4 also discusses the relationship between GMM estimation and maximum likelihood estimation in more detail and explains quasi-maximum likelihood estimation. This is relevant for Section 7.3, where count data models are discussed, and for Section 8.11, where models for conditional heteroskedasticity are presented.

6.1.3 An Example (Continued)

To clarify the general formulae in the previous subsection, let us reconsider the example concerning the pool of red and yellow balls. In this model, the loglikelihood contribution of observation i can be written as

$$\log L_i(p) = y_i \log p + (1 - y_i) \log(1 - p),$$

with a first derivative

$$\frac{\partial \log L_i(p)}{\partial p} = \frac{y_i}{p} - \frac{1-y_i}{1-p}.$$

Note that the expected value of the first derivative is zero, using $E\{y_i\} = p$. The negative of the second derivative is

$$-\frac{\partial^2 \log L_i(p)}{\partial p^2} = \frac{y_i}{p^2} + \frac{1-y_i}{(1-p)^2},$$

which has an expected value of

$$E\left\{-\frac{\partial^2 \log L_i(p)}{\partial p^2}\right\} = \frac{E\{y_i\}}{p^2} + \frac{1-E\{y_i\}}{(1-p)^2} = \frac{1}{p} + \frac{1}{1-p} = \frac{1}{p(1-p)}.$$

From this it follows that the asymptotic variance of the maximum likelihood estimator $\hat{p}$ is given by $V = p(1-p)$, and we have

$$\sqrt{N}(\hat{p} - p) \rightarrow \mathcal{N}(0, p(1-p)).$$

This result can be used to construct confidence intervals or to test hypotheses. For example, the hypothesis H_0: $p = p_0$ can be tested using the test statistic

$$\frac{\hat{p} - p_0}{\text{se}(\hat{p})},$$

where $\text{se}(\hat{p}) = \sqrt{\hat{p}(1-\hat{p})/N}$. Under the null hypothesis, the test statistic has an asymptotic standard normal distribution. This is similar to the usual t-tests discussed in the context of the linear model. A 95% confidence interval is given by

$$\hat{p} - 1.96\ \text{se}(\hat{p}),\ \hat{p} + 1.96\ \text{se}(\hat{p})$$

so that, with a sample of 100 balls of which 44 are red ($\hat{p} = 0.44$), we can conclude with 95% confidence that p is between 0.343 and 0.537. When $N = 1000$ with 440 red balls, the interval reduces to (0.409, 0.471). In this particular application it is clear that the normal distribution is an approximation based on large-sample theory and will never hold in small samples. In any finite sample, $\hat{p}$ can only take a finite number of different outcomes in the range [0, 1]. In fact, in this example the small-sample distribution of $N_1 = N\hat{p}$ is known to be binomial with parameters N and p, and this result could be employed instead.

6.1.4 The Normal Linear Regression Model

In this subsection we consider the linear regression model with normal i.i.d. errors (independent of all x_i). This is the model considered in Chapter 2, combined with assumptions (A1)–(A5). Writing

$$y_i = x_i'\beta + \varepsilon_i, \quad \varepsilon_i \sim NID(0, \sigma^2),$$

this imposes that (conditional upon the exogenous variables) y_i is normal with mean $x_i'\beta$ and a constant variance σ^2. Generalizing (6.9), the loglikelihood function for this model can be written as

$$\log L(\beta, \sigma^2) = \sum_{i=1}^{N} \log L_i(\beta, \sigma^2) = -\frac{N}{2}\log(2\pi\sigma^2) - \frac{1}{2}\sum_{i=1}^{N}\frac{(y_i - x_i'\beta)^2}{\sigma^2}. \tag{6.22}$$

The score contributions are given by

$$s_i(\beta, \sigma^2) = \begin{pmatrix} \dfrac{\partial \log L_i(\beta, \sigma^2)}{\partial \beta} \\ \dfrac{\partial \log L_i(\beta, \sigma^2)}{\partial \sigma^2} \end{pmatrix} = \begin{pmatrix} \dfrac{(y_i - x_i'\beta)}{\sigma^2} x_i \\ -\dfrac{1}{2\sigma^2} + \dfrac{1}{2}\dfrac{(y_i - x_i'\beta)^2}{\sigma^4} \end{pmatrix},$$

and the maximum likelihood estimates $\hat{\beta}, \hat{\sigma}^2$ will satisfy the first-order conditions

$$\sum_{i=1}^{N} \frac{(y_i - x_i'\hat{\beta})}{\hat{\sigma}^2} x_i = 0$$

and

$$-\frac{N}{2\hat{\sigma}^2} + \frac{1}{2}\sum_{i=1}^{N} \frac{(y_i - x_i'\hat{\beta})^2}{\hat{\sigma}^4} = 0.$$

It is easily verified that the solutions to these equations are given by

$$\hat{\beta} = \left(\sum_{i=1}^{N} x_i x_i'\right)^{-1} \sum_{i=1}^{N} x_i y_i \quad \text{and} \quad \hat{\sigma}^2 = \frac{1}{N}\sum_{i=1}^{N} (y_i - x_i'\hat{\beta})^2.$$

The estimator for the vector of slope coefficients is identical to the familiar OLS estimator, while the estimator for the variance differs from the OLS value s^2 because it divides by N rather than by $N - K$.

To obtain the asymptotic covariance matrix of the maximum likelihood estimator for β and σ^2, we use

$$I_i(\beta, \sigma^2) = E\{s_i(\beta, \sigma^2)s_i(\beta, \sigma^2)'\}.$$

Using the fact that for a normal distribution $E\{\varepsilon_i\} = 0, E\{\varepsilon_i^2\} = \sigma^2, E\{\varepsilon_i^3\} = 0$ and $E\{\varepsilon_i^4\} = 3\sigma^4$ (see Appendix B), this expression can be shown to equal

$$I_i(\beta, \sigma^2) = \begin{pmatrix} \dfrac{1}{\sigma^2} x_i x_i' & 0 \\ 0 & \dfrac{1}{2\sigma^4} \end{pmatrix},$$

if we take expectations conditional upon x_i. Using this, the asymptotic covariance matrix is given by

$$V = I(\beta, \sigma^2)^{-1} = \begin{pmatrix} \sigma^2 \Sigma_{xx}^{-1} & 0 \\ 0 & 2\sigma^4 \end{pmatrix},$$

where

$$\Sigma_{xx} = \lim_{N \to \infty} \frac{1}{N} \sum_{i=1}^{N} x_i x_i'.$$

From this it follows that $\hat{\beta}$ and $\hat{\sigma}^2$ are asymptotically normally distributed according to

$$\sqrt{N}(\hat{\beta} - \beta) \to \mathcal{N}(0, \sigma^2 \Sigma_{xx}^{-1})$$
$$\sqrt{N}(\hat{\sigma}^2 - \sigma^2) \to \mathcal{N}(0, 2\sigma^4).$$

The fact that the information matrix is block diagonal implies that the ML estimators for β and σ^2 are (asymptotically) independent. In finite samples, $\hat{\beta}$ is approximately normally distributed, with mean β, and with a covariance matrix that can be estimated as

$$\hat{\sigma}^2\left(\sum_{i=1}^{N} x_i x_i'\right)^{-1}.$$

Note that this corresponds quite closely to the results that are familiar for the OLS estimator.

6.1.5 The Stochastic Frontier Model

In some cases there are good reasons not to impose a normal (symmetric) distribution upon an equation's error term. In such cases, the model can still be estimated by maximum likelihood when other distributional assumptions are made, even though the resulting ML estimator will be different from OLS. In this subsection we discuss an example of this, often used to estimate the (production or cost) inefficiency of a firm.

A production function specifies the maximum possible amount of output that can be produced with a given combination of inputs. Theoretically, this can be written as $y = f(x)$, where x is a vector of inputs (labour, capital), and f denotes the production function. Not every firm can produce the maximum amount of output. The actually produced output of firm i with inputs x_i differs from $f(x_i)$ due to technical inefficiencies, and $y_i \leq f(x_i)$. In addition, there are many other uncontrollable factors that affect output. To model this, Aigner, Lovell and Schmidt (1977) have proposed a stochastic production frontier model, which is given by

$$y_i = x_i'\beta - u_i + v_i, \tag{6.23}$$

where y_i denotes log output and x_i is a vector of log inputs. The error term in this model consists of two components. The term v_i is the usual disturbance term, often assumed to have a mean zero normal distribution. The term $u_i \geq 0$ captures inefficiency. The model in (6.23) can be interpreted as describing a stochastic production frontier, where the frontier for any particular firm is given by $x_i'\beta + v_i$, and where u_i reflects the fact that each firm's output must lie on or below its frontier. The magnitude of u_i corresponds to the percentage by which a firm fails to achieve the production frontier.

Estimation of this model is possible by maximum likelihood based on a random sample of firms (with similar technology) provided that distributional assumptions are made upon both v_i and u_i. For example, one can assume that v_i has a normal distribution with mean 0 and variance σ_v^2, whereas u_i is the absolute value of a normal distribution with mean 0 and variance σ_u^2, both independent of x_i. The latter is referred to as a half-normal distribution. As a result, (6.23) presents a linear regression model with an asymmetric error term. Moreover, the combined error term is not mean zero.

Let us write the model under the above assumptions as

$$y_i = x_i'\beta + \varepsilon_i. \tag{6.24}$$

The loglikelihood contribution of observation i for this model is (see Greene, 2012, Chapter 16)

$$\log L_i(\beta, \sigma_u^2, \sigma_v^2) = -\log\sigma + \frac{1}{2}\log\frac{2}{\pi} + \log\Phi\left(\frac{-\lambda(y_i - x_i'\beta)}{\sigma}\right) - \frac{1}{2}\frac{(y_i - x_i'\beta)^2}{\sigma^2},$$

where $\sigma^2 = \sigma_u^2 + \sigma_v^2$, $\lambda = \sigma_u/\sigma_v$ and Φ denotes the standard normal distribution function. Once the loglikelihood function is known, estimation of the model parameters is straightforward, although in this case numerical optimization is required. Because the error term ε_i, though having a nonzero mean, is uncorrelated with the regressors in (6.24), the partial slope coefficients in the model can be estimated consistently by OLS. However, OLS is inefficient, and it does not directly provide consistent estimators for the error variances. Note that the loglikelihood contributions for this model reduce to those of the normal linear regression model (see (6.22)) when $\sigma_u^2 = 0$.

Given estimates for the unknown parameters, it is possible to estimate the average level of technical inefficiency of all firms in the sample, using $E\{\varepsilon_i\} = E\{-u_i\} = -\sigma_u\sqrt{(2/\pi)}$. It is also possible to estimate the inefficiency of each firm in the sample. This, for example, can be used to rank producers or to determine best practices; see Parmeter and Kumbhakar (2014) for more details and a recent survey.

6.2 Specification Tests

6.2.1 Three Test Principles

On the basis of the maximum likelihood estimator, a large number of alternative tests can be constructed. Such tests are typically based upon one out of three different principles: the Wald, the likelihood ratio or the Lagrange multiplier principle. Although any of the three principles can be used to construct a test for a given hypothesis, each of them has its own merits and advantages. The Wald test is used a number of times in the previous chapters and is generally applicable to any estimator that is consistent and asymptotically normal. The likelihood ratio (LR) principle provides an easy way to compare two alternative nested models, whereas the Lagrange multiplier (LM) tests allow one to test restrictions that are imposed in estimation. This makes the LM approach particularly suited for misspecification tests where a chosen specification of the model is tested for misspecification in several directions (like heteroskedasticity, non-normality, or omitted variables).

Consider again the general problem where we estimate a K-dimensional parameter vector θ by maximizing the loglikelihood function, that is,

$$\max_{\theta} \log L(\theta) = \max_{\theta} \sum_{i=1}^{N} \log L_i(\theta).$$

Suppose that we are interested in testing one or more linear restrictions on the parameter vector $\theta = (\theta_1, \ldots, \theta_K)'$. These restrictions can be summarized as H_0: $R\theta = q$ for some fixed J-dimensional vector q, where R is a $J \times K$ matrix. It is assumed that the J rows of R are linearly independent, so that the restrictions are not in conflict with each other or redundant. The three test principles can be summarized as follows:

1. **Wald test.** Estimate θ by maximum likelihood and check whether the difference $R\hat{\theta} - q$ is close to zero, using its (asymptotic) covariance matrix. This is the idea that underlies the well-known t- and F-tests.
2. **Likelihood ratio test.** Estimate the model twice – once without the restriction imposed (giving $\hat{\theta}$) and once with the null hypothesis imposed (giving the

constrained maximum likelihood estimator $\tilde{\theta}$, where $R\tilde{\theta} = q$) – and check whether the difference in loglikelihood values $\log L(\hat{\theta}) - \log L(\tilde{\theta})$ is significantly different from zero. This implies the comparison of an unrestricted and a restricted maximum of $\log L(\theta)$.

3. **Lagrange multiplier test.** Estimate the model with the restriction from the null hypothesis imposed (giving $\tilde{\theta}$) and check whether the first-order conditions from the general model are significantly violated. That is, check whether $\partial \log L(\theta)/\partial\theta_{|\tilde{\theta}}$ is significantly different from zero.

While the three tests look at different aspects of the likelihood function, they are, in general, asymptotically equivalent (i.e. the test statistics have the same asymptotic distribution, even if the null hypothesis is violated), and in a few very special cases they even give the same numerical outcomes. In finite samples, the (actual) size and power of the tests may differ (see Exercise 6.1). Most of the time, however, we will choose the test that is most easily computed from the results that we have. For example, the Wald test requires estimating the model without the restriction imposed, while the Lagrange multiplier (LM) test requires only that the model is estimated under the null hypothesis. As a result, the LM test may be particularly attractive when relaxing the null hypothesis substantially complicates model estimation. It is also attractive when the number of different hypotheses one wants to test is large, as the model has to be estimated only once. The likelihood ratio test requires the model to be estimated with and without the restriction, but, as we shall see, is easily computed from the loglikelihood values.

The **Wald test** starts from the result that

$$\sqrt{N}(\hat{\theta} - \theta) \to \mathcal{N}(0, V),$$

from which it follows that the J-dimensional vector $R\hat{\theta}$ also has an asymptotic normal distribution, given by (see Appendix B)

$$\sqrt{N}(R\hat{\theta} - R\theta) \to \mathcal{N}(0, RVR').$$

Under the null hypothesis, $R\theta$ equals the known vector q, so that we can construct a test statistic by forming the quadratic form

$$\xi_W = N(R\hat{\theta} - q)'[R\hat{V}R']^{-1}(R\hat{\theta} - q), \tag{6.25}$$

where $\hat{V}$ is a consistent estimator for V (see above). Under H_0 this test statistic approximately follows a Chi-squared distribution with J degrees of freedom, so that large values for ξ_W lead us to reject the null hypothesis.

The **likelihood ratio test** is even simpler to compute, provided the model is estimated with and without the restrictions imposed. This means that we have two different estimators: the unrestricted ML estimator $\hat{\theta}$ and the constrained ML estimator $\tilde{\theta}$, obtained by maximizing the loglikelihood function $\log L(\theta)$ subject to the restrictions $R\theta = q$. Clearly, maximizing a function subject to a restriction will not lead to a larger maximum compared with the case without the restriction. Thus it follows that $\log L(\hat{\theta}) - \log L(\tilde{\theta}) \geq 0$. If this difference is small, the consequences of imposing the restrictions $R\theta = q$ are limited, suggesting that the restrictions are correct. If the difference is large, the restrictions are likely to be incorrect. The LR test statistic is simply computed as

$$\xi_{LR} = 2[\log L(\hat{\theta}) - \log L(\tilde{\theta})],$$

which, under the null hypothesis, has an approximate Chi-squared distribution with J degrees of freedom. This shows that, if we have estimated two specifications of a model, we can easily test the restrictive specification against the more general one by comparing loglikelihood values. It is important to stress that the use of this test is only appropriate if the two models are nested (see Chapter 3). An attractive feature of the test is that it is easily employed when testing nonlinear restrictions and that the result is not sensitive to the way in which we formulate these restrictions. In contrast, the Wald test can handle nonlinear restrictions but is sensitive to the way they are formulated. For example, it will matter whether we test $\theta_k = 1$ or $\log \theta_k = 0$. See Gregory and Veall (1985), Lafontaine and White (1986) or Phillips and Park (1988) for a discussion.

6.2.2 Lagrange Multiplier Tests

Some of the tests discussed in the previous chapters, like the Breusch–Pagan test for heteroskedasticity, are **Lagrange multiplier tests** (LM tests). To introduce the general idea of an LM test, suppose the null hypothesis restricts some elements in the parameter vector θ to equal a set of given values. To stress this, let us write $\theta' = (\theta_1', \theta_2')$, where the null hypothesis now says that $\theta_2 = q$, where θ_2 has dimension J. The term 'Lagrange multiplier' comes from the fact that it is implicitly based upon the value of the Lagrange multiplier in the constrained maximization problem. The first-order conditions of the Lagrangian,

$$H(\theta, \lambda) = \left[\sum_{i=1}^{N} \log L_i(\theta) - \lambda'(\theta_2 - q) \right], \tag{6.26}$$

yield the constrained ML estimator $\tilde{\theta} = (\tilde{\theta}_1', q')'$ and $\tilde{\lambda}$. The vector $\tilde{\lambda}$ can be interpreted as a vector of shadow prices of the restrictions $\theta_2 = q$. If the shadow prices are high, we would like to reject the restrictions. If they are close to zero, the restrictions are relatively 'innocent'. To derive a test statistic, we would therefore like to consider the distribution of $\tilde{\lambda}$. From the first-order conditions of (6.26) it follows that

$$\sum_{i=1}^{N} \left. \frac{\partial \log L_i(\theta)}{\partial \theta_1} \right|_{\tilde{\theta}} = \sum_{i=1}^{N} s_{i1}(\tilde{\theta}) = 0 \tag{6.27}$$

and

$$\tilde{\lambda} = \sum_{i=1}^{N} \left. \frac{\partial \log L_i(\theta)}{\partial \theta_2} \right|_{\tilde{\theta}} = \sum_{i=1}^{N} s_{i2}(\tilde{\theta}), \tag{6.28}$$

where the vector of score contributions $s_i(\theta)$ is decomposed into the subvectors $s_{i1}(\theta)$ and $s_{i2}(\theta)$, corresponding to θ_1 and θ_2, respectively. The result in (6.28) shows that the vector of Lagrange multipliers $\tilde{\lambda}$ equals the vector of first derivatives with respect to the restricted parameters θ_2, evaluated at the *constrained* estimator $\tilde{\theta}$. Consequently, the vector of shadow prices of the restrictions $\theta_2 = q$ also has the interpretation of measuring the extent to which the first-order conditions with respect to θ_2 are violated, if we evaluate them at the constrained estimates $\tilde{\theta} = (\tilde{\theta}_1', q')'$. As the first derivatives are also referred to as scores, the Lagrange multiplier test is also known as the **score test**.

To determine an appropriate test statistic, we exploit the fact that it can be shown that the sample average $N^{-1}\tilde{\lambda}$ is asymptotically normal with covariance matrix

$$V_\lambda = I_{22}(\theta) - I_{21}(\theta)I_{11}(\theta)^{-1}I_{12}(\theta), \tag{6.29}$$

where $I_{jk}(\theta)$ are blocks in the information matrix $I(\theta)$, as defined below (6.17), that is,

$$I(\theta) = \begin{pmatrix} I_{11}(\theta) & I_{12}(\theta) \\ I_{21}(\theta) & I_{22}(\theta) \end{pmatrix},$$

where $I_{22}(\theta)$ is of dimension $J \times J$. Computationally, we can make use of the fact[4] that (6.29) is the inverse of the lower right $J \times J$ block of the inverse of $I(\theta)$,

$$I(\theta)^{-1} = \begin{pmatrix} I^{11}(\theta) & I^{12}(\theta) \\ I^{21}(\theta) & I^{22}(\theta) \end{pmatrix},$$

that is, $V_\lambda = I^{22}(\theta)^{-1}$. The Lagrange multiplier test statistic can be derived as

$$\xi_{LM} = N^{-1}\tilde{\lambda}'\hat{I}^{22}(\tilde{\theta})\tilde{\lambda}, \tag{6.30}$$

which under the null hypothesis has an asymptotic Chi-squared distribution with J degrees of freedom, and where $\hat{I}(\tilde{\theta})$ denotes an estimate of the information matrix based upon the constrained estimator $\tilde{\theta}$. Only if $I_{12}(\theta) = 0$ and the information matrix is block diagonal, it holds that $I^{22}(\theta) = I(\theta)_{22}^{-1}$. In general, the other blocks of the information matrix are required to compute the appropriate covariance matrix of $N^{-1}\tilde{\lambda}$.

Computation of the LM test statistic is particularly attractive if the information matrix is estimated on the basis of the first derivatives of the loglikelihood function as

$$\hat{I}_G(\tilde{\theta}) = \frac{1}{N}\sum_{i=1}^{N} s_i(\tilde{\theta})s_i(\tilde{\theta})', \tag{6.31}$$

that is, the average outer product of the vector of first derivatives, evaluated under the constrained ML estimates $\tilde{\theta}$. Using (6.27) and (6.28), we can write an LM test statistic as

$$\xi_{LM} = \sum_{i=1}^{N} s_i(\tilde{\theta})'\left(\sum_{i=1}^{N} s_i(\tilde{\theta})s_i(\tilde{\theta})'\right)^{-1}\sum_{i=1}^{N} s_i(\tilde{\theta}). \tag{6.32}$$

Note that the first K–J elements in the vector of score contributions $s_i(\tilde{\theta})$ sum to zero because of (6.27). Nevertheless, these elements are generally important for computing the correct covariance matrix. Only in the case of block diagonality it holds that $I_{12}(\theta) = 0$ and the other block of the information matrix is irrelevant. An asymptotically equivalent version of the LM test statistic in the block diagonal case can be written as

$$\xi_{LM} = \sum_{i=1}^{N} s_{i2}(\tilde{\theta})'\left(\sum_{i=1}^{N} s_{i2}(\tilde{\theta})s_{i2}(\tilde{\theta})'\right)^{-1}\sum_{i=1}^{N} s_{i2}(\tilde{\theta}). \tag{6.33}$$

[4] This result is generally true and follows using partitioned inverses (see Davidson and MacKinnon, 1993, Appendix A; or Greene, 2012, Appendix A).

The expression in (6.32) suggests an easy way to compute a Lagrange multiplier test statistic. Let us denote the $N \times K$ matrix of first derivatives as S, such that

$$S = \begin{pmatrix} s_1(\tilde{\theta})' \\ s_2(\tilde{\theta})' \\ \vdots \\ s_N(\tilde{\theta})' \end{pmatrix}. \tag{6.34}$$

In this matrix, each row corresponds to an observation, and each column corresponds to the derivative with respect to one of the parameters. Consequently, we can write

$$\sum_{i=1}^{N} s_i(\tilde{\theta}) = S'\iota,$$

where $\iota = (1, 1, 1, \ldots, 1)'$ of dimension N. Moreover

$$\sum_{i=1}^{N} s_i(\tilde{\theta}) s_i(\tilde{\theta})' = S'S.$$

This allows us to rewrite (6.32) as

$$\xi_{LM} = \iota' S(S'S)^{-1} S'\iota = N \frac{\iota' S(S'S)^{-1} S'\iota}{\iota'\iota}. \tag{6.35}$$

Now, consider an auxiliary regression of a column of ones upon the columns of the matrix S. From the standard expression for the OLS estimator, $(S'S)^{-1}S'\iota$, we obtain predicted values of this regression as $S(S'S)^{-1}S'\iota$. The explained sum of squares, therefore, is given by

$$\iota' S(S'S)^{-1} S' S(S'S)^{-1} S'\iota = \iota' S(S'S)^{-1} S'\iota,$$

while the total (uncentred) sum of squares of this regression is $\iota'\iota$. Consequently, it follows that one version of the Lagrange multiplier test statistic can be computed as

$$\xi_{LM} = NR^2, \tag{6.36}$$

where R^2 is the uncentred R^2 (see Section 2.4) of an auxiliary regression of a vector of ones upon the score contributions (in S).[5] Under the null hypothesis, the test statistic is asymptotically Chi-squared distributed with J degrees of freedom, where J is the number of restrictions imposed upon θ. Note that the auxiliary regression should not include an intercept term.

The formulae in (6.32) or (6.36) provide one way of computing the Lagrange multiplier test statistic, often referred to as the **outer product gradient** (OPG) version of the LM test statistic (see Godfrey, 1988, p. 15). Unfortunately, tests based on the OPG estimate of the covariance matrix typically have small sample properties that are quite different from those asymptotic theory predicts. Several Monte Carlo experiments suggest that the OPG-based tests tend to reject the null hypothesis too often in cases where it happens to be true. That is, the actual size of the tests may be much larger than the asymptotic size

[5] If your software does not report uncentred R^2s, the same result is obtained by computing N–RSS, where RSS denotes the residual sum of squares.

(typically 5%). This means that one has to be careful in rejecting the null hypothesis when the test statistic exceeds the asymptotic critical value. See Davidson and MacKinnon (1993, Chapter 13) for additional discussion. Alternative ways are available to compute LM test statistics, for example using (6.30) and the matrix of second derivatives of the loglikelihood function, or on the basis of other auxiliary regressions; see Davidson and MacKinnon (2001). Some of these will be discussed in Section 6.3.

Despite the above reservations, we shall focus our discussion mostly upon the NR^2 approach of the LM test. This is because computation is convenient as it requires only the first derivatives. A test for any hypothesis can easily be constructed in this approach, while the columns of S are often determined fairly easily on the basis of the estimation results. When implementing the OPG version of the test, it is recommended to check your programming by also running a regression of a vector of ones upon the columns in S that correspond to the unconstrained parameters. This should result in an R^2 of zero.

In Section 6.3 we discuss the implementation of the Lagrange multiplier principle to test for omitted variables, heteroskedasticity, autocorrelation and non-normality, all in the context of the linear regression model with normal errors. Chapter 7 will cover several applications of LM tests in different types of model. First, however, we shall consider our simple example again.

6.2.3 An Example (Continued)

Let us again consider the simple example concerning the pool of red and yellow balls. This example is particularly simple as it involves only one unknown coefficient. Suppose we are interested in testing the hypothesis H_0: $p = p_0$ for a given value p_0. The (unrestricted) maximum likelihood estimator was seen to equal

$$\hat{p} = \frac{1}{N}\sum_{i=1}^{N} y_i = \frac{N_1}{N},$$

while the constrained 'estimator' is simply $\tilde{p} = p_0$. The Wald test for H_0, in its quadratic form, is based upon the test statistic

$$\xi_W = N(\hat{p} - p_0)[\hat{p}(1 - \hat{p})]^{-1}(\hat{p} - p_0),$$

which is simply the square of the test statistic presented in Subsection 6.1.3.

For the likelihood ratio test we need to compare the maximum loglikelihood values of the unrestricted and the restricted model, that is,

$$\log L(\hat{p}) = N_1 \log(N_1/N) + (N - N_1)\log(1 - N_1/N) \tag{6.37}$$

and

$$\log L(\tilde{p}) = N_1 \log(p_0) + (N - N_1)\log(1 - p_0).$$

The test statistic is simply computed as

$$\xi_{LR} = 2(\log L(\hat{p}) - \log L(\tilde{p})).$$

Finally, we consider the Lagrange multiplier test. With a single coefficient we establish that the Lagrange multiplier $N^{-1}\tilde{\lambda}$ (expressed as a sample average) is asymptotically normal with variance $I(p) = [p(1-p)]^{-1}$. Furthermore,

$$\tilde{\lambda} = \sum_{i=1}^{N} \frac{\partial \log L_i(p)}{\partial p}\bigg|_{p_0} = \frac{N_1}{p_0} - \frac{N - N_1}{1 - p_0}.$$

We can thus compute the LM test statistic as

$$\begin{aligned}\xi_{LM} &= N^{-1}\tilde{\lambda}[p_0(1-p_0)]\tilde{\lambda} \\ &= N^{-1}(N_1 - Np_0)[p_0(1-p_0)]^{-1}(N_1 - Np_0) \\ &= N(\hat{p} - p_0)[p_0(1-p_0)]^{-1}(\hat{p} - p_0).\end{aligned}$$

This shows that in this case the LM test statistic is very similar to the Wald test statistic: the only difference is that the information matrix is estimated using the restricted estimator p_0 rather than the unrestricted estimator $\hat{p}$.

As an illustration, suppose that we have a sample of $N = 100$ balls, of which 44% are red. If we test the hypothesis that $p = 0.5$, we obtain Wald, LR and LM test statistics of 1.46, 1.44 and 1.44, respectively. The 5% critical value taken from the asymptotic Chi-squared distribution with one degree of freedom is 3.84, so that the null hypothesis is not rejected at the 5% level with each of the three tests.

6.3 Tests in the Normal Linear Regression Model

Let us again consider the normal linear regression model, as discussed in Subsection 6.1.4,

$$y_i = x_i'\beta + \varepsilon_i, \quad \varepsilon_i \sim NID(0, \sigma^2),$$

where ε_i is independent of x_i. Suppose we are interested in testing whether the current specification is misspecified. Misspecification could reflect the omission of relevant variables, the presence of heteroskedasticity or autocorrelation or non-normality of the error terms. It is relatively easy to test for such misspecifications using the Lagrange multiplier framework, where the current model is considered to be the restricted model and the ML estimates are the constrained ML estimates. We then consider more general models that allow, for example, for heteroskedasticity, and test whether the current estimates significantly violate the first-order conditions of the more general model.

6.3.1 Testing for Omitted Variables

The first specification test that we consider is testing for omitted variables. In this case, the more general model is

$$y_i = x_i'\beta + z_i'\gamma + \varepsilon_i,$$

where the same assumptions are made about ε_i as before, and z_i is a J-dimensional vector of explanatory variables, independent of ε_i. The null hypothesis states H_0: $\gamma = 0$. Note that, under the assumptions above, the F-test discussed in Subsection 2.5.4 provides an exact test for $\gamma = 0$ and there is no real need to look at asymptotic tests. We discuss the Lagrange multiplier test for $\gamma = 0$ for illustrative purposes, as it can be readily extended to nonlinear models in which the F-test is not available (see Chapter 7). The first-order conditions for the more general model imply that the following derivatives are all equal to zero:

$$\sum_{i=1}^{N} \frac{(y_i - x_i'\beta - z_i'\gamma)}{\sigma^2} x_i,$$

$$\sum_{i=1}^{N} \frac{(y_i - x_i'\beta - z_i'\gamma)}{\sigma^2} z_i$$

and

$$-\frac{N}{2\sigma^2} + \frac{1}{2}\sum_{i=1}^{N} \frac{(y_i - x_i'\beta - z_i'\gamma)^2}{\sigma^4}.$$

Evaluating these derivatives at the (constrained) maximum likelihood estimates $\hat{\beta}$, $\hat{\sigma}^2$ (and $\gamma = 0$) while defining residuals $\hat{\varepsilon}_i = y_i - x_i'\hat{\beta}$, we can write the derivatives as

$$\sum_{i=1}^{N} \frac{\hat{\varepsilon}_i}{\hat{\sigma}^2} x_i; \quad \sum_{i=1}^{N} \frac{\hat{\varepsilon}_i}{\hat{\sigma}^2} z_i; \quad -\frac{N}{2\hat{\sigma}^2} + \frac{1}{2}\sum_{i=1}^{N} \frac{\hat{\varepsilon}_i^2}{\hat{\sigma}^4},$$

where the first and third expressions are zero by construction.[6] The Lagrange multiplier test should thus check whether $\sum_{i=1}^{N} \hat{\varepsilon}_i z_i / \hat{\sigma}^2$ differs significantly from zero. The LM test statistic can be computed as (6.35), where S has typical row

$$[\hat{\varepsilon}_i x_i' \quad \hat{\varepsilon}_i z_i']. \tag{6.38}$$

Because of the block diagonality of the information matrix, the derivatives with respect to σ^2 can be omitted here, although it would not be incorrect to include them in the matrix S as well. Furthermore, irrelevant proportionality factors are eliminated in S. This is allowed because such constants do not affect the outcome of (6.35). In summary, we compute the LM test statistic by regressing a vector of ones upon the (ML or OLS) residuals interacted with the included explanatory variables x_i and the omitted variables z_i, and multiplying the uncentred R^2 by the sample size N. Under the null hypothesis, the resulting test statistic NR^2 has an asymptotic Chi-squared distribution with J degrees of freedom. An asymptotically equivalent version of the test statistic can be obtained as NR^2, where R^2 is the R^2 of an auxiliary regression of the ML (or OLS) residuals upon the complete set of regressors, x_i and z_i. If z_i is taken to be a nonlinear function of x_i, this approach can straightforwardly be used to test the functional form of the model (against a well-defined alternative).

[6] These two expressions correspond to the first-order conditions of the restricted model and define $\hat{\beta}$ and $\hat{\sigma}^2$.

6.3.2 Testing for Heteroskedasticity

Now suppose that the variance of ε_i may not be constant but a function of some variables z_i, typically a subset or function of x_i. This is formalized in (4.37) from Chapter 4, which says that

$$V\{\varepsilon_i\} = \sigma_i^2 = \sigma^2 h(z_i'\alpha), \tag{6.39}$$

where h is an unknown, continuously differentiable function (that does not depend on i), such that $h(.) > 0, h'(.) \neq 0$ and $h(0) = 1$, and where z_i is a J-dimensional vector of explanatory variables (not including a constant). The null hypothesis of homoskedastic errors corresponds to H_0: $\alpha = 0$ (and we have $V\{\varepsilon_i\} = \sigma^2$). The loglikelihood contribution for observation i in the more general model is given by

$$\log L_i(\beta, \sigma^2, \alpha) = -\frac{1}{2}\log(2\pi) - \frac{1}{2}\log \sigma^2 h(z_i'\alpha) - \frac{1}{2}\frac{(y_i - x_i'\beta)^2}{\sigma^2 h(z_i'\alpha)}. \tag{6.40}$$

The score with respect to α is given by

$$\frac{\partial \log L_i(\beta, \sigma^2, \alpha)}{\partial \alpha} = \left[-\frac{1}{2}\frac{1}{h(z_i'\alpha)} + \frac{1}{2}\frac{(y_i - x_i'\beta)^2}{\sigma^2 h(z_i'\alpha)^2}\right]\frac{\partial h(z_i'\alpha)}{\partial \alpha},$$

where

$$\frac{\partial h(z_i'\alpha)}{\partial \alpha} = h'(z_i'\alpha)z_i,$$

where h' is the derivative of h. If we evaluate this under the constrained ML estimates $\hat{\beta}$ and $\hat{\sigma}^2$, this reduces to

$$\left[-\frac{1}{2} + \frac{1}{2}\frac{(y_i - x_i'\hat{\beta})^2}{\hat{\sigma}^2}\right]\kappa z_i = \frac{1}{2\hat{\sigma}^2}\left[(y_i - x_i'\hat{\beta})^2 - \hat{\sigma}^2\right]\kappa z_i,$$

where $\kappa = h'(0) \neq 0$ is an irrelevant constant. This explains the surprising result that the test does not require us to specify the function h.

Because the information matrix is block diagonal with respect to β and (σ^2, α), the OPG version of the Lagrange multiplier test for heteroskedasticity is obtained by computing (6.35), where S has typical row

$$[\hat{\varepsilon}_i^2 - \hat{\sigma}^2 \quad (\hat{\varepsilon}_i^2 - \hat{\sigma}^2)z_i'],$$

where irrelevant proportionality factors are again eliminated. In the auxiliary regression, we thus include the variables that we suspect to affect heteroskedasticity interacted with the squared residuals in deviation from the error variance estimated under the null hypothesis. With J variables in z_i, the resulting test statistic NR^2 has an asymptotic Chi-squared distribution with J degrees of freedom (under the null hypothesis).

The above approach presents a way to compute the Breusch–Pagan test for heteroskedasticity corresponding to our general computation rule given in (6.35). There are alternative ways to compute (asymptotically equivalent) versions of the Breusch–Pagan test statistic, for example, by computing N times the R^2 of an auxiliary regression of $\hat{\varepsilon}_i^2$ (the squared OLS or maximum likelihood residuals) on z_i and a constant.

This was discussed in Chapter 4. See Engle (1984) or Godfrey (1988, Section 4.5) for additional discussion.

If the null hypothesis of homoskedasticity is rejected, one option is to estimate a more general model that allows for heteroskedasticity. This can be based upon (6.40), with a particular choice for $h(.)$, for example, the exponential function. Because heteroskedasticity, in this particular model, does not result in an inconsistent maximum likelihood (OLS) estimator for β, it is also appropriate to compute heteroskedasticity-consistent standard errors; see Chapter 4 and Section 6.4.

6.3.3 Testing for Autocorrelation

In a time series context, the error term in a regression model may suffer from autocorrelation. Consider the linear model

$$y_t = x_t'\beta + \varepsilon_t, \quad t = 1, 2, \ldots, T,$$

with assumptions as stated above. The alternative hypothesis of first-order autocorrelation states that

$$\varepsilon_t = \rho\varepsilon_{t-1} + \upsilon_t,$$

such that the null hypothesis corresponds to H_0: $\rho = 0$. If we rewrite the model as

$$y_t = x_t'\beta + \rho\varepsilon_{t-1} + \upsilon_t,$$

it follows that testing for autocorrelation is similar to testing for an omitted variable, namely, $\varepsilon_{t-1} = y_{t-1} - x_{t-1}'\beta$. Consequently, one can compute a version of the Lagrange multiplier test for autocorrelation using (6.33), where S has typical row

$$[\hat{\varepsilon}_t x_t' \quad \hat{\varepsilon}_t\hat{\varepsilon}_{t-1}]$$

and the number of observations is $T - 1$. If x_t does not contain a lagged dependent variable, the information matrix is block diagonal with respect to β and (σ^2, ρ), and the scores with respect to β, corresponding to $\hat{\varepsilon}_t x_t'$, may be dropped from S. This gives the following test statistic:

$$\xi_{LM} = \sum_{t=2}^{T} \hat{\varepsilon}_t\hat{\varepsilon}_{t-1}\left(\sum_{t=2}^{T} \hat{\varepsilon}_t^2\hat{\varepsilon}_{t-1}^2\right)^{-1} \sum_{t=2}^{T} \hat{\varepsilon}_t\hat{\varepsilon}_{t-1}.$$

Because under the null hypothesis ε_t and ε_{t-1} are independent,[7] it holds that $E\{\varepsilon_t^2\varepsilon_{t-1}^2\} = E\{\varepsilon_t^2\}E\{\varepsilon_{t-1}^2\}$. This indicates that an asymptotically equivalent test statistic is obtained by replacing $1/(T-1)\sum_t \hat{\varepsilon}_t^2\hat{\varepsilon}_{t-1}^2$ with

$$\left(\frac{1}{T-1}\sum_t \hat{\varepsilon}_t^2\right)\left(\frac{1}{T-1}\sum_t \hat{\varepsilon}_{t-1}^2\right).$$

[7] Recall that, under normality, zero correlation implies independence (see Appendix B).

This gives

$$\xi_{LM} = (T-1)\frac{\sum_{t=2}^{T}\hat{\varepsilon}_t\hat{\varepsilon}_{t-1}\left(\sum_{t=2}^{T}\hat{\varepsilon}_{t-1}^2\right)^{-1}\sum_{t=2}^{T}\hat{\varepsilon}_t\hat{\varepsilon}_{t-1}}{\sum_{t=2}^{T}\hat{\varepsilon}_t^2} = (T-1)R^2,$$

where R^2 is the R^2 of an auxiliary regression of the OLS or ML residual $\hat{\varepsilon}_t$ upon its lag $\hat{\varepsilon}_{t-1}$. This corresponds to the Breusch–Godfrey test for autocorrelation as discussed in Chapter 4. If x_t contains a lagged dependent variable, the appropriate auxiliary regression is of $\hat{\varepsilon}_t$ upon $\hat{\varepsilon}_{t-1}$ and x_t. Tests for pth order autocorrelation are obtained by augmenting the rows of S with $\hat{\varepsilon}_t\hat{\varepsilon}_{t-2}$ up to $\hat{\varepsilon}_t\hat{\varepsilon}_{t-p}$, or – for the latter computation – by adding $\hat{\varepsilon}_{t-2}$ up to $\hat{\varepsilon}_{t-p}$ in the auxiliary regression explaining $\hat{\varepsilon}_t$. Engle (1984) and Godfrey (1988, Section 4.4) provide additional discussion.

6.4 Quasi-maximum Likelihood and Moment Conditions Tests

It is typically the case that maximum likelihood requires researchers to make full distributional assumptions, while the generalized method of moments (GMM) discussed in Chapter 5 only makes assumptions about moments of the distribution. However, it is possible that the moment conditions employed in a GMM approach are based upon assumptions about the shape of the distribution as well. This allows us to rederive the maximum likelihood estimator as a GMM estimator with moment conditions corresponding to the first-order conditions of maximum likelihood. This is a useful generalization as it allows us to argue that in some cases the maximum likelihood estimator is consistent, even if the likelihood function is not entirely correct (but the first-order conditions are). Moreover, it allows us to extend the class of Lagrange multiplier tests to (conditional) moment tests.

6.4.1 Quasi-maximum Likelihood

In this subsection we shall see that the maximum likelihood estimator can be interpreted as a GMM estimator by noting that the first-order conditions of the maximum likelihood problem correspond to sample averages based upon theoretical moment conditions. The starting point is that it holds that

$$E\{s_i(\theta)\} = 0 \tag{6.41}$$

for the true K-dimensional parameter vector θ, under the assumption that the likelihood function is correct. The proof of this is relatively easy and instructive. If we consider the density function of y_i given x_i, $f(y_i|x_i;\theta)$, it holds by construction that (see Appendix B)

$$\int f(y_i|x_i;\theta)\,dy_i = 1,$$

where integration is over the support of y_i. Differentiating this with respect to θ gives

$$\int \frac{\partial f(y_i|x_i;\theta)}{\partial\theta}\,dy_i = 0.$$

Because

$$\frac{\partial f(y_i|x_i;\theta)}{\partial\theta} = \frac{\partial \log f(y_i|x_i;\theta)}{\partial\theta} f(y_i|x_i;\theta) = s_i(\theta)\, f(y_i|x_i;\theta),$$

it follows that

$$\int s_i(\theta)\, f(y_i|x_i;\theta)\, dy_i = E\{s_i(\theta)\} = 0,$$

where the first equality follows from the definition of the expectation operator.

Let us assume that θ is uniquely defined by these conditions. That is, there is only one vector θ that satisfies (6.41). Then (6.41) is a set of valid moment conditions, and we can use the GMM approach to estimate θ. Because the number of parameters is equal to the number of moment conditions, this involves solving the first-order conditions

$$\frac{1}{N}\sum_{i=1}^{N} s_i(\theta) = 0.$$

Of course, this reproduces the maximum likelihood estimator $\hat{\theta}$. However, it shows that the resulting estimator is consistent for θ provided that (6.41) is correct, which may be weaker than the requirement that the entire distribution is correctly specified. In the linear regression model with normal errors, the first-order conditions with respect to β are easily seen to correspond to

$$E\{(y_i - x_i'\beta)x_i\} = 0,$$

which corresponds to the set of moment conditions imposed by the OLS estimator. This explains why the maximum likelihood estimator for β in the normal linear regression model is consistent even if the distribution of ε_i is not normal.

If the maximum likelihood estimator is based upon a wrong likelihood function, but can be argued to be consistent on the basis of the validity of (6.41), the estimator is sometimes referred to as a **quasi-maximum likelihood estimator** or pseudo-maximum likelihood estimator (see White, 1982, or Gouriéroux, Monfort and Trognon, 1984). The asymptotic distribution of the quasi-ML estimator may differ from that of the ML estimator. In particular, the result in (6.18) may no longer be valid. Using our general formulae for the GMM estimator, it is possible to derive the asymptotic covariance matrix of the quasi-ML estimator for θ, assuming that (6.41) is correct. Using (5.74)–(5.76), it follows that the quasi-maximum likelihood estimator $\hat{\theta}$ satisfies

$$\sqrt{N}(\hat{\theta} - \theta) \to \mathcal{N}(0, V),$$

where[8]

$$V = I(\theta)^{-1} J(\theta) I(\theta)^{-1}, \tag{6.42}$$

with

$$I(\theta) \equiv \lim_{N\to\infty} \frac{1}{N}\sum_{i=1}^{N} I_i(\theta) \quad \text{and} \quad J(\theta) \equiv \lim_{N\to\infty} \frac{1}{N}\sum_{i=1}^{N} J_i(\theta),$$

[8] The covariance matrix maintains the assumption that observations are mutually independent.

where

$$I_i(\theta) = E\left\{-\frac{\partial s_i(\theta)}{\partial \theta'}\right\} = E\left\{-\frac{\partial^2 \log L_i(\theta)}{\partial \theta \, \partial \theta'}\right\},$$

as defined in (6.16), and

$$J_i(\theta) = E\{s_i(\theta)s_i(\theta)'\},$$

as defined in (6.20). The covariance matrix in (6.42) generalizes the one in (6.18) and is correct whenever the quasi-ML estimator $\hat{\theta}$ is consistent. Its expression is popularly referred to as the 'sandwich formula'. In the case of the linear regression model, estimating the covariance matrix on the basis of (6.42) would reproduce the heteroskedasticity-consistent covariance matrix as discussed in Subsection 4.3.4. Several software packages have the option to compute robust standard errors for the (quasi-)maximum likelihood estimator, based on the covariance matrix in (6.42).

The **information matrix test** (IM test) suggested by White (1982) tests the equality of the two $K \times K$ matrices $I(\theta)$ and $J(\theta)$ by comparing their sample counterparts. Because of the symmetry, a maximum of $K(K+1)/2$ elements have to be compared, so that the number of degrees of freedom for the IM test is potentially very large. Depending on the shape of the likelihood function, the information matrix test checks for misspecification in a number of directions simultaneously (like functional form, heteroskedasticity, skewness and kurtosis). For additional discussion and computational issues, see Davidson and MacKinnon (2004, Section 15.2).

6.4.2 Conditional Moment Tests

The analysis in the previous subsection allows us to generalize the class of Lagrange multiplier tests to so-called **conditional moment tests** (CM tests), as suggested by Newey (1985) and Tauchen (1985). Consider a model characterized by (6.41)

$$E\{s_i(\theta)\} = 0,$$

where the (quasi-)ML estimator $\hat{\theta}$ satisfies

$$\frac{1}{N}\sum_{i=1}^{N} s_i(\hat{\theta}) = 0.$$

Now consider a hypothesis characterized by

$$E\{m_i(\theta)\} = 0, \tag{6.43}$$

where $m_i(\theta)$ is a J-dimensional function of the data and the unknown parameters in θ, just like $s_i(\theta)$. The difference is that (6.43) is not imposed in estimation. It is possible to test the validity of (6.43) by testing whether its sample counterpart

$$\frac{1}{N}\sum_{i=1}^{N} m_i(\hat{\theta}) \tag{6.44}$$

is close to zero. This can be done fairly easily by noting the resemblance between (6.44) and the scores of a more general likelihood function. Consequently, the OPG version of a moment conditions test for (6.43) can be computed by taking N times the uncentred R^2 of a regression of a vector of ones upon the columns of a matrix S, where S now has typical row

$$[s_i(\hat{\theta})' \quad m_i(\hat{\theta})'].$$

Under the null hypothesis that (6.43) is correct, the resulting test statistic has an asymptotic Chi-squared distribution with J degrees of freedom.

The above approach shows that the additional conditions that are tested do not necessarily have to correspond to scores of a more general likelihood function. A particular area where this approach is useful is when testing the hypothesis of normality.

6.4.3 Testing for Normality

Let us consider the linear regression model again with, under the null hypothesis, normal errors. For a continuously observed variable, normality tests usually check for skewness (third moment) and excess kurtosis (fourth moment), because the normal distribution implies that $E\{\varepsilon_i^3\} = 0$ and $E\{\varepsilon_i^4 - 3\sigma^4\} = 0$ (see Appendix B). If $E\{\varepsilon_i^3\} \neq 0$, the distribution of ε_i is not symmetric around zero. If $E\{\varepsilon_i^4 - 3\sigma^4\} > 0$, the distribution of ε_i is said to display **excess kurtosis**. This means that it has fatter tails than the normal distribution. Davidson and MacKinnon (1993, p. 63) provide graphical illustrations of these situations.

Given the discussion in the previous subsection, a test for normality can be obtained by running a regression of a vector of ones upon the columns of the matrix S, which now has typical row

$$[\hat{\varepsilon}_i x_i' \quad \hat{\varepsilon}_i^2 - \hat{\sigma}^2 \quad \hat{\varepsilon}_i^3 \quad \hat{\varepsilon}_i^4 - 3\hat{\sigma}^4],$$

where $\hat{\varepsilon}_i$ denotes the maximum likelihood (or OLS) residual, and then computing N times the uncentred R^2. Although non-normality of ε_i does not invalidate consistency of the OLS estimator or its asymptotic normality, the above test is occasionally of interest. Finding that ε_i has a severely skewed distribution might indicate that it may be advisable to transform the dependent variable prior to estimation (e.g. by considering log wages rather than wages itself). In Chapter 7 we shall see classes of models where normality is far more crucial.

A popular variant of the LM test for normality is the **Jarque–Bera test** (Jarque and Bera, 1980). The test statistic is computed as

$$\xi_{LM} = N\left[\frac{1}{6}\left(\frac{1}{N}\sum_{i=1}^{N}\hat{\varepsilon}_i^3/\hat{\sigma}^3\right)^2 + \frac{1}{24}\left(\frac{1}{N}\sum_{i=1}^{N}\hat{\varepsilon}_i^4/\hat{\sigma}^4 - 3\right)^2\right], \tag{6.45}$$

which is a weighted average of the squared sample moments corresponding to skewness and excess kurtosis, respectively. Under the null hypothesis, it is asymptotically distributed as a Chi-squared with two degrees of freedom; see Godfrey (1988, Section 4.7) for more details.

Wrap-up

Almost any model can be estimated with maximum likelihood provided we are willing to make full distributional assumptions. The ML approach is fully parametric in the sense that the distribution is completely specified, except for a finite number of unknown parameters. Greene (2012, Chapter 14) provides a detailed coverage of the theory of maximum likelihood estimation. In practice, maximum likelihood plays an important role in the estimation of more complicated models, for example the nonlinear models discussed in Chapter 7. Maximum likelihood can be shown to lead to a consistent and asymptotically efficient estimator, which has an asymptotic normal distribution. While the estimator has such attractive properties, these are typically only valid under the condition that the distributional assumptions are satisfied. Accordingly, it is important to pay attention to potential violations of such assumptions. Tests for this can be based upon the Wald, Likelihood Ratio or Lagrange Multiplier principle. Although misspecification tests are readily available, their use in empirical work is relatively limited. In some cases, the first-order conditions of the maximum likelihood problem are more generally valid, and consistency of the maximum likelihood method is obtained under weaker conditions. In such cases, it may be required to estimate the covariance matrix using the more general 'sandwich' formula. Empirical illustrations using the maximum likelihood method are provided in Chapter 7 and some of the subsequent chapters.

Exercises

Exercise 6.1 (The Normal Linear Regression Model)

Consider the following linear regression model:

$$y_i = \beta_1 + \beta_2 x_i + \varepsilon_i,$$

where $\beta = (\beta_1, \beta_2)'$ is a vector of unknown parameters, and x_i is a one-dimensional observable variable. We have a sample of $i = 1, \ldots, N$ independent observations and assume that the error terms ε_i are $NID(0, \sigma^2)$, independent of all x_i. The density function of y_i (for a given x_i) is then given by

$$f(y_i|\beta, \sigma^2) = \frac{1}{\sqrt{2\pi\sigma^2}} \exp\left\{-\frac{1}{2}\frac{(y_i - \beta_1 - \beta_2 x_i)^2}{\sigma^2}\right\}.$$

a. Give an expression for the loglikelihood contribution of observation i, $\log L_i(\beta, \sigma^2)$. Explain why the loglikelihood function of the entire sample is given by

$$\log L(\beta, \sigma^2) = \sum_{i=1}^{N} \log L_i(\beta, \sigma^2).$$

b. Determine expressions for the two elements in $\partial \log L_i(\beta, \sigma^2)/\partial\beta$ and show that both have expectation zero for the true parameter values.

c. Derive an expression for $\partial \log L_i(\beta, \sigma^2)/\partial\sigma^2$ and show that it also has expectation zero for the true parameter values.

Suppose that x_i is a dummy variable equal to 1 for males and 0 for females, such that $x_i = 1$ for $i = 1, \ldots, N_1$ (the first N_1 observations) and $x_i = 0$ for $i = N_1 + 1, \ldots, N$.

d. Derive the first-order conditions for maximum likelihood. Show that the maximum likelihood estimators for β are given by

$$\hat{\beta}_1 = \frac{1}{N - N_1} \sum_{i=N_1+1}^{N} y_i, \quad \hat{\beta}_2 = \frac{1}{N_1} \sum_{i=1}^{N_1} y_i - \hat{\beta}_1.$$

What is the interpretation of these two estimators? What is the interpretation of the true parameter values β_1 and β_2?

e. Show that

$$\partial^2 \log L_i(\beta, \sigma^2)/\partial\beta\partial\sigma^2 = \partial^2 \log L_i(\beta, \sigma^2)/\partial\sigma^2\partial\beta,$$

and show that it has expectation zero. What are the implications of this for the asymptotic covariance matrix of the ML estimator $(\hat{\beta}_1, \hat{\beta}_2, \hat{\sigma}^2)$?

f. Present two ways to estimate the asymptotic covariance matrix of $(\hat{\beta}_1, \hat{\beta}_2)'$ and compare the results.

g. Present an alternative way to estimate the asymptotic covariance matrix of $(\hat{\beta}_1, \hat{\beta}_2)'$ that allows ε_i to be heteroskedastic.

Suppose that we are interested in the hypothesis H_0: $\beta_2 = 0$ with alternative H_1: $\beta_2 \neq 0$. Tests can be based upon the likelihood ratio, Lagrange multiplier or Wald principle.

h. Explain what these three principles are.

i. Discuss for each of the three tests what is required to compute them.

Although the three test statistics have the same asymptotic Chi-squared distribution, it can be shown (see, e.g., Godfrey, 1988, Section 2.3) that in the above model it holds for any finite sample that

$$\xi_W \geq \xi_{LR} \geq \xi_{LM}.$$

j. Explain what is meant by the power of a test. What does this inequality tell us about the powers of the three tests? (Hint: if needed, consult Chapter 2.)

k. Explain what is meant by the (actual) size of a test. What does the inequality tell us about the sizes of the three tests?

l. Would you prefer one of the three tests, knowing the above inequality?

Exercise 6.2 (The Poisson Regression Model)

Let y_i denote the number of times individual i buys tobacco in a given month. Suppose a random sample of N individuals is available, for which we observe values $0, 1, 2, 3, \ldots$. Let x_i be an observed characteristic of these individuals (e.g. gender). If we assume that, for given x_i, y_i has a Poisson distribution with parameter $\lambda_i = \exp\{\beta_1 + \beta_2 x_i\}$, the probability mass function of y_i conditional upon x_i is given by

$$P\{y_i = y|x_i\} = \frac{e^{-\lambda_i}\lambda_i^y}{y!}.$$

a. Write down the loglikelihood function for this so-called Poisson regression model.

b. Derive the score contributions. Using the fact that the Poisson distribution implies that $E\{y_i|x_i\} = \lambda_i$, show that the score contributions have expectation zero.

c. Derive an expression for the information matrix $I(\beta_1, \beta_2)$. Use this to determine the asymptotic covariance matrix of the ML estimator and a consistent estimator for this matrix.

d. Describe how one can test for an omitted variable using the Lagrange multiplier framework. Which auxiliary regression is needed?

More details about the Poisson regression model can be found in Section 7.3.

7 Models with Limited Dependent Variables

In practical applications one often has to cope with the phenomena that are of a discrete or mixed discrete–continuous nature. For example, one could be interested in explaining whether married women have a paid job (yes or no), or how many hours they work (zero or positive). If these types of variables have to be explained, a linear regression model is generally inappropriate. In this chapter we consider alternative models that can be used to model discrete and discrete/continuous variables and pay attention to the estimation and interpretation of their parameters.

Although not exclusively, in many cases the problems analysed with this type of models are of a micro-economic nature, thus requiring data on individuals, households or firms. To stress this, we shall index all variables by i, running from 1 to sample size N. Section 7.1 starts with probably the simplest case of a limited dependent variable model, namely a binary choice model. Extensions to multiple discrete outcomes are discussed in Section 7.2. When the endogenous variable is the frequency of a certain event, for example the number of patents in a given year, count data models are often employed. Section 7.3 introduces several models for count data and presents an empirical illustration. If the distribution of the endogenous variable is continuous with a probability mass at one or more discrete points, the use of tobit models is recommended. The standard tobit model is discussed in Section 7.4, while some extensions, including models with sample selection where a nonrandom proportion of the outcomes is not observed, are contained in Section 7.5. Because sample selection is a problem that often arises with micro data, Section 7.6 contains some additional discussion of the sample selection problem, mainly focusing on the identification problem and under what assumptions it can be solved. An area that has gained interest recently is the estimation of treatment effects, and we discuss this in Section 7.7. Finally, Section 7.8 discusses models in which the dependent variable is a duration, for example the number of weeks it takes for an unemployed person to find a new job. Throughout, a number of empirical illustrations are provided in subsections. Additional discussion of limited dependent variable models in econometrics can be found in two surveys by Amemiya (1981, 1984) and the monographs by Maddala (1983), Franses and Paap (2001), Cameron and Trivedi (2005) and Wooldridge (2010).

7.1 Binary Choice Models

7.1.1 Using Linear Regression?

Suppose we want to explain whether a family possesses a car or not. Let the sole explanatory variable be the family income. We have data on N families ($i = 1, \ldots, N$), with observations on their income, x_{i2}, and whether or not they own a car. This latter element is described by the binary variable y_i, defined as

$$
\begin{aligned}
y_i &= 1 \quad \text{if family } i \text{ owns a car} \\
y_i &= 0 \quad \text{if family } i \text{ does not own a car.}
\end{aligned}
$$

Suppose we were to use a regression model to explain y_i from x_{i2} and an intercept term ($x_{i1} \equiv 1$). This linear model would be given by

$$y_i = \beta_1 + \beta_2 x_{i2} + \varepsilon_i = x_i'\beta + \varepsilon_i, \tag{7.1}$$

where $x_i = (x_{i1}, x_{i2})'$. It seems reasonable to make the standard assumption that $E\{\varepsilon_i|x_i\} = 0$ such that $E\{y_i|x_i\} = x_i'\beta$. This implies that

$$
\begin{aligned}
E\{y_i|x_i\} &= 1.P\{y_i = 1|x_i\} + 0.P\{y_i = 0|x_i\} \\
&= P\{y_i = 1|x_i\} = x_i'\beta.
\end{aligned} \tag{7.2}
$$

Thus, the linear model implies that $x_i'\beta$ is a probability and should therefore lie between 0 and 1. This is only possible if the x_i values are bounded and if certain restrictions on β are satisfied. Usually this is hard to achieve in practice. In addition to this fundamental problem, the error term in (7.1) has a highly non-normal distribution and suffers from heteroskedasticity. Because y_i has only two possible outcomes (0 or 1), the error term, for a given value of x_i, has two possible outcomes as well. In particular, the distribution of ε_i can be summarized as

$$
\begin{aligned}
P\{\varepsilon_i = -x_i'\beta|x_i\} &= P\{y_i = 0|x_i\} = 1 - x_i'\beta \\
P\{\varepsilon_i = 1 - x_i'\beta|x_i\} &= P\{y_i = 1|x_i\} = x_i'\beta.
\end{aligned} \tag{7.3}
$$

This implies that the variance of the error term is not constant but dependent upon the explanatory variables according to $V\{\varepsilon_i|x_i\} = x_i'\beta(1 - x_i'\beta)$. Note that the error variance also depends upon the model parameters β.

7.1.2 Introducing Binary Choice Models

To overcome the problems with the linear model, a class of **binary choice models** (or univariate dichotomous models) exists, designed to model the 'choice' between two discrete alternatives. These models essentially describe the probability that $y_i = 1$ directly, although they are often derived from an underlying latent variable model.

In general, we have

$$P\{y_i = 1|x_i\} = G(x_i, \beta) \tag{7.4}$$

for some function $G(.)$. This equation says that the probability of having $y_i = 1$ depends on the vector x_i containing individual characteristics. For example, the probability that a person owns a house depends on his or her income, education level, age and marital status. Alternatively, the probability that a firm issues dividends depends upon its earnings, market capitalization and some other characteristics. Clearly, the function $G(.)$ in (7.4) should take on values in the interval [0, 1] only. Usually, one restricts attention to functions of the form $G(x_i, \beta) = F(x_i'\beta)$. As $F(.)$ also has to be between 0 and 1, it seems natural to choose F to be some distribution function. Common choices are the standard normal distribution function

$$F(w) = \Phi(w) = \int_{-\infty}^{w} \frac{1}{\sqrt{2\pi}} \exp\left\{-\frac{1}{2}t^2\right\} dt, \tag{7.5}$$

leading to the so-called **probit model**, and the standard logistic distribution function, given by

$$F(w) = L(w) = \frac{e^w}{1 + e^w}, \tag{7.6}$$

which results in the **logit model**. A third choice corresponds to a uniform distribution over the interval [0, 1] with distribution function

$$\begin{aligned} F(w) &= 0, \ w < 0; \\ F(w) &= w, \ 0 \leq w \leq 1; \\ F(w) &= 1, \ w > 1. \end{aligned} \tag{7.7}$$

This results in the so-called **linear probability model**, which is similar to the regression model in (7.1), but the probabilities are set to 0 or 1 if $x_i'\beta$ exceeds the lower or upper limit, respectively. The first two models (probit and logit) are actually more common in applied work. Both a standard normal and a standard logistic random variable have a mean of zero, whereas the latter has a variance of $\pi^2/3$ instead of 1. These two distribution functions are very similar if one corrects for this difference in scaling; the logistic distribution has slightly heavier tails. Accordingly, the probit and logit models typically yield very similar results in empirical work.

Apart from their signs, the coefficients in these binary choice models are not easy to interpret directly. One way to interpret the parameters (and to ease comparison across different models) is to consider the marginal effects of changes in the explanatory variables. For a continuous explanatory variable, x_{ik}, say, the marginal effect is defined as the partial derivative of the probability that y_i equals one. For the three models above, we obtain

$$\begin{aligned} \frac{\partial \Phi(x_i'\beta)}{\partial x_{ik}} &= \phi(x_i'\beta)\beta_k; \\ \frac{\partial L(x_i'\beta)}{\partial x_{ik}} &= \frac{e^{x_i'\beta}}{(1 + e^{x_i'\beta})^2}\beta_k; \\ \frac{\partial x_i'\beta}{\partial x_{ik}} &= \beta_k; \ (\text{or } 0), \end{aligned}$$

where $\phi(.)$ denotes the standard normal density function. Except for the last model, the effect of a change in x_{ik} depends upon the values of x_i. Empirically, marginal effects are typically computed for the 'average' observation, replacing x_i in the previous expressions with the sample averages. Note that in all cases the sign of the effect of a change in x_{ik} corresponds to the sign of its coefficient β_k. For a discrete explanatory variable, for example, a dummy, the effect of a change can be determined from computing the implied probabilities for the two different outcomes, fixing the values of all other explanatory variables. Greene (2012, Section 17.3) provides a discussion on the difference between the average marginal effect and the marginal effect at the average, and on how to calculate standard errors for marginal effects.

When the model of interest contains interaction terms, a subtle issue emerges. Consider, for example, the case where the model of interest contains $\beta_2 x_{i2} + \beta_3 x_{i3} + \beta_4 x_{i2} x_{i3}$. When both β_2 and β_4 are positive, this seems to suggest that $P\{y_i = 1|x_i\}$ increases with x_{i2}, the marginal effect being larger when x_{i3} is bigger. This latter conclusion is not necessarily correct. To see this, note that for the probit model the marginal effect of a change in x_{i2} is now given by

$$\frac{\partial \Phi(x_i'\beta)}{\partial x_{i2}} = \phi(x_i'\beta)(\beta_2 + \beta_4 x_{i3}).$$

Because x_{i3} is correlated with $\phi(x_i'\beta)$, it is possible for the marginal effect to decrease if x_{i3} gets larger, also when $\beta_4 > 0$ (see Ai and Norton, 2003). In general, evaluating the sign and significance of the coefficient β_4 of the interaction term is inappropriate to argue that the likelihood that $y_i = 1$ is more sensitive to x_{i2} when x_{i3} is either larger or smaller. The true interaction effect equals the cross derivative of the conditional probability that $y_i = 1$ with respect to x_{i2} and x_{i3}. That is,

$$\frac{\partial^2 \Phi(x_i'\beta)}{\partial x_{i2} \partial x_{i3}} = \phi(x_i'\beta)\beta_4 + \phi'(x_i'\beta)(\beta_3 + \beta_4 x_{i2})(\beta_2 + \beta_4 x_{i3}),$$

where ϕ' denotes the derivative of ϕ. Even with $\beta_4 = 0$, this interaction may not be negligible. In general, the sign of this interaction effect may differ from the sign of β_4, and its magnitude and sign will depend upon x_i. Moreover, the statistical significance of the interaction effect does not equal the statistical significance of β_4. Similar arguments hold for the logit model. Powers (2005) illustrates this problem in the context of the management turnover literature. Obviously, it is possible to calculate the estimated magnitude of the interaction effect for given values of the explanatory variables, similar to the calculation of (average) marginal effects. Ai and Norton (2003) describe how standard errors should be calculated in this case and provide an illustration.

For the logit model, it is possible to rewrite (7.4) as

$$\log \frac{p_i}{1 - p_i} = x_i'\beta,$$

where $p_i = P\{y_i = 1|x_i\}$ is the probability of observing outcome 1. The left-hand side of this expression is referred to as the log odds ratio. An odds ratio of 3 means that the odds of $y_i = 1$ are 3 times those of $y_i = 0$. Using this equality, the β coefficients can be interpreted as describing the effect upon the odds ratio. For example, if $\beta_k = 0.1$, a one-unit increase of x_{ik} increases the odds ratio by about 10% (ceteris paribus). This interpretation corresponds to a semi-elasticity, as discussed in Section 3.1. See Cameron and Trivedi (2005, Section 14.3.4) for more details.

7.1.3 An Underlying Latent Model

It is possible (but not necessary) to derive a binary choice model from underlying behavioural assumptions. This leads to a latent variable representation of the model, which is in common use even when such behavioural assumptions are not made. Let us look at the decision of a married female to have a paid job or not. The utility difference between having a paid job and not having one depends upon the wage that could be earned but also on other personal characteristics, like the woman's age and education, whether there are young children in the family, etc. Thus, for each person i we can write the utility difference between having a job and not having one as a function of observed characteristics, x_i say, and unobserved characteristics, ε_i say.[1] Assuming a linear additive relationship, we obtain for the utility difference, denoted y_i^*,

$$y_i^* = x_i'\beta + \varepsilon_i. \tag{7.8}$$

Because y_i^* is unobserved, it is referred to as a **latent variable**. In this chapter, latent variables are indicated by an asterisk. Our assumption is that a woman chooses to work if the utility difference exceeds a certain threshold level, which can be set to zero without loss of generality. Consequently, we observe $y_i = 1$ (job) if and only if $y_i^* > 0$, and $y_i = 0$ (no job) otherwise. Thus we have

$$P\{y_i = 1\} = P\{y_i^* > 0\} = P\{x_i'\beta + \varepsilon_i > 0\} = P\{-\varepsilon_i \leq x_i'\beta\} = F(x_i'\beta), \tag{7.9}$$

where F denotes the distribution function of $-\varepsilon_i$, or, in the common case of a symmetric distribution, the distribution function of ε_i. Consequently, we have obtained a binary choice model, the form of which depends upon the distribution that is assumed for ε_i. As the scale of utility is not identified, a normalization on the distribution of ε_i is required. Usually this means that its variance is fixed at a given value. If a *standard* normal distribution is chosen, one obtains the probit model; for the logistic one the logit model is obtained.

Although binary choice models in economics can often be interpreted as being derived from an underlying utility maximization problem, this is certainly not necessary. Usually, one defines the latent variable y_i^* directly, such that the probit model is fully described by

$$\begin{aligned} y_i^* &= x_i'\beta + \varepsilon_i, \quad \varepsilon_i \sim NID(0,1) \\ y_i &= 1 \quad \text{if } y_i^* > 0 \\ &= 0 \quad \text{if } y_i^* \leq 0, \end{aligned} \tag{7.10}$$

where the ε_is are independent of all x_i. For the logit model, the normal distribution is replaced by the standard logistic one. Most commonly, the parameters in binary choice models (or limited dependent variable models in general) are estimated by the method of maximum likelihood.

7.1.4 Estimation

Given our general discussion of maximum likelihood estimation in Chapter 6, we restrict attention to the form of the likelihood function here. In fact, this form is rather simple as it

[1] The error term ε_i should not be confused with the one in the linear model (7.1).

follows immediately from the models given earlier. In general, the likelihood contribution of observation i with $y_i = 1$ is given by $P\{y_i = 1|x_i\}$, considered as a function of the unknown parameter vector β. The likelihood function for the entire sample is thus given by

$$L(\beta) = \prod_{i=1}^{N} P\{y_i = 1|x_i; \beta\}^{y_i} P\{y_i = 0|x_i; \beta\}^{1-y_i}, \tag{7.11}$$

where we included β in the expressions for the probabilities to stress that the likelihood function is a function of β. As usual we prefer to work with the loglikelihood function. Substituting $P\{y_i = 1|x_i; \beta\} = F(x_i'\beta)$, we obtain

$$\log L(\beta) = \sum_{i=1}^{N} y_i \log F(x_i'\beta) + \sum_{i=1}^{N} (1 - y_i) \log(1 - F(x_i'\beta)). \tag{7.12}$$

Substituting the appropriate form for F gives an expression that can be maximized with respect to β. As indicated earlier, the values of β and their interpretation depend upon the distribution function that is chosen. An empirical example in Subsection 7.1.6 will illustrate this.

It is instructive to consider the first-order conditions of the maximum likelihood problem. Differentiating (7.12) with respect to β yields

$$\frac{\partial \log L(\beta)}{\partial \beta} = \sum_{i=1}^{N} \left[\frac{y_i - F(x_i'\beta)}{F(x_i'\beta)(1 - F(x_i'\beta))} f(x_i'\beta) \right] x_i = 0, \tag{7.13}$$

where $f = F'$ is the derivative of the distribution function (so f is the density function). The term in square brackets is often referred to as the **generalized residual** of the model, and we shall see it reappearing when discussing specification tests. It equals $f(x_i'\beta)/F(x_i'\beta)$ for the positive observations ($y_i = 1$) and $-f(x_i'\beta)/(1 - F(x_i'\beta))$ for the zero observations ($y_i = 0$). The first-order conditions thus say that each explanatory variable should be orthogonal to the generalized residual (over the whole sample). This is comparable with the OLS first-order conditions in (2.10), which state that the least squares residuals are orthogonal to each variable in x_i.

For the logit model we can simplify (7.13) to

$$\frac{\partial \log L(\beta)}{\partial \beta} = \sum_{i=1}^{N} \left[y_i - \frac{\exp(x_i'\beta)}{1 + \exp(x_i'\beta)} \right] x_i = 0. \tag{7.14}$$

The solution of (7.14) is the maximum likelihood estimator $\hat{\beta}$. From this estimate we can estimate the probability that $y_i = 1$ for a given x_i as

$$\hat{p}_i = \frac{\exp(x_i'\hat{\beta})}{1 + \exp(x_i'\hat{\beta})}. \tag{7.15}$$

Consequently, the first-order conditions for the logit model imply that

$$\sum_{i=1}^{N} \hat{p}_i x_i = \sum_{i=1}^{N} y_i x_i. \tag{7.16}$$

Thus, if x_i contains a constant term (and there is no reason why it should not), then the sum of the estimated probabilities is equal to $\sum_i y_i$ or the number of observations in the sample for which $y_i = 1$. In other words, the predicted frequency is equal to the actual frequency. Similarly, if x_i includes a dummy variable, say 1 for females, 0 for males, then the predicted frequency will be equal to the actual frequency for each gender group. Although a similar result does not hold exactly for the probit model, it does hold approximately by virtue of the similarity of the logit and probit models.

A look at the second-order conditions of the maximum likelihood problem reveals that the matrix of second-order derivatives is negative definite (unless exact multicollinearity is present). Consequently, the loglikelihood function is globally concave, and convergence of the iterative maximum likelihood algorithm is guaranteed (and usually quite fast).

7.1.5 Goodness-of-Fit

A goodness-of-fit measure is a summary statistic indicating the accuracy with which the model approximates the observed data, like the R^2 measure in the linear regression model. When the dependent variable is qualitative, accuracy can be judged either in terms of the fit between the calculated probabilities and observed response frequencies or in terms of the model's ability to forecast observed responses. Contrary to the linear regression model, there is no single measure for the goodness-of-fit in binary choice models and a variety of measures exists; see Cameron and Trivedi (2005, Section 8.7) for a general discussion of alternative goodness-of-fit measures in nonlinear models.

Often, goodness-of-fit measures are implicitly or explicitly based on comparison with a model that contains only a constant as explanatory variable. Let $\log L_1$ denote the maximum loglikelihood value of the model of interest and let $\log L_0$ denote the maximum value of the loglikelihood function when all parameters, except the intercept, are set to zero. Clearly, $\log L_1 \geq \log L_0$. The larger the difference between the two loglikelihood values, the more the extended model adds to the very restrictive model. (Indeed, a formal likelihood ratio test can be based on the difference between the two values.) A first goodness-of-fit measure is defined as (see Amemiya, 1981, for an extensive list)

$$pseudo\text{-}R^2 = 1 - \frac{1}{1 + 2(\log L_1 - \log L_0)/N}, \tag{7.17}$$

where N denotes the number of observations. An alternative measure is suggested by McFadden (1974),

$$McFadden\ R^2 = 1 - \log L_1 / \log L_0, \tag{7.18}$$

sometimes referred to as the likelihood ratio index. Because the loglikelihood is the sum of log probabilities, it follows that $\log L_0 \leq \log L_1 < 0$, from which it is straightforward to show that both measures take on values in the interval [0, 1] only. If all estimated slope coefficients are equal to zero, we have $\log L_0 = \log L_1$, such that both R^2s are equal to zero. If the model were able to generate (estimated) probabilities that corresponded exactly to the observed values (that is, $\hat{p}_i = y_i$ for all i), all probabilities in the loglikelihood would be equal to one, such that the loglikelihood would be exactly equal to zero. Consequently, the upper limit for the two measures above is obtained for $\log L_1 = 0$. The upper bound of 1 can therefore, in theory, only be attained by McFadden's measure; see Cameron and Windmeijer (1997) for a discussion of the properties of this and alternative measures. In practice, goodness-of-fit measures are usually well below unity.

To compute $\log L_0$ it is not necessary to estimate a probit or logit model with an intercept term only. If there is only a constant term in the model, the distribution function is irrelevant for the implied probabilities and the model essentially says $P\{y_i = 1\} = p$ for some unknown p. The ML estimator for p can easily be shown to be (see (6.4))

$$\hat{p} = N_1/N,$$

where $N_1 = \sum_i y_i$. That is, the estimated probability is equal to the proportion of ones in the sample. The maximum loglikelihood value is therefore given by (compare (6.37))

$$\begin{aligned}\log L_0 &= \sum_{i=1}^{N} y_i \log(N_1/N) + \sum_{i=1}^{N}(1 - y_i)\log(1 - N_1/N) \\ &= N_1 \log(N_1/N) + N_0 \log(N_0/N), \end{aligned} \tag{7.19}$$

where $N_0 = N - N_1$ denotes the number of zeros in the sample. It can be directly computed from the sample size N and the sample frequencies N_0 and N_1. The value of $\log L_1$ is routinely reported by the estimation software. Frequently, the default goodness-of-fit measure, if reported, corresponds to McFadden's R^2.

An alternative way to evaluate the goodness-of-fit is comparing correct and incorrect predictions. To predict whether $y_i = 1$ or not, it seems natural to look at the estimated probability that follows from the model, which is given by $F(x_i'\hat{\beta})$. In general, one predicts that $y_i = 1$ if $F(x_i'\hat{\beta}) > 1/2$. Because $F(0) = 1/2$ for distributions that are symmetric around 0 (like the normal and logistic distributions), this corresponds to $x_i'\hat{\beta} > 0$. Thus, the implied predictions are

$$\begin{aligned}\hat{y}_i &= 1 \quad \text{if } x_i'\hat{\beta} > 0 \\ \hat{y}_i &= 0 \quad \text{if } x_i'\hat{\beta} \leq 0. \end{aligned} \tag{7.20}$$

Now it is possible to construct a cross-tabulation of predictions and actual observations. In Table 7.1, n_{11} denotes the number of correct predictions when the actual outcome is 1, and n_{10} denotes the number of times we predict a zero, while the actual value is 1. Note that $N_1 = n_{11} + n_{10}$ (total number of ones observed) and $n_1 = n_{11} + n_{01}$ (total number of ones predicted). Several goodness-of-fit measures can be computed on the basis of this table. Overall, the proportion of incorrect predictions is

$$wr_1 = \frac{n_{01} + n_{10}}{N},$$

Table 7.1 Cross-tabulation of actual and predicted outcomes

		$\hat{y}_i$		
		0	1	Total
y_i	0	n_{00}	n_{01}	N_0
	1	n_{10}	n_{11}	N_1
	Total	n_0	n_1	N

which can be compared with the proportion of incorrect predictions based on the model with an intercept term only. It is easily seen that for this latter model we will predict a one for all observations if $\hat{p} = N_1/N > 1/2$ and a zero otherwise. The proportion of incorrect predictions is thus given by

$$wr_0 = 1 - \hat{p} \text{ if } \hat{p} > 0.5,$$
$$= \hat{p} \text{ if } \hat{p} \leq 0.5.$$

A goodness-of-fit measure is finally obtained as

$$R_p^2 = 1 - \frac{wr_1}{wr_0}. \tag{7.21}$$

Because it is possible that the model predicts worse than the simple model, one can have $wr_1 > wr_0$, in which case R_p^2 becomes negative. Of course, this is not a good sign for the predictive quality of the model. Also note that $wr_0 \leq 1/2$, that is, even the simplest model will predict at least half of the observations correctly. For example, if 90% of the sample corresponds to $y_i = 1$, we even have $wr_0 = 0.1$. Consequently, in this case any binary choice model needs more than 90% correct predictions to beat the simple model. As a consequence, the overall proportion of correct predictions, $1 - wr_1 = (n_{00} + n_{11})/N$, does not give much information about the quality of the model. It may be more informative to consider the proportions of correct predictions for the two subsamples. From Table 7.1, the proportions of correct predictions for the subsamples with $y_i = 0$ and $y_i = 1$ are given by $p_{00} = n_{00}/N_0$ and $p_{11} = n_{11}/N_1$, respectively. Their sum

$$HM = p_{00} + p_{11}$$

should be larger than 1 for a good model (Henricksson and Merton, 1981). The Kuipers score (originally proposed in the meteorological literature) is equivalent to this and is given by

$$KS = \frac{n_{00}}{N_0} - \frac{n_{10}}{N_1} = \frac{n_{11}}{N_1} - \frac{n_{01}}{N_0},$$

which is the difference between the hit rate (proportion of correct predictions for one outcome) minus the false alarm rate (proportion of wrong predictions for the same outcome). The score has a range of −1 to +1, with 0 representing no predictive power. Negative values would be associated with 'perverse' predictions; see Granger and Pesaran (2000). It is easily verified that $KS = HM - 1$. Unlike the pseudo-R^2 measures based on the log-likelihood function, the last three measures, based on the cross-tabulation of y_i and $\hat{y}_i$, can also be used to evaluate out of sample forecasts. Lahiri and Yang (2013) provide a survey on forecasting binary outcomes and how to evaluate them.

7.1.6 Illustration: The Impact of Unemployment Benefits on Recipiency

As an illustration we consider a sample of 4877 blue-collar workers who lost their jobs in the United States between 1982 and 1991, taken from a study by McCall (1995). Not all unemployed workers eligible for unemployment insurance (UI) benefits apply for it, probably owing to the associated pecuniary and psychological costs. The percentage of eligible unemployed blue-collar workers that actually apply for UI benefits is called the take-up rate, and it was only 68% in the available sample. It is therefore interesting to investigate what makes people decide not to apply.

The amount of UI benefits a person can receive depends upon the state of residence, the year of becoming unemployed and his or her previous earnings. The replacement rate, defined as the ratio of weekly UI benefits to previous weekly earnings, varies from 33% to 54% with a sample average of 44%, and is potentially an important factor for an unemployed worker's choice to apply for unemployment benefits. Of course, other variables may influence the take-up rate as well. Owing to personal characteristics, some people are more able than others to find a new job in a short period of time and will therefore not apply for UI benefits. Indicators of such personal characteristics are schooling, age and, owing to potential (positive or negative) discrimination in the labour market, racial and gender dummies. In addition, preferences and budgetary reasons, as reflected in the family situation, may be of importance. Because of the important differences in the state unemployment rates, the probability of finding a new job varies across states, and we will therefore include the state unemployment rate in the analysis. The last type of variable that could be relevant relates to the reason why the job was lost. In the analysis we will include dummy variables for the reasons: slack work, position abolished and end of seasonal work.

We estimate three different models, the results of which are presented in Table 7.2. The linear probability model is estimated by ordinary least squares, so no corrections for

Table 7.2 Binary choice models for applying for unemployment benefits (blue-collar workers)

	LPM		Logit		Probit	
Variable	Estimate	Standard error	Estimate	Standard error	Estimate	Standard error
constant	−0.077	(0.122)	−2.800	(0.604)	−1.700	(0.363)
replacement rate	0.629	(0.384)	3.068	(1.868)	1.863	(1.127)
replacement rate^2	−1.019	(0.481)	−4.891	(2.334)	−2.980	(1.411)
age	0.0157	(0.0047)	0.068	(0.024)	0.042	(0.014)
age^2/10	−0.0015	(0.0006)	−0.0060	(0.0030)	−0.0038	(0.0018)
tenure	0.0057	(0.0012)	0.0312	(0.0066)	0.0177	(0.0038)
slack work	0.128	(0.014)	0.625	(0.071)	0.375	(0.042)
abolished position	−0.0065	(0.0248)	−0.0362	(0.1178)	−0.0223	(0.0718)
seasonal work	0.058	(0.036)	0.271	(0.171)	0.161	(0.104)
head of household	−0.044	(0.017)	−0.211	(0.081)	−0.125	(0.049)
married	0.049	(0.016)	0.242	(0.079)	0.145	(0.048)
children	−0.031	(0.017)	−0.158	(0.086)	−0.097	(0.052)
young children	0.043	(0.020)	0.206	(0.097)	0.124	(0.059)
live in SMSA	−0.035	(0.014)	−0.170	(0.070)	−0.100	(0.042)
nonwhite	0.017	(0.019)	0.074	(0.093)	0.052	(0.056)
year of displacement	−0.013	(0.008)	−0.064	(0.015)	−0.038	(0.009)
>12 years of school	−0.014	(0.016)	−0.065	(0.082)	−0.042	(0.050)
male	−0.036	(0.018)	−0.180	(0.088)	−0.107	(0.053)
state max. benefits	0.0012	(0.0002)	0.0060	(0.0010)	0.0036	(0.0006)
state unempl. rate	0.018	(0.003)	0.096	(0.016)	0.057	(0.009)
Loglikelihood				−2873.197		−2874.071
Pseudo-R^2				0.066		0.066
McFadden R^2				0.057		0.057
R_p^2		0.035		0.046		0.045

heteroskedasticity are made, and no attempt is made to keep the implied probabilities between 0 and 1. The logit and probit models are both estimated by maximum likelihood. Because the logistic distribution has a variance of $\pi^2/3$, the estimates of β obtained from the logit model are roughly a factor $\pi/\sqrt{3}$ larger than those obtained from the probit model, acknowledging the small differences in the shape of the distributions. Similarly, the estimates for the linear probability model are quite different in magnitude and approximately 4 times as small as those for the logit model (except for the intercept term). Looking at the results in Table 7.2, we see that the signs of the coefficients are identical across the different specifications, while the statistical significance of the explanatory variables is also comparable. This is not an unusual finding. If we would calculate the average marginal effects of the explanatory variables in each of the three models, they are typically very close. For example, the estimated marginal effect, evaluated at the sample averages of the regressors, for *tenure* is 0.0066 for the logit model and 0.0062 for the probit model. This means that the probability of applying for UI benefits increases by a bit more than 0.6 percentage points with one more year of tenure. The estimated effect of being married, for the average person, is 0.0517 and 0.0515 for the logit and probit specifications, respectively, implying that being married increases the probability by about 5%. For the linear probability model, the marginal effects correspond to the estimated coefficients.

For all specifications, the replacement rate has an insignificant positive coefficient, while its square is significantly negative. The ceteris paribus effect of the replacement rate will thus depend upon its value. For the probit model, for example, we can derive that the estimated marginal effect[2] of a change in the replacement rate (rr) equals the value of the normal density function multiplied by $1.863 - 2 \times 2.980rr$, which is negative for 85% of the observations in the sample. This is counterintuitive and suggests that other variables might be more important in explaining the take-up rate.

The dummy variable that indicates whether the job was lost because of slack work is highly significant in all specifications, which is not surprising given that these workers typically will find it hard to get a new job. Many other variables are statistically insignificant or only marginally significant. This is particularly troublesome, as with this large number of observations a significance level of 1% or less may be more appropriate[3] than the traditional 5%. The two variables relating to the state of residence are statistically significant. The higher the state unemployment rate and the higher the maximum benefit level, the more likely it is that individuals will apply for benefits, which is intuitively reasonable. The ceteris paribus effect of being married is estimated to be positive, while, somewhat surprisingly, being head of the household has a negative effect on the probability of take-up.

The fact that the models do not do a very good job in explaining the probability that someone applies for UI benefits is reflected in the goodness-of-fit measures that are computed. Usually, goodness-of-fit is fairly low for discrete choice models. In this application, the alternative goodness-of-fit measures indicate that the specified models perform between 3.5% and 6.6% better than a model that specifies the probability of take-up to be constant. To elaborate upon this, let us consider the R_p^2 criterion for the logit model. If we generate predictions $\hat{y}_i$ on the basis of the estimated logit probabilities by predicting a one if the estimated probability is larger than 0.5 and a 0 otherwise, this results

[2] See Section 3.1 for the computation of marginal effects in the linear model.

[3] See the discussion on this issue in Section 2.5.7.

Table 7.3 Cross-tabulation of actual and predicted outcomes (logit model)

		$\hat{y}$		
		0	1	Total
y_i	0	242	1300	1542
	1	171	3164	3335
	Total	413	4464	4877

in the cross-tabulation in Table 7.3. The off-diagonal elements in this table indicate the number of observations for which the model's prediction is incorrect. It is clear that for the majority of individuals we predict that they will apply for UI benefits, while for 171 individuals we predict that they will not apply whereas in fact they will. The R_p^2 criterion can be computed directly from this table as

$$R_p^2 = 1 - \frac{171 + 1300}{1542},$$

where 1542 corresponds to the number of incorrect predictions from the naive model where the probability of take-up is constant ($\hat{p} = 3335/4877$). The loglikelihood value for the latter model is given by

$$\log L_0 = 3335 \log \frac{3335}{4877} + 1542 \log \frac{1542}{4877} = -3043.028,$$

which allows us to compute the pseudo and McFadden R^2 measures. Finally, we note that $p_{00} + p_{11}$ for this logit model is

$$\text{HM} = \frac{242}{1542} + \frac{3164}{3335} = 1.106,$$

whereas it is 1 for the naive model by construction.

7.1.7 Specification Tests in Binary Choice Models

Although maximum likelihood estimators have the property of being consistent, there is one important condition for this to hold: the likelihood function has to be correctly specified.[4] This means that we must be sure about the entire distribution that we impose upon our data. Deviations will cause inconsistent estimators, and in binary choice models this typically arises when the probability that $y_i = 1$ is misspecified as a function of x_i, that is, when (7.9) is misspecified. Usually, such misspecifications are motivated from the latent variable model and reflect heteroskedasticity or non-normality (in the probit case) of ε_i. In addition, we may want to test for omitted variables without having to re-estimate the model. The most convenient framework for such tests is the Lagrange multiplier (LM) framework as discussed in Section 6.2.

[4] We can relax this requirement somewhat to say that the first-order conditions of the maximum likelihood problem should be valid (in the population). If this is the case, we can obtain consistent estimators even with the incorrect likelihood function. This is referred to as quasi-maximum likelihood estimation (see Section 6.4).

LM tests are based on the first-order conditions from a more general model that specifies the alternative hypothesis, and checking whether these are violated if we evaluate them at the parameter estimates of the current, restricted, model. Thus, if we want to test for J omitted variables z_i, we should evaluate whether

$$\sum_{i=1}^{N}\left[\frac{y_i - F(x_i'\hat{\beta})}{F(x_i'\hat{\beta})(1-F(x_i'\hat{\beta}))}f(x_i'\hat{\beta})\right] z_i \tag{7.22}$$

is significantly different from zero. Denoting the term in square brackets as the generalized residual, $\hat{\varepsilon}_i^G$, this means checking whether $\hat{\varepsilon}_i^G$ and z_i are correlated. As we have seen in Section 6.2, a simple way of computing the LM test statistic is obtained from a regression of a vector of ones upon the $K + J$ variables $\hat{\varepsilon}_i^G x_i'$ and $\hat{\varepsilon}_i^G z_i'$ and computing N times the uncentred R^2 (see Section 2.4) of this auxiliary regression. Under the null hypothesis that z_i enters the model with zero coefficients, the test statistic is asymptotically Chi-squared distributed with J degrees of freedom.

Heteroskedasticity of ε_i will cause the maximum likelihood estimators to be inconsistent, and we can test for it fairly easily. Consider the alternative that the variance of ε_i depends upon exogenous variables[5] z_i as

$$V\{\varepsilon_i\} = kh(z_i'\alpha) \tag{7.23}$$

for some function $h > 0$ with $h(0) = 1$, $k = 1$ or $\pi^2/3$ (depending on whether we have a probit or logit model) and $h'(0) \neq 0$. The loglikelihood function would generalize to

$$\log L(\beta, \alpha) = \sum_{i=1}^{N} y_i \log F\left(\frac{x_i'\beta}{\sqrt{h(z_i'\alpha)}}\right) + \sum_{i=1}^{N}(1-y_i)\log\left(1 - F\left(\frac{x_i'\beta}{\sqrt{h(z_i'\alpha)}}\right)\right). \tag{7.24}$$

The derivatives with respect to α, evaluated under the null hypothesis that $\alpha = 0$, are given by

$$\sum_{i=1}^{N}\left[\frac{y_i - F(x_i'\hat{\beta})}{F(x_i'\hat{\beta})(1-F(x_i'\hat{\beta}))}f(x_i'\hat{\beta})\right](x_i'\hat{\beta})\kappa z_i, \tag{7.25}$$

where κ is a constant that depends upon the form of h. Consequently, it is easy to test H_0: $\alpha = 0$ using the LM test by taking N times the uncentred R^2 of a regression of ones upon $\hat{\varepsilon}_i^G x_i'$ and $(\hat{\varepsilon}_i^G \cdot x_i'\hat{\beta})z_i'$. Again, the test statistic has an asymptotic Chi-squared distribution with J degrees of freedom (the dimension of z_i). Because of the normalization (the variance is not estimated), z_i should not include a constant. Also, note that $\sum_i \hat{\varepsilon}_i^G \cdot x_i'\hat{\beta} = 0$ by construction because of the first-order conditions. Although κ appears in the derivatives in (7.25), it is just a constant and therefore irrelevant in the computation of the test statistic. Consequently, the test for heteroskedasticity does not depend upon the form of the function $h(.)$, only upon the variables z_i that affect the variance (compare Newey,

[5] As the model describes the probability of $y_i = 1$ for a given set of x_i variables, the variables determining the variance of ε_i should be in this conditioning set as well. This means that z_i is a subset of (functions of) x_i. Note that it is possible that a priori restrictions on β are imposed to exclude some x_i variables from the 'mean' function $x_i'\beta$.

1985). This is similar to the Breusch–Pagan test for heteroskedasticity in the linear regression model, as discussed in Subsections 4.4.2 and 6.3.2.

Finally, we discuss a normality test for the probit model. For a continuously observed variable, normality tests usually check for skewness (third moment) and excess kurtosis (fourth moment), that is, they check whether $E\{\varepsilon_i^3\} = 0$ and $E\{\varepsilon_i^4 - 3\sigma^4\} = 0$ (compare Pagan and Vella, 1989). It is possible to derive tests for normality in the case with non-continuous observations in this way. Alternatively, and often equivalently, we can remain within the Lagrange multiplier framework and specify an alternative distribution that is more general than the normal, and test the restrictions implied by the latter. A parameterization of non-normality is obtained by stating that ε_i has the distribution function (compare Bera, Jarque and Lee, 1984; Ruud, 1984; or Newey, 1985)

$$P\{\varepsilon_i \leq t\} = \Phi(t + \gamma_1 t^2 + \gamma_2 t^3), \tag{7.26}$$

which characterizes the Pearson family of distributions (some restrictions on γ_1 and γ_2 apply). This class of distributions allows for skewness ($\gamma_1 \neq 0$) and excess kurtosis (fat tails) ($\gamma_2 \neq 0$) and reduces to the normal distribution if $\gamma_1 = \gamma_2 = 0$. Consequently, a test for normality is simply a test of two parametric restrictions. In the probit model the probability that $y_i = 1$ would more generally be described by

$$P\{y_i = 1|x_i\} = \Phi(x_i'\beta + \gamma_1(x_i'\beta)^2 + \gamma_2(x_i'\beta)^3). \tag{7.27}$$

This shows that a test for normality, in this case, corresponds to a test for the omitted variables $(x_i'\beta)^2$ and $(x_i'\beta)^3$. Consequently, the test statistic for the null hypothesis $\gamma_1 = \gamma_2 = 0$ is easily obtained by running an auxiliary regression of ones upon $\hat{\varepsilon}_i^G x_i'$, $\hat{\varepsilon}_i^G(x_i'\hat{\beta})^2$ and $\hat{\varepsilon}_i^G(x_i'\hat{\beta})^3$ and computing N times R^2. Under the null, the test statistic is Chi-squared distributed with two degrees of freedom. The two additional terms in the regression correspond to skewness and kurtosis, respectively.

7.1.8 Relaxing Some Assumptions in Binary Choice Models

For a given set of x_i variables a binary choice model describes the probability that $y_i = 1$ as a function of these variables. There are several ways in which the restrictions imposed by the model can be relaxed. Almost without exception, these extensions are within the class of single-index models in which there is one function of x_i that determines all probabilities (like $x_i'\beta$). First, it is straightforward, using the results of the previous subsection and analogous to linear regression models, to include nonlinear functions of x_i as additional explanatory variables. For example, if age is included in x_i, you could include age-squared as well.

Most extensions of binary choice models are motivated by the latent variable framework and relax the distributional assumptions on the error term. For example, one could allow that the error term ε_i in (7.8) is heteroskedastic. If the form of heteroskedasticity is known, say $V\{\varepsilon_i\} = \exp\{z_i'\alpha\}$, where z_i contains (functions of) elements in x_i and α is an unknown parameter vector, the essential change is that the probability that $y_i = 1$ also depends upon the error variance, that is,

$$P\{y_i = 1|x_i\} = F\left(x_i'\beta/\sqrt{\exp\{z_i'\alpha\}}\right).$$

The parameters in β and α can be estimated simultaneously by maximizing the loglikelihood function, as given in (7.24), with $h(.)$ as the exponential function. As in the standard homoskedastic case, we have to impose a normalization restriction, which is done most easily by not including an intercept term in z_i. In this case $\alpha = 0$ corresponds to $V\{\varepsilon_i\} = 1$. Alternatively, one can set one of the β coefficients equal to 1 or -1, preferably one corresponding to a variable that is 'known' to have a nonzero effect on y_i, while not imposing a restriction on the variance of ε_i. This is a common normalization constraint when a semi-parametric estimator is employed.

It is also possible to estimate the parameter vector β **semi-parametrically**, that is, without imposing distributional assumptions on the error ε_i, except that it has a median of zero and is independent of x_i. Although the interpretation of the β coefficients without a distribution function F is hard, their signs and significance are of interest. A well-known method is referred to as Manski's **maximum score estimator** (Manski, 1975, 1985). Essentially, it tries to maximize the number of correct predictions based on (7.20). This is equivalent to minimizing the number of incorrect predictions $\sum_i (y_i - \hat{y}_i)^2$ with respect to β, where $\hat{y}_i$ is defined from (7.20). Because this objective function is not differentiable with respect to β, Manski describes a numerical algorithm to solve the maximization problem. Another problem is that the rate of convergence (to get consistency) is not $\sqrt{N}$, as usual, but less ($N^{1/3}$). To some extent, both problems are solved in Horowitz's smooth maximum score estimator (Horowitz, 1992), which is based on a smoothed version of the objective function above. Additional details and discussion can be found in Horowitz (1998), Pagan and Ullah (1999, Chapter 7) and Cameron and Trivedi (2005, Section 14.7).

7.2 Multiresponse Models

In many applications, the number of alternatives that can be chosen is larger than 2. For example, we can distinguish the choice between full-time work, part-time work or not working, or the choice of a company to invest in Europe, Asia or the United States. Some quantitative variables can only be observed to lie in certain ranges. This may be because questionnaire respondents are unwilling to give precise answers, or are unable to do so, perhaps because of conceptual difficulties in answering the question. Examples of this are questions about income, the value of a house or about job or income satisfaction. Multiresponse models are developed to describe the probability of each of the possible outcomes as a function of personal or alternative specific characteristics. An important goal is to describe these probabilities with a limited number of unknown parameters and in a logically consistent way. For example, probabilities should lie between 0 and 1 and, over all alternatives, add up to 1.

An important distinction exists between ordered response models and unordered models. An ordered response model is generally more parsimonious but is only appropriate if there exists a logical ordering of the alternatives. The reason is that it assumes there is one underlying latent variable that drives the choice between the alternatives. In other words, the results will be sensitive to the ordering of the alternatives, so this ordering should make sense. Unordered models are not sensitive to the way in which the alternatives are numbered. In many cases, they can be based upon the assumption that each alternative has a utility level and that individuals choose the alternative that yields highest utility.

7.2.1 Ordered Response Models

Let us consider the choice between M alternatives, numbered from 1 to M. If there is a logical ordering in these alternatives (e.g. no car, one car, more than one car), a so-called **ordered response model** can be used. This model is also based on *one* underlying latent variable but with a different match from the latent variable, y_i^*, to the observed one ($y_i = 1, 2, \ldots, M$). Usually, one says that

$$y_i^* = x_i'\beta + \varepsilon_i \tag{7.28}$$

$$y_i = j \quad \text{if } \gamma_{j-1} < y_i^* \leq \gamma_j, \tag{7.29}$$

for unknown γ_js with $\gamma_0 = -\infty, \gamma_1 = 0$ and $\gamma_M = \infty$. Consequently, the probability that alternative j is chosen is the probability that the latent variable y_i^* is between two boundaries γ_{j-1} and γ_j. Assuming that ε_i is i.i.d. standard normal results in the **ordered probit model**. The logistic distribution gives the **ordered logit model**. For $M = 2$ we are back at the binary choice model.

Consider an example from the labour supply literature. Suppose married females answer the question 'How much would you like to work?' in three categories 'not', 'part-time' and 'full-time'. According to neoclassical theory, desired labour supply, as measured by these answers, will depend upon preferences and a budget constraint. So variables related to age, family composition, partner's income and education level could be of importance. To model the outcomes, $y_i = 1$ (not working), $y_i = 2$ (part-time working) and $y_i = 3$ (full-time working), we note that there appears to be a logical ordering in these answers. To be precise, the question is whether it is reasonable to assume that there exists a single index $x_i'\beta$ such that higher values for this index correspond to, on average, larger values for y_i. If this is the case, we can write an ordered response model as

$$y_i^* = x_i'\beta + \varepsilon_i \tag{7.30}$$

$$\begin{aligned} y_i &= 1 \quad \text{if } y_i^* \leq 0, \\ &= 2 \quad \text{if } 0 < y_i^* \leq \gamma, \\ &= 3 \quad \text{if } y_i^* > \gamma, \end{aligned} \tag{7.31}$$

where we can loosely interpret y_i^* as 'willingness to work' or 'desired hours of work'. One of the boundaries is normalized to zero, which fixes the location, but we also need a normalization on the scale of y_i^*. The most natural one is that ε_i has a fixed variance. In the ordered probit model this means that ε_i is $NID(0, 1)$. The implied probabilities are obtained as

$$P\{y_i = 1|x_i\} = P\{y_i^* \leq 0|x_i\} = \Phi(-x_i'\beta),$$

$$P\{y_i = 3|x_i\} = P\{y_i^* > \gamma|x_i\} = 1 - \Phi(\gamma - x_i'\beta)$$

and

$$P\{y_i = 2|x_i\} = \Phi(\gamma - x_i'\beta) - \Phi(-x_i'\beta),$$

where γ is an unknown parameter that is estimated jointly with β. Estimation is based upon maximum likelihood, where the above probabilities enter the likelihood function. The interpretation of the β coefficients is in terms of the underlying latent variable model (e.g. a positive β means that the corresponding variable increases a woman's willingness to work), or in terms of the effects on the respective probabilities, as we have seen for the binary choice model in Subsection 7.1.2. Suppose that the kth coefficient in (7.30) is positive ($\beta_k > 0$). This means that the latent variable y_i^* increases if x_{ik} increases. Accordingly, the probability that $y_i = 3$ will increase, while the probability that $y_i = 1$ will decrease. The effect on the intermediate categories, however, is ambiguous; the probability that $y_i = 2$ may increase or decrease.

7.2.2 About Normalization

To illustrate the different normalization constraints that are required, let us consider a model where such constraints are not imposed. That is,

$$\begin{aligned} y_i^* &= \beta_1 + x_i'\beta + \varepsilon_i, \quad \varepsilon_i \sim NID(0, \sigma^2), \\ y_i &= 1 \quad \text{if } y_i^* \leq \gamma_1 \\ &= 2 \quad \text{if } \gamma_1 < y_i^* \leq \gamma_2 \\ &= 3 \quad \text{if } y_i^* > \gamma_2, \end{aligned}$$

where the constant is taken out of the x_i vector. As we can only observe whether y_i is 1, 2 or 3, the only elements that the data can identify are the probabilities of these three events, for given values of x_i. Not accidentally, these are exactly the probabilities that enter the likelihood function. To illustrate this, consider the probability that $y_i = 1$ (given x_i), given by

$$P\{y_i = 1|x_i\} = P\{\beta_1 + x_i'\beta + \varepsilon_i \leq \gamma_1|x_i\} = \Phi\left(\frac{\gamma_1 - \beta_1}{\sigma} - x_i'\left(\frac{\beta}{\sigma}\right)\right),$$

which shows that varying β, β_1, σ and γ_1 does not lead to a different probability as long as β/σ and $(\gamma_1 - \beta_1)/\sigma$ remain the same. This reflects an identification problem: different combinations of parameter values lead to the same loglikelihood value and there is no unique maximum. To circumvent this problem, normalization constraints are imposed. The standard model imposes that $\sigma = 1$ and $\gamma_1 = 0$, but, as shown in Subsection 7.2.3, it is also possible to set $\sigma = 1$ and $\beta_1 = 0$. The interpretation of the coefficients is conditional upon a particular normalization constraint, but the probabilities are insensitive to it. In some applications, the boundaries correspond to observed values rather than unknown parameters and it is possible to estimate the variance of ε_i. This is illustrated in Subsection 7.2.4.

7.2.3 Illustration: Explaining Firms' Credit Ratings

Standard and Poor's is one of the leading institutions that provide credit ratings for companies. A credit rating reflects the opinion of a firm's overall creditworthiness and its capacity to satisfy its financial obligations, and plays an important role in the pricing of credit risk. For example, the cost of debt financing varies widely with a firm's credit rating. Standard and Poor's ratings range from AAA (highest rating) to D (lowest rating). We group these debt ratings into seven categories, indexed by a score of 1 (lowest) to 7 (highest); see Ashbaugh-Skaife, Collins and LaFond (2006).

In this illustration, we consider a sample of 921 US firms and try to explain their credit score in 2005 from a set of firm characteristics. The explanatory variables we employ are based on Altman and Rijken (2004) and include working capital of the firm, retained earnings, earnings before interest and taxes (*ebit*), book leverage and log sales (as a proxy for firm size). The first three variables are scaled by total assets. Working capital is a proxy for the short-term liquidity of a firm, retained earnings proxies for historic profitability, while *ebit* proxies for current profitability. Firm size is included because larger firms face lower risk and thus are expected to have higher credit ratings. A firm's book leverage is defined as the ratio of the firm's (book value of) debt to assets. All data are taken from Compustat.

In addition to the debt ratings with seven categories, we also employ an alternative classification scheme that partitions credit ratings into two categories: investment grade and speculative grade (see Ashbaugh-Skaife, Collins and LaFond, 2006). A speculative grade is obtained when the debt rating score is 3 or less (corresponding to a Standard and Poor's credit rating of BB+ or less). Because many bond portfolio managers are not allowed to invest in speculative grade bonds, firms with a speculative rating incur significant costs. Table 7.4 presents some summary statistics for our sample. The average firm has a leverage of 0.293, which indicates that it is financed for 29.3% with debt. Of the 921 firms, only 47.2% have an investment grade rating in 2005. The credit rating varies from 1 to 7, with an average of 3.499 and a median of 3.

We estimate two discrete choice models: an ordered model explaining a firm's credit rating (from 1 to 7), and a binary model explaining the investment grade indicator. Following the majority of the literature in this field, we use a logit specification for both. The results are presented in Table 7.5. Note that both models are consistent with a latent variable equation of the form

$$y_i^* = \beta_1 + x_i'\beta + \varepsilon_i,$$

where ε_i has a logistic distribution, and where the observed variable is either $y_i = I(y_i^* > 0)$ or the discrete variable $y_i = 1, 2, \dots, 7$, corresponding to $y_i^* < \gamma_1$, $\gamma_1 \le y_i^* < \gamma_2, \dots$ and $y_i^* \ge \gamma_6$, respectively. The normalization constraint in the ordered logit model is $\beta_1 = 0$.[6] The coefficient estimates for the five explanatory variables are reasonably

Table 7.4 Summary statistics

	average	median	minimum	maximum
credit rating	3.499	3	1	7
investment grade	0.472	0	0	1
book leverage	0.293	0.264	0.000	0.999
working capital/total assets	0.140	0.123	−0.412	0.748
retained earnings/total assets	0.157	0.180	−0.996	0.980
earnings before interest and taxes/total assets	0.094	0.090	−0.384	0.652
log sales	7.996	7.884	1.100	12.701

[6] The estimation results in Table 7.5 are obtained with Eviews. Other programmes may impose a different normalization constraint (e.g. $\gamma_1 = 0$).

similar across the two models, as well as their statistical significance. With the exception of the working capital variable, all coefficient estimates have the expected sign. The results indicate that larger firms have significantly better credit ratings than smaller firms, ceteris paribus. Higher earnings before interest and taxes as well as higher retained earnings also improve credit ratings. A higher leverage, meaning that a firm is financed relatively more with debt, reduces the expected credit rating. Note that the ordered logit exploits more detailed information about the latent variable and can therefore be expected to yield more efficient estimates than the binary logit model. This is confirmed by the standard errors in Table 7.5.

The likelihood functions are not directly comparable across the two models (because the dependent variable is different), nor are the McFadden R^2s (computed using (7.18) for both models). The likelihood ratio tests strongly reject the hypothesis that all five slope coefficients are jointly equal to zero. To compare the two models, we can compare the implied probability of a given firm to obtain an investment grade rating (i.e. a rating of 4 or more). For the ordered logit model, this probability is given by

$$P\{y_i^* \geq \gamma_3 | x_i\} = P\{\varepsilon_i \geq \gamma_3 - x_i'\beta | x_i\} = \frac{1}{1 + \exp\{\gamma_3 - x_i'\beta\}},$$

where the latter equality follows from the logistic distributional assumption. For the binary logit model, the probability of achieving an investment-grade credit rating is

$$P\{y_i^* \geq 0 | x_i\} = P\{\varepsilon_i \geq -\beta_1 - x_i'\beta | x_i\} = \frac{1}{1 + \exp\{-\beta_1 - x_i'\beta\}}.$$

These two expressions explain why the estimate of γ_3 in the ordered model is close to that of $-\beta_1$ in the binary model.

To obtain some intuition of the economic magnitude of the effects described by the coefficients in Table 7.5, consider what happens for the average firm if its book leverage

Table 7.5 Estimation results binary and ordered logit, MLE

	Binary logit			Ordered logit	
	Estimate	Standard error		Estimate	Standard error
constant	−8.214	0.867		–	–
book leverage	−4.427	0.771		−2.752	0.477
ebit/ta	4.355	1.440		4.731	0.945
log *sales*	1.082	0.096		0.941	0.059
re/ta	4.116	0.489		3.560	0.302
wk/ta	−4.012	0.748		−2.580	0.483
			γ_1	−0.369	0.633
			γ_2	4.881	0.521
			γ_3	7.626	0.551
			γ_4	9.885	0.592
			γ_5	12.883	0.673
			γ_6	14.783	0.784
loglikelihood	−341.08			−965.31	
McFadden R^2	0.465			0.309	
LR test (χ_5^2)	591.8 ($p = 0.000$)			862.9 ($p = 0.000$)	

changes from the 25th to the 75th percentile of the distribution, while holding all other variables fixed at their sample average. For the binary choice model the estimated probability of obtaining an investment grade rating decreases from 54.3% to 31.2%; for the ordered logit, the probability decreases from 51.7% to 37.0%. This means that firms with high leverage face substantially higher costs of debt financing.

7.2.4 Illustration: Willingness to Pay for Natural Areas

An interesting problem in public economics is how to determine the value of a good that is not traded. For example, what is the economic value of a public good like a forest or 'clean air'? In this subsection we consider an example from the contingent valuation literature. In this field, surveys are used to elicit willingness to pay (WTP) values for a hypothetical change in the availability of some nonmarket good, for example a forest. Since the extensive study to measure the welfare loss to US citizens as a result of the massive oil spill due to the grounding of the oil tanker Exxon Valdez in the Gulf of Alaska (March 1989), the contingent valuation method plays an important role in measuring the benefits of a wide range of environmental goods.[7]

In this subsection, we consider a survey that was conducted in 1997 in Portugal. The survey responses capture how much individuals are willing to pay to avoid the commercial and tourism development of the Alentejo Natural Park in southwest Portugal.[8] To find out what an individual's WTP was, it was not directly asked what amount a person would be willing to pay to preserve the park. Instead, each individual i in the sample was faced with a (potentially) different initial bid amount B_i^I and asked whether he or she would be willing to pay this amount or not. The interviewers used a so-called double-bounded procedure: each person was asked about a follow-up bid that was higher (lower) if the initial bid had been accepted (rejected). For each respondent we thus have an initial bid B_i^I and one of the follow-up bids B_i^L or B_i^U, where $B_i^L < B_i^I < B_i^U$. Each person in the sample faced a random initial bid, and the follow-up bid was dependent on this amount according to the following scheme (in euro):

	Initial bid	Increased bid	Decreased bid
Scheme 1	6	18	3
Scheme 2	12	24	6
Scheme 3	24	48	12
Scheme 4	48	120	24

A person's willingness to pay is unobserved and will be denoted by the latent variable B_i^*. To model how B_i^* varies with personal characteristics x_i, we may want to specify a linear relationship

$$B_i^* = x_i'\beta + \varepsilon_i, \tag{7.32}$$

[7] A nontechnical discussion of contingent valuation is given in Portney (1994), Hanemann (1994) and Diamond and Hausman (1994).

[8] I am grateful to Paulo Nunes for providing the data used in this subsection.

where ε_i is an unobserved error term, independent of x_i. Four possible outcomes can be observed, indexed by $y_i = 1, 2, 3, 4$. In particular,

$y_i = 1$ if both bids get rejected ($B_i^* < B_i^L$);

$y_i = 2$ if the first bid gets rejected and the second gets accepted ($B_i^L \leq B_i^* < B_i^I$);

$y_i = 3$ if the first gets accepted while the second gets rejected ($B_i^I \leq B_i^* < B_i^U$);

$y_i = 4$ if both bids get accepted ($B_i^* \geq B_i^U$).

If we assume that ε_i is $NID(0, \sigma^2)$, the above setting corresponds to an ordered probit model. Unlike in the previous subsection, the boundaries B_i^L, B_i^I and B_i^U are observed, so that no normalization is needed on σ^2 and it can be estimated. Note that in this application the latent variable B_i^* has the clear interpretation of a person's willingness to pay, measured in euros. Under the above assumptions, the probability of observing the last outcome ($y_i = 4$) is given by[9]

$$P\{y_i = 4|x_i\} = P\{x_i'\beta + \varepsilon_i \geq B_i^U|x_i\} = 1 - \Phi\left(\frac{B_i^U - x_i'\beta}{\sigma}\right). \tag{7.33}$$

Similarly, the probability of observing the second outcome is

$$\begin{aligned} P\{y_i = 2|x_i\} &= P\{B_i^L \leq x_i'\beta + \varepsilon_i < B_i^I|x_i\} \\ &= \Phi\left(\frac{B_i^I - x_i'\beta}{\sigma}\right) - \Phi\left(\frac{B_i^L - x_i'\beta}{\sigma}\right). \end{aligned} \tag{7.34}$$

The other two probabilities can be derived along the same lines. These probabilities directly enter the loglikelihood function, maximization of which yields consistent estimators for β and σ^2 (under standard assumptions).

The first model we estimate contains an intercept only. This is of interest as it can be interpreted as describing the (unconditional) distribution of the willingness to pay in the population. The second model includes three explanatory variables that may affect people's WTP, corresponding to age, gender and income. Consequently, we estimate two different models using maximum likelihood, one with an intercept only and one that includes variables for age, income and gender. The results are presented in Table 7.6. In the subsample that we use, a total of $N = 312$ people were interviewed, of which 123 (39%) answered no to both bids, 18 answered no–yes, 113 yes–no and 58 answered yes to both questions.

From the model with an intercept only we see that the estimated average WTP is almost 19 euros, with a fairly large standard deviation of 38.6 euros. Because we assumed that the distribution of B_i^* is normal, this implies that 31% of the population have a negative willingness to pay.[10] As this is not possible, we will reinterpret the latent variable as

[9] As B_i^* is continuously distributed, the probability of each outcome is zero. This implies that the places of the equality signs in the inequalities are irrelevant.

[10] Note that $P\{B_i^* < 0\} = \Phi(-\mu/\sigma)$ if B_i^* is normally distributed with mean μ and standard deviation σ. Substituting the estimated values gives a probability of 0.31.

Table 7.6 Ordered probit model for willingness to pay

	I: intercept only		II: with characteristics	
Variable	Estimate	Standard error	Estimate	Standard error
constant	18.74	(2.77)	30.55	(8.59)
age class	–		−6.93	(1.64)
female	–		−5.88	(5.07)
income class	–		4.86	(1.87)
$\hat{\sigma}$	38.61	(2.11)	36.47	(1.89)
Loglikelihood	−409.00		−391.25	
Normality test (χ_2^2)	6.326	($p = 0.042$)	2.419	($p = 0.298$)

'desired WTP', the actual WTP being the maximum of zero and the desired amount.[11] In this case, actual willingness to pay, given that it is positive, is described by a truncated normal distribution, the expected value of which is estimated to be €38.69.[12] The estimate for the expected WTP over the entire sample is then $38.69 \times 0.69 = 26.55$ euros, because 31% have a zero willingness to pay. Multiplying this by the total number of households in the population (about 3 million) produces an estimated total willingness to pay of about 80 million euros.

The inclusion of personal characteristics is not very helpful in eliminating the problem of negative values for B_i^*. Apparently, there is a relatively large group of people that say no to both bids, such that the imposed normal distribution generates substantial probability mass in the negative region. The explanatory variables that are included are age, in six brackets ($< 29, 29–39, \ldots, > 69$), a female dummy and income (in eight brackets). With the inclusion of these variables, the intercept term no longer has the same interpretation as before. Now, for example, the expected willingness to pay for a male in income class 1 ($<$ €375 per month) and aged between 20 and 29 is $30.55 - 6.93 + 4.86 = 28.48$ euros, or, taking into account the censoring, 33.01 euros. We see that the WTP significantly decreases with age and increases with income, whereas there is no statistical evidence of a gender effect.

As in the binary probit model, the assumption of normality is crucial here for consistency of the estimators as well as the interpretation of the parameter estimates (in terms of expected WTP). A test for normality can be computed within the Lagrange multiplier framework discussed in Section 6.2. As before, the alternative is that the appropriate distribution is within the Pearson family of distributions and a test for normality tests two parametric restrictions. Unfortunately, the analytical expressions are rather complicated and will not be presented here (see Glewwe, 1997). Under the null hypothesis of normality, the test statistics have a Chi-squared distribution with two degrees of freedom. The two statistics in the table indicate a marginal rejection of normality in the simple model with an intercept only, but do not lead to rejection of the normality assumption in the extended model.

[11] This interpretation is similar to the one employed in tobit models. See Section 7.4.

[12] If $y \sim \mathcal{N}(\mu, \sigma^2)$, we have that $E\{y|y > c\} = \mu + \sigma\lambda([c - \mu]/\sigma)$, where $\lambda(t) = \phi(-t)/\Phi(-t) \geq 0$. See Appendix B for details.

7.2.5 Multinomial Models

In several cases, there is no natural ordering in the alternatives, and it is not realistic to assume that there is a monotonic relationship between one underlying latent variable and the observed outcomes. Consider, for example, modelling the mode of transportation (bus, train, car, bicycle, walking). In such cases, an alternative framework has to be used to put some structure on the different probabilities. A common starting point is a random utility framework, in which the utility of each alternative is a linear function of observed characteristics (individual and/or alternative specific) plus an additive unobservable disturbance term. Individuals are assumed to choose the alternative that has the highest utility. With appropriate distributional assumptions on the disturbance terms, this approach leads to manageable expressions for the probabilities implied by the model.

To formalize this, suppose there is a choice between M alternatives, indexed $j = 1, 2, \ldots, M$, noting that the order is arbitrary. Next, assume that the utility level that individual i attaches to each of the alternatives is given by U_{ij}, $j = 1, 2, \ldots, M$. Then alternative j is chosen by individual i if it gives highest utility, that is, if $U_{ij} = \max\{U_{i1}, \ldots, U_{iM}\}$. Of course, these utility levels are not observed, and we need to make some additional assumptions to make this set-up operational. Let us assume that $U_{ij} = \mu_{ij} + \varepsilon_{ij}$, where μ_{ij} is a nonstochastic function of observables and a small number of unknown parameters, and ε_{ij} is an unobservable error term. From this, it follows that

$$\begin{aligned} P\{y_i = j\} &= P\{U_{ij} = \max\{U_{i1}, \ldots, U_{iM}\}\} \\ &= P\left\{\mu_{ij} + \varepsilon_{ij} > \max_{k=1,\ldots,M,\ k\neq j} \{\mu_{ik} + \varepsilon_{ik}\}\right\}. \end{aligned} \tag{7.35}$$

To evaluate this probability, we need to be able to say something about the maximum of a number of random variables. In general, this is complicated, but a very convenient result arises if we can assume that all ε_{ij} are mutually independent with a so-called log Weibull distribution (also known as a type I extreme value distribution). In this case, the distribution function of each ε_{ij} is given by

$$F(t) = \exp\{-e^{-t}\}, \tag{7.36}$$

which does not involve unknown parameters. Under these assumptions, it can be shown that

$$P\{y_i = j\} = \frac{\exp\{\mu_{ij}\}}{\exp\{\mu_{i1}\} + \exp\{\mu_{i2}\} + \cdots + \exp\{\mu_{iM}\}}.$$

Notice that this structure automatically implies that $0 \leq P\{y_i = j\} \leq 1$ and that $\sum_{j=1}^{M} P\{y_i = j\} = 1$.

The distribution of ε_{ij} sets the scaling of utility (which is undefined) but not the location. To solve this, it is common to normalize one of the deterministic utility levels to zero, say $\mu_{i1} = 0$. Usually, μ_{ij} is assumed to be a linear function of observable variables, which may depend upon the individual (i), the alternative (j) or both. Thus we write $\mu_{ij} = x_{ij}'\beta$. With this we obtain

$$P\{y_i = j\} = \frac{\exp\{x_{ij}'\beta\}}{1 + \exp\{x_{i2}'\beta\} + \cdots + \exp\{x_{iM}'\beta\}}, \quad j = 1, 2, \ldots, M. \tag{7.37}$$

This constitutes the so-called **conditional logit model**. In this model the probability of an individual choosing alternative j is a simple function of the explanatory variables, by virtue of the convenient assumptions made about the distribution of the unobservables in (7.35). Typical things to include in $x_{ij}'\beta$ are alternative-specific characteristics. When explaining the mode of transportation, this may include variables like travelling time and costs, which may vary from one person to another. A negative β coefficient then means that the utility of an alternative is reduced if travelling time is increased. Consequently, if travelling time of one of the alternatives is reduced (while the other alternatives are not affected), this alternative will get a higher probability of being picked.

In some applications, we may observe the characteristics of the decision-makers, for example their age, gender and income. In this case, it is appropriate to reformulate the above model imposing $\mu_{ij} = x_i'\beta_j$, where x_i is a K-dimensional vector containing the characteristics of individual i (including an intercept term) and β_j denotes a vector of alternative-specific coefficients. Imposing $\mu_{i1} = 0$ as before, this leads to

$$P\{y_i = j\} = \frac{\exp\{x_i'\beta_j\}}{1 + \exp\{x_i'\beta_2\} + \cdots + \exp\{x_i'\beta_M\}}, \quad j = 1, 2, \ldots, M, \tag{7.38}$$

with $\beta_1 = 0$. This model is typically referred to as the **multinomial logit model**. In this case we estimate $K - 1$ slope coefficients plus an intercept term for all but one of the alternatives. It is also possible to combine individual-specific and alternative-specific variables in the model, leading to the mixed logit model. Often, authors refer to all three cases as the multinomial logit model. If there are only two alternatives ($M = 2$), these models reduce to the standard binary logit model.

The conditional logit and multinomial logit model are estimated by maximum likelihood, where the probabilities of the observed outcomes enter the loglikelihood function. Under regularity conditions, and assuming that the model is correctly specified, this provides consistent, efficient and asymptotically normal estimators for the β coefficients. Despite the attractiveness of the analytical expressions given in (7.37) and (7.38), these models have one big drawback, which is due to the assumption that all ε_{ij}s are independent. This implies that (conditional upon observed characteristics) utility levels of any two alternatives are independent. This is particularly troublesome if two or more alternatives are very similar. A typical example would be to decompose the category 'travel by bus' into 'travel by blue bus' and 'travel by red bus'. Clearly, we would expect that a high utility for a red bus implies a high utility for a blue bus. Another way to see the problem is to note that the probability ratio of two alternatives does not depend upon the nature of any of the other alternatives. Suppose that alternative 1 denotes travel by car and alternative 2 denotes travel by (blue) bus. Then the probability ratio (or odds ratio) is given by

$$\frac{P\{y_i = 2\}}{P\{y_i = 1\}} = \exp\{x_{i2}'\beta\} \tag{7.39}$$

irrespective of whether the third alternative is a red bus or a train. Clearly, this is something undesirable. McFadden (1974) called this property of the multinomial logit model **independence of irrelevant alternatives** (IIA). Hausman and McFadden (1984) propose a test for the IIA restriction based on the result that the model parameters can be estimated consistently by applying a multinomial logit model to any subset of alternatives (see Franses and Paap, 2001, Section 5.3, for details). The test compares the estimates from the model with all alternatives to estimates using a subset of alternatives.

Let us consider a simple example from marketing that involves stated preferences (rather than observed choices). Suppose that a number of respondents are asked to pick their preferred coffee-maker from a set of five, say, alternative combinations of characteristics (capacity, price, special filter (yes/no) and thermos flask (yes/no)). Typically, the combinations are not the same for all respondents. Let us refer to these characteristics as x_{ij}. To make sure that $\mu_{i1} = 0$, the x_{ij} are measured in differences from a reference coffee-maker, which without loss of generality corresponds to alternative 1. The probability that a respondent selects alternative j can be (assumed to be) described by a multinomial logit model, with

$$P\{y_i = j\} = \frac{\exp\{x_{ij}'\beta\}}{1 + \exp\{x_{i2}'\beta\} + \cdots + \exp\{x_{i5}'\beta\}}. \tag{7.40}$$

A positive β coefficient implies that people attach positive utility to the corresponding characteristic.

Under appropriate assumptions, the estimated model can be used to predict the probability of an individual choosing an alternative that is not yet on the market, provided this alternative is a (new) combination of existing characteristics. To illustrate this, suppose the current market for coffee-makers consists of two products: a machine for 10 cups without filter and thermos for 25 euros (z_1) and a machine for 15 cups with filter for 35 euros (z_2), while brand X is considering to introduce a new product: a machine for 12 cups with filter and thermos for 33 euros (z_3). If the respondents are representative of those who buy coffee-makers, the expected market share of this new product corresponds to the probability of preferring the new machine to the two existing ones, and could be estimated as

$$\frac{\exp\{(z_3 - z_1)'\hat{\beta}\}}{1 + \exp\{(z_2 - z_1)'\hat{\beta}\} + \exp\{(z_3 - z_1)'\hat{\beta}\}},$$

where $\hat{\beta}$ is the maximum likelihood estimate for β. In fact, it would be possible to select an optimal combination of characteristics in z_3 so as to maximize this estimated market share.[13]

Although it is possible to relax the IIA property, this generally leads to (conceptually and computationally) more complicated models (see, e.g., Amemiya, 1981, or Maddala, 1983). Jones and Hensher (2007) examine three advanced logit models that may overcome the drawbacks of the standard multinomial logit model, and compare the empirical performance of these models in the context of corporate takeover prediction. In some applications, the choice between M alternatives can be decomposed into two or more sequential choices. A popular specification is the **nested logit model**, which is appropriate if the alternatives can be divided into S groups, where the IIA assumption holds within each group but not across groups. To illustrate this, suppose the three relevant alternatives in the mode of transportation example are: travel by car, train or bus. We may divide these alternatives into private and public modes of transportation. Then the first choice is between private and public, while the second one is between train and bus, conditional

[13] This example is clearly oversimplified. In marketing applications the property of independence of irrelevant alternatives is often considered unsatisfactory. Moreover, the model does not take into account observed and unobserved heterogeneity across consumers. See Louviere (1988) or Carroll and Green (1995) for some additional discussion.

upon the first choice being public transport. It is possible to model these two choices by two (bivariate) logit models; see Franses and Paap (2001, Section 5.1), Cameron and Trivedi (2005, Section 15.6) or Wooldridge (2010, Section 16.2) for more details.

7.3 Models for Count Data

In certain applications, we would like to explain the number of times a given event occurs, for example, how often a consumer visits a supermarket in a given week, or the number of patents a firm has obtained in a given year. Clearly, the outcome might be zero for a substantial part of the population. While the outcomes are discrete and ordered, there are two important differences with ordered response outcomes. First, the values of the outcome have a cardinal rather than just an ordinal meaning (4 is twice as much as 2 and 2 is twice as much as 1). Second, there (often) is no natural upper bound to the outcomes. As a result, models for count data are very different from ordered response models.

7.3.1 The Poisson and Negative Binomial Models

Let us denote the outcome variable by y_i, taking values $0, 1, 2, \ldots$. Our goal is to explain the distribution of y_i, or the expected value of y_i, given a set of characteristics x_i. Let us assume that the expected value of y_i, given x_i, is given by

$$E\{y_i|x_i\} = \exp\{x_i'\beta\}, \qquad (7.41)$$

where β is a set of unknown parameters. Because y_i is non-negative, we choose a functional form that produces non-negative conditional expectations. The above assumption relates the expected outcome of y_i to the individual characteristics in x_i, but does not fully describe the distribution. If we want to determine the probability of a given outcome (e.g. $P\{y_i = 1|x_i\}$), additional assumptions are necessary.

A common assumption in count data models is that, for given x_i, the count variable y_i has a **Poisson distribution** with expectation $\lambda_i \equiv \exp\{x_i'\beta\}$. This implies that the probability mass function of y_i conditional upon x_i is given by

$$P\{y_i = y|x_i\} = \frac{\exp\{-\lambda_i\}\lambda_i^y}{y!}, \quad y = 0, 1, 2, \ldots, \qquad (7.42)$$

where $y!$ is short-hand notation for $y \times (y-1) \times \cdots \times 2 \times 1$ (referred to as 'y factorial'), with $0! = 1$. Substituting the appropriate functional form for λ_i produces expressions for the probabilities that can be used to construct the loglikelihood function for this model, referred to as the **Poisson regression model**. Assuming that observations on different individuals are mutually independent, estimation of β by means of maximum likelihood is therefore reasonably simple: the loglikelihood function is the sum of the appropriate log probabilities, interpreted as a function of β. If the Poisson distribution is correct, and assuming we have a random sample of y_i and x_i, this produces a consistent, asymptotically efficient and asymptotically normal estimator for β.

To illustrate the above probabilities, consider an individual characterized by $\lambda_i = 2$. For this person, the probabilities of observing $y_i = 0, 1, 2, 3$ are given by 0.135, 0.271, 0.271 and 0.180, respectively (such that the probability of observing four or more events is 0.143). The expected value of y_i corresponds to the weighted average of all outcomes, weighted by their respective probabilities, and is equal to $\lambda_i = 2$. The specification in (7.41) and (7.42) allows λ_i and the probabilities to vary with x_i. In particular, the parameters in β indicate how the expected value of y_i varies with x_i (taking into account the exponential function). For an individual with expected value $\lambda_i = 3$, the probabilities of $y_i = 0, 1, 2, 3$ change to 0.050, 0.149, 0.224 and 0.224 respectively (with a probability of 0.353 of observing four or more).

An important drawback of the Poisson distribution is that it automatically implies that the conditional variance of y_i is also equal to λ_i. That is, in addition to (7.41), the assumption in (7.42) implies that

$$V\{y_i|x_i\} = \exp\{x_i'\beta\}. \tag{7.43}$$

This condition is referred to as **equidispersion** and illustrates the restrictive nature of the Poisson distribution. In many applications, the equality of the conditional mean and variance of the distribution has been rejected. A wide range of alternative count distributions have been proposed that do not impose (7.43); see Winkelmann (2010) or Cameron and Trivedi (2013) for an overview. Alternatively, it is possible to obtain a consistent estimator for the conditional mean in (7.41) without specifying the conditional distribution, like we did in (7.42). In fact, the Poisson regression model is able to do so even if the Poisson distribution is invalid. This is because the first-order conditions of the maximum likelihood problem are valid more generally, so that we can obtain a consistent estimator for β using the quasi-maximum likelihood approach, as discussed in Section 6.4 (see Wooldridge, 2010, Section 18.2). This means that we solve the usual maximum likelihood problem but adjust the way in which standard errors are computed. Several software packages provide computation of such 'robust' or 'sandwich' standard errors.

To illustrate the (quasi-) maximum likelihood approach, consider the loglikelihood function of the Poisson regression model (assuming a random sample of size N), given by

$$\begin{aligned}\log L(\beta) &= \sum_{i=1}^{N}[-\lambda_i + y_i \log \lambda_i - \log y_i!] \\ &= \sum_{i=1}^{N}[-\exp\{x_i'\beta\} + y_i(x_i'\beta) - \log y_i!].\end{aligned} \tag{7.44}$$

The last term in square brackets is typically dropped, because it does not depend upon the unknown parameters. The first-order conditions of maximizing $\log L(\beta)$ with respect to β are given by

$$\sum_{i=1}^{N}(y_i - \exp\{x_i'\beta\})x_i = \sum_{i=1}^{N} \varepsilon_i x_i = 0, \tag{7.45}$$

where the first equality defines the error term $\varepsilon_i = y_i - \exp\{x_i'\beta\}$. Because (7.41) implies that $E\{\varepsilon_i|x_i\} = 0$, we can interpret (7.45) as the sample moment conditions corresponding to the set of orthogonality conditions $E\{\varepsilon_i x_i\} = 0$. As a result, the estimator that maximizes (7.44) is generally consistent under condition (7.41), even if y_i given x_i does not have a Poisson distribution. In this case, we refer to the estimator as a quasi-maximum likelihood estimator (QMLE).

Using (7.44), and from the general discussion on maximum likelihood estimation in Section 6.1, we can easily derive the asymptotic covariance matrix of the ML estimator. In the i.i.d. case, it is given by

$$V_{MLE} = I(\beta)^{-1} = (E\{\exp\{x_i'\beta\}x_ix_i'\})^{-1}. \tag{7.46}$$

However, for the quasi-maximum likelihood estimator $\hat{\beta}_{QMLE}$, it follows from the results in Section 6.4 that the appropriate asymptotic covariance matrix is

$$V_{QMLE} = I(\beta)^{-1}J(\beta)I(\beta)^{-1}, \tag{7.47}$$

where

$$J(\beta) = E\{[y_i - \exp\{x_i'\beta\}]^2 x_ix_i'\} = E\{\varepsilon_i^2 x_ix_i'\}. \tag{7.48}$$

These covariance matrices can easily be estimated by replacing expectations with sample averages and unknown parameters with their ML estimates. The QMLE covariance matrix is similar to the White covariance matrix used for the linear regression model. If

$$V\{y_i|x_i\} = E\{\varepsilon_i^2|x_i\} > \exp\{x_i'\beta\},$$

we have a case of **overdispersion**, a situation that is often encountered in practice. In such a case, it follows from (7.47) and (7.48) that the variance of the quasi-maximum likelihood estimator may be much larger than suggested by (7.46).

Despite its robustness, a disadvantage of the quasi-maximum likelihood approach is that it does not allow computing of conditional probabilities, as in (7.42). All we impose and estimate is (7.41). Consequently, it is not possible to determine, for example, what the probability is that a given firm has zero patents in a given year, conditional upon its characteristics, unless we are willing to make additional assumptions. Of course, from (7.41) we can determine what the *expected number* of patents is for the above firm. Alternative more general count data models are therefore useful. One alternative is the application of a full maximum likelihood analysis of the NegBin I model of Cameron and Trivedi (1986). NegBin I is a special case of the negative binomial distribution. It imposes that

$$V\{y_i|x_i\} = (1 + \delta^2)\exp\{x_i'\beta\} \tag{7.49}$$

for some $\delta^2 > 0$ to be estimated. As a result, the NegBin I model allows for overdispersion (relative to the Poisson regression model). Unfortunately, the NegBin I maximum likelihood estimators are consistent only if (7.49) is valid and thus do not have the robustness property of the (quasi-) maximum likelihood estimators of the Poisson model. If (7.49) is valid, the NegBin I estimates are more efficient than the Poisson estimates. A further generalization is the NegBin II model, which assumes

$$V\{y_i|x_i\} = (1 + \alpha^2\exp\{x_i'\beta\})\exp\{x_i'\beta\}, \tag{7.50}$$

for some $\alpha^2 > 0$, where the amount of overdispersion is increasing with the conditional mean $E\{y_i|x_i\} = \exp\{x_i'\beta\}$; see Cameron and Trivedi (1986) for more details. In many software packages, the NegBin II model is referred to as the 'negative binomial model'. The NegBin I model is quite popular in the statistics literature, because it is a special case of the 'generalized linear model' (see Cameron and Trivedi, 2013, Section 2.4). Unlike the NegBin I model, the maximum likelihood estimator for the NegBin II model is robust to distributional misspecification. Thus, provided the conditional mean is correctly specified, the NegBin II maximum likelihood estimator is consistent for β. The associated maximum likelihood standard errors, however, will only be correct if the distribution is correctly specified (see Cameron and Trivedi, 2013, Subsection 3.3.4).

Given that maximum likelihood estimation of the negative binomial models is fairly easy using standard software, a test of the Poisson distribution is often carried out by testing $\delta^2 = 0$ or $\alpha^2 = 0$ using a Wald or likelihood ratio test. Rejection is an indication of overdispersion. The alternative hypotheses are one-sided and given by $\delta^2 > 0$ and $\alpha^2 > 0$, respectively. Because δ^2 and α^2 cannot be negative, the distribution of the Wald and LR test statistics is nonstandard (see Cameron and Trivedi, 2013, Section 3.4). In practice, this problem only affects the appropriate critical values. Rather than using the 95% critical value for the Chi-squared distribution, one should use the 90% percentile to test with 95% confidence. That is, the null hypothesis of no overdispersion is rejected with 95% confidence if the test statistic exceeds 2.71 (rather than 3.84).

All three models presented above state that the variance of y_i is larger if the expected value of y_i is larger. The Poisson model is very restrictive in that it imposes that the variance and the mean are equal. The NegBin I model allows the variance to exceed the mean, but imposes that their ratio is the same for all observations (and equals $1 + \delta^2$). The NegBin II model allows the variance to exceed the mean, their ratio being larger for units that have a high mean. In this case, the amount of overdispersion increases with the conditional mean.

The easiest way to interpret the coefficients in count data models is through the conditional expectation in (7.41). Suppose that x_{ik} is a continuous explanatory variable. The impact of a marginal change in x_{ik} upon the expected value of y_i (keeping all other variables fixed) is given by

$$\frac{\partial E\{y_i|x_i\}}{\partial x_{ik}} = \exp\{x_i'\beta\}\beta_k, \tag{7.51}$$

which has the same sign as the coefficient β_k. The exact response depends upon the values of x_i through the conditional expectation of y_i. This expression can be evaluated for the 'average' individual in the sample, using sample averages of x_i, or for each individual in the sample separately. A more attractive approach is to convert this response into a semi-elasticity. Computing

$$\beta_k = \frac{\partial E\{y_i|x_i\}}{\partial x_{ik}} \frac{1}{E\{y_i|x_i\}} \tag{7.52}$$

provides the *relative* change in the conditional mean if the kth regressor changes by one unit (ceteris paribus). If x_{ik} is a logarithm of an explanatory variable, say $x_{ik} = \log(X_{ik})$, then β_k measures the elasticity of y_i with respect to X_{ik}. That is, it measures the relative change in the expected value of y_i if X_{ik} changes by 1%.

For a discrete variable, these calculus methods are inappropriate. Consider a binary variable x_{ik} that only takes the values 0 and 1. Then, we can compare the conditional means of y_i, given $x_{ik} = 0$ and given $x_{ik} = 1$, keeping the other variables in x_i fixed. It is easily verified that

$$\frac{E\{y_i|x_{ik} = 1, x_i^*\}}{E\{y_i|x_{ik} = 0, x_i^*\}} = \exp\{\beta_k\}, \tag{7.53}$$

where x_i^* denotes the vector x_i, excluding its kth element. Thus, the conditional mean is $\exp\{\beta_k\}$ times larger if the binary indicator is equal to one rather than zero, irrespective of the values of the other explanatory variables. For small values of β_k, we have $\exp\{\beta_k\} \approx 1 + \beta_k$. For example, a value of $\beta_k = 0.05$ indicates that the expected value of y_i (e.g. the number of patents) increases by approximately 5% if the indicator variable changes from 0 to 1.

7.3.2 Illustration: Patents and R&D Expenditures

The relationship between research and development expenditures of firms and the number of patents applied for and received by them has received substantial attention in the literature; see Hausman, Hall and Griliches (1984). Because the number of patents is a count variable, ranging from zero to many, count data models are commonly applied to this problem. In this subsection, we consider a sample of 181 international manufacturing firms, taken from Cincera (1997). For each firm, we observe annual expenditures on research and development (R&D), the industrial sector it operates in, the country of its registered office and the total number of patent applications for a number of consecutive years. We shall use the information on 1991 only.

The average number of patent applications in 1991 was 73.6, with a minimum of 0 and a maximum of 925. About 10% of the firms in the sample have zero applications, while the median number is 20. Given the large spread in the number of applications, with a sample standard deviation of 151, the unconditional count distribution is clearly overdispersed and far away from a Poisson distribution. The inclusion of conditioning explanatory variables may reduce the amount of overdispersion. However, given the descriptive statistics, it seems unlikely that it would eliminate it completely.

Each of the models we consider states that the expected number of patents y_i is given by

$$E\{y_i|x_i\} = \exp\{x_i'\beta\}, \tag{7.54}$$

where x_i contains a constant, the log of R&D expenditures, industry and geographical dummies. Despite its restrictive nature, the first model we consider is the Poisson regression model, which assumes that y_i conditional upon x_i follows a Poisson distribution. The maximum likelihood estimation results are presented in Table 7.7. The sector dummies refer to aerospace, chemistry, computers (hardware and software), machinery and instruments, and motor vehicles. These estimates suggest that aerospace and motor vehicles are sectors with a relatively low number of patent applications, whereas the chemistry, computers and machines sectors have relatively high numbers of applications. The reference category for the geographical dummies is Europe, although there is one firm located in 'the rest of the world'. The estimates indicate clear differences between Japan, Europe and the United States in terms of the expected number of applications. The high levels of significance are striking and somewhat suspicious. However, one should keep in mind that the standard errors are only valid if the Poisson distribution is correct, which seems unlikely given the amount of overdispersion in the count variable. Nevertheless, the estimator is consistent as long as (7.54) is correct, even if the Poisson distribution is invalid. In this case, we need to compute standard errors using the more general expression for the covariance matrix (see (7.47)). Such standard errors of the quasi-maximum likelihood estimator are provided in the third column of Table 7.7, and are substantially higher than those in column 2. As a result, statistical significance is reduced considerably.

Table 7.7 Estimation results Poisson model, MLE and QMLE

	MLE		QMLE
	Estimate	Standard error	Robust standard error
constant	−0.8737	0.0659	0.7429
log (*R&D*)	0.8545	0.0084	0.0937
aerospace	−1.4218	0.0956	0.3802
chemistry	0.6363	0.0255	0.2254
computers	0.5953	0.0233	0.3008
machines	0.6890	0.0383	0.4147
vehicles	−1.5297	0.0419	0.2807
Japan	0.2222	0.0275	0.3528
USA	−0.2995	0.0253	0.2736
Loglikelihood	−4950.789		
Pseudo-R^2	0.675		
LR test (χ^2_8)	20587.54 ($p = 0.000$)		
Wald test (χ^2_8)			338.9 ($p = 0.000$)

For example, we no longer find that the Japanese and US firms are significantly different from European ones. The huge difference between the alternative standard errors is a strong indication of model misspecification. That is, the Poisson distribution has to be rejected (even though we did not perform a formal misspecification test). Nevertheless, the conditional mean in (7.54) may still be correctly specified.

The likelihood ratio and Wald test statistics reported in Table 7.7 provide tests for the hypothesis that all coefficients in the model except the intercept term are equal to zero. The Wald test is based on the robust covariance matrix and therefore more appropriate than the likelihood ratio test, which assumes that the Poisson distribution is correct. The Wald test strongly rejects the hypothesis that the conditional mean is constant and independent of the explanatory variables. The pseudo-R^2 reported in the table is the likelihood ratio index (see Subsection 7.1.5), as it is computed by many software packages. As in all nonlinear models, there is no universal definition of a goodness-of-fit measure in models for count data. Cameron and Windmeijer (1996) discuss several alternative measures that are typically considered more appropriate.

Because the coefficient for the log of R&D expenditures has the interpretation of an elasticity, the estimated value of 0.85 implies that the expected number of patents increases by 0.85% if R&D expenditures (ceteris paribus) increase by 1%. The estimated coefficient of −1.42 for *aerospace* indicates that, ceteris paribus, the average number of patents in the aerospace industry is $100[\exp(-1.4218) - 1] = -75.9\%$ less than in the reference industries (food, fuel, metal and others). The computer industry has expected numbers of patents that are $100[\exp(0.5953) - 1] = 81.3\%$ higher. These numbers are statistically significant at the 95% level when using the robust standard errors.

In Table 7.8, we present the estimation results for two alternative specifications: the NegBin I and the NegBin II models. These two models specify a negative binomial distribution for the number of patents and differ in the specification for the conditional variance. The NegBin I model implies a constant dispersion, according to (7.49), whereas the NegBin II allows the dispersion to depend upon the conditional mean according to (7.50). The two models reduce to the Poisson regression model when $\delta^2 = 0$ or $\alpha^2 = 0$,

Table 7.8 Estimation results NegBin I and NegBin II model, MLE

	NegBin I (MLE)			NegBin II (MLE)	
	Estimate	Standard error		Estimate	Standard error
constant	0.6899	0.5069		−0.3246	0.4982
log (*R&D*)	0.5784	0.0676		0.8315	0.0766
aerospace	−0.7865	0.3368		−1.4975	0.3772
chemistry	0.7333	0.1852		0.4886	0.2568
computers	0.1450	0.2063		−0.1736	0.2988
machines	0.1559	0.2550		0.0593	0.2793
vehicles	−0.8176	0.2686		−1.5306	0.3739
Japan	0.4005	0.2573		0.2522	0.4264
USA	0.1588	0.1984		−0.5905	0.2788
δ^2	95.2437	14.0069	α^2	1.3009	0.1375
Loglikelihood	−848.195			−819.596	
Pseudo R^2	0.944			0.946	
LR test (χ^2_8)	88.55 ($p = 0.000$)			145.75 ($p = 0.000$)	

respectively. The two Wald tests for overdispersion, based on δ^2 and α^2, strongly reject the null hypothesis. Again, these results indicate that the Poisson model should be rejected.

Within the maximum likelihood framework, the NegBin II model is preferred here to NegBin I because it has a higher loglikelihood value with the same number of parameters. Note that the loglikelihood values are substantially larger (less negative) than the −4950.789 reported for the Poisson regression model. Interestingly, the estimated coefficients for the NegBin I specification are quite different from those for the NegBin II model, as well as from the Poisson quasi-maximum likelihood estimates. For example, the estimated elasticity of R&D expenditures is as low as 0.58 for the NegBin I model. Given that the NegBin II estimates, unlike the NegBin I estimates, are robust to misspecification of the conditional variance, this finding is also unfavourable to the NegBin I model. If the NegBin II model is correctly specified, we expect that estimation by maximum likelihood is more efficient than the robust quasi-maximum likelihood estimator based upon the Poisson loglikelihood function. The standard errors in Tables 7.7 and 7.8 are consistent with this suggestion.

7.4 Tobit Models

In certain applications the dependent variable is continuous, but its range may be constrained. Most commonly this occurs when the dependent variable is zero for a substantial part of the population but positive (with many different outcomes) for the rest of the population. Examples are: expenditures on durable goods, hours of work and the amount of foreign direct investment of a firm. Tobit models are particularly suited to model this type of variable. The original tobit model was suggested by James Tobin (Tobin, 1958), who analysed household expenditures on durable goods taking into account their non-negativity, while only in 1964 Arthur Goldberger referred to this model as a **tobit model**, because of its similarity to probit models. The original model has been generalized in many ways. Since the survey by Amemiya (1984), economists also refer to these generalizations as tobit models. In this section and the next we present the original tobit model and some of its extensions. More details can be found in Maddala (1983), Amemiya (1984) and Wooldridge (2010).

7.4.1 The Standard Tobit Model

Suppose that we are interested in explaining the expenditures on tobacco of US households in a given year. Let y denote the expenditures on tobacco, while z denotes all other expenditures (both in US$). Total disposable income (or total expenditures) is denoted by x. We can think of a simple utility maximization problem, describing the household's decision problem:

$$\max_{y,z} U(y, z) \tag{7.55}$$

$$y + z \leq x \tag{7.56}$$

$$y, z \geq 0. \tag{7.57}$$

The solution to this problem depends, of course, on the form of the utility function U. As it is unrealistic to assume that some households would spend all their money on tobacco, the corner solution $z = 0$ can be excluded a priori. However, the solution for y will be zero or positive, and we can expect a corner solution for a large proportion of households. Let us denote the solution to (7.55)–(7.56) without the constraint in (7.57) as y^*. Under appropriate assumptions on U, this solution will be linear in x. As economists we do not observe everything that determines the utility that a household attaches to tobacco. We account for this by allowing for unobserved heterogeneity in the utility function and thus for unobserved heterogeneity in the solution as well. Thus we write

$$y^* = \beta_1 + \beta_2 x + \varepsilon, \tag{7.58}$$

where ε corresponds to unobserved heterogeneity.[14] So, if there were no restrictions on y and consumers could spend any amount on tobacco, they would choose to spend y^*. The solution to the original constrained problem will therefore be given by

$$\begin{aligned} y &= y^* \quad \text{if } y^* > 0 \\ y &= 0 \quad \text{if } y^* \leq 0. \end{aligned} \tag{7.59}$$

So, if a household would like to spend a negative amount y^*, it will spend nothing on tobacco. In essence, this gives us the **standard tobit model**, which we formalize as follows:

$$\begin{aligned} y_i^* &= x_i'\beta + \varepsilon_i, \quad i = 1, 2, \ldots, N, \\ y_i &= y_i^* \quad \text{if } y_i^* > 0 \\ &= 0 \quad \text{if } y_i^* \leq 0, \end{aligned} \tag{7.60}$$

where ε_i is assumed to be $NID(0, \sigma^2)$ and independent of x_i. Notice the similarity of this model with the standard probit model as given in (7.10); the difference is in the mapping from the latent variable to the observed variable. (Also note that we can identify the

[14] Alternative interpretations of ε are possible. These may involve optimization errors of the household or measurement errors.

scaling here, so that we do not have to impose a normalization restriction.) The model in (7.60) is also referred to as the **censored regression model**. It is a standard regression model, where all negative values are mapped to zeros. That is, observations are censored (from below) at zero. The model thus describes two things. One is the probability that $y_i = 0$ (given x_i), given by

$$P\{y_i = 0\} = P\{y_i^* \leq 0\} = P\{\varepsilon_i \leq -x_i'\beta\}$$
$$= P\left\{\frac{\varepsilon_i}{\sigma} \leq -\frac{x_i'\beta}{\sigma}\right\} = \Phi\left(-\frac{x_i'\beta}{\sigma}\right) = 1 - \Phi\left(\frac{x_i'\beta}{\sigma}\right), \tag{7.61}$$

where Φ, as before, denotes the standard normal distribution function. The other is the distribution of y_i given that it is positive. This is a truncated normal distribution with expectation

$$E\{y_i|y_i > 0\} = x_i'\beta + E\{\varepsilon_i|\varepsilon_i > -x_i'\beta\} = x_i'\beta + \sigma\frac{\phi(x_i'\beta/\sigma)}{\Phi(x_i'\beta/\sigma)}, \tag{7.62}$$

where ϕ is the standard normal density function. The last term in this expression denotes the conditional expectation of a mean-zero normal variable given that it is larger than $-x_i'\beta$ (see Appendix B). Obviously, this expectation is larger than zero. The result in (7.62) also shows why it is inappropriate to restrict attention to the positive observations only and estimate a linear model from this subsample: the conditional expectation of y_i no longer equals $x_i'\beta$, but also depends nonlinearly on x_i through $\phi(.)/\Phi(.)$.

The coefficients in the tobit model can be interpreted in a number of ways, depending upon one's interest. For example, the tobit model describes the probability of a zero outcome as

$$P\{y_i = 0\} = 1 - \Phi(x_i'\beta/\sigma).$$

This means that β/σ can be interpreted in a similar fashion as β in the probit model to determine the marginal effect of a change in x_{ik} upon the probability of observing a zero outcome (compare Subsection 7.1.2). That is,

$$\frac{\partial P\{y_i = 0\}}{\partial x_{ik}} = -\phi(x_i'\beta/\sigma)\frac{\beta_k}{\sigma}. \tag{7.63}$$

Moreover, as shown in (7.62), the tobit model describes the expected value of y_i given that it is positive. This shows that the marginal effect of a change in x_{ik} upon the value of y_i, given the censoring, will be different from β_k. It will also involve the marginal change in the second term of (7.62), corresponding to the censoring. From (7.62) it follows that the expected value of y_i is given by[15]

$$E\{y_i\} = x_i'\beta\Phi(x_i'\beta/\sigma) + \sigma\phi(x_i'\beta/\sigma). \tag{7.64}$$

From this it follows that the marginal effect on the expected value of y_i of a change in x_{ik} is given by[16]

$$\frac{\partial E\{y_i\}}{\partial x_{ik}} = \beta_k\Phi(x_i'\beta/\sigma). \tag{7.65}$$

---

[15] Use $E\{y\} = E\{y|y > 0\}P\{y > 0\} + 0$.

[16] This is obtained by differentiating with respect to x_{ik}, using the chain rule and using the functional form of ϕ. Several terms cancel out (compare Greene, 2012, Section 19.3).

This tells us that the marginal effect of a change in x_{ik} upon the expected outcome y_i is given by the model's coefficient multiplied by the probability of having a positive outcome. If this probability is close to one for a particular individual, the marginal effect is very close to β_k, as in the linear model. Finally, the marginal effect upon the latent variable is easily obtained as

$$\frac{\partial E\{y_i^*\}}{\partial x_{ik}} = \beta_k. \tag{7.66}$$

Unless the latent variable has a direct interpretation, which is typically not the case, it seems most natural to be interested in (7.65).

7.4.2 Estimation

Estimation of the tobit model is usually done through maximum likelihood. The contribution to the likelihood function of an observation either equals the probability mass (at the observed point $y_i = 0$) or the conditional density of y_i, given that it is positive, times the probability mass of observing $y_i > 0$. The loglikelihood function can thus be written as

$$\begin{aligned}\log L_1(\beta, \sigma^2) &= \sum_{i \in I_0} \log P\{y_i = 0\} + \sum_{i \in I_1} [\log f(y_i | y_i > 0) + \log P\{y_i > 0\}] \\ &= \sum_{i \in I_0} \log P\{y_i = 0\} + \sum_{i \in I_1} \log f(y_i),\end{aligned} \tag{7.67}$$

where $f(.)$ is generic notation for a density function and the last equality follows from the definition of a conditional density.[17] The index sets I_0 and I_1 are defined as the sets of those indices corresponding to the zero and the positive observations, respectively. That is, $I_0 = \{i = 1, \ldots, N\colon y_i = 0\}$. Using the appropriate expressions for the normal distribution, we obtain

$$\begin{aligned}\log L_1(\beta, \sigma^2) &= \sum_{i \in I_0} \log \left[1 - \Phi\left(\frac{x_i'\beta}{\sigma}\right)\right] \\ &+ \sum_{i \in I_1} \log \left[\frac{1}{\sqrt{2\pi\sigma^2}} \exp\left\{-\frac{1}{2}\frac{(y_i - x_i'\beta)^2}{\sigma^2}\right\}\right].\end{aligned} \tag{7.68}$$

Maximization of (7.68) with respect to β and σ^2 yields the maximum likelihood estimates, as usual. Assuming that the model is correctly specified, this gives us consistent and asymptotically efficient estimators for both β and σ^2 (under mild regularity conditions).

The parameters in β have a double interpretation: one as the impact of a change in x_i on the probability of a nonzero expenditure, and one as the impact of a change in x_i on the level of this expenditure. Both effects thus automatically have the same sign. Although we motivated the tobit model above through a utility maximization framework, this is usually not the starting point in applied work: y_i^* could simply be interpreted as 'desired expenditures', with actual expenditures being equal to zero if the desired quantity is negative.

[17] Recall that $f(y|y > c) = f(y)/P\{y > c\}$ for $y > c$ and 0 otherwise (see Appendix B).

In some applications, observations are completely missing if $y_i^* \leq 0$. For example, our sample may be restricted to households with positive expenditures on tobacco only. In this case, we can still assume the same underlying structure but with a slightly different observation rule. This leads to the so-called **truncated regression model**. Formally, it is given by

$$\begin{aligned} y_i^* &= x_i'\beta + \varepsilon_i, \quad i = 1, 2, \ldots, N, \\ y_i &= y_i^* \quad \text{if } y_i^* > 0 \\ (y_i, x_i) &\text{ not observed if } y_i^* \leq 0, \end{aligned} \tag{7.69}$$

where, as before, ε_i is assumed to be $NID(0, \sigma^2)$ and independent of x_i. In this case we no longer have a **random sample** and we have to take this into account when making inferences (e.g. estimating β, σ^2). The likelihood contribution of an observation i is not just the density evaluated at the observed point y_i but the density at y_i conditional upon selection into the sample, that is conditional upon $y_i > 0$. The loglikelihood function for the truncated regression model is thus given by

$$\log L_2(\beta, \sigma^2) = \sum_{i \in I_1} \log f(y_i | y_i > 0) = \sum_{i \in I_1} [\log f(y_i) - \log P\{y_i > 0\}], \tag{7.70}$$

which, for the normal distribution, reduces to

$$\log L_2(\beta, \sigma^2) = \sum_{i \in I_1} \left\{ \log \left[\frac{1}{\sqrt{2\pi\sigma^2}} \exp \left\{ -\frac{1}{2} \frac{(y_i - x_i'\beta)^2}{\sigma^2} \right\} \right] - \log \Phi \left(\frac{x_i'\beta}{\sigma} \right) \right\}. \tag{7.71}$$

Although there is no need to observe what the characteristics of the individuals with $y_i = 0$ are, nor to know how many individuals are 'missing', we have to assume that they are unobserved only because their characteristics and unobservables are such that $y_i^* \leq 0$. Maximizing $\log L_2$ with respect to β and σ^2 again gives consistent estimators. If observations with $y_i = 0$ are really missing, it is the best one can do. However, even if observations with $y_i = 0$ are available, one could still maximize $\log L_2$ instead of $\log L_1$, that is, one could estimate a truncated regression model even if a tobit model would be applicable. It is intuitively obvious that the latter (tobit) approach uses more information and therefore will generally lead to more efficient estimators. In fact, it can be shown that the information contained in the tobit model combines that contained in the truncated regression model with that of the probit model describing the zero/nonzero decision. This fact follows easily from the result that the tobit loglikelihood function is the sum of the truncated regression and probit loglikelihood functions.

7.4.3 *Illustration: Expenditures on Alcohol and Tobacco (Part 1)*

In economics, (systems of) demand equations are often used to analyse the effect of, for example, income, tax or price changes on consumer demand. A practical problem that emerges is that expenditures on particular commodities may be zero, particularly if the goods are not aggregated into broad categories. While this typically occurs with durable goods, we shall concentrate on a different type of commodity here: alcoholic beverages and tobacco.

Starting from the assumption that a consumer maximizes his utility as a function of the quantities of the goods consumed, it is possible to derive (Marshallian) demand functions for each good as

$$q_j = g_j(x, p),$$

where q_j denotes the quantity of good j, x denotes total expenditures and p is a vector of prices of all relevant goods. The function g_j depends upon the consumer's preferences. In the empirical application we shall consider cross-sectional data where prices do not vary across observations. Therefore, p can be absorbed into the functional form to get

$$q_j = g_j^*(x).$$

This relationship is commonly referred to as an **Engel curve** (see, e.g., Deaton and Muellbauer, 1980, Chapter 1). From this, one can define the total expenditure elasticity of q_j, the quantity of good j that is consumed, as

$$\epsilon_j = \frac{\partial g_j^*(x)}{\partial x} \frac{x}{q_j}.$$

This elasticity measures the relative effect of a 1% increase in total expenditures and can be used to classify goods into luxuries, necessities and inferior goods. A good is referred to as a luxury good if the quantity that is consumed increases more than proportionally with total expenditures ($\epsilon_j > 1$), whereas it is a necessity if $\epsilon_j < 1$. If the quantity of a good's purchase decreases when total expenditure increases, the good is said to be inferior, which implies that the elasticity ϵ_j is negative.

A convenient parameterization of the Engel curve is

$$w_j = \alpha_j + \beta_j \log x,$$

where $w_j = p_j q_j / x$ denotes the budget share of good j. It is a simple exercise to derive that the total expenditure elasticities for this functional form are given by

$$\epsilon_j = 1 + \beta_j / w_j, \tag{7.72}$$

such that good j is a necessity if $\epsilon_j < 1$ or $\beta_j < 0$, whereas a luxury good corresponds to $\beta_j > 0$.

Below, we shall focus on two particular goods, alcoholic beverages and tobacco. Moreover, we explicitly focus on heterogeneity across households, and the suffix i will be used to index observations on individual households. The almost ideal demand system of Deaton and Muellbauer (1980, Section 3.4) implies Engel curves of the form

$$w_{ji} = \alpha_{ji} + \beta_{ji} \log x_i + \varepsilon_{ji},$$

where w_{ji} is household i's budget share of commodity j, and x_i denotes total expenditures. The parameters α_{ji} and β_{ji} may depend upon household characteristics, like family composition, age and education of the household head. The random terms ε_{ji} capture unobservable differences between households. Because β_{ji} varies over households, the functional form of the above Engel curve permits goods to be luxuries or necessities depending upon household characteristics.

When we consider expenditures on alcohol or tobacco, the number of zeros is expected to be substantial. A first way to explain these zeros is that they arise from corner solutions when the non-negativity constraint of the budget share ($w_{ji} \geq 0$) becomes binding. This means that households prefer not to buy alcoholic beverages or tobacco at current prices and income, but that a price decrease or income increase would (ultimately) change this. The discussion as to whether or not this is a realistic assumption is deferred to Subsection 7.5.4. As the corner solutions do not satisfy the first-order conditions for an interior optimum of the underlying utility maximization problem, the Engel curve does not apply to observations with $w_{ji} = 0$. Instead, the Engel curve is assumed to describe the solution to the household's utility maximization problem if the non-negativity constraint is not imposed, a negative solution corresponding to zero expenditures on the particular good. This way, we can adjust the model to read

$$\begin{aligned} w_{ji}^* &= \alpha_{ji} + \beta_{ji} \log x_i + \varepsilon_{ji}, \\ w_{ji} &= w_{ji}^* \quad \text{if } w_{ji}^* > 0 \\ &= 0 \quad \text{otherwise,} \end{aligned}$$

which corresponds to a standard tobit model if it is assumed that $\varepsilon_{ji} \sim NID(0, \sigma^2)$ for a given good j. Atkinson, Gomulka and Stern (1990) use a similar approach to estimate an Engel curve for alcohol, but assume that ε_{ji} has a non-normal skewed distribution.

To estimate the above model, we employ data[18] from the Belgian household budget survey of 1995–1996, supplied by the National Institute of Statistics (NIS). The sample contains 2724 households for which expenditures on a broad range of goods are observed as well as a number of background variables, relating to, for example, family composition and occupational status. In this sample, 62% of the households have zero expenditures on tobacco, while 17% do not spend anything on alcoholic beverages. The average budget shares, for the respective subsamples of positive expenditures, are 3.22% and 2.15%.

Below, we shall estimate the two Engel curves for alcohol and tobacco separately. This means that we do not take into account the possibility that a binding non-negativity constraint on tobacco may also affect expenditures on alcohol, or vice versa. We shall assume that α_{ji} is a linear function of the age of the household head,[19] the number of adults in the household and the numbers of children younger than 2 and 2 or older, while β_{ji} is taken to be a linear function of age and the number of adults. This implies that the products of log total expenditures with age and number of adults are included as explanatory variables in the tobit model. The estimation results for the standard tobit models are presented in Table 7.9.

For tobacco, there is substantial evidence that age is an important factor in explaining the budget share, both separately and in combination with total expenditures. For alcoholic beverages, only the number of children and total expenditures are individually significant. As reported in the table, Wald tests for the hypothesis that all coefficients, except the intercept term, are equal to zero produce highly significant values for both goods. Under the null hypothesis, these test statistics, comparable with the F-statistic that is typically computed for the linear model (see Subsection 2.5.4), have an asymptotic Chi-squared distribution with seven degrees of freedom.

[18] I am grateful to the NIS for permission to use these data.

[19] Age is measured in 10-year interval classes ranging from 0 (younger than 30) to 4 (60 or older).

Table 7.9 Tobit models for budget shares alcohol and tobacco

Variable	Alcoholic beverages		Tobacco	
	Estimate	Standard error	Estimate	Standard error
constant	−0.1592	(0.0438)	0.5900	(0.0934)
age class	0.0135	(0.0109)	−0.1259	(0.0242)
nadults	0.0292	(0.0169)	0.0154	(0.0380)
nkids ≥ 2	−0.0026	(0.0006)	0.0043	(0.0013)
nkids < 2	−0.0039	(0.0024)	−0.0100	(0.0055)
$\log(x)$	0.0127	(0.0032)	−0.0444	(0.0069)
age $\times \log(x)$	−0.0008	(0.0088)	0.0088	(0.0018)
nadults $\times \log(x)$	−0.0022	(0.0012)	−0.0006	(0.0028)
$\hat{\sigma}$	0.0244	(0.0004)	0.0480	(0.0012)
Loglikelihood	4755.371		758.701	
Wald test (χ_7^2)	117.86	($p = 0.000$)	170.18	($p = 0.000$)

If we assume that a household under consideration has a sufficiently large budget share to ignore changes in the second term of (7.62), the total expenditure elasticity can be computed on the basis of (7.72) as $1 + \beta_{ji}/w_{ji}$. It measures the total elasticity for those that consume alcohol and those that smoke, respectively. If we evaluate the above elasticities at the sample averages of those households that have positive expenditures, we obtain estimated elasticities[20] of 1.294 and 0.180, respectively. This indicates that alcoholic beverages are a luxury good, whereas tobacco is a necessity. In fact, the total expenditure elasticity of tobacco expenditures is fairly close to zero.

In this application the tobit model assumes that all zero expenditures are the result of corner solutions, and that a sufficiently large change in income or relative prices would ultimately create positive expenditures for any household. In particular for tobacco this seems not really appropriate. Many people do not smoke because of, for example, health or social reasons, and would not smoke even if cigarettes were free. If this is the case, it is more appropriate to model the decision to smoke or not as a process separate from the decision of how much to spend on it. The so-called tobit II model, one of the extensions of the standard tobit model that will be discussed below, could be appropriate for this situation. Therefore, we shall come back to this example in Subsection 7.5.4.

7.4.4 Specification Tests in the Tobit Model

A violation of the distributional assumptions on ε_i will generally lead to inconsistent maximum likelihood estimators for β and σ^2. In particular, non-normality and heteroskedasticity are a concern. We can test for these alternatives, as well as for omitted variables, within the Lagrange multiplier framework. To start the discussion, first note that the first-order conditions of the loglikelihood $\log L_1$ with respect to β are given by

$$\sum_{i \in I_0} \frac{-\phi(x_i'\hat{\beta}/\hat{\sigma})}{1 - \Phi(x_i'\hat{\beta}/\hat{\sigma})} x_i + \sum_{i \in I_1} \frac{\hat{\varepsilon}_i}{\hat{\sigma}} x_i = \sum_{i=1}^{N} \hat{\varepsilon}_i^G x_i = 0, \tag{7.73}$$

[20] We first take averages and then compute the ratio.

where we define the generalized residual $\hat{\varepsilon}_i^G$ as the scaled residual $\hat{\varepsilon}_i/\hat{\sigma} = (y_i - x_i'\hat{\beta})/\hat{\sigma}$ for the positive observations and as $-\phi(.)/(1 - \Phi(.))$, evaluated at $x_i'\hat{\beta}/\hat{\sigma}$, for the zero observations. Thus we obtain first-order conditions that are of the same form as in the probit model or the linear regression model. The only difference is the definition of the appropriate (generalized) residual.

Because σ^2 is also a parameter that is estimated, we also need the first-order condition with respect to σ^2 to derive the specification tests. Apart from an irrelevant scaling factor, this is given by

$$\sum_{i\in I_0} \frac{x_i'\hat{\beta}}{\hat{\sigma}} \frac{\phi(x_i'\hat{\beta}/\hat{\sigma})}{1 - \Phi(x_i'\hat{\beta}/\hat{\sigma})} + \sum_{i\in I_1} \left(\frac{\hat{\varepsilon}_i^2}{\hat{\sigma}^2} - 1 \right) = \sum_{i=1}^{N} \hat{\varepsilon}_i^{G(2)} = 0, \tag{7.74}$$

where we defined $\hat{\varepsilon}_i^{G(2)}$, a second-order generalized residual. The first-order condition with respect to σ^2 says that the sample average of $\hat{\varepsilon}_i^{G(2)}$ should be zero. It can be shown (see Gouriéroux, Monfort, Renault and Trognon, 1987) that the second-order generalized residual is an estimate for $E\{\varepsilon_i^2/\sigma^2 - 1|y_i, x_i\}$, just like the (first-order) generalized residual $\hat{\varepsilon}_i^G$ is an estimate for $E\{\varepsilon_i/\sigma|y_i, x_i\}$. Although it is beyond the scope of this text to derive this, it is intuitively reasonable: if ε_i cannot be determined from y_i, x_i and β, we replace the expressions with the conditional expected values given all we know about y_i^*, as reflected in y_i. This is simply the best guess of what we think the residual should be, given that we only know that it satisfies $\varepsilon_i < -x_i'\beta$.

From (7.73) it is immediately clear how we would test for J omitted variables z_i. As the additional first-order conditions would imply that

$$\sum_{i=1}^{N} \hat{\varepsilon}_i^G z_i = 0,$$

we can simply do a regression of ones upon the $K + 1 + J$ variables $\hat{\varepsilon}_i^G x_i'$, $\hat{\varepsilon}_i^{G(2)}$ and $\hat{\varepsilon}_i^G z_i'$ and compute the test statistic as N times the uncentred R^2. The appropriate asymptotic distribution under the null hypothesis is a Chi-squared with J degrees of freedom. This is similar to the test described in Subsection 6.3.1 for the linear model. The second-order generalized residual is added in the tobit case because the information matrix is no longer block diagonal.

A test for heteroskedasticity can be based upon the alternative that

$$V\{\varepsilon_i\} = \sigma^2 h(z_i'\alpha), \tag{7.75}$$

where $h(.)$ is an unknown differentiable function with $h(0) = 1$ and $h(.) > 0$, and z_i is a J-dimensional vector of explanatory variables, not including an intercept term. The null hypothesis corresponds to $\alpha = 0$, implying that $V\{\varepsilon_i\} = \sigma^2$. The additional scores with respect to α, evaluated under the current set of parameter estimates $\hat{\beta}$, $\hat{\sigma}^2$, are easily obtained as $\kappa\hat{\varepsilon}_i^{G(2)} z_i'$, where κ is an irrelevant constant that depends upon h. Consequently, the LM test statistic for heteroskedasticity is easily obtained as N times the uncentred R^2 of a regression of ones upon the $K + 1 + J$ variables $\hat{\varepsilon}_i^G x_i'$, $\hat{\varepsilon}_i^{G(2)}$ and $\hat{\varepsilon}_i^{G(2)} z_i'$. Note that also in this case the test statistic does not depend upon the form of h, only upon z_i.

If homoskedasticity is rejected, we can estimate a tobit model with heteroskedastic errors if we specify a functional form for h, for example, $h(z_i'\alpha) = \exp\{z_i'\alpha\}$. In the log-likelihood function, we simply replace σ^2 with $\sigma^2 \exp\{z_i'\alpha\}$, and we estimate α jointly with the parameters β and σ^2. Alternatively, it is possible that heteroskedasticity is found because something else is wrong with the model. For example, the functional form may not be appropriate, and nonlinear functions of x_i should be included. Also, a transformation of the dependent variable could eliminate the heteroskedasticity problem. This explains, for example, why in many cases people specify a model for log wages rather than wages themselves.

Finally, we discuss a test for non-normality. This test can be based upon the framework of Pagan and Vella (1989) and implies a test of the following two conditional moment conditions that are implied by normality: $E\{\varepsilon_i^3/\sigma^3|x_i\} = 0$ and $E\{\varepsilon_i^4/\sigma^4 - 3|x_i\} = 0$, corresponding to the absence of skewness and excess kurtosis, respectively (see Section 6.4). Let us first consider the quantities $E\{\varepsilon_i^3/\sigma^3|y_i, x_i\}$ and $E\{\varepsilon_i^4/\sigma^4 - 3|y_i, x_i\}$, noting that taking expectations over y_i (given x_i) produces the two moments of interest. If $y_i > 0$, we can simply estimate the sample equivalents as $\hat{\varepsilon}_i^3/\hat{\sigma}^3$ and $\hat{\varepsilon}_i^4/\hat{\sigma}^4 - 3$ respectively, where $\hat{\varepsilon}_i = y_i - x_i'\hat{\beta}$. For $y_i = 0$ the conditional expectations are more complicated, but they can be computed using the following formulae (Lee and Maddala, 1985):

$$E\left\{\frac{\varepsilon_i^3}{\sigma^3}\middle| x_i, y_i = 0\right\} = \left[2 + \left(\frac{x_i'\beta}{\sigma}\right)^2\right] E\left\{\frac{\varepsilon_i}{\sigma}\middle| x_i, y_i = 0\right\} \tag{7.76}$$

$$E\left\{\frac{\varepsilon_i^4}{\sigma^4} - 3\middle| x_i, y_i = 0\right\} = 3E\left\{\frac{\varepsilon_i^2}{\sigma^2} - 1\middle| x_i, y_i = 0\right\} + \left(\frac{x_i'\beta}{\sigma}\right)^3 E\left\{\frac{\varepsilon_i}{\sigma}\middle| x_i, y_i = 0\right\}. \tag{7.77}$$

These two quantities can easily be estimated from the ML estimates $\hat{\beta}$ and $\hat{\sigma}^2$ and the generalized residuals $\hat{\varepsilon}_i^G$ and $\hat{\varepsilon}_i^{G(2)}$. Let us denote the resulting estimates as $\hat{\varepsilon}_i^{G(3)}$ and $\hat{\varepsilon}_i^{G(4)}$ respectively, such that

$$\begin{aligned}\hat{\varepsilon}_i^{G(3)} &= \hat{\varepsilon}_i^3/\hat{\sigma}^3 && \text{if } y_i > 0\\ &= [2 + (x_i'\hat{\beta}/\hat{\sigma})^2]\hat{\varepsilon}_i^G && \text{otherwise,}\end{aligned} \tag{7.78}$$

and

$$\begin{aligned}\hat{\varepsilon}_i^{G(4)} &= \hat{\varepsilon}_i^4/\hat{\sigma}^4 - 3 && \text{if } y_i > 0\\ &= 3\hat{\varepsilon}_i^{G(2)} + (x_i'\hat{\beta}/\hat{\sigma})^3\hat{\varepsilon}_i^G && \text{otherwise.}\end{aligned} \tag{7.79}$$

By the law of iterated expectations the null hypothesis of normality implies that (asymptotically) $E\{\hat{\varepsilon}_i^{G(3)}|x_i\} = 0$ and $E\{\hat{\varepsilon}_i^{G(4)}|x_i\} = 0$. Consequently, the conditional moment test for non-normality can be obtained by running a regression of a vector of ones upon the $K + 3$ variables $\hat{\varepsilon}_i^G x_i'$, $\hat{\varepsilon}_i^{G(2)}$, $\hat{\varepsilon}_i^{G(3)}$ and $\hat{\varepsilon}_i^{G(4)}$ and computing N times the uncentred R^2. Under the null hypothesis, the asymptotic distribution of the resulting test statistic is Chi-squared with two degrees of freedom.

Although the derivation of the different test statistics may seem complicated, their computation is relatively easy. They can be computed using an auxiliary regression after some straightforward computations involving the maximum likelihood estimates and the data. Because, in general, the maximum likelihood estimator for the tobit model will be inconsistent in case of omitted variables, heteroskedasticity or non-normality, testing for misspecification should be standard routine in empirical work. Although it is possible to calculate 'robust' standard errors using the sandwich formula discussed in Subsection 6.4.1, this is of little help, as it simply means that you are consistently estimating the standard errors of an estimator that is inconsistent itself. There is no such thing as a tobit model with heteroskasticity-consistent standard errors. Instead, the misspecification should be modelled and incorporated explicitly.

7.5 Extensions of Tobit Models

The standard tobit model imposes a structure that is often too restrictive: exactly the same variables affecting the probability of a nonzero observation determine the level of a positive observation and, moreover, with the same sign. This implies, for example, that those who are more likely to spend a positive amount are, on average, also those who spend more on a durable good. In this section, we shall discuss models that relax this restriction. Taking the specific example of holiday expenditures, it is conceivable that households with many children are less likely to have positive expenditures, while, if a holiday is taken up, the expected level of expenditures for such households is higher.

Suppose that we are interested in explaining wages. Obviously, wages are only observed for people who are actually working, but for economic purposes we are often interested in (potential) wages not conditional upon this selection. For example: a change in some exogenous variable may lower someone's wage such that he or she decides to stop working. Consequently, his or her wage would no longer be observed and the effect of this explanatory variable could be underestimated from the available data. Because the sample of workers may not be a random sample of the population (of potential workers) – in particular one can expect that people with lower (potential) wages are more likely to be unemployed – this problem is often referred to as a **sample selection problem**.

7.5.1 The Tobit II Model

The traditional model to describe sample selection problems is the **tobit II model**,[21] also referred to as the **sample selection model**. In this context, it consists of a linear wage equation

$$w_i^* = x_{1i}'\beta_1 + \varepsilon_{1i}, \tag{7.80}$$

where x_{1i} denotes a vector of exogenous characteristics (age, education, gender, ...) and w_i^* denotes person i's wage. The wage w_i^* is not observed for people who are not working (which explains the *). To describe whether a person is working or not, a second equation is specified, which is of the binary choice type. That is,

$$h_i^* = x_{2i}'\beta_2 + \varepsilon_{2i}, \tag{7.81}$$

where we have the following observation rule:

$$w_i = w_i^*, \; h_i = 1 \quad \text{if } h_i^* > 0 \tag{7.82}$$

$$w_i \text{ not observed}, \; h_i = 0 \quad \text{if } h_i^* \leq 0, \tag{7.83}$$

[21] This classification of tobit models is due to Amemiya (1984). The standard tobit model of Section 7.4 is then referred to as tobit I.

where w_i denotes person i's actual wage.[22] The binary variable h_i simply indicates working or not working. The model is completed by a distributional assumption on the unobserved errors $(\varepsilon_{1i}, \varepsilon_{2i})$, usually a bivariate normal distribution with expectations zero, variances σ_1^2 and σ_2^2, respectively, and a covariance σ_{12}. The model in (7.81) is, in fact, a standard probit model, describing the choice between working or not working. Therefore, a normalization restriction is required, and, as before, one usually sets $\sigma_2^2 = 1$. The choice to work is affected by the variables in x_{2i} with coefficients β_2. The equation (7.80) describes (potential) wages as a function of the variables in x_{1i} with coefficients β_1. The signs and magnitude of the β coefficients may differ across the two equations. In principle, the variables in x_1 and x_2 can be different, although one has to be very careful in this respect (see Subsection 7.5.2). If we impose that $x_{1i}'\beta_1 = x_{2i}'\beta_2$ and $\varepsilon_{1i} = \varepsilon_{2i}$, it is easily seen that we are back at the standard tobit model (tobit I).

The conditional expected wage, given that a person *is* working, is given by

$$\begin{aligned} E\{w_i|h_i = 1\} &= x_{1i}'\beta_1 + E\{\varepsilon_{1i}|h_i = 1\} \\ &= x_{1i}'\beta_1 + E\{\varepsilon_{1i}|\varepsilon_{2i} > -x_{2i}'\beta_2\} \\ &= x_{1i}'\beta_1 + \frac{\sigma_{12}}{\sigma_2^2}E\{\varepsilon_{2i}|\varepsilon_{2i} > -x_{2i}'\beta_2\} \\ &= x_{1i}'\beta_1 + \sigma_{12}\frac{\phi(x_{2i}'\beta_2)}{\Phi(x_{2i}'\beta_2)}, \end{aligned} \tag{7.84}$$

where the last equality uses $\sigma_2^2 = 1$ and the expression for the expectation of a truncated standard normal distribution, similar to that used in (7.62). The third equality uses the fact that for two normal random variables $E\{\varepsilon_1|\varepsilon_2\} = (\sigma_{12}/\sigma_2^2)\varepsilon_2$. Appendix B provides more details on these results. Note that we can write $\sigma_{12} = \rho_{12}\sigma_1$, where ρ_{12} is the correlation coefficient between the two errors. Again, this shows the generality of the model in comparison with (7.62). It follows directly from (7.84) that the conditional expected wage equals $x_{1i}'\beta_1$ only if $\sigma_{12} = \rho_{12} = 0$. So, if the error terms from the two equations are uncorrelated, the wage equation can be estimated consistently by ordinary least squares. A sample selection bias in the OLS estimator arises if $\sigma_{12} \neq 0$. The term $\phi(x_{2i}'\beta_2)/\Phi(x_{2i}'\beta_2)$ is known as the inverse Mills ratio (IMR). Because it is denoted $\lambda(x_{2i}'\beta_2)$ by Heckman (1979), it is also referred to as **Heckman's lambda**.

The crucial parameter that makes the sample selection model different from just a regression model and a probit model is the correlation coefficient (or covariance) between the two equations' error terms. If the errors were uncorrelated, we could simply estimate the wage equation by OLS and ignore the selection equation (unless we were interested in it). Now, why can we expect correlation between the two error terms? Although the tobit II model can be motivated in different ways, we shall more or less follow Gronau (1974) in his reasoning. Assume that the utility maximization problem of the individual (in Gronau's case: housewives) can be characterized by a **reservation wage** w_i^r (the value of time). A woman will work if the actual wage she is offered exceeds this reservation wage. The reservation wage of course depends upon personal characteristics, via the utility function and the budget constraint, so that we write (assume)

$$w_i^r = z_i'\gamma + \eta_i,$$

[22] In most applications the model is formulated in terms of log wages.

where z_i is a vector of characteristics and η_i is unobserved. Usually the reservation wage is not observed.

Now assume that the wage a person is offered depends on her personal characteristics (and some job characteristics) as in (7.80), that is

$$w_i^* = x_{1i}'\beta_1 + \varepsilon_{1i}.$$

If this wage is below w_i^r, individual i is assumed not to work. We can thus write her labour supply decision as

$$\begin{aligned} h_i &= 1 \quad \text{if } w_i^* - w_i^r > 0 \\ &= 0 \quad \text{if } w_i^* - w_i^r \leq 0. \end{aligned}$$

The inequality can be written in terms of observed characteristics and unobserved errors as

$$h_i^* \equiv w_i^* - w_i^r = x_{1i}'\beta_1 - z_i'\gamma + (\varepsilon_{1i} - \eta_i) = x_{2i}'\beta_2 + \varepsilon_{2i} \tag{7.85}$$

by appropriately defining x_{2i} and ε_{2i}. Consequently, our simple economic model where labour supply is based on a reservation wage leads to a model of the tobit II form. A few things are worth noting from (7.85). First, the offered wage influences the decision to work or not. This implies that the error term ε_{2i} involves the unobserved heterogeneity influencing the wage offer, that is involves ε_{1i}. If η_i is uncorrelated with ε_{1i}, the correlation between ε_{2i} and ε_{1i} is expected to be positive. Consequently, we can expect a sample selection bias in the least squares estimator from economic arguments. Second, the variables in x_{1i} are all included in x_{2i}, plus all variables in z_i that are not contained in x_{1i}. Economic arguments thus indicate that we should include in x_{2i} at least those variables that are contained in x_{1i}.

Let us repeat the statistical model, the tobit II model, for convenience, substituting y for w to stress generality:

$$y_i^* = x_{1i}'\beta_1 + \varepsilon_{1i} \tag{7.86}$$

$$h_i^* = x_{2i}'\beta_2 + \varepsilon_{2i} \tag{7.87}$$

$$y_i = y_i^*,\ h_i = 1 \quad \text{if } h_i^* > 0 \tag{7.88}$$

$$y_i \text{ not observed},\ h_i = 0 \quad \text{if } h_i^* \leq 0, \tag{7.89}$$

where

$$\begin{pmatrix} \varepsilon_{1i} \\ \varepsilon_{2i} \end{pmatrix} \sim NID\left(\begin{pmatrix} 0 \\ 0 \end{pmatrix}, \begin{pmatrix} \sigma_1^2 & \sigma_{12} \\ \sigma_{12} & 1 \end{pmatrix} \right). \tag{7.90}$$

This model has two observed endogenous variables y_i and h_i. Statistically, it describes the joint distribution of y_i and h_i conditional upon the variables in *both* x_{1i} and x_{2i}. That is, (7.86) should describe the conditional distribution of y_i^* conditional upon *both* x_{1i} and x_{2i}. The only reason not to include a certain variable in x_{1i} that is included in x_{2i} is that we are confident that it has a zero coefficient in the first equation. For example, there could be variables that affect reservation wages only but not the wage itself. Incorrectly omitting a variable from (7.86) while including it in (7.87) may seriously affect the estimation results and may lead to spurious conclusions of the existence of sample selection bias.

In the empirical banking and corporate finance literature, tobit models are increasingly used to identify the presence of private information, corresponding to $\sigma_{12} \neq 0$ (see Li and Prabhala, 2007). As an example, consider a sample of bank loans and assume that y_i denotes the interest rate that a bank charges for a loan. We only observe the interest rate paid on a loan for individuals who are granted a loan, not for those whose loan application is denied. The decision to grant a loan ($h_i = 1$) is taken by a bank on the basis of observable information about the applicant (x_i), but also on the basis of private information that is not observed by the econometrician. When private information is related to the creditworthiness of an individual, it is likely to affect both the probability that a loan is granted and the interest rate charged on the loan. In this case, $\sigma_{12} \neq 0$ is an indication of the presence of such private information.

7.5.2 Estimation

For estimation purposes, the model can be thought of as consisting of two parts. The first part describes the binary choice problem. The contribution to the likelihood function is simply the probability of observing $h_i = 1$ or $h_i = 0$. The second part describes the distribution of y_i for those with $h_i = 1$, so that the likelihood contribution is $f(y_i|h_i = 1)$. The loglikelihood function is then given by

$$\log L_3(\beta, \sigma_1^2, \sigma_{12}) = \sum_{i \in I_0} \log P\{h_i = 0\} + \sum_{i \in I_1} [\log f(y_i|h_i = 1) + \log P\{h_i = 1\}]. \tag{7.91}$$

The binary choice part is standard; the only complicated part is the conditional distribution of y_i given $h_i = 1$. Therefore, it is more common to decompose the joint distribution of y_i and h_i differently, by using

$$f(y_i|h_i = 1)P\{h_i = 1\} = P\{h_i = 1|y_i\}f(y_i). \tag{7.92}$$

The last term on the right-hand side is simply the normal density function, while the first term is a probability from a conditional normal density function, characterized by (see Appendix B)

$$E\{h_i^*|y_i\} = x_{2i}'\beta_2 + \frac{\sigma_{12}}{\sigma_1^2}(y_i - x_{1i}'\beta_1)$$

$$V\{h_i^*|y_i\} = 1 - \sigma_{12}^2/\sigma_1^2,$$

where the latter equality denotes the variance of h_i^* conditional upon y_i and given the exogenous variables. With this we can write the loglikelihood as

$$\log L_3(\beta, \sigma_1^2, \sigma_{12}) = \sum_{i \in I_0} \log P\{h_i = 0\} + \sum_{i \in I_1} [\log f(y_i) + \log P\{h_i = 1|y_i\}] \tag{7.93}$$

with the following equalities

$$P\{h_i = 0\} = 1 - \Phi(x'_{2i}\beta_2) \tag{7.94}$$

$$P\{h_i = 1|y_i\} = \Phi\left(\frac{x'_{2i}\beta_2 + (\sigma_{12}/\sigma_1^2)(y_i - x'_{1i}\beta_1)}{\sqrt{1 - \sigma_{12}^2/\sigma_1^2}}\right) \tag{7.95}$$

$$f(y_i) = \frac{1}{\sqrt{2\pi\sigma_1^2}} \exp\left\{-\frac{1}{2}(y_i - x'_{1i}\beta_1)^2/\sigma_1^2\right\}. \tag{7.96}$$

Maximization of $\log L_3(\beta, \sigma_1^2, \sigma_{12})$ with respect to the unknown parameters leads (under mild regularity conditions) to consistent and asymptotically efficient estimators that have an asymptotic normal distribution.

In empirical work, the sample selection model is often estimated in a two-step way. This is computationally simpler, and it will also provide good starting values for the maximum likelihood procedure. The two-step procedure is due to Heckman (1979) and is based on the following regression (compare (7.84))

$$y_i = x'_{1i}\beta_1 + \sigma_{12}\lambda_i + \eta_i, \tag{7.97}$$

where

$$\lambda_i = \frac{\phi(x'_{2i}\beta_2)}{\Phi(x'_{2i}\beta_2)}.$$

The error term in this model equals $\eta_i = \varepsilon_{1i} - E\{\varepsilon_{1i}|x_i, h_i = 1\}$. Given the assumption that the distribution of ε_{1i} is independent of x_i (but not of h_i), η_i is uncorrelated with x_{1i} and λ_i by construction. This means that we could estimate β_1 and σ_{12} by running a least squares regression of y_i upon the original regressors x_{1i} and the inverse Mills ratio λ_i. The fact that λ_i is not observed is not a real problem because the only unknown element in λ_i is β_2, which can be estimated consistently by probit maximum likelihood applied to the selection model. This means that in the regression (7.97) we replace λ_i with its estimate $\hat{\lambda}_i$ and OLS will still produce consistent estimators of β_1 and σ_{12}. In general, this two-step estimator (sometimes popularly referred to as 'heckit') will not be efficient, but it is computationally simple and consistent.

One problem with the two-step estimator is that routinely computed OLS standard errors are incorrect, unless $\sigma_{12} = 0$. This problem is often ignored because it is still possible to validly test the null hypothesis of no sample selection bias using a standard t-test on $\sigma_{12} = 0$. In general, however, standard errors will have to be adjusted because η_i in (7.97) is heteroskedastic and because β_2 is estimated. If x_{1i} and x_{2i} are identical, the model is only identified through the fact that λ_i is a nonlinear function. Empirically, the two-step approach will therefore not work very well if there is little variation in λ_i and λ_i is close to being linear in x_{2i}. This is the subject of many Monte Carlo studies, for example Yamagata and Orme (2005); see Puhani (2000) for a short overview. The inclusion of variables in x_{2i} in addition to those in x_{1i} can be important for identification in the second step, although often there are no natural candidates and any choice is easily criticized. At the very least, some sensitivity analysis with respect to the imposed exclusion restrictions should be performed, to make sure that the inverse Mills ratio is not incorrectly picking up the effect of omitted variables.

The model that is estimated in the second step describes the conditional expected value of y_i given x_i and given that $h_i = 1$, for example the expected wage given that a person is working. Often, the expected value of y_i given x_i, not conditional upon $h_i = 1$, is the focus of interest, and this is given by $x'_{1i}\beta_1$, which is directly obtained from the last regression. Predicting wages for an arbitrary person can thus be based upon (7.97), but should not include $\sigma_{12}\lambda(x'_{2i}\beta_2)$. A positive covariance σ_{12} indicates that there is unobserved heterogeneity that positively affects both wages and the probability of working. That is, those with a wage that is higher than expected are more likely to be working (conditional on a given set of x_i values).

The two-step estimator of the sample-selection model is one of the most often used estimators in empirical micro-econometric work. There seems to be a strong belief that the inclusion of the inverse Mills ratio in a model eliminates all problems of selection bias. This is certainly not generally true, and the sample selection model should be employed with extreme care. The presence of nonrandom selection induces a fundamental identification problem, and consequently the validity of any solution will depend upon the validity of the assumptions that are made, which can only be partly tested. Much of the concerns raised with instrumental variables estimation (see Chapter 5) translate directly to the sample selection model. If there are no exclusion restrictions in x_{1i}, that is, if all variables in x_{2i} from the selection equation are included in the equation of interest, the two-step estimator is solely identified through the joint normality assumption (leading to the particular functional form of the inverse Mills ratio λ_i). Even if this assumption would be correct, the two-step estimator is very likely to suffer from multicollinearity. One implication of this is that insignificance of the inverse Mills ratio is not a reliable guide as to the absence of selection bias. It is therefore highly recommended to include additional exogenous variables in x_{2i} that do not appear in x_{1i}. This requires a valid exclusion restriction, just as in the case of instrumental variables. The importance of this is often neglected, frequently resulting in studies that either have no exclusion restrictions, or where the specification of the first stage is not reported and thus unclear; see Lennox, Francis and Wang (2012) for a critical survey on the use of the Heckman two-step procedure in the accounting literature. Because identification rests critically upon the exclusion restriction(s), estimation results tend to be very sensitivity to the choices made, and a small difference in the specification of (7.87) can yield wildly different estimates for (7.86). Therefore, exclusion restrictions should be well documented and well motivated. Moreover, a careful sensitivity analysis with respect to robustness and multicollinearity is desirable. Because the sample selection model easily suffers from misspecification problems, a simple first check is to investigate the implied correlated coefficient in the estimate for $\sigma_{12} = \rho_{12}\sigma_1$ to see whether it is well within the $[-1, 1]$ interval. Section 7.6 will pay more attention to sample selection bias and the implied identification problem.

7.5.3 Further Extensions

The structure of a model with one or more latent variables, normal errors and an observation rule mapping the unobserved endogenous variables into observed ones can be used in a variety of applications. Amemiya (1984) characterizes several tobit models by the form of the likelihood function, because different structures may lead to models that are statistically the same. An obvious extension, resulting in the tobit III model, is the one where h_i^* in the earlier labour supply/wage equation model is partially observed as hours of work. In that case we observe

$$y_i = y_i^*, \ h_i = h_i^* \quad \text{if } h_i^* > 0 \tag{7.98}$$

$$y_i \text{ not observed}, \ h_i = 0 \quad \text{if } h_i^* \leq 0 \tag{7.99}$$

with the same underlying latent structure. Essentially, this says that the selection model is not of the probit type but of the standard tobit type. Applications using models of this and more complicated structures can often be found in labour economics, where one explains wages for different sectors, union/nonunion members, etc., taking into account that sectoral choice is probably not exogenous but based upon potential wages in the two sectors, that labour supply is not exogenous or both. Other types of selection model are also possible, including, for example, an ordered response model. See Vella (1998) for more discussion on this topic.

7.5.4 Illustration: Expenditures on Alcohol and Tobacco (Part 2)

In Subsection 7.4.3 we considered the estimation of Engel curves for alcoholic beverages and tobacco, taking into account the problem of zero expenditures. The standard tobit model assumes that these zero expenditures are the result of corner solutions. That is, a household's budget constraint and preferences are such that the optimal budget shares of alcohol and tobacco, as determined by the first-order conditions, and in the absence of a non-negativity constraint, would be negative. As a consequence, the optimal allocation for the household is zero expenditures, which corresponds to a corner solution that is not characterized by the usual first-order conditions. It can be disputed that this is a realistic assumption, and this subsection considers some alternatives to the tobit I model. The alternatives are a simple OLS for the positive observations, possibly combined with a binary choice model that explains whether expenditures are positive or not, and a combined tobit II model that models budget shares jointly with the binary decision to consume or not.

Obviously one can think of reasons other than those implicit in the tobit model why households do not consume tobacco or alcohol. Because of social or health reasons, for example, many nonsmokers would not smoke even if tobacco were available for free. This implies that whether or not we observe zero expenditures may be determined quite differently from the amount of expenditures for those that consume the good. Some commodities are possibly subject to abstention. Keeping this in mind, we can consider alternative specifications to the tobit model. A first alternative is very simple and assumes that abstention is determined randomly in the sense that the unobservables that determine budget shares are independent of the decision to consume or not. If this is the case, we can simply specify an Engel curve that is valid for people who do not abstain and ignore the abstention decision. This would allow us to estimate the total expenditure elasticity for people who have a positive budget share, but would not allow us to analyse possible effects arising through a changing composition of the population with positive values. Statistically, this means that we can estimate the Engel curve simply by ordinary least squares but using only those observations that have positive expenditures. The results of this exercise are reported in Table 7.10. In comparison with the results for the tobit model, reported in Table 7.9, it is surprising that the coefficient for log total expenditures in the Engel curve for alcohol is negative and statistically not significantly different

Table 7.10 Models for budget shares alcohol and tobacco, estimated by OLS using positive observations only

Variable	Alcoholic beverages		Tobacco	
	Estimate	Standard error	Estimate	Standard error
constant	0.0527	(0.0439)	0.4897	(0.0741)
age class	0.0078	(0.0110)	−0.0315	(0.0206)
nadults	−0.0131	(0.0163)	−0.0130	(0.0324)
nkids ≥ 2	−0.0020	(0.0006)	0.0013	(0.0011)
nkids < 2	−0.0024	(0.0023)	−0.0034	(0.0045)
log(x)	−0.0023	(0.0032)	−0.0336	(0.0055)
age × log(x)	−0.0004	(0.0008)	0.0022	(0.0015)
nadults × log(x)	0.0008	(0.0012)	0.0011	(0.0023)
	$R^2 = 0.051$ $s = 0.0215$ $N = 2258$		$R^2 = 0.154$ $s = 0.0291$ $N = 1036$	

from zero. Estimating total expenditure elasticities, as defined in (7.72), on the basis of the OLS estimation results leads to values of 0.923 and 0.177 for alcohol and tobacco, respectively.

The elasticities based on the OLS estimates are valid if abstention is determined on the basis of the observables in the model but not on the basis of the unobservables that are collected in the error term. Moreover they are conditional upon the fact that the household has positive expenditures. To obtain insight in what causes households to consume these two goods or not, we can use a binary choice model, the most obvious choice being a probit model. If all zero expenditures are explained by abstention rather than by corner solutions, the probit model should include variables that determine preferences and should not include variables that determine the household's budget constraint. This is because in this case a changing budget constraint will never induce a household to start consuming alcohol or tobacco. This would imply that total expenditures and relative prices should not be included in the probit model. In the absence of price variation across households, total expenditures are an obvious candidate for exclusion from the probit model. However, it is conceivable that education level is an important determinant of abstention of alcohol or tobacco, while – unfortunately – no information about education is available in our sample. This is why we include total expenditures in the probit model, despite our reservations, but think of total expenditures as a proxy for education level, social status or other variables that affect household preferences. In addition to variables included in the Engel curve, the model for abstention also includes two dummy variables for blue- and white-collar workers.[23] It is assumed that these two variables do not affect the budget shares of alcohol and tobacco but only the decision to consume or not. As any exclusion restriction, this one can also be disputed, and we shall return to this issue below when estimating a joint model for budget shares and abstention.

The estimation results for the two probit models are given in Table 7.11. For alcoholic beverages it appears that total expenditures, the number of adults in the household as well as the number of children older than 2 are statistically significant in explaining abstention. For tobacco, total expenditures, number of children older than 2, age and being a

[23] The excluded category (reference group) includes inactive and self-employed people.

Table 7.11 Probit models for abstention of alcohol and tobacco

	Alcoholic beverages		Tobacco	
Variable	Estimate	Standard error	Estimate	Standard error
constant	−15.882	(2.574)	8.244	(2.211)
age	0.6679	(0.6520)	−2.4830	(0.5596)
nadults	2.2554	(1.0250)	0.4852	(0.8717)
nkids ≥ 2	−0.0770	(0.0372)	0.0813	(0.0308)
nkids < 2	−0.1857	(0.1408)	−0.2117	(0.1230)
$\log(x)$	1.2355	(0.1913)	−0.6321	(0.1632)
age $\times \log(x)$	−0.0448	(0.0485)	0.1747	(0.0413)
nadults $\times \log(x)$	−0.1688	(0.0743)	−0.0253	(0.0629)
blue collar	−0.0612	(0.0978)	0.2064	(0.0834)
white collar	0.0506	(0.0847)	0.0215	(0.0694)
Loglikelihood	−1159.865		−1754.886	
Wald test (χ^2_9)	173.18	($p = 0.000$)	108.91	($p = 0.000$)

blue-collar worker are statistically important explanators for abstention. To illustrate the estimation results, consider a household consisting of two adults, the head being a 35-year-old blue-collar worker, and two children older than 2. If the total expenditures of this artificial household are equal to the overall sample average, the implied estimated probabilities of a positive budget share of alcohol and tobacco are given by 86.8% and 51.7%, respectively. A 10% increase in total expenditures changes these probabilities only marginally to 88.5% and 50.4%.

Assuming that the specification of the Engel curve and the abstention model are correct, the estimation results in Tables 7.10 and 7.11 are appropriate provided that the error term in the probit model is independent of the error term in the Engel curve. Correlation between these error terms invalidates the OLS results and would make a tobit II model more appropriate. Put differently, the two-equation model that was estimated is a special case of a tobit II model in which the error terms in the respective equations are uncorrelated. It is possible to test for a nonzero correlation if we estimate the more general model. As discussed earlier, in the tobit II model it is very important which variables are included in which of the two equations. If the same variables are included in both equations, the model is only identified through the normality assumption that was imposed upon the error terms.[24] This is typically considered to be an undesirable situation. The exclusion of variables from the abstention model does not solve this problem. Instead, it is desirable to include variables in the abstention model that we are confident do not determine the budget shares directly. The problem of finding such variables is similar to finding appropriate instruments with endogenous regressors (see Chapter 5), and we should be equally critical and careful in choosing them; our estimation results will critically depend upon the choice that we make. In the above abstention model the dummies for being a blue- or white-collar worker are included to take up this role. If we are confident that these variables do not affect budget shares directly, estimation of the tobit II model may be appropriate.

[24] To see this, note that the functional form of λ is determined by the distributional assumptions of the error term. See the discussion in Section 7.6.

Table 7.12 Two-step estimation of Engel curves for alcohol and tobacco (tobit II model)

Variable	Alcoholic beverages		Tobacco	
	Estimate	Standard error	Estimate	Standard error
constant	0.0543	0.1330)	0.4516	(0.1086)
age class	0.0077	(0.0130)	−0.0173	(0.0359)
nadults	−0.0133	(0.0247)	−0.0174	(0.0340)
$nkids \geq 2$	−0.0020	(0.0008)	0.0008	(0.0015)
$nkids < 2$	−0.0024	(0.0026)	−0.0021	(0.0054)
$\log(x)$	−0.0024	(0.0094)	−0.0301	(0.0090)
$age \times \log(x)$	−0.0004	(0.0009)	0.0012	(0.0025)
$nadults \times \log(x)$	0.0008	(0.0018)	0.0014	(0.0024)
λ	−0.0002	(0.0165)	−0.0090	(0.0186)
$\hat{\sigma}_1$	−0.0215	n.c.	−0.0291	n.c.
Implied ρ	−0.01	n.c.	−0.31	n.c.
	$N = 2258$		$N = 1036$	

Using Heckman's two step-procedure, as described in Subsection 7.5.2, we can re-estimate the two Engel curves taking into account the sample selection problem due to possible endogeneity of the abstention decision. The results of this are presented in Table 7.12, where OLS is used but standard errors are adjusted to take into account heteroskedasticity and the estimation error in λ. For alcoholic beverages the inclusion of $\hat{\lambda}$ does not affect the results very much, and we obtain estimates that are pretty close to those reported in Table 7.10. The t-statistic on the coefficient for $\hat{\lambda}$ does not allow us to reject the null hypothesis of no correlation, while the estimation results imply an estimated correlation coefficient (computed as the ratio of the coefficient for $\hat{\lambda}$ and the standard deviation of the error term $\hat{\sigma}_1$) of only −0.01. Computation of these correlation coefficients is important because the two-step approach may easily imply correlations outside the $[-1, 1]$ range, indicating that the tobit II model may not be appropriate, or indicating that some exclusion restrictions are not appropriate. Note that these estimation results imply that total expenditures have a significant impact on the probability of having positive expenditures on alcohol, but do not significantly affect the budget share of alcohol. For tobacco we also find that the inverse Mills ratio enters the equation insignificantly, although the implied correlation coefficient is as large as −0.31. The estimation results are therefore very similar to those reported in Table 7.10. To conclude we compute the total expenditure elasticities of alcohol and tobacco on the basis of the estimation results in Table 7.12. Using similar computations as before, we obtain estimated elasticities of 0.920 and 0.243, respectively. Apparently and not surprisingly, tobacco is a necessary good for those that smoke. In fact, tobacco expenditures are close to being inelastic.

7.6 Sample Selection Bias

When the sample used in a statistical analysis is not randomly drawn from a larger population, selection bias may arise. We briefly touched upon this problem in Section 2.9. In the presence of selection bias, standard estimators and tests may result in misleading inferences. Because there are many situations where this may be the case, and the tobit II model does not necessarily provide an adequate solution to it, some additional discussion of this problem is warranted.

At the general level, we can say that selection bias arises if the probability of a particular observation to be included in the sample depends upon the phenomenon we are explaining. There are a number of reasons why this may occur. First, it could be due to the sampling frame. For example, if you interview people in the university restaurant and ask how often they visit it, those that go there every day are much more likely to end up in the sample than those that visit every two weeks. Second, **nonresponse** may result in selection bias. For example, people who refuse to report their income are typically those with relatively high or relatively low income levels. Third, it could be due to **self-selection** of economic agents. That is, individuals select themselves into a certain state, for example working, union member, public sector employment, in a nonrandom way on the basis of economic arguments. In general, those who benefit most from being in a certain state will be more likely to be in this state.

7.6.1 The Nature of the Selection Problem

Suppose we are interested in the conditional distribution of a variable y_i given a set of other (exogenous) variables x_i, that is $f(y_i|x_i)$. Usually, we will formulate this as a function of a limited number of parameters, and interest lies in these parameters. Selection is indicated by a dummy variable r_i such that both y_i and x_i are observed if $r_i = 1$ and either y_i is unobserved if $r_i = 0$ or both y_i and x_i are unobserved if $r_i = 0$.

All inferences ignoring the selection rule are (implicitly) conditional upon $r_i = 1$. Interest, however, lies in the conditional distribution of y_i given x_i but not given $r_i = 1$. We can thus say that the selection rule is **ignorable** (Rubin, 1976, Little and Rubin, 1987) if conditioning upon the outcome of the selection process has no effect. That is, if

$$f(y_i|x_i, r_i = 1) = f(y_i|x_i). \tag{7.100}$$

If we are only interested in the conditional expectation of y_i given x_i, we can relax this to

$$E\{y_i|x_i, r_i = 1\} = E\{y_i|x_i\}. \tag{7.101}$$

A statement that is equivalent to (7.100) is that

$$P\{r_i = 1|x_i, y_i\} = P\{r_i = 1|x_i\}, \tag{7.102}$$

which says that the probability of selection into the sample should not depend upon y_i, given that it is allowed to depend upon the variables in x_i. This already shows some important results. First, selection bias does not arise if selection depends upon the exogenous variables only. Thus, if we are estimating a wage equation that has marital status on the right-hand side, it does not matter if married people are more likely to end up in the sample than those who are not married. At a more general level, it follows that whether or not selection bias is a problem depends upon the distribution of interest.

If the selection rule is not ignorable, it should be taken into account when making inferences. As stressed by Manski (1989), a fundamental identification problem arises in this case. To see this, note that

$$E\{y_i|x_i\} = E\{y_i|x_i, r_i = 1\}P\{r_i = 1|x_i\} + E\{y_i|x_i, r_i = 0\}P\{r_i = 0|x_i\}. \tag{7.103}$$

If x_i is observed irrespective of r_i, it is possible to identify the probability that $r_i = 1$ as a function of x_i (e.g. using a binary choice model). Thus, it is possible to identify $P\{r_i = 1|x_i\}$ and $P\{r_i = 0|x_i\}$, while $E\{y_i|x_i, r_i = 1\}$ is also identified (from the selected sample). However, since no information on $E\{y_i|x_i, r_i = 0\}$ is provided by the data, it is *not possible* to identify $E\{y_i|x_i\}$ without additional information or making additional (nontestable) assumptions. As Manski (1989) notes, in the absence of prior information, the selection problem is fatal for inference on $E\{y_i|x_i\}$.

If it is possible to restrict the range of possible values of $E\{y_i|x_i, r_i = 0\}$, it is possible to determine bounds on $E\{y_i|x_i\}$ that may be useful. To illustrate this, suppose we are interested in the unconditional distribution of y_i (so no x_i variables appear) and we happen to know that this distribution is normal with unknown mean μ and unit variance. If 10% is missing, the most extreme cases arise where these 10% are all in the left or all in the right tail of the distribution. Using properties of a truncated normal distribution,[25] one can derive

$$-1.75 \leq E\{y_i|r_i = 0\} \leq 1.75,$$

so that

$$0.9E\{y_i|r_i = 1\} - 0.175 \leq E\{y_i\} \leq 0.9E\{y_i|r_i = 1\} + 0.175,$$

where $E\{y_i|r_i = 1\}$ can be estimated by the sample average in the selected sample. In this way, we can estimate an upper and lower bound for the unconditional mean of y_i, not making any assumptions about the selection rule. The price that we pay for this is that we need to make assumptions about the form of the distribution of y_i, which are not testable. If we shift interest to other aspects of the distribution of y_i, given x_i, rather than its mean, such assumptions may not be needed. For example, if we are interested in the *median* of the distribution, we can derive upper and lower bounds from the probability of selection without assuming anything about the shape of the distribution.[26] Manski (1989, 1994) provides additional details and discussion of these issues, while Manski (2007) provides a general framework for inference in cases where the parameters of interest are only partially identified.

A more common approach in applied work imposes additional structure on the problem to identify the quantities of interest. Let

$$E\{y_i|x_i\} = g_1(x_i) \tag{7.104}$$

and

$$E\{y_i|x_i, r_i = 1\} = g_1(x_i) + g_2(x_i), \tag{7.105}$$

which, as long as we do not make any assumptions about the functions g_1 and g_2, is not restrictive. Assumptions about the form of g_1 and g_2 are required to identify g_1, which is what we are interested in. The most common assumption is the **single index** assumption,

[25] For a standard normal variable y it holds that $P\{y > 1.28\} = 0.10$ and $E\{y|y > 1.28\} = \phi(1.28)/0.10 = 1.75$ (see Appendix B).

[26] Recall that the median of a random variable y is defined as the value m for which $P\{y \leq m\} = 0.5$ (see Appendix B). If 10% of the observations are missing, we know that m is between the (theoretical) 40% and 60% quantiles of the observed distribution. That is, $m_1 \leq m \leq m_2$, with $P\{y \leq m_1|r = 1\} = 0.4$ and $P\{y \leq m_2|r = 1\} = 0.6$.

which says that g_2 depends upon x_i only through a single index, $x_i'\beta_2$, say. This assumption is often motivated from a latent variable model:

$$y_i = g_1(x_i) + \varepsilon_{1i} \tag{7.106}$$

$$r_i^* = x_i'\beta_2 + \varepsilon_{2i} \tag{7.107}$$

$$r_i = 1 \quad \text{if } r_i^* > 0, \quad 0 \text{ otherwise}, \tag{7.108}$$

where $E\{\varepsilon_{1i}|x_i\} = 0$ and ε_{2i} is independent of x_i. Then it holds that

$$E\{y_i|x_i, r_i = 1\} = g_1(x_i) + E\{\varepsilon_{1i}|\varepsilon_{2i} > -x_i'\beta_2\}, \tag{7.109}$$

where the latter term depends upon x_i only through the single index $x_i'\beta_2$. Thus we can write

$$E\{y_i|x_i, r_i = 1\} = g_1(x_i) + g_2^*(x_i'\beta_2), \tag{7.110}$$

for some function g_2^*. Because β_2 can be identified from the selection process, provided observations on x_i are available irrespective of r_i, identification of g_1 is achieved by assuming that it does not depend upon one or more variables in x_i (while these variables have a nonzero coefficient in β_2). This means that exclusion restrictions are imposed upon g_1.

From (7.84), it is easily seen that the tobit II model constitutes a special case of the above framework, where $g_1(x_i) = x_i'\beta_1$ and g_2^* is given by $\sigma_{12}\phi(x_i'\beta_2)/\Phi(x_i'\beta_2)$. The assumption that ε_{1i} and ε_{2i} are i.i.d. jointly normal produces the functional form of g_2^*. Moreover, the restriction that g_1 is linear (while g_2^* is not) implies that the model is identified even in the absence of exclusion restrictions in $g_1(x_i)$. In practice, though, empirical identification may benefit from imposing zero restrictions on β_1. When the distribution of ε_{1i} and ε_{2i} is not normal, (7.101) is still valid, and this is what is exploited in many semi-parametric estimators of the sample selection model.

7.6.2 Semi-parametric Estimation of the Sample Selection Model

Although it is beyond the scope of this text fully to discuss semi-parametric estimators for limited dependent variable models, some intuitive discussion will be provided here. While semi-parametric estimators relax the joint normality assumption of ε_{1i} and ε_{2i}, they generally maintain the single index assumption. That is, the conditional expectation of ε_{1i} given selection into the sample (and given the exogenous variables) depends upon x_i only through $x_i'\beta_2$. This requires that we can model the selection process in a fairly homogeneous way. If observations are missing for a variety of reasons, the single index assumption may no longer be appropriate. For example, individuals who do not have a job may not be working because their reservation wage is too high (a supply-side argument), as in the standard model, but also because employers are not interested in hiring them (a demand-side argument). These two processes are not necessarily well described by a single index model.

The other crucial assumption in all semi-parametric approaches is that there is at least one variable that enters the selection equation ($x_i'\beta_2$) that does not enter the equation of interest $g_1(x_i)$. This means that we need an exclusion restriction in g_1 in order to identify the model. This is obvious as we would never be able to separate g_1 from g_2^*

if both depend upon the same set of variables and no functional form restrictions are imposed. As discussed before, imposing an exclusion restriction is similar to finding a valid instrument and needs to be well motivated on economic grounds.

Most semi-parametric estimators are two-step estimators, just like Heckman's (1979). In the first step, the single-index parameter β_2 is estimated semi-parametrically, that is, without imposing a particular distribution upon ε_{2i}. From this, an estimate for the single index is constructed, so that in the second step the unknown function g_2^* is estimated jointly with g_1 (usually imposing some functional form upon g_1, like linearity). A simple way to approximate the unknown function $g_2^*(x_i'\beta_2)$ is the use of a series approximation, for example polynomials or splines in (transformations of) $x_i'\beta_2$; see Newey (2009). An alternative approach is based on the elimination of $g_2^*(x_i'\beta_2)$ from the model by considering differences between observations that have values of $x_i'\hat{\beta}_2$ that are similar.

All semi-parametric methods involve some additional regularity conditions and assumptions. An intuitive survey of alternative estimation methods for the sample-selection model is given in Vella (1998). Pagan and Ullah (1999) provide more details. Empirical implementation is usually not straightforward; see Newey, Powell and Walker (1990) or Martins (2001) for some applications.

7.7 Estimating Treatment Effects

Another area where sample selection plays an important role is in the estimation of treatment effects. A treatment effect refers to the impact of receiving a certain treatment upon a particular outcome variable, for example the effect of participating in a job training programme upon future earnings.[27] Because this effect may be different across individuals and selection into the training programme may be nonrandom, the estimation of treatment effects has received much attention in the recent literature (see, e.g., Angrist, Imbens and Rubin, 1996; Heckman and Vytlacil, 2005; Imbens and Wooldridge, 2009; and Heckman, 2010). In the simplest case, the treatment effect is simply the coefficient for a treatment dummy variable in a regression model. Because interest is in the *causal* effect of the treatment, we need to worry about the potential endogeneity of the treatment dummy. Alternatively, to be more precise, we need to worry about selection into treatment. In this section, we consider the problem of estimating treatment effects in a more general context, where the effect of treatment may differ across individuals and may affect the probability of individuals choosing for treatment. A more extensive discussion can be found in Cameron and Trivedi (2005, Chapter 25), Lee (2005) and Wooldridge (2010, Chapter 21). Imbens (2015) provides a useful practical guide to the estimation of average treatment effects.

Let us start by defining the two potential outcomes for an individual as y_{0i} and y_{1i}, corresponding to the outcome without and with treatment, respectively. At this stage, we think of y_{0i} and y_{1i} as having a continuous distribution (e.g. earnings). The individual specific gains to treatment are given by $y_{1i} - y_{0i}$, which is the difference between an actual outcome and a counterfactual one. There are several important problems in estimating treatment effects. First, only one of the two potential outcomes is observed, depending upon the decision of the individual to participate in the programme or not. In particular,

[27] In what follows, we use the terms 'participating in a programme' and 'receiving treatment' as being equivalent.

if r_i is a binary variable indicating treatment, we only observe

$$y_i \equiv (1 - r_i)y_{0i} + r_i y_{1i}. \tag{7.111}$$

Second, the gains to treatment are typically different across individuals, and several alternative population parameters are proposed to summarize the effect of treatment for a particular group of individuals. A standard one is the **average treatment effect**,[28] defined as

$$ATE \equiv E\{y_{1i} - y_{0i}\} \tag{7.112}$$

or, conditional upon one or more covariates, $E\{y_{1i} - y_{0i}|x_i\}$. The average treatment effect describes the expected effect of treatment for an *arbitrary* person (with characteristics x_i). That is, it measures the effect of randomly assigning a person in the population to the programme. Whereas Heckman (1997) criticizes this parameter of interest by stating that 'picking a millionaire at random to participate in a training programme for low-skilled workers' is not policy relevant or feasible, it may be of interest if the population of interest is appropriately defined (including only those who are eligible for treatment).

Also of interest is the average treatment effect for the treated, defined as

$$ATET \equiv E\{y_{1i} - y_{0i}|r_i = 1\} \tag{7.113}$$

or, conditional upon one or more covariates, $E\{y_{1i} - y_{0i}|x_i, r_i = 1\}$. Thus, $ATET$ is the mean effect for those that actually participate in the programme. As argued by Imbens and Wooldridge (2009), in many cases $ATET$ is the more interesting estimand than the overall average effect. A third parameter of interest is the local average treatment effect (LATE) defined by Imbens and Angrist (1994). This reflects the expected effect of the treatment for those individuals whose behaviour is affected by the instrument used in estimation. Accordingly, the definition of LATE depends upon the instrument. Each instrumental variable estimator of a treatment effect estimates the average treatment effect for a different subgroup of the population, namely for those who change treatment status because they comply with the assignment-to-treatment mechanism implied by the instrument.[29] Ichino and Winter-Ebmer (1999), for example, use this approach to analyse and interpret different IV estimates of the returns to schooling.

Below, we focus on the estimation of ATE and $ATET$. The econometric problem is to identify these measures from observations on y_i, r_i and x_i. Note that it is easy to identify $E\{y_i|r_i = 1\} = E\{y_{1i}|r_i = 1\}$ and $E\{y_i|r_i = 0\} = E\{y_{0i}|r_i = 0\}$ but in general this is insufficient to identify either ATE or $ATET$. In the ideal situation people are randomly selected into the programme, and there is no difference between ATE and $ATET$. In this case, an obvious estimator for the average treatment effect is the difference in the sample averages of y_{1i} and y_{0i}. That is,

$$\hat{\Delta}_{ate} = \bar{y}_1 - \bar{y}_0 = \frac{1}{N_1}\sum_{i=1}^{N} r_i y_{1i} - \frac{1}{N_0}\sum_{i=1}^{N}(1 - r_i)y_{0i}, \tag{7.114}$$

[28] Because the expectation refers to the population of interest, it would be more appropriate to refer to this quantity as the expected treatment effect. The current terminology follows the convention in the literature.

[29] See also Heckman (2010) for a critical discussion of what question LATE is answering.

where $N_1 = \sum_{i=1}^{N} r_i$ and $N_0 = \sum_{i=1}^{N}(1 - r_i)$ and $N_0 + N_1 = N$. This is a consistent estimator for both *ATE* and *ATET* if r_i is independent of both y_{0i} and y_{1i}. That is, if allocation into the programme is completely random.

However, in observational studies the assumption that the treatment decision is independent of the potential outcomes is often hard to maintain. In general, one might expect that the average treatment effect for those who choose to participate in the programme is somewhat larger than the average treatment effect for the entire population. Put differently, one might expect that the decision to participate is partly determined by the gains from treatment. This demands alternative ways to estimate the treatment parameters. A first approach is based on regression models.

7.7.1 Regression-based Estimators

To illustrate the issues, let us assume that both y_{0i} and y_{1i} can be related to x_i by means of a linear model, that is

$$y_{0i} = \alpha_0 + x_i'\beta_0 + \varepsilon_{0i}, \tag{7.115}$$

$$y_{1i} = \alpha_1 + x_i'\beta_1 + \varepsilon_{1i}, \tag{7.116}$$

where the constant is eliminated from x_i, and where ε_{0i} and ε_{1i} are zero mean error terms, satisfying $E\{\varepsilon_{ji}|x_i\} = 0$ for $j = 0, 1$. The linearity assumption is not crucial, and some exclusion restrictions may be imposed upon the covariate vectors in the two equations (see Heckman, 2001). With this, the observed outcome is given by

$$y_i = \alpha_0 + x_i'\beta_0 + \varepsilon_{0i} + r_i[(\alpha_1 - \alpha_0) + x_i'(\beta_1 - \beta_0) + (\varepsilon_{1i} - \varepsilon_{0i})], \tag{7.117}$$

where the term in square brackets denotes the gain from the programme. This is an example of a **switching regression model**, where the outcome equation depends upon the regime ($r_i = 0$ or $r_i = 1$). The individual specific gain from the programme consists of three components: a constant, a component related to observable characteristics and an idiosyncratic component related to unobservables.[30] We can rewrite (7.117) as

$$y_i = \alpha_0 + x_i'\beta_0 + \delta r_i + r_i x_i'\gamma + \varepsilon_i, \tag{7.118}$$

where $\delta \equiv \alpha_1 - \alpha_0$, $\gamma \equiv \beta_1 - \beta_0$ and $\varepsilon_i \equiv (1 - r_i)\varepsilon_{0i} + r_i\varepsilon_{1i}$. In this model, the average treatment effect for individuals with characteristics x_i is given by

$$ATE(x_i) = \delta + x_i'\gamma, \tag{7.119}$$

while the average treatment effect upon the treated is given by

$$ATET(x_i) = \delta + x_i'\gamma + E\{\varepsilon_{1i} - \varepsilon_{0i}|x_i, r_i = 1\}. \tag{7.120}$$

The two concepts are equivalent if the last term in this expression is zero, which happens in two important special cases. The first case arises when there are no unobservable components in the gain from treatment, and it holds that $\varepsilon_{0i} = \varepsilon_{1i}$. The second case arises

[30] Although the unobservable components are not observed by the researcher, they may be (partially) known to the individual.

when the treatment decision is independent of the unobservable gains from the treatment. In this case, $E\{\varepsilon_{1i} - \varepsilon_{0i}|x_i, r_i = 1\} = E\{\varepsilon_{1i} - \varepsilon_{0i}|x_i\} = 0$. This implies that individuals, at the time they make their participation decision, are unaware of $\varepsilon_{1i} - \varepsilon_{0i}$ (or simply ignore it). Note that, even if the last term in (7.120) is zero, the *unconditional* average treatment effect for the treated can differ from the population average treatment effect in cases where the average characteristics in x_i of the treated group differ from those in the population. For example, this happens when the treatment effect depends upon age and the treated group is older than the control group.

To estimate either *ATE* or *ATET*, the first step is to find consistent estimators for δ and γ. This is relatively straightforward if it is assumed that y_{0i}, y_{1i} are independent of r_i, conditional upon x_i, which is referred to as **conditional independence** or **unconfoundedness**. It says that, conditional upon the covariates x_i, selection into treatment is not related to the potential outcomes. Implicitly, this means that the set of covariates x_i is sufficiently large and includes all variables confounding treatment. This assumption implies that

$$E\{\varepsilon_{0i}|x_i, r_i = 0\} = 0$$

and

$$E\{\varepsilon_{1i}|x_i, r_i = 1\} = 0,$$

so that the models in (7.115) and (7.116) can be estimated consistently using standard OLS on the appropriate subsamples. In the special case where the slope coefficients are unaffected by the treatment ($\beta_0 = \beta_1 = \beta$), the average treatment effect reduces to a constant and can be estimated from OLS in

$$y_i = \alpha_0 + x_i'\beta + \delta r_i + \varepsilon_i, \tag{7.121}$$

where δ denotes the average treatment effect, and $\varepsilon_i = (1 - r_i)\varepsilon_{0i} + r_i\varepsilon_{1i}$, as before. This error term satisfies $E\{\varepsilon_i|x_i, r_i\} = 0$ by virtue of the unconfoundedness assumption.

More generally, once we have consistent estimates for the coefficients, we can use the regression models in (7.115) and (7.116) to predict the actual and counterfactual outcomes for each individual in the sample and estimate *ATE* as

$$\hat{\Delta}_{ate,reg} = \frac{1}{N}\sum_{i=1}^{N}(\hat{y}_{1i} - \hat{y}_{0i}), \tag{7.122}$$

where

$$\hat{y}_{1i} = \bar{y}_1 + (x_i - \bar{x}_1)'b_1$$

where b_1 is the OLS estimate for β_1 from (7.116) and where we have used the definition of the OLS estimator for the intercept. A similar expression can be derived for $\hat{y}_{0i}$. Analogously, *ATET* can be estimated using

$$\hat{\Delta}_{atet,reg} = \frac{1}{N_1}\sum_{i=1}^{N} r_i(\hat{y}_{1i} - \hat{y}_{0i}). \tag{7.123}$$

The estimator in (7.122) is referred to as the regression-adjustment estimator for *ATE*. It can be written as

$$\hat{\Delta}_{ate,reg} = \bar{y}_1 - \bar{y}_0 - (\bar{x}_1 - \bar{x}_0)'\left(\frac{N_0}{N}b_1 + \frac{N_1}{N}b_0\right). \tag{7.124}$$

To adjust for the differences in covariates, the simple difference in average outcomes in (7.114) is adjusted by the difference in average covariates multiplied by the weighted average of the regression coefficients. If the average values of the covariates are very different across the subsamples, the adjustment to the sample mean is typically large. It is important to note that the adjustment strongly depends upon the linear regression models being accurate over the entire range of covariate values. If the models are used to predict outcomes far away from where the regression parameters are estimated, the results can be quite sensitive to minor changes in the specification (Imbens and Wooldridge, 2009). This explains why recent empirical work on the estimation of treatment effects has moved away from the regression-based approaches (see Subsection 7.7.3).

The unconfoundedness assumption requires that, conditional upon observed covariates, there are no unobservables that affect both the potential outcomes and the treatment decision. Many recent studies impose such an assumption. For example, Huber, Lechner and Wunsch (2011) argue that they observe all important confounders when investigating the health effects of transitions from welfare to employment and of assignments to welfare-to-work programmes, which justifies a conditional independence assumption. Nevertheless, the assumption is quite restrictive and requires that there are no unobservable components to y_{0i} and y_{1i} that also affect a person's decision to participate in the programme. That is, individuals may decide to participate in the programme on the basis of x_i (e.g. previous education or gender), but not on the basis of unobservables affecting either y_{0i} or y_{1i}. This is similar to condition (7.87) in the previous section.

If the unconfoundedness assumption does not hold, the treatment effects can be estimated consistently provided one is willing to make alternative identifying assumptions. This is often nontrivial. As an illustration, let us assume that the treatment decision can be described by a probit equation

$$r_i^* = x_i'\beta_2 + \eta_i, \tag{7.125}$$

with $r_i = 1$ if $r_i^* > 0$ and 0 otherwise, where η_i is assumed to be $NID(0, 1)$, independent of x_i. Further, assume that the error terms in (7.115) and (7.116) are also normal, with variances σ_0^2 and σ_1^2 and covariances σ_{02} and σ_{12} with η_i. This is a special case of what is referred to as 'selection upon unobservables'. Now we can write

$$E\{\varepsilon_{0i}|x_i, r_i = 0\} = \sigma_{02}E\{\eta_i|x_i, \eta_i \leq -x_i'\beta_2\} = \sigma_{02}\lambda_i(x_i'\beta_2)$$
$$E\{\varepsilon_{1i}|x_i, r_i = 1\} = \sigma_{12}E\{\eta_i|x_i, \eta_i > -x_i'\beta_2\} = \sigma_{12}\lambda_i(x_i'\beta_2),$$

where

$$\lambda_i(x_i'\beta_2) = E\{\eta_i|x_i, r_i\} = \frac{r_i - \Phi(x_i'\beta_2)}{\Phi(x_i'\beta_2)(1 - \Phi(x_i'\beta_2))}\phi(x_i'\beta_2), \tag{7.126}$$

which corresponds to the generalized residual of the probit model (see Subsection 7.1.4). It extends the definition of the inverse Mills ratio of Subsection 7.5.2 to cases with $r_i = 0$. In the general case where σ_{02} or σ_{12} may be nonzero, these results indicate that the parameters in (7.115) and (7.116) can be estimated consistently by maximum likelihood or by using a variant of the two-step approach discussed for the sample selection model, including the inverse Mills ratio $\lambda_i(x_i'\hat{\beta}_2)$ as additional variable. Identification strongly rests upon distributional assumptions[31] and it is advisable to have exclusion

[31] Heckman, Tobias and Vytlacil (2003) extend the above latent variable model to cases where the error terms are not jointly normal.

restrictions in (7.115) and (7.116). That is, ideally an instrumental variable can be found that affects the decision whether to participate in the programme, but not the actual and counterfactual outcomes of y_i. Under these assumptions, the average treatment effect on the treated from (7.120) equals

$$ATET(x_i) = \delta + x_i'\gamma + (\sigma_{12} - \sigma_{02})\lambda_i(x_i'\beta_2),$$

where the last term denotes the selection effect. If it is imposed that $\beta_0 = \beta_1 = \beta$, it follows that

$$E\{y_i|x_i, r_i\} = \alpha_0 + x_i'\beta + \delta r_i + E\{\varepsilon_i|x_i, r_i\} \tag{7.127}$$

$$= \alpha_0 + x_i'\beta + \delta r_i + \sigma_{12} r_i \lambda_i(x_i'\beta_2) + \sigma_{02}(1 - r_i)\lambda_i(x_i'\beta_2),$$

which shows that we can consistently estimate α_0, β and δ from a single regression provided we include the generalized residual *interacted with the treatment dummy*. In the general case, *ATE* and *ATET* can be estimated using (7.122) and (7.123), respectively, but using the extended models (with $\lambda_i(x_i'\hat{\beta}_2)$ as additional regressor) to calculate the fitted values.

If it can be assumed that $\sigma_{02} = \sigma_{12}$, in which case $ATE(x_i)$ and $ATET(x_i)$ are identical, simpler alternative estimation techniques are available. For example, the two-step approach reduces to the standard approach described in (7.83), provided we extend the definition of λ_i to the $r_i = 0$ cases. This is the dummy endogenous variable model of Heckman (1978b). Alternatively, the model parameters can also be estimated consistently by instrumental variables techniques, as discussed in Chapter 5, provided there is a valid exclusion restriction in (7.121). Heckman (1997) and Vella and Verbeek (1999b), among others, stress the behavioural assumptions that are implicitly made in an instrumental variables context. If responses to treatment vary across individuals, the instrumental variables estimator is only consistent for *ATE* if individuals do not select into the programme on the basis of the idiosyncratic component of their response to the programme. Similar arguments can be made in cases where treatment is a multi-valued or continuous variable, like schooling; see Angrist and Imbens (1995) or Card (1999) for examples and discussion. If observations before and after the treatment are available for both treated and untreated individuals, it is possible to use differences-in-differences methods to estimate treatment effects; see Subsection 10.2.2.

The identification of *ATE* and *ATET* within the model specified by equations (7.115), (7.116) and (7.125) may be somewhat fragile. For example, distributional assumptions on the error terms may be inappropriate, the exclusion restrictions in the first two equations may be incorrect, or the instruments in (7.125) may be weak.

7.7.2 Regression Discontinuity Design

In recent years, much attention has been given to regression discontinuity design as an approach to estimate treatment effects, and its popularity in economics appears to be growing; see Imbens and Lemieux (2008) and Lee and Lemieux (2010) for detailed overviews and guidelines for practitioners. The crucial assumption here is that treatment r_i is related to an observable variable, x_i, say, with a discontinuity at a known value c, while the relationship between the outcome variable and x_i is continuous (for both the treated and untreated groups). In the sharp regression discontinuity design we have

$$r_i = I\{x_i \geq c\}, \tag{7.128}$$

where I is the indicator function, equal to 1 if its argument is true (and 0 otherwise). In this case, the assignment to treatment is completely determined by x_i being on either side of a fixed (and known) threshold, c. The general challenge in estimating treatment effects is that we wish to compare the outcome y_i for individuals with and without treatment that are as similar as possible. In the regression discontinuity set-up, it is reasonable to assume that individuals just above and just below the threshold are roughly the same. Accordingly, the treatment effect is estimated by comparing the outcomes y_i of individuals with x_i just below and just above the threshold. This is then the estimated treatment effect for those who are at the margin of receiving treatment (x_i close to c). That is, it estimates $E\{y_{1i} - y_{0i}|x_i = c\}$. Let us, as an illustration, assume that both outcomes are linearly related to x_i, that is $y_{0i} = \mu_0 + \beta_0(x_i - c) + \varepsilon_{0i}$ and $y_{1i} = \mu_1 + \beta_1(x_i - c) + \varepsilon_{1i}$. The only crucial assumption here is that both functions are continuous in x_i. This can be combined into

$$y_i = \mu_0 + \beta_0(x_i - c) + \delta r_i + (\beta_1 - \beta_0) r_i x_i + \varepsilon_i, \tag{7.129}$$

where $\delta = \mu_1 - \mu_0$. Because, conditional upon x_i, r_i is deterministic, the unconfoundedness requirement is trivially satisfied. The estimate of δ is just the jump in the linear function around c. If we are convinced that the linearity assumption is correct, we can easily estimate this by OLS.[32] If not, it makes sense to only estimate this equation for individuals with values of x_i close to c. This is equivalent to estimating two separate regressions, one for values of x_i just below c, one for values of x_i just above c. Because r_i is a deterministic function of x_i, identification of the treatment effect relies on the ability to separate the discontinuous function, $I\{x_i \geq c\}$, from the smooth (and in this case linear) functions of x_i. This approach can be extended to more general functions of x_i entering the conditional expectations of y_{0i} and y_{1i}, and to include additional covariates. Unknown smooth continuous functions of x_i can be reasonably well approximated locally by using polynomials of sufficiently high order.

In the fuzzy regression discontinuity design, there is assumed to be a discrete jump in the probability receiving treatment at $x_i = c$. That is,

$$P\{r_i = 1|x_i\} = g_1(x_i) \text{ if } x_i \geq c, \quad g_0(x_i) \text{ otherwise},$$

where the continuous functions g_0 and g_1 must differ discretely at $x_i = c$. Angrist and Pischke (2009, Chapter 6) argue that estimation of the treatment effect in this case can be interpreted as an instrumental variables approach (estimated in a small neighbourhood around the discontinuity) using $z_i = I\{x_i \geq c\}$, possibly interacted with powers of x_i, as instruments.

The difficulty with regression discontinuity design is that one may not easily come across cases with a clean threshold, and where x_i is observed. A clean threshold requires that there are no other programmes that use the same threshold that may interfere with the one under investigation. Moreover, it requires that individuals are not able to manipulate their x_i to push themselves over the threshold. Convincing cases often relate to institutional settings. For example, Lee, Moretti and Butler (2004) use the fraction of votes to the Democratic candidate in district elections (x_i), where a Democrat is elected ($r_i = 1$) if the fraction exceeds 50%, that is, if $x_i > 0.50$. The regression discontinuity design compares

[32] In some cases, one may wish to impose that the slope coefficients on either side of the jump are identical ($\beta_0 = \beta_1$).

districts where the Democratic candidate barely lost with those where the Democratic candidate barely won. The average voting records of Democrats who are barely elected represent, on average, how Democrats would have voted in the districts that were in actuality barely won by Republicans (and vice versa).

Angrist and Lavy (1999) investigate the impact of class size upon test scores in Israel, where they are using the rule that class sizes in Israeli schools are capped at 40. Compared to the case of 40 students, this implies a sharp drop in class size when 41 students are enrolled, to an average of 20.5. When 80 pupils are enrolled, the average class size will again be 40, but when 81 pupils are enrolled the average class size drops to 27. Accordingly, class size is a nonlinear and nonmonotonic function of the size of enrolment cohorts, with several discontinuities. Angrist and Lavy exploit this exogenous source of variation to estimate the causal impact of class size on test scores.

As a final example, Kerr, Lerner and Schoar (2014) investigate the impact of early stage financiers ('angel investors') on the firms they invest in. They use a regression discontinuity approach because they observe the interest level, the number of angels expressing interest in a given deal. Moreover, they observe a very stark jump in funding probability around a particular interest level. In this case, the discontinuity is due to how critical mass develops within angel groups around prospective deals, rather than institutional settings. Again, identification relies on comparing firms just above the threshold with those just below, which are assumed to have very similar ex ante characteristics.

As stressed by Imbens and Lemieux (2008), the regression discontinuity design, at best, provides estimates for a subpopulation only (individuals with $x_i = c$), which can only be extrapolated under strong assumptions (e.g. homogeneity of the treatment effect).

7.7.3 Weighting and Matching

Given that the results of linear regression can be quite sensitive to small changes in specification, particularly when the distribution of one or more covariates is different among the subsamples with $r_i = 0$ and $r_i = 1$, the recent literature has moved to alternative, more sophisticated, approaches for adjusting differences in covariates. Many of those approaches rely on the **propensity score**, defined as the conditional probability of assignment to a treatment given the vector x_i (Rosenbaum and Rubin, 1983). Mathematically, we write

$$p(x_i) = P\{r_i = 1|x_i\},$$

where it is assumed that $0 < p(x_i) < 1$ for all x_i. This assumption, typically referred to as the overlap assumption, ensures that for each value of x_i there is a positive probability to observe units in both the treatment and the control group. If, for example, there is no chance of observing an individual in the treatment group younger than 30, we will never be able to estimate the average treatment effect over the population that includes people younger than 30. The propensity score can be estimated using the binary choice models from Section 7.1, but it is also possible to use semi-parametric alternatives.

Assuming unconfoundedness, consistent estimators for *ATE* and *ATET* can be derived based upon weighting using the propensity score. To see how this works, consider

$$E\left\{\frac{r_i y_i}{p(x_i)}\right\} = E\left\{\frac{r_i y_{1i}}{p(x_i)}\right\} = E\left\{E\left\{\frac{r_i y_{1i}}{p(x_i)}\middle| x_i\right\}\right\} = E\left\{\frac{p(x_i)E\{y_{1i}|x_i\}}{p(x_i)}\right\} = E\{y_{1i}\},$$

which is the unconditional expected outcome under treatment. The third equality holds by virtue of the unconfoundedness assumption. Similarly, it can be shown that

$$E\left\{\frac{(1-r_i)y_i}{1-p(x_i)}\right\} = E\{y_{0i}\}.$$

Combined, these two expressions suggest an obvious estimator for *ATE* as

$$\hat{\Delta}_{ate,weight} = \frac{1}{N}\sum_{i=1}^{N}\left(\frac{r_i y_i}{\hat{p}(x_i)} - \frac{(1-r_i)y_i}{1-\hat{p}(x_i)}\right), \tag{7.130}$$

where $\hat{p}(x_i)$ is the estimated propensity score. In the simple case where $p(x_i)$ does not depend upon x_i and $\hat{p}(x_i) = N_1/N$, this expression reduces to (7.114). While the estimator in (7.130) can be written as the difference between two weighted averages, it may be less attractive because the weights do not add up to one. A more common version is

$$\hat{\Delta}_{ate,weight2} = \sum_{i=1}^{N}(\hat{w}_i(x_i)y_i - [1-\hat{w}_i(x_i)]y_i), \tag{7.131}$$

where the weights $\hat{w}_i(x_i)$ are given by

$$\hat{w}_i(x_i) = \frac{r_i/\hat{p}(x_i)}{\sum_{j=1}^{N} r_j/\hat{p}(x_j)}.$$

In this estimator, referred to as as the **inverse probability weighting** (IPW) estimator, the weights are normalized to sum to unity. The key input for the calculation of these estimators is the estimated propensity score, and alternative approaches have been proposed for its specification and estimation. Rosenbaum and Rubin (1983) suggest that the propensity score be estimated using a flexible logit model, where squares and interactions of x_i are included. Hirano, Imbens and Ridder (2003) improve upon the efficiency of the estimator using a more flexible logit model where the number of functions of the covariates increases with the sample size. If the estimated propensity scores are very close to zero or one, the weighting estimators for *ATE* may not be very accurate (and this will be reflected in their standard errors).

The final approach we consider is based on **matching**. In this approach, the missing counterfactual observations are imputed using the outcomes of one or more matched cases of the opposite treatment group. The corresponding estimates can be written as

$$\hat{\Delta}_{ate,match} = \frac{1}{N}\sum_{i=1}^{N}(\hat{y}_{1i} - \hat{y}_{0i}),$$

and

$$\hat{\Delta}_{atet,match} = \frac{1}{N_1}\sum_{i=1}^{N} r_i(\hat{y}_{1i} - \hat{y}_{0i}),$$

where $\hat{y}_{1i} = y_{1i}$ if $r_i = 1$ and an imputed value if $r_i = 0$, and, similarly $\hat{y}_{0i} = y_{0i}$ if $r_i = 0$ and an imputed value if $r_i = 1$. There are different ways to calculate the imputed values. For example, one could impute the actual outcome for an individual who has 'the closest' values of x_i but is in the opposite treatment group (the 'nearest neighbour'). Alternatively, the (weighted) average of the m nearest neighbours can be used. Because matching upon the full set of covariates may be a bit cumbersome, Rosenbaum and Rubin (1983) have proposed matching based on the estimated propensity score. This facilitates the matching process because individuals with dissimilar covariate values may nevertheless have similar values for their propensity scores. Propensity score matching has gained popularity recently, see, for example, Deheija and Wahba (2002) and Abadie and Imbens (2016), who derive the large sample distribution. More details on the estimation of treatment effects can also be found in Cameron and Trivedi (2005, Chapter 25) or Wooldridge (2010, Chapter 21).

7.8 Duration Models

In some applications, we are interested in explaining the duration of a certain event. For example, we may be interested in explaining the time it takes for an unemployed person to find a job, the time that elapses between two purchases of the same product, the duration of a strike or the duration of a firm's bank relationships. The data we have contain duration spells, that is, we observe the time elapsed until a certain event (e.g. finding a job) occurs. Usually, duration data are censored in the sense that the event of interest has not occurred for some individuals at the time the data are analysed. Duration models have their origin in survival analysis, where the duration of interest is the survival of a given subject, for example an insect. In economics, duration models are often used in labour market studies, where unemployment spells are analysed. In this section, we will briefly touch upon duration modelling. More details can be found in Jenkins (2005), Wooldridge (2010, Chapter 22), or, more extensively, in Lancaster (1990) or Cameron and Trivedi (2005, Chapters 17–19).

7.8.1 Hazard Rates and Survival Functions

Let T denote the time spent in the initial state. For example, if the initial state is unemployment, T may denote the number of weeks until a person becomes employed. It is most convenient to treat T as a continuous variable. The distribution of T is defined by the cumulative density function

$$F(t) = P\{T \leq t\}, \tag{7.132}$$

which denotes the probability that the event has occurred by duration t. It is typically assumed that $F(t)$ is differentiable, so that the density function of T can be written as $f(t) = F'(t)$. Later on, we will allow the distribution of T to depend upon personal characteristics. The **survivor function** is the probability of surviving past t and is defined as

$$S(t) \equiv 1 - F(t) = P\{T > t\}.$$

The conditional probability of leaving the initial state within the time interval t until $t + h$, given survival up to time t, can be written as

$$P\{t \leq T < t + h | T \geq t\}.$$

If we divide this probability by h, we obtain the average probability of leaving per unit time period over the interval t until $t + h$. Consideration of shorter and shorter intervals results in the so-called **hazard function**, which is formally defined as

$$\lambda(t) = \lim_{h \downarrow 0} \frac{P\{t \leq T < t + h | T \geq t\}}{h}. \tag{7.133}$$

At each time t, the hazard function is the instantaneous rate of leaving the initial state per unit of time. The hazard function can be expressed as a function of the (cumulative) density function of T in a straightforward way. First, write

$$P\{t \leq T < t + h | T \geq t\} = \frac{P\{t \leq T < t + h\}}{P\{T \geq t\}} = \frac{F(t + h) - F(t)}{1 - F(t)}.$$

Because

$$\lim_{h \downarrow 0} \frac{F(t + h) - F(t)}{h} = F'(t) = f(t),$$

it follows directly that

$$\lambda(t) = \frac{f(t)}{1 - F(t)} = \frac{f(t)}{S(t)}. \tag{7.134}$$

The hazard and survival functions provide alternative but equivalent characterizations of the distribution of T, noting that most duration models are based on making particular assumptions about the hazard function.

There is a one-to-one relation between a specification for the hazard function and a specification for the cumulative density function of T. To see this, first note that $\partial \log[1 - F(t)]/\partial t = -F'(t)/[1 - F(t)]$, where $F'(t) = f(t)$. So we can write

$$\lambda(t) = -\frac{\partial \log[1 - F(t)]}{\partial t}.$$

Now integrate both sides over the interval $[0, s]$. This gives

$$\int_0^s \lambda(t)\, dt = -\log[1 - F(s)] + \log[1 - F(0)]$$
$$= -\log[1 - F(s)],$$

because $F(0) = 0$. Consequently, it follows that

$$F(s) = 1 - \exp\left(-\int_0^s \lambda(t)\, dt\right). \tag{7.135}$$

The important result is that, whatever functional form we choose for $\lambda(t)$, we can derive $F(t)$ from it, and vice versa. While most implementations start from a specification of the hazard function, the cumulative density function and survival function are important for constructing the likelihood function of the model.

As a simple case, assume that the hazard rate is constant, that is, $\lambda(t) = \lambda$. This implies that the probability of leaving during the next time interval does not depend upon the duration spent in the initial state. A constant hazard implies

$$F(t) = 1 - \exp(-\lambda t),$$

corresponding to the exponential distribution. In most cases, researchers work with a convenient specification for the hazard function, for example one that leads to closed-form expressions for the survival function $S(t)$. Moreover, the hazard function is typically allowed to depend upon personal characteristics, x_i, say. Let us, in general, denote the hazard function of an individual i with characteristics x_i as $\lambda(t, x_i)$. For the moment, we assume that these characteristics do not vary with survival or calendar time. A popular class of models are the so-called **proportional hazard models**, in which the hazard function can be written as the product of a **baseline hazard function** that does not depend upon x_i and a person-specific non-negative function that describes the effect of the characteristics x_i. In particular,

$$\lambda(t, x_i) = \lambda_0(t) \exp\{x_i'\beta\}. \tag{7.136}$$

In this model, $\lambda_0(t)$ is a baseline hazard function that describes the risk of leaving the initial state for (hypothetical) individuals with $x_i = 0$, who serve as a reference group, and $\exp\{x_i'\beta\}$ is an adjustment factor that depends upon the set of characteristics x_i. Note that the adjustment is the same at all durations t. To identify the baseline hazard, x_i should not include an intercept term. If x_{ik} is a continuous variable, we can derive

$$\frac{\partial \log \lambda(t, x_i)}{\partial x_{ik}} = \beta_k. \tag{7.137}$$

Consequently, the coefficient β_k measures the proportional change in the hazard rate that can be attributed to an absolute change in x_{ik}. Note that this effect does not depend upon duration time t. If $\lambda_0(t)$ is not constant, the model exhibits **duration dependence**. There is positive duration dependence if the hazard rate increases with the duration. In this case, the probability of leaving the initial state increases (ceteris paribus) the longer one is in the initial state.

A wide range of possible functional forms can be chosen for the baseline hazard $\lambda_0(t)$. Some of them impose either positive or negative duration dependence at all durations, whereas others allow the baseline hazard to increase for short durations and to decrease for longer durations. A relatively simple specification is the **Weibull model**, which states that[33]

$$\lambda_0(t) = \gamma\alpha t^{\alpha-1},$$

where $\alpha > 0$ and $\gamma > 0$ are unknown parameters. When $\alpha = 1$, we obtain the exponential distribution with $\gamma = \lambda$. If $\alpha > 1$, the hazard rate is monotonically increasing, whereas for $\alpha < 1$ it is monotonically decreasing. The **log-logistic hazard** function is given by

$$\lambda_0(t) = \frac{\gamma\alpha t^{\alpha-1}}{1 + \gamma t^{\alpha}},$$

where, again, $\alpha > 0$ and $\gamma > 0$ are unknown parameters. When $\alpha \leq 1$, the hazard rate is monotonically decreasing to zero as t increases. If $\alpha > 1$, the hazard is increasing until $t = [(\alpha - 1)/\gamma]^{1-\alpha}$ and then it decreases to zero. With a log-logistic hazard function, it can be shown that the log duration, $\log(T)$, has a logistic distribution. See Franses and Paap (2001, Chapter 8) or Greene (2012, Section 19.4) for a graphical illustration of these hazard functions.

[33] Different authors may use different (but equivalent) normalizations and notations.

7.8.2 Samples and Model Estimation

Before turning to estimation, it is important to consider the types of data that are used for estimation. We assume that the population of interest consists of all individuals who enter the initial state between time 0 and time t_0 (e.g. a given calendar year), where t_0 is a known constant. Two sampling schemes are typically encountered in duration analysis. With **stock sampling**, we randomly sample individuals who are in the initial state at time t_0, while with **flow sampling** we sample individuals who *enter* the initial state between time 0 and t_0. In both cases, we record the length of time each individual is in the initial state. Because after a certain amount of time we stop following individuals in the sample (and start analysing our data), both types of data are typically **right-censored**. That is, for those individuals who are still in the initial state we only know that the duration lasted at least as long as the tracking period. With stock sampling, the data may also be **left-censored** if some or all of the starting times in the initial state are not observed. Moreover, stock sampling introduces a sample selection problem. As we shall see below, the censoring and the sample selection problem can be handled by appropriately adjusting the likelihood function.

Let us, first of all, consider maximum likelihood estimation with right-censored flow data. Assume that we randomly sample individuals who become unemployed (enter the initial state) between time 0 and t_0. Let a_i denote the time at which individual i becomes unemployed, and let t_i^* denote the total unemployment duration. For some individuals, t_i^* will not be observed because of right-censoring (the unemployment duration exceeds the period over which we track the individuals). If c_i denotes the censoring time for individual i, we observe

$$t_i = \min\{t_i^*, c_i\}.$$

That is, for some individuals we observe the exact unemployment duration, whereas for others we only know it exceeds c_i. The censoring time may vary across individuals because censoring often takes place at a fixed calendar date. If, for example, we sample from individuals who become unemployed during 2014 and we stop tracking those individuals by the end of 2015, the censoring time may vary between 1 and 2 years depending upon the moment in 2014 the individual became unemployed.

The contribution to the likelihood function of individual i is given by the conditional density of t_i if the observation is not censored, or the conditional probability that $t_i^* > c_i$ (i.e. $t_i = c_i$) in the case of censoring, in each case, conditional upon the observed characteristics x_i. We assume that the distribution of t_i, given x_i, does not depend upon the starting time a_i. This implies, for example, that unemployment durations that start in summer have the same expected length as those that start in winter. If there are seasonal effects, we may capture them by including calendar dummies in x_i corresponding to different values of a_i (see Wooldridge, 2010, Chapter 22). Thus, the likelihood contribution of individual i is given by

$$f(t_i|x_i;\theta)$$

if the duration is uncensored, where θ denotes the vector of unknown parameters that characterize the distribution. For right-censored observations, the likelihood contribution is

$$P\{t_i = c_i|x_i;\theta\} = P\{t_i^* > c_i|x_i;\theta\} = 1 - F(c_i|x_i;\theta).$$

Given a random sample of size N, the maximum likelihood estimator is obtained by maximizing

$$\log L_1(\theta) = \sum_{i=1}^{N} [d_i \log f(t_i|x_i;\theta) + (1-d_i)\log[1-F(c_i|x_i;\theta)]], \tag{7.138}$$

where d_i is a dummy variable indicating censoring ($d_i = 1$ if uncensored, $d_i = 0$ if censored). The functional form of f and F depend upon the specification of the hazard function.

With stock sampling, the loglikelihood function is slightly more complicated because of the sample selection problem. Suppose our population of interest consists of all individuals who became unemployed during 2014, while we sample from all those who are unemployed by the end of the year. In this case, anyone whose unemployment spell ended before the end of 2014 will not be included in the sample. Because this spell is necessarily less than 1 year, we cannot assume that this observation is missing randomly. Kiefer (1988) refers to this sample selection problem as length-biased sampling. This sample selection problem is similar to the one in the truncated regression model that was discussed in Section 7.4, and we can correct for it in a similar fashion. The likelihood contribution for individual i in the absence of censoring is changed into

$$f(t_i|x_i;\theta, t_i \geq t_0 - a_i) = \frac{f(t_i|x_i;\theta)}{1 - F(t_0 - a_i|x_i;\theta)}.$$

With right-censoring, the likelihood contribution is the conditional probability that t_i^* exceeds c_i, given by

$$P\{t_i^* > c_i|x_i;\theta, t_i \geq t_0 - a_i\} = \frac{1 - F(c_i|x_i;\theta)}{1 - F(t_0 - a_i|x_i;\theta)}.$$

From this, it follows directly that the loglikelihood function with stock sampling can be written as

$$\log L_2(\theta) = \log L_1(\theta) - \sum_{i=1}^{N} \log[1 - F(t_0 - a_i|x_i;\theta)], \tag{7.139}$$

where the additional term takes account of the sample selection problem. Unlike in the case of flow sampling, both the starting dates a_i and the length of the sampling interval t_0 appear in the loglikelihood. The exact functional form of the loglikelihood function depends upon the assumptions that we are making about the distribution of the duration variable. As mentioned earlier, these assumptions are typically stated by specifying a functional form for the hazard function.

When the explanatory variables are time varying, things are a bit more complicated, because it does not make sense to study the distribution of a duration conditional upon the values of the explanatory variables at one point in time. Another extension is the inclusion of unobserved heterogeneity in the model, because the explanatory variables that are included in the model may be insufficient to capture all heterogeneity across individuals. In the proportional hazards model, this implies that the specification for the hazard rate is extended to

$$\lambda(t, x_i, v_i) = v_i \lambda_0(t) \exp\{x_i'\beta\}, \tag{7.140}$$

where v_i is an unobservable positive random variable with $E\{v_i\} = 1$. This expression describes the hazard rate for individual i given his or her characteristics in x_i and given his or her unobserved heterogeneity v_i. Because v_i is unobserved, it is integrated out of the likelihood function by assuming an appropriate parametric distribution.[34] See Wooldridge (2010, Chapter 22) for more details on these extensions.

7.8.3 Illustration: Duration of Bank Relationships

In this subsection, we consider an example from financial economics concerning the duration of firm–bank relationships. A strong bank relationship is typically considered valuable to a firm because it decreases the costs of loans and increases the availability of credit. On the other hand, however, the bank's acquisition of private information during a relationship may have undesirable consequences. For example, banks may be able to extract monopoly rents from the relationship. Ongena and Smith (2001) examine the duration of 383 firm–bank relationships and investigate the presence of positive or negative duration dependence. Moreover, they relate relationship durations to observed firm-specific characteristics, such as size and age. The sample is based upon annual data on bank relationships of Norwegian firms, listed on the Oslo Stock Exchange, for the years 1979–1995, which corresponds to flow sampling as described earlier. A bank relationship is ended when the firm drops a bank from its list of primary bank relationships or replaces one bank by another. The average duration in the sample is 4.1 years. The data are right-censored, because a number of durations are not completed by 1995.

We consider a small subset of the results from Ongena and Smith (2001), corresponding to the proportional hazard model in (7.136), where the baseline hazard function is of the Weibull type. As a special case, the exponential baseline hazard is obtained by imposing $\alpha = 1$. The firm-specific characteristics that are included are: logarithm of year-end sales, time elapsed since the firm's founding date (age at start), profitability, as measured by the ratio of operating income to book value of assets, Tobin's Q, leverage and a dummy for multiple bank relationships. Tobin's Q, defined as the ratio of the value of equity and debt to the book value of assets, is typically interpreted as an indicator for management quality and/or the presence of profitable investment opportunities. Leverage is the book value of debt divided by the sum of market value of equity and book value of debt. Highly leveraged firms are expected to be more dependent on banks.

The maximum likelihood estimation results for the two different models, both adjusted for right-censoring, are presented in Table 7.13. The results are reasonably similar for the exponential and Weibull baseline hazard. The estimated value for α in the latter model is 1.351 and significantly larger than unity. This indicates that the Weibull model is preferred to the exponential one, which is confirmed by the difference in loglikelihood values. Moreover, it implies that bank relationships exhibit positive duration dependence. That is, the probability of ending a bank relationship, ceteris paribus, increases as the duration lengthens. The results for the firm-specific variables indicate that profitable firms end bank relationships earlier, consistent with the idea that such firms are less dependent on bank financing. In particular, firms with 10% higher sales are associated

[34] This approach is similar to using a random effects specification in panel data models with limited dependent variables; see Section 10.7.

Table 7.13 Estimation results proportional hazards model

	Exponential (MLE)		Weibull (MLE)	
	Estimate	Standard error	Estimate	Standard error
constant	−3.601	0.561	−3.260	0.408
log(*sales*)	−0.218	0.053	−0.178	0.038
age at start	−0.00352	0.00259	−0.00344	0.00183
profitability	2.124	0.998	1.752	0.717
Tobin's Q	0.268	0.195	0.238	0.141
leverage	2.281	0.628	1.933	0.444
multiple relationships	0.659	0.231	0.491	0.168
α	1	(fixed)	1.351	0.135
Loglikelihood	−259.1469		−253.5265	

Source: Reprinted from Ongena, S. and Smith, D. C., (2001), The Duration of Bank Relationships, *Journal of Financial Economics*, 61: 449–475, with permission from Elsevier.

with an approximately 2% lower hazard rate. Further, the probability of ending a bank relationship decreases in firm size and increases in firm leverage and when firms maintain multiple bank relationships. Using (7.137), the coefficient estimate of the dummy for multiple relationships in the Weibull model indicates that the hazard rate is about $100[\exp(0.491) - 1] = 63.4\%$ greater for firms that have more than one bank relationship.

Wrap-up

This chapter has covered a wide range of models explaining discrete or limited dependent variables. In addition to univariate nonlinear models, such as probit and logit models for binary outcomes, tobit models for truncated or censored outcomes, count data models and duration models, this chapter also paid attention to issues related to sample selection bias, identification in such cases, and the estimation of treatment effects. Many of the models considered in this chapter are estimated by maximum likelihood, where it should be stressed that the likelihood function depends critically upon the assumed structure of the problem. Frequently, this requires some understanding of how individuals, households or firms are making decisions. Extensive coverage of much of the material in this chapter can be found in Cameron and Trivedi (2005) and Wooldridge (2010). The interpretation of nonlinear models is less straightforward than the linear regression model. The use of probit and logit models is widespread, and typically the two models do not yield very different results in the explanation of a binary variable. In tobit models, distributional assumptions are more critical. A crucial assumption throughout this chapter was that observations in the sample are mutually independent. If the data contain repeated observations on the same individuals or households, this assumption is typically violated and alternative specifications are required. This is discussed in Chapter 10.

Exercises

Exercise 7.1 (Binary Choice Models)

For a sample of 600 married females, we are interested in explaining participation in market employment from exogenous characteristics in x_i (age, family composition, education). Let $y_i = 1$ if person i has a paid job and 0 otherwise. Suppose we estimate a linear regression model

$$y_i = x_i'\beta + \varepsilon_i$$

by ordinary least squares.

a. Give two reasons why this is not really an appropriate model.

As an alternative, we could model the participation decision by a probit model.

b. Explain the probit model.
c. Give an expression for the loglikelihood function of the probit model.
d. How would you interpret a positive β coefficient for education in the probit model?
e. Suppose you have a person with $x_i'\beta = 2$. What is your prediction for her labour market status y_i? Why?
f. To what extent is a logit model different from a probit model?

Now assume that we have a sample of women who are not working ($y_i = 0$), part-time working ($y_i = 1$) or full-time working ($y_i = 2$).

g. Is it appropriate, in this case, to specify a linear model as $y_i = x_i'\beta + \varepsilon_i$?
h. What alternative model could be used instead that exploits the information contained in part-time versus full-time working?
i. How would you interpret a positive β coefficient for education in this latter model?
j. Would it be appropriate to pool the two outcomes $y_i = 1$ and $y_i = 2$ and estimate a binary choice model? Why or why not?

Exercise 7.2 (Probit and Tobit Models)

To predict the demand for its new investment fund, a bank is interested in the question as to whether people invest part of their savings in risky assets. To this end, a tobit model is formulated of the following form:

$$y_i^* = \beta_1 + \beta_2 x_{i2} + \beta_3 x_{i3} + \varepsilon_i,$$

where x_{i2} denotes a person's age, x_{i3} denotes income and the amount of savings invested in risky assets is given by

$$\begin{aligned} y_i &= y_i^* \quad \text{if } y_i^* > 0 \\ &= 0 \quad \text{otherwise.} \end{aligned}$$

It is assumed that ε_i is $NID(0, \sigma^2)$, independent of all explanatory variables.

Initially, the bank is only interested in the question as to whether a person is investing in risky assets, which is indicated by a discrete variable d_i that satisfies

$$d_i = 1 \quad \text{if } y_i^* > 0$$
$$= 0 \quad \text{otherwise.}$$

a. Derive the probability that $d_i = 1$ as a function of $x_i = (1, x_{i2}, x_{i3})'$, according to the above model.

b. Show that the model that describes d_i is a probit model with coefficients $\gamma_1 = \beta_1/\sigma, \gamma_2 = \beta_2/\sigma, \gamma_3 = \beta_3/\sigma$.

c. Write down the loglikelihood function $\log L(\gamma)$ of the probit model for d_i. What are, in general, the properties for the maximum likelihood estimator $\hat{\gamma}$ for $\gamma = (\gamma_1, \gamma_2, \gamma_3)'$?

d. Give a general expression for the asymptotic covariance matrix of the ML estimator. Describe how it can be estimated in a given application.

e. Write down the first-order condition with respect to γ_1 and use this to define the generalized residual of the probit model.

f. Describe how the generalized residual can be used to test the hypothesis that gender does not affect the probability of investing in risky assets. (Formulate the hypothesis first, describe how a test statistic can be computed and what the appropriate distribution or critical values are.) To what class does this test belong?

g. Explain why it is not possible to identify σ^2 using information on d_i and x_i only (as in the probit model).

h. It is possible to estimate $\beta = (\beta_1, \beta_2, \beta_3)'$ and σ^2 from the tobit model (using information on y_i). Write down the loglikelihood function of this model.

i. Suppose we are interested in the hypothesis that age does not affect the amount of risky savings. Formulate this hypothesis. Explain how this hypothesis can be tested using a likelihood ratio test.

j. It is also possible to test the hypothesis from **i** on the basis of the results of the probit model. Why would you prefer the test using the tobit results?

Exercise 7.3 (Tobit Models – Empirical)

Consider the data used in Subsections 7.4.3 and 7.5.4 to estimate Engel curves for alcoholic beverages and tobacco. Banks, Blundell and Lewbel (1997) proposed the quadratic almost ideal demand system, which implies quadratic Engel curves of the form

$$w_{ji} = \alpha_{ji} + \beta_{ji} \log x_i + \gamma_{ji} \log^2 x_i + \varepsilon_{ji}.$$

This form has the nice property that it allows goods to be luxuries at low income levels, while they can become necessities at higher levels of income (total expenditures).

a. Re-estimate the standard tobit model for alcohol from Subsection 7.4.3. Refer to this as model A. Check that your results are the same as those in the text.

b. Extend model A by including the square of log total expenditures, and estimate it by maximum likelihood.

c. Test whether the quadratic term is relevant using a Wald test and a likelihood ratio test.

d. Compute the generalized residual for model A. Check that it has mean zero.

e. Compute the second-order generalized residual for model A, as defined in (7.74). Check that is has mean zero too.

f. Perform a Lagrange multiplier test in model A for the hypothesis that the quadratic term $\log^2 x$ is irrelevant.

g. Perform an LM test for heteroskedasticity in model A related to age and the number of adults.

h. Test for normality in model A.

Exercise 7.4 (Tobit Models)

A top university requires all students that apply to do an entry exam. Students who obtain a score of less than 100 are not admitted. For students who score above 100, the scores are registered, after which the university selects students from this group for admittance. We have a sample of 500 potential students who did their entry exam in 2010. For each student, we observe the result of the exam being:

- 'rejected', if the score is less than 100, or
- the score, if it is 100 or more.

In addition, we observe background characteristics of each candidate, including parents' education, gender and the average grade at high school.

The dean is interested in the relationship between these background characteristics and the score for the entry exam. He specifies the following model

$$\begin{aligned} y_i^* &= \beta_0 + x_i'\beta_1 + \varepsilon_i, \qquad && \varepsilon_i \sim NID(0, \sigma^2), \\ y_i &= y_i^* && \text{if } y_i^* \geq 100 \\ &= \text{'rejected'} && \text{if } y_i^* < 100, \end{aligned}$$

where y_i is the observed score of student i and x_i is the vector of background characteristics (excluding an intercept).

a. Show that the above model can be written as the standard tobit model (tobit I).

b. First, the dean does a regression of y_i upon x_i and a constant (by OLS), using the observed scores of 100 and more ($y_i \geq 100$). Show that this approach does not lead to consistent or unbiased estimators for β_1.

c. Explain in detail how the parameter vector $\beta = (\beta_0, \beta_1')'$ can be estimated consistently, using the observed scores only.

d. Explain how you would estimate this model using all observations. Why is this estimator preferable to the one of **c**? (No proof or derivations are required.)

e. The dean considers specifying a tobit II model (a sample selection model). Describe this model. Is this model adequate for the above problem?

8 Univariate Time Series Models

One objective of analysing economic data is to predict or forecast the future values of economic variables. One approach to do this is to build a more or less structural econometric model, describing the relationship between the variable of interest and other economic quantities, to estimate this model using a sample of data and to use it as the basis for forecasting and inference. Although this approach has the advantage of giving economic content to one's predictions, it is not always very useful. For example, it may be possible to adequately model the contemporaneous relationship between unemployment and the inflation rate, but, as long as we cannot predict future inflation rates, we are also unable to forecast future unemployment.

In this chapter we follow a different route: a pure time series approach. In this approach the current values of an economic variable are related to past values (either directly or indirectly). The emphasis is purely on making use of the information in past values of a variable for forecasting its future. In addition to producing forecasts, time series models also produce the distribution of future values, conditional upon the past, and can thus be used to evaluate the likelihood of certain events.

In this chapter we discuss the class of autoregressive integrated moving average (ARIMA) models, which is developed to model stationary and nonstationary time series processes. In Sections 8.1 and 8.2, we analyse the properties of these models and how they are related. An important issue is whether a time series process is stationary, which implies that the distribution of the variable of interest does not depend upon time. Nonstationarity can arise from different sources, but an important one is the presence of so-called unit roots. Sections 8.3 and 8.4 discuss this problem and how one can test for this type of nonstationarity, while an empirical example concerning exchange rates and prices is provided in Section 8.5. In Section 8.6, we discuss how the model parameters can be estimated, while Section 8.7 explains how an appropriate ARIMA model is chosen. Section 8.8 describes an empirical illustration concerning the estimation of persistence of inflation in the United States using an ARIMA model. Section 8.9

demonstrates how a univariate time series model can be used to forecast future values of an economic variable. To illustrate the use of such forecasts in an economic context, Section 8.10 analyses the expectations theory of the term structure of interest rates. Finally, Section 8.11 presents autoregressive conditional heteroskedasticity models that explain the variance of a series (of error terms) from its history.

The seminal work on the estimation and identification of ARIMA models is the monograph by Box and Jenkins (1976). Additional details and a discussion of more recent topics can be found in many textbooks on time series analysis. Mills and Markellos (2008), Martin, Hurn and Harris (2013) and Enders (2014) are particularly suited for economists. At a more advanced level, Hamilton (1994) and Pesaran (2015) provide excellent expositions.

8.1 Introduction

In general we consider a time series of observations on some variable, for example, the unemployment rate, denoted as $Y_1, \ldots, Y_T$. These observations will be considered realizations of random variables that can be described by some stochastic process. Our aim is to describe the properties of this stochastic process by means of a relatively simple model. It will be of particular importance how observations corresponding to different time periods are related, so that we can exploit the dynamic properties of the series to generate predictions for future periods.

8.1.1 Some Examples

A simple way to model dependence between consecutive observations states that Y_t depends linearly upon its previous value Y_{t-1}. That is,

$$Y_t = \delta + \theta Y_{t-1} + \varepsilon_t, \tag{8.1}$$

where ε_t denotes a serially uncorrelated innovation with a mean of zero and a constant variance. The process in (8.1) is referred to as a first-order **autoregressive process** or $AR(1)$ process. It states that the current value Y_t equals a constant δ plus θ times its previous value plus an unpredictable component ε_t. We have seen processes like this before when discussing (first-order) autocorrelation in the linear regression model. For the moment, we shall assume that $|\theta| < 1$. The process for ε_t is an important building block of time series models and is referred to as a **white noise process**. In this chapter, ε_t will always denote such a process that is mean zero, homoskedastic, and exhibits no autocorrelation.

The expected value of Y_t can be solved from

$$E\{Y_t\} = \delta + \theta E\{Y_{t-1}\},$$

which, assuming that $E\{Y_t\}$ does not depend upon t, allows us to write

$$\mu \equiv E\{Y_t\} = \frac{\delta}{1-\theta}. \tag{8.2}$$

Defining $y_t \equiv Y_t - \mu$, we can write (8.1) as

$$y_t = \theta y_{t-1} + \varepsilon_t. \tag{8.3}$$

Writing time series models in terms of y_t rather than Y_t is often notationally more convenient, and we shall do so frequently in the rest of this chapter. One can allow for nonzero means by adding an intercept term to the model. Whereas Y_t is observable, y_t is only observed if the mean of the series is known. Note that $V\{y_t\} = V\{Y_t\}$.

The model in (8.1) is a relatively simple example of describing a stochastic process for a time series. It tells us how different values for Y_t are generated and how they depend upon each other. In general, the joint distribution of all values of Y_t is characterized by the so-called **autocovariances**, the covariances between Y_t and its lags, Y_{t-k}, $k = 1, 2, 3, \ldots$ For the $AR(1)$ model, the dynamic properties of the Y_t series can easily be determined using (8.1) or (8.3) if we impose that variances and autocovariances do not depend upon the time index t. This is a so-called stationarity assumption, and we return to it in Subsection 8.1.2. Writing

$$V\{Y_t\} = V\{\theta Y_{t-1} + \varepsilon_t\} = \theta^2 V\{Y_{t-1}\} + V\{\varepsilon_t\}$$

and imposing $V\{Y_t\} = V\{Y_{t-1}\}$, we obtain

$$V\{Y_t\} = \frac{\sigma^2}{1-\theta^2}. \tag{8.4}$$

This also requires $|\theta| < 1$, as was assumed before. Furthermore, we can determine that

$$\text{cov}\{Y_t, Y_{t-1}\} = E\{y_t y_{t-1}\} = E\{(\theta y_{t-1} + \varepsilon_t)y_{t-1}\} = \theta V\{y_{t-1}\} = \theta\frac{\sigma^2}{1-\theta^2} \tag{8.5}$$

and, generally (for $k = 1, 2, 3, \ldots$),

$$\text{cov}\{Y_t, Y_{t-k}\} = \theta^k \frac{\sigma^2}{1-\theta^2}. \tag{8.6}$$

As long as θ is nonzero, any two observations on Y_t have a nonzero correlation, while this dependence is smaller (and potentially arbitrary close to zero) if the observations are further apart. Note that the covariance between Y_t and Y_{t-k} depends on k only, not on t. This reflects the stationarity of the process.

Another simple time series model is the first-order **moving average process** or $MA(1)$ process, given by

$$Y_t = \mu + \varepsilon_t + \alpha\varepsilon_{t-1}. \tag{8.7}$$

Apart from the mean μ, this says that Y_1 is a weighted average of ε_1 and ε_0, Y_2 is a weighted average of ε_2 and ε_1, etc. The values of Y_t are defined in terms of drawings from the white noise process ε_t. The variances and autocovariances in the $MA(1)$ case are given by

$$\begin{aligned}
V\{Y_t\} &= E\{(\varepsilon_t + \alpha\varepsilon_{t-1})^2\} = E\{\varepsilon_t^2\} + \alpha^2 E\{\varepsilon_{t-1}^2\} = (1+\alpha^2)\sigma^2 \\
\text{cov}\{Y_t, Y_{t-1}\} &= E\{(\varepsilon_t + \alpha\varepsilon_{t-1})(\varepsilon_{t-1} + \alpha\varepsilon_{t-2})\} = \alpha E\{\varepsilon_{t-1}^2\} = \alpha\sigma^2 \\
\text{cov}\{Y_t, Y_{t-2}\} &= E\{(\varepsilon_t + \alpha\varepsilon_{t-1})(\varepsilon_{t-2} + \alpha\varepsilon_{t-3})\} = 0
\end{aligned}$$

or, in general,

$$\text{cov}\{Y_t, Y_{t-k}\} = 0, \quad \text{for } k = 2, 3, 4, \ldots$$

Consequently, the simple moving average structure implies that observations that are two or more periods apart are uncorrelated. Clearly, the $AR(1)$ and $MA(1)$ processes imply very different autocovariances for Y_t.

As we shall see in Section 8.2, both the autoregressive model and the moving average model can be generalized by including additional lags in (8.1) or (8.7), respectively. Apart from a few exceptions, which we shall address below, there are no fundamental differences between autoregressive and moving average processes. The choice is simply a matter of parsimony. For example, we can rewrite the $AR(1)$ model as an infinite-order moving average process, provided that $|\theta| < 1$. To see this, substitute $Y_{t-1} = \delta + \theta Y_{t-2} + \varepsilon_{t-1}$ into (8.1) to obtain

$$Y_t = \mu + \theta^2(Y_{t-2} - \mu) + \varepsilon_t + \theta\varepsilon_{t-1},$$

which, after repeated substitution, results in

$$Y_t = \mu + \theta^n(Y_{t-n} - \mu) + \sum_{j=0}^{n-1} \theta^j \varepsilon_{t-j}. \tag{8.8}$$

If we allow $n \to \infty$, the second term on the right-hand side will converge to zero (because $|\theta| < 1$) and we obtain

$$Y_t = \mu + \sum_{j=0}^{\infty} \theta^j \varepsilon_{t-j}. \tag{8.9}$$

This expression is referred to as the moving average representation of the autoregressive process: the AR process in (8.1) is written as an infinite-order moving average process. We can do so provided that $|\theta| < 1$. As we shall see below, for some purposes a moving average representation is more convenient than an autoregressive one.

In the previous discussion, we assumed that the process for Y_t is stationary. Before discussing general autoregressive and moving average processes, the next subsection pays attention to the important concept of stationarity.

8.1.2 Stationarity and the Autocorrelation Function

A stochastic process is said to be **strictly stationary** if its probability distribution remains unchanged when time progresses. Effectively, this means that the process is in 'stochastic equilibrium' and realizations over different time intervals would be similar (Pesaran, 2015, Section 12.2). This implies that the distribution of Y_1 is the same as that of any other Y_t, and also, for example, that the covariances between Y_t and Y_{t-k} for any k do not depend upon t. Usually, we will only be concerned with the means, variances and covariances of the series, and it is sufficient to impose that these moments are independent of time, rather than the entire distribution. This is referred to as **weak stationarity** or covariance stationarity. Finally, a process is called trend stationary if it is covariance stationary apart from a perfectly predictable time trend. An example is the process for Y_t if $Y_t - \gamma t$ is covariance stationary (for a fixed value of γ).

Formally, a process $\{Y_t\}$ is defined to be weakly stationary if for all t it holds that

$$E\{Y_t\} = \mu < \infty, \tag{8.10}$$

$$V\{Y_t\} = E\{(Y_t - \mu)^2\} = \gamma_0 < \infty, \tag{8.11}$$

$$\text{cov}\{Y_t, Y_{t-k}\} = E\{(Y_t - \mu)(Y_{t-k} - \mu)\} = \gamma_k, \quad k = 1, 2, 3, \ldots \tag{8.12}$$

Hereafter, the term 'stationary' is taken to mean 'weakly stationary'. Conditions (8.10) and (8.11) require the process to have a constant finite mean and variance, while (8.12) states that the autocovariances of Y_t depend only upon the distance in time between the two observations. The mean, variances and autocovariances are thus independent of time. Under weak stationarity, the kth-order autocovariance γ_k is defined as

$$\gamma_k = \text{cov}\{Y_t, Y_{t-k}\} = \text{cov}\{Y_{t-k}, Y_t\}, \tag{8.13}$$

which, for $k = 0$, gives the variance of Y_t. As the autocovariances are not independent of the units in which the variables are measured, it is common to standardize by defining **autocorrelations** ρ_k as

$$\rho_k = \frac{\text{cov}\{Y_t, Y_{t-k}\}}{V\{Y_t\}} = \frac{\gamma_k}{\gamma_0}. \tag{8.14}$$

Note that $\rho_0 = 1$, while $-1 \leq \rho_k \leq 1$.

The autocorrelations considered as a function of k are referred to as the **autocorrelation function** (ACF) or the correlogram of the series Y_t. The ACF plays a major role in modelling the dependencies among observations because it characterizes the process describing the evolution of Y_t over time. From the ACF we can infer the extent to which one value of the process is correlated with previous values and thus the length and strength of the memory of the process. It indicates how long (and how strongly) a shock in the process (ε_t) affects the values of Y_t. As an example, consider the two processes we have seen previously. For the $AR(1)$ process

$$Y_t = \delta + \theta Y_{t-1} + \varepsilon_t$$

we have autocorrelation coefficients

$$\rho_k = \theta^k, \tag{8.15}$$

while for the $MA(1)$ process

$$Y_t = \mu + \varepsilon_t + \alpha\varepsilon_{t-1}$$

we have

$$\rho_1 = \frac{\alpha}{1 + \alpha^2} \text{ and } \rho_k = 0, \quad k = 2, 3, 4, \ldots \tag{8.16}$$

Consequently, a shock in an $MA(1)$ process affects Y_t in two periods only, whereas a shock in the $AR(1)$ process affects all future observations with a decreasing effect.

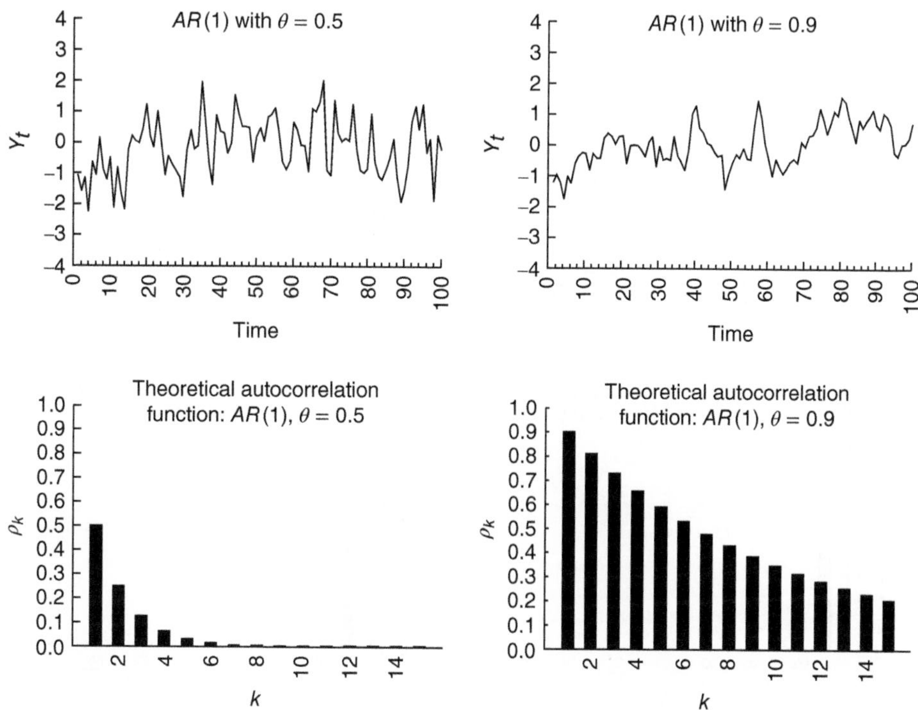

Figure 8.1 First-order autoregressive processes: data series and autocorrelation functions.

To illustrate this, we generated several artificial time series according to a first-order autoregressive process as well as a first-order moving average process. The data for the simulated *AR*(1) processes with parameter θ equal to 0.5 and 0.9 are depicted in Figure 8.1, combined with their autocorrelation functions. All series are standardized to have unit variance and zero mean. If we compare the AR series with $\theta = 0.5$ and $\theta = 0.9$, it appears that the latter process is smoother, that is, has a higher degree of persistence. This means that, after a shock, it takes longer for the series to return to its mean. The autocorrelation functions show an exponential decay in both cases, although it takes large lags for the ACF of the $\theta = 0.9$ series to become close to zero. For example, after 15 periods, the effect of a shock is still $0.9^{15} = 0.21$ of its original effect. For the $\theta = 0.5$ series, the effect at lag 15 is virtually zero.

The data and ACF for two simulated moving average processes, with $\alpha = 0.5$ and $\alpha = 0.9$, are displayed in Figure 8.2. The difference between the two is less pronounced than in the AR case. For both series, shocks only have an effect in two consecutive periods. This means that, in the absence of new shocks, the series are back at their mean after two periods. The first-order autocorrelation coefficients do not differ much, and are 0.40 and 0.50, respectively.

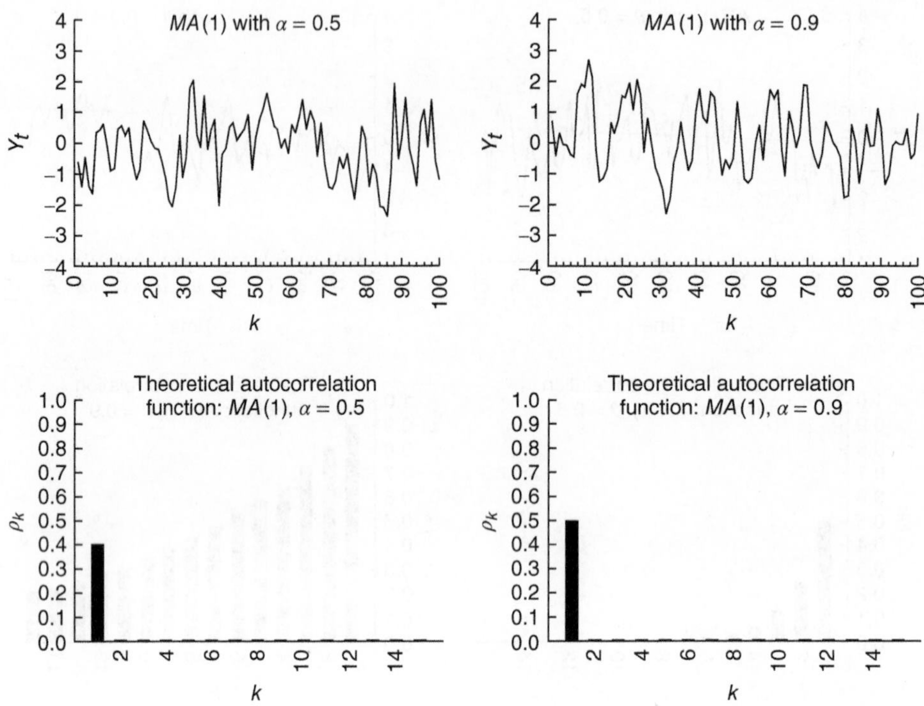

Figure 8.2 First-order moving average processes: data series and autocorrelation functions.

8.2 General ARMA Processes

8.2.1 Formulating ARMA Processes

In this section, we define more general autoregressive and moving average processes. First, we define a moving average process of order q, or in short an $MA(q)$ process, as

$$y_t = \varepsilon_t + \alpha_1\varepsilon_{t-1} + \cdots + \alpha_q\varepsilon_{t-q}, \tag{8.17}$$

where ε_t is a white noise process and $y_t = Y_t - \mu$. That is, the demeaned series y_t is a weighted combination of $q + 1$ white noise terms. An autoregressive process of order p, an $AR(p)$ process, is given by

$$y_t = \theta_1 y_{t-1} + \theta_2 y_{t-2} + \cdots + \theta_p y_{t-p} + \varepsilon_t. \tag{8.18}$$

Obviously, it is possible to combine the autoregressive and moving average specification into an $ARMA(p, q)$ model, which consists of an AR part of order p and an MA part of order q:

$$y_t = \theta_1 y_{t-1} + \cdots + \theta_p y_{t-p} + \varepsilon_t + \alpha_1\varepsilon_{t-1} + \cdots + \alpha_q\varepsilon_{t-q}. \tag{8.19}$$

As mentioned previously, there is no fundamental difference between moving average and autoregressive processes. Under suitable conditions (see Subsection 8.2.2) an AR model can be written as an MA model, and vice versa. The order of one of these is usually quite long, and the choice for an MA, AR or a combined ARMA representation is a matter of parsimony. For example, we have seen previously that an $AR(1)$ model can be written as an $MA(\infty)$, a moving average model of infinite order. For certain purposes, the AR representation of the model is convenient, while for other purposes the MA representation is. This will become clear below.

Often it is convenient to use the **lag operator**, denoted by L. It is defined by

$$Ly_t = y_{t-1}. \tag{8.20}$$

Powers of L are defined as repeated applications of L. For example,

$$L^2 y_t = L(Ly_t) = Ly_{t-1} = y_{t-2},$$

so that, more generally, $L^p y_t = y_{t-p}$ with $L^0 \equiv 1$. Also, $L^{-1} y_t = y_{t+1}$. Operating L on a constant leaves the constant unaffected, for example, $L\mu = \mu$. Using the lag operator allows us to write ARMA models in a concise way. For an $AR(1)$ model we can write

$$y_t = \theta L y_t + \varepsilon_t \tag{8.21}$$

or

$$(1 - \theta L) y_t = \varepsilon_t. \tag{8.22}$$

This says that a combination of y_t and its lag, with weights 1 and $-\theta$, equals a white noise process. Similarly, we can write a general $AR(p)$ model as

$$\theta(L) y_t = \varepsilon_t, \tag{8.23}$$

where $\theta(L)$ is a polynomial of order p in the lag operator L, usually referred to as a **lag polynomial**, given by

$$\theta(L) = 1 - \theta_1 L - \theta_2 L^2 - \cdots - \theta_p L^p. \tag{8.24}$$

We can interpret a lag polynomial as a filter that, if applied to a time series, produces a new series. So the filter $\theta(L)$ applied to an $AR(p)$ process y_t produces a white noise process ε_t. It is relatively easy to manipulate lag polynomials. For example, transforming a series by two such polynomials one after the other is the same as transforming the series once by a polynomial that is the product of the two original ones. This way, we can define the inverse of a filter, which is naturally given by the inverse of the polynomial. Thus the inverse of $\theta(L)$, denoted as $\theta^{-1}(L)$, is defined so as to satisfy $\theta^{-1}(L)\theta(L) = 1$. If $\theta(L)$ is a finite-order polynomial in L, its inverse will be one of infinite order. For the $AR(1)$ case we find

$$(1 - \theta L)^{-1} = \sum_{j=0}^{\infty} \theta^j L^j \tag{8.25}$$

provided that $|\theta| < 1$. This is similar to the result that the infinite sum $\sum_{j=0}^{\infty} \theta^j$ equals $(1 - \theta)^{-1}$ if $|\theta| < 1$, while it does not converge for $|\theta| \geq 1$. In general, the inverse of a polynomial $\theta(L)$ exists if its coefficients satisfy some conditions, in which case we call $\theta(L)$ **invertible**. This is discussed in the following subsection. With (8.25) we can write the $AR(1)$ model as

$$(1 - \theta L)^{-1}(1 - \theta L) y_t = (1 - \theta L)^{-1} \varepsilon_t$$

or

$$y_t = \sum_{j=0}^{\infty} \theta^j L^j \varepsilon_t = \sum_{j=0}^{\infty} \theta^j \varepsilon_{t-j}, \tag{8.26}$$

which corresponds to (8.9).

Under appropriate conditions, the converse is also possible, and we can write a moving average model in autoregressive form. Using the lag operator, we can write the $MA(1)$ process as

$$y_t = (1 + \alpha L)\varepsilon_t$$

and the general $MA(q)$ process as

$$y_t = \alpha(L)\varepsilon_t,$$

where

$$\alpha(L) = 1 + \alpha_1 L + \alpha_2 L^2 + \cdots + \alpha_q L^q. \tag{8.27}$$

Note that we have defined the polynomials such that the MA polynomial has plus signs whereas the AR polynomial has minus signs. Now, if $\alpha^{-1}(L)$ exists, we can write

$$\alpha^{-1}(L)y_t = \varepsilon_t, \tag{8.28}$$

which, in general, will be an AR model of infinite order. For the $MA(1)$ case, we use, similar to (8.25),

$$(1 + \alpha L)^{-1} = \sum_{j=0}^{\infty} (-\alpha)^j L^j, \tag{8.29}$$

provided that $|\alpha| < 1$. Consequently, an $MA(1)$ model can be written as

$$y_t = \alpha \sum_{j=0}^{\infty} (-\alpha)^j y_{t-j-1} + \varepsilon_t. \tag{8.30}$$

A necessary condition for the infinite AR representation ($AR(\infty)$) to exist is that the MA polynomial is invertible, which, in the $MA(1)$ case, requires that $|\alpha| < 1$. Particularly for making forecasts conditional upon an observed past, the AR representations are very convenient (see Section 8.9). The MA representations are often convenient to determine variances and covariances (of forecast errors).

An important result is captured by **Wold's representation theorem**. It states that any covariance stationary process can be represented in the form of an infinite-order moving average process, that is,

$$Y_t = \mu + \sum_{j=0}^{\infty} \alpha_j \varepsilon_{t-j},$$

where $\alpha_0 = 0$ and $\sum_{j=0}^{\infty} \alpha_j^2$ is finite. This implies that any stationary process can be arbitrarily well approximated by a finite-order moving average specification (of sufficiently large order). For a more parsimonious representation, we may want to work with an ARMA model that contains both an autoregressive and a moving average part. The general ARMA model can be written as

$$\theta(L)y_t = \alpha(L)\varepsilon_t, \tag{8.31}$$

which (if the AR lag polynomial is invertible) can be written in $MA(\infty)$ representation as

$$y_t = \theta^{-1}(L)\alpha(L)\varepsilon_t, \tag{8.32}$$

or (if the MA lag polynomial is invertible) in infinite AR form as

$$\alpha^{-1}(L)\theta(L)y_t = \varepsilon_t. \tag{8.33}$$

Both $\theta^{-1}(L)\alpha(L)$ and $\alpha^{-1}(L)\theta(L)$ are lag polynomials of infinite length, with restrictions on the coefficients.

8.2.2 *Invertibility of Lag Polynomials*

As we have seen in Subsection 8.2.1, the first-order lag polynomial $1 - \theta L$ is invertible if $|\theta| < 1$. In this section, we shall generalize this condition to higher-order lag polynomials. Let us first consider the case of a second-order polynomial, given by $1 - \theta_1 L - \theta_2 L^2$. Generally, we can find values ϕ_1 and ϕ_2 such that the polynomial can be written as

$$1 - \theta_1 L - \theta_2 L^2 = (1 - \phi_1 L)(1 - \phi_2 L). \tag{8.34}$$

It is easily verified that ϕ_1 and ϕ_2 can be solved for from[1] $\phi_1 + \phi_2 = \theta_1$ and $-\phi_1\phi_2 = \theta_2$. The conditions for invertibility of the second-order polynomial are just the conditions that both the first-order polynomials $1 - \phi_1 L$ and $1 - \phi_2 L$ are invertible. Thus, the requirement for invertibility is that both $|\phi_1| < 1$ and $|\phi_2| < 1$.

These requirements can also be formulated in terms of the so-called **characteristic equation**

$$(1 - \phi_1 z)(1 - \phi_2 z) = 0. \tag{8.35}$$

This equation has two solutions, z_1 and z_2 say, referred to as the **characteristic roots**. The requirement $|\phi_i| < 1$ corresponds to $|z_i| > 1$. If any solution satisfies $|z_i| \leq 1$, the corresponding polynomial is noninvertible. A solution that equals unity is referred to as a **unit root**.

The presence of a unit root in the lag polynomial $\theta(L)$ can be detected relatively easily, without solving the characteristic equation, by noting that the polynomial $\theta(z)$ evaluated at $z = 1$ is zero if $\sum_{j=1}^{p} \theta_j = 1$. Thus, the presence of a first unit root can be verified by checking whether the sum of the autoregressive coefficients (SARC) equals one. If the SARC exceeds one, the polynomial is not invertible.

As an example, consider the $AR(2)$ model

$$y_t = 1.2y_{t-1} - 0.32y_{t-2} + \varepsilon_t. \tag{8.36}$$

We can write this as

$$(1 - 0.8L)(1 - 0.4L)y_t = \varepsilon_t, \tag{8.37}$$

[1] It is possible that ϕ_1, ϕ_2 is a pair of complex numbers, for example, if $\theta_1 = 0$ and $\theta_2 < 0$. In the text we ignore this possibility.

with characteristic equation

$$1 - 1.2z + 0.32z^2 = (1 - 0.8z)(1 - 0.4z) = 0. \tag{8.38}$$

The solutions (characteristic roots) are 1/0.8 and 1/0.4, which are both larger than one. Consequently, the AR polynomial in (8.36) is invertible. Note that the SARC of this model equals $0.88 < 1$. In contrast, the $AR(1)$ model

$$y_t = 1.2y_{t-1} + \varepsilon_t \tag{8.39}$$

corresponds to a noninvertible lag polynomial.

The issue as to whether or not the lag polynomials are invertible is important for several reasons. For moving average models, or more generally, models with a moving average component, invertibility of the MA polynomial is important for estimation and prediction. For models with an autoregressive part, the AR polynomial is invertible if and only if the process is stationary. Section 8.3 explores this last issue.

8.2.3 Common Roots

Decomposing the moving average and autoregressive polynomials into products of linear functions in L also shows the problem of **common roots** or **cancelling roots**. This means that the AR and the MA parts of the model have roots that are identical and the corresponding linear functions in L cancel out. To illustrate this, let the true model be an $ARMA(2, 1)$ process, described by

$$(1 - \theta_1 L - \theta_2 L^2)y_t = (1 + \alpha L)\varepsilon_t. \tag{8.40}$$

Then, we can write this as

$$(1 - \phi_1 L)(1 - \phi_2 L)y_t = (1 + \alpha L)\varepsilon_t. \tag{8.41}$$

Now, if $\alpha = -\phi_1$, we can divide both sides by $(1 + \alpha L)$ to obtain

$$(1 - \phi_2 L)y_t = \varepsilon_t,$$

which is exactly the same as (8.41). Thus, in the case of one cancelling root, an $ARMA(p, q)$ model can be written equivalently as an $ARMA(p - 1, q - 1)$ model.

As an example, consider the model

$$y_t = y_{t-1} - 0.25y_{t-2} + \varepsilon_t - 0.5\varepsilon_{t-1}, \tag{8.42}$$

which can be rewritten as

$$(1 - 0.5L)(1 - 0.5L)y_t = (1 - 0.5L)\varepsilon_t.$$

Clearly, this can be reduced to an $AR(1)$ model as

$$(1 - 0.5L)y_t = \varepsilon_t$$

or

$$y_t = 0.5y_{t-1} + \varepsilon_t,$$

which describes exactly the same process as (8.42).

The problem of common roots illustrates why it may be problematic, in practice, to estimate an ARMA model with an AR part and an MA part of a high order. The reason is that identification and estimation are hard if roots of the MA and AR polynomials are almost identical. Empirically, it is therefore recommended to choose the orders of the ARMA(p, q) model as small as possible. We shall return to this in Section 8.7.

In Section 8.6, we shall discuss estimation of ARMA models. First, however, we pay more attention to stationarity and unit roots in Section 8.3 and discuss several tests for the presence of a unit root in Section 8.4. An empirical illustration concerning long-run purchasing power parity is provided in Section 8.5.

8.3 Stationarity and Unit Roots

Stationarity of a stochastic process requires that the variances and autocovariances are finite and independent of time. It is easily verified that finite-order MA processes are stationary by construction because they correspond to a weighted sum of a fixed number of stationary white noise processes. Stationarity of autoregressive or ARMA processes is less trivial. Consider, for example, the $AR(1)$ process

$$y_t = \theta y_{t-1} + \varepsilon_t, \tag{8.43}$$

with $\theta = 1$. Taking variances on both sides gives $V\{y_t\} = V\{y_{t-1}\} + \sigma^2$, which has no solution for the variance of the process consistent with stationarity, unless $\sigma^2 = 0$, in which case an infinity of solutions exists. The process in (8.43) is a first-order autoregressive process with a unit root ($\theta = 1$), usually referred to as a **random walk**. The unconditional variance of y_t does not exist, that is, is infinite, and the process is nonstationary. In fact, for any value of θ with $|\theta| \geq 1$, (8.43) describes a nonstationary process.

We can formalize the above results as follows. The $AR(1)$ process is stationary if and only if the polynomial $1 - \theta L$ is invertible, that is, if the root of the characteristic equation $1 - \theta z = 0$ is larger than unity. This result is straightforwardly generalized to arbitrary ARMA models. The $ARMA(p, q)$ model

$$\theta(L)y_t = \alpha(L)\varepsilon_t \tag{8.44}$$

corresponds to a stationary process if and only if the solutions $z_1, \dots, z_p$ to $\theta(z) = 0$ are larger than one (in absolute value), that is, when the AR polynomial is invertible. For example, the $ARMA(2, 1)$ process given by

$$y_t = 1.2y_{t-1} - 0.2y_{t-2} + \varepsilon_t - 0.5\varepsilon_{t-1} \tag{8.45}$$

is nonstationary because $z = 1$ is a solution to $1 - 1.2z + 0.2z^2 = 0$.

A special case that is of particular interest arises when one root is exactly equal to one, while the other roots are larger than one. If this arises, we can write the process for y_t as

$$\theta^*(L)(1 - L)y_t = \theta^*(L)\Delta y_t = \alpha(L)\varepsilon_t, \tag{8.46}$$

where $\theta^*(L)$ is an invertible polynomial in L of order $p - 1$, and $\Delta \equiv 1 - L$ is the first-difference operator. Because the roots of the AR polynomial are the solutions to $\theta^*(z)$

$(1 - z) = 0$, there is one solution $z = 1$, or in other words a single unit root. Equation (8.46) thus shows that Δy_t can be described by a stationary ARMA model if the process for y_t has one unit root. Consequently, we can eliminate the nonstationarity by transforming the series into first-differences (changes). Writing the process in (8.45) as

$$(1 - 0.2L)(1 - L)y_t = (1 - 0.5L)\varepsilon_t$$

shows that it implies that Δy_t is described by a stationary $ARMA(1, 1)$ process given by

$$\Delta y_t = 0.2\Delta y_{t-1} + \varepsilon_t - 0.5\varepsilon_{t-1}.$$

A series that becomes stationary after first-differencing is said to be **integrated of order one**, denoted $I(1)$. If Δy_t is described by a stationary $ARMA(p, q)$ model, we say that y_t is described by an autoregressive *integrated* moving average (ARIMA) model of order p, 1, q, or in short an $ARIMA(p, 1, q)$ model.

First-differencing quite often can transform a nonstationary series into a stationary one. In particular this may be the case for aggregate economic series or their natural logarithms. Note that, when Y_t is, for example, the log of national income, ΔY_t corresponds to the income growth rate, which is not unlikely to be stationary. Note that the AR polynomial is required to have an *exact* unit root. If the true model is an $AR(1)$ with $\theta = 1.01$, we have $\Delta y_t = 0.01y_{t-1} + \varepsilon_t$, which is nonstationary, as it depends upon the nonstationary process y_t. Consequently, an $AR(1)$ process with $\theta = 1.01$ is not integrated of order one.

In some cases, taking first-differences is insufficient to obtain stationarity and another differencing step is required. In this case the stationary series is given by $\Delta(\Delta Y_t) = \Delta Y_t - \Delta Y_{t-1}$, corresponding to the change in the growth rate for logarithmic variables. If a series must be differenced twice before it becomes stationary, then it is said to be **integrated of order two**, denoted $I(2)$, and it must have two unit roots. Accordingly, a series Y_t is $I(2)$ if ΔY_t is nonstationary but $\Delta^2 Y_t$ is stationary. A more formal definition of integration is given in Engle and Granger (1987). Thus, a time series integrated of order zero is stationary in levels, while for a time series integrated of order one the first-difference is stationary. A white noise series and a stable $AR(1)$ process are examples of $I(0)$ series, while a random walk process, as described by (8.43) with $\theta = 1$, is an example of an $I(1)$ series.

In the long run, it can make a surprising amount of difference whether the series has an exact unit root or whether the root is slightly larger than one. It is the difference between being $I(0)$ and being $I(1)$. In general, the main differences between processes that are $I(0)$ and $I(1)$ can be summarized as follows. An $I(0)$ series fluctuates around its mean with a finite variance that does not depend on time, whereas an $I(1)$ series wanders widely. Typically, it is said that an $I(0)$ series is **mean reverting**, as there is a tendency in the long run to return to its mean. Furthermore, an $I(0)$ series has a limited memory of its past behaviour (implying that the effects of a particular random innovation are only transitory), whereas an $I(1)$ process has an infinitely long memory (implying that an innovation will permanently affect the process). This last aspect becomes clear from the autocorrelation functions: for an $I(0)$ series the autocorrelations decline rapidly as the lag increases, whereas for the $I(1)$ process the estimated autocorrelation coefficients decay to zero only very slowly (and almost linearly).

The last property makes the presence of a unit root an interesting question from an economic point of view. In models with unit roots, shocks (which may be due to policy interventions) have persistent effects that last forever, whereas in the case of stationary models, shocks can only have a temporary effect. Of course, the long-run effect of a shock is not necessarily of the same magnitude as the short-run effect. Consequently, starting in the early 1980s, a vast amount of literature has appeared[2] on the presence of unit roots in many macro-economic time series, with – depending upon the particular technique applied – sometimes conflicting conclusions. The fact that the autocorrelations of a stationary series taper off or die out rapidly may help in determining the degree of differencing needed to achieve stationarity (usually referred to as d). In addition, a number of formal unit root tests has been proposed in the literature, some of which we shall discuss in Section 8.4.

Empirical series where the choice between a unit root (nonstationarity) and a 'near unit root' (stationarity) is particularly ambiguous are interest rate series (see, e.g., Rose, 1988). The high degree of persistence in (real or nominal) interest rates quite often makes the unit root hypothesis *statistically* not rejectable, although nonstationary interest rates do not seem to be very plausible from an *economic* point of view. The empirical example in Section 8.10 illustrates this issue.

8.4 Testing for Unit Roots

To introduce the testing procedures for a unit root, we concentrate on autoregressive models. This may not be particularly restrictive since any ARMA model will always have an AR representation (provided the MA polynomial $\alpha(L)$ is invertible).

8.4.1 Testing for Unit Roots in a First-order Autoregressive Model

Let us first consider the $AR(1)$ process

$$Y_t = \delta + \theta Y_{t-1} + \varepsilon_t, \tag{8.47}$$

where $\theta = 1$ corresponds to a unit root. As the constant in a stationary $AR(1)$ model satisfies $\delta = (1 - \theta)\mu$, where μ is the mean of the series, the null hypothesis of a unit root also implies that the intercept term should be zero. Although it is possible to jointly test the two restrictions $\delta = 0$ and $\theta = 1$, it is easier (and more common) to test only that $\theta = 1$. It seems obvious to use the estimate $\hat{\theta}$ for θ from an ordinary least squares procedure (which is consistent, irrespective of the true value of θ) and the corresponding standard error to test the null hypothesis. However, as was shown in the seminal paper of Dickey and Fuller (1979), under the null that $\theta = 1$ the standard t-ratio does not have a t distribution, not even asymptotically. The reason for this is that the nonstationarity of the process invalidates standard results on the distribution of the OLS estimator $\hat{\theta}$ (as discussed in Chapter 2). For example, if $\theta = 1$, the variance of Y_t, denoted by γ_0, is not defined (or, if you want, is infinitely large). For any finite sample size, however, a finite estimate of the variance for Y_t will be obtained.

[2] The most influential study is Nelson and Plosser (1982), which argues that many economic time series are better characterized by unit roots than by deterministic trends.

To test the null hypothesis that $\theta = 1$, it is possible to use the standard t-statistic given by

$$DF = \frac{\hat{\theta} - 1}{se(\hat{\theta})}, \tag{8.48}$$

where $se(\hat{\theta})$ denotes the usual OLS standard error. Critical values, however, have to be taken from the appropriate distribution, which under the null hypothesis of nonstationarity is nonstandard. In particular, the distribution is skewed to the left (with a long left-hand tail) so that critical values are smaller than those for (the normal approximation of) the t distribution. Using a 5% significance level in a one-tailed test of H_0: $\theta = 1$ (a unit root) against H_1: $|\theta| < 1$ (stationarity), the correct critical value in large samples is −2.86 rather than −1.65 for the normal approximation. Consequently, if you use the standard t tables you may reject a unit root too often. Selected percentiles of the appropriate distribution are published in several works by Dickey and Fuller. In columns 2 and 3 of Table 8.1 we present 1% and 5% critical values for this test, usually referred to as the **Dickey–Fuller test**, for a range of different sample sizes.

Usually, a slightly more convenient regression procedure is used. In this case, the model is rewritten as

$$\Delta Y_t = \delta + (\theta - 1)Y_{t-1} + \varepsilon_t, \tag{8.49}$$

from which the t-statistic for $\theta - 1 = 0$ is identical to DF in (8.48). The reason for this is that the least squares method is invariant to linear transformations.

It is possible that (8.49) holds with $\theta = 1$ and a nonzero intercept $\delta \neq 0$. Because in this case δ cannot equal $(1 - \theta)\mu$, (8.49) cannot be derived from a pure $AR(1)$ model. This is seen by considering the resulting process

$$\Delta Y_t = \delta + \varepsilon_t, \tag{8.50}$$

which is known as a **random walk with drift**, where δ is the drift parameter. In the model for the level variable Y_t, δ corresponds to a linear time trend. Because (8.50) implies that $E\{\Delta Y_t\} = \delta$, it is the case that (for a given starting value Y_0) $E\{Y_t\} = Y_0 + \delta t$. This shows that the interpretation of the intercept term in (8.49) depends heavily upon the presence of a unit root. In the stationary case, δ reflects the nonzero mean of the series; in the unit root case, it reflects a **deterministic trend** in Y_t. Because in the latter case first-differencing produces a stationary time series, the process for Y_t is referred to as

Table 8.1 1% and 5% critical values for Dickey–Fuller tests

	Without trend		With trend	
Sample size	1%	5%	1%	5%
$T = 25$	−3.75	−3.00	−4.38	−3.60
$T = 50$	−3.58	−2.93	−4.15	−3.50
$T = 100$	−3.51	−2.89	−4.04	−3.45
$T = 250$	−3.46	−2.88	−3.99	−3.43
$T = 500$	−3.44	−2.87	−3.98	−3.42
$T = \infty$	−3.43	−2.86	−3.96	−3.41

Source: Fuller, W. A., (1976), *Introduction to Statistical Time-Series*, p. 373, John Wiley & Sons, Inc., New York. Reprinted with permission.

difference stationary. In general, a difference stationary process is a process that can be made stationary by differencing.

It is also possible that nonstationarity is caused by the presence of a deterministic time trend in the process, rather than by the presence of a unit root. This happens when the $AR(1)$ model is extended to

$$Y_t = \delta + \theta Y_{t-1} + \gamma t + \varepsilon_t, \tag{8.51}$$

with $|\theta| < 1$ and $\gamma \neq 0$. In this case, we have a nonstationary process because of the linear trend γt. This nonstationarity can be removed by regressing Y_t upon a constant and t, and then considering the residuals of this regression, or by simply including t as an additional variable in the model. As defined previously, in this case the process for Y_t is trend stationary. In contrast to the unit root case, shocks to a trend stationary process are transitory, and their effects die out over time. Nonstationary processes may thus be characterized by the presence of a deterministic trend, like γt, a stochastic trend implied by the presence of a unit root, or both.

It is possible to test whether Y_t follows a random walk against the alternative that it follows the trend stationary process in (8.51). This can be tested by running the regression

$$\Delta Y_t = \delta + (\theta - 1)Y_{t-1} + \gamma t + \varepsilon_t. \tag{8.52}$$

The null hypothesis one would like to test is that the process is a random walk rather than trend stationary and corresponds to H_0: $\delta = \gamma = \theta - 1 = 0$. Instead of testing this joint hypothesis, it is quite common to use the t-ratio corresponding to $\hat{\theta} - 1$, denoted by DF_τ, assuming that the other restrictions in the null hypotheses are satisfied. Although the null hypothesis is still the same as in the previous unit root test, the testing regression is different and thus we have a different distribution of the test statistic. The critical values for DF_τ, given in the last two columns of Table 8.1, are still smaller than those for DF. In fact, with an intercept and a deterministic trend included, the probability that $\hat{\theta} - 1$ is positive (given that the true value $\theta - 1$ equals zero) is negligibly small. It should be noted, however, that, if the unit root hypothesis, $\theta - 1 = 0$ is rejected, we cannot conclude that the process for Y_t is likely to be stationary. Under the alternative hypothesis, γ may be nonzero so that the process for Y_t is not stationary (but only trend stationary).

The phrase Dickey–Fuller test, or simply DF test, is used for any of the tests described here and can thus be based upon a regression with or without a trend.[3] If a graphical inspection of the series indicates a clear positive or negative trend, it is most appropriate to perform the Dickey–Fuller test with a trend. This implies that the alternative hypothesis allows the process to exhibit a linear deterministic trend. Note, however, that unnecessarily including a time trend may result in a loss of power. It is important to stress that the unit root hypothesis corresponds to the *null* hypothesis. If we are unable to reject the presence of a unit root, it does not necessarily mean that it is true. It could just be that there is insufficient information in the data to reject it. Of course, this is simply the general difference between accepting a hypothesis and not rejecting it. Because the long-run properties of the process depend crucially upon the imposition of a unit root or not, this is something to be aware of. Not all series for which we *cannot reject* the unit root hypothesis are necessarily integrated of order one.

[3] If the mean of the series is known to be zero, the intercept term may be dropped from the regressions, leading to a third variant of the Dickey–Fuller test. This test is rarely used in practice.

To circumvent the problem that unit root tests often have low power, Kwiatkowski et al. (1992) propose an alternative test where stationarity is the null hypothesis and the existence of a unit root is the alternative. This test is usually referred to as the **KPSS test**. The basic idea is that a time series is decomposed into the sum of a deterministic time trend, a random walk and a stationary error term (typically not white noise). The null hypothesis (of trend stationarity) specifies that the variance of the random walk component is zero. The test is actually a Lagrange multiplier test (see Chapter 6), and computation of the test statistic is fairly simple. First, run an auxiliary regression of Y_t upon an intercept and a time trend t. Next, save the OLS residuals e_t and compute the partial sums $S_t = \sum_{s=1}^{t} e_s$ for all t. Then the test statistic is given by

$$KPSS = T^{-2} \sum_{t=1}^{T} S_t^2/\hat{\sigma}^2, \tag{8.53}$$

where $\hat{\sigma}^2$ is an estimator for the 'long-run variance' $\sigma^2 = \sum_{j=-\infty}^{\infty} E\{\varepsilon_t \varepsilon_{t-j}\}$. This estimator is a weighted average of the sample autocovariances and several alternative weighting schemes have been proposed. Most popular are the Bartlett weights used by KPSS (see Subsection 4.10.2) and the quadratic spectral kernel (Andrews, 1991). In practice, the KPSS test appears to be quite sensitive to the choices made to estimate σ^2. The asymptotic distribution is nonstandard, and Kwiatkowski et al. (1992) report a 5% critical value of 0.146. If the null hypothesis is stationarity rather than trend stationarity, the trend term should be omitted from the auxiliary regression. The test statistic is then computed in the same fashion, but the 5% critical value is 0.463.

8.4.2 Testing for Unit Roots in Higher-Order Autoregressive Models

A test for a single unit root in higher-order AR processes can easily be obtained by extending the Dickey–Fuller test procedure. The general strategy is that lagged differences, such as $\Delta Y_{t-1}, \Delta Y_{t-2}, \ldots$, are included in the regression, such that its error term corresponds to white noise. This leads to the so-called **augmented Dickey–Fuller tests** (ADF tests), for which the same *asymptotic* critical values hold as those shown in Table 8.1.

Consider the $AR(2)$ model

$$Y_t = \delta + \theta_1 Y_{t-1} + \theta_2 Y_{t-2} + \varepsilon_t \tag{8.54}$$

which can be written in factorized form as

$$(1 - \phi_1 L)(1 - \phi_2 L)(Y_t - \mu) = \varepsilon_t. \tag{8.55}$$

The stationarity condition requires that ϕ_1 and ϕ_2 are both less than one in absolute value, but, if $\phi_1 = 1$ and $|\phi_2| < 1$, we have a single unit root, $\theta_1 + \theta_2 = 1$ and $\theta_2 = -\phi_2$. Equation (8.54) can be used to test the unit root hypothesis by testing $\theta_1 + \theta_2 = 1$, given $|\theta_2| < 1$. This is conveniently done be rewriting (8.54) as

$$\Delta Y_t = \delta + (\theta_1 + \theta_2 - 1)Y_{t-1} - \theta_2 \Delta Y_{t-1} + \varepsilon_t. \tag{8.56}$$

The coefficients in (8.56) can be consistently estimated by ordinary least squares, and the estimate of the coefficient for Y_{t-1} provides a means for testing the null hypothesis $\pi \equiv \theta_1 + \theta_2 - 1 = 0$. The resulting t-ratio, $\hat{\pi}/\text{se}(\hat{\pi})$, has the same (approximate) distribution as DF. In the spirit of the Dickey–Fuller procedure, one might add a time trend to the test regression. Depending on which variant is used, the resulting test statistic has to be compared with a critical value taken from the appropriate column of Table 8.1.

This procedure can easily be generalized to the testing of a *single* unit root in an $AR(p)$ process. The trick is that any $AR(p)$ process can be written as

$$\Delta Y_t = \delta + \pi Y_{t-1} + c_1 \Delta Y_{t-1} + \cdots + c_{p-1} \Delta Y_{t-p+1} + \varepsilon_t, \tag{8.57}$$

with $\pi = \theta_1 + \cdots + \theta_p - 1$ (the sum of the autoregressive coefficients minus one), and suitably chosen constants $c_1, \ldots, c_{p-1}$. As $\pi = 0$ implies $\theta(1) = 0$, it also implies that $z = 1$ is a solution to the characteristic equation $\theta(z) = 0$. Thus, as before, the hypothesis that $\pi = 0$ corresponds to a unit root, and we can test it using the corresponding t-ratio. If the $AR(p)$ assumption is correct, and under the null hypothesis of a unit root, the asymptotic distributions of the DF or DF_τ statistics, calculated from (8.57) (including a time trend, where appropriate), are the same as before. The small-sample critical values are somewhat different from the tabulated ones and are provided by, for example, MacKinnon (1991).

Thus, when Y_t follows an $AR(p)$ process, a test for a single unit root can be constructed from a regression of ΔY_t on Y_{t-1} and $\Delta Y_{t-1}, \ldots, \Delta Y_{t-p+1}$ by testing the significance of the 'level' variable Y_{t-1} (using the one-sided appropriate critical values). It is interesting to note that, under the null hypothesis of a single unit root, all variables in (8.57) are stationary, except Y_{t-1}. Therefore, the equality in (8.57) can only make sense if Y_{t-1} does not appear and $\pi = 0$, which explains intuitively why the unit root hypothesis corresponds to $\pi = 0$. The inclusion of the additional lags, in comparison with the standard Dickey–Fuller test, is done to make the error term in (8.57) asymptotically a white noise process, which is required for the distributional results to be valid. As it will generally be the case that p is unknown, it is advisable to choose a fairly high value of p. If too many lags are included, this will somewhat reduce the power of the tests, but, if too few lags are included, the asymptotic distributions from the table are simply not valid (because of autocorrelation in the residuals), and the tests may lead to seriously biased conclusions. It is possible to use statistical significance of the additional variables to select the maximum lag length $p + 1$, as is done with the recursive t-statistic procedure of Campbell and Perron (1991). This corresponds to a general-to-specific approach where one starts with a reasonably large upper bound on p and the order of the autoregression is reduced by one until the last included lag is significant. Alternatively, it is possible to employ model selection criteria like the Akaike and Schwarz Information Criteria (see Subsection 8.7.4), as advocated by Hall (1994). Ng and Perron (2001) propose a class of Modified Information Criteria for the purpose of unit root testing, where the penalty factor is sample dependent.

A regression of the form (8.57) can also be used to test for a unit root in a general (invertible) ARMA model. Said and Dickey (1984) argue that when, theoretically, one lets the number of lags in the regression grow with the sample size (at a cleverly chosen rate), the same asymptotic distributions hold and the ADF tests are also valid for an ARMA model with a moving average component. The argument essentially is, as we have seen before, that any ARMA model (with invertible MA polynomial) can be written as an infinite autoregressive process. This explains why, when testing for unit roots, people usually do not worry about MA components.

Phillips and Perron (1988) have suggested an alternative to the augmented Dickey–Fuller tests. Instead of adding additional lags in the regressions to obtain an error term that has no autocorrelation, they stick to the original Dickey–Fuller regressions but adjust the DF-statistics to take into account the (potential) autocorrelation pattern in the errors. These adjustments, based on corrections similar to those applied to compute Newey–West (HAC) standard errors (see Chapter 4), are quite complicated and will not be discussed here. The (asymptotic) critical values are again the same as those reported in Table 8.1. The Phillips–Perron test, sometimes referred to as a nonparametric test for a unit root, is, like the Said–Dickey (or ADF) test, applicable for general ARMA models. Monte Carlo studies do not show a clear ranking of the two tests regarding their power (probability to reject the null if it is false) in finite samples.

If the ADF test does not allow rejection of the null hypothesis of one unit root, the presence of a second unit root may be tested by estimating the regression of $\Delta^2 Y_t$ on $\Delta Y_{t-1}, \Delta^2 Y_{t-1}, \ldots, \Delta^2 Y_{t-p+1}$, and comparing the t-ratio of the coefficient on ΔY_{t-1} with the appropriate critical value from Table 8.1. Alternatively, the presence of two unit roots may be tested *jointly* by estimating the regression of $\Delta^2 Y_t$ on $Y_{t-1}, \Delta Y_{t-1}, \Delta^2 Y_{t-1}, \ldots, \Delta^2 Y_{t-p+1}$, and computing the usual F-statistic for testing the joint significance of Y_{t-1} and ΔY_{t-1}. Again, though, this test statistic has a distribution under the null hypothesis of a double unit root that is not the usual F distribution. Percentiles of this distribution are given by Hasza and Fuller (1979).

8.4.3 Extensions

Before moving to an illustration, let us stress that a stochastic process may be nonstationary for other reasons than the presence of one or two unit roots. A linear deterministic trend is one example, but many other forms of nonstationarity are possible. To illustrate this, note that, if the process for Y_t is nonstationary, so will be the process for $\log Y_t$. However, at most one of these processes will be characterized by a unit root. Without going into details, it may be mentioned that the recent literature on unit roots also includes discussions of stochastic unit roots, seasonal unit roots, fractional integration and panel data unit root tests. A stochastic unit root implies that a process is characterized by a root that is not constant but stochastic and varying around unity. Such a process can be stationary for some periods and mildly explosive for others (see Granger and Swanson, 1997; or Gouriéroux and Robert, 2006). A seasonal unit root arises if a series becomes stationary after seasonal differencing (Hylleberg et al., 1993). For example, if the monthly series $Y_t - Y_{t-12}$ is stationary whereas Y_t is not (see Patterson, 2000, Section 7.7, for an intuitive discussion). Fractional integration starts from the idea that a series may be integrated of order d, where d is not an integer. If $d \geq 0.5$, the process is nonstationary and said to be fractionally integrated. By allowing d to take any value between 0 and 1, the gap between stationary and nonstationary processes is closed; see Bailey (1996) and Gouriéroux and Jasiak (2001, Chapter 5); a recent application on stock market volatility is provided in Bollerslev et al. (2013). Finally, panel data unit root tests involve tests for unit roots in multiple series, for example, GDP in 10 different countries. This extension is discussed in Chapter 10.

8.4.4 Illustration: Stock Prices and Earnings

In this subsection we consider annual data on the S&P Composite Stock Price Index and S&P Composite Earnings over the period 1871–2009 ($T = 139$), both corrected for inflation. The stock price index reflects the price level at the end of the year, while the earnings index aggregates corporate profits per share over the entire calender year. Because the US inflation rate varied substantially over this period of almost 140 years, adjusting for the consumer price index is important to obtain a good impression of the real increase in the stock market over this period. Because stock prices and earnings can be expected to grow exponentially over time, we take the natural logarithm of both series. Figure 8.3 plots the price and earnings indexes over time.

While it is clear from the figure that both series are not stationary in the sense of fluctuating around a long-run mean, it is not clear from a visual inspection whether the nonstationarity is due to the presence of a deterministic trend or due to one or more unit roots. To test for a unit root, it therefore makes sense to include a linear trend in the equation, as well as a constant. First, let us consider a standard Dickey–Fuller regression for the log price series, which gives

$$\Delta Y_t = \underset{(0.038)}{0.437} + \underset{(0.0074)}{0.00176}\, t - \underset{(0.0376)}{0.0984}\, Y_{t-1} + e_t, \tag{8.58}$$

resulting in a DF test statistic of −2.621. As the appropriate critical value at the 5% level is −3.44, this does not allow us to reject the null hypothesis of a unit root. However, we need to be sure that the number of lags in the testing regression is sufficiently large to make the error term white noise. Thus, it is advisable to perform a range of augmented Dickey–Fuller tests as well, implying that we add additional lags of ΔY_t to the right-hand

Figure 8.3 Log stock price and earnings, 1871–2009.

side. Restricting attention to the test statistics, the results with up to six additional lags are as follows:

DF	$ADF(1)$	$ADF(2)$	$ADF(3)$	$ADF(4)$	$ADF(5)$	$ADF(6)$
−2.621	−2.744	−2.273	−2.618	−2.255	−2.154	−2.345

None of these tests implies a rejection of the null hypothesis of a unit root. An alternative way to remove the serial correlation is the use of the non-parametric Phillips-Perron (1988) test. Using a lag length of 6 for the Newey–West correction for serial correlation leads to a value of −2.663 for the test statistic, which again implies that the unit root is not rejected.

The KPSS test is developed to test the null hypothesis of stationarity or trend stationarity. To calculate the test statistic we have to choose the weighting scheme to estimate the long-run variance ('kernel'), as well as the number of lags ('bandwidth'). Sticking to a lag length of 6, the KPSS test for stationarity produces a value of 0.223 when Bartlett weights are used, and of 0.203 when the quadratic spectral kernel is used. These values are well above the 5% critical value of 0.146 and therefore reject trend stationarity in favour of a unit root. This implies that shocks to the series, like the severe credit crisis in 2008, tend to have a permanent effect on the stock price level, rather than transitory. That is, there is no evidence that in the years after a shock stock prices will convert back to a deterministic long-term trend.

If we impose a first unit root on the log price series, we can test for the presence of a second unit root, even though this does not make too much sense economically. Note that first-differencing the log price series produces relative price changes or returns. Testing for a second unit root by means of an augmented Dickey–Fuller test implies regressions of the form

$$\Delta^2 Y_t = \delta + \pi \Delta Y_{t-1} + c_1 \Delta^2 Y_{t-1} + \cdots + \varepsilon_t,$$

and the null hypothesis corresponds to $\pi = 0$. We have omitted a trend term in the regressions because it seems unlikely that stock returns exhibit a deterministic trend. If we restrict attention to tests using a lag length of 6, the augmented Dickey–Fuller test produces a test statistic of −4.106, which is strongly rejecting the unit root hypothesis. The KPSS test for stationarity, with a Bartlett kernel, produces a value of 0.054, which is much smaller than the 5% critical value of 0.463. Both tests clearly indicate that the first-differenced price series is likely to be stationary.

We can repeat all tests for the log earnings series, and the conclusions are similar, although the evidence is a bit mixed. For example, the ADF(6) test statistic for the augmented Dickey–Fuller regression with an intercept and time trend is −2.778, which means that a unit root is not rejected. The KPSS(6) test statistics for trend stationarity are 0.158 (Bartlett kernel) and 0.148 (quadratic spectral kernel), which are (marginal) rejections of trend stationarity at the 5% level. The Phillips–Perron test statistic (with a lag length of 6), however, produces a test statistic of −4.908, which would imply a clear rejection of a unit root.

To conclude this subsection, we consider the log of the price/earnings ratio, which is simply the difference between the log stock price and the log earnings series. The question as to whether valuation ratios, like the price/earnings ratio, are mean reverting has received considerable attention in the literature and has interesting implications for forecasting future stock prices. For example, Campbell and Shiller (1998) argue that the

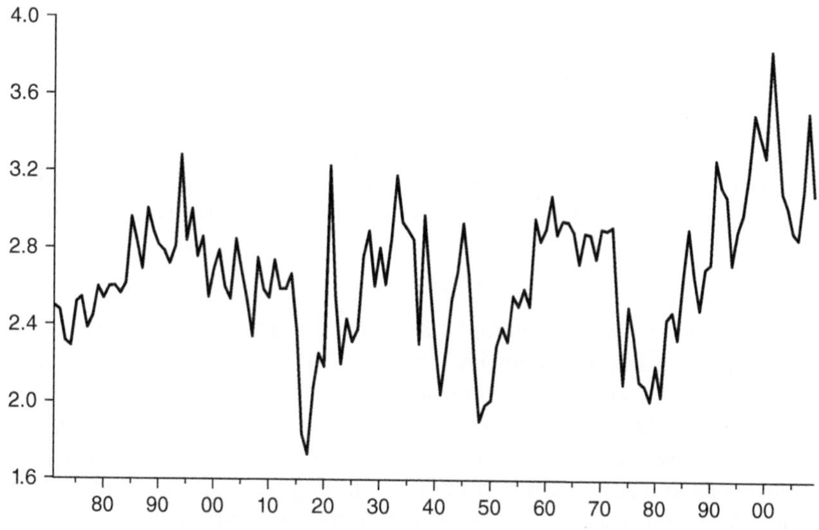

Figure 8.4 Log price/earnings ratio, 1871–2009.

high price/earnings ratios observed in the late 1990s imply a decline in future stock prices to bring the ratio into line with its historical level. First, we plot the log price/earnings ratio in Figure 8.4. Seemingly, the series fluctuates around a long-run average, although it sometimes takes many years for the series to revert to its mean.

Using the previous tests, the standard Dickey–Fuller regression (excluding a time trend) results in

$$\Delta Y_t = \underset{(0.155)}{0.685} - \underset{(0.058)}{0.255}\, Y_{t-1} + e_t,$$

corresponding to a test statistic of −4.424. This clearly rejects the null hypothesis of a unit root. However, with two or more lags included in the regression, the augmented Dickey–Fuller tests typically do not reject a unit root. For example, with a lag length of 6, the test statistic is −2.208, and including a time trend does not make much difference. The KPSS test for stationarity, using the Bartlett kernel and 6 lags, produces a value of 0.331 and does not reject either. Unfortunately, it is not uncommon for the unit root tests and the stationarity tests to yield conflicting results (see Kwiatskowski et al., 1992, for some examples). The appropriate conclusion in this case is that the data are not sufficiently informative to distinguish between these two hypotheses. Apparently, mean reversion in the log price/earnings series, if present, is very slow.

8.5 Illustration: Long-run Purchasing Power Parity (Part 1)

In this section we pay attention to an empirical example concerning prices in two countries and the exchange rate between these countries. If two countries produce tradeable goods, and there are no impediments to international trade, such as tariffs or transaction costs, then the law of one price should hold, that is,

$$S_t = P_t / P_t^*, \tag{8.59}$$

where S_t is the spot exchange rate (home currency price of a unit of foreign exchange), P_t is the (aggregate) price in the domestic country and P_t^* the price in the foreign country. The law of one price implies that exchange rates are such that a good sells at the same price in two different countries when expressed in the same currency. In logarithms, we can write

$$s_t = p_t - p_t^* \tag{8.60}$$

(where lowercase letters denote natural logarithms). Condition (8.60), which is referred to as absolute **purchasing power parity** (absolute PPP), implies that a unit of currency in one country has the same purchasing power in a foreign country. Few economists would believe that (8.60) holds exactly at every point in time, and usually PPP is seen as determining the exchange rate in the long-run. In the empirical literature there is an ongoing debate as to whether some form of purchasing power parity holds (see Taylor and Taylor, 2004). In this section, we shall analyse the question whether (8.60) is 'valid' in the long-run. A first necessary step is an analysis of the properties of the variables involved in (8.60).

Our empirical example concerns the United Kingdom and the euro area over the period January 1988 until December 2010 ($T = 276$). We analyse the consumer price index series (CPI) for both currency areas, where the price index for the euro is based on a weighted average of its participating countries. Because the Sterling/euro rate is only available from January 1999, we use the 'synthetic' euro as provided by the European Central Bank for the first part of the sample period. First, in Figure 8.5, we plot the log of the two price series (where January 1988 is set to 100 for both series). Clearly, this figure indicates nonstationarity of the two series, while it seems be the case that the two series have different growth rates, particularly in some subperiods (like 1988–1992). We start by

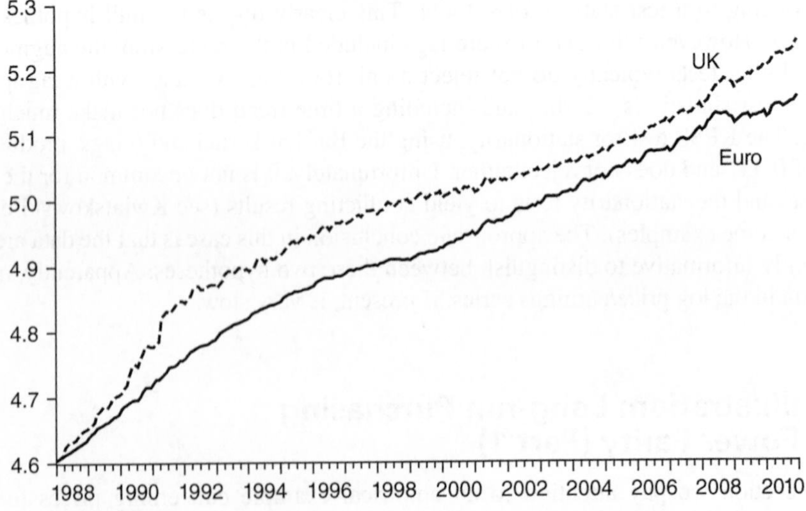

Figure 8.5 Log consumer price index UK and euro area, Jan 1988–Dec 2010.

applying a number of unit root tests on the two (log) price series. The null hypothesis in this case is that the series have a unit root, while the alternative is that the series are trend stationary. Accordingly, we allow for both an intercept and a deterministic trend in the test regressions. For p_t, the log of the euro consumer price index, we obtain the following results, including a constant and time trend, but no lagged differences in the model:

$$\Delta p_t = \underset{(0.0042)}{0.101} + \underset{(0.000014)}{0.000033}\ t - \underset{(0.0075)}{0.0211}\ p_{t-1} + e_t.$$

The implied estimate for the first-order autoregressive coefficient θ equals 0.9789 with a standard error of 0.0075. The Dickey–Fuller test statistic is −2.821, while the 5% critical value is −3.43, suggesting that the null hypothesis of a unit root is not rejected. If we, inappropriately, eliminate the time trend from the model, the Dickey–Fuller test statistic is −3.476, and the null hypothesis of a unit root is marginally rejected at the 1% level. It is quite likely that the simple $AR(1)$ model employed in the test regression is too restrictive. The augmented Dickey-Fuller tests include additional lags of Δp_t in the model to capture any remaining serial correlation. While it is possible to use significance tests or model selection criteria to select the optimal lag length, we will simply calculate a range of ADF test statistics for different lag lengths. This gives the results in Table 8.2, where the maximum lag length is fixed at 36. This choice makes sense given that monthly price series tend to have some seasonal component. In fact, in all cases the 12th, 24th and 36th lagged differences are statistically highly significant. The appropriate critical values for the ADF test statistics are −3.43 at the 5% level and −3.99 at the 1% level. The variation in the ADF test statistics is limited, although the values occasionally shift from insignificant to significant or vice versa. From the test results we conclude that a unit root in the log euro price series is not rejected, particularly when we focus on the tests with a sufficiently large number of lags. The finding that prices are driven by a unit root, rather than a deterministic trend, implies that price shocks have a permanent effect, rather than transitory.

Table 8.2 Unit root tests for log price index euro area and the United Kingdom

	Euro (p_t)	UK (p_t^*)
Statistic	With intercept and trend	
DF	−2.821	−3.587
ADF(1)	−2.810	−3.535
ADF(2)	−2.912	−3.697
ADF(3)	−3.029	−3.706
ADF(4)	−3.241	−3.785
ADF(5)	−3.402	−3.936
ADF(6)	−3.173	−3.316
ADF(7)	−3.368	−3.439
ADF(8)	−3.518	−3.401
ADF(9)	−3.600	−3.763
ADF(10)	−3.704	−3.816
ADF(11)	−3.730	−3.840
ADF(12)	−3.506	−3.678
ADF(24)	−3.098	−4.068
ADF(36)	−3.361	−2.262

Table 8.3 Unit root tests for log exchange rate euro/UK

Statistic	Without trend	With trend
DF	−1.268	−1.235
ADF(1)	−1.203	−1.164
ADF(2)	−1.234	−1.199
ADF(3)	−1.318	−1.286
ADF(4)	−1.450	−1.462
ADF(5)	−1.405	−1.366
ADF(6)	−1.294	−1.246

For the log of the consumer price index in the United Kingdom, p_t^*, we find a similar set of results, as shown in the last column of Table 8.2. Here, the inclusion of the 36th lag has an important impact on the test statistics. Again we do not reject the null hypothesis that the log price series contains a unit root.

For the log of the exchange rate s_t, measured as euros per pound, the Dickey–Fuller and augmented Dickey–Fuller tests give the results in Table 8.3, where we only report the ADF tests up to lag 6. The results here are quite clear. In none of the cases we can reject the null hypothesis of a unit root.

If purchasing power parity between the euro area and the United Kingdom holds in the long-run, one can expect that short-run deviations, $s_t - (p_t - p_t^*)$, corresponding to the real exchange rate, are limited and do not wander widely. In other words, one can expect $s_t - (p_t - p_t^*)$ to be stationary (but not trend stationary). A test for PPP can thus be based on the analysis of the log real exchange rate $rs_t = s_t - (p_t - p_t^*)$. The series is plotted in Figure 8.6, while the results for the augmented Dickey–Fuller tests for this variable are given in Table 8.4.

Figure 8.6 Log real exchange rate euro area/UK, Jan 1988–Dec 2010.

Table 8.4 Unit root tests for log real exchange rate euro area/UK

Statistic	Without trend	With trend
DF	−1.492	−1.490
ADF(1)	−1.473	−1.469
ADF(2)	−1.427	−1.418
ADF(3)	−1.476	−1.466
ADF(4)	−1.627	−1.616
ADF(5)	−1.520	−1.504
ADF(6)	−1.389	−1.367
ADF(12)	−1.993	−1.966

The results show that the null hypothesis of a unit root in rs_t (corresponding to nonstationarity) cannot be rejected. Consequently, there is no evidence for PPP to hold in this form. One reason why we may not be able to reject the null hypothesis is simply that our sample contains insufficient information: the sample period is too short and standard errors are simply too high to reject the unit root hypothesis. This is a problem often found in tests for purchasing power parity. As stressed by Taylor and Taylor (2004), statistical tests to examine the long-run properties of the real exchange rate easily suffer from low power. That is, it may be very hard to reject the null hypothesis of a unit root with a relatively short sample, when in reality the real exchange rate reverts only slowly towards its mean over long periods of time. If we reverse the null and alternative hypothesis, and employ the KPSS test with a lag length of 6, we obtain values 0.579 (Bartlett kernel) and 0.537 (quadratic spectral kernel), both of which are marginal rejections at the 5% level.

Based on the results from the standard Dickey-Fuller regression (without a trend) from Table 8.4, we find an estimated autocorrelation coefficient of $\hat{\theta} = 0.982$. Accordingly, a proportion of 0.982 of any shock in the real exchange rate will still remain after one month, while $\hat{\theta}^2 = 0.964$ of it remains after two months. The **half-life** of a shock tells us how long it would take for the effect of a shock to die out by 50%, and can be solved from $h = \log(0.5)/\log(\theta)$. The current estimates imply a half-life of about 38 months, which is consistent with the observation in Rogoff (1996) that the estimated half-lives mostly fall into the range of 3–5 years. The term 'purchasing power parity puzzle' is often used to refer to the difficulty of reconciling high short-term volatility of real exchange rates with very slow rates of mean reversion. In Chapter 9, we shall investigate the empirical evidence for some weaker forms of PPP.

8.6 Estimation of ARMA Models

Suppose that we know that the data series $Y_1, Y_2, \dots, Y_T$ is generated by an ARMA process of order p, q. Depending upon the specification of the model, and the distributional assumptions we are willing to make, we can estimate the unknown parameters by ordinary or nonlinear least squares, or by maximum likelihood.

8.6.1 Least Squares

The least squares approach chooses the model parameters such that the residual sum of squares is minimal. This is particularly easy for models in autoregressive form. Consider the $AR(p)$ model

$$Y_t = \delta + \theta_1 Y_{t-1} + \theta_2 Y_{t-2} + \cdots + \theta_p Y_{t-p} + \varepsilon_t, \tag{8.61}$$

where ε_t is a white noise error term that is uncorrelated with anything dated $t-1$ or before. Consequently, we have

$$E\{Y_{t-j}\varepsilon_t\} = 0 \quad \text{for } j = 1, 2, 3, \ldots, p,$$

that is, error terms and explanatory variables are contemporaneously uncorrelated and OLS applied to (8.61) provides consistent estimators. Estimation of an autoregressive model is thus no different than that of a linear regression model with a lagged dependent variable. Clearly, assumption (A2) as introduced in Chapter 2 will not be satisfied in an autoregressive model, and the OLS estimator exhibits a small sample bias. For example, in the $AR(1)$ model it can be shown that the estimator for the autoregressive coefficient is biased towards zero, particularly when the true autoregressive coefficient is close to one. For higher-order models, the direction of the bias is less clear. Bias-correction methods that have found their way in empirical work are proposed by Shaman and Stine (1988) and Andrews and Chen (1994).

For moving average models, estimation is somewhat more complicated. Suppose that we have an $MA(1)$ model

$$Y_t = \mu + \varepsilon_t + \alpha\varepsilon_{t-1}.$$

Because ε_{t-1} is not observed, we cannot apply regression techniques here. In theory, ordinary least squares would minimize

$$S(\alpha, \mu) = \sum_{t=2}^{T} (Y_t - \mu - \alpha\varepsilon_{t-1})^2.$$

A possible solution arises if we write ε_{t-1} in this expression as a function of observed Y_ts. This is possible only if the MA polynomial is *invertible*. In this case we can use

$$\varepsilon_{t-1} = \sum_{j=0}^{\infty} (-\alpha)^j (Y_{t-j-1} - \mu)$$

(see Subsection 8.2.1) and write

$$S(\alpha, \mu) = \sum_{t=2}^{T} \left(Y_t - \mu - \alpha \sum_{j=0}^{\infty} (-\alpha)^j (Y_{t-j-1} - \mu) \right)^2.$$

In practice, Y_t is not observed for $t = 0, -1, \ldots$, so we have to cut off the infinite sum in this expression to obtain an approximate sum of squares

$$\tilde{S}(\alpha, \mu) = \sum_{t=2}^{T} \left(Y_t - \mu - \alpha \sum_{j=0}^{t-2} (-\alpha)^j (Y_{t-j-1} - \mu) \right)^2. \tag{8.62}$$

This corresponds to equating the pre-sample values of Y_t to the unconditional mean μ. Because, asymptotically, if T goes to infinity the difference between $S(\alpha, \mu)$ and $\tilde{S}(\alpha, \mu)$ disappears, minimizing (8.62) with respect to α and μ gives consistent estimators $\hat{\alpha}$ and $\hat{\mu}$. Unfortunately, (8.62) is a high-order polynomial in α and thus has very many local minima. Therefore, numerically minimizing (8.62) is complicated. However, as we know that $-1 < \alpha < 1$, a grid search (e.g. $-0.99, -0.98, -0.97, \ldots, 0.98, 0.99$) can be performed. The resulting nonlinear least squares estimators for α and μ are consistent and asymptotically normal.

8.6.2 Maximum Likelihood

An alternative estimator for ARMA models is provided by maximum likelihood. This requires that an assumption is made about the distribution of ε_t, most commonly normality. Although the normality assumption is strong, the ML estimators are very often consistent even in cases where ε_t is not normal. Conditional upon an initial value, the loglikelihood function can be written as

$$\log L(\alpha, \theta, \mu, \sigma^2) = -\frac{T-1}{2}\log(2\pi\sigma^2) - \frac{1}{2}\sum_{t=2}^{T}\varepsilon_t^2/\sigma^2,$$

where ε_t is a function of the coefficients α, θ and μ and of y_t and its history. For an $AR(1)$ model it holds that $\varepsilon_t = y_t - \theta y_{t-1}$, where $y_t = Y_t - \mu$, and for the $MA(1)$ model we have

$$\varepsilon_t = y_t - \alpha\sum_{j=0}^{t-2}(-\alpha)^j y_{t-j-1} = \sum_{j=0}^{t-1}(-\alpha)^j y_{t-j}.$$

Both of the implied loglikelihood functions are conditional upon an initial value. For the $AR(1)$ case, y_1 is treated as given, while for the $MA(1)$ case the initial condition is $\varepsilon_0 = 0$. The resulting estimators are therefore referred to as **conditional maximum likelihood** estimators. The conditional ML estimators for α, θ and μ are easily seen to be identical to the least squares estimators.

The *exact* maximum likelihood estimator combines the conditional likelihood with the likelihood from the initial observations. In the $AR(1)$ case, for example, the following term is added to the loglikelihood:

$$-\frac{1}{2}\log(2\pi) - \frac{1}{2}\log[\sigma^2/(1-\theta^2)] - \frac{1}{2}\frac{y_1^2}{\sigma^2/(1-\theta^2)},$$

which follows from the fact that the marginal density of y_1 is normal with mean zero and variance $\sigma^2/(1-\theta^2)$. For a moving average process, the exact likelihood function is somewhat more complex. If T is large, the way we treat the initial values has negligible impact, so that the conditional and exact maximum likelihood estimators are asymptotically equivalent in cases where the AR and MA polynomials are invertible. More details can be found in Hamilton (1994, Chapter 5) and Pesaran (2015, Chapter 14).

It will be clear from the previous discussion that estimating autoregressive models is simpler than estimating moving average models. Estimating ARMA models, which combine an autoregressive part with a moving average part, closely follows the lines of ML estimation of the MA parameters. As any (invertible) ARMA model can be approximated by an autoregressive model of infinite order, it has become more and more common practice to use autoregressive specifications instead of MA or ARMA ones, and allowing for a sufficient number of lags. Particularly if the number of observations is not too small, this approach may work pretty well in practice. Of course, an MA representation of the same process may be more parsimonious. Another advantage of autoregressive models is that they are easily generalized to multivariate time series where one wants to model a set of economic variables jointly. This leads to so-called **vector autoregressive models** (VAR models), which are discussed in Chapter 9.

8.7 Choosing a Model

Most of the time there are no economic reasons to choose a particular specification for an ARMA model. Consequently, to a large extent the data will determine which time series model is appropriate. Before estimating any model, it is common to estimate autocorrelation and partial autocorrelation coefficients directly from the data, which may give some idea about which model might be appropriate. After one or more models are estimated, their quality can be judged by checking whether the residuals are white noise, and by comparing them with alternative specifications. These comparisons can be based on statistical tests or the use of model selection criteria.

8.7.1 The Autocorrelation Function

The autocorrelation function (ACF) describes the correlation between Y_t and its lag Y_{t-k} as a function of k. Recall that the kth-order autocorrelation coefficient is defined as

$$\rho_k = \frac{\text{cov}\{Y_t, Y_{t-k}\}}{V\{Y_t\}} = \frac{\gamma_k}{\gamma_0},$$

noting that $\text{cov}\{Y_t, Y_{t-k}\} = E\{y_t y_{t-k}\}$.

For the $MA(1)$ model we have seen that

$$\rho_1 = \frac{\alpha}{1+\alpha^2}, \quad \rho_2 = 0, \quad \rho_3 = 0, \ldots,$$

that is, only the first autocorrelation coefficient is nonzero. For the $MA(2)$ model

$$y_t = \varepsilon_t + \alpha_1\varepsilon_{t-1} + \alpha_2\varepsilon_{t-2},$$

we have

$$\begin{aligned}
E\{y_t^2\} &= (1+\alpha_1^2+\alpha_2^2)\sigma^2,\\
E\{y_t y_{t-1}\} &= (\alpha_1+\alpha_1\alpha_2)\sigma^2,\\
E\{y_t y_{t-2}\} &= \alpha_2\sigma^2,\\
E\{y_t y_{t-k}\} &= 0, \quad k = 3, 4, 5, \ldots
\end{aligned}$$

It follows directly from this that the ACF is zero after two lags. This is a general result for moving average models: for an $MA(q)$ model the ACF is zero after q lags.

The *sample* autocorrelation function gives the *estimated* autocorrelation coefficients as a function of k. The coefficient ρ_k can be estimated by

$$\hat{\rho}_k = \frac{\frac{1}{T-k}\sum_{t=k+1}^{T}(Y_t - \bar{Y})(Y_{t-k} - \bar{Y})}{\frac{1}{T}\sum_{t=1}^{T}(Y_t - \bar{Y})^2}, \tag{8.63}$$

where $\bar{Y} = (1/T)\sum_{t=1}^{T} Y_t$ denotes the sample average. That is, the population variance and covariance in the ratio are replaced by their sample estimates. Alternatively, ρ_k can be estimated by regressing Y_t upon Y_{t-k} and a constant, which will give a slightly different estimator, because the summation in the numerator and denominator will be over the same set of observations. We can use $\hat{\rho}_k$ to test the hypothesis that $\rho_k = 0$. To do this, we employ the result that asymptotically

$$\sqrt{T}(\hat{\rho}_k - \rho_k) \to \mathcal{N}(0, \upsilon_k),$$

where

$$\upsilon_k = 1 + 2\rho_1^2 + 2\rho_2^2 + \cdots + 2\rho_q^2 \quad \text{if } q < k.$$

So, to test the hypothesis that the true model is $MA(0)$ versus the alternative that it is $MA(1)$, we can test $\rho_1 = 0$ by comparing the test statistic $\sqrt{T}\hat{\rho}_1$ with the critical values of a standard normal distribution. Testing $MA(k-1)$ versus $MA(k)$ is done by testing $\rho_k = 0$ and comparing the test statistic

$$\sqrt{T}\frac{\hat{\rho}_k}{\sqrt{1 + 2\hat{\rho}_1^2 + \cdots + 2\hat{\rho}_{k-1}^2}} \tag{8.64}$$

with critical values from the standard normal distribution. Typically, two-standard error bounds for $\hat{\rho}_k$ based on the estimated variance $1 + 2\hat{\rho}_1^2 + \cdots + 2\hat{\rho}_{k-1}^2$ are graphically displayed in the plot of the sample autocorrelation function (see the example in Section 8.8). The order of a moving average model can in this way be determined from an inspection of the sample ACF. At least it will give us a reasonable value for q to start with, and diagnostic checking, as discussed in Subsection 8.7.3, should indicate whether it is appropriate or not.

For autoregressive models the ACF is less helpful. For the $AR(1)$ model we have seen that the autocorrelation coefficients do not cut off at a finite lag length. Instead, they go to zero exponentially corresponding to $\rho_k = \theta^k$. For higher-order autoregressive models, the autocorrelation function is more complex. Consider the general $AR(2)$ model

$$Y_t = \delta + \theta_1 Y_{t-1} + \theta_2 Y_{t-2} + \varepsilon_t.$$

To derive the autocovariances, it is convenient to take the covariance of both sides with Y_{t-k} to obtain

$$\text{cov}\{Y_t, Y_{t-k}\} = \theta_1 \text{cov}\{Y_{t-1}, Y_{t-k}\} + \theta_2 \text{cov}\{Y_{t-2}, Y_{t-k}\} + \text{cov}\{\varepsilon_t, Y_{t-k}\}.$$

For $k = 0, 1, 2$, this gives

$$\gamma_0 = \theta_1\gamma_1 + \theta_2\gamma_2 + \sigma^2,$$
$$\gamma_1 = \theta_1\gamma_0 + \theta_2\gamma_1,$$
$$\gamma_2 = \theta_1\gamma_1 + \theta_2\gamma_0.$$

This set of equations, known as the **Yule–Walker equations**, can be solved for the autocovariances γ_0, γ_1 and γ_2 as a function of the model parameters θ_1, θ_2 and σ^2. The higher-order covariances can be determined recursively from

$$\gamma_k = \theta_1\gamma_{k-1} + \theta_2\gamma_{k-2} \quad (k = 2, 3, \ldots),$$

which corresponds to a second-order differential equation. Depending on θ_1 and θ_2, the patterns of the ACF can be very different. Consequently, in general only a real expert may be able to identify an $AR(2)$ process from the ACF pattern, let alone from the sample ACF pattern. An alternative source of information that is helpful is provided by the *partial* autocorrelation function.

8.7.2 The Partial Autocorrelation Function

We define the kth-order sample **partial autocorrelation coefficient** as the estimate for θ_k in an $AR(k)$ model. We denote this by $\hat{\theta}_{kk}$. So, estimating

$$Y_t = \delta + \theta_1 Y_{t-1} + \varepsilon_t$$

gives us $\hat{\theta}_{11}$, while estimating

$$Y_t = \delta + \theta_1 Y_{t-1} + \theta_2 Y_{t-2} + \varepsilon_t$$

yields $\hat{\theta}_{22}$, the estimated coefficient for Y_{t-2} in the $AR(2)$ model. The partial autocorrelation $\hat{\theta}_{kk}$ measures the additional correlation between Y_t and Y_{t-k} after adjustments have been made for the intermediate values $Y_{t-1}, \ldots, Y_{t-k+1}$.

Obviously, if the true model is an $AR(p)$ process, then estimating an $AR(k)$ model by OLS gives consistent estimators for the model parameters if $k \geq p$. Consequently, we have

$$\text{plim}\ \hat{\theta}_{kk} = 0 \quad \text{if } k > p. \tag{8.65}$$

Moreover, it can be shown that the asymptotic distribution is standard normal, that is,

$$\sqrt{T}(\hat{\theta}_{kk} - 0) \rightarrow \mathcal{N}(0, 1) \quad \text{if } k > p. \tag{8.66}$$

Consequently, the partial autocorrelation coefficients (or the partial autocorrelation function (PACF)) can be used to determine the order of an AR process. Testing an $AR(k-1)$ model versus an $AR(k)$ model implies testing the null hypothesis that $\theta_{kk} = 0$. Under the null hypothesis that the model is $AR(k-1)$, the approximate standard error of $\hat{\theta}_{kk}$ based on (8.66) is $1/\sqrt{T}$, so that $\theta_{kk} = 0$ is rejected if $|\sqrt{T}\hat{\theta}_{kk}| > 1.96$. This way one can look at the PACF and test for each lag whether the partial autocorrelation coefficient is zero. For a genuine $AR(p)$ model the partial autocorrelations will be close to zero after the pth lag.

For moving average models it can be shown that the partial autocorrelations do not have a cut-off point but tail off to zero, just like the autocorrelations in an autoregressive model. In summary, an *AR(p)* process is described by:

1. an ACF that is infinite in extent (it tails off);
2. a PACF that is (close to) zero for lags larger than p.

For an *MA(q)* process we have:

1. an ACF that is (close to) zero for lags larger than q;
2. a PACF that is infinite in extent (it tails off).

In the absence of any of these two situations, a combined ARMA model may provide a parsimonious representation of the data.

8.7.3 Diagnostic Checking

As a last step in the model-building cycle, some checks on the model adequacy are required. Possibilities are doing a **residual analysis** and **overfitting** the specified model. For example, if an $ARMA(p, q)$ model is chosen (on the basis of the sample ACF and PACF), we could also estimate an $ARMA(p+1, q)$ and an $ARMA(p, q+1)$ model and test the significance of the additional parameters.

A residual analysis is usually based on the fact that the residuals of an adequate model should be approximately white noise. A plot of the residuals can be a useful tool in checking for outliers. Moreover, the estimated residual autocorrelations are usually examined. Recall that for a white noise series the autocorrelations are zero. Therefore the significance of the residual autocorrelations is often checked by comparing with approximate two-standard error bounds $\pm 2/\sqrt{T}$. To check the overall acceptability of the residual autocorrelations, the Ljung–Box (1978) portmanteau test statistic,

$$Q_K = T(T+2) \sum_{k=1}^{K} \frac{1}{T-k} r_k^2, \tag{8.67}$$

is often used. Here, the r_ks are the estimated autocorrelation coefficients of the residuals $\hat{\varepsilon}_t$ and K is a number chosen by the researcher. Values of Q for different K may be computed in a residual analysis. For an $ARMA(p, q)$ process, the statistic Q_K is approximately Chi-squared distributed with $K - p - q$ degrees of freedom (under the null hypothesis that the $ARMA(p, q)$ is correctly specified). If a model is rejected at this stage, the model-building cycle has to be repeated. Note that this test only makes sense if $K > p + q$.

8.7.4 Criteria for Model Selection

Because economic theory does not provide any guidance on the appropriate choice of model, some additional criteria can be used to choose from alternative models that are acceptable from a statistical point of view. As a more general model will always provide a better fit (within the sample) than a restricted version of it, all such criteria provide a trade-off between goodness-of-fit and the number of parameters used to obtain that fit.

For example, if an $MA(2)$ model would provide the same fit as an $AR(10)$ model, we would prefer the first as it is more parsimonious. As discussed in Chapter 3, a well-known criterion is **Akaike's information criterion** (AIC) (Akaike, 1973). In the current context it is given by

$$AIC = \log \hat{\sigma}^2 + 2\frac{p+q+1}{T}, \tag{8.68}$$

where $\hat{\sigma}^2$ is the estimated variance of ε_t. An alternative is Schwarz's **Bayesian information criterion** (BIC or SIC), proposed by Schwarz (1978), which is given by

$$BIC = \log \hat{\sigma}^2 + \frac{p+q+1}{T} \log T. \tag{8.69}$$

Both criteria are likelihood based and represent a different trade-off between 'fit', as measured by the loglikelihood value, and 'parsimony', as measured by the number of free parameters, $p+q+1$ (assuming that a constant is included in the model). Usually, the model with the smallest AIC or BIC value is preferred, although one can choose to deviate from this if the differences in criterion values are small for a subset of the models.

While the two criteria differ in their trade-off between fit and parsimony, the BIC criterion can be preferred because it has the property that it will almost surely select the true model, if $T \to \infty$, provided that the true model is in the class of $ARMA(p, q)$ models for relatively small values of p and q. In this case, the AIC criterion tends to result asymptotically in overparameterized models (see Hannan, 1980). On the other hand, it has been argued that the AIC performs well in cases where the true model is not in the class of models under consideration because the extra parameters may approximate the misspecification.

8.8 Illustration: The Persistence of Inflation

Inflation is one of the key variables in monetary economics. Several studies investigate the persistence of inflation in the United States (e.g. Fuhrer and Moore, 1995; or Pivetta and Reis, 2007). Persistence, in this case, refers to the long-run effect of a shock to inflation. How long and how strongly does a 1% shock to inflation today affect future inflation rates? And how long does it take for the inflation rate to return to its previous level, if ever? To investigate this, we investigate the dynamic properties of the quarterly inflation rate in the United States by means of unit root tests and ARIMA models. The data we have are seasonally adjusted inflation rates from 1960 to 2010 ($T = 204$ quarters), based on the Consumer Price Index (CPI) provided by the Bureau of Labor Statistics. The inflation rate is the annualized quarterly change in the CPI calculated as $Y_t = 400 \log(CPI_t/CPI_{t-1})$. A graph of the resulting series is provided in Figure 8.7.

The figure shows that inflation was relatively low in the 1960s, whereas it rose steadily in the 1970s, with peaks around 1974 and 1980. At the beginning of the 1980s, the Federal Reserve enforced its policy to reduce inflation rates, leading to lower and more stable inflation rates until the 1990s. The first decade of the new century exhibits increased variation in inflation rates, partly attributable to the recession and the high variation in commodity prices, like crude oil, in this period.

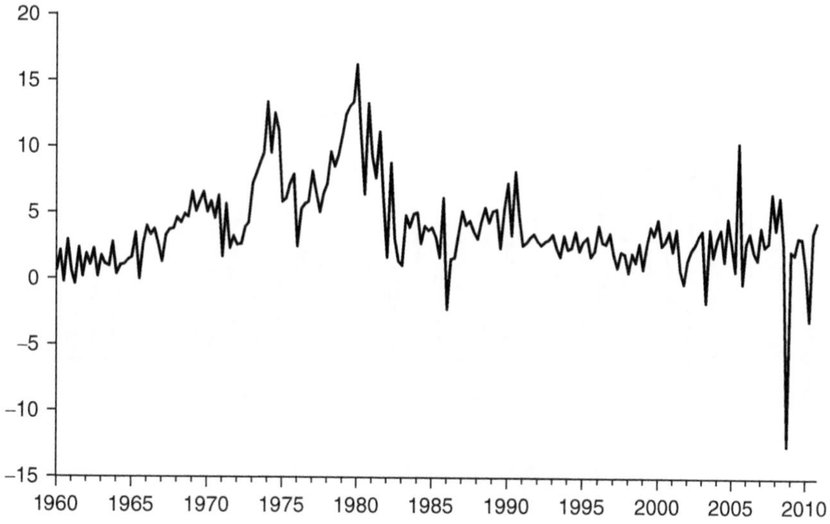

Figure 8.7 Quarterly inflation in the United States, 1960–2010.

As a first step, we test for the presence of a unit root in the quarterly inflation series using the augmented Dickey–Fuller test. With an intercept in the test regression the ADF test with two lags results in a value for the test statistic of −3.078, which is a marginal rejection at the 5% level. With four lags, the test statistic reduces to −2.764, which is only a marginal rejection at the 10% level. When more lags are added, it becomes increasingly less likely to reject the null hypothesis of unit root. Using the KPSS test to test the null hypothesis of stationarity also provides conflicting conclusions depending upon the number of lags that is included in the Newey–West correction. These results suggest that inflation is either $I(1)$ or $I(0)$ with a high degree of persistence. Our next look at the data involves an inspection of the sample autocorrelation and partial autocorrelation functions, which are presented in Figures 8.8 and 8.9, respectively. The ACF confirms that inflation is highly persistent, with the first seven autocorrelation coefficients being statistically significantly different from zero. The PACF indicates statistical significance of the first three partial autocorrelation coefficients, after which the PACF is close to zero, with an occasional peak in either direction.

To continue our analysis, we shall assume that inflation is $I(0)$, as is done in Fuhrer and Moore (1995), and analyse the persistence of inflation after estimating one or more ARMA models. Based on the sample autocorrelation function and partial autocorrelation function, the first model we estimate is a third-order autoregressive model (because the PACF becomes insignificant at lag 4). Estimating the $AR(3)$ model by OLS we obtain

$$\begin{aligned} y_t = \underset{(0.068)}{0.292}\, y_{t-1} + \underset{(0.069)}{0.227}\, y_{t-2} + \underset{(0.069)}{0.300}\, y_{t-3} + \hat{\varepsilon}_t; \\ AIC = 4.577476; \quad BIC = 4.642537; \quad s = 2.36338. \end{aligned}$$

For brevity, we do not report the estimated intercepts. The Ljung–Box test statistics are $Q_6 = 10.568$ ($p = 0.014$) and $Q_{12} = 16.961$ ($p = 0.049$), which suggest that residual

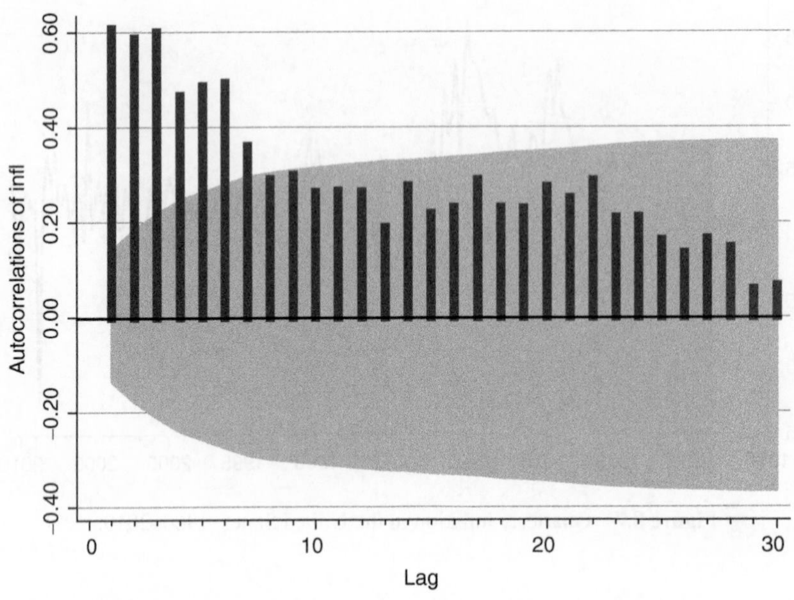

Figure 8.8 Sample autocorrelation function of inflation rate.

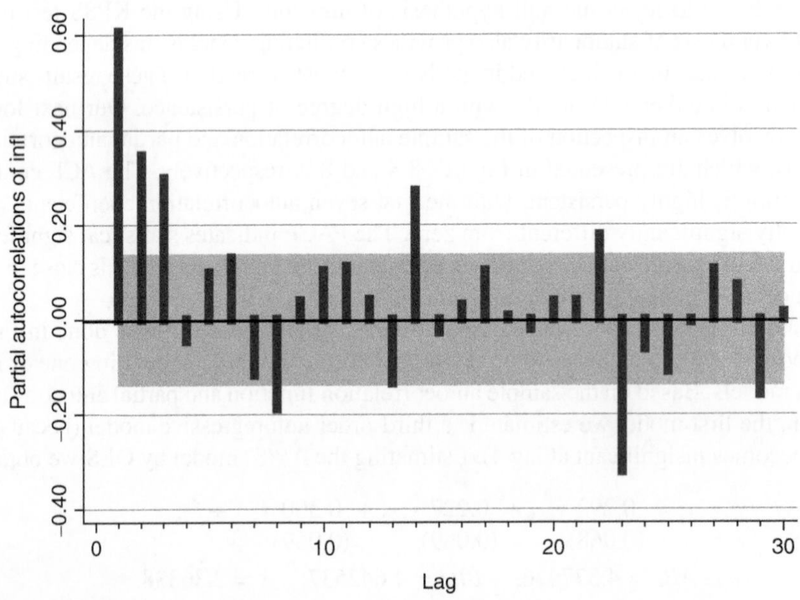

Figure 8.9 Sample partial autocorrelation function of inflation rate.

autocorrelation is still present and marginally significant. In an attempt to accommodate this we consider two extensions. First, we extend the model by adding an additional autoregressive term. The estimated $AR(4)$ model is given by

$$\begin{aligned} y_t = &\underset{(0.071)}{0.305}\, y_{t-1} + \underset{(0.071)}{0.328}\, y_{t-2} + \underset{(0.072)}{0.313}\, y_{t-3} - \underset{(0.072)}{0.043}\, y_{t-4} + \hat{\varepsilon}_t; \\ AIC &= 4.585499; \quad BIC = 4.666825; \quad s = 2.36720. \end{aligned}$$

The Ljung–Box statistics are $Q_6 = 11.143$ ($p = 0.004$) and $Q_{12} = 17.505$ ($p = 0.025$). Alternatively, we add a moving average term to the $AR(3)$ model, which results in

$$\begin{aligned} y_t = &\underset{(0.212)}{0.104}\, y_{t-1} + \underset{(0.108)}{0.303}\, y_{t-2} + \underset{(0.089)}{0.365}\, y_{t-3} + \underset{(0.227)}{0.207}\, \hat{\varepsilon}_{t-1} + \hat{\varepsilon}_t; \\ AIC &= 4.584362; \quad BIC = 4.665689; \quad s = 2.36586; \\ Q_6 &= 10.882\ (p = 0.004), \quad Q_{12} = 17.286\ (p = 0.027). \end{aligned}$$

Neither of these two extended specifications is superior to the original $AR(3)$ model. Nevertheless, each of the three models estimated so far still exhibit some residual serial correlation. An inspection of the residual ACF and PACF suggests that including a 6th lag may be appropriate. Therefore, as a next specification, we consider an $AR(6)$ model. The estimation results are as follows:

$$\begin{aligned} y_t = &\underset{(0.071)}{0.297}\, y_{t-1} + \underset{(0.074)}{0.218}\, y_{t-2} + \underset{(0.077)}{0.248}\, y_{t-3} \\ &-\underset{(0.077)}{0.106}\, y_{t-4} + \underset{(0.075)}{0.062}\, y_{t-5} + \underset{(0.072)}{0.132}\, y_{t-6} + \hat{\varepsilon}_t; \\ AIC &= 4.577884; \quad BIC = 4.691741; \quad s = 2.34702; \\ Q_{12} &= 13.605\ (p = 0.034). \end{aligned}$$

The three additional lags of y_t in this model are individually insignificant at the 5% level. The AIC is slightly better than for the $AR(3)$ model, but the BIC, which has a larger punishment for the additional parameters, favours the more parsimonious $AR(3)$ specification. The Ljung–Box test marginally rejects the null hypothesis of no residual autocorrelation at the 5% level. As a final specification, we estimate an $AR(6)$ model, but exclude the intermediate lags 4 and 5. This results in

$$\begin{aligned} y_t = &\underset{(0.068)}{0.270}\, y_{t-1} + \underset{(0.069)}{0.216}\, y_{t-2} + \underset{(0.075)}{0.242}\, y_{t-3} + \underset{(0.066)}{0.125}\, y_{t-6} + \hat{\varepsilon}_t; \\ AIC &= 4.569353; \quad BIC = 4.650680; \quad s = 2.34817; \\ Q_6 &= 5.174\ (p = 0.075), \quad Q_{12} = 15.106\ (p = 0.057). \end{aligned}$$

This specification (marginally) satisfies the Ljung–Box portmanteau tests. The 6th lag, however, is only marginally significant. The AIC favours the latter specification to the $AR(3)$ model, whereas the BIC favours the $AR(3)$.

The results of our specification search are not clear-cut, and either the $AR(3)$ or the (reduced) $AR(6)$ model can be defended. We shall now analyse to what extent these models give different answers to the question of persistence of inflation. Following Pivetta and Reis (2007) we distinguish three scalar measures for persistence. The first measure is the sum of the coefficients in the autoregressive process (SARC). The rationale for this measure comes from the fact that the cumulative effect of a shock to inflation is measured by $1/(1 - \sum_{j=1}^{p} \theta_j)$. Note that we have seen before that $\sum_{j=1}^{p} \theta_j = 1$ corresponds to a unit root and infinite persistence. The second measure we consider is the largest root of the autoregressive polynomial. Again, when the largest root is one (a unit root), the process is infinitely persistent and inflation never returns to its initial level after a shock. The final measure is the half-life of a shock and measures the number of periods required for a shock to inflation to dissipate by one-half. We estimate it using $h = \log(0.5)/\log(\sum_{j=1}^{p} \theta_j)$, which is a simple transformation of the SARC. Alternative estimators have been proposed for estimating the half-life in higher-order autoregressive models (see, e.g., Rossi, 2005).

For the $AR(3)$ model the SARC is 0.814, while for the reduced $AR(6)$ model it is somewhat higher at 0.845. The estimated largest roots for the two models are 0.90 and 0.94, respectively. Finally, the estimated half-life is 3.37 for the $AR(3)$ model and 4.11 quarters for the $AR(6)$ model. We conclude that persistence of inflation is quite high, irrespective of which of the two models is used.

8.9 Forecasting with ARMA Models

A main goal of building a time series model is predicting the future path of economic variables. Empirically, ARMA models usually perform quite well in this respect and often outperform more complicated structural models. Of course, ARMA models do not provide any economic insight in the forecasts and are unable to forecast under alternative economic scenarios. In case there is no model uncertainty and the model parameters are known, forecasting is relatively straightforward, and it is easy to derive the optimal forecast, which is simply the conditional expectation of a future value, given the available information. In the next subsection, we discuss the optimal forecast and how it can be derived in ARMA models. Subsection 8.9.2 pays attention to forecast accuracy, again in the situation where model uncertainty does not play a role. Subsection 8.9.3 focuses on genuine out-of-sample forecasting, where the forecasting model is not a priori given and may change over time, and model parameters must be estimated. An extensive treatment of the economics and statistics of forecasting is provided in Elliott and Timmermann (2016).

8.9.1 The Optimal Forecast

Suppose we are at time T and are interested in predicting Y_{T+h}, the value of Y_t h periods ahead. A forecast for Y_{T+h} will be based on an **information set**, denoted by $\mathcal{I}_T$, that contains the information that is available and potentially used at the time of making the forecast. Ideally, it contains all the information that is observed and known at time T. In univariate time series modelling we will usually assume that the information set at any point t in time contains the values of Y_t and all its lags. Thus we have

$$\mathcal{I}_T = \{Y_{-\infty}, \ldots, Y_{T-1}, Y_T\}. \tag{8.70}$$

In general, the forecast $\hat{Y}_{T+h|T}$ (the forecast for Y_{T+h} as constructed at time T) is a function of (variables in) the information set $\mathcal{I}_T$. Our criterion for choosing a forecast from the many possible ones is to minimize the expected quadratic forecast error

$$E\{(Y_{T+h} - \hat{Y}_{T+h|T})^2|\mathcal{I}_T\}, \tag{8.71}$$

where $E\{.|\mathcal{I}_T\}$ denotes the conditional expectation given the information set $\mathcal{I}_T$. It is not very hard to show that the best forecast for Y_{T+h} given the information set at time T is the conditional expectation of Y_{T+h} given the information $\mathcal{I}_T$. We denote this optimal forecast as

$$Y_{T+h|T} \equiv E\{Y_{T+h}|\mathcal{I}_T\}. \tag{8.72}$$

Because the optimal forecast is a conditional expectation, it satisfies the usual properties of expectation operators. Most importantly, the conditional expectation of a sum is the sum of conditional expectations. Further, it holds that the conditional expectation of Y_{T+h} given an information set $\mathcal{I}'_T$, where $\mathcal{I}'_T$ is a subset of $\mathcal{I}_T$, is at best as good as $Y_{T+h|T}$ based on $\mathcal{I}_T$. In line with our intuition, it holds that, the more information one uses to determine the forecast (the larger $\mathcal{I}_T$ is), the better the forecast will be. For example, $E\{Y_{T+h}|Y_T, Y_{T-1}, Y_{T-2}, \dots\}$ will usually be a better forecast than $E\{Y_{T+h}|Y_T\}$ or $E\{Y_{T+h}\}$ (an empty information set).

For simplicity, we shall, below, assume that the parameters in the ARMA model for Y_t are known. In practice one would simply replace the unknown parameters with their consistent estimates. Now, how do we determine these conditional expectations when Y_t follows an ARMA process? We consider forecasting y_{T+h}, noting that $Y_{T+h|T} = \mu + y_{T+h|T}$. As a first example, consider an $AR(1)$ process where it holds by assumption that

$$y_{T+1} = \theta y_T + \varepsilon_{T+1}.$$

Consequently,

$$y_{T+1|T} = E\{y_{T+1}|y_T, y_{T-1}, \dots\} = \theta y_T + E\{\varepsilon_{T+1}|y_T, y_{T-1}, \dots\} = \theta y_T, \tag{8.73}$$

where the latter equality follows from the fact that the white noise process is unpredictable. To predict two periods ahead ($h = 2$), we write

$$y_{T+2} = \theta y_{T+1} + \varepsilon_{T+2},$$

from which it follows that

$$E\{y_{T+2}|y_T, y_{T-1}, \dots\} = \theta E\{y_{T+1}|y_T, y_{T-1}, \dots\} = \theta^2 y_T. \tag{8.74}$$

In general, we obtain $y_{T+h|T} = \theta^h y_T$. Thus, the last observed value y_T contains all the information to determine the predictor for any future value. When h is large, the forecast of y_{T+h} converges to 0 (the unconditional expectation of y_t), provided (of course) that $|\theta| < 1$. With a nonzero mean, the best forecast for Y_{T+h} is directly obtained as $\mu + y_{T+h|T} = \mu + \theta^h(Y_T - \mu)$. Note that this differs from $\theta^h Y_T$.

As a second example, consider an $MA(1)$ process where

$$y_t = \varepsilon_t + \alpha\varepsilon_{t-1}.$$

Then we have

$$E\{y_{T+1}|y_T, y_{T-1}, \dots\} = \alpha E\{\varepsilon_T|y_T, y_{T-1}, \dots\} = \alpha\varepsilon_T,$$

where, implicitly, we assume that ε_T is observed (contained in $\mathcal{I}_T$). This is an innocent assumption *provided the MA process is invertible*. In that case we can write

$$\varepsilon_T = \sum_{j=0}^{\infty} (-\alpha)^j y_{T-j},$$

and determine the one-period-ahead forecast as

$$y_{T+1|T} = \alpha \sum_{j=0}^{\infty} (-\alpha)^j y_{T-j}. \tag{8.75}$$

Predicting two periods ahead gives

$$y_{T+2|T} = E\{\varepsilon_{T+2}|y_T, y_{T-1}, \dots\} + \alpha E\{\varepsilon_{T+1}|y_T, y_{T-1}, \dots\} = 0, \tag{8.76}$$

which shows that the $MA(1)$ model is uninformative for forecasting two periods ahead: the best forecast is simply the (unconditional) expected value of y_t, normalized at 0. This also follows from the autocorrelation function of the process, because the ACF is zero after one lag. That is, the 'memory' of the process is only one period.

For the general $ARMA(p, q)$ model

$$y_t = \theta_1 y_{t-1} + \dots + \theta_p y_{t-p} + \varepsilon_t + \alpha_1 \varepsilon_{t-1} + \dots + \alpha_q \varepsilon_{t-q},$$

we can derive the following recursive formula to determine the optimal forecasts

$$\begin{aligned} y_{T+h|T} = {} & \theta_1 y_{T+h-1|T} + \dots + \theta_p y_{T+h-p|T} + \varepsilon_{T+h|T} + \alpha_1 \varepsilon_{T+h-1|T} \\ & + \dots + \alpha_q \varepsilon_{T+h-q|T}, \end{aligned} \tag{8.77}$$

where $\varepsilon_{T+K|T}$ is the optimal forecasts for ε_{T+K} at time T, and

$$\begin{aligned} y_{T+k|T} &= y_{T+k} && \text{if } k \leq 0 \\ \varepsilon_{T+k|T} &= 0 && \text{if } k > 0 \\ \varepsilon_{T+k|T} &= \varepsilon_{T+k} && \text{if } k \leq 0, \end{aligned}$$

where the latter innovation can be solved from the autoregressive representation of the model. For this we have used the fact that the process is stationary and invertible, in which case the information set $\{y_T, y_{T-1}, \dots\}$ is equivalent to $\{\varepsilon_T, \varepsilon_{T-1}, \dots\}$. That is, if all ε_ts are known from $-\infty$ to T, then all y_ts are known from $-\infty$ to T, and vice versa.

To illustrate this, consider an $ARMA(1, 1)$ model where

$$y_t = \theta y_{t-1} + \varepsilon_t + \alpha \varepsilon_{t-1}$$

such that

$$y_{T+1|T} = \theta y_{T|T} + \varepsilon_{T+1|T} + \alpha \varepsilon_{T|T} = \theta y_T + \alpha \varepsilon_T.$$

Using the fact that (assuming invertibility)

$$y_t - \theta y_{t-1} = (1 + \alpha L)\varepsilon_t$$

can be rewritten as

$$\varepsilon_t = (1 + \alpha L)^{-1}(y_t - \theta y_{t-1}) = \sum_{j=0}^{\infty} (-\alpha)^j L^j (y_t - \theta y_{t-1}),$$

we can write for the one-period-ahead forecast

$$y_{T+1|T} = \theta y_T + \alpha \sum_{j=0}^{\infty} (-\alpha)^j (y_{T-j} - \theta y_{T-j-1}). \tag{8.78}$$

Forecasting two periods ahead gives

$$y_{T+2|T} = \theta y_{T+1|T} + \varepsilon_{T+2|T} + \alpha \varepsilon_{T+1|T} = \theta y_{T+1|T}. \tag{8.79}$$

Note that this does not equal $\theta^2 y_T$.

8.9.2 Forecast Accuracy

In addition to the forecast itself, it is important (sometimes even more important) to know how accurate this forecast is. To judge forecasting precision, we define the **forecast error** as $Y_{T+h} - Y_{T+h|T} = y_{T+h} - y_{T+h|T}$ and the expected quadratic forecast error as

$$C_h^2 \equiv E\{(y_{T+h} - y_{T+h|T})^2\} = V\{y_{T+h}|\mathcal{I}_T\}, \tag{8.80}$$

where the latter step follows from the fact that $y_{T+h|T} = E\{y_{T+h}|\mathcal{I}_T\}$. Determining C_h^2, corresponding to the variance of the h-period-ahead forecast error, is relatively easy with the moving average representation.

To start with the simplest case, consider an $MA(1)$ model. Then we have

$$C_1^2 = V\{y_{T+1}|y_T, y_{T-1}, \ldots\} = V\{\varepsilon_{T+1} + \alpha\varepsilon_T|\varepsilon_T, \varepsilon_{T-1}, \ldots\} = V\{\varepsilon_{T+1}\} = \sigma^2.$$

Alternatively, we explicitly solve for the forecast, which is $y_{T+1|T} = \alpha\varepsilon_T$, and determine the variance of $y_{T+1} - y_{T+1|T} = \varepsilon_{T+1}$, which gives the same result. For the two-period-ahead forecast we have

$$C_2^2 = V\{y_{T+2}|y_T, y_{T-1}, \ldots\} = V\{\varepsilon_{T+2} + \alpha\varepsilon_{T+1}|\varepsilon_T, \varepsilon_{T-1}, \ldots\} = (1 + \alpha^2)\sigma^2.$$

As expected, the accuracy of the forecast decreases if we predict further into the future. It will not, however, increase any further if h is increased beyond 2. This becomes clear if we compare the expected quadratic forecast error with that of a simple unconditional forecast:

$$\hat{y}_{T+h|T} = E\{y_{T+h}\} = 0$$

(empty information set). For this forecast we have

$$C_h^2 = E\{(y_{T+h} - 0)^2\} = V\{y_{T+h}\} = (1 + \alpha^2)\sigma^2.$$

Consequently, this gives an upper bound on the inaccuracy of the forecast. The $MA(1)$ model thus gives more efficient forecast only if one predicts one period ahead. More general ARMA models, however, will yield efficiency gains also in further-ahead forecast.

Suppose the general model is $ARMA(p, q)$, which we write as an $MA(\infty)$ model, with α_j coefficients to be determined:

$$y_t = \sum_{j=0}^{\infty} \alpha_j \varepsilon_{t-j} \quad \text{with } \alpha_0 \equiv 1.$$

The h-period-ahead forecast (in terms of ε_ts) is given by

$$y_{T+h|T} = E\{y_{T+h}|y_T, y_{T-1}, \dots\} = \sum_{j=0}^{\infty} \alpha_j E\{\varepsilon_{T+h-j}|\varepsilon_T, \varepsilon_{T-1}, \dots\} = \sum_{j=h}^{\infty} \alpha_j \varepsilon_{T+h-j},$$

such that

$$y_{T+h} - y_{T+h|T} = \sum_{j=0}^{h-1} \alpha_j \varepsilon_{T+h-j}.$$

Consequently, we have

$$E\{(y_{T+h} - y_{T+h|T})^2\} = \sigma^2 \sum_{j=0}^{h-1} \alpha_j^2. \tag{8.81}$$

This shows how the variances of the forecast errors can easily be determined from the coefficients in the moving average representation of the model. Recall that, for the computation of the forecast, the autoregressive representation was most convenient.

The previous results can be used to construct confidence intervals around the forecasts. For example, a 95% confidence interval for predicting one-period ahead is given by

$$y_{T+1|T} - 1.96c_1, \quad y_{T+1|T} + 1.96c_1,$$

where the normal distribution is imposed. For h-period ahead prediction, the interval is

$$y_{T+h|T} - 1.96c_h, \quad y_{T+h|T} + 1.96c_h.$$

The forecast uncertainty is reflected in the width of the interval.

As an illustration, consider the $AR(1)$ model where $\alpha_j = \theta^j$. The expected quadratic forecast errors are given by

$$c_1^2 = \sigma^2, \quad c_2^2 = \sigma^2(1 + \theta^2), \quad c_3^2 = \sigma^2(1 + \theta^2 + \theta^4),$$

etc. For h going to infinity, we have $c_\infty^2 = \sigma^2(1 + \theta^2 + \theta^4 + \cdots) = \sigma^2/(1 - \theta^2)$, which is the unconditional variance of y_t and therefore the expected quadratic forecast error of a constant predictor $\hat{y}_{T+h|T} = E\{y_{T+h}\} = 0$. Consequently, the informational value contained in an $AR(1)$ process slowly decays over time. In the long run the forecast equals the unconditional forecast, being the mean of the y_t series (as is the case in all stationary time series models). Note that for a random walk, with $\theta = 1$, the forecast error variance increases linearly with the forecast horizon.

8.9.3 Evaluating Forecasts

The results of Subsection 8.9.2 provide theoretical benchmarks for the forecasting accuracy in the case where the model of interest is known and there is no parameter uncertainty. In Section 3.5 we already discovered that for genuine out-of-sample forecasting, things may be less optimistic. If we are to generate a series of forecasts using an ARMA model that are genuinely out-of-sample, we should base the forecasts on a model whose specification and estimation is based upon information that was available at the time of making the forecast. In these cases, it is not necessarily the case that a model that provides the best in-sample fit, or the lowest value for either the *AIC* or *BIC* criterion, has the best out-of-sample forecasting performance. A first reason is that the forecasts are subject to parameter uncertainty. Replacing the unknown parameters by the estimated counterparts introduces additional uncertainty that will be extrapolated into the future. This problem is particularly severe with overparametrized models. In this case the estimated specification may pick up accidental patterns in the estimation sample that have no structural meaning. A second related reason is that the forecasts are subject to model uncertainty. Any errors made in the specification search process may translate into additional forecast inaccuracy. A third reason is that the true process that generates the data may vary over time, due to structural breaks or otherwise. Accordingly, a forecasting relationship that worked well over a particular historical period, does not necessarily work in the future.

Let us denote the period over which forecasts are available as $T + 1$ to $T + H$. Let the forecasts be denoted by $\hat{y}_{T+h}$, $h = 1, 2, \ldots, H$, while the actual outcomes are given by y_{T+h}. To test whether the forecasts are unbiased, it is possible to use a regression model that relates the actual (out-of-sample) values to the forecasts. Suppose we estimate the following model

$$y_{T+h} = \beta_1 + \beta_2 \hat{y}_{T+h} + v_{T+h}, \quad h = 1, 2, \ldots, H. \tag{8.82}$$

If the forecasts are unbiased, it should be that $\beta_2 = 1$ and $\beta_1 = 0$. It is straightforward to test this by means of an F-test (or two t-tests). The R^2 of this regression provides a measure to assess the forecast quality and corresponds to R^2_{os2} introduced in Section 3.5. Note that a biased forecast may still produce a high out-of-sample R^2.

In Section 3.5 we discussed a number of criteria that can be used to evaluate the out-of-sample forecasting performance of any model or procedure. These criteria are based on a comparison of the forecasts with the realized values. While this means that these measures can only be calculated ex post, they may be informative for future forecasts as well. Denoting the forecast errors by $e_{T+h} = y_{T+h} - \hat{y}_{T+h}$, two common criteria are the mean absolute deviation, given by

$$MAD = \frac{1}{H} \sum_{h=1}^{H} |e_{T+h}|,$$

and the root mean squared error given by

$$RMSE = \sqrt{\frac{1}{H} \sum_{h=1}^{H} e^2_{T+h}}.$$

The lower these measures, the more accurate the forecasts.

More generally, one can define a loss function (or cost function), which describes the 'loss' of making (and acting upon) a wrong forecast. Let us, in general, denote this by $L(e_{T+h}) \geq 0$, which assumes that the loss does not depend upon y_{T+h} and not on the time period itself. A quadratic loss function corresponds to $L(e_{T+h}) = e_{T+h}^2$ and is quite common in empirical work, but it is also possible to use asymmetric loss functions, for example, when the consequences of a positive forecast error are more severe than those of a negative forecast error of the same magnitude; see Elliott and Timmermann (2016, Chapter 2) for more discussion.

To compare two or more competing forecasting models, Diebold and Mariano (1995) propose to compare the average difference in the loss functions of the two forecasts. Let $e_{1,T+h}$ denote the forecast errors from model 1, and $e_{2,T+h}$ those from model 2. Then the **Diebold-Mariano test** is based on the difference

$$\bar{d} = \frac{1}{H}\sum_{h=1}^{H}[L(e_{1,T+h}) - L(e_{2,T+h})].$$

Under the null hypothesis of equal forecast accuracy, the expected value of $\bar{d}$ is 0, and Diebold and Mariano (1995) show that $\bar{d}/\text{se}(\bar{d})$ has an asymptotic standard normal distribution, where $\text{se}(\bar{d})$ is a standard error, typically allowing for serial correlation. With the test it is possible to compare the predictive accuracy of two competing forecast series; see Enders (2014, Section 2.9), Pesaran (2015, Section 17.11) or Elliot and Timmermann (2016, Chapter 17). It is also possible to evaluate forecasting performance in a conditional sense. For example, it may be of interest to know whether model 1 forecasts better in a recession than does model 2; see Clark and McCracken (2013) for more discussion.

8.10 Illustration: The Expectations Theory of the Term Structure

Quite often, building a time series model is not a goal in itself, but a necessary ingredient in an economic analysis. To illustrate this, we shall in this section pay attention to the term structure of interest rates. The term structure has attracted considerable attention in both the macro-economics and finance literature (see, e.g., Pagan, Hall and Martin, 1996), and the expectations hypothesis plays a central role in many of these studies.

To introduce the problem, we consider an n-period discount bond, which is simply a claim to one dollar paid to you n periods from today. The (market) price at time t (today) of this discount bond is denoted as p_{nt}. The implied interest rate r_{nt} can then be solved from

$$p_{nt} = \frac{1}{(1 + r_{nt})^n}.$$

The **yield curve** describes r_{nt} as a function of its maturity n, and may vary from one period t to another. This depicts the term structure of interest rates. Models for the term structure try simultaneously to model how the different interest rates are linked and how the yield curve moves over time.

The **pure expectations hypothesis**, in a linearized form, can be written as

$$r_{nt} = \frac{1}{n}\sum_{h=0}^{n-1} E\{r_{1,t+h}|\mathcal{I}_t\}, \tag{8.83}$$

where $\mathcal{I}_t$ denotes the information set containing all information available at time t. This says that the long-term interest rate is the average of the expected short-term rates over the same interval. The left-hand side of this can be interpreted as the certain yield of an n-period investment, while the right-hand side corresponds to the *expected*[4] yield from investing in one-period bonds over an n-period horizon. Thus, expected returns on bonds of different maturities are assumed to be equal.

The **expectations hypothesis**, in a more general form, allows for risk premia by assuming that expected returns on different bonds can differ by constants, which can depend on maturity but not on time. This extends (8.83) to

$$r_{nt} = \frac{1}{n}\sum_{h=0}^{n-1} E\{r_{1,t+h}|\mathcal{I}_t\} + \Phi_n, \tag{8.84}$$

where Φ_n denotes a risk or term premium that varies with maturity n. Instead of testing the expectations hypothesis in this form, which is the subject of many studies (see Campbell and Shiller, 1991), we shall look at a simple implementation of (8.84). Given that the term premia are constant, we can complete the model by making assumptions about the relevant information set $\mathcal{I}_t$ and the time series process of the one-period interest rate.

Let us assume, for simplicity, that

$$\mathcal{I}_t = \{r_{1t}, r_{1,t-1}, r_{1,t-2}, \ldots.\},$$

such that the relevant information set contains the current and lagged short interest rates only. If r_{1t} can be described by an $AR(1)$ process,

$$r_{1t} - \mu = \theta(r_{1,t-1} - \mu) + \varepsilon_t,$$

with $0 < \theta \leq 1$, the optimal s-period-ahead predictor (see (8.74)) is given by

$$E\{r_{1,t+h}|\mathcal{I}_t\} = \mu + \theta^h(r_{1t} - \mu).$$

Substituting this into (8.84) results in

$$\begin{aligned} r_{n,t} &= \frac{1}{n}\sum_{h=0}^{n-1}[\mu + \theta^h(r_{1t} - \mu)] + \Phi_n \\ &= \mu + \xi_n(r_{1t} - \mu) + \Phi_n, \end{aligned} \tag{8.85}$$

where, for $0 < \theta < 1$,

$$\xi_n = \frac{1}{n}\sum_{h=0}^{n-1}\theta^h = \frac{1}{n}\frac{1-\theta^n}{1-\theta} < \xi_{n-1} < 1, \tag{8.86}$$

while for $\theta = 1$ we have $\xi_n = 1$ for each maturity n.

[4] We impose *rational* expectations, which means that economic agents have expectations that correspond to mathematical expectations, conditional upon some information set.

The rather simple model of the term structure in (8.85) implies that long rates depend linearly on short rates and that short rate changes have less impact on longer rates than on shorter rates since ξ_n is decreasing with n if $0 < \theta < 1$. Note, for example, that

$$V\{r_{nt}\} = \xi_n^2 V\{r_{1t}\}, \tag{8.87}$$

which, with $0 < \theta < 1$, implies that short rates are more volatile than long rates. The result in (8.85) also implies that there is just one factor that drives interest rates at any maturity and thus one factor that shifts the term structure.

If all risk premia are zero ($\Phi_n = 0$), an inverted yield curve (with short rates exceeding long rates) occurs if the short rate is above its mean μ, which – when the distribution of ε_t is symmetric around zero (e.g. normal) – happens in 50% of cases. The reason is that, when the short rate is below its average, it is expected to increase to its average again, which increases the long rates. In practice, we see inverted yield curves in less than 50% of the periods. For the United States,[5] for example, we displayed the 1-month and the 5-year bond yields from January 1970 to February 1991 in Figure 8.10 ($T = 254$). Usually, the long rate is above the short rate, but there are a few periods of inversion where this is not the case, for example, from June 1973 to March 1974.

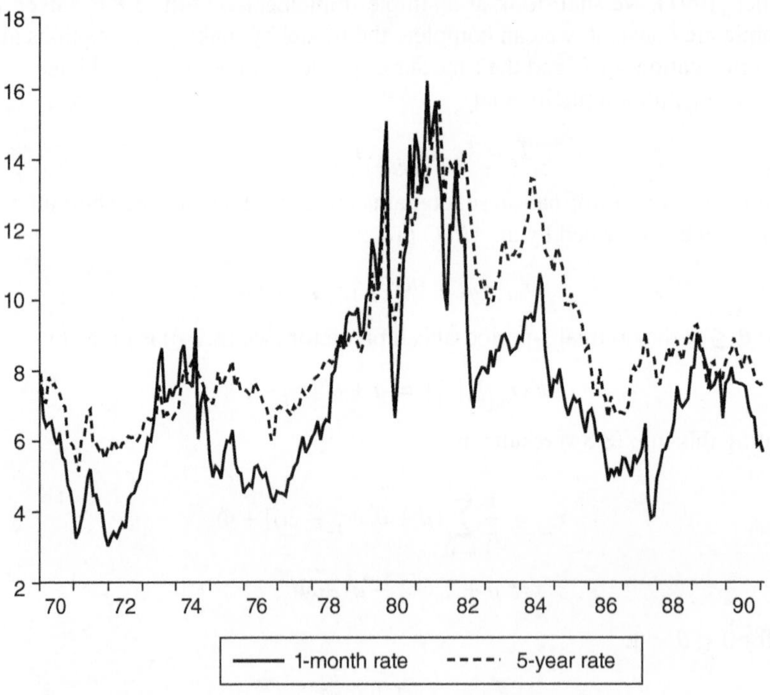

Figure 8.10 1-month and 5-year interest rates (in %), 1970:1–1991:2.

[5] The data used in this section are taken from the McCulloch and Kwon data set (see McCulloch and Kwon, 1993).

Clearly the time series properties of the short-term interest rate are important for the cross-sectional relationships between the interest rates at different maturities. If the short rate follows an $AR(1)$ process, we obtain the fairly simple expression in (8.85), for which we can note that the values of ξ_n are very sensitive to the precise value of θ, particularly for large maturities, if θ is close to unity. For more general time series processes we obtain similar expressions, but the result will not just involve the current short rate r_{1t}. Because the optimal forecast for an $AR(2)$ model, for example, depends upon the two last observations, an $AR(2)$ process for the short rate would give an expression similar to (8.85) that involves r_{1t} and $r_{1,t-1}$.

A debatable issue is that of stationarity. In many cases, the presence of a unit root in the short-term interest rate cannot be rejected *statistically*, but this does not necessarily mean that we have to accept the unit root hypothesis. *Economically*, it seems hard to defend nonstationarity of interest rates, although their persistence is known to be high. That is, even with stationarity it takes a very long time for the series to go back to its mean. Different authors make different judgements on this issue, and you will find empirical studies on the term structure of interest rates that choose either way. Let us first estimate an $AR(1)$ model for the 1-month interest rate. Estimation by OLS gives (standard errors in parentheses):

$$\underset{}{r_{1t}} = \underset{(0.152)}{0.350} + \underset{(0.020)}{0.951}\; r_{1,t-1} + e_t, \quad \hat{\sigma} = 0.820. \tag{8.88}$$

The implied estimate for μ is 0.350/(1 − 0.951), which corresponds to approximately 7.2%, while the sample average is 7.3%. We can determine the Dickey–Fuller test statistic from this regression as $(0.951 - 1)/0.020 = -2.49$, which means that we cannot reject the null hypothesis of a unit root at the 5% level.[6] Because the $AR(1)$ model may be too restrictive, we also performed a number of augmented Dickey–Fuller tests with one, three and six additional lags included. The resulting test statistics were −2.63, −2.29 and −1.88, respectively. Only the first test implies a rejection at the 10% level. Thus, similar to Rose (1988) we find that a unit root in the short-term interest rate cannot be rejected statistically. Despite this, we will not impose it a priori below.

The short-term interest rate is fairly well described by the first-order autoregressive process in (8.88). Estimating $AR(2)$ or $ARMA(1, 1)$ specifications, for example, does not result in a significant improvement. The estimated autocorrelation function of the residuals of the $AR(1)$ model is given in Figure 8.11. The first significant residual autocorrelation coefficient occurs at lag 8, which provides only weak evidence against the hypothesis that the error term in (8.88) is a white noise process. Moreover, none of the Ljung–Box tests rejects.

A way to test the expectations hypothesis is to regress a long-interest rate on the short rate, that is,

$$r_{nt} = \beta_1 + \beta_2 r_{1t} + u_t. \tag{8.89}$$

If (8.85) is taken to be literally true, the error term in this regression should be negligibly small (i.e. the R^2 should be rather close to unity) and the true value of β_2 should

[6] From Table 8.1, the appropriate critical value is −2.88.

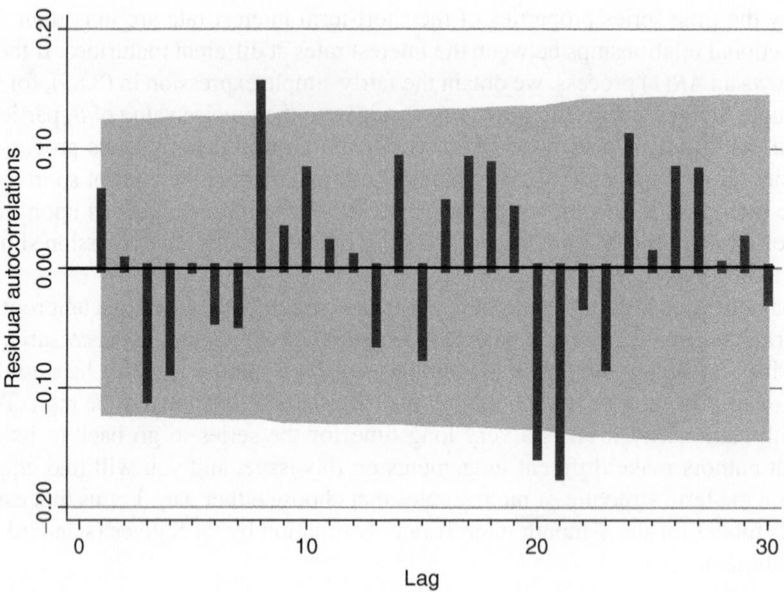

Figure 8.11 Residual autocorrelation function, $AR(1)$ model, 1970:1–1991:2.

equal ξ_n. The results of these regressions for maturities $n = 3$, 12 and 60 are given in Table 8.5. Given the high sensitivity of ξ_n with respect to θ, which was not significantly different from one, the estimated values for ξ_n do not, a priori, seem in conflict with the time series model for the short rate. It must be mentioned, however, that the R^2 of the regression with the 5-year bond yield is fairly low. This implies that other factors affect the long-term yield in addition to the short rate. One explanation is time variation in the risk premium Φ_n. Alternatively, the presence of measurement errors in the interest rates may reduce their cross-sectional correlations.

At a more general level, the previous example illustrates the delicate dependence of long-run forecasts on the imposition of a unit root. Although the estimated value of 0.95 is not significantly different from one, imposing the unit root hypothesis would imply that interest rates follow a random walk and that the forecast for *any* future period is equal to the most recent observation, in this case 5.68%. Using $\theta = 0.95$, the optimal forecast 10 periods ahead is 6.3%, while the forecast for a 5-year horizon is virtually identical to the unconditional mean of the series, 7.2%.

Table 8.5 The term structure of interest rates

	Quarterly $n = 3$	Annual $n = 12$	5-year $n = 60$
value of ξ_n with $\theta = 0.95$	0.951	0.766	0.318
value of ξ_n with $\theta = 1$	1	1	1
OLS estimate of ξ_n	1.009	0.947	0.739
(standard error)	(0.009)	(0.017)	(0.028)
R^2 of regression	0.982	0.929	0.735

8.11 Autoregressive Conditional Heteroskedasticity

In financial time series one often observes what is referred to as **volatility clustering**. In this case big shocks (residuals) tend to be followed by big shocks in either direction, and small shocks tend to follow small shocks. For example, stock markets are typically characterized by periods of high volatility and more 'relaxed' periods of low volatility. This is particularly true at high frequencies, for example, with daily or weekly returns, but less clear at lower frequencies. One way to model such patterns is to allow the variance of ε_t to depend upon its history.

8.11.1 ARCH and GARCH Models

The seminal paper in this area is Engle (1982), which proposes the concept of **autoregressive conditional heteroskedasticity (ARCH)**. It says that the variance of the error term at time t depends upon the squared error terms from previous periods. The most simple form is

$$\sigma_t^2 \equiv E\{\varepsilon_t^2|\mathcal{I}_{t-1}\} = \varpi + \alpha\varepsilon_{t-1}^2, \tag{8.90}$$

where $\mathcal{I}_{t-1}$ denotes the information set, typically including ε_{t-1} and its entire history. This specification is called an **ARCH(1)** process. To ensure that $\sigma_t^2 \geq 0$ irrespective of ε_{t-1}^2, we need to impose $\varpi \geq 0$ and $\alpha \geq 0$. The ARCH(1) model says that, when a big shock happens in period $t-1$, it is more likely that ε_t has a large (absolute) value as well. That is, when ε_{t-1}^2 is large, the variance of the next innovation ε_t is also large.

The specification in (8.90) does not imply that the process for ε_t is nonstationary. It just says that the squared values ε_t^2 and ε_{t-1}^2 are correlated. The *unconditional* variance of ε_t is given by

$$\sigma^2 = E\{\varepsilon_t^2\} = \varpi + \alpha E\{\varepsilon_{t-1}^2\}$$

and has a stationary solution

$$\sigma^2 = \frac{\varpi}{1-\alpha} \tag{8.91}$$

provided that $0 \leq \alpha < 1$. Note that the unconditional variance does not depend upon t.

The ARCH(1) model is easily extended to an **ARCH(p)** process, which we can write as

$$\sigma_t^2 = \varpi + \alpha_1\varepsilon_{t-1}^2 + \alpha_2\varepsilon_{t-2}^2 + \cdots + \alpha_p\varepsilon_{t-p}^2 = \varpi + \alpha(L)\varepsilon_{t-1}^2, \tag{8.92}$$

where $\alpha(L)$ is a lag polynomial of order $p-1$. To ensure that the conditional variance is non-negative, ϖ and the coefficients in $\alpha(L)$ must be non-negative. To ensure that the process is stationary, it is also required that $\alpha(1) < 1$. The effect of a shock j periods ago on current volatility is determined by the coefficient α_j. In an ARCH(p) model, old shocks of more than p periods ago have no effect on current volatility.

The presence of ARCH errors in a regression or autoregressive model does not invalidate OLS estimation. It does imply, however, that more efficient (nonlinear) estimators exist than OLS. More importantly, it may be of interest to predict future variances, for example, because they correspond to the riskiness of an investment. Consequently, it is relevant to test for the presence of ARCH effects and, if needed, to estimate the model allowing for it. Testing for pth-order autoregressive heteroskedasticity can be done along the lines of the Breusch–Pagan test for heteroskedasticity discussed in Chapter 4. It suffices to run an auxiliary regression of squared OLS residuals e_t^2 upon lagged squares

$e_{t-1}^2, \ldots, e_{t-p}^2$ and a constant and compute T times the R^2. Under the null hypothesis of homoskedasticity ($\alpha_1 = \cdots = \alpha_p = 0$) the resulting test statistic asymptotically follows a Chi-squared distribution with p degrees of freedom. Accordingly, testing homoskedasticity against the alternative that the errors follow an ARCH(p) process is very straightforward.

In empirical applications, the use of the ARCH model from (8.92) is quite uncommon and the basic model has been generalized in many different ways. A widely employed variant, proposed by Bollerslev (1986), is the generalized ARCH or **GARCH** model. In its general form, a GARCH(p, q) model can be written as

$$\sigma_t^2 = \varpi + \sum_{j=1}^{p} \alpha_j \varepsilon_{t-j}^2 + \sum_{j=1}^{q} \beta_j \sigma_{t-j}^2 \tag{8.93}$$

or

$$\sigma_t^2 = \varpi + \alpha(L)\varepsilon_{t-1}^2 + \beta(L)\sigma_{t-1}^2, \tag{8.94}$$

where $\alpha(L)$ and $\beta(L)$ are lag polynomials. In practice a GARCH(1,1) specification often performs very well. It can be written as

$$\sigma_t^2 = \varpi + \alpha\varepsilon_{t-1}^2 + \beta\sigma_{t-1}^2, \tag{8.95}$$

which has only three unknown parameters to estimate. Non-negativity of σ_t^2 requires that ϖ, α and β are non-negative. If we define the surprise in the squared innovations as $\upsilon_t \equiv \varepsilon_t^2 - \sigma_t^2$, the GARCH(1, 1) process can be rewritten as

$$\varepsilon_t^2 = \varpi + (\alpha + \beta)\varepsilon_{t-1}^2 + \upsilon_t - \beta\upsilon_{t-1},$$

which shows that the squared errors follow an *ARMA*(1, 1) process. While the error υ_t is uncorrelated over time (because it is a surprise term), it does exhibit heteroskedasticity. The root of the autoregressive part is $\alpha + \beta$, so that stationarity requires that $\alpha + \beta < 1$. Values of $\alpha + \beta$ close to unity imply that the persistence in volatility is high. When $\alpha + \beta = 1$ we obtain the **integrated GARCH** or IGARCH model (see Engle and Bollerslev, 1986), in which volatility shocks have a permanent effect. Noting that,[7] under stationarity, $E\{\varepsilon_{t-1}^2\} = E\{\sigma_{t-1}^2\} = \sigma^2$, the unconditional variance of ε_t can be written as

$$\sigma^2 = \varpi + \alpha\sigma^2 + \beta\sigma^2$$

or

$$\sigma^2 = \frac{\varpi}{1 - \alpha - \beta}. \tag{8.96}$$

We can recursively substitute lags of (8.95) into itself to obtain

$$\begin{aligned}\sigma_t^2 &= \varpi(1 + \beta + \beta^2 + \cdots) + \alpha(\varepsilon_{t-1}^2 + \beta\varepsilon_{t-2}^2 + \beta^2\varepsilon_{t-3}^2 + \cdots)\\ &= \frac{\varpi}{1-\beta} + \alpha\sum_{j=1}^{\infty} \beta^{j-1}\varepsilon_{t-j}^2,\end{aligned} \tag{8.97}$$

which shows that the GARCH(1,1) specification is equivalent to an infinite-order ARCH model with geometrically declining coefficients. It implies that the effect of a shock

[7] The equality that follows only holds if ε_t does not exhibit autocorrelation.

on current volatility decreases over time. Consequently, a GARCH specification may provide a parsimonious alternative to a higher-order ARCH process. Equation (8.97) can also be rewritten as

$$\sigma_t^2 - \sigma^2 = \alpha \sum_{j=1}^{\infty} \beta^{j-1}(\varepsilon_{t-j}^2 - \sigma^2), \tag{8.98}$$

which is convenient for forecasting.

Given that the GARCH(p, q) model corresponds to an *ARMA*(p, q) model for ε_t^2, the Box–Jenkins approach of analysing autocorrelations and partial autocorrelations, as discussed in Sections 8.1 and 8.7, can be applied to the squared OLS residuals. This way it is possible to obtain some idea about the strength of the GARCH effects and the appropriate number of lags (see Bollerslev, 1988).

Over the years a plethora of variants and generalizations of ARCH and GARCH models have been developed, leading to 'a perplexing alphabet-soup of acronyms and abbreviations' (Bollerslev, 2010). Reviews can be found in, among others, Bollerslev, Chou and Kroner (1992), Bera and Higgins (1993), Bollerslev, Engle and Nelson (1994), Li, Ling and McAleer (2002) and Andersen et al. (2006). Multivariate extensions are covered extensively in Bauwens, Laurent and Rombouts (2006) and Silvennoinen and Teräsvirta (2009). An important restriction of the ARCH and GARCH specifications above is their symmetry: only the absolute values of the innovations matter, not their sign. That is, a big negative shock has the same impact on future volatility as a big positive shock of the same magnitude. An interesting extension is towards asymmetric volatility models, in which good news and bad news have a different impact on future volatility. Note that the distinction between good and bad news is more sensible for stock markets than for exchange rates, where agents typically are on both sides of the market. That is, good news for one agent may be bad news for another.

An asymmetric model should allow for the possibility that an unexpected drop in price ('bad news') has a larger impact on future volatility than an unexpected increase in price ('good news') of similar magnitude. Two popular asymmetric specifications are the **threshold GARCH** model (or GJR model), proposed by Glosten, Jagannathan and Runkle (1993) and the **exponential GARCH** (or EGARCH) model, proposed by Nelson (1991). The GJR model is a simple extension of the standard GARCH(1,1) model, which specifies the conditional variance as

$$\sigma_t^2 = \varpi + \alpha\varepsilon_{t-1}^2 + \beta\sigma_{t-1}^2 + \gamma I_{t-1}\varepsilon_{t-1}^2, \tag{8.99}$$

where $I_{t-1} = 1$ if $\varepsilon_{t-1} > 0$ and zero otherwise. When $\gamma < 0$ negative shocks have a larger impact on future volatility than do positive shocks of the same magnitude. The EGARCH model of Nelson (1991) is given by

$$\log \sigma_t^2 = \varpi + \beta \log \sigma_{t-1}^2 + \gamma \frac{\varepsilon_{t-1}}{\sigma_{t-1}} + \alpha \frac{|\varepsilon_{t-1}|}{\sigma_{t-1}}, \tag{8.100}$$

where α, β and γ are constant parameters. Because the level $\varepsilon_{t-1}/\sigma_{t-1}$ is included, the EGARCH model is asymmetric as long as $\gamma \neq 0$. Also in this model, when $\gamma < 0$, positive shocks generate less volatility than negative shocks ('bad news'). Both the GJR model and the EGARCH model can be extended by including additional lags. Note that we can rewrite (8.100) as

$$\log \sigma_t^2 = \varpi + \beta \log \sigma_{t-1}^2 + (\gamma + \alpha)\frac{\varepsilon_{t-1}}{\sigma_{t-1}} \quad \text{if } \varepsilon_{t-1} > 0$$
$$= \varpi + \beta \log \sigma_{t-1}^2 + (\gamma - \alpha)\frac{\varepsilon_{t-1}}{\sigma_{t-1}} \quad \text{if } \varepsilon_{t-1} < 0.$$

The logarithmic transformation guarantees that variances will never become negative. Typically, one would expect that $\gamma + \alpha > 0$ while $\gamma < 0$.

Engle and Ng (1993) characterize a range of alternative models for conditional volatility by a so-called **news impact curve**, which describes the impact of the last return shock (news) on current volatility (keeping all information dated $t-2$ or before constant and fixing all lagged conditional variances at the unconditional variance σ^2). Compared with GARCH(1,1), the EGARCH and GJR models have asymmetric news impact curves (with a larger impact for negative shocks when $\gamma < 0$). Because the effect of a shock upon σ_t^2 is exponential in the EGARCH model, rather than quadratic, its news impact curve typically has larger slopes (see Engle and Ng, 1993).

Financial theory tells us that certain sources of risk are priced by the market. That is, assets with more 'risk' may provide higher average returns to compensate for it. If σ_t^2 is an appropriate measure of risk, the conditional variance may enter the conditional mean function of y_t. One variant of the **ARCH-in-mean** or **ARCH-M** model of Engle, Lilien and Robins (1987) specifies that

$$y_t = x_t'\theta + \delta\sigma_t^2 + \varepsilon_t,$$

where ε_t is described by an ARCH(p) process (with conditional variance σ_t^2). Campbell, Lo and MacKinlay (1997, Section 12.2) provide additional discussion on the links between ARCH-M models and asset pricing models, like the CAPM discussed in Section 2.7.

8.11.2 Estimation and Prediction

The models in (8.92), (8.93), (8.99) and (8.100) are partial models describing the conditional volatility of a series. Before they can be estimated we also need to specify the conditional mean. Let us, in general, specify a linear model for the conditional mean as

$$y_t = x_t'\theta + \varepsilon_t,$$

where x_t may include lagged values of y_t (as in an autoregressive model) and/or exogenous variables (e.g. seasonal dummies).[8] As a special case, x_t is just a constant. Furthermore, let the conditional variance of ε_t be described by an ARCH(p) process. If we make assumptions about the (conditional) distribution of ε_t, we can estimate the model by maximum likelihood. To see how, let

$$\varepsilon_t = \sigma_t \upsilon_t \quad \text{with} \quad \upsilon_t \sim NID(0, 1).$$

[8] To avoid confusion with the GARCH parameters, the regression coefficients are referred to as θ.

This implies that, *conditional* upon the information in $\mathcal{I}_{t-1}$, the innovation ε_t is normal with mean zero and variance σ_t^2. It does not imply, however, that the *unconditional* distribution of ε_t is normal, because σ_t becomes a random variable if we do not condition upon $\mathcal{I}_{t-1}$. Typically, the unconditional distribution has fatter tails than a normal one. From this, we can write down the conditional distribution of y_t as

$$f(y_t|x_t, \mathcal{I}_{t-1}) = \frac{1}{\sqrt{2\pi\sigma_t^2}} \exp\left\{-\frac{1}{2}(\varepsilon_t^2/\sigma_t^2)\right\}$$

where $\sigma_t^2 = \varpi + \alpha_1\varepsilon_{t-1}^2 + \cdots + \alpha_p\varepsilon_{t-p}^2$ and $\varepsilon_t = y_t - x_t'\theta$. From this, the loglikelihood function can be determined as the sum over all t of the log of the above expression, substituting the appropriate expressions for σ_t^2 and ε_t. The result can be maximized in the usual way with respect to $\theta, \alpha_1, \ldots, \alpha_p$ and ϖ. Imposing the stationarity condition ($\sum_{j=1}^{p} \alpha_j < 1$) and the non-negativity condition ($\alpha_j \geq 0$ for all j) may be difficult in practice, so that large values for p are not recommended.

If v_t does not have a standard normal distribution, the above maximum likelihood procedure may provide consistent estimators for the model parameters, even though the likelihood function is incorrectly specified. The reason is that, under some fairly weak assumptions, the first-order conditions of the maximum likelihood procedure are also valid when v_t is not normally distributed. This is referred to as **quasi-maximum likelihood estimation** (see Section 6.4). Some adjustments have to be made, however, for the computation of the standard errors (see Hamilton, 1994, p. 663, for details). It is also possible to estimate a GARCH model by maximum likelihood making alternative distributional assumptions for v_t. Common choices are a standardized t distribution with s degrees of freedom ($s > 2$) and the Generalized Error Distribution (GED) with tail parameter $\kappa > 0$. The parameters s and κ can be treated as unknown parameters and estimated jointly with the other parameters in the model, or can be fixed a priori (which is less common). Both distributions allow for fatter tails than the normal distribution. For $\kappa = 2$, the GED is a normal distribution, for $\kappa < 2$ it is fat-tailed, and for $v \to \infty$ the t distribution converges to a normal distribution; see Mills and Markellos (2008, Subsection 5.5.5) for more details.

A computationally simpler approach is the use of feasible GLS (see Chapter 4). In this case, θ is first estimated consistently by applying OLS. Second, a regression is done of the squared OLS residuals e_t^2 upon $e_{t-1}^2, \ldots, e_{t-p}^2$ and a constant. This is the same regression that was used for the heteroskedasticity test described previously. The fitted values from this regression are estimates for σ_t^2 and can be used to transform the model and compute a weighted least squares (EGLS) estimator for θ. This approach only works well if the fitted values for σ_t^2 are all strictly positive. Moreover, it does not provide asymptotically efficient estimators for the ARCH parameters.

In financial markets, GARCH models are frequently used to forecast volatility of returns, which is an important input for investment, option pricing, risk management and financial market regulation (see Poon and Granger, 2003, for a review). Forecasting the conditional variance from an ARCH(p) model is straightforward. To see this, rewrite the model 'in deviations from means' as

$$\sigma_t^2 - \sigma^2 = \alpha_1(\varepsilon_{t-1}^2 - \sigma^2) + \cdots + \alpha_p(\varepsilon_{t-p}^2 - \alpha^2)$$

with $\sigma^2 = \varpi/(1 - \alpha_1 \cdots - \alpha_p)$. Assuming for notational convenience that the model parameters are known, the one-period ahead forecast follows as

$$\sigma^2_{t+1|t} \equiv E\{\varepsilon^2_{t+1}|\mathcal{I}_t\} = \sigma^2 + \alpha_1(\varepsilon^2_t - \sigma^2) + \cdots + \alpha_p(\varepsilon^2_{t-p+1} - \sigma^2).$$

This is analogous to predicting from an $AR(p)$ model for y_t as discussed in Section 8.9. Elliott and Timmermann (2016, Chapter 13) provide more discussion on volatility forecasting. Forecasting the conditional volatility more than one period-ahead can be done using the recursive formula

$$\sigma^2_{t+h|t} \equiv E\{\varepsilon^2_{t+h}|\mathcal{I}_t\} = \sigma^2 + \alpha_1(\sigma^2_{t+h-1|t} - \sigma^2) + \cdots + \alpha_p(\sigma^2_{t+h-p|t} - \sigma^2),$$

where $\sigma^2_{t+j|t} = \varepsilon^2_{t+j}$ if $j \leq 0$. The h-period-ahead forecast converges to the unconditional variance σ^2 if h becomes large (assuming that $\alpha_1 + \cdots + \alpha_p < 1$).

For a GARCH model, prediction and estimation can take place along the same lines if we use (8.97), (8.98) or a higher-order generalization. For example, the one-period-ahead forecast for a GARCH(1, 1) model is given by

$$\sigma^2_{t+1|t} = \sigma^2 + \alpha(\varepsilon^2_t - \sigma^2) + \beta(\sigma^2_t - \sigma^2),$$

where $\sigma^2_t = \sigma^2 + \alpha \sum_{j=1}^{\infty} \beta^{j-1}(\varepsilon^2_{t-j} - \sigma^2)$. The h-period-ahead forecast can be written as

$$\begin{aligned}\sigma^2_{t+h|t} &= \sigma^2 + (\alpha + \beta)[\sigma^2_{t+h-1|t} - \sigma^2] \\ &= \sigma^2 + (\alpha + \beta)^{h-1}[\alpha(\varepsilon^2_t - \sigma^2) + \beta(\sigma^2_t - \sigma^2)],\end{aligned}$$

which shows that the volatility forecasts converge to the unconditional variance at a rate $\alpha + \beta$. For EGARCH models, estimation can also be done by maximum likelihood, although simple closed-form expressions for multiperiod forecasts are not available. Empirically the likelihood function for an EGARCH model is more difficult to maximize, and problems of nonconvergence occasionally occur. Zivot (2009) discusses the empirical analysis of univariate GARCH models for financial time series and pays particular attention to practical issues.

8.11.3 Illustration: Volatility in Daily Exchange Rates

To illustrate some of the volatility models discussed previously, we consider a series of daily exchange rates between the US dollar and the euro from 4 January 1999 to 28 February 2011. Excluding days for which no prices are quoted (New Year's day, etc.), this results in a total of $T = 3109$ observations. As a first step, we take the natural logarithm of the exchange rate, which has the advantage that the results are insensitive to whether we work in dollars per euro or euros per dollar. Applying the standard set of tests to this series provides strong evidence for the presence of a unit root. In fact, log exchange rates are very well described by a random walk (see, e.g., Meese and Rogoff, 1983), so we consider a model where y_t is the daily change in the log exchange rate and the conditional mean of y_t is assumed to be constant. The time series of the change in the log exchange rate (in \$/€), multiplied by 100, is depicted in Figure 8.12. Clearly, the figure shows the existence of periods with low volatility (e.g. 2006/07) and periods with high volatility (e.g. 2008/09).

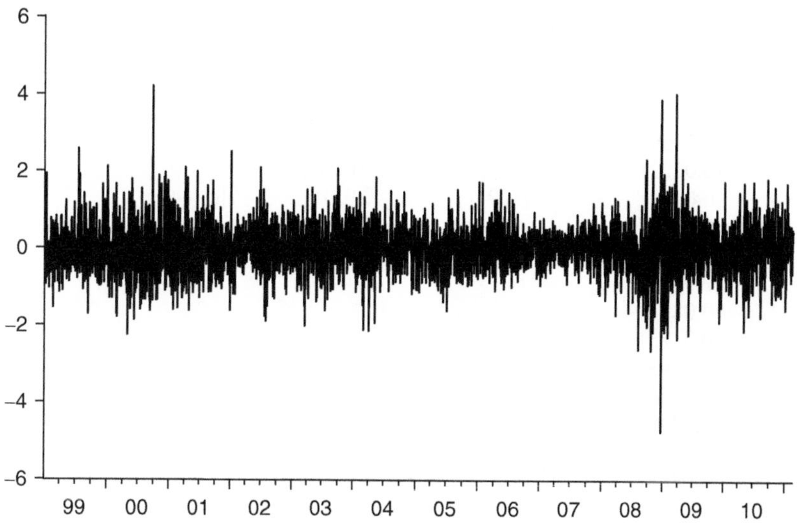

Figure 8.12 Daily change in log exchange rate \$/€, 4 January 1999–18 February 2011.

The descriptive statistics reveal that the average daily change is fairly close to zero, but also tell us that the unconditional distribution of y_t is characterized by fat tails, reflected in a highly significant Jarque-Bera test statistic (see Subsection 6.4.3). The OLS residuals e_t obtained from regressing y_t upon a constant correspond, of course, to y_t minus its sample average. On the basis of these residuals we can perform tests for ARCH effects, by regressing e_t^2 upon a constant and p of its lags. A test of homoskedasticity against ARCH(1) errors produces a test statistic (computed as T times the R^2 of the auxiliary regression) of 136.3, which is highly significant for a Chi-squared distribution with one degree of freedom. Similarly, we can test against ARCH(6) errors, which results in a test statistic of 208.2. Clearly, conditional homoskedasticity is strongly rejected.

The following four models are estimated: an ARCH(6), a GARCH(1,1), an EGARCH (1,1) and a GARCH(1,1) model with t-distributed errors. The first three models are estimated assuming that the conditional distribution of the errors is normal. The estimation results based on maximum likelihood are presented in Table 8.6. For the ARCH(6) specification, most lags have a significant and positive impact. (Note that non-negativity is imposed in estimation.) The more parsimonious GARCH(1,1) model also indicates that the effect of lagged shocks dies out only very slowly. The estimated value of $\alpha + \beta$ is 0.9967, so that the estimated process is very close to being nonstationary. This is a typical finding in empirical applications, and one could consider imposing a unit root ($\alpha + \beta = 1$) and work with an IGARCH model. When a t distribution is imposed the estimated value of $\alpha + \beta$ is only slightly smaller. For the EGARCH model we find very weak evidence of asymmetry as the γ coefficient has a t-ratio of only −1.64. As mentioned previously, this is not an unusual result for exchange rates. The large coefficient for $\log \sigma_{t-1}^2$ also reflects the high persistence in exchange rate volatility. Comparing the two versions of the GARCH(1,1) model, it appears that the model assuming a t distribution performs better. The estimated degrees of freedom parameter is slightly above 11, which indicates fatter

Table 8.6 GARCH estimates for change in log exchange rate

	ARCH(6) Normal	GARCH(1,1) Normal	GARCH(1,1) t distribution		EGARCH(1,1) Normal
Constant	0.2359	0.0016	0.0018		−0.0622
	(0.0122)	(0.0007)	(0.0009)		(0.0076)
ε^2_{t-1}	0.0739	0.0309	0.0310	$\lvert\varepsilon_{t-1}\rvert/\sigma_{t-1}$	0.0745
	(0.0158)	(0.0040)	(0.0055)		(0.0090)
ε^2_{t-2}	0.0258	–	–		
	(0.0171)				
ε^2_{t-3}	0.0857	–	–		
	(0.0173)				
ε^2_{t-4}	0.1143	–	–		
	(0.0194)				
ε^2_{t-5}	0.0965	–	–		
	(0.0207)				
ε^2_{t-6}	0.0786	–	–		
	(0.0182)				
σ^2_{t-1}	–	0.9658	0.9650	$\log(\sigma^2_{t-1})$	0.9950
		(0.0044)	(0.0062)		(0.00173)
			$\hat{s} = 11.02$	$\varepsilon_{t-1}/\sigma_{t-1}$	−0.0078
			(1.77)		(0.0048)
$\log L$	−3044.86	−2977.88	−2952.04		−2974.81

tails than the normal distribution. Moreover, the loglikelihood value of GARCH(1,1) with a t distribution is well above that of GARCH(1,1) with normality. If the error terms actually have a t distribution, the standard errors for the GARCH(1,1) assuming normality are incorrect and, given the results in Table 8.6, probably too optimistic.

8.12 What about Multivariate Models?

This chapter has concentrated on a more or less pure statistical approach of fitting an adequate time series model (from the class of ARMA models) to an observed time series. This is what we referred to as univariate time series modelling. In real life, it is obvious that many economic variables are related to each other. This, however, does not imply that a pure time series analysis is wrong. Building structural models in which variables are linked to each other (often based on economic theory) is a different branch. It gives insight into the interrelationships between variables and *how* a certain policy (shock) affects the economy (not just what its final effect is). Of course, these advantages do require a 'correct' representation of the underlying economy. In the time series approach, one is more concerned with predicting future values, including future uncertainty (variances). To this end (in univariate time series analysis), only the history of the variable under concern is taken into account. As said before, from the predictive point of view, a pure time series approach often outperforms a more structural approach.

To illustrate the relationships, assume that the following regression model describes the relationship between two (demeaned) variables y_t and x_t,

$$y_t = \beta x_t + \varepsilon_t,$$

where ε_t is a white noise error term. If x_t can be described by some ARMA model, then y_t is the sum of an ARMA process and a white noise process and will therefore also follow an ARMA process. For example, if x_t can be described by a first-order moving average model

$$x_t = u_t + \alpha u_{t-1},$$

where u_t is a white noise error independent of ε_t, then we can write

$$y_t = \beta u_t + \alpha\beta u_{t-1} + \varepsilon_t.$$

From this, we can easily derive that the autocovariances of y_t are $V\{y_t\} = \sigma_\varepsilon^2 + \beta^2 (1+\alpha^2)\sigma_u^2$, $\text{cov}\{y_t, y_{t-1}\} = \beta^2\alpha\sigma_u^2$ and $\text{cov}\{y_t, y_{t-k}\} = 0$ for $k = 2, 3, \ldots$. Consequently, y_t follows a first-order moving average process, with parameters that can be solved from the above covariances. Thus, the fact that two variables are related does not imply that a pure times series approach is invalid.

In Chapter 9, we shall extend the univariate time series approach to a multivariate setting. This allows us to consider the time series properties of a number of series simultaneously, along with their short- and long-run dependencies.

Wrap-up

Univariate time series models aim to capture the dynamics of a single time series process. The length and strength of the persistence of a series over time are summarized by the autocorrelation function and the partial autocorrelation function. Unit root process are nonstationary and have infinite persistence, that is, shocks have a permanent effect on the level of the series. The presence of a unit root can be tested empirically by the parametric augmented Dickey–Fuller tests or alternatives like the Phillips–Perron test. The class of autoregressive moving average models is able to describe the dynamics of any stationary time series. Autoregressive models can be estimated by ordinary least squares, while moving average can be estimated using nonlinear least squares. Both can also be estimated by maximum likelihood assuming normal innovations. Univariate time series models provide a convenient way to generate one or more period ahead forecasts. When a series is characterized by time-varying conditional volatility, ARCH models and their many extensions can be used. The current chapter only presented a brief introduction to time series analysis, and many specialized textbooks are available (e.g. Enders, 2014; or Pesaran, 2015). An important topic that we did not cover is the potential presence of structural breaks. There is also a wide range of nonlinear time series models, often going under the names of fancy acronyms; Franses and van Dijk (2000) provide a good starting point.

Exercises

Exercise 8.1 (ARMA Models and Unit Roots)

A researcher uses a sample of 200 quarterly observations on Y_t, the number (in 1000s) of unemployed persons, to model the time series behaviour of the series and to generate predictions. First, he computes the sample autocorrelation function, with the following results:

k	1	2	3	4	5	6	7	8	9	10
$\hat{\rho}_k$	0.83	0.71	0.60	0.45	0.44	0.35	0.29	0.20	0.11	−0.01

a. What do we mean by the sample autocorrelation function? Does the above pattern indicate that an autoregressive or moving average representation is more appropriate? Why?

Next, the sample partial autocorrelation function is determined. It is given by

k	1	2	3	4	5	6	7	8	9	10
$\hat{\theta}_{kk}$	0.83	0.16	−0.09	0.05	0.04	−0.05	0.01	0.10	−0.03	−0.01

b. What do we mean by the sample partial autocorrelation function? Why is the first partial autocorrelation equal to the first autocorrelation coefficient (0.83)?

c. Does the above pattern indicate that an autoregressive or moving average representation is more appropriate? Why?
The researcher decides to estimate, as a first attempt, a first-order autoregressive model given by

$$Y_t = \delta + \theta Y_{t-1} + \varepsilon_t. \tag{8.101}$$

The estimated value for θ_1 is 0.83 with a standard error of 0.07.

d. Which estimation method is appropriate for estimating the $AR(1)$ model? Explain why it is consistent.

e. The researcher wants to test for a unit root. What is meant by 'a unit root'? What are the implications of the presence of a unit root? Why are we interested in it? (Give statistical or economic reasons.)

f. Formulate the hypothesis of a unit root and perform a unit root test based on the above regression.

g. Perform a test for the null hypothesis that $\theta = 0.90$.

Next, the researcher extends the model to an $AR(2)$, with the following results (standard errors in parentheses):

$$\underset{}{Y_t =} \underset{(5.67)}{50.0} + \underset{(0.07)}{0.74}\, Y_{t-1} + \underset{(0.07)}{0.16}\, Y_{t-2} + \hat{\varepsilon}_t. \tag{8.102}$$

h. Would you prefer the $AR(2)$ model to the $AR(1)$ model? How would you check whether an $ARMA(2, 1)$ model may be more appropriate?

i. What do the above results tell you about the validity of the unit root test of **f**?

j. How would you test for the presence of a unit root in the $AR(2)$ model?

k. From the above estimates, compute an estimate for the average number of unemployed $E\{Y_t\}$.

l. Suppose the last two quarterly unemployment levels for 2016:III and 2016:IV were 550 and 600, respectively. Compute forecasts for 2017:I and 2017:II.

m. Can you say anything sensible about the forecasted value for the quarter 2037:I? (And its accuracy?)

Exercise 8.2 (Modelling Daily Returns – Empirical)

For this exercise, daily returns on the S&P 500 index are available from January 1981 to April 1991 ($T = 2783$). Returns are computed as first-differences of the log of the S&P 500 US stock price index.

a. Plot the series, and determine the sample autocorrelation and partial autocorrelation function.

b. Estimate an $AR(1)$ up to $AR(7)$ model, and test the individual and joint significance of the AR coefficients. Why would a significance level of 1% or less be more appropriate than the usual 5%?

c. Perform Ljung–Box tests on residual autocorrelation in these seven models for $K = 6$ (when appropriate), 12 and 18.

d. Compare AIC and BIC values. Use them, along with the results of the statistical tests, to choose a preferred specification.

For the next questions, use your preferred specification.

e. Save the residuals of your model, and test against pth-order autoregressive heteroskedasticity (choose several alternative values for p).

f. Re-estimate your model allowing for ARCH(p) errors (where p is chosen on the basis of the above tests). Compare the estimates with those of the test regressions.

g. Re-estimate your model allowing for GARCH(1,1) errors. Is there any indication of nonstationarity?

h. Re-estimate your model allowing for EGARCH errors. (Be sure to check that the programme has converged.) Is there any evidence for asymmetry?

Exercise 8.3 (Modelling Quarterly Income – Empirical)

For this exercise we use data on quarterly disposable income in the United Kingdom for the quarters 1971:I to 1985:II, measured in million pounds and current prices ($T = 58$).

a. Produce a graph of the natural logarithm of quarterly income. Estimate a standard Dickey–Fuller regression, with an intercept term, for log income and compute the Dickey–Fuller test statistic for a unit root. What do you conclude? Repeat the test while including a linear time trend.

b. Perform augmented Dickey–Fuller tests including one up to six lags, with and without including a linear trend. What do you conclude about the presence of a unit root in log income?

c. Transform the series into first-differences and produce a graph. Perform augmented Dickey–Fuller tests on the change in log income including one up to six lags. What do you conclude? Motivate why you did or did not include a time trend.

d. Determine the sample ACF and PACF for the change in log income. Is there an obvious model suggested by these graphs?

e. Estimate an $AR(4)$ and an $MA(4)$ model for the change in log income.

f. Test for serial correlation in the residuals of these two models. Can you reject the null hypothesis of white noise errors?

g. Find a parsimonious model that adequately describes the process generating the change in log income. Motivate the steps that you take.

h. Use the model to forecast quarterly disposable income in 1985:III.

Exercise 8.4 (Purchasing Power Parity – Empirical)

For this exercise, we use time series data for the exchange rate between the US dollar and the UK pound sterling, as well as aggregate price series for both countries. The sample period is Jan 1988–Dec 2010 ($T = 276$).

a. Present a graph of the log price index for the United States. Test for the presence of a unit root in this series using augmented Dickey–Fuller tests. Why does it make sense to include an intercept and deterministic time trend in the test regressions?

b. Test for the presence of a unit root using the Phillips–Perron test using the Bartlett kernel (following Newey and West, 1987). Investigate the sensitivity of the test for different choices for the bandwidth (number of lags).

c. Test the null hypothesis of trend stationarity against the alternative of a unit root using the KPSS test. Investigate the sensitivity of the test for different choices for the bandwidth and kernel. Overall, what is your conclusion on the (trend) stationarity of the log US price series?

d. Construct the (log) real exchange rate between the United States and the United Kingdom, and display its development over time in a graph. What does long-run purchasing power parity imply for the time series properties of this series?

e. Test whether the log real exchange rate is stationary, using a variety of tests. Explain why you would or would not include an intercept term in the test regressions. And a deterministic time trend?

Exercise 8.5 (ARMA modelling – Empirical)

In Subsection 2.7.3 we considered the fraudulent returns of Bernard Madoff's investment fund. Another red flag for possible hedge fund fraud suggested by Bollen and Pool (2012) is the presence of serial correlation in returns. In this exercise you are asked to analyse the returns of Fairfield Sentry Ltd and specify and estimate an ARMA model for them. Use model selection criteria and specification tests to find an appropriate ARMA specification. As a comparison, you may also want to find an ARMA model for the stock market index return.

9 Multivariate Time Series Models

In Chapter 8 we considered models describing the stochastic process of a single time series. One reason why it may be more interesting to consider several series simultaneously is that it may improve forecasts. For example, the history of a second variable, X_t say, may help forecasting future values of Y_t. It is also possible that particular values of X_t are associated with particular movements in the Y_t variable. For example, oil price shocks may be helpful in explaining gasoline consumption. In addition to the forecasting issue, this also allows us to consider 'what-if' questions. For example, what is the expected future development of gasoline consumption if oil prices are increasing by 10% over the next couple of years?

In this chapter we consider multivariate time series models. In Section 9.1, we consider explaining one variable from its own past including current or lagged values of a second variable. This way, the dynamic effects of a change in X_t upon Y_t can be modelled and estimated. To apply standard estimation or testing procedures in a dynamic time series model, it is typically required that the various variables are stationary, since the majority of econometric theory is built upon the assumption of stationarity. For example, regressing a nonstationary variable Y_t upon a nonstationary variable X_t may lead to a so-called **spurious regression**, in which estimators and test statistics are misleading. The use of nonstationary variables does not necessarily result in invalid estimators. An important exception arises when two or more $I(1)$ variables are **cointegrated**, that is, if there exists a particular linear combination of these *nonstationary* variables that is *stationary*. In such cases a long-run relationship between these variables exists. Often, economic theory suggests the existence of such long-run or equilibrium relationships, for example, purchasing power parity or the quantity theory of money. The existence of a long-run relationship also has its implications for the short-run behaviour of the $I(1)$ variables because there has to be some mechanism that drives the variables to their long-run equilibrium relationship. This mechanism is modelled by an **error-correction mechanism**, in which the 'equilibrium error' also drives the short-run dynamics of the series. Section 9.2

introduces the concept of cointegration when only two variables are involved, and relates it to error-correction models. In Section 9.3 an empirical illustration is provided on purchasing power parity, which can be characterized as corresponding to a long-run cointegrating relationship.

Another starting point of multivariate time series analysis is the multivariate generalization of the ARMA processes of Chapter 8. This is the topic of Section 9.4, where particular emphasis is placed on **vector autoregressive models** (VARs). The existence of cointegrating relationships between the variables in the VAR has important implications on the way the model can be estimated and represented. Section 9.5 discusses how hypotheses regarding the number of cointegrating relationships can be tested, and how an error-correction model representing the data can be estimated. Finally, Section 9.6 concludes with an empirical illustration concerning money demand and inflation.

There exists a fairly large number of textbooks on time series analysis that discuss cointegration, vector autoregressions and error-correction models. For economists, attractive choices are Patterson (2000), Mills and Markellos (2008), Enders (2014) and Tsay (2014). More technical detail is provided in, for example, Banerjee et al. (1993), Hamilton (1994), Johansen (1995), Maddala and Kim (1998), Gouriéroux and Jasiak (2001), Lütkepohl (2005), Juselius (2006) and Pesaran (2015). Most of these texts also discuss topics that are not covered in this chapter, including structural VARs, seasonality and structural breaks.

9.1 Dynamic Models with Stationary Variables

Considering an economic time series in isolation and applying techniques from Chapter 8 to model it may provide good forecasts in many cases. It does not, however, allow us to determine what the effects are of, for example, a change in a policy variable. To do so, it is possible to include additional variables in the model. Let us consider two (stationary) variables,[1] Y_t and X_t, and assume that it holds that

$$Y_t = \delta + \theta Y_{t-1} + \phi_0 X_t + \phi_1 X_{t-1} + \varepsilon_t. \tag{9.1}$$

As an illustration, we can think of Y_t as 'company sales' and X_t as 'advertising', both in month t. If we assume that ε_t is a white noise process, independent of $X_t, X_{t-1}, \ldots$ and $Y_{t-1}, Y_{t-2}, \ldots$, the above relation is sometimes referred to as an **autoregressive distributed lag** model. To estimate it consistently, we can simply use ordinary least squares.

The interesting element in (9.1) is that it describes the dynamic effects of a change in X_t upon current and future values of Y_t. Taking partial derivatives, we can derive that the immediate response is given by

$$\partial Y_t / \partial X_t = \phi_0. \tag{9.2}$$

Sometimes this is referred to as the **impact multiplier**. An increase in X with one unit has an immediate impact on Y of ϕ_0 units. The effect after one period is

$$\partial Y_{t+1} / \partial X_t = \theta \partial Y_t / \partial X_t + \phi_1 = \theta \phi_0 + \phi_1, \tag{9.3}$$

[1] In line with Chapter 8, we use capital letters to denote the original series and small letters for deviations from the mean.

and after two periods

$$\partial Y_{t+2}/\partial X_t = \theta \partial Y_{t+1}/\partial X_t = \theta(\theta\phi_0 + \phi_1) \tag{9.4}$$

and so on. This shows that, after the first period, the effect is decreasing if $|\theta| < 1$. Imposing this so-called stability condition allows us to determine the long-run effect of a unit change in X_t. It is given by the **long-run multiplier** (or equilibrium multiplier)

$$\begin{aligned} &\phi_0 + (\theta\phi_0 + \phi_1) + \theta(\theta\phi_0 + \phi_1) + \cdots \\ &= \phi_0 + (1 + \theta + \theta^2 + \cdots)(\theta\phi_0 + \phi_1) = \frac{\phi_0 + \phi_1}{1 - \theta}. \end{aligned} \tag{9.5}$$

This says that, if advertising X_t increases with one unit, the expected cumulative increase in sales is given by $(\phi_0 + \phi_1)/(1 - \theta)$. If the increase in X_t is permanent, the long-run multiplier also has the interpretation of the expected long-run permanent increase in Y_t. From (9.1) the long-run equilibrium relation between Y and X can be seen to be (imposing $E\{Y_t\} = E\{Y_{t-1}\}$)

$$E\{Y_t\} = \delta + \theta E\{Y_t\} + \phi_0 E\{X_t\} + \phi_1 E\{X_t\} \tag{9.6}$$

or

$$E\{Y_t\} = \frac{\delta}{1 - \theta} + \frac{\phi_0 + \phi_1}{1 - \theta} E\{X_t\}, \tag{9.7}$$

which presents an alternative derivation of the long-run multiplier. We shall write (9.7) concisely as $E\{Y_t\} = \alpha + \beta E\{X_t\}$, with obvious definitions of α and β.

There is an alternative way to formulate the autoregressive distributed lag model in (9.1). Subtracting Y_{t-1} from both sides of (9.1) and some rewriting gives

$$\Delta Y_t = \delta - (1 - \theta)Y_{t-1} + \phi_0 \Delta X_t + (\phi_0 + \phi_1)X_{t-1} + \varepsilon_t$$

or

$$\Delta Y_t = \phi_0 \Delta X_t - (1 - \theta)[Y_{t-1} - \alpha - \beta X_{t-1}] + \varepsilon_t. \tag{9.8}$$

This formulation is an example of an **error-correction model**. It says that the change in Y_t is due to the current change in X_t plus an error-correction term. If Y_{t-1} is above the equilibrium value that corresponds to X_{t-1}, that is, if the 'equilibrium error' in square brackets is positive, an additional negative adjustment in Y_t is generated. The speed of adjustment is determined by $1 - \theta$, which is the adjustment parameter. Assuming stability ensures that $1 - \theta > 0$.

It is also possible to consistently estimate the error-correction model by least squares. Because the residual sum of squares that is minimized with (9.8) is the same as that of (9.1), the resulting estimates are numerically identical.[2] The residuals are also identical, but the R^2s will differ because the dependent variables in (9.1) and (9.8) are different.

Both the autoregressive distributed lag model in (9.1) and the error-correction model in (9.8) assume that the values of X_t can be treated as given, that is, as being uncorrelated with the equations' error terms. Essentially this says that (9.1) is appropriately describing the expected value of Y_t given its own history and conditional upon current and lagged

[2] The model in (9.8) can be estimated by nonlinear least squares or by OLS after reparameterization and solving for the original parameters from the resulting estimates. The results are the same.

values of X_t. If X_t is simultaneously determined with Y_t and $E\{X_t\varepsilon_t\} \neq 0$, OLS in either (9.1) or (9.8) would be inconsistent. The typical solution in this context is to consider a bivariate model for both Y_t and X_t (see Section 9.5).

Special cases of the model in (9.1) can be derived from alternative models that have some economic interpretation. For example, let Y_t^* denote the optimal or desired level of Y_t and assume that

$$Y_t^* = \alpha + \beta X_t + \eta_t \tag{9.9}$$

for some unknown coefficients α and β, and where η_t is an error term independent of $X_t, X_{t-1}, \ldots$. The actual value Y_t differs from Y_t^* because adjustment to its optimal level corresponding to X_t is not immediate. Suppose that the adjustment is only partial in the sense that

$$Y_t - Y_{t-1} = (1-\theta)(Y_t^* - Y_{t-1}), \tag{9.10}$$

where $0 < \theta < 1$. Substituting (9.9) we obtain

$$\begin{aligned} Y_t &= Y_{t-1} + (1-\theta)\alpha + (1-\theta)\beta X_t - (1-\theta)Y_{t-1} + (1-\theta)\eta_t \\ &= \delta + \theta Y_{t-1} + \phi_0 X_t + \varepsilon_t, \end{aligned} \tag{9.11}$$

where $\delta = (1-\theta)\alpha, \phi_0 = (1-\theta)\beta$ and $\varepsilon_t = (1-\theta)\eta_t$. This is a special case of (9.1) as it does not include X_{t-1}. The model given by (9.9) and (9.10) is referred to as a **partial adjustment model**.

The autoregressive distributed lag model in (9.1) can be easily generalized. Restricting attention to two variables only, we can write a general form as

$$\theta(L)Y_t = \delta + \phi(L)X_t + \varepsilon_t, \tag{9.12}$$

where

$$\theta(L) = 1 - \theta_1 L - \cdots - \theta_p L^p$$
$$\phi(L) = \phi_0 + \phi_1 L + \cdots + \phi_q L^q$$

are two lag polynomials. Note that the constant in $\phi(L)$ is not restricted to be one. Assuming that $\theta(L)$ is invertible (see Subsection 8.2.2), we can write

$$Y_t = \theta^{-1}(1)\delta + \theta^{-1}(L)\phi(L)X_t + \theta^{-1}(L)\varepsilon_t. \tag{9.13}$$

The coefficients in the lag polynomial $\theta^{-1}(L)\phi(L)$ describe the dynamic effects of X_t upon current and future values of Y_t. The long-run effect of X_t is obtained as

$$\theta^{-1}(1)\phi(1) = \frac{\phi_0 + \phi_1 + \cdots + \phi_q}{1 - \theta_1 - \cdots - \theta_p}, \tag{9.14}$$

which generalizes the result in (9.5). Recall from Subsection 8.2.2 that invertibility of $\theta(L)$ requires that $\theta_1 + \theta_2 + \cdots + \theta_p < 1$, which guarantees that the denominator in (9.14) is nonzero. A special case arises if $\theta(L) = 1$, so that the model in (9.12) does not contain any lags of Y_t. This is referred to as a distributed lag model.

As long as it can be assumed that the error term ε_t is a white noise process, or – more generally – is stationary and independent of $X_t, X_{t-1}, \ldots$ and $Y_{t-1}, Y_{t-2}, \ldots$, the distributed lag models can be estimated consistently by ordinary least squares. Problems may arise, however, if along with Y_t and X_t the implied ε_t is also nonstationary. This is discussed in Section 9.2.

9.2 Models with Nonstationary Variables

9.2.1 Spurious Regressions

The assumption that the Y_t and X_t variables are stationary is crucial for the properties of standard estimation and testing procedures. To show consistency of the OLS estimator, for example, we typically use the result that, when the sample size increases, sample (co)variances converge to population (co)variances. Unfortunately, when the series are nonstationary, population (co)variances are ill-defined because the series are not fluctuating around a constant mean.

Consider two variables, Y_t and X_t, generated by two independent random walks,

$$Y_t = Y_{t-1} + \varepsilon_{1t}, \qquad \varepsilon_{1t} \sim IID(0, \sigma_1^2) \tag{9.15}$$

$$X_t = X_{t-1} + \varepsilon_{2t}, \qquad \varepsilon_{2t} \sim IID(0, \sigma_2^2), \tag{9.16}$$

where ε_{1t} and ε_{2t} are mutually independent. There is nothing in this data-generating mechanism that leads to a relationship between Y_t and X_t. A researcher unfamiliar with these processes may want to estimate a regression model explaining Y_t from X_t and a constant,[3]

$$Y_t = \alpha + \beta X_t + \varepsilon_t. \tag{9.17}$$

The results from this regression are likely to be characterized by a fairly high R^2 statistic, highly autocorrelated residuals and a significant value for β. This phenomenon is the well-known problem of nonsense or **spurious regressions** (see Granger and Newbold, 1974). In this case, two independent nonstationary series are spuriously related owing to the fact that they are both trended. As argued by Granger and Newbold, in these situations, characterized by a high R^2 and a low Durbin–Watson (*dw*) statistic, the usual t- and F-tests on the regression parameters may be very misleading. The reason for this is that the distributions of the conventional test statistics are very different from those derived under the assumption of stationarity. In particular, as shown by Phillips (1986), the OLS estimator does not converge in probability as the sample size increases, the t- and F-test statistics do not have well-defined asymptotic distributions and the *dw* statistic converges to zero. The reason is that, with Y_t and X_t being $I(1)$ variables, the error term ε_t will also be a nonstationary $I(1)$ variable.

To illustrate the spurious regression result, we generated two series of 200 observations according to (9.15) and (9.16) with normal error terms, starting with $Y_0 = X_0 = 0$ and setting $\sigma_1^2 = \sigma_2^2 = 1$. The results of a standard OLS regression of Y_t upon X_t and a constant are presented in Table 9.1. Although the parameter estimates in this table would be completely different from one simulation to the next, the t-ratios, R^2 and *dw* statistic show a very typical pattern: using the usual significance levels, both the constant term and X_t are highly significant, the R^2 of 31% seems reasonable, while the Durbin–Watson statistic is extremely low. (Remember from Chapter 4 that values close to 2 correspond to the null hypothesis of no autocorrelation.) *Estimation results like this should not be taken seriously*. Because both Y_t and X_t contain a stochastic trend, the OLS estimator tends to find a significant correlation between the two series, even if they are completely unrelated. Statistically, the problem is that ε_t is nonstationary.

[3] To ensure consistent notation throughout this chapter, the constant term is denoted by α and the slope coefficient by β. It will be clear from what follows that the role of the constant is often fundamentally different from the slope coefficients when variables are nonstationary.

Table 9.1 Spurious regression: OLS involving two independent random walks

Dependent variable: Y			
Variable	Estimate	Standard error	t-ratio
constant	3.9097	0.2462	15.881
X	−0.4435	0.0473	−9.370
$s = 3.2698$	$R^2 = 0.3072$	$\bar{R}^2 = 0.3037$	$F = 87.7987$
$dw = 0.1331$			

If lagged values of both the dependent and independent variables are included in the regression, as in (9.1), no spurious regression problem arises because there exist parameter values (namely $\theta = 1$ and $\phi_0 = \phi_1 = 0$) such that the error term ε_t is $I(0)$, even if Y_t and/or X_t are $I(1)$. In this case the OLS estimator is consistent for all parameters. Thus, including lagged values in the regression is sufficient to solve many of the problems associated with spurious regression (see Hamilton, 1994, p. 562). Alternatively, it is legitimate to estimate a regression model using the first-differenced series ΔY_t and ΔX_t.

9.2.2 Cointegration

An important exception to the results in Subsection 9.2.1 arises when the two nonstationary series have the same stochastic trend in common. Consider two series, integrated of order one, Y_t and X_t, and suppose that a linear relationship exists between them. This is reflected in the proposition that there exists some value β such that $Y_t - \beta X_t$ is $I(0)$, although Y_t and X_t are both $I(1)$. In such a case it is said that Y_t and X_t are **cointegrated**, and that they share a **common trend**. Although the relevant asymptotic theory is nonstandard, it can be shown that one can consistently estimate β from an OLS regression of Y_t on X_t as in (9.17). In fact, in this case, the OLS estimator b is said to be **super consistent** for β because it converges to β at a much faster rate than with conventional asymptotics. In the standard case, $\sqrt{T}(b - \beta)$ is asymptotically normal, and we say that b is $\sqrt{T}$-consistent for β. In the cointegration case, $\sqrt{T}(b - \beta)$ is degenerate, which means that b converges to β at such a fast rate that the difference $b - \beta$, multiplied by an increasing $\sqrt{T}$ factor, still converges to zero. Instead, the appropriate asymptotic distribution is that of $T(b - \beta)$. Consequently, conventional inference procedures do not apply.

The intuition behind the super consistency result is quite straightforward. Suppose the estimated regression model is

$$Y_t = a + bX_t + e_t. \tag{9.18}$$

For the true value of β, $Y_t - \beta X_t$ is $I(0)$. Clearly, for $b \neq \beta$, the OLS residual e_t will be nonstationary and hence will have a very large variance in any finite sample. For $b = \beta$, however, the estimated variance of e_t will be much smaller. Since ordinary least squares chooses a and b to minimize the sample variance of e_t, it is extremely good in finding an estimate close to β.

If Y_t and X_t are both $I(1)$ and there exists a β such that $Z_t = Y_t - \beta X_t$ is $I(0)$, Y_t and X_t are cointegrated, with β being called the cointegrating parameter, or, more generally,

$(1, -\beta)'$ being called the **cointegrating vector**. When this occurs, a special constraint operates on the long-run components of Y_t and X_t. Since both Y_t and X_t are $I(1)$, they will be dominated by 'long-wave' components, but the linear combination Z_t, being $I(0)$, will not be: Y_t and βX_t must therefore have long-run components that virtually cancel out to produce Z_t.

This idea is related to the concept of a **long-run equilibrium**. Suppose that such an equilibrium is defined by the relationship

$$Y_t = \alpha + \beta X_t. \tag{9.19}$$

Then $z_t = Z_t - \alpha$ is the 'equilibrium error', which measures the extent to which the value of Y_t deviates from its 'equilibrium value' $\alpha + \beta X_t$. If z_t is $I(0)$, the equilibrium error is stationary and fluctuating around zero. Consequently, the system will, on average, be in equilibrium. However, if Y_t and X_t are not cointegrated and, consequently, z_t is $I(1)$, the equilibrium error can wander widely and zero-crossings would be very rare. Under such circumstances, it does not make sense to refer to $Y_t = \alpha + \beta X_t$ as a long-run equilibrium. Consequently, the presence of a cointegrating vector can be interpreted as the presence of a long-run equilibrium relationship.

It is important to distinguish cases where there is a cointegrating relationship between Y_t and X_t and spurious regression cases. Suppose we know from previous results that Y_t and X_t are integrated of order one, and suppose we estimate the 'cointegrating regression'

$$Y_t = \alpha + \beta X_t + \varepsilon_t. \tag{9.20}$$

If Y_t and X_t are cointegrated, the error term in (9.20) is $I(0)$. If not, ε_t will be $I(1)$. Hence, one can test for the presence of a cointegrating relationship by testing for a unit root in the OLS residuals e_t from (9.20). It seems that this can be done by using the Dickey–Fuller tests of the previous section. For example, one can run the regression

$$\Delta e_t = \gamma_0 + \gamma_1 e_{t-1} + u_t \tag{9.21}$$

and test whether $\gamma_1 = 0$ (a unit root). There is, however, an additional complication in testing for unit roots in OLS residuals rather than in observed time series. Because the OLS estimator 'chooses' the residuals in the cointegrating regression (9.20) to have as small a sample variance as possible, even if the variables are not cointegrated, the OLS estimator will make the residuals 'look' as stationary as possible. Thus, using standard DF or ADF tests, we may reject the null hypothesis of nonstationarity too often. As a result, the appropriate critical values are more negative than those for the standard Dickey–Fuller tests and are presented in Table 9.2. If e_t is not appropriately described by a first-order autoregressive process, one should add lagged values of Δe_t to (9.21), leading to the augmented Dickey–Fuller (ADF) tests, with the same asymptotic critical values. This test can be extended to test for cointegration between three or more variables. If more than a single X_t variable is included in the cointegrating regression, the critical values shift further to the left. This is reflected in the additional rows in Table 9.2. An alternative approach to take into account serial correlation in the regression residuals employs standard errors based on the Newey–West methodology and leads to the Phillips–Ouliaris (1990) test for no cointegration. In essence, this is the Phillips–Perron test but then applied to the regression residuals.

Table 9.2 Asymptotic critical values residual-based unit root tests for no cointegration (with constant term)

Number of variables (incl. Y_t)	Significance level 1%	5%	10%
2	−3.90	−3.34	−3.04
3	−4.29	−3.74	−3.45
4	−4.64	−4.10	−3.81
5	−4.96	−4.42	−4.13

Source: Davidson, R. and MacKinnon, J. G., (1993), *Estimation and Inference in Econometrics*, Oxford University Press, Oxford. By permission of Oxford University Press.

An alternative test for cointegration is based on the usual Durbin–Watson statistic from (9.20). Note that the presence of a unit root in ε_t asymptotically corresponds to a zero value for the *dw* statistic. Thus, under the null hypothesis of a unit root, the appropriate test is whether *dw* is significantly larger than *zero*. Unfortunately, critical values for this test, commonly referred to as the **cointegrating regression Durbin–Watson test** or **CRDW test** (see Sargan and Bhargava, 1983), depend upon the process that generated the data. Nevertheless, the value of the Durbin–Watson statistic often suggests the presence or absence of a cointegrating relationship. When the data are generated by a random walk, 5% critical values are given in Table 9.3 for a number of different sample sizes. Note that, when T goes to infinity, and Y_t and X_t are not cointegrated, the *dw* statistic converges to zero (in probability).

The cointegration tests discussed here test the presence of a unit root in regression residuals. This implies that the null hypothesis of a unit root corresponds to *no* cointegration. So, if we cannot reject the presence of a unit root in the OLS residuals, this implies that we *cannot reject* that Y_t and X_t are *not* cointegrated. Sometimes, it may be more appropriate to test the null hypothesis that two or more variables are cointegrated against the alternative that they are not. Several authors have suggested tests for the null of cointegration; see Maddala and Kim (1998, Section 4.5) for a review, or Gabriel (2003) for a Monte Carlo comparison.

Table 9.3 5% Critical values CRDW tests for no cointegration

Number of variables (incl. Y_t)	Number of observations 50	100	200
2	0.72	0.38	0.20
3	0.89	0.48	0.25
4	1.05	0.58	0.30
5	1.19	0.68	0.35

Source: Banerjee et al., (1993), *Co-Integration, Error Correction, and the Econometric Analysis of Non-Stationary Data*, Oxford University Press, Oxford. By permission of Oxford University Press.

If Y_t and X_t are cointegrated, OLS applied to (9.20) produces a superconsistent estimator of the cointegrating vector, even if short-run dynamics are incorrectly omitted. The reason for this is that the nonstationarity asymptotically dominates all forms of misspecification in the stationary part of (9.20). Thus, incomplete short-run dynamics, autocorrelation in ε_t, omitted (stationary) variables and endogeneity of X_t are all problems in the stationary part of the regression that can be neglected (i.e. are of lower order) when looking at the asymptotic distribution of the superconsistent estimator b. In general, however, the OLS estimator for the cointegrating parameter has a non-normal distribution, and inferences based on its t-statistic tend to be misleading.

Another problem with the OLS estimator is that, despite the superconsistency property, Monte Carlo studies indicate that in small samples the bias in the estimated cointegrating relation may be substantial (see Banerjee et al., 1993, Section 7.4). Typically these biases are small if the R^2 of the cointegrating regression is close to unity. A large number of alternative estimators have been proposed in the literature (see Hargreaves, 1994, for a review). A simple alternative is the so-called dynamic OLS estimator, suggested by Stock and Watson (1993), based on extending the cointegrating regression by adding leads and lags of ΔX_t. Under appropriate conditions, the resulting estimator for β has an approximate normal distribution, and standard t-statistics (based on HAC standard errors) are valid. A more complicated alternative is the so-called fully modified OLS estimator, suggested by Phillips and Hansen (1990); see Patterson (2000, Chapter 9) for discussion. Pesaran, Shin and Smith (2001) propose a bounds testing approach when it is not known with certainty whether the regressors are $I(1)$ or trend stationary.

Asymptotically, one can interchange the role of Y_t and X_t and estimate

$$X_t = \alpha^* + \beta^* Y_t + u_t^* \tag{9.22}$$

to get superconsistent estimates of $\alpha^* = -\alpha/\beta$ and $\beta^* = 1/\beta$. Note that this would not occur if Y_t and X_t were stationary, in which case the distinction between endogenous and exogenous variables is crucial. For example, if (Y_t, X_t) is i.i.d. bivariate normal with expectations zero, variances σ_y^2, σ_x^2 and covariance σ_{xy}, the conditional expectation of Y_t given X_t equals $\sigma_{xy}/\sigma_x^2 X_t = \beta X_t$ and the conditional expectation of X_t given Y_t is $\sigma_{xy}/\sigma_y^2 Y_t = \beta^* Y_t$ (see Appendix B). Note that $\beta^* \neq 1/\beta$, unless Y_t and X_t are perfectly correlated ($\sigma_{xy} = \sigma_x \sigma_y$). As perfect correlation also implies that the R^2 equals unity, this also suggests that the R^2 obtained from a cointegrating regression should be quite high (as it converges to one if the sample size increases).

Although the existence of a long-run relationship between two variables is of interest, it may be even more relevant to analyse the short-run properties of the two series. This can be done using the result that the presence of a cointegrating relationship implies that there exists an error-correction model that describes the short-run dynamics consistently with the long-run relationship.

9.2.3 Cointegration and Error-correction Mechanisms

The Granger representation theorem (Granger, 1983; Engle and Granger, 1987) states that, if a set of variables are cointegrated, then there exists a valid **error-correction representation** of the data. Thus, if Y_t and X_t are both $I(1)$ and have a cointegrating vector $(1, -\beta)'$, there exists an error-correction representation, with $Z_t = Y_t - \beta X_t$, of the form

$$\theta(L)\Delta Y_t = \delta + \phi(L)\Delta X_{t-1} - \gamma Z_{t-1} + \alpha(L)\varepsilon_t, \tag{9.23}$$

where ε_t is white noise[4] and where $\theta(L)$, $\phi(L)$ and $\alpha(L)$ are polynomials in the lag operator L (with $\theta_0 \equiv 1$). Let us consider a special case of (9.23),

$$\Delta Y_t = \delta + \phi_1 \Delta X_{t-1} - \gamma(Y_{t-1} - \beta X_{t-1}) + \varepsilon_t, \tag{9.24}$$

where the error term has no moving average part and the other dynamics are kept as simple as possible. Intuitively, it is clear why the Granger representation theorem should hold. If Y_t and X_t are both $I(1)$ but have a long-run relationship, there must be some force that pulls the equilibrium error back towards zero. The error-correction model does exactly this: it describes how Y_t and X_t behave in the short-run consistent with a long-run cointegrating relationship. If the cointegrating parameter β is known, all terms in (9.24) are $I(0)$ and no inferential problems arise: we can estimate it by OLS in the usual way.

When $\Delta Y_t = \Delta X_{t-1} = 0$, we obtain the 'no change' steady state equilibrium

$$Y_t - \beta X_t = \frac{\delta}{\gamma}, \tag{9.25}$$

which corresponds with (9.19) if $\alpha = \delta/\gamma$. In this case the error-correction model can be written as

$$\Delta Y_t = \phi_1 \Delta X_{t-1} - \gamma(Y_{t-1} - \alpha - \beta X_{t-1}) + \varepsilon_t, \tag{9.26}$$

where the constant is only present in the long-run relationship. If, however, the error-correction model (9.24) contains a constant that equals $\delta = \alpha\gamma + \lambda$, with $\lambda \neq 0$, this implies deterministic trends in both Y_t and X_t and the long-run equilibrium corresponds to a steady state growth path with $\Delta Y_t = \Delta X_{t-1} = \lambda/(1 - \phi_1)$. Recall from Chapter 8 that a nonzero intercept in a univariate ARMA model with a unit root also implies that the series has a deterministic trend.

In some cases it makes sense to assume that the cointegrating vector is known a priori (e.g. when the only sensible equilibrium is $Y_t = X_t$). In that case, inferences in (9.23) or (9.24) can be made in a standard way. If β is unknown, the cointegrating vector can be estimated (super)consistently from the cointegrating regression (9.20). Consequently, with standard $\sqrt{T}$ asymptotics, one can ignore the fact that β is estimated and apply conventional theory to the estimation of the parameters in (9.23).

Note that the precise lag structure in (9.23) is not specified by the theorem, so we probably need to do some specification analysis on this issue. Moreover, the theory is symmetric in its treatment of Y_t and X_t, so that there should also exist an error-correction representation with ΔX_t as the left-hand side variable. Because at least one of the variables has to adjust to deviations from the long-run equilibrium, at least one of the adjustment parameters γ in the two error-correction equations has to be nonzero. If X_t does not adjust to the equilibrium error (has a zero adjustment parameter), it is weakly exogenous for β (as defined by Engle, Hendry and Richard, 1983). This means that we can include ΔX_t in the right-hand side of (9.24) without affecting the error-correction term

[4] The white noise term ε_t is assumed to be independent of both $Y_{t-1}, Y_{t-2}, \ldots$ and $X_{t-1}, X_{t-2}, \ldots$.

$-\gamma(Y_{t-1} - \beta X_{t-1})$. That is, we can condition upon X_t in the error-correction model for Y_t (see Section 9.5).

The representation theorem also holds conversely, i.e. if Y_t and X_t are both $I(1)$ and have an error-correction representation, then they are necessarily cointegrated. It is important to realize that the concept of cointegration can be applied to (nonstationary) integrated time series only. If Y_t and X_t are $I(0)$, the generating process can always be written in an error-correction form (see Section 9.1).

9.3 Illustration: Long-run Purchasing Power Parity (Part 2)

In Section 8.5, we introduced the topic of purchasing power parity (PPP), which requires the exchange rate between two currencies to equal the ratio of the two countries' price levels. In logarithms, absolute PPP can be written as

$$s_t = p_t - p_t^*, \tag{9.27}$$

where s_t is the log of the spot exchange rate, p_t the log of domestic prices and p_t^* the log of foreign prices. Few proponents of PPP would argue for a strict adherence to PPP. Rather, PPP is usually seen as determining the exchange rate in the long-run, while a variety of other factors, such as trading restrictions, productivity and preference changes, may influence the exchange rate in conditions of disequilibrium (see Taylor and Taylor, 2004). Consequently, (9.27) is viewed as an equilibrium or cointegrating relationship.

Using monthly observations for the euro area and the United Kingdom from January 1988 until December 2010, as before, we are thus looking for a cointegrating relationship between p_t, p_t^* and s_t. In Section 8.5 we already concluded that nonstationarity of the real exchange rate $rs_t \equiv s_t - p_t + p_t^*$ could not be rejected. This implies that $(1, -1, 1)'$ is rejected as a cointegrating vector. In this section we test whether another cointegrating relationship exists, initially using only two variables: s_t, the log exchange rate, and $ratio_t \equiv p_t - p_t^*$, the log of the price ratio. Intuitively, such relationship would imply that a change in relative prices corresponds to a less than (or more than) proportionate change in the exchange rate, while imposing symmetry. The corresponding cointegrating regression is

$$s_t = \alpha + \beta ratio_t + \varepsilon_t, \tag{9.28}$$

where $\beta = 1$ corresponds to (9.27). Note that p_t and p_t^* are not based on prices but price indices. Therefore, one may expect that the constant in (9.28) is different from zero. Consequently, we can only test for relative PPP instead of absolute PPP.

The evidence in Section 8.5 suggested that s_t was $I(1)$. For the log price ratio, $ratio_t$, the results of the (augmented) Dickey–Fuller tests are given in Table 9.4. On the basis of these results, we do not reject the null hypothesis of a unit root in $ratio_t$, although the ADF(24) statistic, without trend, is marginally significant.

We are now ready to estimate the cointegrating regression and test for cointegration between s_t and $p_t - p_t^*$. First, we estimate (9.28) by ordinary least squares. This gives the results in Table 9.5. The test for the existence of a cointegrating relationship is a test for stationarity of the residuals in this regression. Note that the R^2 of this regression is very low, which is inconsistent with it being a cointegrating regression. We can formally test

Table 9.4 Unit root tests for log price ratio euro zone versus UK

Statistic	Without trend	With trend
DF	−2.487	−2.564
ADF(1)	−2.533	−2.622
ADF(2)	−2.518	−2.639
ADF(3)	−2.137	−2.288
ADF(4)	−2.070	−2.229
ADF(5)	−2.037	−2.213
ADF(6)	−2.103	−2.227
ADF(12)	−2.989	−3.041
ADF(24)	−3.131	−3.424
ADF(36)	−2.027	−1.975

Table 9.5 OLS results

Dependent variable: s_t (log exchange rate)

Variable	Estimate	Standard error	t-ratio
constant	0.3825	0.0181	21.17
$ratio_t = p_t - p_t^*$	1.0166	0.2813	3.61

$s = 0.1045$ $R^2 = 0.0455$ $\bar{R}^2 = 0.0420$ $F = 13.064$
$dw = 0.0412$ $T = 276$

for a unit root in the residuals by means of the CRDW test, based on the Durbin–Watson statistic. Clearly, the value of 0.0412 is not significant at any reasonable level of significance and consequently, we cannot reject the null hypothesis of a unit root in the residuals. Instead of the CRDW test we can also apply the augmented Dickey–Fuller tests, the results of which are given in Table 9.6. The appropriate 5% critical value is −3.34 (see Table 9.2). Again, the null hypothesis of a unit root cannot be rejected and, consequently, there is no evidence in the data that the spot exchange rate and the price ratio are cointegrated. This conclusion corresponds with that in, for example, Corbae and Ouliaris (1988), who conclude that there is no long-run tendency for exchange rates and relative prices to settle down on an equilibrium track.

A potential explanation for this rejection is that the restriction imposed, viz. that p_t and p_t^* enter (9.28) with coefficient β and $-\beta$, respectively, is invalid, owing to, for example, transportation costs or measurement error. We can estimate (9.28) with unconstrained coefficients, so that we can test the existence of a more general cointegrating relationship between the three variables, s_t, p_t and p_t^*. However, when we consider more than

Table 9.6 ADF (cointegration) tests of residuals

DF	−1.497		
ADF(1)	−1.478	ADF(4)	−1.628
ADF(2)	−1.431	ADF(5)	−1.522
ADF(3)	−1.479	ADF(6)	−1.391

Table 9.7 OLS results

Dependent variable: s_t (log exchange rate)			
Variable	Estimate	Standard error	t-ratio
constant	0.4193	0.2082	2.014
p_t	1.0076	0.2863	3.520
p_t^*	1.0150	0.2819	3.602

$s = 0.1047$ $R^2 = 0.0456$ $\bar{R}^2 = 0.0386$ $F = 6.525$
$dw = 0.0412$ $T = 276$

Table 9.8 ADF (cointegration) tests of residuals

DF	−1.508		
ADF(1)	−1.489	ADF(4)	−1.633
ADF(2)	−1.439	ADF(5)	−1.528
ADF(3)	−1.485	ADF(6)	−1.399

two-dimensional systems, the number of cointegrating relationships may be more than one. For example, there may be two different cointegrating relationships between three $I(1)$ variables, which makes the analysis somewhat more complicated than in the two-dimensional case. Section 9.5 will pay attention to the more general case.

When there exists only one cointegrating vector, we can estimate the cointegrating relationship, as before, by regressing one variable upon the other variables. This does require, however, that the cointegrating vector involves the left-hand side variable of this regression, because its coefficient is implicitly normalized to minus one. In our example, we regress s_t upon p_t and p_t^* to obtain the results reported in Table 9.7. The results are very close to those reported in Table 9.5, and the value of the Durbin-Watson statistic has not changed after relaxing the restriction imposed in (9.28). The ADF tests on the residuals are also similar and are reported in Table 9.8, where the appropriate 5% critical value is −3.74 (see Table 9.2). Again, we cannot reject the null hypothesis that there is no cointegrating relationship between the log exchange rate and the log price indices of the UK and euro area. It does not appear that some (weak) form of purchasing power parity holds for these two currency regions. Of course, it could be the case that our sample period is just not long enough to find sufficient evidence for a cointegrating relationship. This seems to be in line with what people find in the literature. With longer samples, up to a century or more, the evidence is more in favour of some long-run tendency to PPP (see Froot and Rogoff, 1995; or Taylor and Taylor, 2004).

9.4 Vector Autoregressive Models

The autoregressive moving average models of the previous chapter can be readily extended to the multivariate case, in which the stochastic process that generates the time series of a *vector* of variables is modelled. The most common approach is to consider a **vector autoregressive (VAR)** model. A VAR describes the dynamic evolution of a number of variables from their common history. If we consider two variables, Y_t and X_t, say, the VAR consists of two equations. A first-order VAR is given by

$$Y_t = \delta_1 + \theta_{11} Y_{t-1} + \theta_{12} X_{t-1} + \varepsilon_{1t} \tag{9.29}$$

$$X_t = \delta_2 + \theta_{21} Y_{t-1} + \theta_{22} X_{t-1} + \varepsilon_{2t}, \tag{9.30}$$

where ε_{1t} and ε_{2t} are two white noise processes (independent of the history of Y and X) that may be correlated. If, for example, $\theta_{12} \neq 0$, it means that the history of X helps explaining Y. The system (9.29)–(9.30) can be written as

$$\begin{pmatrix} Y_t \\ X_t \end{pmatrix} = \begin{pmatrix} \delta_1 \\ \delta_2 \end{pmatrix} + \begin{pmatrix} \theta_{11} & \theta_{12} \\ \theta_{21} & \theta_{22} \end{pmatrix} \begin{pmatrix} Y_{t-1} \\ X_{t-1} \end{pmatrix} + \begin{pmatrix} \varepsilon_{1t} \\ \varepsilon_{2t} \end{pmatrix} \tag{9.31}$$

or, with appropriate definitions, as[5]

$$\vec{Y}_t = \delta + \Theta_1 \vec{Y}_{t-1} + \vec{\varepsilon}_t, \tag{9.32}$$

where $\vec{Y}_t = (Y_t, X_t)'$ and $\vec{\varepsilon}_t = (\varepsilon_{1t}, \varepsilon_{2t})'$. This extends the first-order autoregressive model from Chapter 8 to the more-dimensional case. In general, a *VAR*(p) model for a k-dimensional vector $\vec{Y}_t$ is given by

$$\vec{Y}_t = \delta + \Theta_1 \vec{Y}_{t-1} + \cdots + \Theta_p \vec{Y}_{t-p} + \vec{\varepsilon}_t, \tag{9.33}$$

where each Θ_j is a $k \times k$ matrix and $\vec{\varepsilon}_t$ is a k-dimensional vector of white noise terms with covariance matrix Σ. We can use the lag operator to define a matrix lag polynomial

$$\Theta(L) = I_k - \Theta_1 L - \cdots - \Theta_p L^p,$$

where I_k is the k-dimensional identity matrix, so that we can write the VAR as

$$\Theta(L)\vec{Y}_t = \delta + \vec{\varepsilon}_t.$$

The matrix lag polynomial is a $k \times k$ matrix where each element corresponds to a pth-order polynomial in L. Extensions to vectorial ARMA (VARMA) models can be obtained by premultiplying $\vec{\varepsilon}_t$ with a (matrix) lag polynomial.

The VAR model implies univariate ARMA models for each of its components. The advantages of considering the components simultaneously include that the model may be more parsimonious and have fewer lags, and that more accurate forecasting is possible, because the information set is extended also to include the history of the other variables. From a different perspective, Sims (1980) has advocated the use of VAR models instead of structural simultaneous equation models because the distinction between endogenous and exogenous variables does not have to be made a priori, and 'arbitrary' constraints to ensure identification are not required (see, e.g., Canova, 1995, for a discussion). Like a reduced form, a VAR is always identified. For the purpose of structural inference and policy analysis, however, the standard reduced form VAR in (9.33) may not perform very well, because it does not allow differentiating between correlation and causation (Stock and Watson, 2001). To remedy this, structural VARs can be developed that incorporate economic theory or institutional

[5] Despite the fact that the use of arrows to denote vectors is somewhat uncommon, we will use it in this section and the next to avoid confusion with the scalar random variables.

knowledge by imposing assumedly credible restrictions (see Enders, 2014, Chapter 5, for more discussion).

The expected value of $\vec{Y}_t$ in (9.33) can be determined if we impose stationarity. This gives

$$E\{\vec{Y}_t\} = \delta + \Theta_1 E\{\vec{Y}_t\} + \cdots + \Theta_p E\{\vec{Y}_t\}$$

or

$$\mu = E\{\vec{Y}_t\} = (I - \Theta_1 - \cdots - \Theta_p)^{-1}\delta = \Theta(1)^{-1}\delta,$$

which shows that stationarity will require that the $k \times k$ matrix $\Theta(1)$ is invertible.[6] For the moment we shall assume that this is the case. As before, we can subtract the mean and consider $\vec{y}_t = \vec{Y}_t - \mu$, for which we have

$$\vec{y}_t = \Theta_1 \vec{y}_{t-1} + \cdots + \Theta_p \vec{y}_{t-p} + \vec{\varepsilon}_t. \tag{9.34}$$

We can use the VAR model for forecasting in a straightforward way. For forecasting from the end of the sample period (period T), the relevant information set now includes the vectors $\vec{y}_T, \vec{y}_{T-1}, \ldots$, and we obtain for the optimal one-period-ahead forecast

$$\vec{y}_{T+1|T} = E\{\vec{y}_{T+1}|\vec{y}_T, \vec{y}_{T-1}, \ldots\} = \Theta_1 \vec{y}_T + \cdots + \Theta_p \vec{y}_{T-p+1}. \tag{9.35}$$

The one-period-ahead forecast error variance is simply $V\{\vec{y}_{T+1}|\vec{y}_T, \vec{y}_{T-1}, \ldots\} = \Sigma$. Forecasts more than one period ahead can be obtained recursively. For example,

$$\begin{aligned}\vec{y}_{T+2|T} &= \Theta_1 \vec{y}_{T+1|T} + \cdots + \Theta_p \vec{y}_{T-p+2} \\ &= \Theta_1(\Theta_1 \vec{y}_T + \cdots + \Theta_p \vec{y}_{T-p+1}) + \cdots + \Theta_p \vec{y}_{T-p+2}.\end{aligned} \tag{9.36}$$

To estimate a vector autoregressive model, we can simply use ordinary least squares equation by equation,[7] which is consistent because the white noise terms are assumed to be independent of the history of $\vec{y}_t$. From the residuals of each of the k equations, $e_{1t}, \ldots, e_{kt}$, we can estimate the (i,j)-element in Σ as[8]

$$\hat{\sigma}_{ij} = \frac{1}{T-p} \sum_{t=p+1}^{T} e_{it} e_{jt}, \tag{9.37}$$

so that

$$\hat{\Sigma} = \frac{1}{T-p} \sum_{t=p+1}^{T} \vec{e}_t \vec{e}_t', \tag{9.38}$$

where $\vec{e}_t = (e_{1t}, \ldots, e_{kt})'$.

Determining the lag length p in an empirical application is not always easy, and univariate autocorrelation or partial autocorrelation functions will not help; see Canova (1995)

[6] Recall from Chapter 8 that, in the $AR(p)$ case, stationarity requires that $\theta(1) \neq 0$, so that $\theta(1)^{-1}$ exists.

[7] Because the explanatory variables are the same for each equation, a system estimator, like SUR (see Greene, 2012, Section 10.2), provides the same estimates as OLS applied to each equation separately. If different restrictions are imposed upon the equations, SUR estimation will be more efficient than OLS, though OLS remains consistent.

[8] Assuming that observations are available from $t = 1, \ldots, T$, the number of useful observations is $T - p$. Note that a degrees of freedom correction can be applied, as in the linear regression model (see Chapter 2).

for a discussion. A reasonable strategy is to estimate a VAR model for different values of p and then select on the basis of the Akaike or Schwarz information criteria, as discussed in Chapters 3 and 8, or on the basis of statistical significance; see Lütkepohl (2005, Chapter 4) for alternative approaches.

The **Granger causality test** (Granger, 1969) examines whether lagged values of one variable in the VAR help to predict another variable. A time series Y_{1t} is said to Granger cause Y_{2t} if past values of Y_{1t} help predicting Y_{2t} beyond information contained in past values of Y_{2t} alone. Put differently, Y_{1t} is said to Granger cause Y_{2t} if lagged values of Y_{1t} are statistically significant in the equation explaining Y_{2t}. Granger causality does not imply causality in the more common sense of the term, as used in, for example, Chapter 5. The null hypothesis that Y_{1t} 'does not Granger cause' Y_{2t} implies that all coefficients for the lagged values of Y_{1t} are zero in the equation for Y_{2t} and can be tested using the results of the OLS estimates by means of an F-test or a likelihood ratio test. If a variable in the VAR does not Granger cause any of the other variables, it can be dropped from the VAR. Note that it is possible that Y_{1t} Granger causes Y_{2t} while Y_{2t} Granger causes Y_{1t}. Often, the results of Granger causality tests are more informative than the potentially large number of coefficient estimates from the k^2 lag polynomials in $\Theta(L)$.

If $\Theta(1)$ is invertible, it means that we can write the vector autoregressive model as a vector moving average (VMA) model by premultiplying with $\Theta(L)^{-1}$. This is similar to deriving the moving average representation of a univariate autoregressive model. This gives

$$\vec{Y}_t = \Theta(1)^{-1}\delta + \Theta(L)^{-1}\vec{\varepsilon}_t = \mu + \Theta(L)^{-1}\vec{\varepsilon}_t, \tag{9.39}$$

which describes each element in $\vec{Y}_t$ as a weighted sum of all current and past shocks in the system. Writing $\Theta(L)^{-1} = I_k + A_1L + A_2L^2 + \cdots$, we have

$$\vec{Y}_t = \mu + \vec{\varepsilon}_t + A_1\vec{\varepsilon}_{t-1} + A_2\vec{\varepsilon}_{t-2} + \cdots \tag{9.40}$$

If the white noise vector $\vec{\varepsilon}_t$ increases by a vector d, the effect upon $\vec{Y}_{t+s}$ $(s > 0)$ is given by A_sd. Thus the matrix

$$A_s = \frac{\partial \vec{Y}_{t+s}}{\partial \vec{\varepsilon}_t'} \tag{9.41}$$

has the interpretation that its (i,j)-element measures the effect of a one-unit increase in ε_{jt} upon $Y_{i,t+s}$. If only the first element ε_{1t} of $\vec{\varepsilon}_t$ changes, the effects are given by the first column of A_s. The dynamic effects upon the jth variable of such a one-unit increase are given by the elements in the first column and jth row of $I_k, A_1, A_2, \ldots$. A plot of these elements as a function of s is called the **impulse-response function**. It measures the response of $Y_{j,t+s}$ to an impulse in Y_{1t}, keeping constant all other variables dated t and before. Although it may be hard to derive expressions for the elements in $\Theta(L)^{-1}$, the impulse responses can be determined fairly easily by simulation methods (see Hamilton, 1994). Canova (2007, Section 4.4) provides more details.

If $\Theta(1)$ is not invertible, it cannot be the case that all variables in $\vec{Y}_t$ are stationary $I(0)$ series. At least one stochastic trend must be present. In the extreme case where we have k independent stochastic trends, all k variables are integrated of order one, while no cointegrating relationships exist. In this case, $\Theta(1)$ is equal to a null matrix. The intermediate cases are more interesting: the rank of the matrix $\Theta(1)$ equals the number of linear combinations of variables in $\vec{Y}_t$ that are $I(0)$, that is, determines the number of cointegrating vectors. This is the topic of the next section.

9.5 Cointegration: the Multivariate Case

When more than two variables are involved, cointegration analysis is somewhat more complex because the cointegrating vector generalizes to a **cointegrating space**, the dimension of which is not known a priori. That is, when we have a set of k $I(1)$ variables, there may exist up to $k-1$ independent linear relationships that are $I(0)$, while any linear combination of these relationships is – by construction – also $I(0)$. This implies that individual cointegrating vectors are no longer identified; only the space spanned by these vectors is. Ideally, vectors in the cointegrating space can be found that have an economic interpretation and can be interpreted as representing long-run equilibria.

9.5.1 Cointegration in a VAR

If the elements in the k-dimensional vector $\vec{Y}_t$ are $I(1)$ there may be different vectors β such that $Z_t = \beta'\vec{Y}_t$ is $I(0)$. That is, there may be more than one cointegrating vector β. It is clearly possible for several equilibrium relations to govern the long-run behaviour of the k variables. In general, there can be $r \leq k-1$ linearly independent cointegrating vectors,[9] which are gathered together into the $k \times r$ **cointegrating matrix**[10] β. By construction, the rank of the matrix[11] β is r, which will be called the **cointegrating rank** of $\vec{Y}_t$. This means that each element in the r-dimensional vector $\vec{Z}_t = \beta'\vec{Y}_t$ is $I(0)$, whereas each element in the k-dimensional vector $\vec{Y}_t$ is $I(1)$.

The Granger representation theorem (Engle and Granger, 1987) directly extends to this more general case and claims that, if $\vec{Y}_t$ is cointegrated, there exists a valid error-correction representation of the data. Although there are different ways to derive and describe such a representation, we start from the vector autoregressive model for $\vec{Y}_t$ introduced in the previous section:

$$\vec{Y}_t = \delta + \Theta_1\vec{Y}_{t-1} + \cdots + \Theta_p\vec{Y}_{t-p} + \vec{\varepsilon}_t \tag{9.42}$$

or

$$\Theta(L)\vec{Y}_t = \delta + \vec{\varepsilon}_t. \tag{9.43}$$

For the case with $p = 3$ we can write this as

$$\begin{aligned}\Delta\vec{Y}_t &= \delta + (\Theta_1 + \Theta_2 - I_k)\vec{Y}_{t-1} - \Theta_2\Delta\vec{Y}_{t-1} + \Theta_3\vec{Y}_{t-3} + \vec{\varepsilon}_t \\ &= \delta + (\Theta_1 + \Theta_2 + \Theta_3 - I_k)\vec{Y}_{t-1} - \Theta_2\Delta\vec{Y}_{t-1} - \Theta_3(\Delta\vec{Y}_{t-1} + \Delta\vec{Y}_{t-2}) + \vec{\varepsilon}_t\end{aligned}$$

---

[9] The existence of k cointegrating relationships between the k elements in $\vec{Y}_t$ would imply that there exist k independent linear combinations that are $I(0)$, such that, necessarily, all individual elements in $\vec{Y}_t$ must be $I(0)$. Clearly, this is in conflict with the definition of cointegration as a property of $I(1)$ variables, and it follows that $r \leq k-1$.

[10] We follow the convention in the cointegration literature to denote the cointegrating *matrix* by a Greek lowercase β.

[11] See Appendix A for the definition of the rank of a matrix.

or

$$\Delta\vec{Y}_t = \delta + \Gamma_1 \Delta\vec{Y}_{t-1} + \Gamma_2 \Delta\vec{Y}_{t-2} + (\Theta_1 + \Theta_2 + \Theta_3 - I_k)\vec{Y}_{t-1} + \vec{\varepsilon}_t,$$

where $\Gamma_1 = -\Theta_2 - \Theta_3$ and $\Gamma_2 = -\Theta_3$. This rewrites the VAR in first-differences plus a term involving levels. For general values of p we can write[12]

$$\Delta\vec{Y}_t = \delta + \Gamma_1 \Delta\vec{Y}_{t-1} + \cdots + \Gamma_{p-1} \Delta\vec{Y}_{t-p+1} + \Pi\vec{Y}_{t-1} + \vec{\varepsilon}_t, \tag{9.44}$$

where the 'long-run matrix'

$$\Pi \equiv -\Theta(1) = -(I_k - \Theta_1 - \cdots - \Theta_p) \tag{9.45}$$

determines the long-run dynamic properties of $\vec{Y}_t$.[13] This equation is a direct generalization of the regressions used in the augmented Dickey–Fuller test. Because $\Delta\vec{Y}_t$ and $\vec{\varepsilon}_t$ are stationary (by assumption), it must be the case that $\Pi\vec{Y}_{t-1}$ in (9.44) is also stationary. This could reflect three different situations. First, if all elements in $\vec{Y}_t$ are integrated of order one and no cointegrating relationships exist, it must be the case that $\Pi = 0$ and (9.44) presents a (stationary) VAR model for $\Delta\vec{Y}_t$. Second, if all elements in $\vec{Y}_t$ are stationary $I(0)$ variables, the matrix $\Pi = -\Theta(1)$ must be of full rank and invertible so that we can write a vector moving average representation $\vec{Y}_t = \Theta^{-1}(L)(\delta + \vec{\varepsilon}_t)$. Third, if Π is of rank r $(0 < r < k)$, the elements in $\Pi\vec{Y}_{t-1}$ are linear combinations that are stationary. If the variables in $\vec{Y}_t$ are $I(1)$, these linear combinations must correspond to cointegrating vectors. The latter case is the most interesting one. If Π has a reduced rank of $r \leq k - 1$, this means that there are r independent linear combinations of the k elements in $\vec{Y}_t$ that are stationary, that is: there exist r cointegrating relationships. Note that the existence of k cointegrating relationships is impossible: if k independent linear combinations produce stationary series, all k variables themselves must be stationary.

If Π has reduced rank it can be written as the product of a $k \times r$ matrix γ and an $r \times k$ matrix β' that both have rank r.[14] That is, $\Pi = \gamma\beta'$. Substituting this produces the model in error-correction form

$$\Delta\vec{Y}_t = \delta + \Gamma_1 \Delta\vec{Y}_{t-1} + \cdots + \Gamma_{p-1} \Delta\vec{Y}_{t-p+1} + \gamma\beta'\vec{Y}_{t-1} + \vec{\varepsilon}_t. \tag{9.46}$$

The linear combinations $\beta'\vec{Y}_{t-1}$ present the r cointegrating relationships. The coefficients in γ measure how the elements in $\Delta\vec{Y}_t$ are adjusted to the r 'equilibrium errors' $\vec{Z}_{t-1} = \beta'\vec{Y}_{t-1}$. Thus, (9.46) is a generalization of (9.24) and is referred to as a **vector error-correction model (VECM)**.

If we take expectations in the error-correction model, we can derive

$$(I - \Gamma_1 - \cdots - \Gamma_{p-1})E\{\Delta\vec{Y}_t\} = \delta + \gamma E\{\vec{Z}_{t-1}\}. \tag{9.47}$$

---

[12] It is possible to rewrite the VAR such that any lag appears in levels on the right-hand side, with the same coefficients in the 'long-run matrix' Π. For comparison with the univariate case, we prefer to include the first lag; see Juselius (2006, Section 4.2) for more discussion and examples.

[13] In the univariate case, the long-run properties are determined by $\theta(1)$, where $\theta(L)$ is the AR polynomial (see Chapter 8).

[14] This means that the r columns in γ are linearly independent, and that the r rows in β' are independent (see Appendix A).

There is no deterministic trend in any of the variables if $E\{\Delta\vec{Y}_t\} = 0$. Under the assumption that the matrix $(I - \Gamma_1 - \cdots - \Gamma_{p-1})$ is nonsingular, this requires that $\delta + \gamma E\{\vec{Z}_{t-1}\} = 0$ (compare Subsection 9.2.3), where $E\{\vec{Z}_{t-1}\}$ corresponds to the vector of intercepts in the cointegrating relations. If we impose this restriction, intercepts appear in the cointegrating relationships only, and we can rewrite the error-correction model to include $\vec{z}_t = \vec{Z}_{t-1} - E\{\vec{Z}_{t-1}\}$ and have no intercepts, that is,

$$\Delta\vec{Y}_t = \Gamma_1\Delta\vec{Y}_{t-1} + \cdots + \Gamma_{p-1}\Delta\vec{Y}_{t-p+1} + \gamma(-\alpha + \beta'\vec{Y}_{t-1}) + \vec{\varepsilon}_t,$$

where α is an r-dimensional vector of constants, satisfying $E\{\beta'\vec{Y}_{t-1}\} = E\{\vec{Z}_{t-1}\} = \alpha$. As a result, all terms in this expression have mean zero, and no deterministic trends exist. In this situation (typically referred to as case II: restricted intercepts), each of the long-run equilibria implied by the cointegrating relationships involves an intercept.

If we add one common constant to the vector error-correction model, we obtain

$$\Delta\vec{Y}_t = \lambda + \Gamma_1\Delta\vec{Y}_{t-1} + \cdots + \Gamma_{p-1}\Delta\vec{Y}_{t-p+1} + \gamma(-\alpha + \beta'\vec{Y}_{t-1}) + \vec{\varepsilon}_t,$$

where λ is a k-dimensional vector with identical elements λ_1. Now the long-run equilibrium corresponds to a steady state growth path with growth rates for all variables given by

$$E\{\Delta\vec{Y}_t\} = (I - \Gamma_1 - \cdots - \Gamma_{p-1})^{-1}\lambda.$$

The deterministic trends in each Y_{jt} are assumed to cancel out in the long run, so that no deterministic trend is included in the error-correction term. We can go as far as allowing for $k - r$ separate deterministic trends that cancel out in the cointegrating relationships, in which case we are back at specification (9.46) without restrictions on δ. In this case (case III: unrestricted intercepts) δ is capturing r intercept terms in the long-run relationships and $k - r$ different deterministic trends in the variables in $\vec{Y}_t$. This implies that the long-run equilibria involve intercept terms, while the underlying variables exhibit deterministic trends (in addition to a unit root). If there are more than $k - r$ separate deterministic trends, they cannot cancel out in $\beta'\vec{Y}_{t-1}$ and we should include a deterministic trend in the cointegrating equations. It depends upon the context whether a time trend in a long-run equilibrium relationship makes sense. See Juselius (2006, Chapter 6) and Pesaran (2015, Section 22.9) for additional discussion and some alternatives. It is very uncommon to have time trends in the first-differenced part of the model (as well as in the cointegrating relationships), as this would imply a quadratic time trend in the data.

9.5.2 Example: Cointegration in a Bivariate VAR

As an example, consider the case where $k = 2$. In this case the number of cointegrating vectors may be zero or one ($r = 0, 1$). Let us consider a first-order (nonstationary) VAR for $\vec{Y}_t = (Y_t, X_t)'$. That is,

$$\begin{pmatrix} Y_t \\ X_t \end{pmatrix} = \begin{pmatrix} \theta_{11} & \theta_{12} \\ \theta_{21} & \theta_{22} \end{pmatrix}\begin{pmatrix} Y_{t-1} \\ X_{t-1} \end{pmatrix} + \begin{pmatrix} \varepsilon_{1t} \\ \varepsilon_{2t} \end{pmatrix},$$

where, for simplicity, we do not include intercept terms. The matrix Π is given by

$$\Pi = -\Theta(1) = \begin{pmatrix} \theta_{11} - 1 & \theta_{12} \\ \theta_{21} & \theta_{22} - 1 \end{pmatrix}.$$

This matrix is a zero matrix if $\theta_{11} = \theta_{22} = 1$ and $\theta_{12} = \theta_{21} = 0$. This corresponds to the case where Y_t and X_t are two random walks. The matrix Π has reduced rank if

$$(\theta_{11} - 1)(\theta_{22} - 1) - \theta_{21}\theta_{12} = 0. \tag{9.48}$$

If this is the case,

$$\beta' = \begin{pmatrix} \theta_{11} - 1 \, \theta_{12} \end{pmatrix}$$

is a cointegrating vector (where we choose an arbitrary normalization) and we can write

$$\Pi = \gamma\beta' = \begin{pmatrix} 1 \\ \theta_{21}/(\theta_{11} - 1) \end{pmatrix} \begin{pmatrix} \theta_{11} - 1 \, \theta_{12} \end{pmatrix}.$$

Using this, we can write the model in error-correction form. First, write

$$\begin{pmatrix} Y_t \\ X_t \end{pmatrix} = \begin{pmatrix} Y_{t-1} \\ X_{t-1} \end{pmatrix} + \begin{pmatrix} \theta_{11} - 1 & \theta_{12} \\ \theta_{21} & \theta_{22} - 1 \end{pmatrix} \begin{pmatrix} Y_{t-1} \\ X_{t-1} \end{pmatrix} + \begin{pmatrix} \varepsilon_{1t} \\ \varepsilon_{2t} \end{pmatrix}.$$

Next, we rewrite this as

$$\begin{pmatrix} \Delta Y_t \\ \Delta X_t \end{pmatrix} = \begin{pmatrix} 1 \\ \theta_{21}/(\theta_{11} - 1) \end{pmatrix} ((\theta_{11} - 1)Y_{t-1} + \theta_{12}X_{t-1}) + \begin{pmatrix} \varepsilon_{1t} \\ \varepsilon_{2t} \end{pmatrix}. \tag{9.49}$$

The resulting error-correction form is thus quite simple, as it excludes any dynamics. Note that both Y_t and X_t adjust to the equilibrium error, because $\theta_{21} = 0$ is excluded. (Also note that $\theta_{21} = 0$ would imply $\theta_{11} = \theta_{22} = 1$ and no cointegration.)

The fact that the linear combination $Z_t = (\theta_{11} - 1)Y_t + \theta_{12}X_t$ is $I(0)$ also follows from this result. Note that we can write

$$\Delta Z_t = (\theta_{11} - 1 \quad \theta_{12}) \begin{pmatrix} 1 \\ \theta_{21}/(\theta_{11} - 1) \end{pmatrix} Z_{t-1} + (\theta_{11} - 1 \quad \theta_{12}) \begin{pmatrix} \varepsilon_{1t} \\ \varepsilon_{2t} \end{pmatrix}$$

or, using (9.48),

$$Z_t = Z_{t-1} + (\theta_{11} - 1 + \theta_{22} - 1)Z_{t-1} + v_t = (\theta_{11} + \theta_{22} - 1)Z_{t-1} + v_t,$$

where $v_t = (\theta_{11} - 1)\varepsilon_{1t} + \theta_{12}\varepsilon_{2t}$ is a white noise error term. Consequently, Z_t is described by a stationary $AR(1)$ process unless $\theta_{11} = 1$ and $\theta_{22} = 1$, which is excluded.

9.5.3 Testing for Cointegration

If it is known that there exists at most one cointegrating vector, a simple approach to testing for the existence of cointegration is the Engle–Granger approach described in Section 9.2.2. It requires running a regression of Y_{1t} (being the first element of $\vec{Y}_t$) on the other $k - 1$ variables $Y_{2t}, \ldots, Y_{kt}$ and testing for a unit root in the residuals. This can be done using the ADF tests on the OLS residuals, applying the critical values from Table 9.2. If the unit root hypothesis is rejected, the hypothesis of no cointegration is also rejected. In this case, the static regression gives consistent estimates of the cointegrating vector, while in a second stage the error-correction model can be estimated using the estimated cointegrating vector from the first stage.

There are some problems with this Engle–Granger approach. First, the results of the tests are sensitive to the left-hand side variable of the regression, that is, to the normalization applied to the cointegrating vector. Second, if the cointegrating vector happens not to involve Y_{1t} but only $Y_{2t}, \ldots, Y_{kt}$, the test is not appropriate and the cointegrating vector will not be consistently estimated by a regression of Y_{1t} upon $Y_{2t}, \ldots, Y_{kt}$. Third, the residual-based test tends to lack power because it does not exploit all the available information about the dynamic interactions of the variables. Fourth, it is possible that more than one cointegrating relationship exists between the variables $Y_{1t}, \ldots, Y_{kt}$. If, for example, two distinct cointegrating relationships exist, OLS typically estimates a linear combination of them. Fortunately, as the null hypothesis for the cointegration tests is that there is *no* cointegration, the tests are still appropriate for their purpose.

An alternative approach that does not suffer from these drawbacks was proposed by Johansen (1988), who developed a maximum likelihood estimation procedure that also allows one to test for the number of cointegrating relations. The details of the Johansen procedure are very complex, and we shall only focus on a few aspects. Further details can be found in Johansen and Juselius (1990) and Johansen (1991), or in textbooks like Banerjee et al. (1993, Chapter 8), Hamilton (1994, Chapter 20), Johansen (1995, Chapter 11), Lütkepohl (2005, Chapter 8), Juselius (2006) and Pesaran (2015, Chapter 22). The starting point of the Johansen procedure is the VAR representation of $\vec{Y}_t$ given in (9.44) and reproduced here:

$$\Delta \vec{Y}_t = \delta + \Gamma_1 \Delta \vec{Y}_{t-1} + \cdots + \Gamma_{p-1} \Delta \vec{Y}_{t-p+1} + \Pi \vec{Y}_{t-1} + \vec{\varepsilon}_t, \tag{9.50}$$

where $\vec{\varepsilon}_t$ is $NID(0, \Sigma)$. Note that the use of maximum likelihood requires us to impose a particular distribution (normality) for the white noise terms. Assuming that $\vec{Y}_t$ is a vector of $I(1)$ variables, while r linear combinations of $\vec{Y}_t$ are stationary, we can write

$$\Pi = \gamma \beta', \tag{9.51}$$

where, as before, γ and β are of dimension $k \times r$. Again, β denotes the matrix of cointegrating vectors, while γ represents the matrix of weights with which each cointegrating vector enters each of the $\Delta \vec{Y}_t$ equations. The approach of Johansen is based on the estimation of the system (9.50) by maximum likelihood while imposing the restriction in (9.51) for a given value of r.

The first step in the Johansen approach involves testing hypotheses about the rank of the long-run matrix Π, or – equivalently – the number of columns in β. For a given r, it can be shown (see, e.g., Hamilton, 1994, Section 20.2) that the ML estimate for β equals the matrix containing the r eigenvectors corresponding to the r largest (estimated) eigenvalues of a $k \times k$ matrix that can be estimated fairly easily using an OLS package. Let us denote the (theoretical) eigenvalues of this matrix in decreasing order as $\lambda_1 \geq \lambda_2 \geq \cdots \geq \lambda_k$. If there are r cointegrating relationships (and Π has rank r), it must be the case that $\log(1 - \lambda_j) = 0$ for the smallest $k - r$ eigenvalues, that is, for $j = r + 1, r + 2, \ldots, k$. We can use the (estimated) eigenvalues, say $\hat{\lambda}_1 > \hat{\lambda}_2 > \cdots > \hat{\lambda}_k$, to test hypotheses about the rank of Π. For example, the hypothesis H_0: $r \leq r_0$ versus the alternative H_1: $r_0 < r \leq k$, can be tested using the statistic

$$\lambda_{\text{trace}}(r_0) = -T \sum_{j=r_0+1}^{k} \log(1 - \hat{\lambda}_j). \tag{9.52}$$

This test is the so-called **trace test**. It checks whether the smallest $k - r_0$ eigenvalues are significantly different from zero. Furthermore, we can test $H_0\colon r \leq r_0$ versus the more restrictive alternative $H_1\colon r = r_0 + 1$ using

$$\lambda_{\max}(r_0) = -T\log(1 - \hat{\lambda}_{r_0+1}). \tag{9.53}$$

This alternative test is called the **maximum eigenvalue test**, as it is based on the estimated $(r_0 + 1)$th largest eigenvalue.

The two tests described here are likelihood ratio tests (see Chapter 6), but do not have the usual Chi-squared distributions. Instead, the appropriate distributions are multivariate extensions of the Dickey–Fuller distributions. As with the unit root tests, the percentiles of the distributions depend on whether a constant and a time trend are included. Critical values for the three most relevant cases are presented in Table 9.9. Using standard numbering (e.g. Pesaran, 2015, Section 22.9), Case II assumes that there are no deterministic trends and includes r intercepts in the cointegrating relationships. This is the appropriate choice if none of the data series appears to have a trend. Case III is most common and is based on the inclusion of k unrestricted intercepts in the VAR, which implies $k - r$ separate deterministic trends and r intercepts in the cointegrating vectors. Case IV has unrestricted intercepts and r restricted trends (in the cointegrating relationships). Case I (not included) has no deterministic components in the model and is highly uncommon. The critical values depend upon $k - r_0$, the number of nonstationary components under the null hypothesis. Note that when $k - r_0 = 1$ the two test statistics are identical and thus have the same distribution.

Table 9.9 Critical values Johansen's LR tests for cointegration (Pesaran, Shin and Smith, 2000)

	λ_{trace}-statistic $H_0\colon r \leq r_0$ vs $H_1\colon r > r_0$		λ_{max}-statistic $H_0\colon r \leq r_0$ vs $H_1\colon r = r_0 + 1$	
$k - r_0$	5%	10%	5%	10%
Case II: restricted intercepts in VAR (in cointegrating relations only)				
1	9.16	7.53	9.16	7.53
2	20.18	17.88	15.87	13.81
3	34.87	31.93	22.04	19.86
4	53.48	49.95	28.27	25.80
5	75.98	71.81	34.40	31.73
Case III: unrestricted intercepts in VAR				
1	8.07	6.50	8.07	6.50
2	17.86	15.75	14.88	12.98
3	31.54	28.78	21.12	19.02
4	48.88	45.70	27.42	24.99
5	70.49	66.23	33.64	31.02
Case IV: unrestricted intercepts and restricted trends in VAR				
1	12.39	10.55	12.39	10.55
2	25.77	23.08	19.22	17.18
3	42.34	39.34	25.42	27.10
4	63.00	59.16	31.79	29.13
5	87.17	82.88	37.86	35.04

There are many studies that show that the small sample properties of the test statistics in (9.52) and (9.53) differ substantially from the asymptotic properties. As a result, the tests are biased towards finding cointegration too often when asymptotic critical values are used (see Cheung and Lai, 1993). A small sample correction, which is now commonly used, was suggested by Ahn and Reinsel (1990) and Reimers (1992) and implies that the test statistics are multiplied by a factor $(T - pk)/T$, where p denotes the number of lags in the VAR model. A more accurate correction factor is derived in Johansen (2002).

The outcomes of the trace test or maximum eigenvalue test should be used to decide upon the cointegrating rank r in the VAR. Given a value of r, the model parameters are then estimated by maximum likelihood, imposing the reduced rank restriction in (9.51). In practice, choosing r is often a difficult decision. In addition to the lag length p, the test outcomes will depend upon the deterministic components that are included in the VAR (see Hjelm and Johansson, 2005, for a discussion of pitfalls and a Monte Carlo study). Moreover, even though the short-run dynamics in (9.50) are asymptotically irrelevant, they are often important in small samples. Also note that the null hypothesis of a unit root is not always reasonable from an economic point of view. Finally, all results are only valid under the assumption of constant model parameters, which excludes the possibility of structural breaks or other sources of parameter nonconstancy. Juselius (2006, Chapter 8) provides more discussion on these issues. For empirical work, she advises that as much additional information as possible be used deciding upon the cointegrating rank, for example by making a graph of the (supposedly) cointegrating relations and taking the economic interpretability of the results into account.

It is important to realize that the parameters γ and β are not uniquely identified in the sense that different combinations of γ and β can produce the same matrix $\Pi = \gamma\beta'$. This is because $\gamma\beta' = \gamma PP^{-1}\beta'$ for any invertible $r \times r$ matrix P. In other words, what the data can determine is the space spanned by the columns of β, the cointegration space and the space spanned by γ. Consequently, the cointegrating vectors in β have to be normalized in some way to obtain unique cointegrating relationships. Often, it is hoped that these relationships are so-called 'structural' cointegrating relationships that have a sensible economic interpretation. In general, it may not be possible statistically to identify these structural cointegrating relationships from the estimated β matrix; see Davidson (2000, Section 16.6) for a discussion.

9.5.4 Illustration: Long-run Purchasing Power Parity (Part 3)

In this subsection we continue our previous analysis concerning long-run purchasing power parity. We shall analyse the existence of one or more cointegrating relationships between the three variables s_t, p_t and p_t^*, using Johansen's technique described above. The first step in this procedure is the determination of p, the maximum order of the lags in the autoregressive representation given in (9.42). It appears that, in general, too few lags in the model lead to rejection of the null hypotheses too easily, whereas too many lags in the model decrease the power of the tests. This indicates that there is some optimal lag length. In addition to p, we have to decide upon whether to include a time trend in (9.42) or not. Given that the two log price series are clearly trended, it makes sense to include one or more deterministic trends in the model. On the other hand, the inclusion of a deterministic trend in the cointegrating relationship itself does not seem to be sensible from an economic point of view. We therefore include three unrestricted intercepts in the VAR.

Table 9.10 Maximum eigenvalue tests for cointegration

Null hypothesis	Alternative	λ_{max}-statistic	5% critical value
$H_0: r = 0$	$H_1: r = 1$	26.759	21.132
$H_0: r \leq 1$	$H_1: r = 2$	6.708	14.265
$H_0: r \leq 2$	$H_1: r = 3$	4.054	3.841

lag length $p = 3$ unrestricted intercepts included $T = 273$
Estimated eigenvalues: 0.0934, 0.0243, 0.0147

In the presence of one cointegrating relationship this would correspond to an intercept in the cointegrating vector and two separate deterministic trends in the VAR. In the absence of cointegration, the intercepts correspond to three deterministic trends. Let us start by considering the case with $p = 3$. (Note that this implies two lags in the first-differenced equation (9.50).) The first step in Johansen's procedure yields the results in Table 9.10. These results present the estimated eigenvalues $\hat{\lambda}_1, \ldots, \hat{\lambda}_k$ $(k = 3)$ in descending order. Recall that each nonzero eigenvalue corresponds to a cointegrating vector. A range of test statistics based on these estimated eigenvalues is given as well. These results indicate that

1. The null hypothesis of no cointegration ($r = 0$) has to be rejected at a 5% level, when tested against the hypothesis of one cointegrating vector ($r = 1$), because 26.759 exceeds the critical value of 21.132.
2. The null hypothesis of zero or one cointegrating vector ($r \leq 1$) cannot be rejected against the alternative of two cointegrating relationships ($r = 2$).
3. The null hypothesis of two or fewer cointegrating vectors is marginally rejected against the alternative of $r = 3$. Recall that $r = 3$ corresponds to stationarity of each of the three series.

Given our experience with the univariate tests in Section 8.5, we are aware that the test results may be sensitive to the number of lags that is included. Most importantly, a 12th lag often appears important when dealing with monthly price series. We therefore repeat the Johansen test procedure, but now we choose $p = 13$. What is quite clear from the results in Table 9.11 is that the evidence in favour of one or two cointegrating vectors is weak. The first test that considers the null hypothesis of no cointegration ($r = 0$) versus the alternative of one cointegrating relationship ($r = 1$) does not lead to rejection of the null. Suppose we continue our analysis despite our reservations, while we decide that the number of cointegrating vectors is equal to one ($r = 1$). The next part of the results

Table 9.11 Maximum eigenvalue tests for cointegration

Null hypothesis	Alternative	λ_{max}-statistic	5% critical value
$H_0: r = 0$	$H_1: r = 1$	16.942	21.132
$H_0: r \leq 1$	$H_1: r = 2$	5.087	14.265
$H_0: r \leq 2$	$H_1: r = 3$	3.359	3.841

lag length $p = 13$ unrestricted intercepts included $T = 263$
Estimated eigenvalues: 0.0624; 0.0192; 0.0127

Table 9.12 Johansen estimation results

Estimated cointegrating vector		
Variable		Normalized
s_t	6.191	1.000
p_t	−59.782	−9.657
p_t^*	62.989	10.174

based on VAR with $p = 13$

consists of the estimated cointegrating vector β, presented in Table 9.12. The normalized cointegrating vector is given in the third column and corresponds to

$$s_t = 9.656p_t - 10.174p_t^*, \tag{9.54}$$

which does not seem to correspond to an economically interpretable long-run relationship.

As the conclusion that there exists one cointegrating relationship between our three variables is most probably incorrect, we do not pursue this example any further. To appropriately test for long-run purchasing power parity via the Johansen procedure, we will probably need longer time series. Alternatively, some authors use several sets of countries simultaneously and apply panel data cointegration techniques (see Chapter 10). Another problem may lie in measuring the two price indices in an accurate way, comparable across the two countries.

9.6 Illustration: Money Demand and Inflation

One of the advantages of cointegration in multivariate time series models is that it may help improving forecasts. The reason is that forecasts from a cointegrated system are tied together by virtue of the existence of one or more long-run relationships. Typically, this advantage is realized when forecasting over medium or long horizons (compare Engle and Yoo, 1987). Hoffman and Rasche (1996) and Lin and Tsay (1996) empirically examine the forecast performance in a cointegrated system. In this section, based on the Hoffman and Rasche study, we consider an empirical example concerning a five-dimensional vector process. The empirical work is based on quarterly data for the United States from 1954:I to 1994:IV ($T = 164$) for the following variables:

m_t	log of real M1 money balances
$infl_t$	quarterly inflation rate (in% per year)
cpr_t	commercial paper rate
y_t	log real GDP (in billions of 1987 dollars)
tbr_t	treasury bill rate

The commercial paper rate and the treasury bill rate are considered as risky and risk-free returns on a quarterly horizon, respectively. The series for M1 and GDP are seasonally adjusted. Although one may dispute the presence of a unit root in some of these series, we shall follow Hoffman and Rasche (1996) and assume that these five variables are all well described by an $I(1)$ process.

A priori one could think of three possible cointegrating relationships governing the long-run behaviour of these variables. First, we can specify an equation for *money demand* as

$$m_t = \alpha_1 + \beta_{14} y_t + \beta_{15} tbr_t + \varepsilon_{1t},$$

where β_{14} denotes the income elasticity and β_{15} the interest rate elasticity. It can be expected that β_{14} is close to unity, corresponding to a unitary income elasticity, and that $\beta_{15} < 0$. Second, if *real* interest rates are stationary, we can expect that

$$infl_t = \alpha_2 + \beta_{25} tbr_t + \varepsilon_{2t}$$

corresponds to a cointegrating relationship with $\beta_{25} = 1$. This is referred to as the Fisher relation, where we are using actual inflation as a proxy for expected inflation.[15] Third, it can be expected that the risk premium, as measured by the difference between the commercial paper rate and the treasury bill rate, is stationary, so that a third cointegrating relationship is given by

$$cpr_t = \alpha_3 + \beta_{35} tbr_t + \varepsilon_{3t}$$

with $\beta_{35} = 1$.

Before proceeding to the vector process of these five variables, let us consider the OLS estimates of the above three regressions. These are presented in Table 9.13. To ease comparison with later results, the layout stresses that the left-hand side variables are included in the cointegrating vector (if it exists) with a coefficient of −1. Note that the OLS standard errors are inappropriate if the variables in the regression are integrated. Except for the risk premium equation, the R^2s are not close to unity, which is an informal requirement for a cointegrating regression. The Durbin–Watson statistics are small, and, if the critical values from Table 9.3 are appropriate, we would reject the null hypothesis of no cointegration at the 5% level for the last two equations but not for the money demand equation. Recall that the critical values in Table 9.3 are based on the assumption that all series are random walks, which may be correct for interest rate series but may be incorrect for money supply and GDP. Alternatively, we can test for a unit root in the

Table 9.13 Univariate cointegrating regressions by OLS (standard errors in parentheses), intercept estimates not reported

	Money demand	Fisher equation	Risk premium
m_t	−1	0	0
$infl_t$	0	−1	0
cpr_t	0	0	−1
y_t	0.423	0	0
	(0.016)		
tbr_t	−0.031	0.558	1.038
	(0.002)	(0.053)	(0.010)
R^2	0.815	0.409	0.984
dw	0.199	0.784	0.705
$ADF(6)$	−3.164	−1.888	−3.975

[15] The real interest rate is defined as the nominal interest rate minus the *expected* inflation rate.

residuals of these regressions by the augmented Dickey–Fuller tests. The results are not very sensitive to the number of lags that are included, and the test statistics for six lags are reported in Table 9.13. The 5% asymptotic critical value from Table 9.2 is given by −3.77 for the regression involving three variables and −3.37 for the regressions with two variables. Only for the risk premium equation can we thus reject the null hypothesis of no cointegration.

So far, the empirical evidence for the existence of the suggested cointegrating relationships between the five variables is somewhat mixed. Only for the risk premium equation do we find an R^2 close to unity, a sufficiently high Durbin–Watson statistic and a significant rejection of the ADF test for a unit root in the residuals. For the two other regressions there is little reason to reject the null hypothesis of no cointegration. Potentially this is caused by a lack of power of the tests that we employ, and it is possible that a multivariate vector analysis provides stronger evidence for the existence of cointegrating relationships between these five variables. Some additional information is provided if we plot the residuals from these three regressions. If the regressions correspond to cointegration, these residuals can be interpreted as long-run equilibrium errors and should be stationary and fluctuating around zero. For the three regressions, the residuals are displayed in Figures 9.1, 9.2 and 9.3, respectively. Although a visual inspection of these graphs is ambiguous, the residuals of the money demand and risk premium regressions could be argued to be stationary on the basis of these graphs. For the Fisher equation, the current sample period provides less evidence of mean reversion.

The first step in the Johansen approach involves testing for the cointegrating rank r. To compute these tests we need to choose the maximum lag length p in the vector autoregressive model. Choosing p too small will invalidate the tests, and choosing p too large

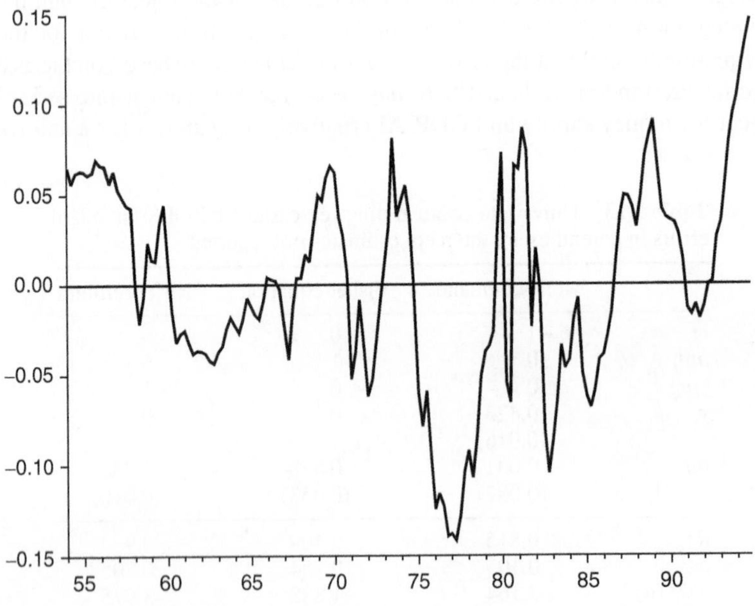

Figure 9.1 Residuals of money demand regression.

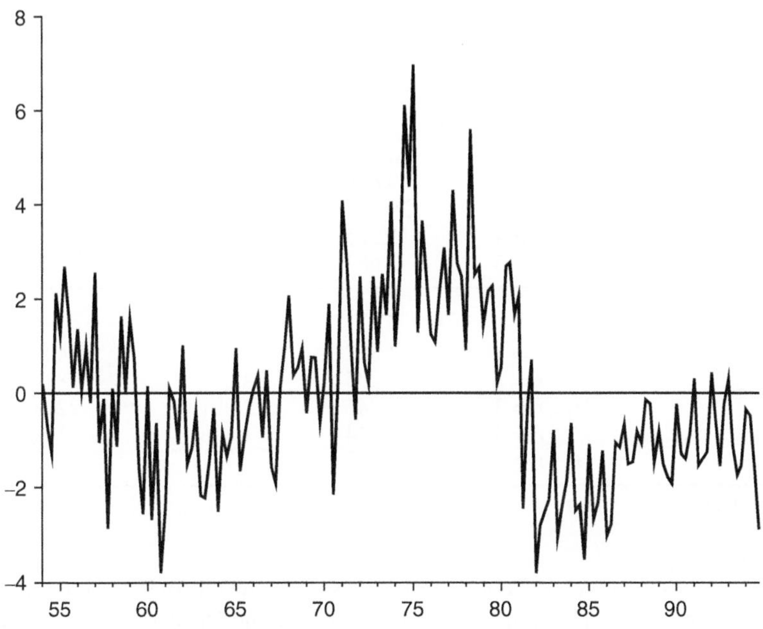

Figure 9.2 Residuals of Fisher regression.

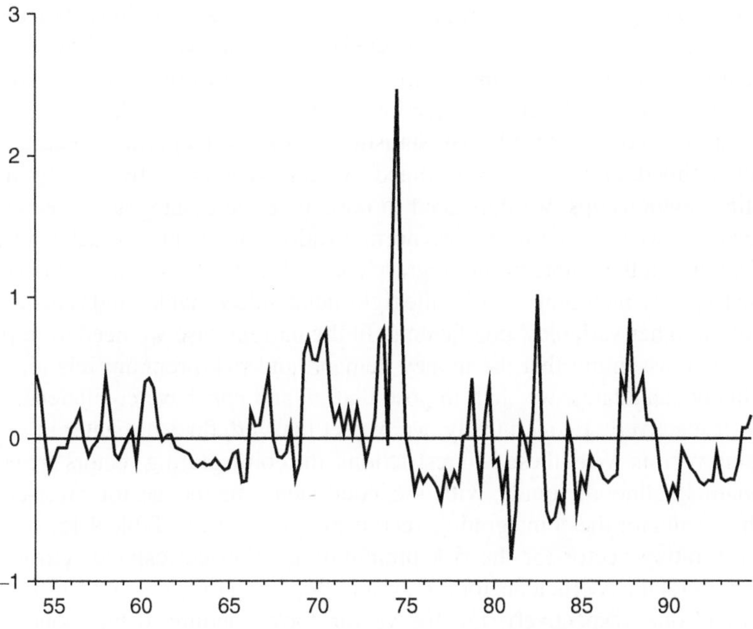

Figure 9.3 Residuals of risk premium regression.

Table 9.14 Trace and maximum eigenvalue tests for cointegration

Null hypothesis	Alternative	Test statistic $p = 5$	$p = 6$	5% critical value
		λ_{trace}-statistic		
$H_0: r = 0$	$H_1: r \geq 1$	104.263	120.861	76.97
$H_0: r \leq 1$	$H_1: r \geq 2$	59.406	71.347	54.07
$H_0: r \leq 2$	$H_1: r \geq 3$	29.171	36.660	34.19
$H_0: r \leq 3$	$H_1: r \geq 4$	11.925	14.659	20.26
$H_0: r \leq 4$	$H_1: r = 5$	3.602	2.761	9.16
		λ_{max}-statistic		
$H_0: r = 0$	$H_1: r = 1$	44.857	49.513	34.81
$H_0: r \leq 1$	$H_1: r = 2$	30.235	34.687	28.59
$H_0: r \leq 2$	$H_1: r = 3$	17.246	22.001	22.30
$H_0: r \leq 3$	$H_1: r = 4$	8.324	11.898	15.89
$H_0: r \leq 4$	$H_1: r = 5$	3.602	2.761	9.16

restricted intercepts included $T = 159$ (158)

may result in a loss of power. In Table 9.14 we present the results of the cointegrating rank tests for $p = 5$ and $p = 6$. The results show that there is some sensitivity with respect to the choice of the maximum lag length in the vector autoregressions, although qualitatively the conclusion changes only marginally. At the 5% level all tests reject the null hypotheses of no or one cointegrating relationship. The tests do not reject the null hypothesis that $r \leq 2$, with a marginal exception for the trace statistic when $p = 6$. As before, we need to choose the cointegrating rank r from these results. The most obvious choice is $r = 2$, although one could consider $r = 3$ as well (see Hoffman and Rasche, 1996).

If we restrict the rank of the long-run matrix to be equal to two, we can estimate the cointegrating vectors and the error-correction model by maximum likelihood, following the Johansen procedure. Recall that statistically the cointegrating vectors are not individually defined, only the space spanned by these vectors is. To identify individual cointegrating relationships, we thus need to normalize the cointegrating vectors somehow. When $r = 2$ we need to impose two normalization constraints on each cointegrating vector. Note that in the cointegrating regressions in Table 9.13 a number of constraints are imposed a priori, including a -1 for the right-hand-side variables and zero restrictions on some of the other variables' coefficients. In the current case we need to impose two restrictions and, assuming that the money demand and risk premium relationships are the most likely candidates, we shall impose that m_t and cpr_t have coefficients of -1, 0 and 0, -1, respectively. Economically, we expect that $infl_t$ does not enter in any of the cointegrating vectors. With these two restrictions, the cointegrating vectors are estimated by maximum likelihood, jointly with the coefficients in the vector error-correction model. The results for the cointegrating vectors are presented in Table 9.15.

The cointegrating vector for the risk premium equation corresponds closely to our expectations, with the coefficients for $infl_t$, y_t and tbr_t being insignificantly different from zero, zero and one, respectively. For the vector corresponding to the money demand equation, $infl_t$ appears to enter the equation significantly. Recall that m_t corresponds

Table 9.15 ML estimates of cointegrating vectors (after normalization) based on VAR with $p = 6$ (standard errors in parentheses), intercept estimates not reported

	Money demand	Risk premium
m_t	−1	0
$infl_t$	−0.023	0.037
	(0.006)	(0.028)
cpr_t	0	−1
y_t	0.424	−0.122
	(0.037)	(0.174)
tbr_t	−0.028	1.018
	(0.005)	(0.023)

loglikelihood value: 773.0678

to *real* money demand, which should normally not depend upon the inflation rate. The coefficient estimate of −0.023 implies that, ceteris paribus, *nominal* money demand ($m_t + infl_t$) increases somewhat less than proportionally with the inflation rate.

It is possible to test our a priori cointegrating vectors by using likelihood ratio tests. These tests require that the model is re-estimated, imposing some additional restrictions on the cointegrating vectors. This way we can test the following hypotheses:[16]

$$H_0^a: \beta_{12} = 0, \quad \beta_{14} = 1;$$
$$H_0^b: \beta_{22} = \beta_{24} = 0, \quad \beta_{25} = 1; \text{ and}$$
$$H_0^c: \beta_{12} = \beta_{22} = \beta_{24} = 0, \quad \beta_{14} = \beta_{25} = 1,$$

where β_{12} denotes the coefficient for $infl_t$ in the money demand equation and β_{22} and β_{24} are the coefficients for inflation and GDP in the risk premium equation, respectively. The loglikelihood values for the complete model, estimated imposing H_0^a, H_0^b and H_0^c respectively, are given by 766.9174, 763.7389, 770.3043. The likelihood ratio test statistics, defined as twice the difference in loglikelihood values, for the three null hypotheses are thus given by 12.301, 18.658 and 5.527. The asymptotic distributions under the null hypotheses of the test statistics are the usual Chi-squared distributions, with degrees of freedom given by the number of restrictions that are tested (see Chapter 6). The restrictions imposed by the risk premium equation, as reflected in H_0^b, are not rejected by the likelihood ratio test. On the other hand, the restrictions imposed by the money demand equation in H_0^a are clearly rejected and, as a result, also the joint set of restrictions in H_0^c is rejected.

As a last step we consider the vector error-correction model for this system. This corresponds to a VAR of order $p - 1 = 5$ for the first-differenced series, with the inclusion of two error-correction terms in each equation, one for each cointegrating vector. Note that the number of parameters estimated in this vector error-correction model is well

[16] The tests here are actually overidentifying restrictions tests (see Chapter 5). We interpret them as regular hypotheses tests, taking the a priori restrictions in Table 9.15 as given.

Table 9.16 Estimated matrix of adjustment coefficients (standard errors in parentheses), $*$ indicates significance at the 5% level

	Error-correction term	
Equation	$ecm1_{t-1}$	$ecm2_{t-1}$
Δm_t	0.022*	0.009*
	(0.011)	(0.003)
$\Delta infl_t$	1.672	−1.216*
	(2.367)	(0.557)
Δcpr_t	−2.591*	0.732*
	(1.199)	(0.282)
Δy_t	0.066*	−0.001
	(0.014)	(0.003)
Δtbr_t	−1.577	0.340
	(1.082)	(0.255)

above 100, so we shall concentrate on a limited part of the results only. The two error-correction terms are given by

$$ecm1_t = -m_t - 0.023\,infl_t + 0.424y_t - 0.028tbr_t + 3.376;$$

$$ecm2_t = -cpr_t + 0.037\,infl_t - 0.122y_t + 1.018tbr_t + 1.456.$$

The adjustment coefficients in the 5×2 matrix γ, with their associated standard errors, are reported in Table 9.16. The long-run money demand equation contributes significantly to the short-run movements of money demand, income and the commercial paper rate. The short-run behaviour of money demand, inflation and the commercial paper rate appears to be significantly affected by the long-run risk premium relationship. There is no statistical evidence that the treasury bill rate adjusts to any deviation from long-run equilibria, so that it could be treated as weakly exogenous.

Wrap-up

Dynamic models with stationary variables can be parametrized in different ways, corresponding to, for example, an error-correction mechanism or a partial adjustment model. In fact, such models arise as restrictions on a general vector autoregressive (VAR) model, where the entire set of variables is explained from their past. When the variables are nonstationary due to the presence of a unit root, care is warranted. For example, one has to be careful to prevent spurious relationships, which arise when two or more independent nonstationary series are spuriously related owing to the fact they are both trended. A low Durbin–Watson statistic is an important flag. Whereas first-differencing may produce stationary series, modelling the first-differenced series may ignore important information contained in the levels of the series. This occurs when the series are cointegrated. That is, if a linear relationship exists between two or more nonstationary variables that is stationary. This means that the series share one or more common trends. In these cases, a vector autoregressive model of the level variables can be rewritten as an error-correction model for the first-differenced series. The error-correction terms capture the deviations from the long-run equilibria. The Johansen procedure is the most common approach used for testing for the number of cointegrating relationships and for estimating the vector error-correction model. Juselius (2006) provides an excellent discussion of this approach.

Exercises

Exercise 9.1 (Cointegration Theory)

a. Assume that the two series y_t and x_t are $I(1)$ and assume that both $y_t - \beta_1 x_t$ and $y_t - \beta_2 x_t$ are $I(0)$. Show that this implies that $\beta_1 = \beta_2$, i.e. there can be only one unique cointegrating parameter.

b. Explain intuitively why the Durbin-Watson statistic in a regression of the $I(1)$ variables y_t upon x_t is informative about the question of cointegration between y_t and x_t.

c. Explain what is meant by 'superconsistency'.

d. Consider three $I(1)$ variables y_t, x_t and z_t. Assume that y_t and x_t are cointegrated, and that x_t and z_t are cointegrated. Does this imply that y_t and z_t are also cointegrated? Why (not)?

Exercise 9.2 (Cointegration)

Consider the following very simple relationship between aggregate savings S_t and aggregate income Y_t:

$$S_t = \alpha + \beta Y_t + \varepsilon_t, \quad t = 1, \ldots, T. \tag{9.55}$$

For some country this relationship is estimated by OLS over the years 1956–2005 ($T = 50$). The results are given in Table 9.17.

Table 9.17 Aggregate savings explained from aggregate income; OLS results

Variable	Coefficient	Standard error	t-ratio
constant	38.90	4.570	8.51
income	0.098	0.009	10.77

$T = 50 \quad s = 22.57 \quad R^2 = 0.93 \quad dw = 0.70$

Assume, for the moment, that the series S_t and Y_t are *stationary*. (Hint: if needed, consult Chapter 4 for the first set of questions.)

a. How would you interpret the coefficient estimate of 0.098 for the income variable?

b. Explain why the results indicate that there may be a problem of positive autocorrelation. Can you give arguments why, in economic models, positive autocorrelation is more likely than negative autocorrelation?

c. What are the effects of autocorrelation on the properties of the OLS estimator? Think about unbiasedness, consistency and the BLUE property.

d. Describe two different approaches to handle the autocorrelation problem in the above case. Which one would you prefer?

From now on, assume that S_t and Y_t are nonstationary $I(1)$ series.

e. Are there indications that the relationship between the two variables is 'spurious'?

f. Explain what we mean by 'spurious regressions'.

g. Are there indications that there is a cointegrating relationship between S_t and Y_t?

h. Explain what we mean by a 'cointegrating relationship'.

i. Describe two different tests that can be used to test the null hypothesis that S_t and Y_t are not cointegrated.

j. How do you interpret the coefficient estimate of 0.098 under the hypothesis that S_t and Y_t are cointegrated?

k. Are there reasons to correct for autocorrelation in the error term when we estimate a cointegrating regression?

l. Explain intuitively why the estimator for a cointegrating parameter is superconsistent.

m. Assuming that S_t and Y_t are cointegrated, describe what we mean by an error-correction mechanism. Give an example. What do we learn from it?

n. How can we consistently estimate an error-correction model?

Exercise 9.3 (Cointegration – Empirical)

In this exercise we employ quarterly data on UK nominal consumption and income, for 1971:I to 1985:II ($T = 58$). Part of these data was used in Exercise 8.3.

a. Test for a unit root in the consumption series using several augmented Dickey–Fuller tests.

b. Perform a regression by OLS explaining consumption from income. Test for cointegration using two different tests.

c. Perform a regression by OLS explaining income from consumption. Test for cointegration.

d. Compare the estimation results and R^2s from the last two regressions.

e. Determine the error-correction term from one of the two regressions and estimate an error-correction model for the change in consumption. Test whether the adjustment coefficient is zero.

f. Repeat the last question for the change in income. What do you conclude?

Exercise 9.4 (Cointegration – Empirical)

This exercise uses monthly data on the exchange rate between the US dollar and UK pound sterling and the price indexes for these two countries, also used in Exercise 8.4.

a. Test whether the log of the CPI ratio is stationary using a variety of unit root tests.

b. Test for cointegration between the log exchange rate and the log of the CPI ratio using the Engle–Granger methodology (along the lines of Section 9.3). Be careful on the choice of the number of lags.

c. Reverse the role of the two variables in the previous question, and repeat the analysis. Interpret and compare.

d. Test for cointegration between the log exchange rate, and the logs of the two price indexes, using the Engle–Granger methodology.

e. Use the Johansen approach to test for the number of cointegrating relationships between the three variables. Motivate the inclusion of (restricted or unrestricted) intercepts.

f. What is your conclusion on the validity of long-run purchasing power parity between the United Kingdom and the USA? Depending upon our results of **d** and **e** you may want to estimate or test additional specifications.

10 Models Based on Panel Data

A panel data set contains repeated observations over the same units (individuals, households and firms), collected over a number of periods. Although panel data are typically collected at the micro-economic level, it has become increasingly common to pool individual time series of a number of countries or industries and analyse them simultaneously. The availability of repeated observations on the same units allows economists to specify and estimate more complicated and more realistic models than a single cross-section or a single time series would do. The disadvantages are more of a practical nature: because we repeatedly observe the same units, it is usually no longer appropriate to assume that different observations are independent. This may complicate the analysis, particularly in nonlinear and dynamic models. Furthermore, panel data sets very often suffer from missing observations. Even if these observations are missing in a random way, the standard analysis has to be adjusted (see Section 10.8).

This chapter provides an introduction to the analysis of panel data. A simple linear panel data model is presented in Section 10.1, and some advantages compared with cross-sectional or time series data are discussed in the context of this model. Section 10.2 focuses on the static linear model and discusses estimation under fixed effects and random effects assumptions, including instrumental variables estimators and the Fama–MacBeth approach. Attention is also given to heteroskedasticity and serial correlation in the error terms. An empirical illustration concerning the estimation of a wage equation is provided in Section 10.3. The introduction of a lagged dependent variable in the linear model complicates consistent estimation, and, as will be discussed in Section 10.4, instrumental variables procedures or GMM provide interesting alternatives. Section 10.5 provides an empirical example on the estimation of a partial adjustment model for a firm's capital structure. Increasingly, panel data approaches are used in a macro-economic context to investigate the dynamic properties of economic variables. Section 10.6 discusses the recent literature on unit root and cointegration tests in heterogeneous panels. In micro-economic applications, the model of interest often involves limited dependent variables, and panel data extensions of logit, probit and tobit models are discussed in Section 10.7. The problems associated with incomplete panel data and selection bias are discussed in Section 10.8, while Section 10.9 concludes this chapter with a discussion on pseudo panel data and repeated cross-sections. Extensive discussions of the econometrics of panel data can be found in Arellano (2003), Cameron and Trivedi (2005), Wooldridge (2010), Baltagi (2013), Hsiao (2014) and Pesaran (2015).

10.1 Introduction to Panel Data Modelling

An important advantage of panel data compared with time series or cross-sectional data sets is that they allow identification of certain parameters or questions, without the need to make restrictive assumptions. For example, panel data make it possible to analyse *changes* on an *individual* level. Consider a situation in which the average consumption level rises by 2% from one year to another. Panel data can identify whether this rise is the result of, for example, an increase of 2% for all individuals or an increase of 4% for approximately one-half of the individuals and no change for the other half (or any other combination). That is, panel data are suitable not only to model or explain why individual units behave differently but also to model why a given unit behaves differently at different time periods (e.g. because of a different past).

We shall, hereafter, index all variables with an i for the individual[1] ($i = 1, \ldots, N$) and a t for the time period ($t = 1, \ldots, T$). The standard linear regression model can then be written as

$$y_{it} = \beta_0 + x_{it}'\beta + \varepsilon_{it}, \tag{10.1}$$

where x_{it} is a K-dimensional vector of explanatory variables, which – for reasons that will become clear later – does not contain an intercept term.[2] This model imposes that the intercept β_0 and the slope coefficients in β are identical for all individuals and time periods. The error term in (10.1) varies over individuals and time and captures all unobservable factors that affect y_{it}. To estimate this model by OLS, the usual conditions are required to achieve unbiasedness, consistency or efficiency (see Chapters 2, 4 and 5). For example, if $E\{\varepsilon_{it}\} = 0$ and $E\{x_{it}\varepsilon_{it}\} = 0$, the OLS estimator is consistent for β_0 and β under weak regularity conditions. Given that we repeatedly observe the same individuals, however, it is typically unrealistic to assume that the error terms from different periods are uncorrelated. For example, a person's wage will be affected by unobservable characteristics that vary little over time. As a result, routinely computed standard errors for OLS, based on the assumption of i.i.d. error terms, tend to be misleading in panel data applications. Moreover, OLS is likely to be inefficient relative to an estimator that exploits the correlation over time in ε_{it}.

A frequently employed panel data model assumes that

$$\varepsilon_{it} = \alpha_i + u_{it}, \tag{10.2}$$

where u_{it} is assumed to be homoskedastic and not correlated over time. The component α_i is time invariant and homoskedastic across individuals. The model specified by

[1] While we refer to the cross-sectional units as individuals, they could also refer to other units like firms, countries, industries, households or assets.

[2] The elements in β are indexed as β_1 to β_K, where the first element, unlike in the previous chapters, does not refer to the intercept.

(10.1) and (10.2) is referred to as a one-way error components or **random effects model**, and we shall discuss it in more detail later. Estimation by (feasible) generalized least squares exploiting the imposed error structure (which implies that the serial correlation in ε_{it} can completely be attributed to α_i) typically leads to a more efficient estimator for β_0 and β than ordinary least squares.

The assumption that $E\{x_{it}\varepsilon_{it}\} = 0$ states that the observable regressors in x_{it} are uncorrelated with the unobservable characteristics in both α_i and u_{it}. This means that the explanatory variables are exogenous. In many applications this assumption is considered restrictive, and there are reasons to believe that $E\{x_{it}\alpha_i\} \neq 0$. That is, the unobserved heterogeneity in α_i is correlated with one or more of the explanatory variables. For example, in a wage equation a person's unobserved ability is likely to affect wages (y_{it}), but also a person's education level (included in x_{it}). In a firm-level investment equation, unobserved firm characteristics (e.g. managerial quality) may affect investment decisions (y_{it}) as well as characteristics in x_{it} (e.g. the cost of capital). In a cross-sectional context, the standard approach to handle this problem is the use of instrumental variables (see Chapter 5). With panel data, it is possible to exploit the particular nature of the data owing to the availability of repeated observations on the same individuals.

In a **fixed effects model**, this problem is addressed by including individual-specific intercept terms in the model. In this case, we write the model as

$$y_{it} = \alpha_i + x_{it}'\beta + u_{it}, \tag{10.3}$$

where α_i ($i = 1, \ldots, N$) are fixed unknown constants that are estimated along with β, and where u_{it} is typically assumed to be i.i.d. over individuals and time. The overall intercept term β_0 is omitted, as it is subsumed by the individual intercepts α_i. It is common to refer to α_i as fixed (individual) effects. The fixed effects α_i capture all (un)observable time-invariant differences across individuals. In this approach, consistent estimation does not impose that α_i and x_{it} are uncorrelated.

The possibility of treating the α_is as fixed parameters has some great advantages, but also some disadvantages. Most panel data models are estimated under either the fixed effects or the random effects assumption, and we shall discuss this extensively in Section 10.2. First, the next two subsections discuss some potential advantages of panel data in more detail.

10.1.1 Efficiency of Parameter Estimators

Because panel data sets are typically larger than cross-sectional or time series data sets, and explanatory variables vary over two dimensions (individuals and time) rather than one, estimators based on panel data are quite often more accurate than from other sources. Even with identical sample sizes, the use of a panel data set will often yield more efficient estimators than a series of independent cross-sections (where different units are sampled in each period). To illustrate this, consider the following special case of the random effects model in (10.1) and (10.2) where we only include time dummies, that is,

$$y_{it} = \mu_t + \alpha_i + u_{it}, \tag{10.4}$$

where each μ_t is an unknown parameter corresponding to the population mean in period t. Suppose we are not interested in the mean μ_t in a particular period, but in the change of μ_t from one period to another. In general the variance of the efficient estimator for $\mu_t - \mu_s (s \neq t)$, $\hat{\mu}_t - \hat{\mu}_s$, is given by

$$V\{\hat{\mu}_t - \hat{\mu}_s\} = V\{\hat{\mu}_t\} + V\{\hat{\mu}_s\} - 2\,\text{cov}\{\hat{\mu}_t, \hat{\mu}_s\}$$

with $\hat{\mu}_t = 1/N \sum_{i=1}^{N} y_{it}$ $(t = 1, \ldots, T)$. Typically, if a panel data set is used, the covariance between $\hat{\mu}_t$ and $\hat{\mu}_s$ will be positive. For example, under the random effects assumptions of (10.2) it equals σ_α^2/N. However, if two independent cross-sectional data sets are used, different periods will contain different individuals, so $\hat{\mu}_t$ and $\hat{\mu}_s$ will have zero covariance. In other words, if one is interested in changes from one period to another, a panel will yield more efficient estimators than a series of cross-sections.

Note, however, that the reverse is also true, in the sense that repeated cross-sections will be more informative than a panel when one is interested in a sum or average of μ_t over several periods. At a more intuitive level, panel data may provide better information because the *same* individuals are repeatedly observed. On the other hand, having the same individuals rather than different ones may imply less variation in the explanatory variables and thus relatively inefficient estimators. A comprehensive analysis on the choice between a pure panel, a pure cross-section and a combination of these two data sources is provided in Nijman and Verbeek (1990). Their results indicate that, when exogenous variables are included in the model and one is interested in the parameters that measure the effects of these variables, a panel data set will typically yield more efficient estimators than a series of cross-sections with the same number of observations.

10.1.2 Identification of Parameters

A second advantage of the availability of panel data is that it reduces identification problems. Although this advantage may come under different headings, in many cases it involves identification in the presence of endogenous regressors or measurement error, robustness to omitted variables and the identification of individual dynamics.

Let us start with an illustration of the last of these. There are two alternative explanations for the often observed phenomenon that individuals who have experienced an event in the past are more likely to experience that event in the future. The first explanation is that the fact that an individual has experienced the event changes his or her preferences, constraints, etc., in such a way that he or she is more likely to experience that event in the future. The second explanation says that individuals may differ in unobserved characteristics that influence the probability of experiencing the event (but are not influenced by the experience of the event). Heckman (1978a) terms the former explanation 'true state dependence' and the latter 'spurious state dependence'. A well-known example concerns the 'event' of being unemployed. The availability of panel data will ease the problem of distinguishing between true and spurious state dependence, because individual histories are observed and can be incorporated in the model.

As discussed in Section 3.2, omitted variable bias arises if a variable that is correlated with the included variables is excluded from the model. A classical example is the estimation of production functions (Mundlak, 1961). In many cases, especially in the case of small firms, it is desirable to include management quality as an input in the production function. In general, however, management quality is unobservable. Suppose that a production function of the Cobb–Douglas type is given by

$$y_{it} = \beta_0 + x_{it}'\beta + m_i\gamma + u_{it}, \tag{10.5}$$

where y_{it} denotes log output, x_{it} is a K-dimensional vector of log inputs, both for firm i at time t, and m_i denotes the management quality for firm i (which is assumed to be constant over time). The unobserved variable m_i is expected to be negatively correlated with the other inputs in x_{it}, since a high-quality management will probably result in a more efficient use of inputs. Therefore, unless $\gamma = 0$, deletion of m_i from (10.5) will lead to biased estimates of the other parameters in the model. If panel data are available, this problem can be resolved by introducing a firm-specific effect $\alpha_i = \beta_0 + m_i\gamma$ and considering this as a fixed unknown parameter. In a similar way, a fixed time effect can be included in the model to capture the effect of all (observed and unobserved) variables that do not vary over the individual units. This illustrates the proposition that panel data can reduce the effects of omitted variable bias, or – in other words – estimators from a panel data set may be more robust to an incomplete model specification.

Finally, in many cases panel data will provide 'internal' instruments for regressors that are endogenous or subject to measurement error. This is because transformations of the original variables can often be argued to be uncorrelated with the model's error term and correlated with the explanatory variables themselves and no external instruments are needed. For example, if x_{it} is correlated with α_i, it can be argued that $x_{it} - \bar{x}_i$, where $\bar{x}_i$ is the time average for individual i, is uncorrelated with α_i and provides a valid instrument for x_{it}. More generally, estimating the model under the fixed effects assumption eliminates α_i from the error term and, consequently, eliminates all endogeneity problems relating to it. This will be illustrated in the next section. An extensive discussion of the benefits and limitations of panel data is provided in Hsiao (2014, Chapter 13).

10.2 The Static Linear Model

This section presents the static linear model in a panel data setting. We start with the fixed effects model, and pay attention to the within estimator and the first-difference estimator. Next, we present the random effects model. Subsequently, we discuss the choice between fixed effects and random effects, as well as alternative estimation procedures that can be considered to be somewhere between a fixed effects and random effects treatment. This section also pays attention to goodness-of-fit, heteroskedasticity and autocorrelation, and to robust covariance matrix estimation. Finally, we discuss the Fama–MacBeth approach, which has become popular in finance applications.

10.2.1 The Fixed Effects Model

The fixed effects model is simply a linear regression model in which the intercept terms vary over the individual units i, that is,

$$y_{it} = \alpha_i + x_{it}'\beta + u_{it}, \quad u_{it} \sim IID(0, \sigma_u^2), \tag{10.6}$$

where it is usually assumed that all x_{it} are independent of all u_{it}. We can write this in the usual regression framework by including a dummy variable for each unit i in the model. That is,

$$y_{it} = \sum_{j=1}^{N} \alpha_j d_{ij} + x_{it}'\beta + u_{it}, \tag{10.7}$$

where $d_{ij} = 1$ if $i = j$ and 0 elsewhere. We thus have a set of N dummy variables in the model. The parameters $\alpha_1, \ldots, \alpha_N$ and β can be estimated by ordinary least squares in (10.7). The implied estimator for β is referred to as the **least squares dummy variable (LSDV) estimator**. It may, however, be numerically unattractive to have a regression model with so many regressors. Fortunately one can compute the estimator for β in a simpler way. It can be shown that exactly the same estimate for β is obtained if the regression is performed in deviations from individual means. Essentially, this implies that we eliminate the individual effects α_i first by transforming the data. To see this, first note that

$$\bar{y}_i = \alpha_i + \bar{x}_i'\beta + \bar{u}_i, \tag{10.8}$$

where $\bar{y}_i = T^{-1}\sum_t y_{it}$ and $\bar{x}_i$ and $\bar{u}_i$ are defined in a similar way. Consequently, we can write

$$y_{it} - \bar{y}_i = (x_{it} - \bar{x}_i)'\beta + (u_{it} - \bar{u}_i). \tag{10.9}$$

This is a regression model in deviations from individual means, which does not include the individual effects α_i. The transformation that produces observations in deviations from individual means, as in (10.9), is called the **within transformation**. The OLS estimator for β obtained from this transformed model is often called the **within estimator** or **fixed effects estimator**, and it is exactly identical to the LSDV estimator described earlier. It is given by

$$\hat{\beta}_{FE} = \left(\sum_{i=1}^{N} \sum_{t=1}^{T} (x_{it} - \bar{x}_i)(x_{it} - \bar{x}_i)' \right)^{-1} \sum_{i=1}^{N} \sum_{t=1}^{T} (x_{it} - \bar{x}_i)(y_{it} - \bar{y}_i). \tag{10.10}$$

If it is assumed that *all* x_{it} are independent of *all* u_{it} (compare assumption (A2) from Chapter 2), the fixed effects estimator can be shown to be unbiased for β. If, in addition, normality of u_{it} is imposed, $\hat{\beta}_{FE}$ also has a normal distribution. For consistency,[3] it is required that

$$E\{(x_{it} - \bar{x}_i)u_{it}\} = 0 \tag{10.11}$$

(compare assumption (A7) in Chapters 2 and 5). Sufficient for this is that x_{it} is uncorrelated with u_{it} and that $\bar{x}_i$ has no correlation with the error term. These conditions are in turn implied by

$$E\{x_{it}u_{is}\} = 0 \quad \text{for all } s, t, \tag{10.12}$$

in which case we call x_{it} **strictly exogenous**. A strictly exogenous variable is not allowed to depend upon current, future and past values of the error term. In some applications this may be restrictive. Clearly, it excludes the inclusion of lagged dependent variables in x_{it}, but any x_{it} variable that depends upon the history of y_{it} would also violate the condition. For example, if we are explaining labour supply of an individual, we may want to include years of experience in the model, although obviously experience depends upon the person's labour history. Thus, experience is not strictly exogenous in this context.

With explanatory variables independent of all errors, the N intercepts are estimated unbiasedly as

$$\hat{\alpha}_i = \bar{y}_i - \bar{x}_i'\hat{\beta}_{FE}, \quad i = 1, \ldots, N.$$

[3] Unless stated otherwise, we consider in this chapter consistency for the number of individuals N going to infinity. This corresponds to the common situation that we have panels with large N and small T.

Under assumption (10.11) these estimators are consistent for the fixed effects α_i provided T goes to infinity. The reason why $\hat{\alpha}_i$ is inconsistent for fixed T is clear: when T is fixed, the individual averages $\bar{y}_i$ and $\bar{x}_i$ do not converge to anything if the number of individuals increases.

The covariance matrix for the fixed effects estimator $\hat{\beta}_{FE}$, assuming that u_{it} is i.i.d. across individuals and time with variance σ_u^2, is given by

$$V\{\hat{\beta}_{FE}\} = \sigma_u^2 \left(\sum_{i=1}^{N} \sum_{t=1}^{T} (x_{it} - \bar{x}_i)(x_{it} - \bar{x}_i)' \right)^{-1}. \quad (10.13)$$

Unless T is large, using the standard OLS estimate for the covariance matrix based upon the within regression in (10.9) will underestimate the true variance. The reason is that in this transformed regression the error covariance matrix is singular (as the T transformed errors of each individual add up to zero) and the variance of $u_{it} - \bar{u}_i$ is $(T-1)/T\sigma_u^2$ rather than σ_u^2. A consistent estimator for σ_u^2 is obtained from the sum of squared residuals from the within estimator, divided by $N(T-1)$. Defining

$$\hat{u}_{it} = y_{it} - \hat{\alpha}_i - x_{it}'\hat{\beta}_{FE} = y_{it} - \bar{y}_i - (x_{it} - \bar{x}_i)'\hat{\beta}_{FE},$$

we estimate σ_u^2 as

$$\hat{\sigma}_u^2 = \frac{1}{N(T-1)} \sum_{i=1}^{N} \sum_{t=1}^{T} \hat{u}_{it}^2. \quad (10.14)$$

It is possible to apply the usual degrees of freedom correction, in which case K is subtracted from the denominator. Note that using the standard OLS covariance matrix in model (10.7) with N individual dummies is reliable, because the degrees of freedom correction involves N additional unknown parameters corresponding to the individual intercept terms. Under weak regularity conditions, the fixed effects estimator is asymptotically normal, so that the usual inference procedures can be used (like t and Wald tests).

Essentially, the fixed effects model concentrates on differences 'within' individuals. That is, it is explaining to what extent y_{it} differs from $\bar{y}_i$ and does not explain why $\bar{y}_i$ is different from $\bar{y}_j$. The parametric assumptions about β, on the other hand, impose that a change in a regressor has the same (ceteris paribus) effect, whether it is a change from one period to the other or a change from one individual to another. When interpreting the results, however, from a fixed effects regression, it may be important to realize that the parameters are identified only through the within dimension of the data, that is, through time variation.

10.2.2 The First-difference Estimator

Instead of using the within transformation, the individual effects α_i can also be eliminated by first-differencing (10.6). This results in

$$y_{it} - y_{i,t-1} = (x_{it} - x_{i,t-1})'\beta + (u_{it} - u_{i,t-1})$$

or

$$\Delta y_{it} = \Delta x_{it}'\beta + \Delta u_{it}, \quad (10.15)$$

where $\Delta y_{it} = y_{it} - y_{i,t-1}$. Applying OLS to this equation yields the **first-difference estimator**

$$\hat{\beta}_{FD} = \left(\sum_{i=1}^{N} \sum_{t=2}^{T} \Delta x_{it} \Delta x_{it}' \right)^{-1} \sum_{i=1}^{N} \sum_{t=2}^{T} \Delta x_{it} \Delta y_{it}. \tag{10.16}$$

Consistency of this estimator requires that

$$E\{\Delta x_{it} \Delta u_{it}\} = 0$$

or

$$E\{(x_{it} - x_{i,t-1})(u_{it} - u_{i,t-1})\} = 0. \tag{10.17}$$

This condition is weaker than the strict exogeneity condition in (10.12). For example, it would allow correlation between x_{it} and $u_{i,t-2}$. To compute the standard errors for $\hat{\beta}_{FD}$, it should be taken into account that Δu_{it} exhibits serial correlation. Whereas the conditions for consistency of the first-differences estimator are slightly weaker than those for the within estimator, it is, in general, somewhat less efficient. For $T = 2$, both estimators are identical (see Exercise 10.1). If the two estimators provide very different results, this indicates some kind of misspecification, resulting in violation of assumption (10.12). Laporte and Windmeijer (2005), for example, show that the first-difference estimator and the within estimator can lead to very different estimates of treatment effects when these are time-varying and treatment is a state that only changes occasionally.

A simple and sometimes attractive estimator is the **differences-in-differences estimator**. Because it is an intuitively attractive approach, it also helps us to understand the merits of panel data. Suppose we are interested in estimating the impact of a certain 'treatment' upon a given outcome variable (see Section 7.7). While the terminology comes from medical sciences, treatment may also refer to social or economic interventions, for example, enrolment into a labour training programme, receipt of a transfer payment from a social programme or being a member of a trade union. A typical outcome variable is 'earnings'. Let the binary regressor of interest be

$$\begin{aligned} r_{it} &= 1 \text{ if individual } i \text{ receives a treatment in period } t; \\ &= 0 \text{ otherwise.} \end{aligned}$$

Let us assume a fixed effects model for y_{it} as

$$y_{it} = \delta r_{it} + \mu_t + \alpha_i + u_{it},$$

where μ_t is a time-specific fixed effect. For simplicity, the only regressor is r_{it} (in addition to the time and individual fixed effects). In general, the impact of a treatment can be inferred from a comparison of people receiving treatment with those who do not and by a comparison of people before and after the treatment. Panel data combines both.

The individual effects can be eliminated by a first-difference transformation. That is,

$$\Delta y_{it} = \delta \Delta r_{it} + \Delta \mu_t + \Delta u_{it}. \tag{10.18}$$

Assuming that $E\{\Delta r_{it} \Delta u_{it}\} = 0$, the treatment effect δ can be estimated consistently by OLS of Δy_{it} upon Δr_{it} and a set of time dummies. Because the individual effects α_i are eliminated, this procedure allows correlation between α_i and the treatment indicator.

This is important, because in many applications one can argue that individuals with certain (unobserved) characteristics are more likely to receive treatment (or to participate in some programme). Obviously, this approach is very similar to the fixed effects estimator, with the only difference that the first-difference transformation is employed rather than the within transformation.

Let us consider a situation in which there are only two time periods and individuals may receive a treatment in period 2. Thus $r_{i1} = 0$ for all i, while $r_{i2} = 1$ for a subset of the individuals. OLS in (10.18) corresponds to a regression of $y_{i2} - y_{i1}$ upon the treatment dummy and a constant (corresponding to the time effect). The resulting estimate for δ corresponds to the sample average of $y_{i2} - y_{i1}$ for the treated minus the average for the nontreated. Defining $\Delta\bar{y}_{i2}^{treated}$ as the average for the treated ($r_{i2} = 1$) and $\Delta\bar{y}_{i2}^{nontreated}$ as the average for the nontreated ($r_{i2} = 0$), the OLS estimate is simply

$$\hat{\delta} = \Delta\bar{y}_{i2}^{treated} - \Delta\bar{y}_{i2}^{nontreated}.$$

This estimator is called the **differences-in-differences estimator**, because one estimates the time difference for the treated and untreated groups and then takes the difference between the two. The first-differencing takes care of unobservable fixed effects and controls for unobservable (time-invariant) differences between individuals (e.g. health status, ability, intelligence, . . .). The second difference compares treated with untreated individuals. A classic example of a differences-in-differences approach is Card and Krueger (1996), who analyse the effect of a minimum wage increase in New Jersey (using Pennsylvania as a control). The formulation of the model in (10.18) makes clear that we need to assume that the time effects μ_t are common across treated and untreated individuals. This important assumption is typically referred to as the parallel trends assumption. It requires that, in the absence of treatment, both groups would follow the same time trend.

In economics the above methodology is often applied when the data arise from a natural experiment. A natural experiment occurs when some exogenous event (often a change in government policy or the passage of a law) changes the environment in which individuals, families or firms operate. A natural experiment always has a control group, which is not affected by the policy change, and a treatment group, which is thought to be affected by the policy change. Unlike with a true experiment where treatment and control groups can be randomly chosen, in a natural experiment these two groups arise from a particular policy change. In order to control for systematic differences between the control and treatment group, we need two periods of data, one before and one after the treatment. Thus the sample consists of four (sub)groups: the control group before and after the treatment and the treatment group before and after the treatment. Averages within these four subsamples are the building blocks of the differences-in-differences estimator; see Cameron and Trivedi (2005, Chapter 22) for more discussion.

10.2.3 The Random Effects Model

It is commonly assumed in regression analysis that all factors that affect the dependent variable, but that have not been included as regressors, can be appropriately summarized by a random error term. In our case, this leads to the assumption that the α_i are random factors, independently and identically distributed over individuals. Thus we write the random effects model as

$$y_{it} = \beta_0 + x_{it}'\beta + \alpha_i + u_{it}, \quad u_{it} \sim IID(0, \sigma_u^2); \quad \alpha_i \sim IID(0, \sigma_\alpha^2), \tag{10.19}$$

where $\alpha_i + u_{it}$ is treated as an error term consisting of two components: an individual-specific component, which does not vary over time, and a remainder component, which is assumed to be uncorrelated over time.[4] That is, all correlation of the error terms over time is attributed to the individual effects α_i. It is assumed that α_i and u_{it} are mutually independent and independent of x_{js} (for all j and s). This implies that the OLS estimator for β_0 and β from (10.19) is unbiased and consistent. The error components structure implies that the composite error term $\alpha_i + u_{it}$ exhibits a particular form of autocorrelation (unless $\sigma_\alpha^2 = 0$). Consequently, routinely computed standard errors for the OLS estimator are incorrect and a more efficient (GLS) estimator can be obtained by exploiting the structure of the error covariance matrix.

To derive the GLS estimator,[5] first note that for individual i all error terms can be stacked as $\alpha_i \iota_T + u_i$, where $\iota_T = (1, 1, \ldots, 1)'$ of dimension T (a vector of ones) and $u_i = (u_{i1}, \ldots, u_{iT})'$. The covariance matrix of this vector is

$$V\{\alpha_i \iota_T + u_i\} = \Omega = \sigma_\alpha^2 \iota_T \iota_T' + \sigma_u^2 I_T,$$

where I_T is the T-dimensional identity matrix and $\iota_T \iota_T'$ denotes a matrix full of ones. This can be used to derive the generalized least squares (GLS) estimator for the parameters in (10.19). For each individual, we can transform the data by premultiplying the vectors $y_i = (y_{i1}, \ldots, y_{iT})'$, etc., by Ω^{-1}, which is given by

$$\Omega^{-1} = \sigma_u^{-2} \left[I_T - \frac{\sigma_\alpha^2}{\sigma_u^2 + T\sigma_\alpha^2} \iota_T \iota_T' \right],$$

which can also be written as

$$\Omega^{-1} = \sigma_u^{-2} \left[\left(I_T - \frac{1}{T} \iota_T \iota_T' \right) + \psi \frac{1}{T} \iota_T \iota_T' \right],$$

where

$$\psi = \frac{\sigma_u^2}{\sigma_u^2 + T\sigma_\alpha^2}.$$

Noting that $I_T - (1/T)\iota_T \iota_T'$ transforms the data in deviations from individual means and $(1/T)\iota_T \iota_T'$ takes individual means, the GLS estimator for β can be written as

$$\hat{\beta}_{GLS} = \left(\sum_{i=1}^{N} \sum_{t=1}^{T} (x_{it} - \bar{x}_i)(x_{it} - \bar{x}_i)' + \psi T \sum_{i=1}^{N} (\bar{x}_i - \bar{x})(\bar{x}_i - \bar{x})' \right)^{-1}$$

$$\times \left(\sum_{i=1}^{N} \sum_{t=1}^{T} (x_{it} - \bar{x}_i)(y_{it} - \bar{y}_i) + \psi T \sum_{i=1}^{N} (\bar{x}_i - \bar{x})(\bar{y}_i - \bar{y}) \right), \tag{10.20}$$

---

[4] This model is sometimes referred to as a (one-way) error components model.

[5] It may be instructive to re-read the general introduction to GLS estimation in Section 4.2.

where $\bar{x} = (1/NT)\sum_{i,t} x_{it}$ denotes the overall average of x_{it}. It is easy to see that for $\psi = 0$ the fixed effects estimator arises. Because $\psi \to 0$ if $T \to \infty$, it follows that the fixed and random effects estimators are equivalent for large T. If $\psi = 1$, the GLS estimator is just the OLS estimator (and Ω is diagonal). From the general formula for the GLS estimator it can be derived that

$$\hat{\beta}_{GLS} = W\hat{\beta}_B + (I_K - W)\hat{\beta}_{FE},$$

where

$$\hat{\beta}_B = \left(\sum_{i=1}^{N}(\bar{x}_i - \bar{x})(\bar{x}_i - \bar{x})'\right)^{-1}\sum_{i=1}^{N}(\bar{x}_i - \bar{x})(\bar{y}_i - \bar{y})$$

is the so-called **between estimator** for β. It is the OLS estimator in the model for individual means

$$\bar{y}_i = \beta_0 + \bar{x}_i'\beta + \alpha_i + \bar{u}_i, \quad i = 1, \ldots, N. \tag{10.21}$$

The matrix W is a weighting matrix and is proportional to the inverse of the covariance matrix of $\hat{\beta}_B$ (Hsiao, 2014, Section 3.3). That is, the GLS estimator is a matrix-weighted average of the between estimator and the within estimator, where the weights depend upon the relative variances of the two estimators. (The more accurate one gets the higher weight.)

The between estimator effectively discards the time series information in the data set. The GLS estimator, under the current assumptions, is the optimal combination of the within estimator and the between estimator, and is therefore more efficient than either of these two estimators. The OLS estimator (with $\psi = 1$) is also a linear combination of the two estimators, but not the efficient one. Thus, GLS will be more efficient than OLS, as usual. If the explanatory variables are independent of all u_{it} and all α_i, the GLS estimator is unbiased. It is a consistent estimator for N or T or both, tending to infinity if, in addition to (10.11), it also holds that $E\{\bar{x}_i u_{it}\} = 0$ and most importantly that

$$E\{\bar{x}_i \alpha_i\} = 0. \tag{10.22}$$

Note that these conditions are also required for the between estimator to be consistent.

An easy way to compute the GLS estimator is obtained by noting that it can be determined as the OLS estimator in a transformed model (compare Chapter 4), given by

$$(y_{it} - \vartheta\bar{y}_i) = \beta_0(1 - \vartheta) + (x_{it} - \vartheta\bar{x}_i)'\beta + v_{it}, \tag{10.23}$$

where $\vartheta = 1 - \psi^{1/2}$. The error term in this transformed regression is i.i.d. over individuals and time. Note again that $\psi = 0$ corresponds to the within estimator ($\vartheta = 1$). In general, a fixed proportion ϑ of the individual means is subtracted from the data to obtain this transformed model ($0 \leq \vartheta \leq 1$).

Of course, the variance components σ_α^2 and σ_u^2 are unknown in practice. To address this, we can use the feasible GLS estimator (EGLS), where the unknown variances are consistently estimated in a first step. The estimator for σ_u^2 is easily obtained from the within residuals, as given in (10.14). For the between regression the error variance is $\sigma_\alpha^2 + (1/T)\sigma_u^2$, which we can estimate consistently by

$$\hat{\sigma}_B^2 = \frac{1}{N}\sum_{i=1}^{N}(\bar{y}_i - \hat{\beta}_{0B} - \bar{x}_i'\hat{\beta}_B)^2, \tag{10.24}$$

where $\hat{\beta}_{0B}$ is the between estimator for β_0. From this, a consistent estimator for σ_α^2 follows as

$$\hat{\sigma}_\alpha^2 = \hat{\sigma}_B^2 - \frac{1}{T}\hat{\sigma}_u^2. \tag{10.25}$$

Again, it is possible to adjust this estimator by applying a degrees of freedom correction, implying that the number of regressors $K + 1$ is subtracted in the denominator of (10.24). The resulting EGLS estimator is referred to as the **random effects estimator** for β (and β_0), denoted below as $\hat{\beta}_{RE}$. It is also known as the Balestra–Nerlove estimator.

Under weak regularity conditions, the random effects estimator is asymptotically normal. Its covariance matrix is given by

$$V\{\hat{\beta}_{RE}\} = \sigma_u^2\left(\sum_{i=1}^{N}\sum_{t=1}^{T}(x_{it} - \bar{x}_i)(x_{it} - \bar{x}_i)' + \psi T\sum_{i=1}^{N}(\bar{x}_i - \bar{x})(\bar{x}_i - \bar{x})'\right)^{-1}, \tag{10.26}$$

which shows that the random effects estimator is more efficient than the fixed effects estimator as long as $\psi > 0$. The gain in efficiency is due to the use of the between variation in the data $(\bar{x}_i - \bar{x})$. The covariance matrix in (10.26) is routinely estimated from the standard OLS expressions in the transformed model (10.23).

In summary, we have seen a range of estimators for the parameter vector β. The basic two are:

1. The **between estimator**, exploiting the between dimension of the data (differences between individuals), determined as the OLS estimator in a regression of individual averages of y on individual averages of x (and a constant). Consistency, for $N \to \infty$, requires that $E\{\bar{x}_i\alpha_i\} = 0$ and $E\{\bar{x}_i\bar{u}_i\} = 0$. Typically this means that the explanatory variables are strictly exogenous and uncorrelated with the individual-specific effect α_i.
2. The **fixed effects (within) estimator**, exploiting the within dimension of the data (differences within individuals), determined as the OLS estimator in a regression in deviations from individual means. It is consistent for β for $T \to \infty$ or $N \to \infty$, provided that $E\{(x_{it} - \bar{x}_i)u_{it}\} = 0$. Again this requires the explanatory variables to be strictly exogenous, but it does not impose any restrictions upon the relationship between α_i and x_{it}.

Two estimators that combine the within and between dimension of the data are:

3. The **OLS estimator**, exploiting both dimensions (within and between) but not efficiently. Determined (of course) as OLS in the original model given in (10.19). Consistency for $T \to \infty$ or $N \to \infty$ requires that $E\{x_{it}(u_{it} + \alpha_i)\} = 0$. This requires the explanatory variables to be uncorrelated with α_i but does not impose that they are strictly exogenous. It suffices that x_{it} and u_{it} are contemporaneously uncorrelated.
4. The **random effects (EGLS) estimator**, combining the information from the between and within dimensions in an efficient way. It is consistent for $T \to \infty$ or $N \to \infty$ under the combined conditions of 1 and 2. It can be determined as a weighted average of the between and within estimator or as the OLS estimator in a regression where the variables are transformed as $y_{it} - \hat{\vartheta}\bar{y}_i$, where $\hat{\vartheta}$ is an estimate for $\vartheta = 1 - \psi^{1/2}$ with $\psi = \sigma_u^2/(\sigma_u^2 + T\sigma_\alpha^2)$.

Further, we have also considered:

5. The **first-difference (FD) estimator**, determined as OLS after first-differencing the equation of interest. This estimator is an alternative to the fixed effects estimator based on the within transformation, and it also only exploits the time variation in the data. Consistency requires that $E\{(x_{it} - x_{i,t-1})(u_{it} - u_{i,t-1})\} = 0$. If u_{it} is i.i.d., the first-difference estimator is less efficient than the within estimator; for $T = 2$ they are identical.

10.2.4 Fixed Effects or Random Effects?

The choice between a fixed effects and a random effects approach is not easy, and in many applications, particularly when T is small, the differences in the estimates for β appear to be substantial. The most common view is that the discussion should not be about the 'true nature' of the effects α_i. The appropriate interpretation is that the fixed effects approach is conditional upon the values for α_i. That is, it essentially considers the distribution of y_{it} given α_i, where the α_is can be estimated. This makes sense intuitively if the individuals in the sample are 'one of a kind', and cannot be viewed as a random draw from some underlying population. This interpretation is probably most appropriate when i denotes countries, (large) companies or industries, and predictions we want to make are for a particular country, company or industry. Inferences are thus with respect to the effects that are in the sample.

However, even if we are interested in the larger population of individual units, and a random effects framework seems appropriate, the fixed effects estimator may be preferred. The reason for this is that it may be the case that α_i and x_{it} are correlated, in which case the random effects approach, ignoring this correlation, leads to inconsistent estimators. We saw an example of this previously, where α_i included management quality and was argued to be correlated with the other inputs included in the production function. The problem of correlation between the individual effects α_i and the explanatory variables in x_{it} can be handled by using the fixed effects approach, which essentially eliminates the α_i from the model, and thus eliminates any problems that they may cause.

Hausman (1978) has proposed a test for the null hypothesis that x_{it} and α_i are uncorrelated. The general idea of a **Hausman test** is that two estimators are compared: one that is consistent under both the null and alternative hypotheses and one that is consistent (and typically efficient) under the null hypothesis only. A significant difference between the two estimators indicates that the null hypothesis is unlikely to hold. In the present case, assume that $E\{u_{it}x_{is}\} = 0$ for all s, t, so that the fixed effects estimator $\hat{\beta}_{FE}$ is consistent for β irrespective of the question as to whether x_{it} and α_i are uncorrelated, whereas the random effects estimator $\hat{\beta}_{RE}$ is consistent and efficient only if x_{it} and α_i are not correlated. Let us consider the difference vector $\hat{\beta}_{FE} - \hat{\beta}_{RE}$. To evaluate the significance of this difference, we need its covariance matrix. In general this would require us to estimate the covariance between $\hat{\beta}_{FE}$ and $\hat{\beta}_{RE}$, but, because the latter estimator is efficient under the null hypothesis, it can be shown that (under the null)

$$V\{\hat{\beta}_{FE} - \hat{\beta}_{RE}\} = V\{\hat{\beta}_{FE}\} - V\{\hat{\beta}_{RE}\}. \tag{10.27}$$

Consequently, we can compute the Hausman test statistic as

$$\xi_H = (\hat{\beta}_{FE} - \hat{\beta}_{RE})'[\hat{V}\{\hat{\beta}_{FE}\} - \hat{V}\{\hat{\beta}_{RE}\}]^{-1}(\hat{\beta}_{FE} - \hat{\beta}_{RE}), \tag{10.28}$$

where the $\hat{V}$s denote estimates of the true covariance matrices. Under the null hypothesis, which implicitly says that plim$(\hat{\beta}_{FE} - \hat{\beta}_{RE}) = 0$, the statistic ξ_H has an asymptotic Chi-squared distribution with K degrees of freedom, where K is the number of elements in β.

The Hausman test thus tests whether the fixed effects and random effects estimators are significantly different. Computationally, this is relatively easy because the covariance matrix satisfies (10.27). An important reason why the two estimators would be different is the existence of correlation between x_{it} and α_i, although other sorts of misspecification can also lead to rejection (we shall see an example of this below). A practical problem when computing (10.28) is that the covariance matrix in square brackets may not be positive definite in finite samples, such that its inverse cannot be computed. As an alternative, it is possible to test for a subset of the elements in β.

Although the Hausman test is commonly used as a tool to decide between the random effects and fixed effects estimators, it should be used with caution. Rejection should not automatically be interpreted as evidence that the fixed effects model is appropriate. Conversely, if the Hausman test does not reject it is not necessarily the case that the random effects model should be preferred. One problem is that the Hausman test may have low power, leading to severe pre-test biases (see Guggenberger, 2010). Another problem is that the test does not apply if u_{it} is heteroskedastic or exhibits serial correlation. This is because the random effects estimator is no longer efficient in this more general setting and (10.27) fails; Pesaran (2015, Section 26.9) presents an alternative test based on comparing the OLS estimator and the fixed effects estimator for β. Alternative estimators, that bridge the gap between random effects and fixed effects estimators, are also possible; see Subsection 10.2.6.

10.2.5 Goodness-of-Fit

The computation of goodness-of-fit measures in panel data applications is somewhat uncommon. One reason is the fact that one may attach different importance to explaining the within and between variation in the data. Another reason is that the usual R^2 or adjusted R^2 criteria are only appropriate if the model is estimated by OLS.

Our starting point here is the definition of the R^2 in terms of the squared correlation coefficient between actual and fitted values, as presented in Section 2.4. This definition has the advantage that it produces values within the [0, 1] interval, irrespective of the estimator that is used to generate the fitted values. Recall that it corresponds to the standard definition of the R^2 (in terms of sums of squares) if the model is estimated by OLS (provided that an intercept term is included). In the current context, the total variation in y_{it} can be written as the sum of the within variation and the between variation, that is,

$$\frac{1}{NT}\sum_{i,t}(y_{it} - \bar{y})^2 = \frac{1}{NT}\sum_{i,t}(y_{it} - \bar{y}_i)^2 + \frac{1}{N}\sum_{i}(\bar{y}_i - \bar{y})^2,$$

where $\bar{y}$ denotes the overall sample average. Now, we can define alternative versions of an R^2 measure, depending upon the dimension of the data that we are interested in.

For example, the fixed effects estimator is chosen to explain the within variation as well as possible, and thus maximizes the 'within R^2' given by

$$R^2_{within}(\hat{\beta}_{FE}) = \text{corr}^2\{\hat{y}^{FE}_{it} - \hat{y}^{FE}_i, y_{it} - \bar{y}_i\}, \tag{10.29}$$

where $\hat{y}_{it}^{FE} - \hat{y}_i^{FE} = (x_{it} - \bar{x}_i)'\hat{\beta}_{FE}$ and corr^2 denotes the squared correlation coefficient. The between estimator, being an OLS estimator in the model in terms of individual means, maximizes the 'between R^2', which we define as

$$R^2_{between}(\hat{\beta}_B) = \text{corr}^2\{\hat{y}_i^B, \bar{y}_i\}, \tag{10.30}$$

where $\hat{y}_i^B = \bar{x}_i'\hat{\beta}_B$. The OLS estimator maximizes the overall goodness-of-fit and thus the overall R^2, which is defined as

$$R^2_{overall}(\hat{\beta}) = \text{corr}^2\{\hat{y}_{it}, y_{it}\}, \tag{10.31}$$

with $\hat{y}_{it} = x_{it}'b$. It is possible to define within, between and overall R^2s for an arbitrary estimator $\hat{\beta}$ for β by using as fitted values $\hat{y}_{it} = x_{it}'\hat{\beta}$, $\hat{y}_i = (1/T)\sum_t \hat{y}_{it}$ and $\hat{y} = (1/(NT))\sum_{i,t}\hat{y}_{it}$, where the intercept terms are omitted (and irrelevant).[6] For the fixed effects estimator this ignores the variation captured by the $\hat{\alpha}_i$s. If we take into account the variation explained by the N estimated intercepts $\hat{\alpha}_i$, the fixed effects model perfectly fits the between variation. This is somewhat unsatisfactory, though, as it is hard to argue that the fixed effects $\hat{\alpha}_i$ *explain* the variation between individuals, they just capture it. Put differently, if we ask ourselves: why does individual i consume on average more than another individual, the answer provided by $\hat{\alpha}_i$ is simply: because it is individual i. Given this argument, and because the $\hat{\alpha}_i$s are often not computed, it seems appropriate to ignore this part of the model.

Taking the definition in terms of the squared correlation coefficients, the three measures above can be computed for any of the estimators that we considered. If we take the random effects estimator, which is (asymptotically) the most efficient estimator if the assumptions of the random effects model are valid, the within, between and overall R^2s are necessarily smaller than for the fixed effects, between and OLS estimator, respectively. This, again, stresses that goodness-of-fit measures are not adequate to choose between alternative estimators. They provide, however, possible criteria for choosing between alternative (potentially non-nested) specifications of the model.

10.2.6 Alternative Instrumental Variables Estimators

The fixed effects estimator eliminates anything that is time invariant from the model. This may be a high price to pay for allowing the explanatory variables to be correlated with the individual-specific heterogeneity α_i. For example, we may be interested in the effect of time-invariant variables (like gender) on a person's wage. Actually, there is no need to restrict attention to the fixed and random effects assumptions only, as it is possible to derive instrumental variables estimators that can be considered to be in between a fixed and random effects approach.

To see this, let us first of all note that we can write the fixed effects estimator as

$$\hat{\beta}_{FE} = \left(\sum_{i=1}^{N}\sum_{t=1}^{T}(x_{it} - \bar{x}_i)(x_{it} - \bar{x}_i)'\right)^{-1}\sum_{i=1}^{N}\sum_{t=1}^{T}(x_{it} - \bar{x}_i)(y_{it} - \bar{y}_i)$$

$$= \left(\sum_{i=1}^{N}\sum_{t=1}^{T}(x_{it} - \bar{x}_i)x_{it}'\right)^{-1}\sum_{i=1}^{N}\sum_{t=1}^{T}(x_{it} - \bar{x}_i)y_{it}. \tag{10.32}$$

[6] These definitions correspond to the R^2 measures as computed in Stata.

Writing the estimator like this shows that it has the interpretation of an instrumental variables estimator[7] for β in the model

$$y_{it} = \beta_0 + x_{it}'\beta + \alpha_i + u_{it},$$

where each explanatory variable is instrumented by its value in deviation from the individual-specific mean. That is, x_{it} is instrumented by $x_{it} - \bar{x}_i$. Note that $E\{(x_{it} - \bar{x}_i)\alpha_i\} = 0$ by construction (if we take expectations over i and t), so that the IV estimator is consistent provided $E\{(x_{it} - \bar{x}_i)u_{it}\} = 0$, which is implied by the strict exogeneity of x_{it}. Clearly, if a particular element in x_{it} is known to be uncorrelated with α_i there is no need to instrument it; that is, this variable can be used as its own instrument. This route may also allow us to estimate the effect of time-invariant variables.

To describe the general approach, let us consider a linear model with four groups of explanatory variables (Hausman and Taylor, 1981):

$$y_{it} = \beta_0 + x_{1,it}'\beta_1 + x_{2,it}'\beta_2 + w_{1i}'\gamma_1 + w_{2i}'\gamma_2 + \alpha_i + u_{it}, \tag{10.33}$$

where the x variables are time varying and the w variables are time invariant. The variables with index 1 are assumed to be uncorrelated with both α_i and all u_{is}. The variables $x_{2,it}$ and w_{2i} are correlated with α_i but not with any u_{is}. Under these assumptions, the fixed effects estimator would be consistent for β_1 and β_2, but would not estimate the coefficients for the time-invariant variables. Moreover, it is inefficient because $x_{1,it}$ is needlessly instrumented. Hausman and Taylor (1981) suggest that (10.33) be estimated by instrumental variables using the following variables as instruments: $x_{1,it}, w_{1i}$ and $x_{2,it} - \bar{x}_{2i}, \bar{x}_{1i}$. That is, the exogenous variables serve as their own instruments, $x_{2,it}$ is instrumented by its deviation from individual means (as in the fixed effects approach) and w_{2i} is instrumented by the individual average of $x_{1,it}$. Obviously, identification requires that the number of variables in $x_{1,it}$ is at least as large as that in w_{2i}. The resulting estimator, the **Hausman–Taylor estimator**, allows us to estimate the effect of time-invariant variables, even though the time-varying regressors are correlated with α_i. The trick here is to use the time averages of those time-varying regressors that are uncorrelated with α_i as instruments for the time-invariant regressors. Clearly, this requires that sufficient time-varying variables are included that have no correlation with α_i. Of course, it is a straightforward extension to include additional instruments in the procedure that are not based on variables included in the model. This is what one is forced to do in the cross-sectional case, where no transformations are available that can be argued to produce valid instruments. The strong advantage of the Hausman–Taylor approach is that one does not have to use external instruments. With sufficient assumptions, instruments can be derived within the model. Despite this important advantage, the Hausman–Taylor estimator plays a minor role in empirical work. A notable exception is Chowdhury and Nickell (1985).

Hausman and Taylor (1981) also show that the instrument set is equivalent to using $x_{1,it} - \bar{x}_{1i}, x_{2,it} - \bar{x}_{2i}$ and $x_{1,it}, w_{1i}$. This follows directly from the fact that taking different linear combinations of the original instruments does not affect the estimator. They also discuss how the nondiagonal covariance matrix of the error term in (10.33) can be exploited to improve the efficiency of the estimator. Nowadays, this would typically be handled in a GMM framework, as we shall see in Section 10.4 (see Arellano and Bover, 1995).

[7] It may be instructive to re-read Section 5.3 for a general discussion of instrumental variables estimation.

Two subsequent papers try to improve upon the efficiency of the Hausman–Taylor instrumental variables estimator by proposing a larger set of instruments. Amemiya and MaCurdy (1986) suggest the use of the *time-invariant* instruments $x_{1,i1} - \bar{x}_{1i}$ up to $x_{1,iT} - \bar{x}_{1i}$. This requires that $E\{(x_{1,it} - \bar{x}_{1i})\alpha_i\} = 0$ for *each t*. This assumption makes sense if the correlation between α_i and $x_{1,it}$ is due to a time-invariant component in $x_{1,it}$, such that $E\{x_{1,it}\alpha_i\}$ for a given t does not depend upon t. Breusch, Mizon and Schmidt (1989) nicely summarize this literature and suggest as additional instruments the use of the time-invariant variables $x_{2,i1} - \bar{x}_{2i}$ up to $x_{2,iT} - \bar{x}_{2i}$.

10.2.7 Robust Inference

Both the random effects and the fixed effects models assume that the presence of α_i captures all correlation between the unobservables in different time periods. That is, u_{it} is assumed to be uncorrelated over individuals and time. Provided that the x_{it} variables are strictly exogenous, the presence of autocorrelation in u_{it} does not result in inconsistency of the standard estimators. It does, however, invalidate the standard errors and resulting tests, just as we saw in Chapter 4. Moreover, it implies that the estimators are no longer efficient. For example, if the true covariance matrix Ω does have an error components structure, the random effects estimator no longer corresponds to the feasible GLS estimator for β. As we know, the presence of heteroskedasticity in u_{it} or – for the random effects model – in α_i has similar consequences.

One way to avoid misleading inferences, without the need to impose alternative assumptions on the structure of the covariance matrix Ω, is the use of the OLS, random effects or fixed effects estimators for β, while adjusting their standard errors for general forms of heteroskedasticity and autocorrelation. Consider the model[8]

$$y_{it} = x_{it}'\beta + \varepsilon_{it}, \tag{10.34}$$

without the assumption that ε_{it} has an error components structure. Consistency of the (pooled) OLS estimator

$$b = \left(\sum_{i=1}^{N} \sum_{t=1}^{T} x_{it}x_{it}' \right)^{-1} \sum_{i=1}^{N} \sum_{t=1}^{T} x_{it}y_{it} \tag{10.35}$$

for β requires that

$$E\{x_{it}\varepsilon_{it}\} = 0. \tag{10.36}$$

Assuming that error terms of different individuals are uncorrelated ($E\{\varepsilon_{it}\varepsilon_{js}\} = 0$ for all $i \neq j$), the OLS covariance matrix can be estimated by a variant of the Newey–West estimator from Chapter 4, given by

$$\hat{V}\{b\} = \left(\sum_{i=1}^{N} \sum_{t=1}^{T} x_{it}x_{it}' \right)^{-1} \sum_{i=1}^{N} \sum_{t=1}^{T} \sum_{s=1}^{T} e_{it}e_{is}x_{it}x_{is}' \left(\sum_{i=1}^{N} \sum_{t=1}^{T} x_{it}x_{it}' \right)^{-1}, \tag{10.37}$$

where e_{it} denotes the OLS residual. As argued by Petersen (2009), the use of Bartlett weights, as is done in the single time series case discussed in Subsection 4.10.2, is unnecessary in the panel data case and leads to biased standard errors (for finite T).

[8] For notational convenience, the constant is assumed to be included in x_{it} (when relevant).

The estimator in (10.37) allows for general forms of heteroskedasticity as well as arbitrary autocorrelation (within a given individual). Accordingly, (10.37) is referred to as a **panel-robust** estimate for the covariance matrix of the pooled OLS estimator. It is also known as a **cluster-robust** covariance matrix (where the identifier i indexing the individuals is the cluster variable). Clustering standard errors by individuals does not allow for time effects (correlation between ε_{it} and ε_{jt} for $i \neq j$) and persistent common shocks. Thompson (2011) argues that this is potentially relevant for firm level data sets, where market-wide shocks induce correlation between firms at a moment in time, and persistent common shocks, like business cycles, can induce correlation between different firms in different years. Provided that condition (10.36) is satisfied, this can be addressed by calculating standard errors that are robust to simultaneous correlation among two dimensions. In the case without persistent common shocks, the covariance matrix estimator appears equal to the estimator that clusters by individual (10.37), plus the estimator that clusters by time, minus the usual heteroskedasticity-robust OLS covariance matrix (similar to (4.30) but summing over both i and t). The second covariance matrix estimate is similar to (10.37) and given by

$$\hat{V}\{b\} = \left(\sum_{i=1}^{N}\sum_{t=1}^{T} x_{it}x_{it}'\right)^{-1} \sum_{i=1}^{N}\sum_{j=1}^{N}\sum_{t=1}^{T} e_{it}e_{jt}x_{it}x_{jt}' \left(\sum_{i=1}^{N}\sum_{t=1}^{T} x_{it}x_{it}'\right)^{-1}.$$

This works well with reasonably long panels (with T being 25 or more). When T is small, it is preferable to include fixed time effects to control for market-wide shocks. Thompson (2011) shows how the above approach can be extended in a fairly straightforward fashion to allow for correlation between different firms in different time periods, up to a maximum lag length. For this, even larger T is recommended.

Similar to (10.37), it is also possible to construct a robust estimator for the covariance matrix of the random effects estimator $\hat{\beta}_{RE}$ using the transformed model in (10.23); see Wooldridge (2010, Subsection 7.5.1) or Cameron and Miller (2015) for a general discussion. Even though the random effects estimator is not the appropriate EGLS estimator under these weaker conditions, it is still consistent and asymptotically normal, and for interesting departures from the full random effects assumptions, the random effects estimator is likely to be more efficient than pooled OLS (Wooldridge, 2003).

When the model is estimated by the fixed effects estimator, a robust covariance matrix is obtained in a similar way, by replacing the regressors x_{it} in (10.37) with their within transformed counterparts, $\tilde{x}_{it} = x_{it} - \bar{x}_i$, and the OLS residuals with the residuals from the within regression (Arellano, 1987). That is,

$$\hat{V}\{\hat{\beta}_{FE}\} = \left(\sum_{i=1}^{N}\sum_{t=1}^{T} \tilde{x}_{it}\tilde{x}_{it}'\right)^{-1} \sum_{i=1}^{N}\sum_{t=1}^{T}\sum_{s=1}^{T} \hat{u}_{it}\hat{u}_{is}\tilde{x}_{it}\tilde{x}_{is}' \left(\sum_{i=1}^{N}\sum_{t=1}^{T} \tilde{x}_{it}\tilde{x}_{it}'\right)^{-1}, \qquad (10.38)$$

where $\hat{u}_{it} = y_{it} - \hat{\alpha}_i - x_{it}'\hat{\beta}_{FE}$ denotes the within residual. For the first-difference estimator $\hat{\beta}_{FD}$ the first-differenced variables are employed (and the summation is from $t, s = 2$ to T). If the absence of serial correlation is imposed, the cross terms in (10.38) can be omitted and a heteroskedasticity-robust covariance matrix estimator is given by

$$\hat{V}\{\hat{\beta}_{FE}\} = \left(\sum_{i=1}^{N}\sum_{t=1}^{T} \tilde{x}_{it}\tilde{x}_{it}'\right)^{-1} \sum_{i=1}^{N}\sum_{t=1}^{T} \hat{u}_{it}^2\tilde{x}_{it}\tilde{x}_{is}' \left(\sum_{i=1}^{N}\sum_{t=1}^{T} \tilde{x}_{it}\tilde{x}_{it}'\right)^{-1}. \qquad (10.39)$$

Despite the fact that this estimator is frequently used in empirical work, Stock and Watson (2008) show that it is inconsistent for $N \to \infty$ and fixed $T > 2$, and propose a bias-adjustment. The bias is caused by the fact that the individual-specific means cannot be estimated consistently for fixed T. Bertrand, Duflo and Mullainathan (2004) provide a critical discussion on the computation of standard errors for the differences-in-differences estimator and, among other things, conclude that the panel-robust approach works reasonably well for moderate N. Similarly, Petersen (2009) advocates the use of panel-robust standard errors clustered by firms for sufficiently large N. If, on the other hand, N is small and $T \to \infty$, consistency can be achieved by using Bartlett weights in (10.37) as discussed in Subsection 4.10.2; see Arellano (2003, Section 2.3) for more details. Cameron and Miller (2015) provide a useful guide for practitioners to the use of clustered standard errors.

If one is willing to make specific assumptions about the form of heteroskedasticity or autocorrelation, it is possible to improve upon the efficiency of the OLS, random effects or fixed effects estimators by exploiting the structure of the error covariance matrix using a feasible GLS or maximum likelihood approach. An overview of a number of such estimators, which are typically computationally unattractive, is provided in Baltagi (2013, Chapter 5). Kmenta (1986) suggests a relatively simple feasible GLS estimator that allows for first-order autocorrelation in ε_{it} combined with individual-specific heteroskedasticity, but does not allow for a time-invariant component in ε_{it}. Kiefer (1980) proposes a GLS estimator for the fixed effects model that allows for arbitrary covariances between u_{it} and u_{is}; see Arellano (2003, Section 2.3) or Hsiao (2014, Section 3.8) for more details. Wooldridge (2010, Subsection 10.4.3) describes a feasible GLS estimator where the covariance matrix Ω is estimated unrestrictedly from the pooled OLS residuals. Consistency of this estimator basically requires the same conditions as required by the random effects estimator, but it does not impose the error components structure. When N is sufficiently large relative to T, this feasible GLS estimator may provide an attractive alternative to the random effects approach.

10.2.8 Testing for Heteroskedasticity and Autocorrelation

Most of the tests that can be used for heteroskedasticity or autocorrelation in the random effects model are computationally burdensome. For the fixed effects model, which is essentially estimated by OLS, things are relatively less complex. Fortunately, as the fixed effects estimator can be applied even if we make the random effects assumption that α_i is i.i.d. and independent of the explanatory variables, the tests for the fixed effects model can also be used in the random effects case.

A fairly simple test for autocorrelation in the fixed effects model is based upon the Durbin–Watson test discussed in Chapter 4. The alternative hypothesis is that

$$u_{it} = \rho u_{i,t-1} + v_{it}, \tag{10.40}$$

where v_{it} is i.i.d. across individuals and time. This allows for autocorrelation over time with the restriction that each individual has the same autocorrelation coefficient ρ. The null hypothesis under test is $H_0: \rho = 0$ against the one-sided alternative $\rho < 0$ or $\rho > 0$. Let $\hat{u}_{it}$ denote the *residuals from the within regression* (10.9) or – equivalently – from

Table 10.1 5% lower and upper bounds panel Durbin–Watson test

		$N = 100$		$N = 500$		$N = 1000$	
		d_L	d_U	d_L	d_U	d_L	d_U
$T = 6$	$K = 3$	1.859	1.880	1.939	1.943	1.957	1.959
	$K = 9$	1.839	1.902	1.935	1.947	1.954	1.961
$T = 10$	$K = 3$	1.891	1.904	1.952	1.954	1.967	1.968
	$K = 9$	1.878	1.916	1.949	1.957	1.965	1.970

Source: Bhargava, A., Franzini, L. and Narendranathan, W., (1983), Serial Correlation and the Fixed Effects Model, *The Review of Economic Studies* (49): 533–549. Reprinted by permission of Blackwell Publishing.

(10.7). Then Bhargava, Franzini and Narendranathan (1983) suggest the following generalization of the Durbin–Watson statistic:

$$dw_p = \frac{\sum_{i=1}^{N} \sum_{t=2}^{T} (\hat{u}_{it} - \hat{u}_{i,t-1})^2}{\sum_{i=1}^{N} \sum_{t=1}^{T} \hat{u}_{it}^2}. \tag{10.41}$$

Using similar derivations as Durbin and Watson, the authors are able to derive lower and upper bounds on the true critical values that depend upon N, T and K only. Unlike the true time series case, the inconclusive region for the panel data Durbin–Watson test is very small, particularly when the number of individuals in the panel is large. In Table 10.1 we present some selected lower and upper bounds for the true 5% critical values that can be used to test against the alternative of positive autocorrelation. The numbers in the table confirm that the inconclusive regions are small and also indicate that the variation with K, N or T is limited. In a model with three explanatory variables estimated over six time periods, we reject H_0: $\rho = 0$ at the 5% level if dw_p is smaller than 1.859 for $N = 100$ and 1.957 for $N = 1000$, both against the one-sided alternative of $\rho > 0$. For panels with very large N, Bhargava, Franzini and Narendranathan (1983) suggest simply to test if the computed statistic dw_p is less than two, when testing against positive autocorrelation. Because the fixed effects estimator is also consistent in the random effects model, it is also possible to use this panel data Durbin–Watson test in the latter model.

An alternative test for serial correlation can be derived from the residuals from the first-difference estimator. If u_{it} is homoskedastic and exhibits no serial correlation, the correlation between Δu_{it} and $\Delta u_{i,t-1}$ is -0.5. Accordingly, a simple test for serial correlation is obtained by regressing the residuals from (10.15) upon their lags, and testing whether the coefficient on the lagged residual equals -0.5 using a t-test based on clustered standard errors (see Wooldridge, 2010, Subsection 10.6.3).

To test for heteroskedasticity in u_{it}, we can again use the fixed effects residuals $\hat{u}_{it}$. The auxiliary regression of the test regresses the squared within residuals $\hat{u}_{it}^2$ upon a constant and the J variables z_{it} that we think may affect heteroskedasticity. This is a variant of the Breusch–Pagan test[9] for heteroskedasticity discussed in Chapter 4. Its alternative

[9] In a panel data context, the term Breusch–Pagan test is usually associated with a Lagrange multiplier test in the random effects model for the null hypothesis that there are no individual-specific effects ($\sigma_\alpha^2 = 0$); see Wooldridge (2010, Section 10.4.4) or Baltagi (2013, Section 4.2). In applications, this test almost always rejects the null hypothesis.

hypothesis is that

$$V\{u_{it}\} = \sigma^2 h(z_{it}'\alpha),$$

where h is an unknown continuously differentiable function with $h(0) = 1$, so that the null hypothesis that is tested is given by H_0: $\alpha = 0$. Under the null hypothesis, the test statistic, computed as $N(T - 1)$ times the R^2 of the auxiliary regression, will have an asymptotic Chi-squared distribution, with J degrees of freedom. An alternative test can be computed from the residuals of the between regression and is based upon N times the R^2 of an auxiliary regression of the between residuals upon $\bar{z}_i$ or, more generally, upon $z_{i1}, \ldots, z_{iT}$. Under the null hypothesis of homoskedastic errors, the test statistic has an asymptotic Chi-squared distribution, with degrees of freedom equal to the number of variables included in the auxiliary regression (excluding the intercept). The alternative hypothesis of the latter test is less well defined.

10.2.9 The Fama–MacBeth Approach

In the empirical finance literature an alternative approach to deal with large panel data sets is quite common, usually referred to as Fama–MacBeth (1973) regressions. The influential paper by Fama and French (1992) uses this methodology to show that the Capital Asset Pricing Model does a poor job in explaining the cross-section of expected stock returns. The dependent variable in such regressions is often the return on an asset i in period t, and the explanatory variables are (possibly time-varying) characteristics of the stocks (observed before the start of period t). Let us denote the corresponding model as

$$y_{it} = \alpha_t + x_{it}'\beta_t + \varepsilon_{it}, \quad t = 1, 2, \ldots, T, \tag{10.42}$$

where α_t, β_t are unknown coefficients, possibly different across periods. Typically the panel is unbalanced in the sense that the number of stocks per period, N_t, varies over time. Because variances of rates of return differ and because asset returns tend to be correlated with each other, even after controlling for a common time effect it can typically be expected that ε_{it} is heteroskedastic across assets and cross-sectionally correlated. Stacking all error terms for period t in the vector ε_t, we can write this as

$$V\{\varepsilon_t\} = \Omega_t,$$

where Ω_t is an $N_t \times N_t$ positive definite (nondiagonal) covariance matrix. As a result of this, the estimation of α_t and β_t by ordinary least squares using all observations from period t is inefficient and potentially inconsistent for $N_t \to \infty$. The inconsistency arises if the cross-sectional correlation in ε_{it} is due to one or more common factors which do not 'average out' when the OLS estimator is calculated. In addition, the estimation of a sensible standard error for the OLS estimator is hampered by the fact that the covariance matrix of the error terms cannot be estimated with a single cross-section.

The solution proposed by Fama and MacBeth (1973) is remarkably simple, and it is appropriate if it can be assumed that the parameters of interest are time invariant ($\beta_t = \beta$), and, moreover, the error terms are not serially correlated. The model in (10.42) is estimated for each period t by OLS. This leads to time series of estimates $\hat{\alpha}_t$ and $\hat{\beta}_t$, $t = 1, 2, \ldots, T$. Subsequently, hypotheses are tested using the time series averages of the cross-sectional estimates, denoted $\bar{\alpha}$ and $\bar{\beta}$. For $T \to \infty$ these averages provide consistent estimators for the population parameters α and β. The standard errors on $\bar{\beta}$ are simply calculated from the sample standard deviations of the $\hat{\beta}_t$s treating them as independent drawings from a common distribution. Accordingly, the hypothesis that one of the coefficients, β_2 say, is zero can be tested using the t-test statistic

$$t = \frac{\bar{\beta}_2}{\text{se}(\bar{\beta}_2)},$$

which, under the null hypothesis, is approximately standard normally distributed, where $\text{se}(\bar{\beta}_2)$ is the square root of the sample variance of $\hat{\beta}_{2t}$, divided by the number of time periods T. That is,

$$\text{se}(\bar{\beta}_2) = \sqrt{\frac{1}{T^2}\sum_{t=1}^{T}(\hat{\beta}_{2t} - \bar{\beta}_2)^2}.$$

The standard error calculated in this way allows for arbitrary cross-sectional correlation and heteroskedasticity in ε_{it}. This result may seem surprising, as it does not use any of the distributional results of the estimators that are used in calculating $\bar{\beta}$. On second thoughts, however, it is an intuitively appealing procedure. We simply infer the sample variance of $\bar{\beta}_2$ from how the estimates $\hat{\beta}_{2t}$ vary over different subsamples (one for each t). The asymptotic properties of the Fama–MacBeth procedure were first documented in Shanken (1992), almost 20 years after its first use. An important restriction is that the error terms in (10.41) are not allowed to exhibit serial correlation. Petersen (2009) demonstrates that the Fama–MacBeth standard errors are biased in the presence of a firm effect in ε_{it} or other forms of serial correlation. This issue is often overlooked, even in published articles (see Wu, 2004; or Choe, Kho and Stulz, 2005, for some recent examples). Adjustments that allow for serial correlation do not appear to perform very well; see Petersen (2009) for an extensive discussion and Monte Carlo evidence.

In the absence of serial correlation, the Fama–MacBeth procedure implicitly computes a correct, heteroskedasticity-consistent covariance matrix, and therefore results in appropriate t-tests. Different from a pooled OLS estimator, the Fama–MacBeth approach gives the same weight to each period in the sample, irrespective of the number of observations in each period. There are also variants where the first-step regressions are based on weighted least squares or generalized least squares. In asset pricing tests, some of the explanatory variables in (10.42) are often exposures to risk factors, which have to be estimated first. This generates some additional errors-in-variables issues that we will not go into here; see Cochrane (2005, Chapter 12). The small sample properties of the Fama–MacBeth procedure and some alternative approaches (maximum likelihood, GMM) are discussed in Shanken and Zhou (2007).

10.3 Illustration: Explaining Individual Wages

In this section we apply a number of the above estimators when estimating an individual wage equation. The data are taken from the Youth Sample of the National Longitudinal Survey held in the United States and comprise a sample of 545 full-time working males who completed their schooling by 1980 and were then followed over the period 1980–1987. The males in the sample are young, with an age in 1980 ranging from 17 to 23, and have entered the labour market fairly recently, with an average of 3 years of experience in the beginning of the sample period. The data and specifications we choose are similar to those in Vella and Verbeek (1998). Log wages are explained from years of schooling, years of experience and its square, dummy variables for being a union member, working in the public sector and being married and two racial dummies.

The estimation results for the between estimator, based upon individual averages, and the within estimator, based upon deviations from individual means, are given in the first two columns of Table 10.2. First, note that the fixed effects or within estimator eliminates any time-invariant variables from the model. In this case, it means that the effects of schooling and race are wiped out. The differences between the two sets of estimates seem substantial, and we shall come back to this later. In the next column the OLS results are presented applied to the random effects model, where the standard errors are adjusted for heteroskedasticity and arbitrary forms of serial correlation based on the cluster-robust covariance matrix in (10.37). The last column presents the random effects estimator (EGLS). As discussed in Subsection 10.2.3, the variances of the error components α_i and u_{it} can be estimated from the within and between residuals. In particular, we find $\hat{\sigma}_B^2 = 0.1209$ and $\hat{\sigma}_u^2 = 0.1234$. From this, we can consistently estimate σ_α^2 as $\hat{\sigma}_\alpha^2 = 0.1209 - 0.1234/8 = 0.1055$. Consequently, the factor ψ is estimated as

$$\hat{\psi} = \frac{0.1234}{0.1234 + 8 \times 0.1055} = 0.1276,$$

leading to an estimate for ϑ in (10.23) of $\hat{\vartheta} = 1 - \hat{\psi}^{1/2} = 0.6428$. This means that the EGLS estimator can be obtained from a transformed regression where 0.64 times the individual mean is subtracted from the original data. Recall that OLS imposes $\vartheta = 0$ whereas the fixed effects estimator employs $\vartheta = 1$. Note that both the OLS and the random effects estimates are in between the between and fixed effects estimates.

If the assumptions of the random effects model are satisfied, all four estimators in Table 10.2 are consistent, the random effects estimator being the most efficient one. If, however, the individual effects α_i are correlated with one or more of the explanatory variables, the fixed effects estimator is the only one that is consistent. This hypothesis can be tested by comparing the between and within estimators, or the within and random effects estimators, which leads to tests that are equivalent. The simplest one to perform is the Hausman test discussed in Subsection 10.2.4, based upon the latter comparison. The test statistic takes a value of 31.75 and reflects the differences in the coefficients on experience, experience-squared and the union, married and public sector dummies. Under the null hypothesis, the statistic follows a Chi-squared distribution with five degrees of freedom, so that we have to reject the null at any reasonable level of significance.

Marital status is a variable that is likely to be correlated with the unobserved heterogeneity in α_i. Typically one would not expect an important *causal* effect of being married upon one's wage, so that the marital dummy is typically capturing other (unobservable) differences between married and unmarried workers. This is confirmed by the results in the table. If we eliminate the individual effects from the model and consider the fixed effects estimator, the effect of being married reduces to 4.5%, whereas for the between estimator, for example, it is almost 15%. Note that the effect of being married in the fixed effects approach is identified only through people who change marital status over the sample period. Similar remarks can be made for the effect of union status upon a person's wage. Recall, however, that all estimators assume that the explanatory variables

Table 10.2 Estimation results wage equation, males 1980–1987 (standard errors in parentheses)

Dependent variable: log(*wage*)				
Variable	Between	Fixed effects	OLS	Random effects
constant	0.490	–	−0.034	−0.104
	(0.221)		(0.120)	(0.111)
schooling	0.095	–	0.099	0.101
	(0.011)		(0.009)	(0.009)
experience	−0.050	0.116	0.089	0.112
	(0.050)	(0.008)	(0.012)	(0.008)
experience^2	0.0051	−0.0043	−0.0028	−0.0041
	(0.0032)	(0.0006)	(0.0009)	(0.0006)
union member	0.274	0.081	0.180	0.106
	(0.047)	(0.019)	(0.028)	(0.018)
married	0.145	0.045	0.108	0.063
	(0.041)	(0.018)	(0.026)	(0.017)
black	−0.139	–	−0.144	−0.144
	(0.049)		(0.050)	(0.048)
hispanic	0.005	–	0.016	0.020
	(0.043)		(0.039)	(0.043)
public sector	−0.056	0.035	0.004	0.030
	(0.109)	(0.039)	(0.050)	(0.036)
within R^2	0.0470	0.1782	0.1679	0.1776
between R^2	0.2196	0.0006	0.2027	0.1835
overall R^2	0.1371	0.0642	0.1866	0.1808

are uncorrelated with the idiosyncratic error term u_{it}. If such correlations were to exist, even the fixed effects estimator would be inconsistent. Vella and Verbeek (1998) concentrate on the impact of endogenous union status on wages for this group of workers and consider alternative, more complicated, estimators.

The goodness-of-fit measures confirm that the fixed effects estimator results in the largest within R^2 and thus explains the within variation as well as possible. The OLS estimator maximizes the usual (overall) R^2, while the random effects estimator results in reasonable R^2s in all dimensions. Recall that the OLS standard errors in Table 10.2 are adjusted for heteroskedasticity and arbitrary forms of serial correlation in the error terms. Routinely computed standard errors assuming i.i.d. error terms are inappropriate, and – in this application – sometimes less than half of the correct ones.

10.4 Dynamic Linear Models

Among the major advantages of panel data is the ability to model individual dynamics. Many economic models suggest that current behaviour depends upon past behaviour (persistence, habit formation, partial adjustment, etc.), so in many cases we would like to estimate a dynamic model on an individual level. The ability to do so is unique for panel data.

10.4.1 An Autoregressive Panel Data Model

Consider the linear dynamic model with exogenous variables and a lagged dependent variable, that is,

$$y_{it} = x_{it}'\beta + \gamma y_{i,t-1} + \alpha_i + u_{it},$$

where it is assumed that u_{it} is $IID(0, \sigma_u^2)$. In the static model, we have seen arguments of consistency (robustness) and efficiency for choosing between a fixed or random effects treatment of the α_i. In a dynamic model the situation is substantially different, because $y_{i,t-1}$ will depend upon α_i, irrespective of the way we treat α_i. To illustrate the problems that this causes, we first consider the case where there are no exogenous variables included and the model reads

$$y_{it} = \gamma y_{i,t-1} + \alpha_i + u_{it}, \quad |\gamma| < 1. \tag{10.43}$$

Assume that we have observations on y_{it} for periods $t = 0, 1, \ldots, T$. Because $y_{i,t-1}$ and α_i are positively correlated, applying OLS to (10.43) is inconsistent, overestimating the true autoregressive coefficient (in the typical case where $\gamma > 0$). Similarly, the random effects approach is inconsistent.

The fixed effects estimator for γ is given by

$$\hat{\gamma}_{FE} = \frac{\sum_{i=1}^N \sum_{t=1}^T (y_{it} - \bar{y}_i)(y_{i,t-1} - \bar{y}_{i,-1})}{\sum_{i=1}^N \sum_{t=1}^T (y_{i,t-1} - \bar{y}_{i,-1})^2}, \tag{10.44}$$

where $\bar{y}_i = (1/T)\sum_{t=1}^T y_{it}$ and $\bar{y}_{i,-1} = (1/T)\sum_{t=1}^T y_{i,t-1}$. To analyse the properties of $\hat{\gamma}_{FE}$, we can substitute (10.43) into (10.44) to obtain

$$\hat{\gamma}_{FE} = \gamma + \frac{1/(NT)\sum_{i=1}^N \sum_{t=1}^T (u_{it} - \bar{u}_i)(y_{i,t-1} - \bar{y}_{i,-1})}{1/(NT)\sum_{i=1}^N \sum_{i=1}^T (y_{i,t-1} - \bar{y}_{i,-1})^2}. \tag{10.45}$$

This estimator, however, is biased and inconsistent for $N \to \infty$ and fixed T, as the last term on the right-hand side of (10.45) does not have expectation zero and does not converge to zero if N goes to infinity. In particular, it can be shown that (see Nickell, 1981; or Hsiao, 2014, Section 4.2)

$$\operatorname*{plim}_{N\to\infty} \frac{1}{NT} \sum_{i=1}^N \sum_{t=1}^T (u_{it} - \bar{u}_i)(y_{i,t-1} - \bar{y}_{i,-1}) = -\frac{\sigma_u^2}{T^2} \cdot \frac{(T-1) - T\gamma + \gamma^T}{(1-\gamma)^2} \neq 0. \tag{10.46}$$

Thus, for fixed T we have an inconsistent estimator. Note that this inconsistency is not caused by anything we assumed about the α_is, as these are eliminated in estimation. The problem is that the within transformed lagged dependent variable is correlated with the within transformed error. If $T \to \infty$, (10.46) converges to 0 so that the fixed effects estimator is consistent for γ if both $T \to \infty$ and $N \to \infty$.

One could think that the asymptotic bias for fixed T is quite small and therefore not a real problem. This is certainly not the case, as for finite T the bias can hardly be ignored. For example, if the true value of γ equals 0.5, it can easily be computed that (for $N \to \infty$)

$$\begin{aligned}
\text{plim } \hat{\gamma}_{FE} &= -0.25 \quad \text{if } T = 2,\\
\text{plim } \hat{\gamma}_{FE} &= -0.04 \quad \text{if } T = 3,\\
\text{plim } \hat{\gamma}_{FE} &= 0.33 \quad \text{if } T = 10,
\end{aligned}$$

so even for moderate values of T the bias is substantial. Fortunately, there are relatively easy ways to avoid these biases.

To solve the inconsistency problem, we first of all start with a different transformation to eliminate the individual effects α_i, in particular we take first differences. This gives

$$y_{it} - y_{i,t-1} = \gamma(y_{i,t-1} - y_{i,t-2}) + (u_{it} - u_{i,t-1}), \quad t = 2, \ldots, T. \tag{10.47}$$

If we estimate this by OLS, we do not obtain a consistent estimator for γ because $y_{i,t-1}$ and $u_{i,t-1}$ are, by definition, correlated, even if $T \to \infty$. In many applications, this first-difference estimator appears to be severely biased. However, this transformed specification suggests an instrumental variables approach. For example, $y_{i,t-2}$ is correlated with $y_{i,t-1} - y_{i,t-2}$ but not with $u_{i,t-1}$, unless u_{it} exhibits autocorrelation (which we excluded by assumption). This suggests an instrumental variables estimator[10] for γ as

$$\hat{\gamma}_{IV} = \frac{\sum_{i=1}^{N} \sum_{t=2}^{T} y_{i,t-2}(y_{it} - y_{i,t-1})}{\sum_{i=1}^{N} \sum_{t=2}^{T} y_{i,t-2}(y_{i,t-1} - y_{i,t-2})}. \tag{10.48}$$

A necessary condition for consistency of this estimator is that

$$\text{plim} \; \frac{1}{N(T-1)} \sum_{i=1}^{N} \sum_{t=2}^{T} (u_{it} - u_{i,t-1}) y_{i,t-2} = 0 \tag{10.49}$$

for T or N or both going to infinity. The estimator in (10.48) is one of the estimators proposed by Anderson and Hsiao (1981). They also proposed an alternative, where $y_{i,t-2} - y_{i,t-3}$ is used as an instrument. This gives

$$\hat{\gamma}_{IV}^{(2)} = \frac{\sum_{i=1}^{N} \sum_{t=3}^{T} (y_{i,t-2} - y_{i,t-3})(y_{it} - y_{i,t-1})}{\sum_{i=1}^{N} \sum_{t=3}^{T} (y_{i,t-2} - y_{i,t-3})(y_{i,t-1} - y_{i,t-2})}, \tag{10.50}$$

which is consistent (under regularity conditions) if

$$\text{plim} \; \frac{1}{N(T-2)} \sum_{i=1}^{N} \sum_{t=3}^{T} (u_{it} - u_{i,t-1})(y_{i,t-2} - y_{i,t-3}) = 0. \tag{10.51}$$

Note that the second instrumental variables estimator requires an additional lag to construct the instrument, such that the effective number of observations used in estimation is reduced (one sample period is 'lost').

Consistency of both Anderson–Hsiao estimators is achieved under the assumption that u_{it} has no autocorrelation. However, Arellano (1989) has shown that the estimator that uses the first-differenced instrument, when exogenous variables are added to the model, suffers from large variances over a wide range of values for γ. In addition, Monte Carlo evidence by Arellano and Bover (1995) shows that the levels version of the Anderson–Hsiao estimator can have large biases and large standard errors, particularly when γ is close to one. Alternative estimators have been developed that build upon the Anderson–Hsiao approach. These approaches, formulated in a method of moments

[10] See Section 5.3 for a general introduction to instrumental variables estimation.

framework, unify the previous estimators and eliminate the disadvantages of reduced sample sizes. The first step is to note that

$$\text{plim} \frac{1}{N(T-1)} \sum_{i=1}^{N} \sum_{t=2}^{T} (u_{it} - u_{i,t-1}) y_{i,t-2} = E\{(u_{it} - u_{i,t-1}) y_{i,t-2}\} = 0 \tag{10.52}$$

is a moment condition (compare Chapter 5). Similarly,

$$\begin{aligned} \text{plim} & \frac{1}{N(T-2)} \sum_{i=1}^{N} \sum_{t=3}^{T} (u_{it} - u_{i,t-1})(y_{i,t-2} - y_{i,t-3}) \\ & = E\{(u_{it} - u_{i,t-1})(y_{i,t-2} - y_{i,t-3})\} = 0 \end{aligned} \tag{10.53}$$

is a moment condition. Both IV estimators thus impose one moment condition in estimation. It is well known that imposing more moment conditions increases the efficiency of the estimators (provided the additional conditions are valid, of course). Arellano and Bond (1991) suggest that the list of instruments can be extended by exploiting additional moment conditions and letting their number vary with t. To do this, they keep T fixed. For example, when $T = 4$, we have

$$E\{(u_{i2} - u_{i1}) y_{i0}\} = 0$$

as the moment condition for $t = 2$. For $t = 3$, we have

$$E\{(u_{i3} - u_{i2}) y_{i1}\} = 0,$$

but it also holds that

$$E\{(u_{i3} - u_{i2}) y_{i0}\} = 0.$$

For period $t = 4$, we have three moment conditions and three valid instruments:

$$\begin{aligned} E\{(u_{i4} - u_{i3}) y_{i0}\} &= 0, \\ E\{(u_{i4} - u_{i3}) y_{i1}\} &= 0, \\ E\{(u_{i4} - u_{i3}) y_{i2}\} &= 0. \end{aligned}$$

All these moment conditions can be exploited in a GMM framework. To introduce the GMM estimator, define for general sample size T

$$\Delta \varepsilon_i = \begin{pmatrix} u_{i2} - u_{i1} \\ \cdots \\ u_{i,T} - u_{i,T-1} \end{pmatrix} \tag{10.54}$$

as the vector of transformed error terms, and

$$Z_i = \begin{pmatrix} [y_{i0}] & 0 & \cdots & 0 \\ 0 & [y_{i0}, y_{i1}] & & 0 \\ \vdots & & \ddots & 0 \\ 0 & \cdots & 0 & [y_{i0}, \ldots, y_{i,T-2}] \end{pmatrix} \tag{10.55}$$

as the matrix of instruments. Each row in the matrix Z_i contains the instruments that are valid for a given period. Consequently, the set of all moment conditions can be written concisely as

$$E\{Z_i'\Delta u_i\} = 0. \tag{10.56}$$

Note that these are $1 + 2 + 3 + \cdots + T - 1$ conditions. To derive the GMM estimator, write this as

$$E\{Z_i'(\Delta y_i - \gamma \Delta y_{i,-1})\} = 0. \tag{10.57}$$

Because the number of moment conditions will typically exceed the number of unknown coefficients, we estimate γ by minimizing a quadratic expression in terms of the corresponding sample moments (compare Chapter 5), that is,

$$\min_{\gamma} \left[\frac{1}{N}\sum_{i=1}^{N} Z_i'(\Delta y_i - \gamma \Delta y_{i,-1})\right]' W_N \left[\frac{1}{N}\sum_{i=1}^{N} Z_i'(\Delta y_i - \gamma \Delta y_{i,-1})\right], \tag{10.58}$$

where W_N is a symmetric positive definite weighting matrix.[11] Differentiating this with respect to γ and solving for γ gives

$$\hat{\gamma}_{GMM} = \left(\left(\sum_{i=1}^{N} \Delta y_{i,-1}' Z_i\right) W_N \left(\sum_{i=1}^{N} Z_i' \Delta y_{i,-1}\right)\right)^{-1} \times \left(\sum_{i=1}^{N} \Delta y_{i,-1}' Z_i\right) W_N \left(\sum_{i=1}^{N} Z_i' \Delta y_i\right). \tag{10.59}$$

The properties of this estimator, referred to as **first-difference GMM**, depend upon the choice for W_N, although it is consistent as long as W_N is positive definite, for example, for $W_N = I$, the identity matrix.

The **optimal weighting matrix** is the one that gives the most efficient estimator, that is, that gives the smallest asymptotic covariance matrix for $\hat{\gamma}_{GMM}$. From the general theory of GMM in Chapter 5, we know that the optimal weighting matrix is (asymptotically) proportional to the inverse of the covariance matrix of the sample moments. In this case, this means that the optimal weighting matrix should satisfy

$$\operatorname*{plim}_{N\to\infty} W_N = V\{Z_i'\Delta u_i\}^{-1} = E\{Z_i'\Delta u_i \Delta u_i' Z_i\}^{-1}. \tag{10.60}$$

In the standard case where no restrictions are imposed upon the covariance matrix of u_i, this can be estimated using a first-step consistent estimator of γ and replacing the expectation operator with a sample average. This gives

$$\hat{W}_N^{opt} = \left(\frac{1}{N}\sum_{i=1}^{N} Z_i'\Delta\hat{u}_i \Delta\hat{u}_i' Z_i\right)^{-1}, \tag{10.61}$$

where $\Delta\hat{u}_i$ is a residual vector from a first-step consistent estimator, for example, using $W_N = I$.

[11] The suffix N reflects that W_N can depend upon the sample size N and does not reflect the dimension of the matrix.

The general GMM approach does not impose that u_{it} is i.i.d. over individuals and time, and the optimal weighting matrix is thus estimated without imposing these restrictions. In the current model, however, the absence of autocorrelation is required to guarantee the validity of the moment conditions. Instead of estimating the optimal weighting matrix unrestrictedly, it is also possible (and potentially advisable in small samples) to impose the absence of autocorrelation in u_{it}, combined with a homoskedasticity assumption. Noting that under these restrictions

$$E\{\Delta u_i \Delta u_i'\} = \sigma_u^2 G = \sigma_u^2 \begin{pmatrix} 2 & -1 & 0 & \cdots \\ -1 & 2 & \ddots & 0 \\ 0 & \ddots & \ddots & -1 \\ \vdots & 0 & -1 & 2 \end{pmatrix}, \tag{10.62}$$

the optimal weighting matrix can be determined as

$$W_N^{opt} = \left(\frac{1}{N} \sum_{i=1}^{N} Z_i' G Z_i \right)^{-1}. \tag{10.63}$$

Note that this matrix does not involve unknown parameters, so that the optimal GMM estimator can be computed in one step if the original errors u_{it} are assumed to be homoskedastic and exhibit no autocorrelation.

Under weak regularity conditions, the first-difference GMM estimator for γ is consistent and asymptotically normal for $N \to \infty$ and fixed T, with its covariance matrix given by

$$\operatorname*{plim}_{N\to\infty} \left(\left(\frac{1}{N} \sum_{i=1}^{N} \Delta y_{i,-1}' Z_i \right) \left(\frac{1}{N} \sum_{i=1}^{N} Z_i' \Delta u_i \Delta u_i' Z_i \right)^{-1} \left(\frac{1}{N} \sum_{i=1}^{N} Z_i' \Delta y_{i,-1} \right) \right)^{-1}. \tag{10.64}$$

This follows from the more general expressions in Section 5.8. With i.i.d. errors the middle term reduces to

$$\sigma_u^2 W_N^{opt} = \sigma_u^2 \left(\frac{1}{N} \sum_{i=1}^{N} Z_i' G Z_i \right)^{-1}.$$

Alvarez and Arellano (2003) show that, in general, the first-difference GMM estimator is also consistent when both N and T tend to infinity, despite the fact that the number of moment conditions tends to infinity with the sample size. For large T, however, the first-difference GMM estimator will be close to the fixed effects estimator, which provides a more attractive alternative.

Importantly, the IV and first-difference GMM estimators discussed above break down when $\gamma = 1$, a case referred to as a 'unit root'. This is because the instruments $y_{i,t-2}$, $y_{i,t-3}, \ldots$ are no longer correlated with the first-differenced regressor $\Delta y_{i,t-1}$. In this case, the estimators are inconsistent and have a nonstandard asymptotic distribution.

Despite its theoretical appeal, the empirical implementation of the first-difference GMM estimator quite often suffers from poor small sample properties, mostly attributable to the large number of, potentially weak, instruments. In Subsection 10.4.3 we discuss this issue in more detail, including some ways to control the problem of instrument proliferation.

10.4.2 Dynamic Models with Exogenous Variables

If the model also contains exogenous variables, we have

$$y_{it} = x_{it}'\beta + \gamma y_{i,t-1} + \alpha_i + u_{it}, \tag{10.65}$$

which can also be estimated by the generalized instrumental variables or GMM approach. Depending upon the assumptions made about x_{it}, different sets of additional instruments can be constructed. If the x_{it} are *strictly exogenous* in the sense that they are uncorrelated with any of the u_{is} error terms, we also have

$$E\{x_{is}\Delta u_{it}\} = 0 \quad \text{for each } s, t, \tag{10.66}$$

so that $x_{i1}, \ldots, x_{iT}$ can be added to the instruments list for the first-differenced equation in each period. This would make the number of rows in Z_i quite large. Instead, almost the same level of information may be retained when the first-differenced x_{it}s are used as their own instruments.[12] In this case, we impose the moment conditions

$$E\{\Delta x_{it}\Delta u_{it}\} = 0 \quad \text{for each } t \tag{10.67}$$

and the instrument matrix can be written as

$$Z_i = \begin{pmatrix} [y_{i0}, \Delta x_{i2}'] & 0 & \cdots & 0 \\ 0 & [y_{i0}, y_{i1}, \Delta x_{i3}'] & & 0 \\ \vdots & & \ddots & 0 \\ 0 & \cdots & 0 & [y_{i0}, \ldots, y_{i,T-2}, \Delta x_{iT}'] \end{pmatrix}.$$

If the x_{it} variables are not strictly exogenous but **predetermined**, in which case current and lagged x_{it}s are uncorrelated with current error terms, we only have $E\{x_{it}u_{is}\} = 0$ for $s \geq t$. In this case, only $x_{i,t-1}, \ldots, x_{i1}$ are valid instruments for the first-differenced equation in period t. Thus, the moment conditions that can be imposed are

$$E\{x_{i,t-j}\Delta u_{it}\} = 0 \quad \text{for } j = 1, \ldots, t-1 \quad (\text{for each } t). \tag{10.68}$$

In practice, a combination of strictly exogenous and predetermined x variables may occur rather than one of these two extreme cases. The matrix Z_i should then be adjusted accordingly. Baltagi (2013, Chapter 8) provides additional discussion and examples.

Arellano and Bover (1995) provide a framework to integrate the above approach with the instrumental variables estimators of Hausman and Taylor (1981) and others discussed in Subsection 10.2.6. Most importantly, they discuss how information in levels can also be exploited in estimation. That is, in addition to the moment conditions presented above, it is also possible to exploit the presence of valid instruments for the levels equation (10.43) or (10.65), or their averages over time (the between regression). This is of particular importance when the individual series are highly persistent and γ is close to one. In this case, the first-difference GMM estimator may suffer from severe finite sample biases because the instruments are weak; see Blundell and Bond (1998), Blundell, Bond and Windmeijer (2000) and Arellano (2003, Section 6.6). Under certain assumptions, suitably lagged differences of y_{it} can be used to instrument the equation in levels, in addition to the

[12] We give up potential efficiency gains if some x_{it} variables help 'explaining' the lagged endogenous variables.

instruments for the first-differenced equation. For example, if $E\{\Delta y_{i,t-1}\alpha_i\} = 0$, $\Delta y_{i,t-1}$ can be used to instrument $y_{i,t-1}$ in (10.43) and

$$E\{(y_{it} - \gamma y_{i,t-1})(y_{i,t-1} - y_{i,t-2})\} = 0$$

is a valid moment condition that can be added (in the absence of serial correlation in u_{it}). Estimators that use moment conditions based on both levels and first-differences are typically referred to as **system GMM**. The validity of the additional instrument depends upon the assumption that changes in y_{it} are uncorrelated with the fixed effects. This means that individuals are in a kind of steady state, in the sense that deviations from long-term values, conditional upon the exogenous variables, are not systematically related to α_i. Unfortunately, when γ is close to one this assumption is the least likely to be satisfied, given that it takes many periods for deviations from the steady state to decay away. As stressed by Roodman (2009), in situations where system GMM offers the most hope, it may offer the least help.

10.4.3 Too Many Instruments

In Subsections 5.6.4 and 5.8.4 we discussed the problems of weak instruments and weak identification in a GMM context. When instruments are weak, they provide only very little information about the parameters of interest, which leads to poor small sample properties of the GMM estimator. Another, but related, problem arises when the number of instruments (moment conditions) is too large relative to the sample size. The estimation of dynamic panel data models is a situation that can easily suffer from having too many instruments. Note, for example, that for both the first-difference GMM and system GMM estimators, the number of instruments increases quadratically with T. The consequence is that the GMM estimator has very poor small sample properties, and traditional misspecification tests, like the test for overidentifying restrictions, tend to be misleading. This may be particularly the case for the two-step estimator, which relies upon the estimation of a potentially high dimensional optimal weighting matrix.

Roodman (2009) discusses the two main symptoms of instrument proliferation. The first one, which applies to instrumental variable estimators in general, is that numerous instruments can overfit endogenous variables. In finite samples, instruments never have exactly zero correlation with the endogenous components of the instrumented variables, because of sampling variability. Having many instruments therefore results in a small sample bias in the direction of OLS. To illustrate this, consider the extreme case where the number of instruments equals the number of observations. In this case, the first stage (reduced form) regressions (see Subsection 5.6.4) will produce an R^2 of 1, and the instrumental variables estimator reduces to OLS. Accordingly, it is recommendable to reduce the number of instruments, even if they are all theoretically valid and relevant, to reduce the small sample bias in the GMM estimator (see, e.g., Windmeijer, 2005).

The second problem is specific for the two-step GMM estimator that employs an optimal weighting matrix, which needs to be estimated. The number of elements in this matrix is quadratic in the number of instruments, and therefore extremely large when the number of instruments is large.[13] As a result, estimates for the optimal weighting matrix tend to be very imprecise when there are many instruments (see Roodman, 2009,

[13] For example, to estimate (10.43) with $T = 15$, (10.55) and (10.56) result in 105 moment conditions giving 5565 unique elements in the optimal weighting matrix (10.61).

for more details). This has two consequences. First, the standard errors for two-step GMM estimators tend to be severely downward biased. Second, the overidentifying restrictions test, as discussed in Subsection 5.8.2, is far too optimistic in the sense that it rejects the null hypothesis in far too few cases. Bowsher (2002), for example, shows that the overidentifying restrictions test for first-difference GMM, using the full set of instruments in (10.55), almost never rejects when T becomes too large for a given value of N, under both the null hypothesis and many relevant alternatives. When the number of instruments is large, the overidentifying restrictions test may therefore fail to indicate any misspecification or invalid instrumentation. Windmeijer (2005) derives a correction to improve the estimator for the GMM covariance matrix.

A general conclusion from the discussion above is that it is recommendable to reduce the instrument count in the estimation of dynamic panel data models. An obvious way of doing so is to use only certain lags instead of all available lags of the instruments. This way the number of columns in (10.55) can be substantially reduced. An alternative approach is presented in Roodman (2009). He suggests to combine instruments through addition into smaller sets. This has the potential advantage of retaining more information, as no instruments are dropped. Instead of imposing

$$E\{(u_{it} - u_{i,t-1})y_{i,t-s}\} = 0, \quad t = 2, 3, \ldots, T, \; s = 2, 3, \ldots$$

we impose

$$E\{(u_{it} - u_{i,t-1})y_{i,t-s}\} = 0, \quad s = 2, 3, \ldots$$

The new moment conditions embody the same belief about the orthogonality of $u_{it} - u_{i,t-1}$ and $y_{i,t-s}$, but we do not separate the sample moments for each time period. The matrix of instruments then collapses to

$$Z_i^* = \begin{pmatrix} y_{i0} & 0 & 0 & \cdots & 0 \\ y_{i0} & y_{i1} & 0 & \cdots & 0 \\ y_{i0} & y_{i1} & y_{i2} & \cdots & 0 \\ \vdots & \vdots & \vdots & \ddots & \vdots \\ y_{i0} & y_{i1} & \cdots & y_{i,T-3} & y_{i,T-2} \end{pmatrix}. \tag{10.69}$$

These ways of reducing the number of instruments provides some relevant robustness checks for the coefficient estimates, standard errors and misspecification tests. Roodman (2009) presents Monte Carlo evidence showing that reducing and/or collapsing instruments helps to reduce the bias in first-difference and system GMM estimators and to increase the ability of the overidentifying restrictions tests to detect misspecification. In general, he recommends that 'results should be aggressively tested for sensitivity to reductions in the number of instruments'.

In Section 10.5 we continue with an empirical example on the estimation of a dynamic panel data model for a firm's capital structure, using a maximum of 15 years of data. Section 10.6 focuses on the recent literature on panel time series, including tests for unit roots and cointegration. Typically this literature assumes that the number of time periods is sufficiently large, such that the small sample bias in the within estimator for the dynamic panel data model is of secondary importance. Readers who are more interested in micro-econometric applications can continue with Section 10.7, which discusses panel data models with limited dependent variables.

10.5 Illustration: Explaining Capital Structure

The capital structure of a firm tells us how a firm finances its operations, the most important sources being debt and equity. In their seminal paper, Modigliani and Miller (1958) show that in a frictionless world with efficient capital markets a firm's capital structure is irrelevant for its value. In reality, however, market imperfections, like taxes and bankruptcy costs, may make firm value depend on capital structure, and it can be argued that firms select optimal target debt ratios on the basis of a trade-off between the costs and benefits of debt. For example, firms would make a trade-off between the tax benefits of debt financing[14] and the costs of financial distress when they have borrowed too much. In this section, we follow Flannery and Rangan (2006) and investigate the explanatory power of the trade-off theory taking into account that firms may adjust only partially towards their target capital structure. This leads to a dynamic panel data model for the firm's debt ratio.

A firm's debt ratio measures the portion of a firm's capitalization financed with debt and can be defined as

$$MDR_{it} = \frac{D_{it}}{D_{it} + S_{it}P_{it}},$$

where D_{it} is the book value of a firm's interest-bearing debt, S_{it} is the number of common shares outstanding and P_{it} denotes the price per share, all at time t. If a firm is financed by a relatively great deal of debt, it is said to be highly leveraged. The optimal or target debt ratio of a firm at time t is assumed to depend upon firm characteristics, known at time $t-1$ and related to the costs and benefits of operating with various leverage ratios. Accordingly, the target debt ratio is assumed to satisfy

$$MDR^*_{it} = x'_{i,t-1}\beta + \eta_{it},$$

where η_{it} is a mean zero error term accounting for unobserved heterogeneity.

Adjustment costs may prevent firms from choosing their target debt ratio at each point in time. To accommodate this, we specify a target adjustment model as

$$MDR_{it} - MDR_{i,t-1} = (1-\gamma)(MDR^*_{it} - MDR_{i,t-1}),$$

where $0 \leq \gamma \leq 1$ (compare (9.10)). The coefficient γ measures the adjustment speed and is assumed to be identical across firms. If $\gamma = 0$, firms adjust immediately and completely to their target debt ratio. Combining the previous two equations, we can write

$$MDR_{it} = \gamma MDR_{i,t-1} + x'_{i,t-1}\beta(1-\gamma) + \varepsilon_{it},$$

where $\varepsilon_{it} = (1-\gamma)\eta_{it}$. Because it is likely that time-invariant unobserved firm-specific heterogeneity plays a role, our final specification is written as

$$MDR_{it} = \gamma MDR_{i,t-1} + x'_{i,t-1}\beta^* + \alpha_i + u_{it}, \qquad (10.70)$$

which corresponds to a standard dynamic panel data model as discussed in the previous section.

The data we use and the choice of explanatory variables are similar to those in Flannery and Rangan (2006). Our sample of firms is taken from the Compustat Industrial Annual

[14] In most countries interest payments are tax deductible.

Tapes and covers the years 1987 to 2001 ($T = 15$), where we exclude financial firms and regulated utilities whose financing decisions may reflect special factors. Our final sample contains a random subsample of the larger panel covering $N = 3777$ firms and 19 573 firm-year observations. The panel is unbalanced, with the average firm being observed for 5.2 years. To model the target debt ratio, the following variables are used:

ebit_ta	earnings before interest payments and taxes, divided by total assets
mb	ratio of market value to book value of assets
dep_ta	depreciation expenses as a proportion of fixed assets
log(*ta*)	log of total assets
fa_ta	proportion of fixed assets
rd_ta	research and development expenditures, divided by total assets (0 if missing)
rd_dum	dummy indicating whether *rd_ta* is missing
indmedian	industry median debt ratio
rated	dummy indicating whether the firm has a public debt rating

Because information on R&D expenditures is missing for a substantial proportion of the firm-years, we follow Flannery and Rangan (2006)'s pragmatic solution to add a dummy variable to the model equal to one if R&D information is missing.[15] We first estimate the dynamic model in (10.70) by three estimators that are known to be inconsistent for $N \to \infty$ and fixed T: OLS, the within estimator from Subsection 10.2.1 and the first-difference estimator from Subsection 10.2.2. The results are presented in Table 10.3, where all standard errors are calculated in the panel-robust way.[16] That is, standard errors are adjusted for heteroskedasticity and arbitrary forms of within-firm serial correlation (see Subsection 10.2.7). From Subsection 10.4.1, we expect that the OLS estimator for γ overestimates the true coefficient on the lagged dependent variable, whereas the within (fixed effects) estimator will underestimate it (see also Bond, 2002). The first-difference estimator is expected substantially to underestimate the true impact of the lagged dependent variable, particularly if γ is large. This can be understood from (10.47), noting that the first-difference estimator and the within estimator are identical for $T = 2$. These expectations are confirmed in Table 10.3.

The differences between the OLS, within and first-difference results are substantial. The OLS coefficient on lagged *MDR* of 0.883 implies that firms close only 11.7% of the gap between the current and target debt ratio within 1 year. This slow adjustment is consistent with the hypothesis that other considerations outweigh the cost of deviation from optimal leverage. However, the fixed effects approach estimates adjustment to be much faster, with an estimated adjustment speed of 46.5%. The first-difference estimate of −0.110 is simply ridiculous and is mainly presented here to show that inappropriate estimation techniques may yield strongly conflicting and economically senseless results. Given that the OLS and within estimates are probably biased in the opposite direction, we would expect the true adjustment speed to be between 0.535 and 0.884 (ignoring sampling error). Another notable difference between the columns in Table 10.3 is the

[15] In Subsection 2.9.3 we argued that this approach may lead to biased estimation results. This problem is ignored here.

[16] All first-difference estimation results in this section are based on a specification excluding an intercept.

Table 10.3 OLS, within and OLS-FD estimation results dynamic model (panel-robust standard errors in parentheses)

Variable	OLS	Within	First-difference
MDR_{t-1}	0.884	0.535	−0.110
	(0.005)	(0.012)	(0.012)
ebit_ta	−0.032	−0.050	−0.046
	(0.007)	(0.011)	(0.010)
mb	0.0016	0.0023	0.0028
	(0.0007)	(0.0010)	(0.0011)
dep_ta	−0.261	−0.124	0.184
	(0.035)	(0.071)	(0.079)
log(*ta*)	−0.0007	0.038	0.073
	(0.0006)	(0.003)	(0.005)
fa_ta	0.020	0.059	0.101
	(0.006)	(0.017)	(0.018)
rd_dum	0.007	0.0001	−0.017
	(0.002)	(0.0081)	(0.009)
rd_ta	−0.120	−0.066	−0.052
	(0.013)	(0.026)	(0.029)
indmedian	0.032	0.167	0.179
	(0.010)	(0.022)	(0.026)
rated	0.007	0.021	0.011
	(0.003)	(0.006)	(0.007)
within R^2		0.340	
between R^2		0.641	
overall R^2	0.741	0.563	0.033

estimated impact of firm size. The OLS estimate is statistically insignificant, whereas the within and first-difference estimates both yield a highly significant positive coefficient ($t = 12.39$ and $t = 4.89$, respectively). The latter results seem to make more sense, because large firms tend to operate with more leverage, for example, because they have better access to public debt markets. The industry median is included to control for industry characteristics that are not captured by the other explanatory variables and is expected to have a positive coefficient. The magnitude of the coefficient for *indmedian* is larger for the within and first-difference results than for OLS, and so is its statistical significance. The variable *rated* is potentially endogenous, as a firm's credit rating may depend upon its capital structure. We follow Flannery and Rangan (2006) and simply include *rated* as additional explanatory variable, noting that its inclusion or exclusion has little impact on the other coefficient estimates. Note that for most coefficients the OLS robust-standard errors are smaller than the within and first-difference ones. This makes sense as the latter two approaches allow for fixed effects and only identify the coefficients from the within variation in the data. For example, *rd_dum* exhibits very little time variation, and therefore its effect is not very accurately estimated with the fixed effects approaches.

As mentioned before, all estimators in Table 10.3 are inconsistent. The first-difference estimator, while allowing for correlation between α_i and the explanatory variables, is severely biased because the first-differenced lagged dependent variable is highly negatively correlated with the first-differenced error term. The OLS results are inconsistent because of the correlation between the lagged debt ratio and α_i. Both biases do not disappear for $T \to \infty$. The within estimates also allow for fixed effects and thus for correlation between the unobservables in α_i and the explanatory variables, but they suffer from a small-T bias. Despite this, the latter results appear to make more sense than the OLS ones, suggesting that controlling for firm-specific fixed effects in the target debt ratio is important.

To estimate the current dynamic panel data model consistently for $N \to \infty$ and fixed T, the Anderson–Hsiao instrumental variables estimators and the Arellano–Bond GMM estimators are potential candidates. Table 10.4 presents the estimation results of the different approaches. All estimators presented in this table are based on exploiting instruments for the first-differenced equation. The first column presents the results for the Anderson–Hsiao estimator when $\Delta MDR_{i,t-2}$ is used as an instrument for $\Delta MDR_{i,t-1}$, while the second column presents the results when the level $MDR_{i,t-2}$ is used to instrument $\Delta MDR_{i,t-1}$. The differences between the two columns are striking. The estimator using the first-differenced instrument suffers from very high standard errors and extremely unrealistic parameter estimates. For example, the estimated value for γ is as high as 8.56 with a (panel-robust) standard error of 11.4. The estimator using the level instrument seems to produce a bit more realistic results, although the estimated coefficient on the lagged dependent variable is larger than one. A potential explanation for the poor performance of the first-difference Anderson–Hsiao estimator is a weak

Table 10.4 IV and GMM estimation results dynamic model

	Anderson–Hsiao IV		Arellano–Bond GMM	
Variable	Robust s.e.	Robust s.e.	One-step	Two-step
MDR_{t-1}	8.555	1.125	0.472	0.382
	(11.418)	(0.219)	(0.037)	(0.044)
ebit_ta	1.481	0.163	0.050	0.036
	(2.037)	(0.042)	(0.011)	(0.014)
mb	0.296	0.040	0.021	0.015
	(0.385)	(0.007)	(0.002)	(0.002)
dep_ta	−2.439	−0.151	−0.038	0.065
	(3.489)	(0.139)	(0.077)	(0.091)
log(*ta*)	−0.669	−0.032	0.025	0.030
	(0.981)	(0.019)	(0.005)	(0.006)
fa_ta	−1.337	−0.124	−0.005	0.015
	(1.906)	(0.051)	(0.019)	(0.022)
rd_dum	−0.023	−0.021	−0.018	−0.018
	(0.096)	(0.015)	(0.009)	(0.010)
rd_ta	1.068	0.099	0.019	0.001
	(1.560)	(0.052)	(0.033)	(0.031)
indmedian	−4.118	−0.463	0.101	0.092
	(5.681)	(0.121)	(0.034)	(0.034)
rated	−0.338	−0.042	−0.009	−0.007
	(0.464)	(0.013)	(0.082)	(0.007)
Overidentifying restrictions test ($df = 104$)			972.41	436.39
			($p = 0.0000$)	($p = 0.0000$)
Test for second-order autocorrelation in Δu_{it}			−3.287	−3.560
			($p = 0.0010$)	($p = 0.0003$)
Instruments:	ΔMDR_{t-2}	MDR_{t-2}	$MDR_{t-2}, MDR_{t-3}, \ldots$ (for each t)	

instrument problem.[17] We can easily check this by inspecting the underlying reduced-form equations (compare Subsection 5.6.4). In a regression explaining $\Delta MDR_{i,t-1}$ from the first-differenced variables $\Delta x_{i,t-1}$ as well as the proposed instrument $\Delta MDR_{i,t-2}$, the panel-robust t-value of the latter variable is only −1.02. This suggest that the instrument $\Delta MDR_{i,t-2}$ is basically irrelevant and we should not take the corresponding results seriously. For the reduced form containing the instrument $MDR_{i,t-2}$, the corresponding t-value is −5.38. Although this indicates that the Anderson–Hsiao results using the level instrument do not suffer from a weak instrument problem, they yield an economically unappealing estimate of 1.125 for the lagged dependent variable. A potential explanation for this outcome is that the exogeneity of the instrument $MDR_{i,t-2}$ is violated because of the presence of serial correlation in u_{it}.

An alternative approach is the use of the Arellano and Bond (1991) estimator, where further lags of *MDR* are used as instruments for lagged *MDR* (in the first-differenced equation). The results of this are also presented in Table 10.4, where we assume that the explanatory variables are strictly exogenous. The one-step estimates are based on the optimal weighting matrix under the assumption of homoskedasticity given in (10.63), while the two-step estimates use the more generally valid weighting matrix from (10.61). Although several studies have reported that the two-step (optimal GMM) standard errors are biased downwards in small samples and recommend using the one-step estimates, in the current application they appear to be larger than the one-step ones. The one-step GMM results correspond to an adjustment speed of 52.8%, whereas the two-step estimates imply an annual adjustment of 61.8%. Overall, the standard errors of the GMM estimates are relatively high, and a substantial number of explanatory variables are individually statistically insignificant. Further, the GMM results suffer from two additional problems. First, the Sargan test of overidentifying restrictions based on the one-step estimates produces a highly significant test statistic of 972.41. Note, however, that this test is only valid under homoskedasticity. The two-step estimates produce a lower value for the test of overidentifying restrictions, but still highly significant. Second, the hypothesis of no serial correlation in u_{it}, which is required for the instruments to be valid, is strongly rejected for both GMM estimators.[18]

In summary, none of the reported estimates for the dynamic model to explain firms' debt ratios is entirely convincing. The (inconsistent) OLS and within results from Table 10.3 suggest that the true γ coefficient should be in the range 0.535–0.884 (although this ignores the estimation error in both estimates). The GMM estimation results produce γ estimates less than 0.5, while the overidentifying restrictions tests reject both for the one-step and for the two-step results and the coefficient estimates for several other variables are economically unappealing. Recently, Elsas and Florysiak (2015) stress that leverage is a fractional variable, bounded by 0 and 1 and propose an alternative estimator taking this into account. For the current sample, almost 10% of the observations on market leverage is 0, and ignoring this may bias standard estimators. Their proposed maximum

[17] An alternative interpretation to this problem is given by Arellano (1989), who shows that with an autoregressive exogenous variable the Anderson–Hsiao estimator that uses first-differenced instruments has a singularity point and very large variances over a wide range of parameter values. The estimator that uses instruments in levels does not suffer from this problem.

[18] Along this line, Atanasov and Black (2017) argue that lagged endogenous variables are implausible instruments in corporate finance applications. In their words: 'If the lagged variable is time-persistent, the lagged version is not exogenous; if one moves to longer lags to avoid this problem, the lagged variable won't predict the nonlagged value well enough to be usable.'

likelihood estimator is based on an extension of the dynamic random effects tobit model discussed in Section 10.7.

It should be noted here that, if the true coefficient on the lagged dependent variable is close to unity, lagged levels as employed in the Arellano–Bond procedure are poor instruments for first differences. Arellano and Bover (1995) and Blundell and Bond (1998) develop alternative estimators that are based on adding the original equation in levels to the system and using suitably lagged first differences as instruments. Obviously, these first differences should then be orthogonal to α_i.

10.6 Panel Time Series

The recent literature exhibits an increasing integration of techniques and ideas from time series analysis, like unit roots and cointegration, into the area of panel data modelling. The underlying reason for this development is that researchers increasingly realize that cross-sectional information is a useful additional source of information that should be exploited. To analyse the effect of a certain policy measure, for example, adopting a road tax or a pollution tax, it may be more fruitful to compare with other countries than to try to extract information about these effects from the country's own history. Pooling data from different countries may also help to overcome the problem that sample sizes of time series are fairly small, so that tests regarding long-run properties are not very powerful.

A large number of recent articles discuss issues relating to unit roots, spurious regressions and cointegration in panel data. Most of this literature focuses upon the case in which the number of time periods T is fairly large, while the number of cross-sectional units N is small or moderate. As a consequence, it is quite important to deal with potential nonstationarity of the data series, while the presence of a unit root or cointegration may be of specific economic interest. For example, a wide range of applications exists concerning purchasing power parity, focusing on (non)stationarity of real exchange rates for a set of countries, or on testing for cointegration between nominal exchange rates and prices (compare Sections 8.5, 9.3, and Subsection 9.5.4).

In this section we consider panel time series analysis. For ease of discussion, we shall refer below to the cross-sectional units as countries, although they may also correspond to firms, industries or regions. The assumption is that T is sufficiently large to sensibly estimate a different time series model for each country. Because of this, it is natural to think of the possibility that model parameters are different across countries, a case commonly referred to as 'heterogeneous panels'. Pooling the data, by assuming (partial) homogeneity across countries, is potentially efficient and avoids the problem of large numbers of inaccurate country-specific coefficient estimates. How we deal with this issue can make much difference, particularly in dynamic models. For example, Baltagi and Griffin (1997) compare the performance of a wide range of homogeneous and heterogeneous parameter estimators in a dynamic model for gasoline demand in 18 OECD countries, and find surprising variability in the results. Robertson and Symons (1992) and Pesaran and Smith (1995) stress the importance of parameter heterogeneity in dynamic panel data models and analyse the potentially severe biases that may arise from handling it in an inappropriate manner; see also Canova (2007, Chapter 8) and Pesaran (2015, Chapter 28). Such biases are particularly misleading in a nonstationary world as the relationships of the individual series may be completely destroyed.

As long as we consider each time series individually, and the series are of sufficient length, there is not much wrong with applying the time series techniques from Chapters 8 and 9. However, if we pool different series, we have to be aware of the possibility that their processes do not all have the same characteristics or are described by the same parameters. For example, it is conceivable that y_{it} is stationary for country 1 but integrated of order one for country 2. Even when all variables are integrated of order one in each country, heterogeneity in cointegration properties may lead to problems. For example, if for each country i the variables y_{it} and x_{it} are cointegrated with parameter β_i, it holds that $y_{it} - \beta_i x_{it}$ is $I(0)$ for each i, but in general there does not exist a common cointegrating parameter β that makes $y_{it} - \beta x_{it}$ stationary for all i. Similarly, there is no guarantee that the cross-sectional averages $\bar{y}_t = \frac{1}{N}\sum_i y_{it}$ and $\bar{x}_t$ are cointegrated, even if all underlying individual series are cointegrated.

Another important issue is that of cross-sectional dependence. When we pool time series of different countries we have to be aware that these countries are likely to be affected by some common factors, such as global cycles. If the cross-sectional dependence is nonnegligible it has to be dealt with appropriately to make sure that there is any serious gain from pooling data from different countries.

In Subsection 10.6.1 we discuss the issue of cross-sectional heterogeneity, and illustrate some of the biases that can arise if pooling the data and assuming homogenous coefficients is inappropriate. The subsequent two subsections discuss panel unit root tests. These tests are directed at testing the joint null hypothesis of a unit root for each of the countries. Subsection 10.6.3 presents the most recent generation of panel unit root tests that allow for cross-sectional dependence. Finally, Subsection 10.6.4 pays attention to panel cointegration.

10.6.1 Heterogeneity

A common starting point in panel time series is to allow the model coefficients to differ across the units in the sample. For the static model, this implies

$$y_{it} = \alpha_i + x_{it}'\beta_i + u_{it}, \quad i = 1, \ldots, N, \tag{10.71}$$

where it is typically assumed that $u_{it} \sim IID(0, \sigma_{u,i}^2)$. This also allows the error variance to differ with i. With sufficiently large T it makes sense to separately estimate (10.71) for each country i. The question of whether to pool the data or not depends upon whether homogeneity of slope coefficients can be imposed. Tests for the joint hypothesis that $\beta_i = \beta$, $i = 1, \ldots, N$, are typically referred to as tests for **poolability** of the data (see Baltagi, 2013, Section 4.1). If $\beta_i = \beta$ and $\sigma_{u,i}^2 = \sigma_u^2$ for all i, the model reduces to the standard fixed or random effects model, depending upon the assumptions one is willing to make about α_i, and assuming that the error terms u_{it} are independent across units.

In **random coefficient models** it is assumed that, in addition to the intercept terms α_i the slope coefficients β_i also vary randomly across countries, independently from the regressors; see Hsiao and Pesaran (2008) for an overview. This states that $\beta_i = \beta + \eta_i$, where η_i is a vector of zero mean i.i.d. random variables, independent of $x_{i1}, \ldots, x_{iT}$. There exists a wide variety of estimators for $\beta = E\{\beta_i\}$, the average effect of x_{it}. The simplest one is to estimate (10.71) by OLS for each country and then take the average. This is referred to as the **mean group estimator** (Pesaran and Smith, 1995). Swamy (1970) proposes a feasible GLS estimator which produces a weighted average of the individual OLS estimates, where the weights are inversely proportional to their covariance matrices (see Hsiao and Pesaran, 2008). For sufficiently large T, the mean group and Swamy estimators are equivalent. An alternative estimator for β is the fixed effects estimator after pooling the data. Under (10.71) this corresponds to

$$y_{it} = \alpha_i + x_{it}'\beta + [x_{it}'(\beta_i - \beta) + u_{it}], \quad i = 1, \ldots, N. \tag{10.72}$$

When the regressors in (10.71) are strictly exogenous and the coefficients vary independently of the regressors, all these estimators will provide consistent estimators for β. However, this nice result does not carry over to dynamic models, and severe biases may arise if homogeneity is inappropriately imposed (Pesaran and Smith, 1995).

To illustrate the poor performance of pooled estimators in dynamic models with heterogeneity, consider the dynamic model of Section 10.4, given by

$$y_{it} = \alpha_i + x_{it}'\beta + \gamma y_{i,t-1} + u_{it}. \tag{10.73}$$

While we have seen that the fixed effects estimator is biased for fixed T, it is consistent for $T \to \infty$, so that, with T sufficiently large, we can ignore the small sample bias. Let us, however, assume that the true model involves heterogeneous parameters, and is given by

$$y_{it} = \alpha_i + x_{it}'\beta_i + \gamma_i y_{i,t-1} + u_{it}, \quad i = 1, \ldots, N. \tag{10.74}$$

Under standard assumptions, this model can be consistently estimated for a given country i using ordinary least squares (for $T \to \infty$). However, even if the slope coefficients vary randomly across countries, the fixed effects estimator for $\beta = E\{\beta_i\}$ and $\gamma = E\{\gamma_i\}$ based on (10.73) can be severely biased, even for large T. The reason is that under heterogeneity the error term in (10.73) contains $x_{it}'(\beta_i - \beta)$ and $(\gamma_i - \gamma)y_{i,t-1}$. Even with $\gamma_i = \gamma$, the first term will introduce serial correlation in the equation's error term, which, in combination with the lagged dependent variable, leads to inconsistency (see Subsection 5.2.1 and Section 10.4). How severe this problem is depends upon the dynamic properties of x_{it}. As an extreme case, Robertson and Symons (1992) show that if the regressors are random walks, the parameter estimate on a fitted lagged dependent variable has a probability limit of unity, and that on the regressor a probability limit of zero, irrespective of the true values of β and γ. This bias is commonly referred to as **heterogeneity bias**. Robertson and Symons (1992) also show that the Anderson–Hsiao estimators for (10.73) considered in Section 10.4 do not do much better in case of parameter heterogeneity. Fortunately, average estimators or the Swamy estimator do a much better job for sufficiently large N and T.[19]

10.6.2 First Generation Panel Unit Root Tests

To introduce panel data unit root tests, consider the autoregressive model

$$y_{it} = \alpha_i + \gamma_i y_{i,t-1} + u_{it}, \tag{10.75}$$

which we can rewrite as

$$\Delta y_{it} = \alpha_i + \pi_i y_{i,t-1} + u_{it}, \tag{10.76}$$

[19] We need T to be large for the small sample bias to be unimportant. We need N to be large to make sure that the averaging across countries approaches the population means.

where $\pi_i = \gamma_i - 1$. The null hypothesis that all series have a unit root corresponds to H_0: $\pi_i = 0$ for all i. Two alternative hypotheses are considered. The first one imposes homogeneity and states that all series are stationary with the same mean-reversion parameter, that is, H_{1a}: $\pi_i = \pi < 0$ for each country i. The second one allows the mean reversion parameters to be potentially different across countries and states that H_{1b}: $\pi_i < 0$ for at least one country i.[20] The first generation of panel unit root tests impose cross-sectional independence. The main reason for doing so is that it considerably simplifies the derivations of the asymptotic distributions.

Levin and Lin (1992)[21] and Harris and Tzavalis (1999) base their tests upon the OLS estimator for π, imposing homogeneity and assuming that u_{it} is i.i.d. across countries and time. Depending upon the deterministic regressors included, the OLS estimator may be biased, even asymptotically. When fixed effects are included, the estimator corresponds to the fixed effects estimator for π based on (10.76), which is biased for fixed T (see Section 10.4). With appropriate correction and standardization factors, test statistics can be derived that are asymptotically normal for $N \to \infty$ and fixed T (Harris and Tzavalis, 1999) or both $N, T \to \infty$ (Levin and Lin), see Baltagi (2013, Section 12.2) or Pesaran (2015, Section 31.3). Similar to the augmented Dickey–Fuller tests, the test statistics can be modified to allow for serial correlation in u_{it} by including lagged values of Δy_{it} in (10.76). As in the time series case discussed in Chapter 8, the properties of the test statistics (and their computation) depend crucially upon the deterministic regressors included in the test equation. For example, in (10.76) we have included a dummy for each country, corresponding to the fixed effect. Alternative tests are available in cases where the equation includes a common intercept, or in cases where a deterministic trend or time fixed effects are added to the country fixed effects.

The above tests are restrictive because they assume that π_i is the same across all countries, also under the alternative hypothesis. The heterogeneous alternative hypothesis H_{1b} is used by Im, Pesaran and Shin (2003).[22] Their test is based on averaging the augmented Dickey–Fuller (ADF) test statistics (see Section 8.4) over the cross-sectional units, while allowing for different orders of serial correlation. They also propose a test based on the N Lagrange multiplier statistics for $\pi_i = 0$, averaged over all countries. The idea underlying these tests is quite simple: if you have N independent test statistics their average will be asymptotically normally distributed, for $N \to \infty$. Consequently, the tests are based on comparison of appropriately scaled cross-sectional average test statistics with critical values from a standard normal distribution.

An alternative approach to combine information from individual unit root tests is employed by Maddala and Wu (1999) and Choi (2001), who propose panel data unit root tests based on combining the p-values of the N cross-sectional tests. Let p_i denote the p-value of the (augmented) Dickey–Fuller test for unit i. Under the null hypothesis, p_i will have a uniform distribution over the interval [0, 1], small values corresponding to rejection. The combined test statistic is given by

$$P = -2 \sum_{i=1}^{N} \log p_i. \tag{10.77}$$

[20] The typical formulation is that the fraction of the individual processes that are stationary is nonzero and tends to some fixed value p, $0 < p \leq 1$, as $N \to \infty$.

[21] A revised version of the Levin and Lin (1992) paper is available in Levin, Lin and Chu (2002).

[22] A first version of this paper dates back to 1995.

For fixed N, this test statistic will have a Chi-squared distribution with $2N$ degrees of freedom as $T \to \infty$, so that large values of P lead us to reject the null hypothesis. While this test (sometimes referred to as the Fisher test) is attractive because it allows the use of different ADF tests and different time series lengths per unit, a disadvantage is that it requires individual p-values that have to be derived by Monte Carlo simulations.

While the latter tests may seem attractive and easy to use, a word of caution is appropriate. Before one can apply the individual ADF tests underlying the Maddala and Wu (1999) and Im, Pesaran and Shin (2003) approaches, one has to determine the number of lags, and determine whether a trend should be included. It is not obvious how this should be done. For a single time series, a common approach is to perform the ADF test for a range of alternative lag values. For example, in Table 8.2 we presented 15 different (augmented) Dickey–Fuller test statistics for the log price index. If we were to combine the ADF tests for N different countries, in whatever way, this creates a wide range of possible combinations. Smith and Fuertes (2016) warn for pre-test biases in this context.

For all tests, the null hypothesis is that the time series of *all* individual countries have a unit root. This implies that the null hypothesis can be rejected (in sufficiently large samples) if any one of the N coefficients π_i is less than zero. Rejection of the null hypothesis therefore does not indicate that all series are stationary. As Smith and Fuertes (2016) note, if the hypothesis of interest is that all series are stationary (e.g. real exchange rates under purchasing power parity), it would be more appropriate to employ tests where stationarity is the null hypothesis rather than the alternative. Hadri (2000) proposes a panel extension of the KPSS test, discussed in Section 8.4, where the null hypothesis is stationarity of all series, and the alternative is nonstationarity of all series. Hadri and Larsson (2005) extend this by considering the case for fixed T. However, a stationarity test may reject if just one series is nonstationary, which may not be interesting either. Because of these issues, Maddala, Wu and Liu (2000) argue that for purchasing power parity, panel data unit root tests are the wrong answer to the low power of unit root tests in a single time series. Pesaran (2012) clarifies that rejection of the panel unit root hypothesis should be interpreted as evidence that a significant proportion of the units are stationary. He advocates to also estimate the proportion of cross-sectional units for which individual unit root tests are rejected, which is possible for sufficiently large T. The magnitude of this proportion serves as a measure of the importance of the rejection.

Asymptotic properties of estimators and tests depend crucially upon the way in which N, the number of cross-sectional units, and T, the number of time periods, tend to infinity (see Phillips and Moon, 1999). Some tests assume that either T or N is fixed and assume that the other dimension tends to infinity. Many tests are based on a sequential limit, where first T tends to infinity, for fixed N, and subsequently N tends to infinity. Alternatively, some tests assume that both N and T tend to infinity along a specific path (e.g. T/N being fixed). While the type of asymptotics that is applied may seem a theoretical issue, remember that we are using asymptotic theory to approximate the properties of estimators and tests in the finite sample that we happen to have. Although it is hard to make general statements on this matter, some asymptotic approximations are simply better than others. Many papers in this area therefore also contain a Monte Carlo study to analyse the finite sample behaviour of the proposed tests, under controlled circumstances. A common finding for many of the tests above is that they tend to be over-sized. That is, when the null hypothesis is true the tests tend to reject more frequently than their nominal size (say, 5%)

suggests. Further, many tests do not perform very well when the error terms are cross-sectionally correlated, or in the presence of cross-country cointegration. For example, when real exchange rates are $I(1)$ and cointegrated across countries the null hypothesis tends to be rejected too often (see Banerjee, Marcellino and Osbat, 2005, for an illustration). Hlouskova and Wagner (2006) perform a large scale simulation study to investigate the performance of many alternative first generation panel unit root and stationarity tests. One of their main conclusions is that the panel stationarity tests of Hadri (2000) and Hadri and Larsson (2005) perform very poorly. Westerlund and Breitung (2013) summarize a number of critical issues of panel unit roots test, with particular emphasis on the tests of Levin, Lin and Chu (2002) and Im, Pesaran and Shin (2003). These issues mainly relate to the role of deterministic components, serial correlation, cross-sectional dependence and cross-unit cointegration.

10.6.3 Second Generation Panel Unit Root Tests

Imposing cross-sectional independence is quite restrictive and in many applications time series data of different countries tend to be contemporaneously correlated. As stressed by O'Connell 1998 in a panel study on purchasing power parity, allowing for cross-sectional dependence may substantially affect inferences about the presence of a unit root. Baltagi, Bresson and Pirotte (2007) also find that ignoring spatial dependence can seriously bias the size of panel unit root tests. Because individual observations in a panel typically have no natural ordering, modelling cross-sectional dependence is not obvious. The literature on modelling cross-sectional dependence in panel data is evolving very rapidly, and I will only present a brief discussion here.

To illustrate the issue, let us consider a case where the cross-sectional dependence is due to one common factor in the error term (Pesaran, 2007)

$$y_{it} = (1 - \gamma_i)\mu_i + \gamma_i y_{i,t-1} + u_{it}, \tag{10.78}$$

$$u_{it} = \delta_i f_t + \xi_{it}, \tag{10.79}$$

where f_t is a serially uncorrelated unobserved common factor. The coefficients δ_i are referred to as factor loadings. If $\delta_i = \delta$ then $\delta_i f_t$ is a conventional time effect that can be removed by subtracting the cross-sectional means from the data, or by including time dummies. Typically it is assumed that δ_is are random drawings from a given distribution.

Pesaran (2007) argues that the common factor f_t can be proxied by the cross-sectional mean of y_{it} and its lags, when N is sufficiently large. His proposal is to employ the **cross-sectionally augmented** Dickey–Fuller (CADF) regressions, given by

$$\Delta y_{it} = \alpha_i + \pi_i y_{i,t-1} + c_{1i}\bar{y}_t + c_{2i}\,\Delta\bar{y}_t + u_{it}, \tag{10.80}$$

where $\bar{y}_t = N^{-1}\sum_i y_{it}$, and c_{1i}, c_{2i} are nuisance parameters. To test the unit root hypothesis ($\pi_i = 0$ for all i), the average of the N individual CADF t-statistics on π_i can be used (after suitable normalization). One can also consider combining the p-values of the individual tests. Serial correlation can be captured by augmenting (10.80) with additional lags of Δy_{it} and $\Delta\bar{y}_t$.

Pesaran, Smith and Yamagata (2013) extend the CADF regressions to the case of a multifactor error structure. The extension is based on the idea that extending (10.80) by including the cross-sectional averages of a set of variables x_{it} is able to capture the common factors in the model. This assumes the variables in x_{it} share the factors with the variable of interest y_{it}. Moon and Perron (2004) also consider the model in (10.78) but assume that the error terms have J common factors, that is,

$$u_{it} = f_t'\delta_i + \xi_{it},$$

where f_t is a $(J \times 1)$ vector of stationary common factors and δ_i is the corresponding vector of factor loadings. The null hypothesis is tested using (nonstandard) t-statistics based on the pooled OLS estimator, after an orthogonalization procedure to asymptotically eliminate the common factors.

Bai and Ng (2004) consider a more general set-up and allow for the possibility of unit roots (and cointegration) in the common factors. For example, if f_t is nonstationary and integrated of order one, its presence in the individual series y_{it} implies long-run dependence. In this approach, y_{it} can be nonstationary because of its idiosyncratic component ($\gamma_i = 1$) or because of one or more common (nonstationary) factors. As in Chapter 9, the number of nonstationary common factors is inversely related to the number of (cross-sectional) cointegrating relationships between $y_{1t}, \ldots, y_{Nt}$. Bai and Ng (2004) apply a principal component procedure to the first-differenced version of the model, and estimate the factor loadings and the first differences of the common factors. Standard unit root tests are then applied to the factors and the individual 'de-factored' series.

Gengenbach, Palm and Urbain (2010) discuss a number of practical issues in the calculation of several second generation panel unit root tests, combined with a Monte Carlo study examining their small sample properties. More details on the tests discussed above can also be found in, for example, Banerjee and Wagner (2009), Baltagi (2013, Chapter 13), Pesaran (2015, Chapter 31) or Smith and Fuertes (2016).

10.6.4 Panel Cointegration Tests

A wide range of alternative tests is available to test for cointegration in a dynamic panel data setting, and research in this area is evolving rapidly. A substantial number of these tests are based on testing for a unit root in the residuals of a panel cointegrating regression. The drawbacks and complexities associated with the panel unit root tests are also relevant in the cointegration case. Several additional issues are of potential importance when testing for cointegration: heterogeneity in the parameters of the cointegrating relationships, heterogeneity in the number of cointegrating relationships across countries, and the possibility of cointegration between the series from different countries. A final issue is that of estimating the cointegrating vectors, for which several alternative estimators are available, with different small and large sample properties (depending upon the type of asymptotics that is chosen).

When the cointegrating relationship is unknown, which is almost always the case, most cointegration tests start with estimating the cointegrating regression. Let us focus on the bivariate case and write the panel regression as

$$y_{it} = \alpha_i + \beta_i x_{it} + u_{it}, \tag{10.81}$$

where both y_{it} and x_{it} are integrated of order one. Cointegration implies that u_{it} is stationary for each i. Homogeneous cointegration, in addition, requires that $\beta_i = \beta$. If the cointegrating parameter is heterogeneous, and homogeneity is imposed, one estimates

$$y_{it} = \alpha_i + \beta x_{it} + [(\beta_i - \beta)x_{it} + u_{it}], \tag{10.82}$$

and in general the composite error term is integrated of order one, even if u_{it} is stationary. However, the problem of spurious regressions may be less relevant in this situation. This is because a pooled estimator will also average over i, so that the noise in the equation will be attenuated. In many circumstances, when $N \to \infty$, the fixed effects estimator for β is actually consistent for the long-run average relation parameter, as well as asymptotically normal, despite the absence of cointegration (see Phillips and Moon, 1999). With heterogeneous cointegration, the long-run average estimated from the pooled regression may differ substantially from the average of the cointegration parameters, averaged over countries (see Pesaran and Smith, 1995). Consequently, if there is heterogeneous cointegration, it is much better to estimate the individual cointegrating regressions, rather than using a pooled estimator. Obviously, this requires $T \to \infty$.

To test for cointegration, the panel data unit root tests from the previous subsections can be applied to the residuals from these regressions, provided that the critical values are appropriately adjusted (see Pedroni, 1999, or Kao, 1999). Recall that many tests assume cross-sectional independence. Some tests assume homogeneity of the cointegrating parameter and use a pooled OLS or dynamic OLS estimator (see Subsection 9.2.2). Pedroni (2004) suggests two different test statistics for models with heterogeneous cointegration. Wagner and Hlouskova (2010) compare the performance of alternative panel cointegration tests in a large scale simulation study and conclude, among other things, that the tests of Pedroni (2004) perform relatively well.

With more than two variables an additional complication may arise because more than one cointegrating relationship may exist, for one or more of the countries. Further, even with one cointegrating vector per country, the results will be sensitive to the normalization constraint (left-hand side variable) that is chosen. Finally, the existence of between country cointegration may seriously distort the results of within country cointegration tests (see Banerjee, Marcellino and Osbat, 2005). Several of the drawbacks of the single equation methods for panel cointegration can be avoided using a system approach, similar to the cointegrated VAR discussion in Section 9.5; see Binder, Hsiao and Pesaran (2005) or Breitung (2005) for some approaches. To take into account cross-sectional dependence, imposing a common factor structure is potentially helpful. In this case, the error terms are cross-sectionally correlated due to one or more unobserved common factors; see Westerlund (2007) for an example.

The literature in this area is expanding rapidly. Additional discussion on panel cointegration tests can be found in Banerjee (1999), Banerjee and Wagner (2009), Baltagi (2013, Section 12.5), Pesaran (2015, Chapter 31) or Smith and Fuertes (2016).

10.7 Models with Limited Dependent Variables

Panel data are relatively often used in micro-economic problems where the models of interest involve nonlinearities. Discrete or limited dependent variables are an important phenomenon in this area (see Chapter 7), and their combination with panel data usually complicates estimation. The reason is that with panel data it can usually not be argued that different observations on the same unit are independent. Correlations between different error terms typically complicate the likelihood functions of such models and therefore complicate their estimation. In this section we discuss the estimation of panel data logit, probit and tobit models. More details on panel data models with limited dependent variables can be found in Maddala (1987), Wooldridge (2010, Chapters 15–19) or Hsiao (2014, Chapters 7–8).

10.7.1 Binary Choice Models

As in the cross-sectional case, the binary choice model is usually formulated in terms of an underlying latent model. Typically, we write[23]

$$y_{it}^* = x_{it}'\beta + \alpha_i + u_{it}, \tag{10.83}$$

where we observe $y_{it} = 1$ if $y_{it}^* > 0$ and $y_{it} = 0$ otherwise. For example, y_{it} may indicate whether person i is working in period t or not. Let us assume that the idiosyncratic error term u_{it} has a symmetric distribution with distribution function $F(.)$, i.i.d. across individuals and time and independent of all x_{is}. Even in this case the presence of α_i complicates estimation, both when we treat them as fixed unknown parameters and when we treat them as random error terms.

If we treat α_i as fixed unknown parameters, we are essentially including N dummy variables in the model. The loglikelihood function is then given by (compare (7.12))

$$\log L(\beta, \alpha_1, \ldots, \alpha_N) = \sum_{i,t} y_{it} \log F(\alpha_i + x_{it}'\beta) + \sum_{i,t} (1 - y_{it}) \log [1 - F(\alpha_i + x_{it}'\beta)]. \tag{10.84}$$

Maximizing this with respect to β and α_i $(i = 1, \ldots, N)$ results in consistent estimators *provided that the number of time periods T goes to infinity*. For fixed T and $N \to \infty$, the estimators are inconsistent. The reason is that, for fixed T, the number of parameters grows with sample size N, and we have what is known as an 'incidental parameter' problem. Clearly, we can only estimate α_i consistently if the number of observations for individual i grows, which requires that T tends to infinity. In general, the inconsistency of $\hat{\alpha}_i$ for fixed T will carry over to the estimator for β. Greene (2004) provides a Monte Carlo study examining the small sample properties of fixed effects maximum likelihood estimators for a variety of nonlinear models and shows that the bias in estimating β is often substantial.

The incidental parameter problem, where the number of parameters increases with the number of observations, arises in any fixed effects model, including the linear model; see Lancaster (2000) for a recent discussion. For the linear case, however, it was possible to eliminate the α_is, such that β could be estimated consistently, even though all the α_i parameters could not. For most nonlinear models, however, the inconsistency of $\hat{\alpha}_i$ leads to inconsistency of the other parameter estimators as well. Also note that, from a practical point of view, the estimation of more than N parameters may not be very attractive if N is large; see Greene (2004) for more details on computational issues.

Although it is possible to transform the *latent* model such that the individual effects α_i are eliminated, this does not help in this context because there is no mapping from, for example, $y_{it}^* - y_{i,t-1}^*$ to observables like $y_{it} - y_{i,t-1}$. An alternative strategy is the use of **conditional maximum likelihood** (see Andersen, 1970; or Chamberlain, 1980). In this

[23] To simplify the notation, we shall assume that x_{it} includes a constant, whenever appropriate.

case, we consider the likelihood function conditional upon a set of statistics t_i that are sufficient for α_i. This means that, conditional upon t_i, an individual's likelihood contribution no longer depends upon α_i but still depends upon the other parameters β. In the panel data binary choice model, the existence of a sufficient statistic depends upon the functional form of F, that is, depends upon the distribution we impose upon u_{it}.

At the general level let us write the joint density or probability mass function of $y_{i1}, \ldots, y_{iT}$ as $f(y_{i1}, \ldots, y_{iT}|\alpha_i, \beta)$, which depends upon the parameters β and α_i. If a sufficient statistic t_i exists, this means that there exists an observable variable t_i such that $f(y_{i1}, \ldots, y_{iT}|t_i, \alpha_i, \beta) = f(y_{i1}, \ldots, y_{iT}|t_i, \beta)$ and so does not depend upon α_i. Consequently, we can maximize the **conditional likelihood function**, based upon $f(y_{i1}, \ldots, y_{iT}|t_i, \beta)$, to get a consistent estimator for β. Moreover, we can use all the distributional results from Chapter 6 if we replace the loglikelihood with the conditional loglikelihood function. For the *linear* model with normal errors, a sufficient statistic for α_i is $\bar{y}_i$. That is, the conditional distribution of y_{it} given $\bar{y}_i$ does not depend upon α_i, and maximizing the conditional likelihood function can be shown to reproduce the fixed effects estimator for β. Unfortunately, this result does not automatically extend to nonlinear models. For the probit model, for example, it has been shown that no sufficient statistic for α_i exists. This means that we cannot estimate a fixed effects probit model consistently for fixed T.

10.7.2 The Fixed Effects Logit Model

For the fixed effects logit model, the situation is different. In this model $t_i = \bar{y}_i$ is a sufficient statistic for α_i and consistent estimation is possible by conditional maximum likelihood. Note that the conditional distribution of $y_{i1}, \ldots, y_{iT}$ is degenerate if $t_i = 0$ or $t_i = 1$. Consequently, individuals for whom y_{it} does not vary over time do not contribute to the conditional likelihood and should be discarded in estimation. Put differently, their behaviour would be completely captured by their individual effect α_i. This means that only individuals that change status at least once are relevant for estimating β. To illustrate the fixed effects logit model, we consider the case with $T = 2$.

By conditioning upon $t_i = 1/2$, we restrict the sample to the observations for which y_{it} changes, and the two possible outcome sequences are (0, 1) and (1, 0). The conditional probability of the first outcome is

$$P\{(0,1)|t_i = 1/2, \alpha_i, \beta\} = \frac{P\{(0,1)|\alpha_i, \beta\}}{P\{(0,1)|\alpha_i, \beta\} + P\{(1,0)|\alpha_i, \beta\}}.$$

Using

$$P\{(0,1)|\alpha_i, \beta\} = P\{y_{i1} = 0|\alpha_i, \beta\}P\{y_{i2} = 1|\alpha_i, \beta\}$$

with[24]

$$P\{y_{i2} = 1|\alpha_i, \beta\} = \frac{\exp\{\alpha_i + x_{i2}'\beta\}}{1 + \exp\{\alpha_i + x_{i2}'\beta\}},$$

it follows that the conditional probability is given by

$$P\{(0,1)|t_i = 1/2, \alpha_i, \beta\} = \frac{\exp\{(x_{i2} - x_{i1})'\beta\}}{1 + \exp\{(x_{i2} - x_{i1})'\beta\}},$$

[24] See (7.6) in Chapter 7 for the logistic distribution function.

which indeed does not depend upon α_i. Similarly,

$$P\{(1,0)|t_i = 1/2, \alpha_i, \beta\} = \frac{1}{1 + \exp\{(x_{i2} - x_{i1})'\beta\}}.$$

These results show that the conditional distribution of (y_{i1}, y_{i2}), given t_i and α_i, is independent of the individual-specific effects. Accordingly, we can estimate the fixed effects logit model for $T = 2$ using a standard logit with $x_{i2} - x_{i1}$ as explanatory variables and the change in y_{it} as the endogenous event (1 for a positive change, 0 for a negative one). In a sense, conditioning upon $t_i = 1/2$ has the same effect as first differencing (or within transforming) the data in a linear panel data model. Note that in this fixed effects binary choice model it is even more clear than in the linear case that the model is only identified through the 'within dimension' of the data; individuals who do not change status are simply discarded in estimation as they provide no information whatsoever about β. For the case with larger T, it is a bit more cumbersome to derive all the necessary conditional probabilities, but in principle it is a straightforward extension of the above case (see Chamberlain, 1980; or Maddala, 1987). Chamberlain (1980) also discusses how the conditional maximum likelihood approach can be extended to the multinomial logit model. More recently, Ferrer-i-Carbonell and Frijters (2004) have developed a conditional estimator for the fixed-effect ordered logit model, and use it to estimate the determinants of happiness (coded in a number of categories, for example, $0, 1, 2, \ldots, 10$).

If it can be assumed that the α_i are independent of the explanatory variables in x_{it}, a random effects treatment seems more appropriate. This is most easily achieved in the context of a probit model.

10.7.3 The Random Effects Probit Model

Let us start with the latent variable specification

$$y_{it}^* = x_{it}'\beta + \varepsilon_{it}, \tag{10.85}$$

with

$$\begin{aligned} y_{it} &= 1 \quad \text{if } y_{it}^* > 0, \\ y_{it} &= 0 \quad \text{if } y_{it}^* \leq 0, \end{aligned} \tag{10.86}$$

where ε_{it} is an error term with mean zero and unit variance, independent of $(x_{i1}, \ldots, x_{iT})$. To estimate β by maximum likelihood, we will have to complement this with an assumption about the joint distribution of $\varepsilon_{i1}, \ldots, \varepsilon_{iT}$. The likelihood contribution of individual i is the (joint) probability of observing the T outcomes $y_{i1}, \ldots, y_{iT}$. This joint probability is determined from the joint distribution of the latent variables $y_{i1}^*, \ldots, y_{iT}^*$ by integrating over the appropriate intervals. In general, this will thus imply T integrals, which in estimation are typically to be computed numerically. When $T = 4$ or more, this makes maximum likelihood estimation infeasible. It is possible to circumvent this 'curse of dimensionality' by using simulation-based estimators, as discussed in, for example, Keane (1993), Weeks (1995), Hajivassiliou and McFadden (1998) and, more recently, in Liesenfeld and Richard (2010). Their discussion is beyond the scope of this text.

Clearly, if it can be assumed that all ε_{it} are independent, we have $f(y_{i1}, \ldots, y_{iT}|x_{i1}, \ldots, x_{iT}, \beta) = \prod_t f(y_{it}|x_{it}, \beta)$, which involves T one-dimensional integrals only (as in the cross-sectional case). If we make an error components assumption, and assume that $\varepsilon_{it} = \alpha_i + u_{it}$, where u_{it} is independent over time (and individuals), we can write the joint probability as

$$\begin{aligned} f(y_{i1},\ldots,y_{iT}|x_{i1},\ldots,x_{iT},\beta) &= \int_{-\infty}^{\infty} f(y_{i1},\ldots,y_{iT}|x_{i1},\ldots,x_{iT},\alpha_i,\beta)f(\alpha_i)d\alpha_i \\ &= \int_{-\infty}^{\infty}\left[\prod_t f(y_{it}|x_{it},\alpha_i,\beta)\right] f(\alpha_i)d\alpha_i, \end{aligned} \tag{10.87}$$

which requires numerical integration over one dimension. This is a feasible specification that allows the error terms to be correlated across different periods, albeit in a restrictive way. The crucial step in (10.87) is that, conditional upon α_i, the errors from different periods are independent.

In principle, arbitrary assumptions can be made about the distributions of α_i and u_{it}. For example, one could assume that u_{it} has an i.i.d. logistic distribution, while α_i has a normal distribution,[25] or that both components have a logistic distribution. However, this may lead to distributions for $\alpha_i + u_{it}$ that are nonstandard. For example, the sum of two logistically distributed variables in general does not have a logistic distribution. This implies that individual probabilities, like $f(y_{it}|x_{it},\beta)$, are hard to compute and do not correspond to a cross-sectional probit or logit model. Therefore, it is more common to start from the joint distribution of $\varepsilon_{i1},\ldots,\varepsilon_{iT}$. The multivariate logistic distribution has the disadvantage that all correlations are restricted to be 1/2 (see Maddala, 1987), so that it is not very attractive in practice. Consequently, the most common approach is to start from a multivariate normal distribution, which leads to the **random effects probit model**.

Let us assume that the joint distribution of $\varepsilon_{i1},\ldots,\varepsilon_{iT}$ is normal with zero means and variances equal to 1 and $\text{cov}\{\varepsilon_{it},\varepsilon_{is}\} = \sigma_\alpha^2, s \neq t$. This corresponds to assuming that α_i is $NID(0,\sigma_\alpha^2)$ and u_{it} is $NID(0, 1-\sigma_\alpha^2)$. Recall that, as in the cross-sectional case, we need a normalization on the errors' variances. The normalization chosen here implies that the error variance in a given period is unity, such that the estimated β coefficients are directly comparable with estimates obtained from estimating the model from one wave of the panel using cross-sectional probit maximum likelihood. For the random effects probit model, the expressions in the likelihood function are given by

$$\begin{aligned} f(y_{it}|x_{it},\alpha_i,\beta) &= \Phi\left(\frac{x_{it}'\beta+\alpha_i}{\sqrt{1-\sigma_\alpha^2}}\right) && \text{if } y_{it}=1 \\ &= 1-\Phi\left(\frac{x_{it}'\beta+\alpha_i}{\sqrt{1-\sigma_\alpha^2}}\right) && \text{if } y_{it}=0, \end{aligned} \tag{10.88}$$

where Φ denotes the cumulative density function of the standard normal distribution. The density of α_i is given by

$$f(\alpha_i) = \frac{1}{\sqrt{2\pi\sigma_\alpha^2}}\exp\left\{-\frac{1}{2}\frac{\alpha_i^2}{\sigma_\alpha^2}\right\}. \tag{10.89}$$

[25] This is what Stata refers to as a random effects logit model.

The integral in (10.87) has to be computed numerically, which can be done using the algorithm described in Butler and Moffitt (1982). Several software packages have standard routines for estimating the random effects probit model.

It can be shown (Robinson, 1982) that ignoring the correlations across periods and estimating the β coefficients using standard probit maximum likelihood on the pooled data is consistent, though inefficient. This is a special case of quasi-maximum likelihood, as discussed in Subsection 6.4.1. Correct standard errors can be computed using a robust covariance matrix estimator based on the sandwich formula in (6.42).

10.7.4 Tobit Models

The random effects tobit model is very similar to the random effects probit model, the only difference being in the observation rule. Consequently, we can be fairly brief here. Let us start with

$$y_{it}^* = x_{it}'\beta + \alpha_i + u_{it}, \tag{10.90}$$

while

$$\begin{aligned} y_{it} &= y_{it}^* \qquad \text{if } y_{it}^* > 0, \\ y_{it} &= 0 \qquad \text{if } y_{it}^* \leq 0. \end{aligned} \tag{10.91}$$

We make the usual random effects assumption that α_i and u_{it} are i.i.d. normally distributed, independent of $x_{i1}, \ldots, x_{iT}$, with zero means and variances σ_α^2 and σ_u^2, respectively. Using f as generic notation for a density or probability mass function, the likelihood function can be written as in (10.87):

$$f(y_{i1}, \ldots, y_{iT}|x_{i1}, \ldots, x_{iT}, \beta) = \int_{-\infty}^{\infty} \prod_t f(y_{it}|x_{it}, \alpha_i, \beta) f(\alpha_i) d\alpha_i,$$

where $f(\alpha_i)$ is given by (10.89) and $f(y_{it}|x_{it}, \alpha_i, \beta)$ is given by

$$\begin{aligned} f(y_{it}|x_{it}, \alpha_i, \beta) &= \frac{1}{\sqrt{2\pi\sigma_u^2}} \exp\left\{-\frac{1}{2}\frac{(y_{it} - x_{it}'\beta - \alpha_i)^2}{\sigma_u^2}\right\} \qquad \text{if } y_{it} > 0 \\ &= 1 - \Phi\left(\frac{x_{it}'\beta + \alpha_i}{\sigma_u}\right) \qquad \text{if } y_{it} = 0. \end{aligned} \tag{10.92}$$

Note that the latter two expressions are similar to the likelihood contributions in the cross-sectional case, as discussed in Chapter 7. The only difference is the inclusion of α_i in the conditional mean.

In a completely similar fashion, other forms of censoring can be considered, to obtain, for example, the random effects ordered probit model. In all cases, the integration over α_i has to be done numerically.

10.7.5 Dynamics and the Problem of Initial Conditions

The possibility of including a lagged dependent variable in the above models is of economic interest. For example, suppose we are explaining whether or not an individual is unemployed over a number of consecutive months. It is typically the case that individuals who have a longer history of being unemployed are less likely to leave the state of unemployment. As discussed in the introductory section of this chapter, there are two explanations for this: an individual with a longer unemployment history may be discouraged in looking for a job or may (for whatever reason) be less attractive for an employer to hire. This is referred to as **state dependence**: the longer you are in a certain state, the less likely you are to leave it. Alternatively, it is possible that **unobserved heterogeneity** is present such that individuals with certain unobserved characteristics are less likely to leave unemployment. The fact that we observe a spurious state dependence in the data is simply due to a selection mechanism: the long-term unemployed have certain unobservable (time-invariant) characteristics that make it less likely for them to find a job anyhow. In the binary choice models discussed above, the individual effects α_i capture the unobserved heterogeneity. If we include a lagged dependent variable, we can distinguish between the above two explanations.

Let us consider the random effect probit model, although similar results hold for the random effects tobit case. Suppose the latent variable specification is changed into

$$y_{it}^* = x_{it}'\beta + \gamma y_{i,t-1} + \alpha_i + u_{it}, \tag{10.93}$$

with $y_{it} = 1$ if $y_{it}^* > 0$ and 0 otherwise. In this model $\gamma > 0$ indicates positive state dependence: the ceteris paribus probability that $y_{it} = 1$ is larger if $y_{i,t-1}$ is also one. Let us consider maximum likelihood estimation of this dynamic random effects probit model, making the same distributional assumptions as before. In general terms, the likelihood contribution of individual i is given by[26]

$$\begin{aligned} f(y_{i1},\dots,y_{iT}|x_{i1},\dots,x_{iT},\beta) &= \int_{-\infty}^{\infty} f(y_{i1},\dots,y_{iT}|x_{i1},\dots,x_{iT},\alpha_i,\beta)\,f(\alpha_i)d\alpha_i \\ &= \int_{-\infty}^{\infty}\left[\prod_{t=2}^{T} f(y_{it}|y_{i,t-1},x_{it},\alpha_i,\beta)\right] f(y_{i1}|x_{i1},\alpha_i,\beta)\,f(\alpha_i)d\alpha_i, \end{aligned} \tag{10.94}$$

where

$$\begin{aligned} f(y_{it}|y_{i,t-1},x_{it},\alpha_i,\beta) &= \Phi\left(\frac{x_{it}'\beta + \gamma y_{i,t-1} + \alpha_i}{\sqrt{1-\sigma_\alpha^2}}\right) && \text{if } y_{it} = 1, \\ &= 1 - \Phi\left(\frac{x_{it}'\beta + \gamma y_{i,t-1} + \alpha_i}{\sqrt{1-\sigma_\alpha^2}}\right) && \text{if } y_{it} = 0. \end{aligned}$$

This is completely analogous to the static case, and $y_{i,t-1}$ is simply included as an additional explanatory variable. However, the term $f(y_{i1}|x_{i1},\alpha_i,\beta)$ in the likelihood function may cause problems. It gives the probability of observing $y_{i1} = 1$ or 0 without knowing the previous state but conditional upon the unobserved heterogeneity term α_i.

If the initial value is exogenous in the sense that its distribution does not depend upon α_i, we can put the term $f(y_{i1}|x_{i1},\alpha_i,\beta) = f(y_{i1}|x_{i1},\beta)$ outside the integral. In this case, we can simply consider the likelihood function conditional upon y_{i1} and ignore the term $f(y_{i1}|x_{i1},\beta)$ in estimation. The only consequence may be a loss of efficiency if $f(y_{i1}|x_{i1},\beta)$ provides information about β. This approach would be appropriate if the initial state is the same for all individuals or if it is randomly assigned to individuals. An example of the first situation is given in Nijman and Verbeek (1992), who model nonresponse with

[26] For notational convenience, the time index is defined such that the first observation is (y_{i1}, x_{i1}').

respect to consumption. In their application the initial period refers to the month before the panel and no nonresponse was necessarily present.

However, it may be hard to argue in many applications that the initial value y_{i1} is exogenous and does not depend upon a person's unobserved heterogeneity. In that case we need an expression for $f(y_{i1}|x_{i1}, \alpha_i, \beta)$, and this is problematic. If the process we are estimating has been going on for a number of periods before the current sample period, $f(y_{i1}|x_{i1}, \alpha_i, \beta)$ is a complicated function that depends upon person i's unobserved history. This means that it is typically impossible to derive an expression for the marginal probability $f(y_{i1}|x_{i1}, \alpha_i, \beta)$ that is consistent with the rest of the model. Heckman (1981) suggests an approximate solution to this **initial conditions problem** that appears to work reasonably well in practice. It requires an approximation for the marginal probability of the initial state by a probit function, using as much presample information as available, without imposing restrictions between its coefficients and the structural β and γ parameters. Hyslop (1999) employs this approach to estimate a dynamic model of female labour force participation; Vella and Verbeek (1999a) provide an illustration in the context of a dynamic random effects tobit model. The impact of the initial conditions diminishes if the number of sample periods T increases, so one may decide to ignore the problem when T is fairly large; see Hsiao (2014, Subsection 7.5.2) for more discussion.

10.7.6 Semi-parametric Alternatives

The binary choice and censored regression models discussed above suffer from two important drawbacks. First, the distribution of u_{it} conditional upon x_{it} (and α_i) needs to be specified, and second, with the exception of the fixed effects logit model, there is no simple way to estimate the models treating α_i as fixed unknown parameters. Several semi-parametric approaches have been suggested for these models that do not require strong distributional assumptions on u_{it} and somehow allow α_i to be eliminated before estimation.

In the binary choice model, it is possible to obtain semi-parametric estimators for β that are consistent up to a scaling factor whether or not α_i is treated as fixed or random. For example, Manski (1987) suggests a maximum score estimator (compare Subsection 7.1.8), while Lee (1999) provides a $\sqrt{N}$-consistent estimator for the static binary choice model; see Hsiao (2014, Section 7.4) for more details. Honoré and Kyriazidou (2000) propose a semi-parametric estimator for discrete choice models with a lagged dependent variable.

A tobit model as well as a truncated regression model with fixed effects can be estimated consistently using the generalized method of moments exploiting the moment conditions given by Honoré (1992) or Honoré (1993) for the dynamic model. The essential trick of these estimators is that a first-difference transformation, for appropriate subsets of the observations, no longer involves the incidental parameters α_i; see Hsiao (2014, Sections 8.4 and 8.6) for more discussion.

10.8 Incomplete Panels and Selection Bias

For a variety of reasons, empirical panel data sets are often incomplete. For example, after a few waves of the panel, people may refuse cooperation, households may not be located again or may have split up, firms may have finished business or may have merged with another firm or investment funds may be closed down. On the other hand, firms may enter business at a later stage, refreshment samples may have been drawn to compensate attrition or the panel may be collected as a rotating panel. In a rotating panel, each period a fixed proportion of the units is replaced. A consequence of all these events is that the resulting panel data set is no longer rectangular. If the total number of individuals equals N and the number of time periods is T, then the total number of observations is substantially smaller than NT.

A first consequence of working with an incomplete panel is a computational one. Most of the expressions for the estimators given above are no longer appropriate if observations are missing. A simple 'solution' is to discard any individual from the panel that has incomplete information and to work with the completely observed units only. In this approach, estimation uses the **balanced subpanel** only. This is computationally attractive but potentially highly inefficient: a substantial amount of information may be 'thrown away'. This loss in efficiency can be prevented by using all observations including those on individuals that are not observed in all T periods. This way, one uses the **unbalanced panel**. In principle this is straightforward, but computationally it requires some adjustments to the formulae in the previous sections. We shall discuss some of these adjustments in Subsection 10.8.1. Fortunately, most software that can handle panel data also allows for unbalanced data.

Another potential and even more serious consequence of using incomplete panel data is the danger of **selection bias**. If individuals are incompletely observed for an endogenous reason, the use of either the balanced subpanel or the unbalanced panel may lead to biased estimators and misleading tests. To elaborate upon this, suppose that the model of interest is given by

$$y_{it} = x_{it}'\beta + \alpha_i + u_{it}. \tag{10.95}$$

Furthermore, define the indicator variable r_{it} ('response') as $r_{it} = 1$ if (x_{it}, y_{it}) is observed and 0 otherwise. The observations on (x_{it}, y_{it}) are **missing at random** if r_{it} is independent of α_i and u_{it}. This means that conditioning upon the outcome of the selection process does not affect the conditional distribution of y_{it} given x_{it}. If we want to concentrate upon the balanced subpanel, the conditioning is upon $r_{i1} = \cdots = r_{iT} = 1$ and we require that r_{it} is independent of α_i and $u_{i1}, \ldots, u_{iT}$. In these cases, the usual consistency properties of the estimators are not affected if we restrict attention to the available or complete observations only. If selection depends upon the equations' error terms, the OLS, random effects and fixed effects estimators may suffer from selection bias (compare Chapter 7). Subsection 10.8.2 provides additional details on this issue, including some simple tests. In cases with selection bias, alternative estimators have to be used, which are typically computationally unattractive. This is discussed in Subsection 10.8.3. Additional details and discussion on incomplete panels and selection bias can be found in Verbeek and Nijman (1992a, 1996), and Baltagi and Song (2006).

10.8.1 Estimation with Randomly Missing Data

The expressions for the fixed and random effects estimators are easily extended to the unbalanced case. The fixed effects estimator, as before, can be determined as the OLS estimator in the linear model where each individual has its own intercept term. Alternatively, the resulting estimator for β can be obtained directly by applying OLS to the within transformed model, where now all variables are in deviation from the mean *over the available observations*. Individuals that are observed only once provide no information on β and should be discarded in estimation. Defining 'available means' as[27]

$$\bar{y}_i = \frac{\sum_{t=1}^{T} r_{it} y_{it}}{\sum_{t=1}^{T} r_{it}}; \quad \bar{x}_i = \frac{\sum_{t=1}^{T} r_{it} x_{it}}{\sum_{t=1}^{T} r_{it}},$$

the fixed effects estimator can be concisely written as

$$\hat{\beta}_{FE} = \left(\sum_{i=1}^{N} \sum_{t=1}^{T} r_{it}(x_{it} - \bar{x}_i)(x_{it} - \bar{x}_i)' \right)^{-1} \sum_{i=1}^{N} \sum_{t=1}^{T} r_{it}(x_{it} - \bar{x}_i)(y_{it} - \bar{y}_i). \tag{10.96}$$

That is, all sums are simply over the available observations only.

In a similar way, the random effects estimator can be generalized. The random effects estimator for the unbalanced case can be obtained from

$$\hat{\beta}_{GLS} = \left(\sum_{i=1}^{N} \sum_{t=1}^{T} r_{it}(x_{it} - \bar{x}_i)(x_{it} - \bar{x}_i)' + \sum_{i=1}^{N} \psi_i T_i(\bar{x}_i - \bar{x})(\bar{x}_i - \bar{x})' \right)^{-1}$$
$$\times \left(\sum_{i=1}^{N} \sum_{t=1}^{T} r_{it}(x_{it} - \bar{x}_i)(y_{it} - \bar{y}_i) + \sum_{i=1}^{N} \psi_i T_i(\bar{x}_i - \bar{x})(\bar{y}_i - \bar{y}) \right), \tag{10.97}$$

where $T_i = \sum_{t=1}^{T} r_{it}$ denotes the number of periods individual i is observed and

$$\psi_i = \frac{\sigma_u^2}{\sigma_u^2 + T_i \sigma_\alpha^2}.$$

Alternatively, it is obtained by applying OLS to the following transformed model:

$$(y_{it} - \vartheta_i \bar{y}_i) = \beta_0(1 - \vartheta_i) + (x_{it} - \vartheta_i \bar{x}_i)'\beta + v_{it}, \tag{10.98}$$

where $\vartheta_i = 1 - \psi_i^{1/2}$. Note that the transformation applied here is individual-specific and depends upon the number of observations for individual i.

Essentially, the more general formulae for the fixed effects and random effects estimators are characterized by the fact that all summations and means are over the available observations only and that T_i replaces T. Completely analogous adjustments apply to the expressions for the covariance matrices of the two estimators given in (10.13) and (10.26). Consistent estimators for the unknown variances σ_α^2 and σ_u^2 are given by

$$\hat{\sigma}_u^2 = \frac{1}{\sum_{i=1}^{N} T_i - N} \sum_{i=1}^{N} \sum_{t=1}^{T} r_{it}(y_{it} - \bar{y}_i - (x_{it} - \bar{x}_i)'\hat{\beta}_{FE})^2 \tag{10.99}$$

and

$$\hat{\sigma}_\alpha^2 = \frac{1}{N} \sum_{i=1}^{N} \left[(\bar{y}_i - \hat{\beta}_{0B} - \bar{x}_i'\hat{\beta}_B)^2 - \frac{1}{T_i}\hat{\sigma}_u^2 \right], \tag{10.100}$$

[27] We assume that $\sum_{t=1}^{T} r_{it} \geq 1$, that is, each individual is observed at least once.

respectively, where $\hat{\beta}_B$ is the between estimator for β, and $\hat{\beta}_{0B}$ is the between estimator for the intercept (both computed as the OLS estimator in (10.21), where the means now reflect 'available means'). Because the efficiency of the estimators for σ_α^2 and σ_u^2 asymptotically has no impact on the efficiency of the random effects estimator, it is possible to use computationally simpler estimators for σ_α^2 and σ_u^2 that are consistent. For example, one could use the standard estimators computed from the residuals obtained from estimating with the balanced subpanel only, and then use (10.97) or (10.98) to compute the random effects estimator.

10.8.2 Selection Bias and Some Simple Tests

In addition to the usual conditions for consistency of the random effects and fixed effects estimators, based on either the balanced subpanel or the unbalanced panel, it was assumed above that the response indicator variable r_{it} was independent of all unobservables in the model. This assumption may be unrealistic. For example, explaining the performance of hedge funds may suffer from the fact that funds with a bad performance are less likely to survive (Baquero, ter Horst and Verbeek, 2005), analysing the effect of an income policy experiment may suffer from biases if people that benefit less from the experiment are more likely to drop out of the panel (Hausman and Wise, 1979) or estimating the impact of the unemployment rate on individual wages may be disturbed by the possibility that people with relatively high wages are more likely to leave the labour market in case of increasing unemployment (Keane, Moffitt and Runkle, 1988).

If r_{it} depends upon α_i or u_{it}, **selection bias** may arise in the standard estimators (see Chapter 7). This means that the distribution of y given x and conditional upon selection (into the sample) is different from the distribution of y given x (which is what we are interested in). For consistency of the fixed effects estimator it is now required that

$$E\{(x_{it} - \bar{x}_i)u_{it}|r_{i1}, \ldots, r_{iT}\} = 0. \tag{10.101}$$

This means that the fixed effects estimator is inconsistent if whether an individual is in the sample or not tells us something about the expected value of the error term that is related with x_{it}. Clearly, if (10.11) holds and r_{it} is independent of α_i and all u_{is} (for given x_{is}), the above condition is satisfied. Note that sample selection may depend upon α_i without affecting consistency of the fixed effects estimator for β. In fact, u_{it} may even depend upon r_{it} as long as their relationship is time invariant (see Verbeek and Nijman, 1992a, 1996, for additional details).

In addition to (10.101), the conditions for consistency of the random effects estimator are now given by $E\{\bar{x}_i u_{it}|r_{i1}, \ldots, r_{iT}\} = 0$ and

$$E\{\bar{x}_i \alpha_i|r_{i1}, \ldots, r_{iT}\} = 0. \tag{10.102}$$

This does not allow the expected value of either error component to depend on the selection indicators. If individuals with certain values for their unobserved heterogeneity α_i are less likely to be observed in some wave of the panel, this will typically bias the random effects estimator. Similarly, if individuals with certain shocks u_{it} are more likely to drop out, the random effects estimator is typically inconsistent. Note that, because the fixed effects estimator allows selection to depend upon α_i and upon u_{it} in a time-invariant way, it is more robust against selection bias than the random effects estimator. Another important observation made by Verbeek and Nijman (1992a) is that estimators from the unbalanced panel do not necessarily suffer less from selection bias than those from the balanced subpanel. In general, the selection biases in the estimators from the unbalanced and balanced samples need not be the same, and their relative magnitude is not known a priori.

Verbeek and Nijman (1992a) suggest a number of simple tests for selection bias based upon the above observations. First, as the conditions for consistency state that the error terms should – in one sense or another – not depend upon the selection indicators, one can test this by simply including some function of $r_{i1}, \ldots, r_{iT}$ in the model and checking its significance. The relevant null hypothesis states that whether an individual was observed in any of the periods 1 to T should not give us any information about his or her unobservables in the model. Obviously, adding r_{it} to the model in (10.95) leads to multicollinearity as $r_{it} = 1$ for all observations in the sample. Instead, one could add functions of $r_{i1}, \ldots, r_{iT}$, like $r_{i,t-1}, c_i = \Pi_{t=1}^{T} r_{it}$ or $T_i = \Sigma_{t=1}^{T} r_{it}$, indicating whether unit i was observed in the previous period, whether it was observed over all periods and the total number of periods unit i is observed, respectively. Note that in the balanced subpanel all variables are identical for all individuals and thus incorporated in the intercept term. Verbeek and Nijman (1992a) suggest that the inclusion of c_i and T_i may provide a reasonable procedure to check for the presence of selection bias. Note that this requires that the model be estimated under the random effects assumption, as the within transformation would wipe out both c_i and T_i. Of course, if the tests do not reject, there is no reason to accept the null hypothesis of no selection bias, because the power of the tests may be low.

Another group of tests is based upon the idea that the four different estimators, random effects and fixed effects, using either the balanced subpanel or unbalanced panel, usually all suffer differently from selection bias. A comparison of these estimators may therefore give an indication for the likelihood of selection bias. Although any pair of estimators can be compared (see Verbeek and Nijman, 1992a; or Baltagi, 2013, Section 11.4), it is known that fixed effects and random effects estimators may be different for other reasons than selection bias (see Subsection 10.2.4). Therefore, it is most natural to compare either the fixed effects or the random effects estimator using the balanced subpanel, with its counterpart using the unbalanced panel. If different samples, selected on the basis of $r_{i1}, \ldots, r_{iT}$, lead to significantly different estimators, it must be the case that the selection process tells us something about the unobservables in the model. That is, it indicates the presence of selection bias. As the estimators using the unbalanced panel are efficient within a particular class of estimators, we can use the result of Hausman again and derive a test statistic based upon the random effects estimator as (compare (10.28))

$$\xi_{H,RE} = (\hat{\beta}_{RE}^{B} - \hat{\beta}_{RE}^{U})'[\hat{V}\{\hat{\beta}_{RE}^{B}\} - \hat{V}\{\hat{\beta}_{RE}^{U}\}]^{-1}(\hat{\beta}_{RE}^{B} - \hat{\beta}_{RE}^{U}), \tag{10.103}$$

where the $\hat{V}$s denote estimates of the covariance matrices and the superscripts B and U refer to the balanced and unbalanced sample, respectively. Similarly, a test based on the two fixed effects estimators can be derived. Under the null hypothesis, the test statistic follows a Chi-squared distribution with K degrees of freedom. Note that the implicit null hypothesis for the test is that $\text{plim}(\hat{\beta}_{RE}^{B} - \hat{\beta}_{RE}^{U}) = 0$. If this is approximately true and the two estimators suffer similarly from selection bias, the test has no power.[28] Again, it is possible to test for a subset of the elements in β.

10.8.3 Estimation with Nonrandomly Missing Data

As in the cross-sectional case (see Section 7.6), selection bias introduces an identification problem. As a result, it is not possible to obtain consistent estimators for the model parameters in the presence of selection bias, unless additional assumptions are imposed. As an illustration, let us assume that the selection indicator r_{it} can be explained by a random effects probit model, that is

$$r_{it}^* = z_{it}'\gamma + \xi_i + \eta_{it}, \tag{10.104}$$

where $r_{it} = 1$ if $r_{it}^* > 0$ and 0 otherwise, and z_{it} is a (well-motivated) vector of exogenous variables that includes x_{it}. The model of interest is given by

$$y_{it} = x_{it}'\beta + \alpha_i + u_{it}. \tag{10.105}$$

Let us assume that the error components in the two equations have a joint normal distribution. This is a generalization of the cross-sectional sample-selection model considered in Subsection 7.5.1. The effect of sample selection in (10.105) is reflected in the expected values of the unobservables, conditional upon the exogenous variables and the selection indicators, that is

$$E\{\alpha_i | z_{i1}, \ldots, z_{iT}, r_{i1}, \ldots, r_{iT}\} \tag{10.106}$$

and

$$E\{u_{it} | z_{i1}, \ldots, z_{iT}, r_{i1}, \ldots, r_{iT}\}. \tag{10.107}$$

It can be shown (Verbeek and Nijman, 1992a) that (10.107) is time invariant if $\text{cov}\{u_{it}, \eta_{it}\} = 0$ or if $z_{it}'\gamma$ is time invariant. This is required for consistency of the fixed effects estimator. Further, (10.106) is zero if $\text{cov}\{\alpha_i, \xi_i\} = 0$, while (10.107) is zero if $\text{cov}\{u_{it}, \eta_{it}\} = 0$, so that the random effects estimator is consistent if the unobservables in the primary equation and the selection equation are uncorrelated.

Estimation in the more general case is relatively complicated. Hausman and Wise (1979) consider a case where the panel has two periods and attrition only takes place in the second period. In the more general case, using maximum likelihood to estimate the two equations simultaneously requires numerical integration over two dimensions (to integrate out the two individual effects). Nijman and Verbeek (1992) and Vella and Verbeek (1999a) present alternative estimators based upon the two-step estimation method for the cross-sectional sample-selection model. Essentially, the idea is that the terms in (10.106) and (10.107), apart from a constant, can be determined from the probit model in (10.104), so that estimates of these terms can be included in the primary equation. Wooldridge (1995) presents some alternative estimators based on somewhat different assumptions. Das (2004) extends these approaches to cover flexible functional forms in both (10.104) and (10.105) and unknown distributions for the unobserved

[28] The test suggested here is not a real Hausman test because none of the estimators is consistent under the alternative hypothesis. This does not invalidate the test as such but may result in limited power in certain directions.

components. Dustmann and Rochina-Barrachina (2007) apply several alternative estimators to the estimation of a female wage equation and show that the estimation results are considerably sensitive to the particular estimator that is used. Semykina and Wooldridge (2010) propose two estimation procedures that correct for selection bias when some elements in x_{it} are correlated with u_{it} (endogenous regressors).

Identification of (10.105) with attrition or selection bias using the approaches discussed above depends crucially upon the availability of one or more instruments in (10.104). That is, the variables in z_{it} that are not included in (10.105) should be orthogonal to the unobservables in α_i and (most importantly) u_{it}. In this case, the occurrence of selection bias is driven by the correlations between the unobservables in both equations, a case that is sometimes referred to as 'selection upon unobservables'. An alternative approach to handle nonrandom attrition in panel data requires that z_{it} in (10.104) can be chosen in such a way that the unobservables ξ_i and η_{it} are unrelated to the unobservables in (10.105), while z_{it} may depend upon α_i and u_{it}. This says that a (potentially large) set of observables can be found that are relevant for the selection process such that, conditional upon those variables, selection no longer depends upon the unobservables in (10.105). This case is referred to as 'selection upon observables' and is exploited in Fitzgerald, Gottschalk and Moffitt (1998) to evaluate attrition bias in the Panel Study of Income Dynamics (PSID). In their case, z_{it} contains all available lags of y_{it}. Consistent estimation of (10.105) is achieved by attaching weights to each observation in the panel, where the weights depend upon the selection probability (propensity score). Because the two approaches impose different identification conditions, they cannot be tested against each other. Hirano, Imbens, Ridder and Rubin (2001) show how the availability of refreshment samples (new units randomly sampled from the original population) can be used to distinguish between selection upon unobservables and selection upon observables.

10.9 Pseudo Panels and Repeated Cross-sections

In many countries there is a lack of genuine panel data where specific individuals or firms are followed over time. However, repeated cross-sectional surveys may be available, where a random sample is taken from the population at consecutive points in time. Important examples of this are the Current Population Survey in the United States and the Family Expenditure Survey in the United Kingdom. While many types of model can be estimated on the basis of a series of independent cross-sections in a standard way, several models that seemingly require the availability of panel data can also be identified with repeated cross-sections under appropriate conditions. Most importantly, this concerns models with individual dynamics and models with fixed individual-specific effects.

Obviously, the major limitation of repeated cross-sectional data is that the same individuals are not followed over time, so that individual histories are not available for inclusion in a model, for constructing instruments or for transforming a model to first-differences or in deviations from individual means. All of these are often applied with genuine panel data. On the other hand, repeated cross-sections suffer much less from typical panel data problems like attrition and nonresponse, and are very often substantially larger, both in number of individuals or households and in the time period that they span.

10.9.1 The Fixed Effects Model

Consider the linear model with individual effects given by

$$y_{it} = x_{it}'\beta + \alpha_i + u_{it}, \quad t = 1, \ldots, T. \tag{10.108}$$

Unlike the previous sections, the available data set is a series of independent cross-sections, such that observations on N different individuals are available in each period.[29] For simplicity, we shall assume that $E\{x_{it}u_{it}\} = 0$ for each t. If the individual effects α_i are uncorrelated with the explanatory variables in x_{it}, the model in (10.108) can easily be estimated consistently from repeated cross-sections by pooling all observations and performing ordinary least squares treating $\alpha_i + u_{it}$ as a composite error term and including an overall intercept term. However, in many applications the individual effects are likely to be correlated with some or all of the explanatory variables, and OLS is inconsistent. When genuine panel data are available, this can be solved using the within or first-difference transformation to eliminate α_i. Obviously, when repeated observations on the same individuals are not available, such an approach cannot be used.

Deaton (1985) suggests the use of cohorts to obtain consistent estimators for β in (10.108) when repeated cross-sections are available, even if α_i is correlated with one or more of the explanatory variables. Let us define C cohorts, which are groups of individuals sharing some common characteristics. These groups are defined such that each individual is a member of exactly one cohort, which is the same for all periods. For example, a particular cohort can consist of all males born in the period 1950–1954. It is important to realize that the variables on which cohorts are defined should be observed for all individuals in the sample. This rules out time-varying variables (e.g. earnings), because these variables are observed at different points in time for the individuals in the sample. The seminal study of Browning, Deaton and Irish (1985) employs cohorts of households defined on the basis of 5-year age bands subdivided as to whether the head of the household is a manual or nonmanual worker. Propper, Rees and Green (2001) employ year of birth cohorts, subdivided in 10 regions, to examine the determinants of the demand for private health insurance. More recently, Meng et al. (2014) use a pseudo panel with 72 subgroups defined by twelve birth cohorts, gender, and three socioeconomic groups, to estimate price elasticities of demand for alcohol.

If we aggregate all observations to cohort level, the resulting model can be written as

$$\bar{y}_{ct} = \bar{x}_{ct}'\beta + \bar{\alpha}_{ct} + \bar{u}_{ct}, \quad c = 1, \ldots, C; \quad t = 1, \ldots, T, \tag{10.109}$$

where $\bar{y}_{ct}$ is the average value of all observed y_{it}s in cohort c in period t, and similarly for the other variables in the model. The resulting data set is a **pseudo panel** or synthetic panel with repeated observations over T periods and C cohorts. The main problem with estimating β from (10.109) is that $\bar{\alpha}_{ct}$ depends on t, is unobserved and is likely to be correlated with $\bar{x}_{ct}$ (if α_i is correlated with x_{it}). Therefore, treating $\bar{\alpha}_{ct}$ as part of the random error term is likely to lead to inconsistent estimators. Alternatively, one can treat $\bar{\alpha}_{ct}$ as fixed unknown parameters assuming that variation over time can be ignored ($\bar{\alpha}_{ct} = \alpha_c$). If cohort averages are based on a large number of individual observations, this assumption

[29] Because different individuals are observed in each period, this implies that i does not run from 1 to N for each t.

seems reasonable, and a natural estimator for β is the within estimator on the pseudo panel, given by

$$\hat{\beta}_W = \left(\sum_{c=1}^{C} \sum_{t=1}^{T} (\bar{x}_{ct} - \bar{x}_c)(\bar{x}_{ct} - \bar{x}_c)' \right)^{-1} \sum_{c=1}^{C} \sum_{t=1}^{T} (\bar{x}_{ct} - \bar{x}_c)(\bar{y}_{ct} - \bar{y}_c), \tag{10.110}$$

where $\bar{x}_c = T^{-1} \sum_{t=1}^{T} \bar{x}_{ct}$ is the time average of the observed cohort means for cohort c. The properties of this estimator depend, among other things, upon the type of asymptotics that one is willing to employ. In addition to the two dimensions in genuine panel data (N and T), there are two additional dimensions: the number of cohorts C and the number of observations per cohort n_c. A convenient choice is to let $N \to \infty$, with C fixed, so that $n_c \to \infty$. Then the fixed effects estimator based on the pseudo panel, $\hat{\beta}_W$, is consistent for β, provided that

$$\operatorname*{plim}_{n_c \to \infty} \frac{1}{CT} \sum_{c=1}^{C} \sum_{t=1}^{T} (\bar{x}_{ct} - \bar{x}_c)(\bar{x}_{ct} - \bar{x}_c)' \tag{10.111}$$

is finite and invertible, and that

$$\operatorname*{plim}_{n_c \to \infty} \frac{1}{CT} \sum_{c=1}^{C} \sum_{t=1}^{T} (\bar{x}_{ct} - \bar{x}_c)\bar{\alpha}_{ct} = 0. \tag{10.112}$$

Although the first of these two conditions is similar to a standard regularity condition (compare assumption (A6) in Section 2.6), in this context it is somewhat less innocent. It states that the cohort averages exhibit genuine time variation, even with very large cohorts. Whether or not this condition is satisfied depends upon the way the cohorts are constructed, a point to which we shall return later.

Because $\bar{\alpha}_{ct} \to \alpha_c$, for some α_c, if the number of observations per cohort tends to infinity, (10.112) will be satisfied automatically. Consequently, letting $n_c \to \infty$ is a convenient choice to arrive at a consistent estimator for β; see Moffitt (1993) and Ridder and Moffitt (2007). However, as argued by Verbeek and Nijman (1992b) and Devereux (2007), even if cohort sizes are large, the small-sample bias in the within estimator on the pseudo panel may still be substantial. Deaton (1985) considers alternative errors-in-variables estimators for β that do not depend upon $n_c \to \infty$ but instead impose that $N \to \infty$ and $C \to \infty$, with n_c fixed.

10.9.2 An Instrumental Variables Interpretation

To appreciate the role of the way in which the cohorts are constructed, it is useful to reformulate the above estimator as an instrumental variables estimator based on a simple extension of (10.108). The idea advocated by Moffitt (1993) is that grouping can be viewed as an instrumental variables procedure. First, decompose each individual effect α_i into a cohort effect α_c and individual i's deviation from this effect. Letting $z_{ci} = 1$ ($c = 1, \ldots, C$) if individual i is a member of cohort c and 0 otherwise, we can write

$$\alpha_i = \sum_{c=1}^{C} \alpha_c z_{ci} + v_i, \tag{10.113}$$

which can be interpreted as an orthogonal projection. Defining $\alpha = (\alpha_1, \ldots, \alpha_C)'$ and $z_i = (z_{1i}, \ldots, z_{Ci})'$ and substituting (10.113) into (10.108), we obtain

$$y_{it} = x_{it}'\beta + z_i'\alpha + v_i + u_{it}. \tag{10.114}$$

If α_i and x_{it} are correlated, we may also expect that v_i and x_{it} are correlated. Consequently, estimating (10.114) by ordinary least squares would not result in consistent estimators. Now, suppose that instruments for x_{it} can be found that are uncorrelated with $v_i + u_{it}$. In this case, an instrumental variables estimator would typically produce a consistent estimator for β and α_c. A natural choice is to choose the cohort dummies in z_i, interacted with time, as instruments, in which case we derive linear predictors from the K reduced forms:

$$x_{k,it} = z_i'\delta_{kt} + w_{k,it}, \quad k = 1, \ldots, K, \quad t = 1, \ldots, T, \tag{10.115}$$

where δ_{kt} is a vector of unknown parameters. The linear predictor for x_{it} by construction equals $\bar{x}_{ct}$, the vector of averages within cohort c in period t. The resulting instrumental variables estimator for β is then given by

$$\hat{\beta}_{IV1} = \left(\sum_{i=1}^{N} \sum_{t=1}^{T} (\bar{x}_{ct} - \bar{x}_c)x_{it}' \right)^{-1} \sum_{i=1}^{N} \sum_{t=1}^{T} (\bar{x}_{ct} - \bar{x}_c)y_{it}, \tag{10.116}$$

which is numerically identical to the standard within estimator based on the pseudo panel of cohort averages, given in (10.110).

The instrumental variables interpretation is useful because it illustrates that alternative estimators may be constructed using other sets of instruments. For example, z_i may include (smooth) functions of year of birth, rather than a set of dummy variables. Further, the instrument set in (10.115) can be extended to include additional variables. Most importantly, however, the instrumental variables approach stresses that grouping data into cohorts requires grouping variables that should satisfy the typical requirements for instrument exogeneity and relevance.

In practice, cohorts should be defined on the basis of variables that do not vary over time and that are observed for all individuals in the sample. This is a serious restriction. Possible choices include variables like age (date of birth), gender, race or region.[30] Identification of the parameters in the model requires that the reduced forms in (10.115) generate sufficient variation over time. This requirement puts a heavy burden on the cohort identifying variables. In particular, it requires that groups are defined whose explanatory variables all have changed differentially over time. Suppose, as an extreme example, that cohorts are defined on the basis of a variable that is independent of the variables in the model. That is, cohorts are constructed by randomly grouping individuals. In this case, the true population cohort means x_{ct} would be identical for each cohort c (and equal the overall population mean). This leaves only the time variation in x_{ct} to identify the parameters of interest.

10.9.3 Dynamic Models

An important situation where the availability of panel data seems essential to identify and estimate the model of interest is the case where a lagged dependent variable enters the

[30] Note that residential location may be endogenous in certain applications.

model. Let us consider a simple extension of (10.108) given by

$$y_{it} = \gamma y_{i,t-1} + x_{it}'\beta + \alpha_i + u_{it}, \quad t = 1, \ldots, T, \tag{10.117}$$

where the K-dimensional vector x_{it} may include time-invariant and time-varying variables. When genuine panel data are available, the parameters γ and β can be estimated consistently (for fixed T and $N \to \infty$) using the instrumental variables estimators and GMM estimators discussed in Section 10.4. These estimators are based on first-differencing (10.117) and then using lagged values of $y_{i,t-1}$ as instruments.

In the present context, $y_{i,t-1}$ refers to the value of y at $t - 1$ for an individual who is only observed in cross-section t. Thus, an observation for $y_{i,t-1}$ is unavailable. Therefore, the first step is to construct an estimate by using information on the y values of other individuals observed at $t - 1$. A convenient approach is to use the average value of $y_{i,t-1}$ from individuals in the same cohort, $\bar{y}_{c,t-1}$, say. Inserting these predicted values into the original model, we obtain

$$y_{it} = \gamma \bar{y}_{c,t-1} + x_{it}'\beta + \xi_{i,t}, \quad t = 1, \ldots, T, \tag{10.118}$$

where

$$\xi_{it} = \alpha_i + u_{it} + \gamma(y_{i,t-1} - \bar{y}_{c,t-1}). \tag{10.119}$$

The unobserved prediction error $y_{i,t-1} - \bar{y}_{c,t-1}$ is part of the error term and is also likely to be correlated with x_{it}. As a result, OLS estimation of (10.118) is typically inconsistent (see Verbeek and Vella, 2005, for more discussion and exceptions). To overcome this problem, one can use an instrumental variables approach. Note that now we need instruments for x_{it} even though these variables are exogenous in the original model. As before, a natural choice is to use the cohort dummies, interacted with time, as instruments for x_{it}. These instruments are uncorrelated with $y_{i,t-1} - \bar{y}_{c,t-1}$ by construction.

When the instruments z_i are a set of cohort dummies, estimation of (10.118) by instrumental variables is identical to applying OLS to the original model where all variables are replaced by their (time-specific) cohort sample averages. We can write this as

$$\bar{y}_{ct} = \gamma \bar{y}_{c,t-1} + \bar{x}_{ct}'\beta + \bar{\xi}_{ct}, \quad c = 1, \ldots, C, \quad t = 1, \ldots, T, \tag{10.120}$$

where all variables denote period-by-period averages within each cohort. For this approach to be appropriate, we need $\bar{y}_{c,t-1}$ and $\bar{x}_{ct}$ not to be collinear, which requires the instruments to capture variation in $y_{i,t-1}$ independently of the variation in x_{it}. It is possible to include cohort fixed effects in essentially the same way as in the static linear model by including the cohort dummies in the equation of interest, with time-invariant coefficients. This imposes (10.113) and results in

$$\bar{y}_{ct} = \gamma \bar{y}_{c,t-1} + \bar{x}_{ct}'\beta + \alpha_c + \bar{u}_{c,t}, \tag{10.121}$$

where α_c denotes a cohort-specific fixed effect. Applying OLS to (10.121) corresponds to the standard within estimator for γ and β based upon treating the cohort-level data as a panel, which is consistent under the given assumptions (and some regularity conditions) when $n_c \to \infty$ and C is fixed. The usual problem with estimating dynamic panel data models with short T (see Section 10.4), does not arise because the error term, which is a within cohort average of individual error terms that are uncorrelated with z_i, is asymptotically zero.[31] However, it remains to be seen whether suitable instruments can be found that satisfy the earlier conditions, because the rank condition for identification requires that the time-invariant instruments have time-varying relationships with the exogenous variables and the lagged dependent variable, whereas they should not have any time-varying relationship with the equation's error term. While this seems unlikely, it is not impossible. When z_i is uncorrelated with u_{it}, it is typically sufficient that the means of the exogenous variables, conditional upon z_i, are time-varying; see Verbeek and Vella (2005) for more details.

McKenzie (2004) considers the linear dynamic model with cohort-specific coefficients in (10.117). While this extension will typically only make sense if there is a fairly small number of well-defined cohorts, it arises naturally from the existing literature on dynamic heterogeneous panels. For example, Robertson and Symons (1992) and Pesaran and Smith (1995) stress the importance of parameter heterogeneity in dynamic panel data models and analyse the potentially severe biases that may arise from handling it in an inappropriate manner. In many practical applications, investigating whether there are systematic differences between, for example, age cohorts is an interesting question. Obviously, relaxing specification (10.117) by having cohort-specific coefficients puts an additional burden upon the identifying conditions. Verbeek (2008) provides additional discussion and references on pseudo panel data. The analyses in Inoue (2008) also highlight that uncritical application of the inference methods for genuine panels to pseudo panels is potentially misleading.

Wrap-up

When repeated observations on the same units are available the panel nature of the data requires adjustments in standard econometric models. The static linear model is typically estimated under a random effects or a fixed effects assumption. The first allows for time-invariant heterogeneity in the error term, while the second allows this heterogeneity to be correlated with the explanatory variables in the model. This results in more robust estimators. A Hausman test is derived from the difference between the two estimators. A key advantage of panel data is that dynamic models can be estimated at the individual level. When the time dimension of the panel is limited, standard estimators are inconsistent in dynamic models. Instead, one usually employs an instrumental variables or GMM approach (see Arellano, 2003). In models explaining discrete of limited dependent variables the panel nature of the data complicates estimation. Depending upon the distributional assumptions made, fixed effects or random effects estimation is possible based upon a (conditional) maximum likelihood approach. In macro panels, the time dimension is relatively large while the number of cross-sectional units is limited. In these cases, it may be of interest to test for unit roots or cointegration, and a wide range of tests is available extending the time-series tests discussed in Chapters 8 and 9. Wooldridge (2010), Baltagi (2013) and Hsiao (2014) are textbooks specializing in panel data econometrics; Pesaran (2015) focuses on macro panels and panel time series.

[31] Recall that, asymptotically, the number of cohorts is fixed and the number of individuals goes to infinity.

Exercises

Exercise 10.1 (Linear Model)

Consider the following simple panel data model

$$y_{it} = x_{it}\beta + \alpha_i^* + u_{it}, \quad i = 1, \ldots, N, \quad t = 1, \ldots, T, \tag{10.122}$$

where β is one-dimensional, and where it is assumed that

$$\alpha_i^* = \bar{x}_i\lambda + \alpha_i, \quad \text{with} \quad \alpha_i \sim NID(0, \sigma_\alpha^2), \quad u_{it} \sim NID(0, \sigma_u^2).$$

The two error components α_i and u_{it} are mutually independent and independent of all x_{it}s.

The parameter β in (10.122) can be estimated by the fixed effects (or within) estimator given by

$$\hat{\beta}_{FE} = \frac{\sum_{i=1}^N \sum_{t=1}^T (x_{it} - \bar{x}_i)(y_{it} - \bar{y}_i)}{\sum_{i=1}^N \sum_{t=1}^T (x_{it} - \bar{x}_i)^2}.$$

As an alternative, the correlation between the error term $\alpha_i^* + u_{it}$ and x_{it} can be handled by an instrumental variables approach.

a. Give an expression for the IV estimator $\hat{\beta}_{IV}$ for β in (10.122) using $x_{it} - \bar{x}_i$ as an instrument for x_{it}. Show that $\hat{\beta}_{IV}$ and $\hat{\beta}_{FE}$ are identical.

Another way to eliminate the individual effects α_i^* from the model is to take first-differences. This results in

$$y_{it} - y_{i,t-1} = (x_{it} - x_{i,t-1})\beta + (u_{it} - u_{i,t-1}), \quad i = 1, \ldots, N, \quad t = 2, \ldots, T. \tag{10.123}$$

b. Denote the OLS estimator based on (10.123) by $\hat{\beta}_{FD}$. Show that $\hat{\beta}_{FD}$ is identical to $\hat{\beta}_{IV}$ and $\hat{\beta}_{FE}$ if $T = 2$. This identity no longer holds for $T > 2$. Which of the two estimators would you prefer in that case? Explain. (Note: for additional discussion, see Verbeek, 1995.)

c. Consider the between estimator $\hat{\beta}_B$ for β in (10.122). Give an expression for $\hat{\beta}_B$ and show that it is unbiased for $\beta + \lambda$.

d. Finally, suppose we substitute the expression for α_i^* into (10.122), giving

$$y_{it} = x_{it}\beta + \bar{x}_i\lambda + \alpha_i + u_{it}, \quad i = 1, \ldots, N, \quad t = 1, \ldots, T. \tag{10.124}$$

The vector $(\beta, \lambda)'$ can be estimated by GLS (random effects) based on (10.124). It can be shown that the implied estimator for β is identical to $\hat{\beta}_{FE}$. Does this imply that there is no real distinction between the fixed effects and random effects approaches? (Note: for additional discussion, see Hsiao, 2014, Subsection 3.4.2.)

Exercise 10.2 (Hausman–Taylor Model)

Consider the following linear panel data model:

$$y_{it} = x'_{1,it}\beta_1 + x'_{2,it}\beta_2 + w'_{1,i}\gamma_1 + w'_{2,i}\gamma_2 + \alpha_i + u_{it}, \tag{10.125}$$

where $w_{k,i}$ are time invariant and $x_{k,it}$ are time-varying explanatory variables. The variables with index 1 ($x_{1,it}$ and $w_{1,i}$) are strictly exogenous in the sense that $E\{x_{1,it}\alpha_i\} = 0, E\{x_{1,is}u_{it}\} = 0$ for all s, t, $E\{w_{1,i}\alpha_i\} = 0$ and $E\{w_{1,i}u_{it}\} = 0$. It is also assumed that $E\{w_{2,i}u_{it}\} = 0$ and that the usual regularity conditions (for consistency and asymptotic normality) are met.

a. Under which additional assumptions would OLS applied to (10.125) provide a consistent estimator for $\beta = (\beta_1, \beta_2)'$ and $\gamma = (\gamma_1, \gamma_2)'$?

b. Consider the fixed effects (within) estimator. Under which additional assumption(s) would it provide a consistent estimator for β?

c. Consider the OLS estimator for β based upon a regression in first-differences. Under which additional assumption(s) will this provide a consistent estimator for β?

d. Discuss one or more alternative consistent estimators for β and γ if it can be assumed that $E\{x_{2,is}u_{it}\} = 0$ (for all s, t), and $E\{w_{2,i}u_{it}\} = 0$. What are the restrictions, in this case, on the number of variables in each of the categories?

e. Discuss estimation of β if $x_{2,it}$ *equals* $y_{i,t-1}$.

f. Discuss estimation of β if $x_{2,it}$ *includes* $y_{i,t-1}$.

g. Would it be possible to estimate both β and γ consistently if $x_{2,it}$ includes $y_{i,t-1}$? If so, how? If not, why not? (Make additional assumptions, if necessary.)

Exercise 10.3 (Linear Model – Empirical)

This exercise makes use of data for young females from the National Longitudinal Survey (Youth Sample) for the period 1980–1987, available from the book's website. These data are also used in Vella and Verbeek (1999a). We focus on the subsample of 12 039 observations reporting positive hours of work in a given period.

a. Produce summary statistics of the data set and produce a histogram of T_i. How many individuals do you have in the panel? How many of them are continuously working over the entire period 1980–1987?

b. Estimate a simple wage equation using pooled OLS, with clustered (panel-robust) standard errors. Explain a person's log wage from marital status, black, hispanic, schooling, experience and experience-squared, rural and union membership. Estimate another specification that includes time dummies. Compare the results. Test whether the time dummies are jointly significant. Why does the inclusion of time dummies make sense economically?

c. Use the fixed effects and random effects estimators to estimate the same equation. Interpret and compare the results. (You may also want to compare the results with those for males reported in Table 10.2.)

d. Perform a Hausman test, and interpret the result. What exactly is the null hypothesis that you test?

e. On the basis of the random effects results, interpret the estimates for σ_u^2 and σ_α^2, and use them to estimate the transformation factor ϑ in (10.23). How important is the individual effect in this equation?

f. Re-estimate the wage equation, using the random effects estimator, including age and age-squared rather than experience and experience-squared. Compare the results. What happened to the coefficient on schooling? Why?

g. Let us focus on the random effects model including experience and experience-squared. Re-estimate this model including T_i and interpret the results. Evaluate the t-test on the included variable. What does it test? Does the result surprise you? Why doesn't this test work with the fixed effects model? Repeat the estimation but include a dummy for $T_i = 8$. Interpret.

h. Re-estimate the base model (with experience and experience-squared) from **c** using the random effects estimator, using the unbalanced panel and the balanced subpanel (characterized by $T_i = 8$). Compare the results. Does it appear that the loss in efficiency is substantial? What about the coefficient estimates?

i. Perform a Hausman test on the difference between the two estimators in **h** and interpret the results.

j. Repeat the previous test using the fixed effects estimator. Interpret and compare with **i**. If you experience problems calculating the Hausman test statistic, try using panel-robust covariance matrices.

Exercise 10.4 (Dynamic and Binary Choice Models)

Consider the following dynamic wage equation

$$w_{it} = x_{it}'\beta + \gamma w_{i,t-1} + \alpha_i + u_{it}, \tag{10.126}$$

where w_{it} denotes an individual's log hourly wage rate and x_{it} is a vector of personal and job characteristics (age, schooling, gender, industry, etc.).

a. Explain in words why OLS applied to (10.126) is inconsistent.

b. Also explain why the fixed effects estimator applied to (10.126) is inconsistent for $N \to \infty$ and fixed T, but consistent for $N \to \infty$ and $T \to \infty$. (Assume that u_{it} is i.i.d.)

c. Explain why the results from **a** and **b** also imply that the random effects (GLS) estimator in (10.126) is inconsistent for fixed T.

d. Describe a simple consistent (for $N \to \infty$) estimator for β, γ, assuming that α_i and u_{it} are i.i.d. and independent of all x_{it}s.

e. Describe a more efficient estimator for β, γ under the same assumptions.

In addition to the wage equation, assume there is a binary choice model explaining whether an individual is working or not. Let $r_{it} = 1$ if individual i was working in period t and zero otherwise. Then the model can be described as

$$\begin{aligned} r_{it}^* &= z_{it}'\delta + \xi_i + \eta_{it} \\ r_{it} &= 1 \quad \text{if } r_{it}^* > 0 \\ &= 0 \quad \text{otherwise,} \end{aligned} \tag{10.127}$$

where z_{it} is a vector of personal characteristics. Assume that $\xi_i \sim NID(0, \sigma_\xi^2)$ and $\eta_{it} \sim NID(0, 1 - \sigma_\xi^2)$, mutually independent and independent of all z_{it}s. The model in (10.127) can be estimated by maximum likelihood.

f. Give an expression for the probability that $r_{it} = 1$ given z_{it} and ξ_i.

g. Use the expression from **f** to obtain a computationally tractable expression for the likelihood contribution of individual i.

h. Explain why it is not possible to treat the ξ_is as fixed unknown parameters and estimate δ consistently (for fixed T) from this fixed effects probit.

From now on, assume that the appropriate wage equation is static and given by (10.126) with $\gamma = 0$.

i. What are the consequences for the random effects estimator in (10.126) if η_{it} and u_{it} are correlated? Why?

j. What are the consequences for the fixed effects estimator in (10.126) if ξ_i and α_i are correlated (while η_{it} and u_{it} are not)? Why?

Exercise 10.5 (Binary Choice Models – Empirical)

This exercise makes use of data for young females from the National Longitudinal Survey (Youth Sample) for 1980–1987, also used in Exercise 10.3. Our goal is to model union status of working females.

a. Produce summary statistics for union status. How many observations relate to union members? How many females are union members for all periods they are in the panel? How many females are never union members?

b. Estimate a pooled probit model (ignoring the panel nature of the data) explaining union status from age, schooling, hispanic, black, public sector, marital status and a dummy for living in the North East. Interpret the results. Is this estimator consistent? What about its standard errors?

c. Re-estimate the pooled probit using panel-robust standard errors. Compare the results with **b** and interpret.

d. Estimate a pooled logit model explaining union status from the same explanatory variables, also with panel-robust standard errors. Compare the estimated coefficients and their significance with those obtained in **c**. Why are the logit coefficients uniformly bigger than the probit ones?

e. Estimate a random effects probit model based on the previous specification. Can you explain why it is taking so much time to determine the maximum likelihood estimates for this model? Interpret the estimation results. Also report which normalization constraint is imposed upon σ_α^2 and σ_u^2. Use this to compare the coefficient estimates from the random effects probit model with those from the pooled probit model.

f. Perform a likelihood ratio test on the restriction that $\sigma_\alpha^2 = 0$. Interpret.

g. Extend the previous model with a lagged dependent variable (lagged union status). Compare the estimation results with those obtained under **e.** Also compare the estimated value of σ_α^2. Explain. Under what conditions is it appropriate to include a lagged dependent variable in a random effects binary choice model? Are you concerned with the fact that the estimated autoregressive coefficient is bigger than one?

h. Estimate a static fixed effects logit model. Interpret the results. How many individuals are used to estimate this model?

A Vectors and Matrices

In occasional places in this text, use is made of results from linear algebra. This appendix is meant to review the concepts that are used. More details can be found in textbooks on linear algebra or, for example, in Davidson and MacKinnon (1993, Appendix A), Davidson (2000, Appendix A), Greene (2012, Appendix A) or Pesaran (2015, Appendix A). Some of the more complex topics are used in a limited number of places in the text. For example, eigenvalues and the rank of a matrix only play a role in Chapter 9, while the rules of differentiation are only needed in Chapters 2 and 5.

A.1 Terminology

In this book a **vector** is always a *column* of numbers, denoted by

$$a = \begin{pmatrix} a_1 \\ a_2 \\ \vdots \\ a_n \end{pmatrix}.$$

The **transpose** of a vector, denoted by $a' = (a_1, a_2, \ldots, a_n)$, is a row of numbers, sometimes called a row vector. A **matrix** is a rectangular array of numbers. Of dimension $n \times k$, it can be written as

$$A = \begin{pmatrix} a_{11} & a_{12} & \cdots & a_{1k} \\ a_{21} & a_{22} & & \\ & & \ddots & \\ a_{n1} & a_{n2} & \cdots & a_{nk} \end{pmatrix}.$$

The first index of the element a_{ij} refers to the ith row, and the second index to the jth column. Denoting the vector in the jth column of this matrix by a_j, it is seen that A consists of k vectors a_1 to a_k, which we can denote as

$$A = \left[a_1 \; a_2 \; \ldots \; a_k\right].$$

The symbol $'$ denotes the **transpose** of a matrix or vector, obtained as

$$A' = \begin{pmatrix} a_{11} & a_{21} & \cdots & a_{n1} \\ a_{12} & a_{22} & & a_{n2} \\ & & \ddots & \vdots \\ a_{1k} & & \cdots & a_{nk} \end{pmatrix}.$$

The columns of A are the rows of A', and vice versa. A matrix is **square** if $n = k$. A square matrix A is **symmetric** if $A = A'$. A square matrix A is called a **diagonal** matrix if $a_{ij} = 0$ for all $i \neq j$. Note that a diagonal matrix is symmetric by construction. The **identity matrix** I is a diagonal matrix with all diagonal elements equal to one.

A.2 Matrix Manipulations

If two matrices or vectors have the same dimensions, they can be **added** or **subtracted**. Let A and B be two matrices of dimension $n \times k$ with typical elements a_{ij} and b_{ij}, respectively. Then $A + B$ has a typical element $a_{ij} + b_{ij}$, while $A - B$ has a typical element $a_{ij} - b_{ij}$. It easily follows that $A + B = B + A$ and $(A + B)' = A' + B'$.

A matrix A of dimension $n \times k$ and a matrix B of dimension $k \times m$ can be **multiplied** to produce a matrix of dimension $n \times m$. Let us consider the special case of $k = 1$ first. Then $A = a'$ is a row vector and $B = b$ is a column vector. Then we define

$$AB = a'b = (a_1, a_2, \ldots, a_n)\begin{pmatrix} b_1 \\ b_2 \\ \vdots \\ b_n \end{pmatrix} = a_1b_1 + a_2b_2 + \cdots + a_nb_n.$$

We call $a'b$ the **inner product** of the vectors a and b. Note that $a'b = b'a$. Two vectors are called **orthogonal** if $a'b = 0$. For any vector a, except the null vector, we have $a'a > 0$. The **outer product** of a vector a is aa', which is of dimension $n \times n$.

Another special case arises for $m = 1$, in which case A is an $n \times k$ matrix and $B = b$ is a vector of dimension k. Then $c = Ab$ is also a vector, but of dimension n. It has typical elements

$$c_i = a_{i1}b_1 + a_{i2}b_2 + \cdots + a_{ik}b_k,$$

which is the inner product between the vector obtained from the ith row of A and the vector b.

When $m > 1$, B is a matrix and $C = AB$ is a matrix of dimension $n \times m$ with typical elements

$$c_{ij} = a_{i1}b_{1j} + a_{i2}b_{2j} + \cdots + a_{ik}b_{kj}$$

being the inner products between the vectors obtained from the ith row of A and the jth column of B. Note that this can only make sense if the number of columns in A equals the number of rows in B.

As an example, consider

$$A = \begin{pmatrix} 1 & 2 & 3 \\ 4 & 5 & 0 \end{pmatrix}, \quad B = \begin{pmatrix} 1 & 2 \\ 3 & 4 \\ 0 & 5 \end{pmatrix}$$

and

$$AB = \begin{pmatrix} 7 & 25 \\ 19 & 28 \end{pmatrix}.$$

It is important to note that $AB \neq BA$. Even if AB exists, BA may not be defined because the dimensions of B and A do not match. If A is of dimension $n \times k$ and B is of dimension $k \times n$, then AB exists and has dimension $n \times n$, while BA exists with dimension $k \times k$. In the above example, we have

$$BA = \begin{pmatrix} 9 & 12 & 3 \\ 19 & 26 & 9 \\ 20 & 25 & 0 \end{pmatrix}.$$

For the transpose of a product of two matrices, it holds that

$$(AB)' = B'A'.$$

From this (and $(A')' = A$) it follows that both $A'A$ and AA' exist and are symmetric. Finally, multiplying a scalar and a matrix is the same as multiplying each element in the matrix by this scalar. That is, for a scalar c, cA has typical element ca_{ij}.

A.3 Properties of Matrices and Vectors

If we consider a number of vectors a_1 to a_k, we can take a **linear combination** of these vectors. With scalar weights $c_1, \ldots, c_k$ this produces the vector $c_1a_1 + c_2a_2 + \cdots + c_ka_k$, which we can shortly write as Ac, where, as before, $A = [a_1 \cdots a_k]$ and $c = (c_1, \ldots, c_k)'$.

A set of vectors is **linearly dependent** if any of the vectors can be written as a linear combination of the others. That is, if there exist values for $c_1, \ldots, c_k$, not all zero, such that $c_1a_1 + c_2a_2 + \cdots + c_ka_k = 0$ (the null vector). Equivalently, a set of vectors is **linearly independent** if the only solution to

$$c_1a_1 + c_2a_2 + \cdots + c_ka_k = 0$$

is

$$c_1 = c_2 = \cdots = c_k = 0.$$

That is, if the only solution to $Ac = 0$ is $c = 0$.

If we consider all possible vectors that can be obtained as linear combinations of the vectors $a_1, \ldots, a_k$, these vectors form a **vector space**. If the vectors $a_1, \ldots, a_k$ are linearly dependent, we can reduce the number of vectors without changing this vector space. The minimal number of vectors needed to span a vector space is called the **dimension** of that space. This way, we can define the **column space** of a matrix as the space spanned by its columns, and the **column rank** of a matrix as the dimension of its column space. Clearly, the column rank can never exceed the number of columns. A matrix is of **full column rank** if the column rank equals the number of columns. The **row rank** of a matrix is the dimension of the space spanned by the rows of the matrix. In general, it holds that the row rank and the column rank of a matrix are equal, so we can unambiguously define the **rank of a matrix**. Note that this does not imply that a matrix that is of full column rank is automatically of full row rank (this only holds if the matrix is square).

A useful result in regression analysis is that for any A

$$rank(A) = rank(A'A) = rank(AA').$$

A.4 Inverse Matrices

A matrix B, if it exists, is the **inverse** of a matrix A if $AB = I$ and $BA = I$. A necessary requirement for this is that A is a *square* matrix and has *full rank*, in which case A is also called **invertible** or **nonsingular**. In this case, we can define $B = A^{-1}$, and

$$AA^{-1} = I \quad \text{and} \quad A^{-1}A = I.$$

Note that the definition implies that $A = B^{-1}$. Thus we have $(A^{-1})^{-1} = A$. If A^{-1} does not exist, we say that A is **singular**. Analytically, the inverse of a diagonal matrix and the inverse of a 2×2 matrix are easily obtained. For example,

$$\begin{pmatrix} a_{11} & 0 & 0 \\ 0 & a_{22} & 0 \\ 0 & 0 & a_{33} \end{pmatrix}^{-1} = \begin{pmatrix} a_{11}^{-1} & 0 & 0 \\ 0 & a_{22}^{-1} & 0 \\ 0 & 0 & a_{33}^{-1} \end{pmatrix}$$

and

$$\begin{pmatrix} a_{11} & a_{12} \\ a_{21} & a_{22} \end{pmatrix}^{-1} = \frac{1}{a_{11}a_{22} - a_{12}a_{21}} \begin{pmatrix} a_{22} & -a_{12} \\ -a_{21} & a_{11} \end{pmatrix}.$$

If $a_{11}a_{22} - a_{12}a_{21} = 0$, the 2×2 matrix A is singular: its columns are linearly dependent, and so are its rows. We call $a_{11}a_{22} - a_{12}a_{21}$ the determinant of this 2×2 matrix (see below).

Suppose we are asked to solve $Ac = d$ for given A and d, where A is of dimension $n \times n$ and both c and d are n-dimensional vectors. This is a system of n linear equations with n unknowns. If A^{-1} exists, we can write

$$A^{-1}Ac = c = A^{-1}\,d$$

to obtain the solution. If A is not invertible, the system of linear equations has linear dependencies. There are two possibilities. Either more than one vector c satisfies $Ac = d$, so no unique solution exists, or the equations are inconsistent, so there is no solution to the system. If d is the null vector, only the first possibility remains.

It is straightforward to derive that

$$(A^{-1})' = (A')^{-1}$$

and

$$(AB)^{-1} = B^{-1}A^{-1}$$

(assuming that both inverse matrices exist).

A.5 Idempotent Matrices

A special class of matrices is that of symmetric and idempotent matrices. A matrix P is symmetric if $P' = P$ and **idempotent** if $PP = P$. A symmetric idempotent matrix P has the interpretation of a **projection matrix**. This means that the projection vector Px is in the column space of P, while the residual vector $x - Px$ is orthogonal to any vector in the column space of P.

A projection matrix that projects upon the column space of a matrix A can be constructed as $P = A(A'A)^{-1}A'$. Clearly, this matrix is symmetric and idempotent. Projecting twice upon the same space should leave the result unaffected, so we should have $PPx = Px$, which follows directly. The residual from the projection is $x - Px = (I - A(A'A)^{-1}A')x$, so that $M = I - A(A'A)^{-1}A'$ is also a projection matrix with $MP = PM = 0$ and $MM = M = M'$. Thus the vectors Mx and Px are orthogonal.

An interesting projecting matrix (used in Chapter 10) is $Q = I - (1/n)\iota\iota'$, where ι is an n-dimensional vector of ones (so that $\iota\iota'$ is a matrix of ones). The diagonal elements in this matrix are $1 - 1/n$, and all off-diagonal elements are $-1/n$. Now Qx is a vector containing x in deviation from its mean. A vector of means is produced by the transformation matrix $P = (1/n)\iota\iota'$. Note that $PP = P$ and $QP = 0$.

The only nonsingular projection matrix is the identity matrix. All other projection matrices are singular, each having rank equal to the dimension of the space upon which they project.

A.6 Eigenvalues and Eigenvectors

Let A be a symmetric $n \times n$ matrix. Consider the following problem of finding combinations of a vector c (other than the null vector) and a scalar λ that satisfy

$$Ac = \lambda c.$$

In general, there are n solutions $\lambda_1, \ldots, \lambda_n$, called the **eigenvalues** (characteristic roots) of A, corresponding to n vectors $c_1, \ldots, c_n$, called the **eigenvectors** (characteristic vectors). If c_1 is a solution, then so is kc_1 for any constant k, so the eigenvectors are defined up to a constant. The eigenvectors of a symmetric matrix are orthogonal, that is, $c_i'c_j = 0$ for all $i \neq j$.

If an eigenvalue is zero, the corresponding vector c satisfies $Ac = 0$, which implies that A is not of full rank and thus singular. Thus a singular matrix has at least one zero eigenvalue. In general, the rank of a symmetric matrix corresponds to the number of nonzero eigenvalues.

A symmetric matrix is called **positive definite** if all its eigenvalues are positive. It is called **positive semi-definite** if all its eigenvalues are non-negative. A positive definite matrix is invertible. If A is positive definite, it holds for any vector x (not the null vector) that

$$x'Ax > 0.$$

The reason is that any vector x can be written as a linear combination of the eigenvectors as $x = d_1c_1 + \cdots + d_nc_n$ for scalars $d_1, \ldots, d_n$, and we can write

$$\begin{aligned} x'Ax &= (d_1c_1 + \cdots + d_nc_n)'A(d_1c_1 + \cdots + d_nc_n) \\ &= \lambda_1 d_1^2 c_1'c_1 + \cdots + \lambda_n d_n^2 c_n'c_n > 0. \end{aligned}$$

Similarly, for a positive semi-definite matrix A, we have for any vector x

$$x'Ax \geq 0.$$

The **determinant** of a symmetric matrix equals the product of its n eigenvalues. The determinant of a positive definite matrix is positive. A symmetric matrix is singular if the determinant is zero (i.e. if one of the eigenvalues is zero).

A.7 Differentiation

Let x be an n-dimensional column vector. If c is also an n-dimensional column vector, $c'x$ is a scalar. Let us consider $c'x$ as a function of the vector x. Then, we can consider the vector of derivatives of $c'x$ with respect to each of the elements in x, that is

$$\frac{\partial c'x}{\partial x} = c.$$

This is a column vector of n derivatives, the typical element being c_i. More generally, for a vectorial function Ax (where A is a matrix) we have

$$\frac{\partial Ax}{\partial x} = A'.$$

The element in column i, row j of this matrix is the derivative of the jth element in the function Ax with respect to x_i.

Further,

$$\frac{\partial x'Ax}{\partial x} = 2Ax$$

for a symmetric matrix A. If A is not symmetric, we have

$$\frac{\partial x'Ax}{\partial x} = (A + A')x.$$

All these results follow from collecting the results from an element-by-element differentiation.

A.8 Some Least Squares Manipulations

Let $x_i = (x_{i1}, x_{i2}, \ldots, x_{iK})'$ with $x_{i1} \equiv 1$ and $\beta = (\beta_1, \beta_2, \ldots, \beta_K)'$. Then

$$x_i'\beta = \beta_1 + \beta_2 x_{i2} + \cdots + \beta_K x_{iK}.$$

The matrix

$$\sum_{i=1}^N x_i x_i' = \sum_{i=1}^N \begin{pmatrix} x_{i1} \\ x_{i2} \\ \vdots \\ x_{iK} \end{pmatrix} (x_{i1}, x_{i2}, \ldots, x_{iK})$$

$$= \begin{pmatrix} \sum_{i=1}^N x_{i1}^2 & \sum_{i=1}^N x_{i2}x_{i1} & \cdots & \sum_{i=1}^N x_{iK}x_{i1} \\ \vdots & \sum_{i=1}^N x_{i2}^2 & & \\ \vdots & & \ddots & \vdots \\ \sum_{i=1}^N x_{i1}x_{iK} & & \cdots & \sum_{i=1}^N x_{iK}^2 \end{pmatrix}$$

is a $K \times K$ symmetric matrix containing sums of squares and cross-products. The vector

$$\sum_{i=1}^N x_i y_i = \begin{pmatrix} \sum_{i=1}^N x_{i1}y_i \\ \sum_{i=1}^N x_{i2}y_i \\ \vdots \\ \sum_{i=1}^N x_{iK}y_i \end{pmatrix}$$

has length K, so that the system

$$\left(\sum_{i=1}^N x_i x_i' \right) b = \sum_{i=1}^N x_i y_i$$

is a system of K equations with K unknowns (in b). If $\sum_{i=1}^N x_i x_i'$ is invertible, a unique solution exists. Invertibility requires that $\sum_{i=1}^N x_i x_i'$ is of full rank. If it is not full rank, a nonzero K-dimensional vector c exists such that $x_i'c = 0$ for each i and a linear dependence exists between the columns/rows of the matrix $\sum_{i=1}^N x_i x_i'$.

With matrix notation, the $N \times K$ matrix X is defined as

$$X = \begin{pmatrix} x_{11} & x_{12} & \cdots & x_{1K} \\ \vdots & \vdots & \ddots & \vdots \\ x_{N1} & x_{N2} & \cdots & x_{NK} \end{pmatrix}$$

and $y = (y_1, y_2, \ldots, y_N)'$. From this it is easily verified that

$$X'X = \sum_{i=1}^N x_i x_i'$$

and

$$X'y = \sum_{i=1}^{N} x_i y_i.$$

The matrix $X'X$ is not invertible if the matrix X is not of full rank. That is, if a linear dependence exists between the columns of X ('regressors').

B Statistical and Distribution Theory

This appendix briefly reviews some statistical and distribution theory that is used in this text. More details can be found in, for example, Davidson and MacKinnon (1993, Appendix B), Greene (2012, Appendix B) or Pesaran (2015, Appendix B).

B.1 Discrete Random Variables

A **random variable** is a variable that can take different outcomes depending upon 'the state of nature'. For example, the outcome of throwing once with a dice is random, with possible outcomes 1, 2, 3, 4, 5 and 6. Let us denote an arbitrary random variable by Y. If Y denotes the outcome of the dice experiment (and the dice is fair and thrown randomly), the **probability** of each outcome is 1/6. We can denote this as

$$P\{Y = y\} = 1/6 \quad \text{for} \quad y = 1, 2, \ldots, 6.$$

The function that links possible outcomes (in this case $y = 1, 2, \ldots, 6$) to the corresponding probabilities is the **probability mass function** or, more generally, the probability distribution function. We can denote it by

$$f(y) = P\{Y = y\}.$$

Note that $f(y)$ is not a function of the random variable Y, but of all its possible outcomes.

The function $f(y)$ has the property that, if we sum it over all possible outcomes, the result is one. That is

$$\sum_j f(y_j) = 1.$$

The **expected value** of a discrete random variable is a weighted average of all possible outcomes, where the weights correspond to the probability of that particular outcome. We denote

$$E\{Y\} = \sum_j y_j f(y_j).$$

Note that $E\{Y\}$ does not necessarily correspond to one of the possible outcomes. In the dice experiment, for example, the expected value is 3.5.

A distribution is **degenerate** if it is concentrated at one point only, that is, if $P\{Y = y\} = 1$ for one particular value of y and zero for all other values.

B.2 Continuous Random Variables

A **continuous random variable** can take an infinite number of different outcomes, for example, any value in the interval [0, 1]. In this case, each individual outcome has a probability of zero. Instead of a probability mass function, we define the **probability density function** $f(y) \geq 0$ as

$$P\{a \leq Y \leq b\} = \int_a^b f(y)\, dy.$$

In a graph, $P\{a \leq Y \leq b\}$ is the area under the function $f(y)$ between the points a and b. Taking the integral of $f(y)$ over all possible outcomes gives

$$\int_{-\infty}^{\infty} f(y)\, dy = 1.$$

If Y takes values within a certain range only, it is implicitly assumed that $f(y) = 0$ anywhere outside this range.

We can also define the **cumulative density function** (cdf) as

$$F(y) = P\{Y \leq y\} = \int_{-\infty}^{y} f(t)\, dt,$$

such that $f(y) = F'(y)$ (the derivative). The cumulative density function has the property that $0 \leq F(y) \leq 1$, and is monotonically increasing, i.e.

$$F(y) \geq F(x) \quad \text{if } y > x.$$

It easily follows that $P\{a \leq Y \leq b\} = F(b) - F(a)$.

The **expected value** or **mean** of a continuous random variable, often denoted as μ, is defined as

$$\mu = E\{Y\} = \int_{-\infty}^{\infty} y f(y)\, dy.$$

Another measure of location is the **median**, which is the value m for which we have

$$P\{Y \leq m\} \geq 1/2 \quad \text{and} \quad P\{Y \geq m\} \leq 1/2.$$

So 50 % of the observations are below the median and 50 % above. The **mode** is simply the value for which $f(y)$ takes its maximum. It is not often used in econometric applications.

A distribution is **symmetric** around its mean if $f(\mu - y) = f(\mu + y)$. In this case the mean and the median of the distribution are identical.

B.3 Expectations and Moments

If Y and X are random variables and a and b are constants, then it holds that

$$E\{aY + bX\} = aE\{Y\} + bE\{X\},$$

showing that the expectation is a linear operator. Similar results do not necessarily hold if we consider a nonlinear transformation of a random variable. For a nonlinear function g, it does *not* hold in general that $E\{g(Y)\} = g(E\{Y\})$. If g is concave ($g''(Y) < 0$), **Jensen's inequality** says that

$$E\{g(Y)\} \leq g(E\{Y\}).$$

For example, $E\{\log Y\} \leq \log E\{Y\}$. The implication of this is that we cannot determine the expected value of a function of Y from the expected value of Y only. Of course, it holds by definition that

$$E\{g(Y)\} = \int_{-\infty}^{\infty} g(y) f(y)\, dy.$$

The **variance** of a random variable, often denoted by σ^2, is a measure of the dispersion of the distribution. It is defined as

$$\sigma^2 = V\{Y\} = E\{(Y - \mu)^2\}$$

and equals the expected quadratic deviation from the mean. It is sometimes called the **second central moment**. A useful result is that

$$E\{(Y - \mu)^2\} = E\{Y^2\} - 2E\{Y\}\mu + \mu^2 = E\{Y^2\} - \mu^2,$$

where $E\{Y^2\}$ is the second moment. If Y has a discrete distribution, its variance is determined as

$$V\{Y\} = \sum_j (y_j - \mu)^2 f(y_j),$$

where j indexes the different outcomes. For a continuous distribution we have

$$V\{Y\} = \int_{-\infty}^{\infty} (y - \mu)^2 f(y)\, dy.$$

Using these definitions, it is easily verified that

$$V\{aY + b\} = a^2 V\{Y\},$$

where a and b are arbitrary constants. Often we will also use the **standard deviation** of a random variable, denoted by σ, defined as the square root of the variance. The standard deviation is expressed in the same units as Y.

In most cases the distribution of a random variable is not completely described by its mean and variance, and we can define the ***k* th central moment** as

$$E\{(Y - \mu)^k\}, \quad k = 1, 2, 3, \ldots$$

In particular, the third central moment is a measure of the asymmetry of the distribution around its mean, while the fourth central moment measures the peakedness of the distribution. Typically, **skewness** is defined as $S \equiv E\{(Y-\mu)^3\}/\sigma^3$, while **kurtosis** is defined as $K \equiv E\{(Y-\mu)^4\}/\sigma^4$. Kurtosis of a normal distribution is 3, so that $K-3$ is referred to as **excess kurtosis**. A distribution with positive excess kurtosis is called leptokurtic.

B.4 Multivariate Distributions

The **joint density function** of two random variables Y and X, denoted by $f(y, x)$, is defined as

$$P\{a_1 < Y < b_1, a_2 < X < b_2\} = \int_{a_1}^{b_1}\int_{a_2}^{b_2} f(y,x)\, dy\, dx.$$

If Y and X are **independent**, it holds that $f(y,x) = f(y)f(x)$, such that

$$P\{a_1 < Y < b_1, a_2 < X < b_2\} = P\{a_1 < Y < b_1\}P\{a_2 < X < b_2\}.$$

In general, the **marginal distribution** of Y is characterized by the density function

$$f(y) = \int_{-\infty}^{\infty} f(y,x)\, dx.$$

This implies that the expected value of Y is given by

$$E\{Y\} = \int_{-\infty}^{\infty} yf(y)\, dy = \int_{-\infty}^{\infty}\int_{-\infty}^{\infty} yf(y,x)\, dx\, dy.$$

The **covariance** between Y and X is a measure of *linear* dependence between the two variables. It is defined as

$$\sigma_{xy} = \text{cov}\{Y,X\} = E\{(Y-\mu_y)(X-\mu_x)\},$$

where $\mu_y = E\{Y\}$ and $\mu_x = E\{X\}$. The **correlation coefficient** is given by the covariance standardized by the two standard deviations, that is

$$\rho_{yx} = \frac{\text{cov}\{Y,X\}}{\sqrt{V\{Y\}V\{X\}}} = \frac{\sigma_{xy}}{\sigma_x\sigma_y}.$$

The correlation coefficient is always between -1 and 1 and is not affected by the scaling of the variables. The squared correlation coefficient is between 0 and 1 and describes the proportion of the variance in common between Y and X. It can be multiplied by 100 and expressed as a percentage. If $\text{cov}\{Y,X\} = 0$, Y and X are said to be **uncorrelated**. When a, b, c, d are constants, it holds that

$$\text{cov}\{aY+b, cX+d\} = ac\ \text{cov}\{Y,X\}.$$

Further,

$$\text{cov}\{aY+bX, X\} = a\ \text{cov}\{Y,X\} + b\ \text{cov}\{X,X\} = a\ \text{cov}\{Y,X\} + bV\{X\}.$$

It also follows that two variables Y and X are perfectly correlated ($\rho_{yx} = 1$) if $Y = aX$ for some nonzero value of a. If Y and X are correlated, the variance of a linear function of Y and X depends upon their covariance. In particular,

$$V\{aY + bX\} = a^2 V\{Y\} + b^2 V\{X\} + 2ab \operatorname{cov}\{Y, X\}.$$

If we consider a K-dimensional vector of random variables, $\vec{Y} = (Y_1, \ldots, Y_K)'$, we can define its expectation vector as

$$E\{\vec{Y}\} = \begin{pmatrix} E\{Y_1\} \\ \vdots \\ E\{Y_K\} \end{pmatrix}$$

and its variance–covariance matrix (or simply **covariance matrix**) as

$$V\{\vec{Y}\} = \begin{pmatrix} V\{Y_1\} & \cdots & \operatorname{cov}\{Y_1, Y_K\} \\ \vdots & \ddots & \vdots \\ \operatorname{cov}\{Y_K, Y_1\} & \cdots & V\{Y_K\} \end{pmatrix}.$$

Note that this matrix is symmetric. If we consider one or more linear combinations of the elements in $\vec{Y}$, say $R\vec{Y}$, where R is of dimension $J \times K$, it holds that

$$V\{R\vec{Y}\} = RV\{\vec{Y}\}R'.$$

B.5 Conditional Distributions

A conditional distribution describes the distribution of a variable, say Y, given the outcome of another variable X. For example, if we throw with two dice, X could denote the outcome of the first dice and Y could denote the total of the two dice. Then we could be interested in the distribution of Y conditional upon the outcome of the first dice. For example, what is the probability of throwing 7 in total if the first dice had an outcome of 3? Or an outcome of 3 or less? The conditional distribution is implied by the joint distribution of the two variables. We define

$$f(y|X = x) = f(y|x) = \frac{f(y, x)}{f(x)}.$$

If Y and X are independent, it immediately follows that $f(y|x) = f(y)$. From the above definition it follows that

$$f(y, x) = f(y|x)f(x),$$

which says that the joint distribution of two variables can be decomposed in the product of a conditional distribution and a marginal distribution. Similarly, we can write

$$f(y, x) = f(x|y)f(y).$$

The **conditional expectation** of Y given $X = x$ is the expected value of Y from the conditional distribution. That is,

$$E\{Y|X = x\} = E\{Y|x\} = \int yf(y|x)\, dy.$$

The conditional expectation is a function of x, unless Y and X are independent.

Similarly, we can define the conditional variance as

$$V\{Y|x\} = \int (y - E\{Y|x\})^2 f(y|x)\, dy,$$

which can be written as

$$V\{Y|x\} = E\{Y^2|x\} - (E\{Y|x\})^2.$$

It holds that

$$V\{Y\} = E_x\{V\{Y|X\}\} + V_x\{E\{Y|X\}\},$$

where E_x and V_x denote the expected value and variance, respectively, based upon the marginal distribution of X. The terms $V\{Y|X\}$ and $E\{Y|X\}$ are functions of the random variable X and therefore random variables themselves.

Let us consider the relationship between two random variables Y and X, where $E\{Y\} = 0$. Then it follows that Y and X are **uncorrelated** if

$$E\{YX\} = \text{cov}\{Y, X\} = 0.$$

If Y is **conditional mean independent** of X, it means that

$$E\{Y|X\} = E\{Y\} = 0.$$

This is stronger than zero correlation because $E\{Y|X\} = 0$ implies that $E\{Yg(X)\} = 0$ for any function g. If Y and X are **independent**, this is again stronger and it implies that

$$E\{g_1(Y)g_2(X)\} = E\{g_1(Y)\}E\{g_2(X)\}$$

for arbitrary functions g_1 and g_2. It is easily verified that this implies conditional mean independence and zero correlation. Note that $E\{Y|X\} = 0$ does not necessarily imply that $E\{X|Y\} = 0$.

B.6 The Normal Distribution

In econometrics, the **normal distribution** plays a central role. The density function for a normal distribution with mean μ and variance σ^2 is given by

$$f(y) = \frac{1}{\sqrt{2\pi\sigma^2}} \exp\left\{-\frac{1}{2}\frac{(y-\mu)^2}{\sigma^2}\right\},$$

which we write as $Y \sim \mathcal{N}(\mu, \sigma^2)$. It is easily verified that the normal distribution is symmetric. A standard normal distribution is obtained for $\mu = 0$ and $\sigma = 1$. Note that the standardized variable $(Y - \mu)/\sigma$ is $\mathcal{N}(0, 1)$ if $Y \sim \mathcal{N}(\mu, \sigma^2)$. The density of a standard normal distribution, typically denoted by ϕ, is given by

$$\phi(y) = \frac{1}{\sqrt{2\pi}} \exp\left\{-\frac{1}{2}y^2\right\}.$$

A useful property of a normal distribution is that a linear function of a normal variable is also normal. That is, if $Y \sim \mathcal{N}(\mu, \sigma^2)$, then

$$aY + b \sim \mathcal{N}(a\mu + b, a^2\sigma^2).$$

The cumulative density function of the normal distribution does not have a closed-form expression. We have

$$P\{Y \leq y\} = P\left\{\frac{Y-\mu}{\sigma} \leq \frac{y-\mu}{\sigma}\right\} = \Phi\left(\frac{y-\mu}{\sigma}\right) = \int_{-\infty}^{(y-\mu)/\sigma} \phi(t)\, dt,$$

where Φ denotes the cdf of the standard normal distribution. Note that $\Phi(y) = 1 - \Phi(-y)$ owing to the symmetry.

The symmetry also implies that the third central moment of a normal distribution is zero. It can be shown that the fourth central moment of a normal distribution is given by

$$E\{(Y - \mu)^4\} = 3\sigma^4.$$

Typically these properties of the third and fourth central moments are exploited in tests against non-normality.

If (Y, X) have a **bivariate normal distribution** with mean vector $\mu = (\mu_y, \mu_x)'$ and covariance matrix

$$\Sigma = \begin{pmatrix} \sigma_y^2 & \sigma_{yx} \\ \sigma_{yx} & \sigma_x^2 \end{pmatrix}$$

denoted by $(Y, X)' \sim \mathcal{N}(\mu, \Sigma)$, the joint density function is given by

$$f(y, x) = f(y|x)f(x),$$

where both the **conditional density** of Y given X and the **marginal density** of X are normal. The conditional density function is given by

$$f(y|x) = \frac{1}{\sqrt{2\pi\sigma_{y|x}^2}} \exp\left\{-\frac{1}{2}\frac{(y - \mu_{y|x})^2}{\sigma_{y|x}^2}\right\},$$

where $\mu_{y|x}$ is the **conditional expectation** of Y given X, given by

$$\mu_{y|x} = \mu_y + (\sigma_{yx}/\sigma_x^2)(x - \mu_x),$$

and $\sigma_{y|x}^2$ is the conditional variance of Y given X,

$$\sigma_{y|x}^2 = \sigma_y^2 - \sigma_{yx}^2/\sigma_x^2 = \sigma_y^2(1 - \rho_{yx}^2),$$

with ρ_{yx} denoting the correlation coefficient between Y and X. These results have some important implications. First, if two (or more) variables have a joint normal distribution, all marginal distributions and conditional distributions are also normal. Second, the conditional expectation of one variable given the other(s) is a linear function (with an intercept term). Third, if $\rho_{yx} = 0$, it follows that $f(y|x) = f(y)$ so that

$$f(y,x) = f(y)f(x),$$

and Y and X are independent. Thus, if Y and X have a joint normal distribution with zero correlation, then they are automatically independent. Recall that in general independence is a stronger requirement than uncorrelatedness.

Another important result is that a linear function of normal variables is also normal, that is, if $(Y, X)' \sim \mathcal{N}(\mu, \Sigma)$, then

$$aY + bX \sim \mathcal{N}(a\mu_y + b\mu_x, a^2\sigma_y^2 + b^2\sigma_x^2 + 2ab\sigma_{yx}).$$

These results can be generalized to a general K-variate normal distribution. If the K-dimensional vector $\vec{Y}$ has a normal distribution with mean vector μ and covariance matrix Σ, that is

$$\vec{Y} \sim \mathcal{N}(\mu, \Sigma),$$

it holds that the distribution of $R\vec{Y}$, where R is a $J \times K$ matrix, is a J-variate normal distribution, given by

$$R\vec{Y} \sim \mathcal{N}(R\mu, R\Sigma R').$$

In models with limited dependent variables we often encounter forms of **truncation**. If Y has density $f(y)$, the distribution of Y truncated from below at a given point c ($Y \geq c$) is given by

$$f(y|Y \geq c) = \frac{f(y)}{P\{Y \geq c\}} \quad \text{if} \quad y \geq c \quad \text{and 0 otherwise.}$$

If Y is a standard normal variable, the truncated distribution of $Y \geq c$ has mean

$$E\{Y|Y \geq c\} = \lambda_1(c),$$

where

$$\lambda_1(c) = \frac{\phi(c)}{1 - \Phi(c)},$$

and variance

$$V\{Y|Y \geq c\} = 1 - \lambda_1(c)[\lambda_1(c) - c].$$

If the distribution is truncated from above ($Y \leq c$), it holds that

$$E\{Y|Y \leq c\} = \lambda_2(c),$$

with

$$\lambda_2(c) = \frac{-\phi(c)}{\Phi(c)}.$$

If Y has a normal density with mean μ and variance σ^2, the truncated distribution $Y \geq c$ has mean

$$E\{Y|Y \geq c\} = \mu + \sigma\lambda_1(c^*) \geq \mu,$$

where $c^* = (c - \mu)/\sigma$, and, similarly,

$$E\{Y|Y \leq c\} = \mu + \sigma\lambda_2(c^*) \leq \mu.$$

When (Y, X) have a bivariate normal distribution, as above, we obtain

$$E\{Y|X \geq c\} = \mu_y + (\sigma_{yx}/\sigma_x^2)[E\{X|X \geq c\} - \mu_x]$$
$$= \mu_y + (\sigma_{yx}/\sigma_x)\lambda_1(c^*).$$

More details can be found in Maddala (1983, Appendix).

B.7 Related Distributions

Besides the normal distribution, several other distributions are important. First, we define the **Chi-squared distribution** as follows. If $Y_1, \ldots, Y_J$ is a set of independent standard normal variables, it holds that

$$\xi = \sum_{j=1}^{J} Y_j^2$$

has a Chi-squared distribution with J degrees of freedom. We denote $\xi \sim \chi_J^2$. More generally, if $Y_1, \ldots, Y_J$ is a set of independent normal variables with mean μ and variance σ^2, if follows that

$$\xi = \sum_{j=1}^{J} \frac{(Y_j - \mu)^2}{\sigma^2}$$

is Chi-squared with J degrees of freedom. Even more generally, if $\vec{Y} = (Y_1, \ldots, Y_J)'$ is a vector of random variables that has a joint normal distribution with mean vector μ and (nonsingular) covariance matrix Σ, it follows that

$$\xi = (\vec{Y} - \mu)'\Sigma^{-1}(\vec{Y} - \mu) \sim \chi_J^2.$$

If ξ has a Chi-squared distribution with J degrees of freedom, it holds that $E\{\xi\} = J$ and $V\{\xi\} = 2J$.

Next, we consider the ***t* distribution** (or Student distribution). If X has a standard normal distribution, $X \sim \mathcal{N}(0, 1)$, and $\xi \sim \chi_J^2$, and if X and ξ are independent, the ratio

$$t = \frac{X}{\sqrt{\xi/J}}$$

has a **t** distribution with J degrees of freedom. Like the standard normal distribution, the t distribution is symmetric around zero, but it has fatter tails, particularly for small J. If J approaches infinity, the t distribution approaches the normal distribution.

If $\xi_1 \sim \chi^2_{J_1}$ and $\xi_2 \sim \chi^2_{J_2}$, and if ξ_1 and ξ_2 are independent, it follows that the ratio

$$f = \frac{\xi_1/J_1}{\xi_2/J_2}$$

has an ***F* distribution** with J_1 and J_2 degrees of freedom in the numerator and denominator respectively. It easily follows that the inverse ratio

$$\frac{\xi_2/J_2}{\xi_1/J_1}$$

also has an F distribution, but with J_2 and J_1 degrees of freedom respectively. The F distribution is thus the distribution of the ratio of two independent Chi-squared distributed variables, divided by their respective degrees of freedom. When $J_1 = 1, \xi_1$ is a squared normal variable, say $\xi_1 = X^2$, and it follows that

$$t^2 = \left(\frac{X}{\sqrt{\xi_2/J_2}}\right)^2 = \frac{\xi_1}{\xi_2/J_2} = f \sim F^1_{J_2}.$$

Thus, with one degree of freedom in the numerator, the F distribution is just the square of a t distribution. If J_2 is large, the distribution of

$$J_1 f = \frac{\xi_1}{\xi_2/J_2}$$

is well approximated by a Chi-squared distribution with J_1 degrees of freedom. For large J_2 the denominator is thus negligible.

Finally, we consider the **lognormal distribution**. If $\log Y$ has a normal distribution with mean μ and variance σ^2, then $Y > 0$ has a so-called lognormal distribution. The lognormal density is often used to describe the population distribution of (labour) income or the distribution of asset returns (see Campbell, Lo and MacKinlay, 1997). While $E\{\log Y\} = \mu$, it holds that

$$E\{Y\} = \exp\left\{\mu + \frac{1}{2}\sigma^2\right\}$$

(compare Jensen's inequality above).

Bibliography

Abadie, A. and Imbens, G. W. (2016), Matching on the Estimated Propensity Score, *Econometrica*, 84, 781–807.

Abrevaya, J. and Donald, S. G. (2011), A GMM Approach for Dealing with Missing Data on Regressors and Instruments, working paper, University of Texas.

Acemoglu, D., Johnson, S. and Robinson, J. A. (2001), The Colonial Origins of Comparative Development: An Empirical Investigation, *American Economic Review*, 91, 1369–1401.

Acemoglu, D., Johnson, S. and Robinson, J. A. (2005), Institutions as a Fundamental Cause of Growth. In: P. Aghion and S. N. Durlauf, eds, *Handbook of Economic Growth, Volume 1A*, Elsevier Science, Amsterdam, The Netherlands, 386–454.

Ahn, S. K. and Reinsel, C. G. (1990), Estimation for Partially Nonstationary Multivariate Autoregressive Models, *Journal of the American Statistical Association*, 85, 813–823.

Ai, C. and Norton, E. C. (2003), Interaction Terms in Logit and Probit Models, *Economics Letters*, 80, 123–129.

Aigner, D., Lovell C. A. K. and P. Schmidt (1977), Formulation and Estimation of Stochastic Frontier Production Function Models, *Journal of Econometrics*, 6, 21–37.

Akaike, H. (1973), Information Theory and an Extension of the Maximum Likelihood Principle. In: B. N. Petrov and F. Cszaki, eds, *Second International Symposium on Information Theory*, Akademiai Kiado, Budapest, 267–281.

Altman, E. I. and Rijken, H. A. (2004), How Rating Agencies Achieve Rating Stability, *Journal of Banking and Finance*, 28, 2679–2714.

Alvarez, J. and Arellano, M. (2003), The Time Series and Cross-Section Asymptotics of Dynamic Panel Data Estimators, *Econometrica*, 71, 1121–1159.

Amemiya, T. (1981), Qualitative Response Models: A Survey, *Journal of Economic Literature*, 19, 1483–1536.

Amemiya, T. (1984), Tobit Models: A Survey, *Journal of Econometrics*, 24, 3–61.

Amemiya, T. and MaCurdy, T. (1986), Instrumental-Variable Estimation of an Error-Components Model, *Econometrica*, 54, 869–881.

Andersen, E. B. (1970), Asymptotic Properties of Conditional Maximum Likelihood Estimation, *Journal of the Royal Statistical Society, Series B*, 32, 283–301.

Andersen, T. G., Bollerslev, T. Christoffersen, P. and Diebold, F. X. (2006), Volatility and Correlation Forecasting. In: C. W. J. Granger, G. Elliott and A. Timmermann, eds, *Handbook of Economic Forecasting*, North-Holland, Elsevier, Amsterdam, The Netherlands, 777–878.

Anderson, T. W. and Hsiao, C. (1981), Estimation of Dynamic Models with Error Components, *Journal of the American Statistical Association*, 76, 598–606.

Andrews, D. W. K. (1991), Heteroskedasticity and Autocorrelation Consistent Covariance Matrix Estimation, *Econometrica*, 59, 817–858.

Andrews, D. W. K. and Chen, H.-Y. (1994), Approximate Median Unbiased Estimation of Autoregressive Models, *Journal of Business and Economic Statistics*, 12, 187–204.

Anglin, P. M. and Gençay, R. (1996), Semiparametric Estimation of a Hedonic Price Function, *Journal of Applied Econometrics*, 11, 633–648.

Angrist, J. D. and Imbens, G. W. (1995), Two-Stage Least Squares Estimation of Average Causal Effects in Models with Variable Treatment Intensity, *Journal of the American Statistical Association*, 90, 431–442.

Angrist, J. D. and Krueger, A. B. (1991), Does Compulsory School Attendance Affect Schooling and Earnings?, *Quarterly Journal of Economics*, 106, 979–1014.

Angrist, J. D. and Krueger, A. B. (1999), Empirical Strategies in Labor Economics. In: O. Ashenfelter and D. Card, eds, *Handbook of Labor Economics, Volume 3*, Elsevier Science, Amsterdam, The Netherlands, 1277–1366.

Angrist, J. D., Imbens, G. W. and Rubin, D. B. (1996), Identification and Causal Effects Using Instrumental Variables, *Journal of the American Statistical Association*, 91, 444–455.

Angrist, J. D. and Lavy, V. (1999), Using Maimonides' Rule to Estimate the Effect of Class Size on Scholastic Achievement, *Quarterly Journal of Economics*, 114, 533–575.

Angrist, J. D. and Pischke, J.-S. (2009), *Mostly Harmless Econometrics: An Empiricist's Companion*, Princeton University Press, Princeton, NJ.

Angrist, J. D. and Pischke, J.-S. (2015), *Mastering 'Metrics. The Path from Cause to Effect*, Princeton University Press, Princeton, NJ.

Arellano, M. (1987), Computing Robust Standard Errors for Within-Groups Estimators, *Oxford Bulletin of Economics and Statistics*, 49, 431–434.

Arellano, M. (1989), A Note on the Anderson–Hsiao estimator for Panel Data, *Economics Letters*, 31, 337–341.

Arellano, M. (2003), *Panel Data Econometrics*, Oxford University Press, Oxford, UK.

Arellano, M. and Bond, S. (1991), Some Tests of Specification for Panel Data: Monte Carlo Evidence and an Application to Employment Equations, *Review of Economic Studies*, 58, 277–294.

Arellano, M. and Bover, O. (1995), Another Look at the Instrumental Variable Estimation of Error-Components Models, *Journal of Econometrics*, 68, 29–51.

Aron-Dine, A., Einav, L. and Finkelstein, A. (2013), The RAND Health Insurance Experiment, Three Decades Later, *Journal of Economic Perspectives*, 27(1), 197–122.

Ashbaugh-Skaife, H., Collins, D. W. and LaFond, R. (2006), The Effects of Corporate Governance on Firms' Credit Ratings, *Journal of Accounting and Economics*, 42, 203–243.

Ashenfelter, O., Harmon, C. and Oosterbeek, H. (1999), A Review of Estimates of the Schooling/Earnings Relationship, with Tests for Publication Bias, *Labour Economics*, 6, 453–470.

Atanasov, V. and Black, B. (2016), Shock-Based Causal Inference in Corporate Finance and Accounting Research, *Critical Finance Review*, 5, 207–304.

Atanasov, V. and Black, B. (2017), The Trouble with Instruments: Re-Examining Shock-Based IV Designs, working paper, http://ssrn.com/abstract=2417689.

Atkinson, A. B., Gomulka, J. and Stern, N. H. (1990), Spending on Alcohol: Evidence from the Family Expenditure Survey 1970–1983, *The Economic Journal*, 100, 808–827.

Bai, J. and Ng, S. (2004), A PANIC Attack on Unit Roots and Cointegration, *Econometrica*, 72, 1127–1177.

Bailey, R. T. (1996), Long Memory Processes and Fractional Integration in Econometrics, *Journal of Econometrics*, 73, 5–59.

Baltagi, B. H. (2013), *Econometric Analysis of Panel Data*, 5th edition, John Wiley and Sons, Chichester, UK.

Baltagi, B. H. and Griffin, J. M. (1997), Pooled Estimators vs. Their Heterogeneous Counterparts in the Context of Dynamic Demand for Gasoline, *Journal of Econometrics*, 77, 303–327.

Baltagi, B. H. and Song, S. H. (2006), Unbalanced Panel Data: A Survey, *Statistical Papers*, 47, 493–523.

Baltagi, B. H., Bresson, G. and Pirotte, A. (2007), Panel Unit Root Tests and Spatial Dependence, *Journal of Applied Econometrics*, 22, 339–360.

Banerjee, A. (1999), Panel Data Unit Roots and Cointegration: An Overview, *Oxford Bulletin of Economics and Statistics*, 61, 607–629.

Banerjee, A., Marcellino, M. and Osbat, C. (2005), Testing for PPP: Should We Use Panel Methods? *Empirical Economics*, 30, 77–91.

Banerjee, A. and Wagner, M. (2009), Panel Methods to Test for Unit Roots and Cointegration. In: T. C. Mills and K. Patterson, eds, *Palgrave Handbook of Econometrics, Volume 2: Applied Econometrics*, Palgrave MacMillan, 632–728.

Banerjee, A., Dolado, J., Galbraith, J. W. and Hendry, D. F. (1993), *Co-Integration, Error-Correction, and the Econometric Analysis of Non-Stationary Data*, Oxford University Press, Oxford, UK.

Banks, J., Blundell, R. and Lewbel, A. (1997), Quadratic Engel Curves and Consumer Demand, *Review of Economics and Statistics*, 74, 527–539.

Banz, R. (1981), The Relation between Returns and Market Value of Common Stocks, *Journal of Financial Economics*, 9, 3–18.

Baquero, G., ter Horst, J. R. and Verbeek, M. (2005), Survival, Look-Ahead Bias and Persistence in Hedge Fund Performance, *Journal of Financial and Quantitative Analysis*, 40, 493–518.

Bauwens, L., Laurent, S. and Rombouts, J. V. K. (2006), Multivariate GARCH Models: A Survey, *Journal of Applied Econometrics*, 21, 79–109.

Bazzi, S. and Clemens. M. A. (2013), Blunt Instruments: Avoiding Common Pitfalls in Identifying the Causes of Economic Growth, *American Economic Journal: Macroeconomics*, 5, 152–186.

Belsley, D., Kuh, E. and Welsh, R. E. (1980), *Regression Diagnostics: Identifying Influential Data and Sources of Collinearity*, John Wiley and Sons, New York, NY.

Bera, A. K. and Higgins, M. L. (1993), ARCH Models: Properties, Estimation and Testing, *Journal of Economic Surveys*, 7, 305–366.

Bera, A. K., Jarque, C. M. and Lee, L. F. (1984), Testing the Normality Assumption in Limited Dependent Variable Models, *International Economic Review*, 25, 563–578.

Berndt, E. R. (1991), *The Practice of Econometrics, Classic and Contemporary*, Addison-Wesley, Reading, MA.

Berndt, E. R., Hall, B. H., Hall, R. E. and Hausman, J. A. (1974), Estimation and Inference in Nonlinear Structural Models, *Annals of Economic and Social Measurement*, 3, 653–665.

Bertrand, M., Duflo, E. and Mullainathan, S. (2004), How Much Should We Trust Differences in Differences Estimates?, *Quarterly Journal of Economics*, 119, 249–275.

Bhargava, A., Franzini, L. and Narendranathan, W. (1983), Serial Correlation and the Fixed Effects Model, *Review of Economic Studies*, 49, 533–549.

Binder, M., Hsiao, C. and Pesaran, M. H. (2005), Estimation and Inference in Short Panel Vector Autoregressions with Unit Roots and Cointegration, *Econometric Theory*, 21, 795–837.

Blundell, R. and Bond, S. (1998), Initial Conditions and Moment Restrictions in Dynamic Panel Data Models, *Journal of Econometrics*, 87, 115–143.

Blundell, R. W., Bond, S. R. and Windmeijer, F. G. (2000), Estimation in Dynamic Panel Data Models: Improving on the Performance of the Standard GMM Estimator. In: B. H. Baltagi, ed., *Advances in Econometrics, Volume 15, Nonstationary Panels, Panel Cointegration, and Dynamic Panels*, JAI Elsevier, Amsterdam, The Netherlands, 53–92.

Bollen, N. P. B. and Pool, V. K. (2012), Suspicious Patterns in Hedge Fund Returns and the Risk of Fraud, *Review of Financial Studies*, 25, 2673–2702.

Bollerslev, T. (1986), Generalized Autoregressive Conditional Heteroskedasticity, *Journal of Econometrics*, 31, 307–327.

Bollerslev, T. (1988), On the Correlation Structure for the Generalized Autoregressive Conditional Heteroskedastic Process, *Journal of Time Series Analysis*, 9, 121–131.

Bollerslev, T. (2010), Glossary to ARCH (GARCH). In: T. Bollerslev, J. R. Russell and M. Watson, eds, *Volatility and Time Series Econometrics: Essays in Honour of Robert F. Engle*, Oxford University Press, Oxford, UK.

Bollerslev, T., Chou, R. Y. and Kroner, K. F. (1992), ARCH Modeling in Finance. A Review of the Theory and Empirical Evidence, *Journal of Econometrics*, 52, 5–59.

Bollerslev, T., Engle, R. F. and Nelson, D. B. (1994), ARCH Models. In: R. F. Engle and D. L. McFadden, eds, *Handbook of Econometrics, Volume IV*, North-Holland, Elsevier, Amsterdam The Netherlands, 2961–3038.

Bollerslev, T., Osterrieder, D., Sizova, N. and Tauchen, G. (2013), Risk and Return: Long-Run Relations, Fractional Cointegration, and Return Predictability, *Journal of Financial Economics*, 108, 409–424.

Bond, S. (2002), Dynamic Panel Data Models: A Guide to Micro Data Methods and Practice, *Portuguese Economic Journal*, 1, 141–162.

Bouman, S. and Jacobsen, B. (2002), The Halloween Indicator, Sell in May and Go Away: Another Puzzle, *American Economic Review*, 92, 1618–1635.

Bound, J., Jaeger, D. A. and Baker, R. M. (1995), Problems with Instrumental Variables Estimation when the Correlation between the Instrument and the Endogenous Variable is Weak, *Journal of the American Statistical Association*, 90, 443–450.

Bowsher, C. G. (2002), On Testing Overidentifying Restrictions in Dynamic Panel Data Models, *Economics Letters*, 77, 211–220.

Box, G. E. P. and Jenkins, G. M. (1976), *Time Series Analysis: Forecasting and Control*, revised edition, Holden-Day, San Francisco, CA.

Breitung, J. (2005), A Parametric Approach to the Estimation of Cointegration Vectors in Panel Data, *Econometric Reviews*, 24, 151–171.

Breusch, T. (1978), Testing for Autocorrelation in Dynamic Linear Models, *Australian Economic Papers*, 17, 334–355.

Breusch, T. and Pagan, A. (1980), A Simple Test for Heteroskedasticity and Random Coefficient Variation, *Econometrica*, 47, 1287–1294.

Breusch, T., Mizon, G. and Schmidt, P. (1989), Efficient Estimation Using Panel Data, *Econometrica*, 57, 695–700.

Bring, J. (1994), How to Standardize Regression Coefficients, *The American Statistician*, 48, 209–213.

Brodeur, A., Lé, M., Sangnier, M. and Zylberberg, Y. (2016), Star Wars: The Empirics Strike Back, *American Economic Journal: Applied Economics*, 8, 1–32.

Browning, M., Deaton, A. and Irish, M. (1985), A Profitable Approach to Labor Supply and Commodity Demands over the Life Cycle, *Econometrica*, 53, 503–543.

Burbidge, J. B., Magee, L. and Robb, A. L (1988), Alternative Transformations to Handle Extreme Values of the Dependent Variable, *Journal of the American Statistical Association*, 83, 123–127.

Buse, A. (1982), The Likelihood Ratio, Wald, and Lagrange Multiplier Tests: An Expository Note, *The American Statistician*, 36, 153–157.

Butler, J. S. and Moffitt, R. (1982), A Computationally Efficient Quadrature Procedure for the One-Factor Multinomial Probit Model, *Econometrica*, 50, 761–764.

Cameron, A. C. and Miller, D. L. (2015), A Practitioner's Guide to Cluster-Robust Inference, *Journal of Human Resources*, 50, 317–372.

Cameron, A. C. and Trivedi, P. K. (1986), Econometric Models Based on Count Data: Comparisons and Applications of Some Estimators and Tests, *Journal of Applied Econometrics*, 1, 29–53.

Cameron, A. C. and Trivedi, P. K. (2005), *Microeconometrics. Methods and Applications*, Cambridge University Press, Cambridge, New York, NY.

Cameron, A. C. and Trivedi, P. K. (2013), *Regression Analysis of Count Data*, 2nd edition, Cambridge University Press, Cambridge, New York, NY.

Cameron, A. C. and Windmeijer, F. A. G. (1996), *R*-squared Measures for Count Data Regression Models with Applications to Health Care Utilization, *Journal of Business and Economic Statistics*, 14, 209–220.

Cameron, A. C. and Windmeijer, F. A. G. (1997), An *R*-squared Measure of Goodness of Fit for Some Common Nonlinear Regression Models, *Journal of Econometrics*, 77, 329–342.

Campbell, J. Y. and Perron, P. (1991), Pitfalls and Opportunities: What Macroeconomists Should Know about Unit Roots. In: O. Blanchard and S. Fisher, eds, *NBER Macroeconomics Annual*, 6, 141–201, MIT Press, Cambridge.

Campbell, J. Y. and Shiller, R. J. (1991), Yield Spreads and Interest Rate Movements: A Bird's Eye View, *Review of Economic Studies*, 58, 495–514.

Campbell, J. Y. and Shiller, R. J. (1998), Valuation Ratios and the Long-Run Stock Market Outlook, *Journal of Portfolio Management*, 24, 11–26.

Campbell, J. Y. and Thompson, S. B. (2008), Predicting Excess Stock Returns Out of Sample: Can Anything Beat the Historical Average?, *Review of Financial Studies*, 21, 1509–1531.

Campbell, J. Y., Lo, A. W. and MacKinlay, A. C. (1997), *The Econometrics of Financial Markets*, Princeton University Press, Princeton, NJ.

Canova, F. (1995), The Economics of VAR Models. In: K. D. Hoover, ed., *Macroeconometrics: Developments, Tensions and Prospects*, Kluwer Academic Publishers, Boston, MA, 57–97.

Canova, F. (2007), *Methods for Applied Macroeconomic Research*, Princeton University Press, Princeton, NJ.

Card, D. (1995), Using Geographical Variation in College Proximity to Estimate the Return to Schooling. In: L. N. Christofides, E. K. Grant and R. Swidinsky, eds, *Aspects of Labour Market Behaviour: Essays in Honour of John Vanderkamp*, University of Toronto Press, Toronto, Canada, 201–222.

Card, D. (1999), The Causal Effect of Education on Earnings. In: O. Ashenfelter and D. Card, eds, *Handbook of Labor Economics, Volume III, Part A*, North-Holland, Elsevier, Amsterdam, The Netherlands, 1801–1863.

Card, D. and Krueger, A. B. (1994), Minimum Wages and Employment: A Case Study of the Fast-Food Industry in New Jersey and Pennsylvania, *American Economic Review*, 84, 772–793.

Carneiro, P. and Heckman, J. J. (2002), The Evidence on Credit Constraints in Post-Secondary Schooling, *The Economic Journal*, 112, 705–734.

Carroll, J. D. and Green, P. E. (1995), Psychometric Methods in Marketing Research: Part 1 Conjoint Analysis, *Journal of Marketing Research*, 32, 385–391.

Castle, J. L., Qin, X. and Reed, W. R. (2013), Using Model Selection Algorithms to Obtain Reliable Coefficient Estimates, *Journal of Economic Surveys*, 27, 269–296.

Chamberlain, G. (1980), Analysis of Covariance with Qualitative Data, *Review of Economic Studies*, 47, 225–238.

Charemza, W. W. and Deadman, D. F. (1999), *New Directions in Econometric Practice. General to Specific Modelling, Cointegration and Vector Autoregression*, 2nd edition, Edward Elgar, Aldershot, UK.

Cheung, Y.-W. and Lai, K. S. (1993), Finite Sample Sizes of Johansen's Likelihood Ratio Tests for Cointegration, *Oxford Bulletin of Economics and Statistics*, 55, 313–332.

Choe, H., Kho, B. and Stulz, R. M. (2005), Do Domestic Investors Have an Edge? The Trading Experience of Foreign Investors in Korea, *Review of Financial Studies*, 18, 795–829.

Choi, I. (2001), Unit Root Tests for Panel Data, *Journal of International Money and Finance*, 20, 249–272.

Chow, G. (1960), Tests of Equality Between Sets of Coefficients in Two Linear Regressions, *Econometrica*, 28, 591–605.

Chowdhury, G. and Nickell, S. (1985), Hourly Earnings in the United States: Another Look at Unionization, Schooling, Sickness and Unemployment using PSID Data, *Journal of Labor Economics*, 3, 38–69.

Cincera, M. (1997), Patents, R&D, and Technological Spillovers at the Firm Level: Some Evidence from Econometric Count Models for Panel Data, *Journal of Applied Econometrics*, 12, 265–280.

Cochrane, D. and Orcutt, G. (1949), Application of Least Squares Regression to Relationships Containing Autocorrelated Error Terms, *Journal of the American Statistical Association*, 44, 32–61.

Clark, T. and McCracken, M. (2013), Advances in Forecast Evaluation. In: G. Elliott and A. Timmermann, eds, *Handbook of Economic Forecasting, Volume 2B*, Elsevier Science Publishers, Amsterdam, The Netherlands, 1107–1201.

Cochrane, J. H. (2005), *Asset Pricing*, Revised Edition, Princeton University Press, Princeton, NJ.

Cochrane, J. H. (1996), A Cross-Sectional Test of an Investment-Based Asset Pricing Model, *Journal of Political Economy*, 104, 572–621.

Corbae, D. and Ouliaris, S. (1988), Cointegration and Tests of Purchasing Power Parity, *Review of Economics and Statistics*, 70, 508–511.

Cumming, G. (2012), *Understanding The New Statistics: Effect Sizes, Confidence Intervals, and Meta-Analysis*, Routledge, New York, NY.

Dardanoni, V., Modica, S. and Peracchi, F. (2011), Regression with Imputed Covariates: A Generalized Missing-Indicator Approach, *Journal of Econometrics*, 162, 362–368.

Das, M. (2004), Simple Estimators for Nonparametric Panel Data Models with Sample Attrition, *Journal of Econometrics*, 120, 159–180.

Davidson, J. (2000), *Econometric Theory*, Blackwell Publishers, Oxford, UK.

Davidson, R. and MacKinnon, J. G. (1981), Several Tests for Model Specification in the Presence of Alternative Hypotheses, *Econometrica*, 49, 781–793.

Davidson, R. and MacKinnon, J. G. (1993), *Estimation and Inference in Econometrics*, Oxford University Press, Oxford, UK.

Davidson, R. and MacKinnon, J. G. (2001), Artificial Regressions. In: B. H. Baltagi, ed., *A Companion to Econometric Theory*, Blackwell Publishers, Oxford, UK, 16–37.

Davidson, R. and MacKinnon, J. G. (2004), *Econometric Theory and Methods*, Oxford University Press, New York, NY.

Deaton, A. (1985), Panel Data from Time Series of Cross Sections, *Journal of Econometrics*, 30, 109–126.

Deaton, A. and Muellbauer, J. (1980), *Economics and Consumer Behavior*, Cambridge University Press, Cambridge, UK.

Deheija, R. H. and Wahba, S. (2002), Propensity Score-Matching Methods for Nonexperimental Causal Studies, *Review of Economics and Statistics*, 84, 151–161.

Devereux, P. J. (2007), Small Sample Bias in Synthetic Cohort Models of Labor Supply, *Journal of Applied Econometrics*, 22, 839–848.

Diamond, P. A. and Hausman, J. A. (1994), Contingent Valuation: Is Some Number Better than No Number?, *Journal of Economics Perspectives*, 8, 45–64.

Dickey, D. A. and Fuller, W. A. (1979), Distribution of the Estimators for Autoregressive Time Series with a Unit Root, *Journal of the American Statistical Association*, 74, 427–431.

Dickson, M. (2013), The Causal Effect of Education on Wages Revisited, *Oxford Bulletin of Economics and Statistics*, 75, 477–498.

Diebold, F. X. and Mariano, R. (1995), Comparing Predictive Accuracy, *Journal of Business and Economic Statistics*, 13, 253–265.

Donald, S. G. and Newey, W. K. (2001), Choosing the Number of Instruments, *Econometrica*, 69, 1161–1191.

Doornik, J. A. (2008), Encompassing and Automatic Model Selection, *Oxford Bulletin of Economics and Statistics*, 70, 915–925.

Doornik, J. A. (2009), Autometrics. In: J. L. Castle and N. Shephard, eds, *The Methodology and Practice of Econometrics*, Oxford University Press, Oxford, UK.

Durbin, J. and Watson, G. (1950), Testing for Serial Correlation in Least Squares Regression – I, *Biometrika*, 37, 409–428.

Durlauf, S. N., Johnson, P. A. and Temple, J. R. W. (2005), Growth Econometrics. In: P. Aghion and S.N. Durlauf, eds, *Handbook of Economic Growth, Volume 1A*, Elsevier Science, Amsterdam, The Netherlands, 555–677.

Dustmann, C. and Rochina-Barrachina, M. E. (2007), Selection Correction in Panel Data Models: An Application to the Estimation of Females' Wage Equations, *Econometrics Journal*, 10, 263–293.

Eicker, F. (1967), Limit Theorems for Regressions with Unequal and Dependent Errors. In: L. LeCam and J. Neyman, eds, *Proceedings of the Fifth Berkeley Symposium on Mathematical Statistics and Probability*, University of California Press, Berkeley, CA, 59–82.

Elliott, G. and Timmermann, A. (2016), *Economic Forecasting*, Princeton University Press, Princeton, NJ.

Elsas, R. and Florysiak, D. (2015), Dynamic Capital Structure Adjustment and the Impact of Fractional Dependent Variables, *Journal of Financial and Quantitative Analysis*, 50, 1105–1133.

Elton, E. J., Gruber, M. J., Brown, S. J. and Goetzmann, W. N. (2014), *Modern Portfolio Theory and Investment Analysis*, 9th edition, John Wiley and Sons, New York, NY.

Enders, W. (2014), *Applied Econometric Time Series*, 4th edition, John Wiley and Sons, Chichester, UK.

Engle, R. F. (1982), Autoregressive Conditional Heteroskedasticity with Estimates of the Variance of United Kingdom Inflation, *Econometrica*, 50, 987–1007.

Engle, R. F. (1984), Wald, Likelihood Ratio and Lagrange Multiplier Tests in Econometrics. In: Z. Griliches and M. D. Intriligator, eds, *Handbook of Econometrics, Volume II*, North-Holland, Elsevier, Amsterdam, The Netherlands, 775–826.

Engle, R. F. and Bollerslev, T. (1986), Modelling the Persistence of Conditional Variances, *Econometric Reviews*, 5, 1–50.

Engle, R. F. and Granger, C. W. J. (1987), Cointegration and Error Correction: Representation, Estimation and Testing, *Econometrica*, 55, 251–276.

Engle, R. F. and Ng, V. K. (1993), Measuring and Testing the Impact of News on Volatility, *Journal of Finance*, 48, 1749–1778.

Engle, R. F. and Yoo, B. S. (1987), Forecasting and Testing in Co-Integrated Systems, *Journal of Econometrics*, 35, 143–159.

Engle, R. F., Hendry, D. F. and Richard, J.-F. (1983), Exogeneity, *Econometrica*, 51, 277–304.

Engle, R. F., Lilien, D. M. and Robins, R. P. (1987), Estimating Time Varying Risk Premia in the Term Structure: The ARCH-M Model, *Econometrica*, 55, 591–407.

Evans, W. N. and Montgomery, E. (1994), Education and Health: Where there's Smoke there's an Instrument, Working Paper no. 4949, National Bureau of Economic Research, Cambridge, MA.

Fama, E. F. (1991), Efficient Capital Markets II, *Journal of Finance*, 46, 1575–1617.

Fama, E. F. and French, K. R. (1988), Permanent and Temporary Components of Stock Prices, *Journal of Political Economy*, 81, 246–273.

Fama, E. F. and French, K. R. (1992), The Cross-Section of Expected Returns, *Journal of Finance*, 47, 427–465.

Fama, E. F. and MacBeth, J. (1973), Risk, Return and Equilibrium: Empirical Tests, *Journal of Political Economy*, 81, 607–636.

Fernández, A. and Tamayo, C. E. (2017), From Institutions to Financial Development and Growth: What are the Links?, *Journal of Economic Surveys*, 31, 17–57.

Ferrer-i-Carbonell, A. and Frijters, P. (2004), How Important is Methodology for the Estimates of the Determinants of Happiness? *The Economic Journal*, 114, 641–659.

Fitzgerald, J., Gottschalk, P. and Moffitt, R. (1998), An Analysis of Sample Attrition in Panel Data: The Michigan Panel Study of Income Dynamics, *Journal of Human Resources*, 33, 251–299.

Flannery, M. J. and K. P. Rangan (2006), Partial Adjustment toward Target Capital Structures, *Journal of Financial Economics*, 79, 469–506.

Frank, M. Z. and Goyal, V. K. (2008), Trade-off and Pecking Order Theories of Debt. In: B. E. Eckbo, ed., *Handbook of Corporate Finance, Volume 2*, North-Holland, Elsevier, Amsterdam, The Netherlands, 135–202.

Franses, P. H. B. F. and Paap, R. (2001), *Quantitative Models in Marketing Research*, Cambridge University Press, Cambridge, UK.

Franses, P. H. B. F. and van Dijk, D. J. C. (2000), *Nonlinear Time Series Models in Empirical Finance*, Cambridge University Press, Cambridge, UK.

Froot, K. A. and Rogoff, K. (1995), Perspectives on PPP and Long-run Exchange Rates. In: S. Grossman and K. Rogoff, eds, *Handbook of International Economics, Volume III*, North-Holland, Elsevier, Amsterdam, The Netherlands, 1647–1688.

Fuhrer, J. and Moore, G. (1995), Inflation Persistence, *Quarterly Journal of Economics*, 110, 127–159.

Fuller, W. A. (1976), *Introduction to Statistical Time-Series*, John Wiley and Sons, New York, NY.

Gabriel, V. J. (2003), Tests for the Null Hypothesis of Cointegration: A Monte Carlo Comparison, *Econometric Reviews*, 22, 411–435.

Gengenbach, C., Palm, F. C. and Urbain, J.-P. (2010), Panel Unit Root Tests in the Presence of Cross-Sectional Dependencies: Comparison and Implications for Modelling, *Econometric Reviews*, 29, 111–145.

Glewwe, P. (1997), A Test of the Normality Assumption in the Ordered Probit Model, *Econometric Reviews*, 16, 1–19.

Glosten, L. R., Jagannathan, R. and Runkle, R. E. (1993), On the Relation between the Expected Value and the Volatility of the Nominal Excess Return on Stocks, *Journal of Finance*, 48, 1779–1801.

Godfrey, L. (1978), Testing against General Autoregressive and Moving Average Error Models when the Regressors Include Lagged Dependent Variables, *Econometrica*, 46, 1293–1302.

Godfrey, L. (1988), *Misspecification Tests in Econometrics. The Lagrange Multiplier Principle and Other Approaches*, Cambridge University Press, Cambridge, UK.

Gouriéroux, C. and Jasiak, J. (2001), *Financial Econometrics*, Princeton University Press, Princeton, NJ.

Gouriéroux, C. and Robert, C. Y. (2006), Stochastic Unit Root Models, *Econometric Theory*, 22, 1052–1090.

Gouriéroux, C., Monfort, A. and Trognon, A. (1984), Pseudo-maximum Likelihood Methods: Theory, *Econometrica*, 42, 681–700.

Gouriéroux, C., Monfort, A., Renault, E. and Trognon, A. (1987), Generalized Residuals, *Journal of Econometrics*, 34, 5–32.

Goyal, A. and Welch, I. (2008), A Comprehensive Look at the Empirical Performance of Equity Premium Prediction, *Review of Financial Studies*, 21, 1455–1508.

Granger, C. W. J. (1969), Investigating Causal Relations by Econometric Models and Cross-Spectral Methods, *Econometrica*, 37, 424–438.

Granger, C. W. J. (1983), Co-Integrated Variables and Error-Correcting Models, *Unpublished Discussion Paper 83-13*, University of California, San Diego, CA.

Granger, C. W. J. and Newbold, P. (1974), Spurious Regressions in Econometrics, *Journal of Econometrics*, 35, 143–159.

Granger, C. W. J. and Pesaran, M. H. (2000), Economic and Statistical Measures of Forecast Accuracy, *Journal of Forecasting*, 537–560.

Granger, C. W. J. and Swanson, N. R. (1997), An Introduction to Stochastic Unit-Root Processes, *Journal of Econometrics*, 80, 35–62.

Greene, W. H. (2004), The Behaviour of the Maximum Likelihood Estimator of Limited Dependent Variable Models in the Presence of Fixed Effects, *Econometrics Journal*, 7, 98–119.

Greene, W. H. (2012), *Econometric Analysis*, 7th edition, Prentice Hall, Upper Saddle River, NJ.

Gregory, A. W. and Veall, M. R. (1985), On Formulating Wald Tests of Nonlinear Restrictions, *Econometrica*, 53, 1465–1468.

Griliches, Z. (1977), Estimating the Returns to Schooling: Some Econometric Problems, *Econometrica*, 45, 1–22.

Griliches, Z. (1979), Sibling Models and Data in Economics: Beginnings of a Survey, *Journal of Political Economy*, 87, S37–S64.

Gronau, R. (1974), Wage Comparisons: A Selectivity Bias, *Journal of Political Economy*, 82, 1119–1143.

Guggenberger, P. (2010), The Impact of a Hausman Pretest on the Size of a Hypothesis Test: The Panel Data Case, *Journal of Econometrics*, 156, 337–343.

Hadri, K. (2000), Testing for Stationarity in Heterogeneous Panel Data, *Econometrics Journal*, 3, 148–161.

Hadri, K. and Larsson, R. (2005), Testing for Stationarity in Heterogeneous Panel Data Where the Time Dimension is Fixed, *Econometrics Journal*, 8, 55–69.

Hahn, J. and Hausman, J. A. (2003), Weak Instruments: Diagnosis and Cures in Empirical Econometrics, *American Economic Review, Papers and Proceedings*, 93, 118–125.

Hahn, J., Ham, J. C. and Moon, H. R. (2011), The Hausman Test and Weak Instruments, *Journal of Econometrics*, 160, 289–299.

Hajivassiliou, V. A. and McFadden, D. F. (1998), The Method of Simulated Scores for the Estimation of LDV Models, *Econometrica*, 66, 863–896.

Hall, A. R. (1993), Some Aspects of Generalized Method of Moments Estimation. In: G. S. Maddala, C. R. Rao and H. D. Vinod, eds, *Handbook of Statistics, Volume XI*, North-Holland, Elsevier, Amsterdam, The Netherlands, 393–417.

Hall, A. R. (1994), Testing for a Unit Root in Time Series with Pretest Data-Based Model Selection, *Journal of Business and Economic Statistics*, 12, 461–470.

Hall, A. R. (2005), *Generalized Method of Moments*, Oxford University Press, Oxford, UK.

Hamermesh, D. S. and Biddle, J. E. (1994), Beauty and the Labor Market, *American Economic Review*, 84, 1174–1194.

Hamilton, J. D. (1994), *Time Series Analysis*, Princeton University Press, Princeton, NJ.

Hanemann, W. M. (1994), Valuing the Environment through Contingent Valuation, *Journal of Economic Perspectives*, 8, 19–44.

Hannan, E. J. (1980), The Estimation of the Order of an ARMA Process, *Annals of Statistics*, 8, 1071–1081.

Hansen, L. P. (1982), Large Sample Properties of Generalized Method of Moments Estimators, *Econometrica*, 50, 1029–1054.

Hansen, L. P. and Singleton, K. (1982), Generalized Instrumental Variables Estimation of Nonlinear Rational Expectations Models, *Econometrica*, 50, 1269–1286.

Hansen, L. P., Heaton, J. and Yaron, A. (1996), Finite Sample Properties of Some Alternative GMM Estimators, *Journal of Business and Economic Statistics*, 14, 262–280.

Hargreaves, C. P. (1994), A Review of Methods of Estimating Cointegrating Relationships. In: C. P. Hargreaves, ed., *Nonstationary Time Series Analysis and Cointegration*, Oxford University Press, Oxford, UK, 87–131.

Harris, R. D. F. and Tzavalis, E. (1999), Inference for Unit Roots in Dynamic Panels Where the Time Dimension is Fixed, *Journal of Econometrics*, 91, 201–226.

Hasza, D. P. and Fuller, W. A. (1979), Estimation for Autoregressive Processes with Unit Roots, *Annals of Statistics*, 7, 1106–1120.

Hausman, J. A. (1978), Specification Tests in Econometrics, *Econometrica*, 46, 1251–1271.

Hausman, J. A. and McFadden, D. F. (1984), Specification Tests for the Multinomial Logit Model, *Econometrica*, 52, 1219–1240.

Hausman, J. A. and Taylor, W. E. (1981), Panel Data and Unobservable Individual Effects, *Econometrica*, 49, 1377–1398.

Hausman, J. A. and Wise, D. A. (1979), Attrition Bias in Experimental and Panel Data: The Gary Income Maintenance Experiment, *Econometrica*, 47, 455–473.

Hausman, J. A. and Wise, D. A. (1985), eds, *Social Experimentation*, University of Chicago Press, Chicago.

Hausman, J. A., Hall, B. H. and Griliches, Z. (1984), Econometric Models Based on Count Data with an Application to the Patents–R&D Relationship, *Econometrica*, 52, 909–938.

Heckman, J. J. (1978a), Simple Statistical Models for Discrete Panel Data Developed and Applied to Test the Hypothesis of True State Dependence against the Hypothesis of Spurious State Dependence, *Annales de l'INSEE*, 30/31, 227–269.

Heckman, J. J. (1978b), Dummy Endogenous Variables in a Simultaneous Equations System, *Econometrica*, 46, 931–960.

Heckman, J. J. (1979), Sample Selection Bias as a Specification Error, *Econometrica*, 47, 153–161.

Heckman, J. J. (1981), The Incidental Parameters Problem and the Problem of Initial Conditions in Estimating a Discrete Time–Discrete Data Stochastic Process. In: C. F. Manski and D. F. McFadden, eds, *Structural Analysis of Discrete Data with Econometric Applications*, MIT Press, Cambridge, MA, 179–195.

Heckman, J. J. (1990), Varieties of Selection Bias, *American Economic Review*, 80, 313–318.

Heckman, J. J. (1997), Instrumental Variables: A Study of Implicit Behavioral Assumptions Used in Making Program Evaluations, *Journal of Human Resources*, 32, 441–462.

Heckman, J. J. (2001), Micro Data, Heterogeneity, and the Evaluation of Public Policy: Nobel Lecture, *Journal of Political Economy*, 109, 673–748.

Heckman, J. J. (2010), Building Bridges between Structural and Program Evaluation Approaches to Evaluating Policy, *Journal of Economic Literature*, 48, 356–398.

Heckman, J. J., Ichimura, H. and Todd, P. (1998), Matching as an Econometric Evaluation Estimator, *Review of Economic Studies*, 65, 261–294.

Heckman, J. J. and Vytlacil, E. (2005), Structural Equations, Treatment Effects and Econometric Policy Evaluation, *Econometrica*, 73, 669–738.

Heckman, J. J., Tobias, J. L. and Vytlacil, E. (2003), Simple Estimators for Treatment Parameters in a Latent-Variable Framework, *Review of Economics and Statistics*, 85, 748–755.

Hendry, D. F. (2009), The Methodology of Empirical Econometric Modeling: Applied Econometrics Through the Looking Glass. In: T. C. Mills and K. Patterson, eds, *Palgrave Handbook of Econometrics, Volume 2: Applied Econometrics*, Palgrave MacMillan, 3–67.

Hendry, D. F. and Richard, J. F. (1983), The Econometric Analysis of Economic Time Series, *International Statistical Review*, 51, 111–148.

Henriksson, R. D. and Merton, R. C. (1981), On Market Timing and Investment Performance. II. Statistical Procedures for Evaluating Forecasting Skills, *Journal of Business*, 54, 513–533.

Hildreth, C. and Lu, J. (1960), *Demand Relations with Autocorrelated Disturbances*, Technical Bulletin No. 276, Michigan State University, East Lansing, MI.

Hirano K., Imbens, G. W. and Ridder, G. (2003), Efficient Estimation of Average Treatment Effects Using the Estimated Propensity Score, *Econometrica*, 71, 1161–1189.

Hirano, K., Imbens, G. W., Ridder, G. and Rubin, D. B. (2001), Combining Panel Data Sets with Attrition and Refreshment Samples, *Econometrica*, 69, 1645–1659.

Hlouskova, J. and Wagner, (2006), The Performance of Panel Unit Root and Stationarity Tests: Results from a Large Scale Simulation Study, *Econometric Reviews*, 25, 85–116.

Hjelm, G. and Johansson, M.W. (2005), A Monte Carlo Study on the Pitfalls in Determining Deterministic Components in Cointegrating Models, *Journal of Macroeconomics*, 27, 691–703.

Hoffman, D. L. and Rasche, R. H. (1996), Assessing Forecast Performance in a Cointegrated System, *Journal of Applied Econometrics*, 11, 495–517.

Honoré, B. E. (1992), Trimmed LAD and Least Squares Estimation of Truncated and Censored Regression Models with Fixed Effects, *Econometrica*, 60, 533–565.

Honoré, B. E. (1993), Orthogonality Conditions for Tobit Models with Fixed Effects and Lagged Dependent Variables, *Journal of Econometrics*, 59, 35–61.

Honoré, B. E. and Kyriazidou, E. (2000), Panel Data Discrete Choice Models with Lagged Dependent Variables, *Econometrica*, 68, 839–874.

Hoover, K. D. and Perez, S. J. (1999), Data Mining Reconsidered: Encompassing and the General-to-Specific Approach to Specification Search, *Econometrics Journal*, 2, 167–191.

Horowitz, J. L. (1992), A Smoothed Maximum Score Estimator for the Binary Response Model, *Econometrica*, 60, 505–531.

Horowitz, J. L. (1998), *Semiparametric Methods in Econometrics*, Springer-Verlag, New York, NY.

Hsiao, C. (2014), *Analysis of Panel Data*, 3rd edition, Cambridge University Press, Cambridge, New York, NY.

Hsiao, C. and Pesaran, M. H. (2008), Random Coefficient Panel Data Models. In: L. Mátyás and P. Sevestre, eds, *The Econometrics of Panel Data: Fundamentals and Recent Developments in Theory and Practice*, Springer-Verlag, New York, NY, 185–213.

Huber, M., Lechner, M. and Wunsch, C. (2011), Does Leaving Welfare Improve Health? Evidence for Germany, *Health Economics*, 20, 484–504.

Hylleberg, S., Engle, R. F., Granger, C. W. J. and Yoo, B. (1993), Seasonal Integration and Cointegration, *Journal of Econometrics*, 44, 215–238.

Hyslop, D. R. (1999), State Dependence, Serial Correlation and Heterogeneity in Intertemporal Labor Force Participation of Married Women, *Econometrica*, 67, 1255–1294.

Ichino, A. and Winter-Ebmer, R. (1999), Lower and Upper Bounds of Returns to Schooling: An Exercise in IV Estimation with Different Instruments, *European Economic Review*, 43, 889–901.

Im, K., Pesaran, M. H. and Shin, Y. (2003), Testing for Unit Roots in Heterogeneous Panels, *Journal of Econometrics*, 115, 29–52.

Imbens, G. W. (2015), Matching Methods in Practice: Three Examples, *Journal of Human Resources*, 50, 373–419.

Imbens, G. W. and Angrist, J. D. (1994), Identification and Estimation of Local Average Treatment Effects, *Econometrica*, 62, 467–476.

Imbens, G. W. and Lemieux, T. (2008), Regression Discontinuity Designs: A Guide to Practice, *Journal of Econometrics*, 142, 615–635.

Imbens, G. W. and Wooldridge, J. M. (2009), Recent Developments in the Econometrics of Program Evaluation, *Journal of Economic Literature*, 47, 5–86.

Inoue, A. (2008), Efficient Estimation and Inference in Linear Pseudo-Panel Data Models, *Journal of Econometrics*, 142, 449–466.

Jagannathan, R. and Wang, Y. (2007), Lazy Investors, Discretionary Consumption, and the Cross-Section of Stock Returns, *Journal of Finance*, 62, 1623–1661.

Jarque, C. M. and Bera, A. K. (1980), Efficient Tests for Normality, Homoskedasticity and Serial Independence of Regression Residuals, *Economics Letters*, 6, 255–259.

Jenkins, S. P. (2005), *Survival Analysis*, unpublished manuscript, ISER, University of Essex, Colchester. Downloadable from http://www.iser.essex.ac.uk/teaching/stephenj/ec968/.

Johansen, S. (1988), Statistical Analysis of Cointegration Vectors, *Journal of Economic Dynamics and Control*, 12, 231–254.

Johansen, S. (1991), Estimation and Hypothesis Testing of Cointegrating Vectors in Gaussian Vector Autoregressive Models, *Econometrica*, 59, 1551–1580.

Johansen, S. (1995), *Likelihood-Based Inference in Cointegrated Vector Autoregressive Models*, Oxford University Press, Oxford, UK.

Johansen, S. (2002), A Small Sample Correction for the Test of Cointegrating Rank in the Vector Autoregressive Model, *Econometrica*, 70, 1929–1961.

Johansen, S. and Juselius, K. (1990), Maximum Likelihood Estimation and Inference on Cointegration – with Applications to the Demand for Money, *Oxford Bulletin of Economics and Statistics*, 52, 169–210.

Jones, M. P. (1996), Indicator and Stratification Methods for Missing Explanatory variables in Multiple Linear Regression, *Journal of the American Statistical Association*, 91, 222–230.

Jones, S. and Hensher, D. A. (2007), Evaluating the Behavioural Performance of Alternative Logit Models: An Application to Corporate Takeovers Research, *Journal of Business Finance and Accounting*, 34, 1193–1220.

Juselius, K. (2006), *The Cointegrated VAR Model: Methodology and Applications*, Oxford University Press, Oxford, UK.

Kao, C. (1999), Spurious Regression and Residual-Based Tests for Cointegration in Panel Data, *Journal of Econometrics*, 90, 1–44.

Keane, M. P. (1993), Simulation Estimation for Panel Data Models with Limited Dependent Variables. In: G. S. Maddala, C. R. Rao and H. D. Vinod, eds, *Handbook of Statistics, Volume XI*, North-Holland, Elsevier, Amsterdam, The Netherlands, 545–571.

Keane, M. P., Moffitt, R. and Runkle, D. (1988), Real Wages over the Business Cycle: Estimating the Impact of Heterogeneity with Micro Data, *Journal of Political Economy*, 96, 1232–1266.

Kennedy, P. (2008), *A Guide to Econometrics*, 6th edition, Blackwell Publishing, Malden, MA.

Kerr, W. R., Lerner, J. and Schoar, A. (2014), The Consequences of Entrepreneurial Finance: Evidence from Angel Financings, *Review of Financial Studies*, 27, 20–55.

Kiefer, N. (1980), Estimation of Fixed Effects Models for Time Series of Cross-Sections with Arbitrary Intertemporal Covariance, *Journal of Econometrics*, 14, 195–202.

Kiefer, N. (1988), Economic Duration Data and Hazard Functions, *Journal of Economic Literature*, 26, 646–679.

Kmenta, J. (1986), *Elements of Econometrics*, MacMillan, New York, NY.

Koenker, R. (2005), *Quantile Regression*, Cambridge University Press, Cambridge.

Krolzig, H.-M. and Hendry, D. F. (2001), Computer Automation of General-to-Specific Model Selection Procedures, *Journal of Economic Dynamics and Control*, 25, 831–866.

Kwiatkowski, D., Phillips, P. C. B., Schmidt, P. and Shin, Y. (1992), Testing the Null Hypothesis of Stationarity Against the Alternative of a Unit Root: How Sure Are We That Economic Time Series Have a Unit Root? *Journal of Econometrics*, 54, 159–178.

Lafontaine, F. and White, K. J. (1986), Obtaining Any Wald Statistic You Want, *Economics Letters*, 21, 35–40.

Lahiri, K. and Yang, L. (2013), *Forecasting Binary Outcomes*. In: G. Elliott and A. Timmermann, eds, *Handbook of Economic Forecasting, Volume 2A*, Elsevier Science Publishers, Amsterdam, The Netherlands, 1025–1105.

Lancaster, T. (1990), *The Econometric Analysis of Transition Data*, Cambridge University Press, New York, NY.

Lancaster, T. (2000), The Incidental Parameter Problem Since 1948, *Journal of Econometrics*, 95, 391–413.

Laporte, A. and Windmeijer, F. (2005), Estimation of Panel Data Models with Binary Indicators when Treatment Effects are not Constant over Time, *Economics Letters*, 88, 389–396.

Larcker, D. F. and Rusticus, T. O. (2010), On the Use of Instrumental Variables in Accounting Research, *Journal of Accounting and Economics*, 49, 186–205.

Layard, R. and Nickell, S. J. (1986), Unemployment in Britain, *Economica* (Supplement: Unemployment), 53, S121–S169.

Leamer, E. (1978), *Specification Searches*, John Wiley and Sons, New York, NY.

Lee, D. S. and Lemieux, T. (2010), Regression Discontinuity Designs in Economics, *Journal of Economic Literature*, 48, 281–355.

Lee, D. S., Moretti, E. and Butler, M. (2004), Do Voters Affect or Elect Policies? Evidence from the U.S. House, *Quarterly Journal of Economics*, 119, 807–859.

Lee, L. F. and Maddala, G. S. (1985), The Common Structure of Tests for Selectivity Bias, Serial Correlation, Heteroskedasticity and Non-Normality in the Tobit Model, *International Economic Review*, 26, 1–20.

Lee, M.-J. (1996), *Methods of Moments and Semiparametric Econometrics for Limited Dependent Variable Models*, Springer-Verlag, New York, NY.

Lee, M.-J. (1999), A Root-*N* Consistent Semiparametric Estimator for Related Effects Binary Response Panel Data, *Econometrica*, 67, 427–433.

Lee, M.-J. (2005), *Micro-Econometrics for Policy, Program, and Treatment Effects*, Oxford University Press, Oxford, UK.

LeSage, J. and Pace, R. K. (2009), *Introduction to Spatial Econometrics*, Chapman & Hall/CRC, Boca Raton, Florida.

Lennox, C. S., Francis, J. R. and Wang, Z. (2012), Selection Models in Accounting Research, *The Accounting Review*, 87, 589–616.

Levin, A. and Lin, C.-F. (1993), Unit Root Tests in Panel Data: New Results, Discussion Paper, Department of Economics, University of California, San Diego, CA.

Levin, A., Lin, C.-F. and Chu, S.-S. J. (2002), Unit Root Tests in Panel Data: Asymptotic and Finite-Sample Properties, *Journal of Econometrics*, 108, 1–24.

Levitt, S. D. and List, J. A. (2007), What Do Laboratory Experiments Measuring Social Preferences Reveal about the Real World?, *Journal of Economic Perspectives*, 21(2), 153–174.

Levitt, S. D. and List, J. A. (2009), Field Experiments in Economics: The Past, the Present and the Future, *European Economic Review*, 53, 1–18.

Li, W. K., Ling, S. and McAleer, M. (2002), Recent Theoretical Results for Time Series Models with GARCH Errors, *Journal of Economic Surveys*, 16, 245–269.

Li, K. and Prabhala, N. R. (2007), Self-Selection Models in Corporate Finance. In: B.E. Eckbo, ed., *Handbook of Empirical Corporate Finance, Volume 1*, Elsevier Science, Amsterdam, The Netherlands, 37–86.

Liesenfeld, R. and Richard, J.-F. (2010), Efficient Estimation of Probit Models with Correlated Errors, *Journal of Econometrics*, 156, 367–376.

Lin, J.-L. and Tsay, R. S. (1996), Co-Integration Constraint and Forecasting: An Empirical Examination, *Journal of Applied Econometrics*, 11, 519–538.

List, J. A. (2011), Why Economists Should Conduct Field Experiments and 14 Tips for Pulling One Off, *Journal of Economic Perspectives*, 25(3), 3–16.

Little, R. J. A. and Rubin, D. B. (1987), *Statistical Analysis with Missing Data*, John Wiley and Sons, New York, NY.

Little, R. J. A. and Rubin, D. B. (2002), *Statistical Analysis with Missing Data*, 2nd edition, John Wiley and Sons, Hoboken, NJ.

Ljung, G. M. and Box, G. E. P. (1978), On a Measure of Lack of Fit in Time Series Models, *Biometrika*, 65, 297–303.

Lo, A. and MacKinlay, C. (1990), Data-Snooping Biases in Tests of Financial Asset Pricing Models, *Review of Financial Studies*, 3, 431–468.

Louviere, J. J. (1988), Conjoint Analysis Modeling of Stated Preferences. A Review of Theory, Methods, Recent Developments and External Validity, *Journal of Transport Economics and Policy*, 22, 93–119.

Lovell, M. C. (1983), Data Mining, *Review of Economics and Statistics*, 65, 1–12.

Ludvigson, S. C. (2013), Advances in Consumption-Based Asset Pricing: Empirical Tests. In: G. Constantinides, M. Harris and R. Stulz, eds, *Handbook of the Economics of Finance, Volume 2B*, Elsevier Science, Amsterdam, The Netherlands, 799–906.

Lütkepohl, H. (2005), *New Introduction to Multiple Time Series Analysis*, Springer-Verlag, Berlin, Germany.

MacKinnon, J. G. (1991), Critical Values for Cointegration Tests. In: R. F. Engle and C. W. J. Granger, eds, *Long-Run Economic Relationships: Readings in Cointegration*, Oxford University Press, Oxford, UK, 267–276.

MacKinnon, J. G. and White, H. (1985), Some Heteroskedasticity Consistent Covariance Matrix Estimators with Improved Finite Sample Properties, *Journal of Econometrics*, 29, 305–325.

MacKinnon, J. G., White, H. and Davidson, R. (1983), Test for Model Specification in the Presence of Alternative Hypotheses: Some Further Results, *Journal of Econometrics*, 21, 53–70.

Maddala, G. S. (1983), *Limited-Dependent and Qualitative Variables in Econometrics*, Cambridge University Press, Cambridge, UK.

Maddala, G. S. (1987), Limited Dependent Variable Models Using Panel Data, *The Journal of Human Resources*, 22, 307–338.

Maddala, G. S. and Lahiri, K. (2009), *Introductory Econometrics*, 4th edition, John Wiley and Sons, Chichester, UK.

Maddala, G. S. and Kim, I.-M. (1998), *Unit Roots, Cointegration and Structural Change*, Cambridge University Press, New York, NY.

Maddala, G. S. and Wu, S. (1999), A Comparative Study of Unit Root Tests with Panel Data and a New Simple Test, *Oxford Bulletin of Economics and Statistics*, 61, 631–652.

Maddala, G. S., Wu, S. and Liu, P. C. (2000), Do Panel Data Rescue Purchasing Power Parity (PPP) Theory? In: J. Krishnakumar and E. Ronchetti, eds, *Panel Data Econometrics: Future Directions*, North Holland, Amsterdam, The Netherlands, 35–51.

Malkiel, B. G. (1995), Returns from Investing in Equity Mutual Funds 1971–1991, *Journal of Finance*, 50, 549–572.

Manski, C. F. (1975), Maximum Score Estimation of the Stochastic Utility Model of Choice, *Journal of Econometrics*, 3, 205–228.

Manski, C. F. (1985), Semiparametric Analysis of Discrete Response, *Journal of Econometrics*, 27, 313–333.

Manski, C. F. (1987), Semiparametric Analysis of Random Effects Linear Models from Binary Panel Data, *Econometrica*, 55, 357–362.

Manski, C. F. (1989), Anatomy of the Selection Problem, *The Journal of Human Resources*, 24, 243–260.

Manski, C. F. (1994), The Selection Problem. In: C. A. Sims, ed., *Advances in Econometrics, Sixth World Congress, Volume I*, Cambridge University Press, Cambridge, UK, 143–170.

Manski, C. F. (2007), *Identification for Prediction and Decision*, Harvard University Press, Cambridge, MA.

Markopolos, H. (2010), *No One Would Listen: A True Financial Thriller*, John Wiley and Sons, Hoboken, NJ.

Marquering, W. and Verbeek, M. (2004), The Economic Value of Predicting Stock Index Returns and Volatility, *Journal of Financial and Quantitative Analysis*, 39, 407–429.

Martin, V., Hurn, S. and Harris, D. (2013), *Econometric Modelling with Time Series: Specification, Estimation and Testing*, Cambridge University Press, New York, NY.

Martins, M. (2001), Parametric and Semiparametric Estimation of Sample Selection Models: An Empirical Application to the Female Labour Force in Portugal, *Journal of Applied Econometrics*, 16, 23–40.

Masicampo, E. J. and Lalande, D. R. (2012), A Peculiar Prevalence of *p* Values just below .05, *The Quarterly Journal of Experimental Psychology*, 65, 2271–2279.

McCall, B. P. (1995), The Impact of Unemployment Insurance Benefit Levels on Recipiency, *Journal of Business and Economic Statistics*, 13, 189–198.

McCulloch, J. H. and Kwon, H. C. (1993), *U.S. Term Structure Data*, 1947–1991, Ohio State working paper 93–6, Ohio State University, Columbus, OH.

McFadden, D. F. (1974), Conditional Logit Analysis of Qualitative Choice Behavior. In: P. Zaremba, ed., *Frontiers in Econometrics*, Academic Press, New York, NY, 105–142.

McKenzie, D. J. (2004), Asymptotic Theory for Heterogeneous Dynamic Pseudo-Panels, *Journal of Econometrics*, 120, 235–262.

Meese, R. A. and Rogoff, K. (1983), Empirical Exchange Rate Models of the Seventies Do They Fit Out-Of-Sample?, *Journal of International Economics*, 14, 3–24.

Mehra, R. and Prescott, E. (1985), The Equity Premium: A Puzzle, *Journal of Monetary Economics*, 15, 145–161.

Meng, Y., Brennan, A., Purshouse, R., Hill-McManus, D., Angus, C., Holmes, J. and Meier, P. S. (2014), Estimation of Own and Cross Price Elasticities of Alcohol Demand in the UK - A Pseudo-Panel Approach Using the Living Costs and Food Survey 2001–2009, *Journal of Health Economics*, 34, 96–103.

Mills, T. C. and Markellos, R. N. (2008), *The Econometric Modelling of Financial Time Series*, 3rd edition, Cambridge University Press, New York, NY.

Mizon, G. E. (1984), The Encompassing Approach in Econometrics. In: K. F. Wallis and D. F. Hendry, eds, *Quantitative Economics and Econometric Analysis*, Basil Blackwell, Oxford, UK, 135–172.

Mizon, G. E. (1995), Progressive Modeling of Macroeconomic Time Series: The LSE Methodology. In: K.D. Hoover, ed., *Macroeconometrics: Developments, Tensions and Prospects*, Kluwer Academic Publishers, Dordrecht, 107–180.

Mizon, G. E. and Richard, J. F. (1986), The Encompassing Principle and its Application to Testing Non-Nested Hypotheses, *Econometrica*, 54, 657–678.

Modigliani, F. and Miller, M. (1958), The Cost of Capital, Corporation Finance, and the Theory of Investment, *American Economic Review*, 48, 655–669.

Moffitt, R. (1993), Identification and Estimation of Dynamic Models with a Time Series of Repeated Cross-Sections, *Journal of Econometrics*, 59, 99–123.

Moon H. R. and Perron, B. (2004) Testing for a Unit root in Panels with Dynamic Factors, *Journal of Econometrics*, 122, 81–126.

Mundlak, Y. (1961), Empirical Production Function Free of Management Bias, *Journal of Farm Economics*, 43, 44–56.

Nelson, C. R. and Plosser, C. I. (1982), Trends and Random Walks in Macro-economic Time Series: Some Evidence and Implications, *Journal of Monetary Economics*, 10, 139–162.

Nelson, D. (1991), Conditional Heteroskedasticity in Asset Returns: A New Approach, *Econometrica*, 59, 347–370.

Newey, W. K. (1985), Maximum Likelihood Specification Testing and Conditional Moment Tests, *Econometrica*, 53, 1047–1070.

Newey, W. K. (2009), Two-Step Series Estimation of Sample Selection Models, *Econometrics Journal*, 12, S217–S229.

Newey, W. K. and West, K. (1987), A Simple Positive Semi-Definite, Heteroskedasticity and Autocorrelation Consistent Covariance Matrix, *Econometrica*, 55, 703–708.

Newey, W. K., Powell, J. L. and Walker, J. R. (1990), Semiparametric Estimation of Selection Models: Some Empirical Results, *American Economic Review*, 80, 324–328.

Ng, S. (2013), Variable Selection in Predictive Regressions, In: G. Elliott and A. Timmermann, eds, *Handbook of Economic Forecasting, Volume 2B*, Elsevier Science Publishers, Amsterdam, The Netherlands, 753–789.

Ng, S. and Perron, P. (2001), Lag Selection and the Construction of Unit Root Tests with Good Size and Power, *Econometrica*, 69, 1519–1554.

Nickell, S. (1981), Biases in Dynamic Models with Fixed Effects, *Econometrica*, 49, 1417–1426.

Nijman, Th. E. and Verbeek, M. (1990), Estimation of Time Dependent Parameters in Linear Models Using Cross Sections, Panels or Both, *Journal of Econometrics*, 46, 333–346.

Nijman, Th. E. and Verbeek, M. (1992), Nonresponse in Panel Data: The Impact on Estimates of a Life Cycle Consumption Function, *Journal of Applied Econometrics*, 7, 243–257.

O'Connell, P. G. J. (1998), The Overvaluation of Purchasing Power Parity, *Journal of International Economics*, 44, 1–19.

Ongena, S. and Smith, D. C. (2001), The Duration of Bank Relationships, *Journal of Financial Economics*, 61, 449–475.

Owen, P. D. (2003), General-to-Specific Modelling Using PcGets, *Journal of Economic Surveys*, 17, 609–628.

Pagan, A. and Ullah, A. (1999), *Nonparametric Econometrics*, Cambridge University Press, Cambridge, UK.

Pagan, A. and Vella, F. (1989), Diagnostic Tests for Models Based on Individual Data: A Survey, *Journal of Applied Econometrics*, 4, S29–S59.

Pagan, A., Hall, A. D. and Martin, V. (1996), Modeling the Term Structure. In: G. S. Maddala and C. R. Rao, eds, *Handbook of Statistics, Volume XIV*, North-Holland, Elsevier, Amsterdam, The Netherlands, 91–118.

Parker, J. A. and Julliard, C. (2005), Consumption Risk and the Cross-Section of Expected Returns, *Journal of Political Economy*, 113, 185–222.

Parmeter, C. F. and Kumbhakar, S. C. (2014), Efficiency Analysis: A Primer on Recent Advances, *Foundations and Trends in Econometrics*, 7, 191–385.

Patterson, K. D. (2000), *An Introduction to Applied Econometrics: A Time Series Approach*, MacMillan Press, London, UK.

Pedroni, P. (1999), Critical Values for Cointegration Tests in Heterogeneous Panels with Multiple Regressors, *Oxford Bulletin of Economics and Statistics*, 61, 653–678.

Pedroni, P. (2004), Panel Cointegration: Asymptotic and Finite Sample Properties of Pooled Time Series Tests With an Application to the PPP Hypothesis, *Econometric Theory*, 20, 597–625.

Pesaran, M. H. (2007), A Simple Panel Unit Root Test in the Presence of Cross-Section Dependence, *Journal of Applied Econometrics*, 22, 265–312.

Pesaran, M. H. (2012), On the Interpretation of Panel Unit Root Tests, *Economics Letters*, 116, 545–546.

Pesaran, M. H. (2015), *Time Series and Panel Data Econometrics*, Oxford University Press, Oxford, UK.

Pesaran, M. H., Shin, Y. and Smith, R. J. (2000), Structural Analysis of Vector Error Correction Models with Exogenous $I(1)$ Variables, *Journal of Econometrics*, 97, 293–343.

Pesaran, M. H., Shin, Y. and Smith, R. J. (2001), Bounds Testing Approaches to the Analysis of Level Relationships, *Journal of Applied Econometrics*, 16, 289–326.

Pesaran, M. H., Smith, L. V. and Yamagata, T. (2013), Panel Unit Root Tests in the Presence of a Multifactor Error Structure, *Journal of Econometrics*, 175, 94–115.

Pesaran, M. H. and Smith, R. P. (1995), Estimation of Long-run Relationships from Dynamic Heterogeneous Panels, *Journal of Econometrics*, 68, 79–113.

Pesaran, M. H. and Timmermann, A. (1995), The Robustness and Economic Significance of Predictability of Stock Returns, *Journal of Finance*, 50, 1201–1228.

Pesaran, M. H. and Timmermann, A. (2000), A Recursive Modelling Approach to Predicting UK Stock Returns, *The Economic Journal*, 110, 159–191.

Petersen, M. A. (2009), Estimating Standard Errors in Finance Panel Data Sets: Comparing Approaches, *Review of Financial Studies*, 22, 435–480.

Phillips, P. C. B. (1986), Understanding Spurious Regressions in Econometrics, *Journal of Econometrics*, 33, 311–340.

Phillips, P. C. B. and Hansen, B. E. (1990), Statistical Inference in Instrumental Variables Regression with $I(1)$ Processes, *Review of Economic Studies*, 57, 99–125.

Phillips, P. C. B. and Moon, H. R. (1999), Linear Regression Limit Theory for Nonstationary Panel Data, *Econometrica*, 67, 1057–1111.

Phillips, P. C. B. and Ouliaris, S. (1990), Asymptotic Properties of Residual Based Tests for Cointegration, *Econometrica*, 58, 165–194.

Phillips, P. C. B. and Park, J. Y. (1988), On the Formulation of Wald Tests of Nonlinear Restrictions, *Econometrica*, 56, 1065–1083.

Phillips, P. C. B. and Perron, P. (1988), Testing for a Unit Root in Time Series Regression, *Biometrika*, 75, 335–346.

Pivetta, F. and Reis, R. (2007), The Persistence of Inflation in the United States, *Journal of Economic Dynamics and Control*, 31, 1326–1358.

Poon, S.-H. and Granger, C. W. J. (2003), Forecasting Volatility in Financial Markets: A Review, *Journal of Economic Literature*, 41, 478–539.

Portney, P. R. (1994), The Contingent Valuation Debate: Why Should Economists Care?, *Journal of Economic Perspectives*, 8, 3–18.

Powers, E. A. (2005), Interpreting Logit Regressions with Interaction Terms: An Application to the Management Turnover Literature, *Journal of Corporate Finance*, 11, 504–522.

Prais, S. and Winsten, C. (1954), Trend Estimation and Serial Correlation, Cowles Commission Discussion Paper 383, Chicago, IL.

Propper, C., Rees, H. and Green, K. (2001), The Demand for Private Medical Insurance in the UK: A Cohort Analysis, *The Economic Journal*, 111, C180–C200.

Puhani, P. A. (2000), The Heckman Correction for Sample Selection and its Critique, *Journal of Economic Surveys*, 14, 53–67.

Ramsey, J. B. (1969), Tests for Specification Errors in Classical Linear Least Squares Regression Analysis, *Journal of the Royal Statistical Society, Series B*, 32, 350–371.

Rapach, D. and Zhou, G. (2013), Forecasting Stock Returns. In: G. Elliott and A. Timmermann, eds, *Handbook of Economic Forecasting, Volume 2A*, Elsevier Science Publishers, Amsterdam, The Netherlands, 327–383.

Reimers, H.-E. (1992), Comparison of Tests for Multivariate Cointegration, *Statistical Papers*, 33, 335–359.

Ridder, G. and Moffitt, R. (2007), The Econometrics of Data Combination. In: J. J. Heckman and E. E. Leamer, eds, *Handbook of Econometrics, Volume VI, Part B*, North-Holland, Elsevier, Amsterdam, The Netherlands, 5469–5547.

Roberts, M. R. and Whited, T. M. (2013), Endogeneity in Empirical Corporate Finance. In: G. Constantinides, M. Harris and R. Stulz, eds, *Handbook of the Economics of Finance, Volume 2A*, Elsevier Science, Amsterdam, The Netherlands, 493–572.

Robertson, D. and Symons, J. (1992), Some Strange Properties of Panel Data Estimators, *Journal of Applied Econometrics*, 7, 175–189.

Robinson, P. M. (1982), On the Asymptotic Properties of Estimators of Models Containing Limited Dependent Variables, *Econometrica*, 50, 27–41.

Rogoff, K. (1996), The Purchasing Power Parity Puzzle, *Journal of Economic Literature*, 34, 647–668.

Roodman, D. (2009), A Note on the Theme of Too Many Instruments, *Oxford Bulletin of Economics and Statistics*, 71, 135–158.

Rose, A. K. (1988), Is the Real Interest Rate Stable?, *Journal of Finance*, 43, 1095–1112.

Rosen, S. (1974), Hedonic Prices and Implicit Markets: Product Differentiation in Perfect Competition, *Journal of Political Economy*, 82, 34–55.

Rosenbaum, P. R. and Rubin, D. B. (1983), The Central Role of the Propensity Score in Observational Studies for Causal Effects, *Biometrika*, 70, 41–55.

Rossi, B. (2005), Confidence Intervals for Half-Life Deviations from Purchasing Power Parity, *Journal of Business and Economic Statistics*, 23, 432–442.

Rossi, B. (2013), Advances in Forecasting under Instability. In: G. Elliott and A. Timmermann, eds, *Handbook of Economic Forecasting, Volume 2B*, Elsevier Science Publishers, Amsterdam, The Netherlands, 1203–1324.

Rousseeuw, P. J. and Leroy, A. M. (2003), *Robust Regression and Outlier Detection*, John Wiley and Sons, Hoboken, NJ.

Rubin, D. B. (1976), Inference and Missing Data, *Biometrika*, 63, 581–592.

Ruud, P. A. (1984), Test of Specification in Econometrics, *Econometric Reviews*, 3, 211–242.

Sachs, J. D. (2003), Institutions Don't Rule: Direct Effects of Geography on Per Capita Income, NBER Working Paper No. 9490, Cambridge, MA.

Said, S. E. and Dickey, D. A. (1984), Testing for Unit Roots in Autoregressive Moving Average Models of Unknown Order, *Biometrika*, 71, 599–607.

Sargan, J. D. and Bhargava, A. S. (1983), Testing Residuals from Least Squares Regression for Being Generated by the Gaussian Random Walk, *Econometrica*, 51, 213–248.

Savin, N. E. and White, K. J. (1977), The Durbin–Watson Test for Serial Correlation with Extreme Sample Sizes or Many Regressors, *Econometrica*, 45, 1989–1996.

Savov, A. (2011), Asset Pricing with Garbage, *Journal of Finance*, 66, 177–201.

Schwarz, G. (1978), Estimating the Dimension of a Model, *Annals of Statistics*, 6, 461–464.

Semykina, A. and Wooldridge, J. M. (2010), Estimating Panel Data Models in the Presence of Endogeneity and Selection, *Journal of Econometrics*, 157, 375–380.

Shaman, P. and Stine, R. A. (1988), The Bias of Autoregressive Coefficient Estimators, *Journal of the American Statistical Association*, 83, 842–848.

Shanken, J. (1992), On the Estimation of Beta Pricing models, *Review of Financial Studies*, 5, 1–34.

Shanken, J. and Zhou, G. (2007), Estimating and Testing Beta Pricing Models: Alternative Methods and Their Performance in Simulations, *Journal of Financial Economics*, 84, 40–86.

Silvennoinen, A. and Teräsvirta, T. (2009), Multivariate GARCH Models. In: T. G. Andersen, R. A. Davis, J.-P. Kreiss and T. Mikosch, eds, *Handbook of Financial Time Series*, Springer Verlag, Berlin, 201–229.

Sims, C. A. (1980), Macroeconomics and Reality, *Econometrica*, 48, 1–48.

Smith, R. P. and Fuertes, A.-M. (2016), *Panel Time Series*, working paper, Dept of Economics, Birkbeck College, London, UK.

Sovey, A. J. and Green, D. P. (2011), Instrumental Variables Estimation in Political Science: A Readers' Guide, *American Journal of Political Science*, 55, 188–200.

Staiger, D. and Stock, J. H. (1997), Instrumental Variables Regression with Weak Instruments, *Econometrica*, 65, 557–586.

Starbuck, W. H. (2016), 60th Anniversary Essay: How Journals Could Improve Research Practices in Social Science, *Administrative Science Quarterly*, 61, 165–183.

Stewart, J. and Gill, L. (1998), *Econometrics*, 2nd edition, Prentice Hall, London, UK.

Stock, J. H. and Watson, M. W. (1993), A Simple Estimator of Cointegrating Vectors in Higher Order Integrated Systems, *Econometrica*, 61, 783–820.

Stock, J. H. and Watson, M. W. (2001), Vector Autoregressions, *Journal of Economic Perspectives*, 15, 101–115.

Stock, J. H. and Watson, M. W. (2007), *Introduction to Econometrics*, International 2nd edition, Addison-Wesley (Pearson International edition), Boston, MA.

Stock, J. H. and Watson, M. W. (2008), Heteroskedasticity-Robust Standard Errors for Fixed Effects Panel Data Regression, *Econometrica*, 76, 155–174.

Stock, J. H. and Wright, J. H. (2000), GMM with Weak Identification, *Econometrica*, 68, 1055–1096.

Stock, J. H., Wright, J. H. and Yogo, M. (2002), A Survey of Weak Instruments and Weak Identification in Generalized Method of Moments, *Journal of Business and Economic Statistics*, 20, 518–529.

Stock, J. H. and Yogo, M. (2005), Testing for Weak Instruments in Linear IV Regression. In: D. W. K. Andrews and J. H. Stock, eds, *Identification and Inference for Econometric Models, Essays in Honor of Thomas Rothenberg*, Cambridge University Press, New York, NY, 80–108.

Sullivan, R., Timmermann, A. and White, H. (2001), Dangers of Data-Driven Inference: The Case of Calender Effects in Stock Returns, *Journal of Econometrics*, 105, 249–286.

Swamy, P. A. V. B. (1970), Efficient Inference in a Random Coefficient Regression Model, *Econometrica*, 311–323.

Tauchen, G. E. (1985), Diagnostic Testing and Evaluation of Maximum Likelihood Models, *Journal of Econometrics*, 30, 415–443.

Taylor, A. M. and Taylor, M. P. (2004), The Purchasing Power Parity Debate, *Journal of Economic Perspectives*, 18, 135–158.

Taylor, M. P. (1995), The Economics of Exchange Rates, *Journal of Economic Literature*, 33, 12–47.

Thompson, S. B. (2011), Simple Formulas for Standard Errors that Cluster by Both Firm and Time, *Journal of Financial Economics*, 99, 1–10.

Tibshirani, R. (1996), Regression Shrinkage and Selection via the Lasso, *Journal of the Royal Statistical Society, Series B*, 58, 267–288.

Tobin, J. (1958), Estimation of Relationships for Limited Dependent Variables, *Econometrica*, 26, 24–36.

Tsay, R. S. (2014), *Multivariate Time Series Analysis: With R and Financial Applications*, John Wiley and Sons, Chichester, UK.

Varian, H. R. (2014), Big Data: New Tricks for Econometrics, *Journal of Economic Perspectives*, 28(2), 3–28.

Vella, F. (1998), Estimating Models with Sample Selection Bias: A Survey, *Journal of Human Resources*, 33, 127–169.

Vella, F. and Verbeek, M. (1998), Whose Wages Do Unions Raise? A Dynamic Model of Unionism and Wage Rate Determination for Young Men, *Journal of Applied Econometrics*, 13, 163–183.

Vella, F. and Verbeek, M. (1999a), Two-Step Estimation of Panel Data Models with Censored Endogenous Variables and Selection Bias, *Journal of Econometrics*, 90, 239–263.

Vella, F. and Verbeek, M. (1999b), Estimating and Interpreting Models with Endogenous Treatment Effects, *Journal of Business and Economic Statistics*, 17, 473–478.

Verbeek, M. (1995), Alternative Transformations to Eliminate Fixed Effects, *Econometric Reviews*, 14, 205–211.

Verbeek, M. (2008), Pseudo Panels and Repeated Cross-Sections. In: L. Mátyás and P. Sevestre, eds, *The Econometrics of Panel Data: Fundamentals and Recent Developments in Theory and Practice*, Springer-Verlag, New York, NY, 369–385.

Verbeek, M. and Nijman, Th. E. (1992a), Testing for Selectivity Bias in Panel Data Models, *International Economic Review*, 33, 681–703.

Verbeek, M. and Nijman, Th. E. (1992b), Can Cohort Data Be Treated As Genuine Panel Data?, *Empirical Economics*, 17, 9–23.

Verbeek, M. and Nijman, Th. E. (1996), Incomplete Panels and Selection Bias. In: L. Mátyás and P. Sevestre, eds, *The Econometrics of Panel Data. A Handbook of the Theory with Applications*, 2nd revised edition, Kluwer Academic Publishers, Dordrecht, The Netherlands, 449–490.

Verbeek, M. and Vella, F. (2005), Estimating Dynamic Models from Repeated Cross-Sections, *Journal of Econometrics*, 127, 83–102.

Vigen, T. (2015), *Spurious Correlations*, Hachette Books, New York, NY.

Wagner, M. and Hlouskova, J. (2010), The Performance of Panel Cointegration Methods: Results from a Large Scale Simulation Study, *Econometric Reviews*, 29, 182–223.

Wallis, K. F. (1979), *Topics in Applied Econometrics*, 2nd edition, Basil Blackwell, Oxford, UK.

Wasserstein R. L. and Lazar, N. A. (2016), The ASA's Statement on *p*-Values: Context, Process and Purpose, *The American Statistician*, 70, 129–133.

Weeks, M. (1995), Circumventing the Curse of Dimensionality in Applied Work Using Computer Intensive Methods, *The Economic Journal*, 105, 520–530.

Westerlund, J. (2007), Estimating Cointegrated Panels with Common Factors and the Forward Rate Unbiasedness Hypothesis, *Journal of Financial Econometrics*, 3, 491–522.

Westerlund, J. and Breitung, J. (2013), Lessons from a Decade of IPS and LLC, *Econometric Reviews*, 32, 547–591.

White, H. (1980), A Heteroskedasticity-Consistent Covariance Matrix Estimator and a Direct Test for Heteroskedasticity, *Econometrica*, 48, 817–838.

White, H. (1982), Maximum Likelihood Estimation of Misspecified Models, *Econometrica*, 50, 1–25.

White, H. (1990), A Consistent Model Selection Procedure Based on m-Testing. In: C. W. J. Granger, ed., *Modelling Economic Series: Readings in Econometric Methodology*, Clarendon Press, Oxford, UK, 369–383.

Windmeijer, F. (2005), A Finite Sample Correction for the Variance of Linear Efficient Two-Step GMM, *Journal of Econometrics*, 126, 25–51.

Winkelmann, R. (2010), *Econometric Analysis of Count Data*, 5th edition, Springer-Verlag, Berlin Heidelberg, Germany.

Wooldridge, J. M. (1995), Selection Corrections for Panel Data Models under Conditional Mean Independence Assumptions, *Journal of Econometrics*, 68, 115–132.

Wooldridge, J. M. (2003), Cluster-Sample Methods in Applied Econometrics, *American Economic Review*, 93, 133–138.

Wooldridge, J. M. (2010), *Econometric Analysis of Cross-Section and Panel Data*, 2nd edition, MIT Press, Cambridge, MA.

Wooldridge, J. M. (2012), *Introductory Econometrics. A Modern Approach*, 5th edition, South-Western Cengage Learning, Mason, OH.

Wu, Y. (2004), The Choice of Equity-Selling Mechanisms, *Journal of Financial Economics*, 74, 93–119.

Yamagata, T. and Orme, C. D. (2005), On Testing Sample Selection Bias Under the Multicollinearity Problem, *Econometric Reviews*, 24, 467–481.

Zivot, E. (2009), Practical Issues in the Analysis of Univariate GARCH Models. In: T. G. Andersen, R. A. Davies, J.-P. Kreiß, Th. Mikosch, eds, *Handbook of Financial Time Series*, Springer Verlag, Berlin.

Index

Note: Page numbers in *italics* denote illustrations; page numbers in **bold** denote definitions